# MEMOIRS OF THE LIFE

OF

## VICE-ADMIRAL

# LORD VISCOUNT NELSON, K.B.

DUKE OF BRONTÉ, ETC. ETC. ETC.

BY

## THOMAS JOSEPH PETTIGREW, F.R.S., F.S.A.

DOCTOR OF PHILOSOPHY OF THE UNIVERSITY OF GÖTTINGEN;
ETC. ETC. ETC.

Resplendet gloria Marti
Armati referam vires?
*Claudian de Laud. Stil.*

"A spirit equal to all undertakings, and resources fitted to all occasions."
*Lord Collingwood.*

IN TWO VOLUMES.
VOL. II.

SECOND EDITION.

MDCCCXLIX.

Copyright © 2013 Read Books Ltd.
This book is copyright and may not be
reproduced or copied in any way without
the express permission of the publisher in writing

British Library Cataloguing-in-Publication Data
A catalogue record for this book is available from the
British Library

# Horatio Nelson

Horatio Nelson, 1st Viscount Nelson, was a British flag officer in the Royal Navy. He is famed for the part he played in the Napoleonic Wars, most notable amongst his victories being that at the Battle of Trafalgar in 1805.

Born on 29th September 1758 in Norfolk, England, Nelson was the sixth of eleven children born to the Reverend Edmund Nelson and his wife Catherine. His family were well connected; his mother being the grandniece of Robert Walpole (1676-1745), 1st Earl of Oxford, and the *de facto* first Prime Minister of Great Britain, and his godfather, after whom he was named, being 2nd Baron Walpole, of Wolterton, Horatio Walpole (1723-1809). Young Horatio attended Paston Grammar School until the age of 12 when he began his naval career. As an Ordinary Seaman and coxswain, Nelson started his naval career serving under his uncle, Captain Maurice Suckling, on the third-rate HMS Raissonable. Soon after reporting aboard he began his officer training. Unfortunately, Nelson discovered that he was vulnerable to terrible bouts of sea-sickness, a complaint that he was condemned to endure for the rest of his life.

At the age of 20 Nelson was made a captain, going on to serve in the West Indies, the Baltic, and Canada. On his return, with new bride Frances Nesbet, he found himself without command and reduced to half pay. However, following Britain's entrance to the French Revolutionary Wars, in 1793, Nelson found himself in charge of the Agamemnon. During the campaign in the Mediterranean, he lost the sight in his right eye in a battle at Calvi. Not long after, he lost his right arm at the Battle of Santa Cruz de Tenerife.

Nelson was known for being a bold and fearless commander, often to the dismay of his superiors. On one occasion he even defied orders from senior officers to cease action, putting the telescope to his blind eye and claiming he couldn't see their signals. This self-assured attitude did not prevent him from rising through the ranks however. His victories spoke for themselves. One such victory was the triumph of the Battle of the Nile (in 1798) where Nelson destroyed Napoleon's fleet and thus thwarted his ambition to establish a trade route to India.

Although still married, Nelson fell in love with another woman following his posting to Naples. Emma Hamilton, herself married, and Nelson began a lifelong love affair in which they had a daughter together, Horatia, in 1801. In the same year, Nelson was promoted to vice-admiral. He was supremely successful in his position in charge of the British fleet. The Royal Navy won many battles under his command and averted the threat of invasion from the ambitious Napoleon. It was the naval engagement of the Battle of Trafalgar (21st October 1805) that still cements Nelson's place in the history of British warfare however.

This was the most decisive battle of the campaign to stop the French and Spanish Navies, during the War of the Third Coalition (August-December 1805). Aboard the HMS Victory, Nelson led a fleet of 27 ships into battle against 33 enemy vessels just west of Cape Trafalgar, off the coast of Spain. Nelson deviated from conventional naval strategy, dividing his smaller force into two columns directed perpendicularly against the enemy fleet. The tactic worked and the battle was won. However, Nelson was mortally wounded during the engagement, shot by a French sniper.

He was shot in the left shoulder, with the bullet passing through his back.

Despite this injury, as he was being carried below by his men, Nelson asked them to pause while he gave some advice to the midshipman on the handling of the tiller, and then draped a handkerchief over his face to avoid causing alarm amongst the crew. He died on 21st October, 1805. Nelson's body was transported back to England preserved in brandy, and he was subsequently given a state funeral. The first tribute to Nelson was fittingly offered at sea by sailors of Vice-Admiral Dmitry Senyavin's passing Russian squadron, which saluted on learning of the death.

# LIFE OF LORD NELSON.

## CHAPTER I.

### 1801.

THE attack made by the British upon a Danish 40-gun frigate, the Freja, to enforce the right of searching neutral ships for contraband of war, led to animosity between England and Denmark. The taking of Malta by the British, incensed Paul, the Emperor of all the Russias, and induced him to lay an embargo upon British shipping in his ports, amounting to not less than 200 sail. A convention being entered into between Russia and Sweden, agreeing to an armed neutrality on the part of these powers, Denmark joined the confederacy. This brought matters to a crisis. The three Northern Powers, under the influence of France, thus directed against the naval supremacy of England, rendered no inconsiderable effort necessary; and Sir Hyde Parker, with a competent force was dispatched to the Baltic with Lord Nelson, as second in command. Negotiations, presently to be noticed, failing to effect a reconciliation, an attack upon Copenhagen was made.

Few battles recorded in the naval annals of Great Britain have more redounded to the credit of those engaged, than the Battle of Copenhagen. It was wisely planned, bravely fought, and success was followed by the exhibition of distinguished humanity. In Clarke and McArthur's Life of Lord Nelson, the secret orders issued by the Admiralty to Sir Hyde Parker, the Commander-in-chief, have been printed. **Properly to estimate the following letters, it is necessary to repeat this statement :—**

"The Right Honourable Henry Dundas, one of his Majesty's principal Secretaries of State, having, in his letter of yesterday's date, signified to us his Majesty's pleasure, that whether the discussion, supposed to be now pending with the Court of Denmark, should be terminated by an amicable arrangement, or by actual hostilities, the Officer commanding the fleet in the Baltic should, in either case (as soon as the fleet can be withdrawn from before Copenhagen consistently with the attainment of one or the other of the objects for which he is now instructed to take that station), proceed to Revel; and if he should find the division of the Russian navy, usually stationed at that port, still there, to make an immediate and vigorous attack upon it, provided the measure should appear to him practicable, and such as in his judgment would afford a reasonable prospect of success in destroying the arsenals, or in capturing or destroying the ships, without exposing to too great a risk the fleet under his command.

"And Mr. Dundas having further signified to us his Majesty's pleasure, that, consistently with this precaution, the said Officer should be authorized, and directed to proceed successively, and as the season and other operations will permit, against Cronstadt, and in general, by every means in his power to attack, and endeavour to capture or destroy any ships of war, or others, belonging to Russia, wherever he can meet with them, and to annoy that Power as far as his means will admit in every manner not incompatible with the fair and acknowledged usages of war. And that with respect to Sweden, should the Court of Stockholm persist in her hostile engagements with that of Petersburgh against this country, the same general line of conduct, as hath been stated with respect to the ships and ports of the latter should govern the said Officer commanding the fleet in his proceedings against those of Sweden; but that, in the contrary supposition (conceived not to be impossible) of this power relinquishing her present hostile plans against the rights and interests of this country, and of her renewing, either singly or in concert with

Denmark, her ancient engagements with his Majesty, it will in such case be the duty of the said Officer to afford to Sweden every protection in his power against the resentment and attacks of Russia; and Mr. Dundas having also signified that his Majesty, being no less desirous of bringing the existing dispute with Sweden to this latter issue, than he has shewn himself so disposed with respect to Denmark, and upon the same principles, it will therefore be requisite that the said Officer commanding in the Baltic should make such a disposition of his force as may appear best adapted to facilitate and give weight to the arrangement in question, provided it should be concluded with the Court of Denmark, within the forty-eight hours allowed for this purpose, and the proposal of acceding to it, which will be made to that of Sweden, should be entertained by the latter. You are, in pursuance of his Majesty's pleasure, signified as above mentioned, hereby required and directed to proceed, without a moment's loss of time, into the Baltic, and to govern yourself under the different circumstances before stated to the best of your judgment and discretion in the manner therein pointed out, transmitting from time to time to our Secretary, for our information, an account of your proceedings, and such information as you may conceive to be proper for our knowledge. Given under our hands and seals, the 15th of March, 1801.

"St. Vincent.
"T. Troubridge.
"J. Markham."[1]

Sir Hyde Parker consulted with Lord Nelson on the operations intended to be pursued; and the following letter, in consequence of this consultation, is printed from Nelson's own autograph draft, which differs somewhat, though in no essential particulars, from that which has been given in the work above referred to:—

"St. George, March 25, 1801.

"My dear Sir Hyde,

"The conversation we had yesterday, has naturally, from its importance, been the subject of my thoughts; and the

---

[1] Clarke and McArthur, Vol ii. p. 259.

more I have reflected, the more confirmed I am in opinion, that not a moment should be lost in attacking the enemy. They will every day and hour be stronger; we never shall be so good a match for them as at this moment—the only consideration in my mind is, how to get at them with the least risk to our ships.

"By Mr. Vansittart's account, the Danes have taken every means in their power to prevent our getting to attack Copenhagen by the passage of the Sound. Cronenburg has been strengthened, the Crown Islands fortified (on the outermost 20 guns pointing mostly downwards), only 800 yards from very formidable batteries placed under the citadel, supported by 5 sail of the line, 7 floating batteries of 50 guns each, besides small craft, gun-boats, &c. &c.; also, that the Revel squadron of 12 or 14 sail of the line are soon expected, as also 5 sail of Swedes. It would appear by what you have told me of your instructions that Government took for granted that you would find no difficulty in getting off Copenhagen, and that in the event of the failure of a negotiation, that you might instantly attack, and that there would be scarcely a doubt but that the Danish fleet would be destroyed, and the capital made so hot that Denmark would listen to reason and its true interest. By Mr. Vansittart's account, their state of preparation far exceeds what he conceives our Government thought possible, and that the Danish Government is hostile to us in the greatest possible degree; therefore, here you are, with almost the safety, certainly the honour of England, more entrusted to you than ever yet fell to the lot of any British officer. On your decision depends, whether our country shall be degraded in the eyes of Europe, or whether she shall rear her head higher than ever. Again do I repeat, never did our country depend so much on the success or defeat of any fleet as on this. How best to honour our country and abate the pride of her enemies by defeating their schemes, must be the subject of your deepest consideration, as Commander-in-chief, and if what I have to offer can be the least useful in forming your decision, you are most heartily welcome.

"I shall begin with supposing that you are determined to enter by the passage of the Sound, as there are those that think if you leave that passage open that the Danish fleet may leave Copenhagen and join the Dutch or French. I own I have no fears on that subject, for it is not likely that whilst the capital is menaced with an attack, that 9000 of her best men would be sent out of the kingdom. I will suppose that some damage may arise amongst our masts and yards, but perhaps not one but can be made serviceable again. You are now about Cronenburg, if the wind is fair, and you determine to attack the ships and Crown Islands, you must expect the natural issue of such a battle—ships crippled—perhaps one or two lost, for the wind which carries you in will most probably not bring out a crippled ship. This mode I call taking the bull by the horns. This will not prevent the Revel ships or Swedes from coming down and forming a junction with the Danes. To prevent this from taking effect, in my humble opinion, a measure absolutely necessary, and still to attack Copenhagen, two modes are in my view—one to pass Cronenburg, taking the risk of damage, and to pass up the Channel, the deepest and the straitest above the middle grounds, and to come down the Gaspar, or King's Channel, to attack their floating batteries, &c. &c. as we find it convenient. It must have the effect of preventing a junction between the Russians, Swedes, and Danes, and may give us an opportunity of bombarding Copenhagen. A passage also, I am pretty certain, could be found for all our ships to the north of Southolm, perhaps it might be necessary to warp a small distance in the very narrow part. Supposing this mode of attack ineligible, the passage of the Belt, I have no doubt, would be accomplished in four or five days, then the attack by Draco could be carried into effect, the junction of the Russians prevented, and every probability of success on the Danish floating batteries. What effect a bombardment might have I am not called upon to give an opinion, but I think the way would be cleared for the trial. Supposing us through the Belt, with the wind fresh westerly, would it not be feasible to either go with the fleet (or detach ten ships of two or three decks, with one bomb—two fire-ships, if they could be spared), to Revel, to destroy the Russian squadron at that place? I do not see the great risk of such a detachment, with the remainder to attempt the business of Copenhagen. The measure may be thought bold, but I am of opinion the boldest measures are the safest, and our country demands a most vigorous exertion of her forces directed with judgment. In supporting you through the arduous and important task you have undertaken, no exertion of head and heart shall be wanting, my dear Sir Hyde, from your most obedient and faithful servant,

"NELSON AND BRONTÉ."

Colonel Stewart, in the Narrative before alluded to, says, that when Lord Nelson arrived at Yarmouth, his "plan would have been to have proceeded with the utmost dispatch, and with such ships as were in readiness, to the mouth of Copenhagen harbour; then and there to have insisted on amity or war, and have brought the objects of Messrs. Drummond and Vansittart's negotiation to a speedy decision. He would have left orders for the remainder of the fleet to have followed in succession, as they were ready, and by the rapidity of his proceedings have anticipated the formidable preparations for defence which the Danes had scarcely thought of at that early season. The delay in Yarmouth Roads did not accord with his views." The fleet sailed on the 12th of March, and after encountering a heavy gale of wind, which in some measure scattered the vessels, it did not reach Elsinore until the 24th. On the 29th,[1] he changed his flag from the St. George to the Elephant, a lighter ship, and on the following day proceeded through the Sound, anchoring at noon between Huen and Copenhagen.

On the 1st of April, an anchorage only two miles from Copenhagen was effected, the division of ships under the command of Nelson weighed, and in the evening was off Draco. The following day (April 2nd), the battle was fought, and on the succeeding day he re-hoisted his flag on board the St. George.

In a letter[2] to the Dean of Norwich, Lord Bexley, formerly Mr. Vansittart, says, that upon the reported resignation of Mr. Pitt, and Mr. Addington being appointed Prime Minister in January 7, 1801, he, Mr. Vansittart, was selected by the Premier, and recommended to Lord Hawkesbury, Secretary

[1] See preceding Letter, March 30th. Vol. i. p. 452.
[2] Life and Correspondence of Lord Viscount Sidmouth, Vol. i. p. 368.

of the Foreign Department, to be a confidential Minister to Denmark, the Government having received a secret communication from Prince Charles of Hesse, intimating that the Danish Government might be detached from the Northern Coalition, formed under the Emperor Paul, if a confidential person, with full powers, and conciliatory instructions, were sent to it. Prince Charles being brother-in-law to the King of Denmark, rendered the Government anxious to attend to the suggestion as speedily and as secretly as possible. Mr. Vansittart went, accompanied with Dr. Beeke as his Secretary, and met Prince Charles at Sleswick, who immediately, however, expressed his fears that the French influence, combined with the fear of the Emperor Paul at Copenhagen, would be too great to render the mission successful.

The Danes refused to receive Mr. Vansittart as a Minister, unless he would undertake for the unconditional restitution of the Danish ships, detained under embargo in England, as a preliminary to all negotiation. No intercourse, therefore, took place until the arrival of the Blanche frigate, Captain Drummond, who announced the immediate approach of the British fleet under Sir Hyde Parker and Lord Nelson, and brought instructions to Mr. Vansittart from the British Court, authorising him, in case of non-compliance or delay, to demand his passport, and embark immediately on board the fleet. Sir William Drummond, the resident Minister, who had held no communication for some time with the Danes, was with Mr. Vansittart. They proceeded by land to Elsinore, and then by the Blanche with the British Consul and British subjects to the fleet. On board the Admiral (Sir Hyde Parker's) ship, Mr. Vansittart had a conference with the Admiral and with Lord Nelson, and what is described as "a very interesting conversation" with the latter in the stern gallery, whilst Sir Hyde Parker prepared his letters for England by the Kite which conveyed Mr. Vansittart home.

On the 25th Mr. Vansittart and Mr. Drummond, the British Chargé d'Affaires left for England. Lord Nelson was exceedingly impatient of the several delays which occurred prior to reaching Copenhagen, giving to the enemy so much time for preparation. This appears not to have been neglected, for Colonel Stewart writes: "We soon perceived that our delay had been of important advantage to the enemy, who had lined the northern edge of the shoals near the Crown batteries, and the front of the harbour and arsenal with a formidable flotilla. The Trekroner battery appeared, in particular, to have been strengthened, and all the buoys of the Northern, and of the King's Channels had been removed." The line of defence of the Danes extended no less than four miles, estimating from one extreme point to the other. (See Plate.) On the afternoon of the 31st a Council of War was held, and the mode which might be advisable for the attack was considered, that from the eastward appearing to be preferred. "Lord Nelson (Stewart says) offered his services, requiring ten line-of-battle ships, and the whole of the smaller craft. The Commander-in-chief, with sound discretion, and in a handsome manner, not only left every thing to Lord Nelson for this detached service, but gave two more line-of-battle ships than he demanded. During this Council of War, the energy of Lord Nelson's character was remarked: certain difficulties had been started by some of the members, relative to each of the three Powers, we should either have to engage, in succession, or united, in those seas. The number of the Russians was, in particular, represented as formidable. Lord Nelson kept pacing the cabin, mortified at every thing which savoured either of alarm or irresolution. When the above remark was applied to the Swedes, he sharply observed, 'The more numerous the better;' and when to the Russians, he repeatedly said, 'So much the better, I wish they were twice as many, the easier the victory, depend on it.' He alluded, as he afterwards explained in private, to the total want of *tactique* among the Northern fleets; and to his intention, whenever he should bring either the Swedes or Russians to action, of attacking the head of their line, and confusing their movements as much as possible. He used to say, 'Close with a Frenchman, but out-manœuvre a Russian.'"

Nelson having made his last observations on the morning of the 1st of April, on board the Amazon, returned to the Elephant and made the signal to weigh. The shout with which it was received throughout the division, it is said, was heard to a considerable distance; the ships then weighed, and followed the Amazon in succession through the narrow channel. The wind was light, but favourable, and not one accident occurred.

"On board the Elephant, the night of the 1st of April was an important one. As soon as the fleet was at anchor the gallant Nelson sat down to table with a large party of his comrades in arms. He was in the highest spirits, and drank to a leading wind, and to the success of the ensuing day. Captains Foley, Hardy, Fremantle, Riou, Inman;[1] his Lordship's second in command, Admiral Graves, and a few others to whom he was particularly attached, were of this interesting party; from which every man separated with feelings of admiration for their great leader, and with anxious impatience to follow him to the approaching battle. The signal to prepare for action had been made early in the evening. All the Captains retired to their respective ships, Riou excepted, who, with Lord Nelson and Foley arranged the order of battle, and those instructions that were to be issued to each ship on the succeeding day. These three officers retired between nine and ten to the after-cabin, and drew up

---

[1] Captain Henry Inman was the son of a clergyman, and born near Bristol. He entered the navy in 1776, with Captain, afterwards Lord Hood. He was in the Lark frigate when D'Estaing's squadron appeared off Rhode Island, and his vessel being run on shore, and burnt, he was ordered on board the Pearl, Captain Linzee, and proceeded to the West Indies. Made Lieutenant, in the Santa Monica, he was wrecked off Tortola, and again lost his property. After Sir George Rodney's action of the 12th of April, 1782, he was in the Hector, and narrowly escaped with life from shipwreck, after being attacked by two French frigates. The Hector, although severely crippled by the battle, successfully resisted the attack, drove off the two frigates, L'Aigle and Le Lion, which were afterwards captured. In 1790, Inman was appointed to the Latona, and then to the Pigmy cutter, from which he was removed to the Victory, proceeding for Toulon. His exertions in this service procured for him the command of L'Aurore, and he was made Post-Captain, October 9, 1794. In the Romney he came home with a convoy. After a variety of service, he was engaged on the blockade of Dunkirk, and in a most gallant attack, captured La Desirée, to which he was afterwards appointed, and proceeded in her to the attack on Copenhagen, where his services were conspicuous, and called forth the praises of Nelson. Upon the renewal of the war in 1803, Captain Inman was appointed to the Utrecht, and then to the Triumph, of 74 guns, and joined the Channel fleet. He was ordered to the blockade of Rochfort, whence he was removed to support Sir Robert Calder, in his attack on the Brest fleet. He then cruised with Sir Richard Strachan off the Western Isles, when his health failed, and he was appointed to the Sea Fencibles at Lynn, and afterwards made Naval Commissioner at Madras, whence he sailed, February 22, 1809. He reached Madras on the 4th of July, and on the 15th of the same month expired, at the early age of 47.

those orders that have been generally published, and which ought to be referred to as the best proof of the arduous nature of the enterprise in which the fleet was about to be engaged. From the previous fatigue of this day, and of the two preceding, Lord Nelson was so much exhausted while dictating his instructions, that it was recommended to him by us all, and, indeed, insisted upon by his old servant Allen, who assumed much command on these occasions, that he should go to his cot. It was placed on the floor, but from it he still continued to dictate. Captain Hardy returned about eleven, and reported the practicability of the channel, and the depth of water up to the ships of the enemy's line. Had we abided by this report in lieu of confiding in our masters and pilots, we should have acted better. The orders were completed about one o'clock, when half-a-dozen clerks in the foremost cabin proceeded to transcribe them. Lord Nelson's impatience again shewed itself; for instead of sleeping undisturbedly, as he might have done, he was every half hour calling from his cot to these clerks to hasten their work, for that the wind was becoming fair. He was constantly receiving a report of this during the night. Their work being finished about six in the morning, his Lordship, who was previously up and dressed, breakfasted, and about seven made the signal for all Captains. The instructions were delivered to each by eight o'clock; and a special command was given to Captain Riou to act as circumstances might require. The land forces and a body of 500 seamen were to have been united under the command of Captain Fremantle and the Honorable Colonel Stewart, and as soon as the fire of the Crown Battery should be silenced, they were to storm the work, and destroy it. The division under the Commander-in-chief was to menace the ships at the entrance of the harbour, the intricacy of the channel would, however, have prevented their entering; Captain Murray in the Edgar was to lead."[1]

At five minutes past ten the action commenced, and in about half an hour half the fleet was engaged. By half-past eleven the action was general, and so ardently was the contest carried on by both sides, that at one o'clock the chance of

---

[1] Hon. Colonel Stewart's Narrative.

victory had not declared itself in favour of either country. At this time Colonel Stewart reports—

"The London (Sir Hyde Parker's ship) now made signal for the action to cease.[1] Lord Nelson was, at this time, as he had been during the whole action, walking the starboard side of the quarter-deck; sometimes much animated, and at others heroically fine in his observations. A shot through the mainmast knocked a few splinters about us. He observed to me with a smile, 'It is warm work, and this day may be the last to any of us at a moment;' and then stoping short at the gangway he used an expression never to be erased from my memory, and said with emotion, 'but mark you, I would not be elsewhere for thousands.' When the signal, No. 39 (to discontinue the engagement) was made, the Signal Lieutenant reported it to him. He continued his walk, and did not appear to take notice of it. The Lieutenant meeting his Lordship at the next turn, asked, 'whether he should repeat it?' Lord Nelson answered, 'No, acknowledge it.' On the officer returning to the poop, his Lordship called after him, 'Is No. 16 (for close action) still hoisted?' the Lieutenant answering in the affirmative, Lord Nelson said, 'Mind you keep it so.' He now walked the deck considerably agitated, which was always known by his moving the stump of his right arm. After a turn or two, he said to me, in a quick manner, 'Do you know what's shewn on board of the Commander-in-chief, No. 39?' On asking him what that meant, he answered, 'Why to leave off action.' 'Leave off action,' he repeated, and then added with a shrug, 'Now damn me if I do.' He also observed, I believe to Captain Foley, 'You know, Foley, I have only one eye—I have a right to be blind sometimes;' and then with an archness familiar to his character, putting the glass to his blind eye, he exclaimed, 'I really do not see the signal.' This remarkable signal was, therefore, only acknowledged on board the Elephant, not repeated."[2]

---

[1] Sir Hyde Parker is conceived to have ordered this signal to be made, fearing that under the intensity of the firing the squadron would be defeated, and that from the state of the wind and current, he would be prevented bringing his division to their assistance.

[2] Hon. Colonel Stewart's Narrative.

M. Thiers calls this disregard of Sir Hyde Parker's signal a noble act of imprudence, followed, as it often happens to audacious boldness, by a successful result. " Ce fut là une noble imprudence, suivie, comme il arrive souvent à l'imprudence audacieuse, d'un heureux succès."[1] Dean Pellew, in his Life of Lord Sidmouth, has stated, in reference to the interview which took place between the Premier and Lord Nelson on his return from Copenhagen, that the conversation turning on the circumstance of Nelson having continued the action after the Admiral had made the signal of recall, Mr. Addington told him he was a bold man to disregard the orders of his superior: to which he replied, that any one may be depended upon under ordinary circumstances, but that the man of real value was he who would persevere at all risks, and under the heaviest responsibility; but (he added) in the midst of it all, I depended upon you; for I knew that, happen what might, if I did my duty you would stand by me." The Dean observes, that when relating this anecdote, Mr. Addington used to remark that he felt the confidence thus reposed in him, by such a man, on such an occasion, as one of the highest compliments he had ever received."[2]

Another hour elapsed and the greater part of the Danish line had ceased to fire. The Dannebrog, with which the Elephant had been particularly engaged, was now drifting in flames before the wind, and spreading terror through the enemy's line. At half past three she blew up, but not before our men and boats were actively engaged in endeavouring to save her crew, who were seen throwing themselves from the port-holes. At half past two Lord Nelson sent a Flag of Truce on shore, which was confided to Captain Thesiger, who had a knowledge of Copenhagen and the Danish language.

The firing from the Crown Battery, and from our leading ships did not cease until past three o'clock, when the Danish Adjutant-General Lindholm[3] returning with a Flag of Truce, directed the fire of the battery to be suspended. The action closed after five hours' duration, four of which were warmly contested.

---

[1] Hist. du Consulat. de l'Empire, Tom. ii. Liv. ix. p. 415.
[2] Life of Lord Sidmouth, Vol. i. p. 465.
[3] A Captain in the Danish Navy.

The message sent by Lord Nelson was thus addressed:—

"TO THE BROTHERS OF ENGLISHMEN, THE DANES.

"Lord Nelson has directions to spare Denmark when no longer resisting; but if the firing is continued on the part of Denmark, Lord Nelson will be obliged to set on fire all the floating batteries he has taken, without having the power of saving the brave Danes who have defended them. Dated on board his Britannic Majesty's ship Elephant, Copenhagen Roads, April 2, 1801.

"NELSON AND BRONTÉ.

"Vice-Admiral, under the command of Admiral Sir Hyde Parker."

The Crown Prince of Denmark requested to know more minutely the intention of the message:

"His Royal Highness the Prince Royal of Denmark has sent me, General-Adjutant Lindholm, on board to his Britannic Majesty's Vice-Admiral, the Right Honourable Lord Nelson, to ask the particular object of sending the Flag of Truce."

The Prince received the following reply:—

"TO THE GOVERNMENT OF DENMARK.

"Lord Nelson's object in sending on shore a Flag of Truce is *humanity*; therefore consents that hostilities shall cease till Lord Nelson can take *his* prisoners out of the prizes, and *he* consents to land all the wounded Danes, and to burn or remove *his* prizes. Lord Nelson, with humble duty to his Royal Highness, begs leave to say, that he will ever esteem it the *greatest* victory he ever gained if this Flag of Truce may be the happy forerunner of a lasting and happy union between his most Gracious Sovereign and his Majesty the King of Denmark.

"NELSON AND BRONTÉ.[1]

"Elephant, April 2, 1801."

---

[1] This and the preceding messages are printed from the MS. in Lord Nelson's Papers, and the words in Italics were so marked by Lord Nelson. In connexion with the letter addressed to the Danes, Mr. Ferguson has told an anecdote which must not be omitted here, as it is so strongly characteristic of Nelson's coolness

Lord Nelson also directed the Adjutant-General to the Commander-in-chief, then at anchor four miles off, for conference; by which he gained time for our ships, much crippled, to clear off the shoals. This was an important measure for several of the vessels, and among the rest the Elephant ran aground. Nelson went on board the London, and with the Commander-in-chief, and the Adjutant-General Lindholm was engaged in negotiation for an honourable peace. A suspension of hostilities for twenty-four hours was the result, and the wounded Danes were taken ashore. Nelson, after the conference on board the London, returned to the St. George.

The Surgeon of the Elephant, Mr. Ferguson, has borne his excellent testimony to the conduct of Nelson on this occasion: "At the Battle of Copenhagen (says Mr. Ferguson) I was amongst the companions of the hero. The attempt was arduous in the extreme, no common mind would have dared to conceive it; but it was suited to the exalted enterprise of Lord Nelson. As *his* was the invigorating spirit of the Council that planned the attack, so in the execution *he* only could have commanded success. During the interval that preceded the battle, I could only silently admire, when I saw the first man in all the world spend the hours of the day and night in boats, amidst floating ice, and in the severest weather; and wonder when the light shewed me a path marked by buoys, which had been trackless the preceding evening." Sir Hyde Parker also, in his official dispatch to the Admiralty, says: "Was it possible for me to add any thing to the well-earned renown of Lord Nelson, it would be by asserting, that his exertions, great as they have heretofore been, never were carried to a higher pitch of zeal for his country's service."

The Danish force consisted of six sail of the line, eleven floating batteries, mounting from twenty-six 24-pounders to eighteen 18-pounders, and one bomb-ship, besides schooner gun-vessels. These were supported by the Crown islands, mounting eighty-eight cannon and four sail of the line, moored in the harbour's mouth, and some batteries on the island of

---

and intrepidity. When the writing of it was concluded, a wafer was presented to him to secure it, upon which he immediately remarked, "No; bring me wax, and a match: this is no time to appear hurried and informal."

Amak. Of these vessels, seventeen sail, that is, seven of the line, and ten floating batteries, were sunk, burnt, or taken. Our force consisted of twelve sail of the line, four frigates, four sloops, two fire-ships, and seven bombs. Three of the sail of the line were not in action, being on shore; they were, however, exposed to the fire of the enemy. The killed and wounded on our side amounted to 943. *Killed*: officers, 20; seamen, marines, and soldiers, 234. Total 254. *Wounded*: officers, 48; seamen, marines, and soldiers, 641. Total 689. Among the killed were Captain Mosse[1] of the Monarch, and Captain Riou[2] of the Amazon. For his services in this action Nelson was raised to the dignity of a Viscount. He was also

---

[1] Captain Mosse was the officer commanding the Sandwich at the Nore at the time of the mutiny in 1797. His name is honourably associated with that of Captain Riou on the monument in St. Paul's.

[2] Captain Edward Riou, the officer so highly esteemed by Lord Nelson, was made a Lieutenant, Oct. 28, 1780, and drew upon him deserved attention and regard for his conduct in the Guardian frigate of 44 guns, when conveying stores to the British Settlement at Botany Bay towards the close of the year 1789. This vessel was saved by the cool and intrepid behaviour of her Commander, when she had struck on an island of ice, and was taken, after having been the sport of the wind and waves for three weeks, into the Cape of Good Hope. Several of those who were on board of her had quitted the vessel for the preservation of their lives. Being placed in False Bay for repairs, a hurricane came on, and the ill-fated vessel was destroyed. Lieutenant Riou, upon his return to England, was promoted to the rank of Commander, and made Post Captain in 1791. In 1793, he commanded the Rose, 28 guns, and afterwards distinguished himself in the Beaulieu frigate by his services in the West Indies, whence he was compelled to return by the ill state of his health in August, 1795. His health restored, he was appointed to the Amazon of 38 guns in 1799, and served with Nelson in the attack on Copenhagen. Here death put an end to his career, but his merits have been duly appreciated by his country, and recorded on his monument in St. Paul's Cathedral. Lord Nelson was very much pleased with the order and condition of Captain Riou's frigate, and the very superior discipline and seamanship exhibited by her on the day of action. The Hon. Colonel Stewart tells us the Captain was killed by a raking shot when the Amazon shewed her stern to the Trekroner. "He was sitting on a gun, encouraging his men, and had then been wounded by a splinter. He had expressed himself grieved at being thus obliged to retreat, and nobly observed, 'What will Nelson think of us?' His clerk was killed by his side; and by another shot, several of the marines, while hauling on the mainbrace, shared the same fate. Riou then exclaimed, 'Come then, my boys, let us die all together!' The words were scarcely uttered, when the fatal shot severed him in two. Thus, in an instant, was the British service deprived of one of its greatest ornaments, and society of a character of singular worth, resembling the heroes of romance."

appointed, on the 21st of April, Commander-in-chief in the Baltic, and received the thanks of both Houses of Parliament.

Among the Nelson Papers I find the following certificate of the number of prisoners taken on this occasion:

"These are to certify the principal Officers and Commissioners of his Britannic Majesty's Navy, that there were on board of his Danish Majesty's ships, hulks, and praams, which were taken in the action of the 2nd of April with the British squadron, 3500 men. In witness hereof, signed by us,

"JACOB ARENFELDT,
"HANS LEMMING,
"NIELS WEST ANDRESEN,
"Captains in the service of His Danish Majesty.

"Copenhagen, May 7th, 1801."

On the evening of the battle Lord Nelson wrote a brief account of it to Lady Hamilton:—

"St. George, April 2nd, 1801. 8 o'clock at Night.

"My dearest Friend, that same Deity who has on many occasions protected Nelson, has once more crowned his endeavours with complete success. The difficulty of getting at the Danes from sand-banks was our greatest enemy, for, from that event, it took us between four or five hours to take all their floating batteries—this made the battle severe. The Prince Royal of Denmark was a spectator, and nearly killed. When all the flower of the Danish marine was in the possession of your friend, I sent a flag of truce on shore, with a kind note, which instantly brought off the Adjutant-General of his Royal Highness with a civil message, only wishing to know the precise meaning of my flag of truce, to say that the fire of the State of Denmark was stopped, and that the officer sent would agree to any cessation of hostilities I pleased. This was not very inconvenient to me as the Elephant had run on shore alongside a 74 and two or three floating batteries. All our ships behaved well, and some of them have lost many men. Poor Captain Riou has lost his life. A better officer or better man never existed. In short, of 18 sail, large and

Lord Nelson to his Guardian angel
From my best Cable tho' I'm forc'd to part
I leave my Anchor in my Angels heart
Love like a Pilot shall the pledge defend
and for a Buoy his Sacrament give her And

Answer of Lord N's Guardian angel
Go where you list, each thought of Angels Soul
Shall follow you from Indus to the Pole
East, west, North, South, our minds shall never part
and Angels loadstone shall be Nelsons heart
Farewell and over the wide wide Sea
Bright Glory, course pursue
and adverse winds to Love of me
prove fair to fame and you,

and when the dreaded hour of battle nigh
your Angels heart which trembles at a sigh
by your Superior danger bolder grown
Shall dauntless place itself before your own
happy thrice happy should her fond heart prove
a Shield to Valour Constancy & Love

St George April 2nd 1801 9 o'Clock at night
very tired after a hard fought Battle,

small, some are taken, some sunk, some burnt, in the good old way. I do not know how soon Sir Hyde Parker may send to England, and I must write to several persons, and am not a little tired, for I have scarcely slept one moment from the 24th of last month. May the heavens bless you. Remember me kindly to Sir William, the Duke, Lord William, and all our friends. Ever your affectionate and attached friend,

"NELSON AND BRONTÉ."

Although greatly fatigued by his extraordinary exertions for several days preceding this hard fought engagement, his attachment to Lady Hamilton was exhibited in the following lines, which are printed from his own autograph, having alterations of words, and emendations made in the course of composition.[1] It has been doubted whether some lines formerly published, as having been written by Lord Nelson, were in reality emanations of his muse, no other effusions of the kind from his pen being known. The following lines, however, so peculiarly marked and attested as to the time at which they were written, place his efforts in this line beyond question:—

"LORD NELSON TO HIS GUARDIAN ANGEL.

"From my best cable tho' I'm forced to part,
I leave my anchor in my Angel's heart:
Love, like a pilot, shall the pledge defend,
And for a prong his happiest quiver lend.

"ANSWER OF LORD NELSON'S GUARDIAN ANGEL.

"*Go where you list*, each thought of Angel's (Emma's) soul
Shall follow you from Indus to the Pole:
East, west, north, south, our minds shall never part,
Your Angel's loadstone shall be Nelson's heart.
*Farewell*, and o'er the wide, wide sea,
  Bright glory's course pursue,
And adverse winds to love and me,
  Prove fair to *fame* and you.

"And when the dreaded hour of battle's nigh,
Your Angel's heart, which trembles at a sigh,

---

[1] See Fac-simile.

> By your *superior danger* bolder grown
> Shall dauntless place itself before your own
> Happy, thrice happy, should her fond heart prove
> A shield to *Valour, Constancy,* and *Love.*"

"St. George, April 2nd, 1801, 9 o'clock at night; very tired after a hard fought battle."

On the 3rd, Lord Nelson wrote an account of the battle formally to Sir Hyde Parker, which was printed in the London Gazette of April 15th, together with Sir H. Parker's Dispatches, in which Nelson's services are properly noticed. To the Hon. Henry Addington[1] Lord Nelson wrote a particular detail,[2] in accordance with a wish which the Premier had expressed to his Lordship. It is a document displaying great sagacity and tact in diplomacy with the Crown Prince of Denmark; but the principal points are alluded to in the subsequent private letters to Lady Hamilton:—

"April 5th, 1801.

"My dearest Friend,

"I am really tired out. Would to God it was all over, and I safely landed in England. On the 3rd I was sent on shore to talk to the Prince Royal. I believe I told him such truths as seldom reach the ears of princes. The people received me as they always have done; and even the stairs of the palace were crowded, huzzaing, and saying, God bless Lord Nelson. I rather believe these kind salutations were not very pleasing to the Royal ears, nor Count Bernstorff,[3] to whom I gave a very broad hint that his proceedings were very foolish. However, he was very civil. The Prince, upon many points, seemed to quake; for on his question, 'for what is the British fleet come into the Baltic?' my answer was not to be misunderstood:—'To crush the formidable armament, of which Denmark is to contribute her part, preparing against Great Britain.' However, it has brought forward a negotiation; and if they have not enough, we must try and get at their arsenal and city, that will sicken them if they have not

---

[1] Afterwards Lord Sidmouth.

[2] This will be found in the Dispatches and Letters, Vol. iv. p. 332, printed from an autograph in the Sidmouth Papers.

[3] Danish Minister for Foreign Affairs.

had enough. The carnage was dreadful on board all their vessels. I saw on shore a Captain Biller, now a Commodore, who commanded a Danish frigate at Naples; he inquired kindly after you and Sir William; he had often been at your house; aye, who had not that happiness? for you ever was, and ever I am sure will be good. You must know you have been in the battle: for your two pictures, one done by Miss Knight, crowning the Rostral Column, the other done at Dresden (I call them my Guardian Angels; and I believe there would be more virtue in the prayers of Santa Emma, than any saint in the whole Calendar of Rome), I carried on board the Elephant with me, and they are safe, and so am I, not a scratch. To-day I have been obliged to write a letter to Lord St. Vincent, which I hope will touch his heart. God knows it has mine; it was recommending to his protecting hand the widows and orphans of those brave men who lost their lives for their King and country under my orders. It positively made my heart run out of my eyes—it brought fresh to my recollection, that only when I spoke to them all, and shook hands with every Captain, wishing them all with laurel crowns, alas! too many are covered with cypress. The Commander-in-chief has just told me that the vessel goes to England this night if possible. May the heavens bless you, &c. &c.

"NELSON AND BRONTÉ.

"My best regards to Sir William, the Duke, Lord William, and all my friends. Kindest regards to Mrs. Nelson, if she is with you, which I hope she is."

The statement herein made of the manner in which Lord Nelson was received by the Danish people, is completely at variance with what Colonel Stewart has written. He says, "On the 4th (the 3rd, however, was the day, as seen by Lord Nelson's letter on the 5th to Lady Hamilton) his Lordship left the ship, accompanied by Captains Hardy and Fremantle, and was received with all possible attention from the Prince. The populace shewed a mixture of admiration, curiosity, and displeasure. A strong guard secured his safety, and appeared necessary to keep off the mob, whose rage, although mixed with admiration at his thus trusting himself among them, was necessarily to be expected. The events of the 2nd had plunged the whole town into a state of terror, astonishment, and mourning; the oldest inhabitant had never seen a shot fired in anger at his native country. The battle of that day, and the subsequent return of the wounded to the care of their friends on the 3rd, were certainly not events that could induce the Danish nation to receive their conqueror, on this occasion, with much cordiality. It perhaps savoured of rashness in Lord Nelson thus early to risk himself amongst them; but with him his country's cause was paramount to all personal consideration." But the Hon. Henry Addington, in moving the vote of thanks in the House of Commons, adverts particularly to the reception Lord Nelson received from the populace. He said, "Lord Nelson in consequence went on shore, and was received by a brave and generous people—for brave they had shewn themselves in their defence, and generous in the oblivion of their loss—with the loudest and most general acclamations." And Mr. Sheridan happily remarked:—"On the subject more immediately before the House, only one sentiment could be entertained, that of admiration and gratitude, which words were inadequate to express, particularly towards that noble Lord, who could gain the plaudits and acclamations of a vanquished enemy."

TO LADY HAMILTON.

"My dearest Friend,

"I have just got hold of the verses wrote by Miss Knight; they belong to you; the latter part is a little applicable to my present situation. It is dreadfully cold. I am sure, from our communication with the shore yesterday, that it is only fear of Russia that prevents all our disputes being settled. These people must sooner or later submit, and I long to get to Revel before the Russian fleet can join that of Cronstadt; but my dear friend, we are very lazy. We Mediterranean people are not used to it. Some further propositions are to come off this day, but I fear it blows too hard.

"NELSON AND BRONTÉ.

"April 6th. 7 in the morning. I am obliged to stop, as I know not exactly the moment of the vessel's sailing.

"No. of our Lottery Tickets: —2951—9308—42002—50416. You can send and inquire our luck."

The following is from Mr. Vansittart to Lord Nelson, who, as we have seen, preceded him to negotiate with Denmark, but was unsuccessful in his mission. At the time of his departure for England, it appears that the mode of attack and conduct of affairs had been discussed with the Commander-in-chief, Lord Nelson, and Mr. Vansittart:—

"London, April 8th, 1801.

"My dear Lord,

"The solicitude you expressed that I should undertake the explanation of the reasons which induced you to propose a deviation from the original plan of operation designed for the fleet, would have been a motive with me of the strongest kind to enter into as early and complete a vindication of them as possible, if I had been in no respect personally interested in the question. But as your wish at parting with me, that I should meet with a foul wind, was completely gratified, it was not till last Wednesday that we were able to get ashore at Leith. I got to town on Saturday, and went immediately to the Admiralty, but not finding Lord St. Vincent in town I called on Mr. Addington, to whom I gave a full account of what had passed in Sir Hyde Parker's cabin on the 23rd ulto. I have the pleasure to assure you that he was fully satisfied with the propriety of your advice, and of Sir Hyde Parker's ultimate resolution, and that he considers your readiness to take on yourself the responsibility attaching on a deviation from your instructions, as not the least eminent among the services which you have rendered your country in so many years of glory. Mr. Addington has since communicated the whole affair to Lord St. Vincent, who equally acquiesces in the propriety of the determination, so that whatever may be the event of the plan (which Providence must decide) you will have the satisfaction of meeting with the approbation of those who have the best right to judge of it; and I need not say, may depend on the confidence of the public.

"Had not our attention been necessarily turned to a subject of more immediate importance, I should have been happy in the opportunity of suggesting to your Lordship some ideas more directly connected with the business on which I was sent abroad: I mean the measures which it might be proper to adopt in case Denmark or either of the other Northern Courts should apply to the Commander-in-chief for an armistice, or make any other overtures towards accommodation, either in consequence of those successes which such a fleet under such leaders may be expected to obtain, or of any change of political sentiment. In case the Admiral has received no special instructions on this subject, it appears to me, that he could do no more than receive any proposition which may be made, and transmit them to England; granting at the same time, if he shall think it advisable, a cessation of arms on such conditions as may enforce the observance of good faith, and secure the conclusion of a treaty conformable to the interests of Great Britain. What pledge it might be proper in each instance to require, you will be best able to judge if the case should occur, but it seems to be essential that the fleet of the Power applying should either be directed to take its orders from the British Admiral, or disarmed and laid up in such a situation as to be nearly at your discretion. It might, for instance, be required that the Danish fleet should retire into the harbour at Copenhagen, that the floating batteries and fortified islands at the entrance should be given up, and the battery on Amack Point, and that under the citadel on the beach, together with the guns of the citadel commanding the harbour, should be dismounted. Similar measures with respect to Carlscroon or Cronstadt might be pursued, but as the surrender of those fortresses would not be attended with the disgrace and irritation necessarily consequent on the capitulation of the capital of a kingdom, there would be less objection to insisting on this being absolutely put into your hands. I am the more induced to submit these ideas to your Lordship's consideration, as I think it very probable that some overture may come, either from Denmark or Sweden in case you should be able to give such a blow to the Russian navy, and may deliver them from the fear of their powerful ally, and at the same time add to the terror of the British arms. With respect to an attempt on Cronstadt (judging from such plans as I have), I cannot think the difficulties insuperable, especially if the means taken to choke up the Northern Channel are ineffectual, which, from its breadth, I think they must be. It is true that very shallow water is marked at the eastern end, but from the pains taken by the Russians to destroy the passage, I apprehend they must in reality know it to be practicable for large ships. I was more confirmed in this opinion from finding that Etches, who seems the most active and intelligent adventurer I ever met with, and who served some time in the Russian fleet, thinks an attack there by no means difficult. Of that, however, you will before this time have better means of judging.

"Of domestic affairs I have little to say. The King is getting well; we hope securely, but too slowly for the wishes of the nation. Mr. Addington, who has been very ill, is nearly recovered. Believe me, my Lord, with the sincerest wishes for your success and happy return, faithfully

"Yours,
"N. VANSITTART."

The following "minute of conversation with his Royal Highness the Prince Royal of Denmark" corrected by Nelson himself cannot but be interesting here:—

*"Minute of a Conversation with his Royal Highness, the Prince Royal of Denmark.*

"His Royal Highness began the conversation by saying how happy he was to see me, and thanked me for my humanity to the wounded Danes. I then said, that it was to me, and would be the greatest affliction to every man in England, from the King to the lowest person, to think that Denmark had fired on the British flag, and become leagued with her enemies. His Royal Highness stopped me by saying that Admiral Parker had declared war against Denmark. This I denied, and requested his Royal Highness to send for the papers, and he would find the direct contrary, and that it was the farthest from the thoughts of the British

Admiral. I then asked if his Royal Highness would permit me to speak my mind freely on the present situation of Denmark? to which he having acquiesced, I stated to him the sensation which was caused in England by such an unnatural alliance with, at the present moment, the furious enemy of England. His answer was, that when he made the alliance, it was for the protection of their trade, and that Denmark would never be the enemy of England, and that the Emperor of Russia was not the enemy of England when this treaty was formed—that he never would join Russia against England, and his declaration to that effect was the cause of the Emperor's (I think he said) sending away his Minister,—that Denmark was a trading nation, and had only to look to the protection of its lawful commerce. His Royal Highness then enlarged on the impossibility of Danish ships under convoy having on board any contraband trade; but to be subjected to be stopped, even a Danish fleet, by a pitiful privateer, and that she should search all the ships and take out of the fleet any vessels she might please, was what Denmark could not permit. To this my answer was simply, What occasion for convoy to fair trade? To which he answered, Did you find any thing in the convoy of the Freja? and that no Commander could tell what contraband goods might be in the convoy, &c. &c. and as to merchants, they would always sell what was most saleable; and as to swearing to property, I could get any thing sworn to which I pleased. I then said, Suppose that England, which she never will, was to consent to this freedom and nonsense of navigation, I will tell your Royal Highness what the result would be—ruination to Denmark; for the present commerce of Denmark with the warring powers was half the neutral carrying trade, and any merchant in Copenhagen would tell you the same. If all this freedom was allowed, Denmark would not have more than the sixth part, for the State of Passenburgh was as good as the State of Denmark in that case; and it would soon be said, we will not be stopped in the Sound, our flag is our protection, and Denmark would lose a great source of her present revenue; and that the Baltic would soon change its name to the Russian Sea. He said, this was a delicate subject, to which I replied, That his Royal Highness had permitted me to speak out. He then said, Pray answer me a question. For what is the British fleet come into the Baltic? My answer, To crush a most formidable and unprovoked coalition against Great Britain. He then went on to say, that his uncle (George III.) had been deceived, that it was a misunderstanding, and that nothing should ever make him take a part against Great Britain, for that it could not be his interest to see us crushed, nor, he trusted, ours to see him; to which I acquiesced. I then said, there could be no doubt of the hostility of Denmark, for if her fleet had been joined with Russia and Sweden, they would assuredly have gone into the North Sea, menaced the Court of England, and probably have joined the French if they had been able. His Royal Highness said his ships never should join any power against England, but it required not much argument to satisfy him he could not help it, by his treaty. In speaking of the pretended union of the Northern Powers, I could not help saying that his Royal Highness must be sensible that it was nonsense to talk of a mutual protection of trade with a Power who had none, and that he must be sensible that the Emperor of Russia would never have thought of offering to protect the trade of Denmark, if he had not had hostility against Great Britain. He said repeatedly, I have offered to-day, and do offer, my mediation between Great Britain and Russia. My answer was, A mediator must be at peace with both parties. You must settle your matter with Great Britain. At present you are leagued with our enemies, and are considered naturally as a part of the effective force to fight us. Talking much on this subject, his Royal Highness said, What must I do to make myself equal? Answer,—Sign an alliance with Great Britain, and join your fleet to ours. His Royal Highness then said, Russia will go to war with us, and my desire as a commercial nation is to be at peace with all the world. I told him, he knew the offer of Great Britain, either to join us or disarm. And pray, Lord Nelson, what do you call disarming? My answer was, that I was not authorized to give an opinion on the subject; but I considered it as not having on foot any force beyond the customary establishment. Question: And do you consider the guard-ships in the Sound as beyond that common establishment? Answer: I do not. Question: We have always had five sail of the line in the Cattegat and coast of Norway? Answer: I am not authorized to define what is exactly disarming, but I do not think such a force will be allowed. His Royal Highness: When all Europe is in such a dreadful state of confusion, it is absolutely necessary that States should be on their guard. Answer: Your Royal Highness knows the offers of England to keep 20 sail of the line in the Baltic. He then said, I am sure my intentions are very much misunderstood. To which I replied, that Sir Hyde Parker had authorized me to say that upon certain conditions his Royal Highness might have an opportunity of explaining his sentiments at the Court of London. I am not authorized to say on what conditions exactly. Question: But what do you think? Answer: First, a free entry of the British fleet into Copenhagen, and the free use of every thing we may want from it. Before I could get on, he replied quick, That you shall have with pleasure. The next is, whilst this explanation is going on, a total suspension of your treaties with Russia. These, I believe, are the foundation on which Sir Hyde Parker only can build other articles for his justification in suspending his orders, which are plain and positive. His Royal Highness then desired me to repeat what I had said, which having done, he thanked me for my open conversation; and I having made an apology if I had said any thing which he might think too strong, his Royal Highness very handsomely did the same, and we parted, he saying that he hoped we would cease from hostilities to-morrow, as on such an important occasion he must call a Council."

On the 9th an armistice was agreed upon, and the terms transmitted to the Admiralty by the Hon. Lieutenant-Colonel Stewart. They were printed in the London Gazette of April 21st, and are in autograph in the Sidmouth Papers. The following was adressed by Lord Nelson to Lady Hamilton:

"April 9th, 1801.

"My dearest Friend, you will perceive that I am become a negotiator, a bad one no doubt, but perhaps as upright a one as any England could send. Count Bernstorff has taken to his bed, and was not *able* (willing) to make me a visit. Yesterday he had sent off some vague notes to Sir Hyde Parker, and I sent him a message that I was ashamed of his conduct. Did he take Sir Hyde Parker for a fool, to play off his ministerial duplicity, for it would not suit a British Admiral, who came to treat with their hearts in their hands? My object is to make Denmark our friend by conciliation, now we have shewn we can beat them. In mercy spare. In my opinion, nations like individuals are to be won more by acts of kindness than cruelty. We could burn Copenhagen. Would that win an affection towards England? The Armistice has tied up Denmark, and let us loose against her Allies, for which I think Russia will go to war with her. If our Ministry do not approve of my humane conduct, I have begged they would allow me to retire, and under the shade of a chesnut-tree at BRONTE, where the din of war will not reach my ears, do I hope to solace myself, make my people happy and prosperous, and by giving my advice (if asked), enable his Sicilian Majesty, *my benefactor*, to be more than ever respected in the Mediterranean, and to have peace with all the Barbary States. This, my dear friend, you may write to the Queen, and tell Prince Castelcicala. I hope the King and Acton will take care of my estate. Yesterday I was shut up in a room in the palace half wet through—it was a hard task to make them, in plain terms, suspend the treaty of the famed confederacy against England. What will Paul say to all this? I am worn out, no words can express the horror of my situation. The Prince has been very kind in expressions towards me, and said the world would think my humane conduct, on the late melancholy occasion, placed me higher than all my victories, brilliant as they had been. I dined with the Prince, as did Colonel Stewart, Captains Foley and Fremantle."

"*9 o'clock at night.*

" Having concluded the Treaty of Armistice with Denmark, I got on board between six and seven, and found to my inexpressible satisfaction, all your truly kind and affectionate letters. Colonel Stewart is going home with the Armistice, and I have wrote to Mr. Addington, that if he does not approve of it, I beg to be superseded, and to be allowed to retire, for God knows I want rest, and a true friend to comfort me. I have scarcely time to turn round; all here hang on my shoulders; but I am trying to finish, and hope to be home next month. My health will not allow me to remain here all the summer. I hope, I assure you, to retire. Why should I fag my life out? I am not Commander-in-chief.[1] None of my gallant Lieutenants are promoted, but I enjoy that reward, the approbation of such a friend as you and Sir William, which is all I require. I hope to get Sir Hyde to let me pass the Channel the moment the wind suits, for we are losing time, and I want to be home. With best regards to the Duke, Lord William, &c. &c.

" NELSON AND BRONTÉ."

" Your friend was on shore to-day to receive the ratification of the treaty of armistice. I received, as a warrior, all the praises which could gratify the ambition of the vainest man, and the thanks of the nation from the King downwards for my humanity in saving the town from destruction. Nelson is a warrior, but will not be a butcher. I am sure, could you have seen the adoration and respect, you would have cried for joy."

Lord Nelson also wrote to Lord Minto, and Sir Brooke Boothby, Bart. To the former he says: " Before you condemn the Armistice, hear all the reasons: they are weighty and most important. Without it we should have gone no further this year, and with it not half so far as I wish." To the latter: " I but wish to finish Paul, and then retire for ever." Soon after this Lord Nelson heard of the death of the Emperor Paul, as on the 11th he wrote thus to Lady Hamilton :—

" April 11th, 1801.

" My dearest Friend,

" I have answered the King of Naples's letter, and have told him that in six weeks after the peace, I hope to be at his feet, for that it is my intention to go to Bronté. I can

---

[1] He was appointed only April 21st.

assure you that I am fixed to live a country life, and to have many (I hope) years of comfort, which God knows, I never yet had—only moments of happiness; but the case shall be altered. I tell you, my dear good friend, all my little plans, for I know you did, and I hope always will, take a lively interest in my happiness. The death of Paul may prevent the shedding of more human blood in the north. The moment that is clear I shall not remain one minute, and at all events I hope to be in England in May. We have reports that the Swedish fleet is above the Shallows, distant five or six leagues. All our fellows are longing to be at them, and so do I, as great a boy as any of them, for I consider this as being at school, and going to England as going home for the holidays, therefore I really long to finish my task. I am glad to hear that Sir William's pictures sold so well, but believe me, before I would have sold a picture of you, I would have starved. I wonder Sir William could do it. I cannot write politics, as my letter probably will be read, but I have to beg you will remember me most affectionately to our friends of all ages and sexes, therefore I cannot mention names. I will endeavour and know to-morrow if you may safely write to Copenhagen.

" Ever yours affectionately."

Mr. Osborn, Secretary to the Commander-in-chief, was appointed to the agency of the prizes taken at the battle; but difficulties arising, he declined the appointment. Lord Nelson's friend, and agent for the prizes at the Nile, Mr. Davison, was subsequently appointed sole agent, as appears from the following to Hely Addington, Esq.

"St. James's Square, 8th May, 1801.

" Sir,

" Having been appointed sole agent for the Baltic Squadron under the command of Admiral Sir Hyde Parker, for the prizes taken from the Danes in the engagement of the 2nd April off Copenhagen, I beg the favour of you to inform the Lords Commissioners of his Majesty's Treasury that I am prevented applying in the regular manner to the Navy Board for the usual allowance of head money, for want of the vouchers required, which could not be obtained by reason of the prisoners having been immediately set ashore at Copenhagen, and that the only paper transmitted to me to ascertain the number of persons on board the ships and floating batteries at the commencement of the action is a letter from Lord Nelson, stating that for the reasons above-mentioned their number could not be actually ascertained, but from the best accounts they had been able to obtain, the number of men on board the eighteen ships and vessels which struck to his Majstey's squadron under his Lordship's orders, did not amount to less than six thousand men.

"As it does not appear possible that regular vouchers can now be procured, I beg to solicit on behalf of Admiral Sir Hyde Parker, Vice-Admiral Lord Nelson, Rear-Admiral Graves, the several Commanders, Officers and ships' companies, that their Lordships will be pleased to dispense with the regular vouchers (as was done in the case of the victory of the Nile), and give directions to the Navy Board to pay the head money upon the authority of Lord Nelson's letter.

"I have the honour to be,
"Sir,
"Your most obedient humble servant,
"ALEX. DAVISON,
"Sole Agent.

"Extract from Lord Nelson's letter :—

'St. George, 22nd April, 1801.

'The Danes being all landed without any declaration as to numbers, yet this can easily be got over by a dispensing order—not less than six thousand men can be allowed, and that is under the number.

'NELSON AND BRONTÉ.

'To Alex. Davison, Esq.'
"Hely Addington, Esq. &c. &c. &c. Treasury."

The correspondence with Lady Hamilton continues :—

"April 13th, Copenhagen.

"My dearest Friend,

"All your letters up to the 4th April I received with inexpressible pleasure last night. By this occasion of the post

I only acknowledge them. I wrote you yesterday, but as they go a round it may be a day later before you receive them. As soon as we are over the grounds in about two days, I shall write you fully. I love you for your attachment to your dear Queen,[1] and your resolution to live and die with her—she deserves it all, for her faithful affection to you is beyond all description. I expect to be in England in May, but let what will happen, for I do not believe we shall fire another shot in the Baltic, you will hear that I have been so careful not to increase the strength of our opponents, who certainly *died* hard, that I have only put down six sail of the line instead of seven, but a ship more or a ship less cannot add to my reputation, and it might injure a poor Danish officer, which I do not, thank God, want to do. I cannot write politics. Many thanks for the songs. John Bull has always had faith in me, and I am grateful. I shall write you more by the brig Captain Fancourt[2] desires his regards, as I do mine, to Sir William, the Duke, Lord William, and all our real friends."

"April 14th, 1801.

"My dearest Friend,

"I was in hopes that I should have got off some Copenhagen china to have sent you by Captain Bligh,[3] who was one of my seconds on the 2nd. He is a steady seaman, and a good and brave man. If he calls, I hope you will admit him, I have half promised him that pleasure, and if he can get hold of the china he is to take charge of it. I have this day pressed on Lord St. Vincent my leave to retire, and told him

---

[1] The Queen of Naples.

[2] Robert Devereux Fancourt, in the early part of his career, served in the East Indies, under Sir Richard Bickerton, Bart., and was made Post Captain in 1790. In the revolutionary war he was employed in protection of the trade in the West Indies and the Mediterranean, and in 1797, served with Lord Duncan in the North Sea, after which he joined Vice-Admiral Dickson's squadron, and thence proceeded with Sir Hyde Parker in the Copenhagen expedition. His vessel, the Agamemnon, however, unfortunately struck upon a shoal, and he was thereby deprived the honour of being engaged on that memorable occasion. He was made Rear-Admiral, April 28, 1808, and a Vice-Admiral, August 12, 1812. He lived to the advanced age of 84 years, dying June 7th, 1826, an Admiral of the Blue.

[3] Captain George Miller Bligh, died Oct. 14, 1834.

I hoped it would be before April was out. If we have peace with Russia, nothing shall keep me a moment, and to prepare for it I have sent to the Prince to request that he will give a general order for my free passage through his dominions in case I land at Lubeck, which is only thirty-eight miles from Gluckstadt on the Elbe.

"Yours,

"NELSON AND BRONTÉ.

"I shall write by the brig Sir Hyde Parker is going to send home. Best regards to Sir William, the Duke, &c. &c. I have wrote by the post. Rev. Mr. Comyn[1] has not joined. I hope he was not in the Invincible."[2]

On this day, Sir Thomas Troubridge, then one of the Lords of the Admiralty, wrote to Lady Hamilton to acquaint her with the death of Paul,[3] by which it appears that Nelson was aware of it prior to its reaching the English Government:—

"April 14th, 1801.

"My dear Lady Hamilton,

"Your great and good friend, magnanimous Paul, is dead, and the private letters from Mecklenburg, *via* Hamburgh, say our fleet is near Lubeck, having destroyed the Danish squadron. I sincerely hope it is true. One letter asserts that Lord Nelson said it was warm work while it lasted.

"The death of our inveterate enemy may give a turn to affairs; it is reported our seamen are released from prison in Russia, and a messenger arrived from Russia last night, which looks well. I cannot say more—burn this.

"Yours, most truly,

"T. TROUBRIDGE."

From the following letter, Nelson appears to have been very anxious to reach England:—

---

[1] Lord Nelson's Chaplain on board the Vanguard at the Battle of the Nile. Nelson solicited of the Lord Chancellor, and obtained for him the Rectory of Bridgeham, in Norfolk.

[2] Rear-Admiral Totty's ship, wrecked going out of Yarmouth Roads.

[3] He was murdered March 24, 1801.

"St. George, April 15th, 1801.

"My dearest Friend,

"I can get nothing here worth your acceptance, but as I know you have a valuable collection of china I send you some of the Copenhagen manufacture, it will bring to your recollection that here your attached friend Nelson fought and conquered. Captain Bligh has promised to take charge of it, and I hope it will reach you safe. Our guns are all out of the ship in order to get her over the shallow water. My Commander-in-chief has left me, but if there is any work to do, I dare say they will wait for me. *Nelson will be first.* Who can stop him? I have much to say, and before one month is over, I hope to tell you in person. You may get out by management from Troubridge whether my leave is come out, if it is not, I will go without it, for here I will not stay. I have just got a passport from the Prince, which I shall use when occasion requires.

"Ever yours, most faithfully,
"NELSON AND BRONTÉ."

Adjutant-General Lindholm sent to Lord Nelson the passport alluded to in the preceding letter:—

"Copenhagen, April 15th, 1801.

"Sir,

"I have the honour to send your Lordship a German passport for your intended journey; but I hope to see your Lordship on board the St. George before you set out. His Royal Highness has ordered me to present his compliments to your Lordship.

"We hear to-day the interesting news from Hamburgh, that the Emperor of Russia has offered to give up the English vessels, and the English goods detained in Russia, when England will give up the Russian, Danish, and Swedish vessels in her ports. I hope that the northern business will soon be settled. I am, with the greatest esteem, my Lord,

"Your most obedient humble servant,
"LINDHOLM.

"Right Hon. Lord Nelson,
  "Vice-Admiral."

On the same day he wrote to his brother, Maurice Nelson :—

"April 15th, Copenhagen Roads.

"My dear Brother,

"I am glad to find you are in possession of Mr. Hartwell's place; but the neglect shewn me in not having placed you at the Navy Board, is what I cannot forget. We shall see whether the new Administration treats me as ill as the old. I think very likely. Lord St. Vincent will either take this late business up with a very high hand, or he will depress it; but how they will manage about Sir Hyde I cannot guess. I am afraid much will be said about him in the public papers; but not a word shall be drawn from me, for God knows they may make him Lord Copenhagen if they please, it will not offend me. I only want justice for myself, which I have never yet had, and leave to go home for the re-establishment of my health. What has been done with Peyton?[1] His son is a fine lad, and behaves well; say so if you see him. With my best regards to Mrs. Nelson, believe me ever,

"Your affectionate brother,

"NELSON AND BRONTÉ."

He again removed to the Elephant. To Lady Hamilton he writes :—

"Elephant, Baltic, April 17th, 1801.

"My dearest friend,

"Once more I am shifted to the Elephant, and Captain Foley is so good as to be plagued with me. St. George cannot yet be got over the shallows; and as the Swedish fleet was at sea the 14th, Sir Hyde desired me to shift my flag. For my part, I do not expect to fire another gun; the Swedes cannot be such fools as to wait for us. My mind is fixed to be in England the latter end of May; I hope much sooner. Nothing shall keep me here. I cannot write politics, therefore can only assure you that I am ever yours,

"NELSON AND BRONTÉ."

---

[1] This officer died at Priesland, near Lymington, August 2, 1809, a Rear-Admiral of the Red.

"Elephant, April 20th, off Carlscrona.

"Yesterday, my dearest Friend, we saw the Swedish squadron, not at sea, but shut up very snug in their harbour, inside of their batteries; and what is worse for us, their numerous rocks. Thus all our hopes of getting alongside them is at an end; they will not trust themselves out again this summer. We are, at least I am, anxiously waiting for news from England, and expect that we shall be ordered to abstain from hostilities against Russia. In that case, if a ship cannot be given me to go to England, I shall land at Lubeck, only one day's journey to Hamburgh, and take a packet to convey me over. Should the worst happen, and that we have no cessation with Russia, all must be finished by the middle of May, and then I will not stay half an hour. Why should I? No real friend would advise me to it, and for what others say I care not a farthing. My health, and other circumstances, imperiously demand it. I have given up in reason every thing to my country, but the late Ministers have done less for me than any other man in my situation. The Commanders-in-chief made fortunes by their victories, for which Ministers gave them £1000. a year more than poor Nelson, higher title in the Peerage, and promoted their followers, whilst mine were all neglected, and now, what even the custom of the service and common justice gives me, is attempted to be withheld from me by force of money and influence. The 25th of May is fixed for the day of trial,[1] and it is seriously my interest to be in England on that day. I have this day wrote more pressingly, if possible, to Troubridge, about my leave of absence for home. I will go, that is certain.

"Kindest regards and affections administered to those of our friends and acquaintances as the case requires.

"Yours, &c. &c."

Mr. Brierly, the Master of the Bellona says, "Lord Nelson received advice, per letter, from Sir Hyde Parker, of a Swedish squadron being seen by one of our look-out frigates. The moment he received the account, he ordered a boat to be manned; and without even waiting for a boat cloak (though

[1] The Question of Prize Money with Earl St. Vincent.

you must suppose the weather pretty sharp here at this season of the year), and having to row about twenty-four miles with the wind and current against him, jumped into her, and ordered me to go with him, I having been on board that ship, to remain till she had got over the grounds. All I had ever seen or heard of him could not half so clearly prove to me the singular and unbounded zeal of this truly great man. His anxiety in the boat, for near six hours (lest the fleet should have sailed before he got on board one of them, and lest we should not catch the Swedish squadron) is beyond all conception. I will quote some expressions in his own words. It was extremely cold, and I wished him to put on a great coat of mine which was in the boat :—' No, I am not cold; my anxiety for my country will keep me warm. Do you not think the fleet has sailed ?' 'I should suppose not, my Lord.' ' If they are, we shall follow them to Carlscrona in the boat, by God!' I merely state this to shew how his thoughts must have been employed. The idea of going in a small boat, rowing six oars, without a single morsel of any thing to eat or drink, the distance of about fifty leagues, must convince the world, that every other earthly consideration than that of serving his country was totally banished from his thoughts. We reached our fleet by midnight, and went on board the Elephant, Captain Foley, where I left his Lordship in the morning, and returned to my ship. In our late action, nothing but his superior abilities, as well as bravery, could have given us so decided a victory, when four of our ships ran aground, and in the heat of battle."[1]

[1] Naval Chronicle, Vol. v. p. 452.

## CHAPTER II.

### 1801.

AMONG many letters of congratulation addressed to Lord Nelson on his success at Copenhagen that from his Royal Highness the Duke of Clarence, was not the least acceptable:—

"Bushy House, Monday Night, April 20th, 1801.

" Dear Nelson,

" I am to acknowledge yours of the 4th instant, which business and different engagements prevented me from answering by Captain Otway,[1] and this evening I have received

[1] This gallant officer, a native of Tipperary, evinced strong predilection for the Naval service at an early age, rejected his father's offer to purchase for him a Cornetcy in the Dragoons, and entered the Navy in 1784, at the age of 13, on board the Elizabeth of 74 guns, commanded by Sir Richard Kingsmill, Bart. He served in the West Indies and on the coast of Guinea, and was in 1794 a Lieutenant in the Impregnable in Lord Howe's memorable action, where he so distinguished himself by his intrepidity that he was offered by his Commander, Rear-Admiral Caldwell, the position of First Lieutenant. This, however, he had the modesty and good sense to decline, as it might excite jealous feelings among his deserving messmates with whom he lived on good terms. Rear-Admiral Caldwell being moved into the Majestic, Lieutenant Robert Waller Otway accompanied him. He soon after attained the rank of Commander, took La Belle Creole, a large French schooner, carrying a banditti to be employed against the inhabitants of St. Pierre, and for this capture the French Royalists of Martinique presented him with a sword of the value of 200 guineas. He made other prizes, performed important services, and received the thanks of the House of Assembly. These services are detailed in Marshall's Naval Biography (Vol. i. p. 694, et seq.). In 1798 he served in the Gulf of Mexico with Sir Hyde Parker, and was afterwards on the Jamaica station. Accompanying the expedition to the Baltic he was Captain of the Royal George, and afterwards of the London. He was active in the Copenhagen attack, took home the Dispatches, and afterwards commanded the Edgar of 74 guns, in the Channel fleet. He was employed upon the renewal of the war in 1803, distinguishing himself by his ardour in various ships until his health gave way, and was obliged for a time to retire from active service. In 1813, however, he was in the Channel fleet commanding the Ajax, and employed in covering the siege of St. Sebastian. He was made a Rear-Admiral, June 4, 1814, and succeeded Sir William Johnstone Hope as Commander-in-chief on the coast of Scotland in 1818. He received the Freedom of the City of Edinburgh. In 1830 he was made a Vice-Admiral, and an Admiral in 1841. Sir Robert Waller Otway was made a Baronet in 1831, and G.C.B. in 1845; one of

your letter of the 10th, and with your leave will answer them both. The first gave me the most heartfelt pleasure both for public reasons as well as private. I must ever rejoice at the success of my country, and am fully convinced that this is the most decisive and the most brilliant victory that the navy of Great Britain ever gained: believe me it is to me more acceptable because you *my best and oldest friend* was the *hero* that did the act. I cannot help laughing when I hear the d—d fools of our metropolis exclaiming, 'Why is Lord Nelson so much attached to the Duke of Clarence?' When the thanks were moved in the House of Lords, I endeavoured to impress the public mind with the *very great* services you have so repeatedly rendered the King and Country. I am truly happy my old shipmate Tom Foley was your Captain, and I rejoice to find my élève Brisbane[1] has merited your approbation.

"In answer to your second letter, it is a matter of satisfaction to me to find we think alike upon the Northern Expedition. I was from the beginning convinced, beyond Copenhagen, without a truce, the fleet could not proceed to Revel. I think there will *now* be no necessity, as Paul, thank God, is no more. To the principle of searching neutrals I am a friend, but cannot help lamenting that the arrogance and ignorance of our former Ministers should have brought that matter to issue which ought to have been left at rest.

"I am sorry you complain in both your letters of your health, and hope matters will permit your speedy return home, indeed I sincerely wish on every account for peace, but on no one more than that you may have time to recover, and be ready to head the fleets of this country in a future war. Adieu, and take care of yourself. God bless you, and ever believe me in every situation, my dear Nelson,

"Your best and sincerest friend,

the Grooms in Waiting to Her Majesty in 1837, and died suddenly, May 12, 1846, an Admiral of the White, aged 74 years. See Annual Register for 1846, p. 255.

[1] Rear-Admiral Sir Charles Brisbane, K.C.B. who died in 1829.

The Premier also wrote to Lord Nelson on the same day.

#### HON. HENRY ADDINGTON TO LORD NELSON.

"Downing Street, April 20th, 1801.

"My dear Lord,

"You will have heard from Lord St. Vincent how entirely the whole and every part of your Lordship's conduct is approved of by the King, and you must have been informed from various quarters of the impression it has made upon Parliament and the public. It remains for me only to express the sentiments of admiration and of complete satisfaction, with which I contemplate what has passed, under your Lordship's auspices, in the Baltic and at Copenhagen. The transactions in which you had so distinguished a share, and of which, indeed, you were the life and soul, joined to the late event at Petersburgh will, I trust, lead to an honourable accommodation with the Northern Powers; but whilst we hope and expect the best, we must be prepared for the worst; and I am sure that the minds of the people of this country will be at ease whilst your Lordship continues in the Baltic. I must add, that you have gratified and obliged me by your private communications, which I beg you to repeat as frequently as may be consistent with your avocations and convenience. My best wishes on all accounts ever attend you. Believe me to be, with true attachment, my dear Lord, your sincere friend and faithful servant,

"HENRY ADDINGTON."[1]

The King of Naples also wrote to congratulate Lord Nelson on the victory he had obtained :—

"My dear and much esteemed Lord Nelson, I received your welcome letter dated 10th of April, and I am your debtor from that date, owing to you a new and sincere compliment for that glorious day of the above mentioned month, the memorable 2nd, which also will give such advantages to your brave nation and all Europe; and it gives me confidence and hopes of a general and much desired peace. Therefore,

---

[1] Life and Correspondence of Lord Viscount Sidmouth, Vol. i. p. 379.

again receive my cordial rejoicings, and be assured of the great pleasure I shall have to see you again in my kingdoms, where you will find gratitude, esteem, and affection. I beg you also to believe in my feelings, and the part I take in the well merited distinctions which your magnanimous Sovereign has shewn you, and the sensations it must have produced in his Royal and grateful soul for the important service which you have again rendered, and joined to so many others useful and beneficial to your grateful country. I feel the greatest happiness in expressing to you these deeply engraven sentiments which I hope soon by voice to repeat, and to assure you of the constant affection of your

"FERDINAND."

Lieutenant-Colonel Stewart, the bearer of the armistice to England, wrote to Lady Hamilton on his return to Copenhagen as follows:—

"Nelson Arms, Yarmouth, April 23rd, 1801.

"Dear Madam,

"After your having expressed your intentions yesterday of forwarding under my care the picture to Lord Nelson, I feel quite distressed that it was out of my power to wait longer for it than four o'clock yesterday afternoon, having been dismissed by Lord St. Vincent two hours even previous to that time. I feel alarmed at your Ladyship's not thinking me to be a very civil sort of a gentleman, to have thus left town without again calling on you for poor St. Cecilia,[1] but the close manner in which I was kept occupied at the Admiralty, Downing Street, and War Office, after I had the honour of taking leave of Sir William and your Ladyship, really prevented me from so doing. The Favorite sloop of war is, however, now here, expecting to be dispatched with the duplicate of my dispatches to the fleet, and if your Ladyship will send the picture in question to the care of Mr. Stewart, Agent for the Baltic fleet in this town, with directions for its being forwarded by the Favorite, or first safe conveyance, that gentleman will do so with care and with pleasure, for I have been speaking to him on the subject. I am anxious that Lord Nelson should have in his cabin so pretty a *cadeau*,

---

[1] Lady Hamilton's portrait painted by Geo. Romney, R.A.

as I shall thereby frequently have it in *my* power also to admire this interesting fair one. I shall therefore give our noble friend to expect the receipt of poor Cecilia, and must beg that your Ladyship will forward it, for it will, I am confident, give our hero great pleasure, and if you do not, I shall feel convinced that you are angry with me for not having waited for it. You must excuse this scrawl, written during the hasty moment of embarkation, from an inn, and believe me with much truth,

"Your Ladyship's very faithful servant,
"WM. STEWART."

The Colonel was also the bearer of the following letter to Lord Nelson from Alex. Davison, Esq. :—

"St. James's Square, 22nd April, 1801.

"My dear Friend,

"Colonel Stewart's return to the Baltic affords me the happy opportunity of writing to you, and with the general voice of this nation to repeat again and again our joy on the most important victory at this particular period ever this country could have obtained. I will refer you to Colonel Stewart for our political news, who will communicate more in ten minutes than I could in hours writing. I am grieved to find, though however gratifying the cause, that you are not likely to obtain leave of absence so soon as you expected, or your friends here wished. It is said, the service absolutely requires your aid in the Baltic, and without *you* nothing would have been done, and that nothing will be effected without you. Taking all this for granted, as I believe it to be true, yet I own I should have been much pleased to hear of your return immediately, as I see nothing now to be done, in which you as *second* can possibly claim that distinct pointed approbation you, in every act of your life, so justly merit. Fighting for the honour of another ought not to be your station, and as Sir Hyde is battling for a peerage, in God's name let him have it, and return quietly home, leaving you in the command, if it be determined that you are to remain. I hope it is not true, what I have heard, that it is the intention of the Government to offer you the dignity of

Viscount. *That* you ought to have had long ago, and any additional distinction short of an *Earldom*, in my humble opinion, would be degrading. Your last act of service deserves every acknowledgment which a grateful country (whatever Ministers may think) can bestow. The nation would be gratified to see the highest mark of honour conferred upon you.

"I am truly sorry, my dear friend, to tell you poor Maurice[1] is extremely ill, though within these twenty-four hours appearances have taken a favourable turn. Nine days ago he was seized with violent pains in his head, which terminated in an inflammation in the brain. The instant I was informed of it, I dispatched my own physician, Sir John Hayes,[2] to attend him, in whom I have the most perfect confidence as a professional character. Sir John this morning assures me he is out of danger, but that it will require time and great care to bring him about. I am vexed my own miserable situation deprives me the satisfaction of being with Maurice. I have Sir John Hayes's regular report twice a day, and it gives me pleasure to know your brother highly approved my sending my own physician. My own health is as good as I could wish it, but my limbs and ancles so extremely weakened that I am unable to walk. A very few days will put me to rights, and the fit (of gout) be productive of benefit to me.

"Whilst fighting for your country's honour, I must not let you forget yourself, and as the trial in all probability will come before the court about the end of May, I must entreat you to give the different opinions annexed to the case some serious consideration, making such observations and remarks as you think will weigh in the minds of a jury, for though however confident we may in our own judgments be respecting the probable issue, yet too great precautions cannot possibly be taken, when we reflect with whom we are to take the field against. Your private observations cannot fail operating most forcibly on the minds of men of common sense, such as I hope will be on the jury.

"If you are certain of being in England at the period, the less necessity for this precaution, but it would wound my

---

[1] Lord Nelson's Brother.     [2] Sir John Macnamara Hayes, Bart. M.D.

feelings were we to fall short of every possible means in our power to strengthen and arm one's counsel on this important occasion. It hurts me to write a word on business when your mind is so occupied with public duty, yet your own individual interest must *not* be neglected, and I trust you will excuse me.

"Your plate at Rundell's is finished, and a complete case making to contain the whole. I conclude you now would like that it remain until you return. The inclosed letter will, I presume, tell you how matters *stand* in Piccadilly. Several epistles pass daily between us. I conclude Stewart will call there, and will be the bearer of other packets, as she wrote to me last night, telling me a note had been sent to him to give her a visit.

"May every blessing attend you, and that you may soon return to us, is and always will be the sincere prayer of my dear friend's affectionate

"ALEX. DAVISON."

On the 23rd Lord Nelson wrote to Lady Hamilton :—

"St George, April 23rd, 1801.

"My dearest amiable Friend, this day we sailed from Palermo on our tour to Malta. Ah! those were happy times. How different, how forlorn! alas, no wonder. I severely feel the difference, but as we are retiring to the anchorage near Copenhagen, I hope a very short time will place me in London. Yesterday Sir Hyde Parker wrote me word that the Russian Minister at Copenhagen had sent him a letter, saying the Emperor had ordered his fleet to abstain from all hostilities, therefore Sir Hyde Parker was determined to return to the anchorage near Copenhagen. I am truly anxiously looking out for my leave of absence, or that the whole fleet may be ordered home; stay I will not, if the Admiral would make me Lord High Admiral of the Baltic. Don't you think I am perfectly right? If you were to think the contrary it would break my heart, for I have the very highest opinion of your judgment.

"Read the inclosed, and send it if you approve. Who

should I consult but my friends?[1]  Remember me in the most affectionate manner where proper, and respects and compliments as the person deserves to whom you give them."

He wrote again on the 25th under the influence of her most powerful fascination:—

"St. George, Kioge Bay, April 25th, 1801.

"My dearest Friend,

"Sir Hyde has just sent me word that the Arrow sloop sails for England this day, therefore I have only time to say that I hope in a fortnight to be in London. I am in expectation every moment for the removal of the fleet from the Baltic: be that as it may, I will not remain, *no*, not if I was *sure* of being made a DUKE with £50,000 a year. I wish for *happiness* to be my *reward*, and not titles or money. To-morrow is the birthday of *Santa Emma*. She is my guardian angel. It is not in my power to do much honour to her in this place, but I have invited the Admirals and all the Captains who had the happiness of knowing you, and of course experiencing your kindness when in the Mediterranean. You may rely my saint is more adored in this fleet than all the saints in the Roman Calendar. I know you prayed for me both at the Nile and here, and if the prayers of the good, as we are taught to believe, are of avail at the Throne of Grace, why may not yours have saved my life? I own myself a BELIEVER IN GOD, and if I have any merit in not fearing death, it is because I feel that His power can shelter me when He pleases, and that I must fall whenever it is His good pleasure. May the God of heaven and earth, the Protector of those who truly worship Him, bless and preserve you, my dearest Friend, for the greatest happiness which you can wish for in this world, is the constant prayer of your real, sincere and affectionate friend till death,

"NELSON AND BRONTÉ."

"St. George, April 27th, 1801.

"All your letters, my dearest Friend, to the 17th, came safe on the eve of your natal day. You will readily conceive the

---

[1] This probably alludes to the paper on the Armistice.

pleasure they must have given me to know that you still take an interest in my glory. I transfer it all to my guardian angel, Santa Emma. Yesterday, I had twenty-four at dinner, and drank at dinner in a bumper of champagne, Santa Emma.

"I hope, if the fleet is not ordered home, to go in the Blanche, for both my mind and body are required in England, therefore, unless you are sure that we are ordered to attack the Russian fleet, it is of no use writing more letters. I hope to be in London as soon as this letter, and I should like a good lodging in an airy situation. I have directed Hardy to take care of all my letters, and return them to England. I have so much to tell you that I cannot tell you where to begin. I think we shall have a general peace, and then nothing shall stop my going to Bronté.

"Your affectionate and attached friend,
"NELSON AND BRONTÉ."

"St. George, April 28th, 1801.

"My dearest Friend,

"I had last night one of my dreadful attacks, and this day I have applied to Sir Hyde Parker, and he tells me the Blanche shall carry me to England. I have several letters ready wrote for you, but I do not send them, as it is more than probable this will never reach England. Write no more, I hope to be sailed within a week. Keep this to yourself. Ever your most attached and affectionate.

"A small vessel sails with letters in two days."

Sir Brooke Boothby, Bart.,[1] to whom he had written an account of the engagement, replied as follows:—

"Hamburgh, May 1, 1801.

"A thousand thanks, my dear Lord, for your very kind

---

[1] Sir Brooke Boothby, Bart., a minor poet, formed one of the literary coterie of Lichfield, enriched by the society of Darwin, Seward, and Edgeworth. He published a letter to Mr. Burke, Observations on the Appeal from the New to the Old Whigs, and Paine's Rights of Man; Sorrows sacred to the Memory of Penelope; Britannicus, from the French of Racine, a Tragedy; Fables and Satires; and a series of Elegiac Poems on his Daughter. He died March 17, 1824, and was succeeded in the title by his brother.

note, written on the evening of your glorious victory. I preserve it as a precious relic. It found me just beginning to breathe after a painful illness of four months, and really revived me.

"Of all your great actions, the last seems to be deservedly considered as that in which you have surmounted the most extraordinary difficulties, and rendered your country the most immediate and important service; that of Aboukir not excepted. From all I learn, I cannot help thinking you are the only man who could have performed what you have done.

"The poor Danes have been the dupes of the madness of Paul, and the rascality of Buonaparte, who had promised them Hamburgh and Lubeck; and their swindling seizure of this place well deserved the licking they have got, and more. You cannot conceive what extravagant rhodomontades appeared in the papers here, prophesying confidently, before the action, that all your glories were to be buried in Copenhagen roads; and even afterwards, endeavouring to make out that the completely beaten had the better of it; at least, they seem to content themselves with the honour of having contended with you, of which they have in truth some reason to be proud. If these 'fat and greasy citizens' had been bold enough to shut their gates, you would probably have saved them from disgrace, and what I believe they value more, the loss of 40 or 50,000 marks. The Prince of Hesse had no preparations for a siege, and the town had provision for at least a month, and in the meantime the first gun fired against Hamburgh might have been the signal for the destruction of Altona. The *Bourgeoisie* were earnest for resistance, but the cowardly spirit of riches prevailed. You will find, inclosed, some remarks I made on the Prince of Hesse's profligate and foolish manifesto. He has received a very peremptory note from Berlin to evacuate Hamburgh, but continues to negotiate, probably for the sake of the 6000 marks a-day.

"Your rapid proceeding, and the death of Paul, seem completely to derange the impudent plan of his brother tyrant, whom God confound! I remember when I saw you I thought less ill of this robber than you did, but you knew him best. God send the African expedition, which has commenced so well, may be finally successful, and then, I think, the century opens propitiously for poor Old England. Before the battle of Copenhagen Roads we were a little chop-fallen, but now the carmagnoles are down, and we hold our heads high: the reputation of a country is half its strength."

"May 15.

"Not knowing well how to direct, this letter, with the General's,[1] has lain by. I learn with the greatest anxiety that the state of your health obliges you to return. The good of mankind will neither admit of your being long ill, or of your retreat; your services may indeed be soon wanted at home. The Corsican, whose situation is nothing less than pleasant, and who, it is said, has taken fright, must find employment for his troops, and the restless spirit of his new subjects, and will lead or drive them to the British coasts, to do mischief and to perish; both for his purpose.

"The General is almost the only person I see. He is planting his winter cabbages, and seems really to enjoy the content of a clear conscience. If it were nothing else, I think his understanding is of too high a sort for treachery. He was a good subject of the French (limited) monarchy, and has been cast out by their pretended democracy; is he not at liberty to become a member of any country that might adopt him?

"I rejoice that my friend, Lord St. Helens, goes to St. Petersburgh. He will do all that can be done. Will not what is passing in Italy, Portugal, &c. at last open the eyes of those blinded kings? Nothing but uniting all their powers, on the determined, openly declared ground of putting a stop to those impudent invaders, can ultimately save Europe. These detestable people are, I think, made of rather worse stuff than those of other countries, but when collected and inflamed, they may be resembled to those fulminating powders, which, though composed of very ordinary materials, are formidable in their explosion. Saltpetre may be made from horse-dung, brimstone is used to cure the itch, and charcoal for the basest purposes, yet these combined are the gunpowder which decides the fate of nations.

"Adieu, my dear Lord, I began a long letter, thinking it

[1] General Dumouriez.

would find you aboard, and might fill up a leisure moment. Believe me, ever yours, with the sincerest attachment,

"BROOKE BOOTHBY.

"P.S. Amongst other reports equally true, the papers here gave a circumstantial account of the death of Sir Edward Berry, fighting by your side. I inclose you an epitaph I made for a magnificent monument in Westminster Abbey, which will have the effect, not very flattering, for a serious epitaph to make you smile. I am, I believe, not accurate in the *places*, but that is now, thank God, of no consequence. Pray when you have read it send it to your charming Poet Laureate,[1] who, by the bye, I much wish to hear of. Do have the goodness to tell her so. I am leaving Hamburgh, but anything directed under cover to Sir James Crawfurd will find me."

The following is the letter from General Dumouriez,[2] referred to in the preceding :—

[1] Miss Knight.
[2] Claude Francois Duperier Dumouriez, a French General, was born at Cambrai, Jan. 25, 1739. He served in Germany in the seven years war, and at the age of twenty-two years had attained the rank of Captain, was a Knight of St. Louis, and had received twenty-two wounds. Having travelled in Italy, Belgium, Spain, and Portugal, and acquired considerable knowledge of languages and the manners and customs of different nations, he was appointed Aide-Marechál General to the French expedition for the invasion of Corsica in 1768-9. He rose to the rank of Colonel, and afterwards served in a campaign to Russia. The Duc de Choiseul appointed him Minister to the Confederates of Poland, and Louis XV. sent him on a confidential mission to Sweden, but the Ministers becoming jealous of him from his having received instructions immediately from the King, and unknown to the Foreign Minister, the Duc d'Aguillon, he was arrested at Hamburgh, taken back to Paris, and imprisoned in the Bastille, where, after six months confinement, he was banished to the Castle of Caen for three months, and thence liberated by Louis XVI. on his accession to the throne. He was then intrusted with the command of the country from Nantes to Bordeaux, whilst the religious war raged in La Vendée, and was successful in calming the minds of the people. He furnished to the French Government plans for the conquest of Jersey, Guernsey, and the Isle of Wight, and was at the commencement of the Revolution connected with the Girondists. He was appointed Foreign Minister, and prevailed on the King to declare war against Austria in 1792. The violence of the revolutionary movement alarmed him, and he became an object of hatred to the Jacobins, in consequence of which, he withdrew from politics, and went to serve under General Luchner on the northern frontiers. He replaced La Fayette in the army opposed to the Duke of Brunswick, and successfully checked the advance of the Prussians.

Dumouriez distinguished himself also at the battle of Jemappes, and succeeded

"Ottensen par Altona, No. 43,
le 20 Avril, 1801.

"My dear and glorious Nelson,

"Victory is for ever bounded to your name, as my friendship to your character. I hope the peace with the Northern Powers will give another turn to your constant successes more profitable for the public cause. Paul's foolish brain destroyed our hopes, they revive with the successor. If you have the charge of the Mediterranean sea, we can together deliver Italy and France of the democratic tyranny. I desire nothing else. After that take your leave, and spend the remnant of your life in the calmness, shadowed with the laurels you for yourself implanted. Farewell, dear Nelson, and be constant in friendship as you are in triumphing of internal foes and external ennemys.

"Your for ever affectionate friend,

*Dumourier*

In the month of May, his correspondence with Lady Hamilton was frequent, and he was restless to return to England, as the following letters will shew :—

in taking Liège, Antwerp, and Flanders. The trial of Louis XVI. took him to Paris, and after the execution of the Sovereign he became an ardent advocate of Constitutional Monarchy. Entering into negotiations with Prince Cobourg, he was enabled to withdraw his army from Holland, and retired to Tournay, evacuated Belgium, and established his head-quarters at St. Amand, in 1793. Accused of treason, the Convention of Paris summoned him to their bar, but he refused to obey the mandate, and imprisoned those sent to arrest him as hostages for the safety of the Royal Family. His troops, however, refusing to march upon Paris, he took refuge in the Austrian head-quarters, and afterwards sought an asylum in Switzerland, then wandered about, hated as a Constitutionalist, and, under the fear of being taken prisoner, a reward of 300,000 francs having been offered by the National Convention of Paris for his apprehension, he fled to England; afterwards took up his abode at Hamburgh, and is known as the writer of numerous political works, as well as Memoirs of his own life, which appeared at Hamburgh in 2 vols. 8vo. 1794, and were translated into English, and published in London in 3 vols. 8vo. 1796. He rendered some services to the British Government, and was rewarded with a pension. He enjoyed intimacy with, and was highly esteemed by, His Royal Highness the Duke of Kent. From 1804, he resided in England, and died at the age of eighty-four years at Turville Park, near Henley-upon-Thames, March 14, 1823.

"St. George, May 2nd, 1801.

"My dearest Friend,

"I am waiting for the sailing of the Blanche frigate, which is destined to carry the answers of the next vessel to England, and the vessel we have been expecting every day for this week. I have been so very indifferent, and am still so weak, that I cannot take the journey to Hamburgh by land, or I should have been off long ago. I shall get on shore the first land we make in England, but as it is likely to be Yarmouth, I should rejoice to find a line of your friendly hand at the Wrestlers. I dare not say much, as most probably all my letters are read.

"Ever your faithful and affectionate."

"2 o'clock.

"My dearest Friend, from all I now see, it is not possible that this fleet can be much longer kept here, and I find that although from others, there may be much self, yet Mr. Addington wishes me to have the sweets of seeing this business finished: it must soon happen. We must cheer up for the moment, at present we are in the hands of others. We shall be masters one day or other.

"Blanche just going."

"My dearest Friend, again and again I thank you for all your goodness. I cannot say anything, my heart is full and big. Hardy and Parker are at work scaling up. I hope this will be the last packet I send off—the next shall be myself. In the meantime I send you six bottles of Old Hock, 200 years of age, if you believe it—so says the Prince of Denmark's Aide-de-camp; only ten bottles came, so they stole two. I send you the Danish line of defence,[1] correct in the minutest degree. Have a good glass and frame to put to it. I shall repay you the expense when we meet—'tis to add to the Nelson Room. There is a print coming out something similar. I have wrote Mr. Beckford, pray give him the letter. You may shew the line of defence to Troubridge—it is perfect to one gun and shape of vessel. Ever yours,

"NELSON AND BRONTÉ."

Receiving, however, on the 5th, intelligence of his having

[1] See Plate, *ante*.

been appointed Commander-in-chief in the Baltic, he was necessitated to remain :—

"St. George, May 5th, 1801.

"My dearest Friend,

"All my things were on board the Blanche, and Sir Hyde was to have dismissed me this day, but alas, in the night arrived Colonel Stewart, which has overturned all my plans. Sir Hyde has worked his leave of absence, he is ordered home, and I am appointed Commander-in-chief. To paint or describe my grief is impossible. I have this day wrote to the Admiralty that my health is in such a state that they must send out some person who has strength enough to get on with the business. Sir Hyde sets off in the Blanche. I will write fully by way of Hamburgh to-morrow.

"NELSON AND BRONTÉ."

He wrote on the same day to Mr. Davison and says : " A Command never was, I believe, more unwelcomely received by any person than by myself. It may be at the expense of my life; and therefore, for God's sake, at least for mine, try if I cannot be relieved. The time was, a few months ago, that I should have felt the honour, and I really believe that I should have seen more of the Baltic, the consequence of which I can guess. But nothing, I believe, but change of climate can cure me, and having my mind tranquil."[1] To the Earl of St. Vincent he likewise wrote: "I am, in truth, unable to hold the very honourable station you have conferred upon me." Yet the extraordinary activity of his mind is apparent in the following lines immediately succeeding the above: "If Sir Hyde were gone, I would now be under sail, leave six sail of the line off Bornholm to watch the Swedes, and to cover our communication, and go to Revel, where I should at least, if not too late, prevent the junction of the two squadrons: that I shall never suffer. I will have all the English shipping and property restored; but I will do nothing violently; neither commit my country, nor suffer Russia to mix the affairs of Denmark or Sweden with the detention of our ships. Should I meet the Revel squadron, I shall make them stay with me until all

[1] Dispatches and Letters, Vol. iv. p. 353.

our English ships join; for we must not joke. As the business will be settled in a fortnight, I must entreat that some person may come out to take this command."[1]

The Armistice, which he had been the chief instrument in making, was approved of at home under *all* considerations, and he wrote to the Hon. Henry Addington: "I am sorry that the Armistice is only approved under *all* considerations. Now I own myself of opinion that every part of the *all* was to the advantage of our King and country. I stated many of my reasons for thinking it advantageous. We knew not of the death of Paul, or a change of sentiments in the Court of Russia, if her sentiments are changed. My object was to get at Revel before the frost broke up at Cronstadt, that the twelve sail of the line might be destroyed. I shall now go there as a friend, but the two fleets shall not form a junction, if not already accomplished, unless my orders permit it. My health is gone, and although I should be happy to try and hold out a month or six weeks longer, yet death is no respecter of persons. I own, at present, I should not wish to die a natural death."[2] And again on the 8th: "Forgive me for one moment, but so much having been said, both by friends and enemies, why I sent on shore a Flag of Truce on the 2nd of April, and but few seemed pleased with the Armistice, I take the liberty of sending the reasons why I sent the Flag of Truce, and also my reasons why I think the Armistice was a proper measure. If you and some other friends approve, I care not. I have dispersed the reasons to several hands, for I feel hurt."[3]

One of the papers alluded to was forwarded, together with the following correspondence, to Lady Hamilton:—

"May 8th, 1801.

"My dearest Friend,

"As both my friends and enemies seem not to know why I sent on shore a Flag of Truce, the former, many of them, thought it was a *ruse de guerre,* and not quite justifiable; the latter, I believe, attributed it to a desire to have no more fighting, and few, very few, to the cause that I felt, and

[1] Clarke and McArthur, Vol. ii. p. 285.
[2] From an Autograph in the Sidmouth Papers.
[3] Ibid.

which, I trust in God, I shall retain to the last moment, *humanity*. I know it must to the world be proved, and therefore I will suppose you all the world to me.

"First, no ship was on shore near the Crown batteries, or any where else within reach of any shore when my Flag of Truce went on shore; the Crown batteries, and the batteries on Amack, and in the Dockyard were firing at us, one half their shot necessarily striking the ships who had surrendered, and our fire did the same, and worse, for the surrendered ships had four of them got close together, and it was a massacre, this caused my note. It was a sight which no real man could have enjoyed. I felt when the Danes became my prisoners, I became their protector, and if that had not been a sufficient reason, the moment of a complete victory was surely the proper time to make an opening with the nation we had been fighting with. When the Truce was settled and full possession taken of our prizes, the ships were ordered, except two, to proceed and join Sir Hyde Parker, and in performing this service, the Elephant and Defiance grounded on the middle ground. I give you verbatim an answer to a part of a letter from a person high in rank about the Prince Royal, which will bear testimony to the truth of my assertions, viz. 'As to your Lordship's motives for sending a Flag of Truce to our Government it never can be misconstrued, and your subsequent conduct has sufficiently shewn that humanity is always the companion of true valour. You have done more, you have shewn yourself a friend of the re-establishment of peace and good harmony between this country and Great Britain.'

"If, after this, either pretended friends or open enemies say any thing upon the subject, tell them THEY BE DAMNED. Get Mr. Este, or some other able man, to put these truths before the public. Envious men and enemies wish to hurt me, but truth will stand its ground, and I feel as firm as a *rock*. I have wrote strongly to Mr. Nepean to come home. Why should I stay?

"Your true and faithful,

"NELSON AND BRONTÉ."

### ON THE ARMISTICE.

"Much having been said relative to the bad terms of the Armistice made with Denmark, I wish to observe, first, that the Armistice was only intended a military one, and that all political subjects were left for the discussion of the Ministers of the two powers.

"Peace, Denmark could not, in the moment, make with you, as the moment she made it with you, she would lose all her possessions except the island of Zealand, and that also the moment the frost set in, therefore there was no damage we could do her equal to the loss of every thing; our destruction would have been Copenhagen and her fleet, then we had done our worst, and not much nearer being friends. By the Armistice we tied the arms of Denmark for four months from assisting our enemies and her Allies, whilst we had every part of Denmark and its provinces open to give us every thing we wanted. Great Britain was left the power of taking Danish possessions and ships in all parts of the world, whilst we had locked up the Danish Navy, and put the key in our pocket. Time was afforded the two countries to arrange matters on an amicable footing; besides, to say the truth, I look upon the Northern league to be like a tree, of which *Paul* was the *trunk*, and Sweden and Denmark the branches. If I can get at the *trunk* and hew it down, the branches fall of course, but I may lop the branches, and yet not be able to fell the tree, and my power must be weaker when its greatest strength is required. If we could have cut up the Russian fleet, that was my object. Denmark and Sweden deserved whipping, but *Paul* deserved punishment. I own I consider it as a wise measure, and I wish my reputation to stand upon its merits.

["Duplicate originals sent by way of Rostock this day. Heavens bless you, save our friends; a letter goes this day also by the Danish post, and also by Rostock."]

"May 8th, 1801.

"My dearest Friend,

"I hope you have received my numerous letters sent by the post since April 10th, say six or seven or more, but perhaps they never will arrive. The Post Office in Denmark may stop them, although an English merchant, Mr. Balfour, said he would take care and send them under cover to his merchant. The Cruizer arrived yesterday, and Sir Thomas Troubridge had the nonsense to say, now I was a Commander-in-chief I must be pleased. Does he take me for a greater fool than I am, for if I had ever such good health, that I must soon be a complete beggar if I staid, I will explain to you. Sir Hyde Parker, when he had the command in the Baltic given to him, had the chance of great honours and great riches from the prizes to be taken; but that was not enough for such a great officer; he had the emolument of the whole North Sea command given to him, and taken from Dickson, and of course I had then the honour of sharing one-fifth part as much as Sir Hyde Parker, Dickson, Totty,[1] &c. will share for the Danish battle, and Sir Hyde, I dare say, will get near £5000. Now, what is done for me? Orders not to make prizes in the *Baltic*. My commission as Commander-in-chief does not extend to the North Sea, therefore I can make no prize-money here, and am excluded from sharing with Dickson what may be taken in the North Seas. He shares for my fighting; but if the Dutch come out, and he fights, I am not to have one farthing. I have now all the expenses of a Commander-in-chief, and am stripped even of the little chance of prize-money, which I might have had by being in a subordinate situation. This is the honour, this is my reward—*a prison for debt.* I see no other prospect. I have wrote very strongly by the Arrow, which left us your birth-day. I wrote by Sir Hyde, desiring they would send out another Commander-in-chief, and I have wrote it again this day. Why should I die to do what pleases those who care not a damn about me? I will try and bear up and return; but it breaks my poor heart. My conduct is surely different, or I know not myself.

"Your truly affectionate,
"NELSON AND BRONTÉ."

[1] This officer commanded the Invincible, which was lost, going out of Yarmouth Roads to join the Baltic fleet. He died of an attack of yellow fever in the West Indies, June 2, 1802, a Rear-Admiral.

"St. George, May 8th, 1801. Baltic.

"My dearest Friend,

"Under your kind care I might recover, and I trust in God I shall be supported till that time arrives. You understand every thing in what I have said, for this letter will be read ten times at least before you get it. I trust another Admiral is on his way to supersede me, for it is downright murder to keep me here. If I could fight a battle, the smell of powder and exertion might cheer one for the moment. Had the command been given me in February, many lives would have been saved, and we should have been in a very different situation; but the wise heads at home know every thing. I have wrote this day a packet for you with all my public letters, by way of Rostock and Hamburgh; therefore if you see Troubridge, say I have wrote to him, Nepean, and the Earl, that way. I have wrote you more letters by the Danish post, but I have not heard of one getting to you, therefore I must not say a word. How are all our friends? They may depend I am firm as a rock—'tis not a Dukedom and £50,000. a year could shake me. Whilst I live my honour is sacred.

"Yours truly.

"Damn our enemies—bless our friends.
"Amen—Amen—Amen.
"I am not such a hypocrite as to bless them that hate us, or if a man strike me on the cheek to turn the other—No, *knock* him down, by God.

"Some cruel remarks have been made in some of the papers relative to the first Flag of Truce and the Armistice. All false, for I feel all honourable for me. I have answered them by way of Rostock, and you must get some able friend to fit them out for the public eye, for I will not sit down quietly and have my public character pulled to pieces. Colonel Stewart is now my guest; Hardy, &c. are all well. Thank Lady Malmesbury for her congratulations. George Elliot is very well, but cannot be expected to write. May the heavens bless you."

Sir Hyde Parker had received several letters acquainting him that many vessels with corn for England, from the

Baltic, had been arrested in the ports of Norway; Lord Nelson, therefore, wrote through Adjutant-General Lindholm to Count Bernstorff, to require their freedom of passage. To this application the following replies were given:—

" Copenhagen, May 6th, 1801.<br>7 o'clock in the afternoon.

" My Lord!

" I have had the honour to receive your Lordship's letter of this date. I have delivered the letter to Count Bernstorff, who will inform himself about the corn affair in Norway, and he will have the honour to send your Lordship his answer as soon as possible. Count Bernstorff presents his respects to your Lordship.

" I remember that some Swedish ships laden with corn, and bound to England, were seized in Norway, but they were not seized because they were bound to England, but the reason was, that the people in that part of Norway were in such a want of bread, that the King's officers were obliged to buy it, and paid the cargo to the master of the vessels.

" The Prince Regent presents his compliments to your Lordship, and his Royal Highness is very sensible of the attention and kindness which your Lordship has expressed in the letter which I have had the honour to receive this day. I beg you to receive the assurance of the great esteem with which I have the honour to subscribe myself, my Lord,

" Your Lordship's most obedient,<br>" and humble servant,<br>" H. LINDHOLM.

" Right Hon. Lord Nelson, Duke of Bronté, Vice-Admiral of the Blue, and Knight of the most Honourable Order of the Bath."

"Copenhagen, May 12th, 1801.

" My Lord,

" I have the honour to congratulate your Lordship as Commander-in-chief of the Baltic fleet, and I wish very sincerely that your Lordship may enjoy a perfect health.

" I hear with great satisfaction that Lord St. Helens is appointed Ambassador to the Court of Petersburgh, and that we can soon expect him in our Roads, passing in his way to that capital. I hope that the differences between Great Britain and the Northern Powers will be settled in a short period, and that peace and friendship will be established on a firm basis. The English Ministers have shewn their inclination to settle things in a satisfactory manner to all trading nations, by making a change with the Courts of Vice-Admiralty in the West Indies, whose conduct in many instances has been highly iniquitous.

"I have the honour to send your Lordship a letter from Count Bernstorff, and I am assured that he has given a satisfactory information about the corn ships in Norway.

"The Certificate,[1] signed by three officers, of the number of men who were on board the ships on the 2nd of April, is here inclosed, and some letters found on the coast near Kioge.

"I have the honour to remain with the greatest esteem,
"My Lord,
"Your Lordship's most obedient
"and humble servant,
"H. LINDHOLM.

"Right Hon. Lord Nelson."

The state of things consequent upon the arrangements with Denmark on the accession of the new Czar, and his expressed desire for conciliatory measures and conduct, rendered an extraordinary mission to Petersburgh essential. Lord St. Helens was appointed to this important embassy; and his Majesty George III., in a note to Mr. Addington, dated from Kew, May 12, 1801, states:—"As the King relies on every thing being settled to the mutual advantage of both countries, he shall feel much personally gratified in rewarding Lord St. Helens on the completion of the business, by placing him in the British House of Peers."[2] The embassy was entirely successful; a treaty was signed on the 17th of June, 1801, and the right of searching vessels belonging to the subjects of either of the contracting parties when accompanied by one of their own ships of war, was placed on its proper basis.

---

[1] See page 15, *ante*.   [2] Life of Lord Sidmouth, Vol. i. p. 386.

### COUNT BERNSTORFF TO LORD NELSON.

(Received May 18th, at sea.)

"My Lord,

"I received the day before yesterday the two letters with which your Excellency has honoured me, and learn with much pleasure that his Britannic Majesty has approved of the Armistice concluded here the 9th of last month. My Court will carefully fulfil its stipulations. It is true the inhabitants of Holstein were at first uneasy, their province not being comprised in it. But it appears to me, that the basis of the arrangement for the re-establishment of a good understanding between the two powers is so solidly laid, that the effect of it will speedily be felt in all parts of the dominions of the King, my master. My Court has not delayed to make known its disposition and wishes in that respect to the Court of London, and anticipates a prompt and satisfactory result.

"With respect to the alleged detention of different vessels laden with corn for England in the Norwegian ports, I am ignorant of the fact, unless it applies to some Swedish ships detained in Norway, in consequence of measures taken by their own Government to break off her communication with England; I shall, however, take care to procure some exact explanations on the subject; and I beg your Excellency to believe that my Government values too highly the facilities which Admiral Parker has given to the provisioning of Norway, to feel any wish on her part to present obstacles to the same object for England. If it should be necessary that further or more precise orders should be given to that effect, I pledge myself, my Lord, that those orders shall be given immediately.

"Accept, I beg, the assurance of the high consideration with which I have the honour to be, my Lord,

"Your Excellency's very humble,
"and very obedient servant,
"C. BERNSTORFF.

"Copenhagen, May 8, 1801."

The first part of this letter refers to a communication made by Lord Nelson when conveying to Count Bernstorff the approval of the Armistice, expressing his hope that information would be given in Holstein to assure the inhabitants that the Armistice extended to that province, which it appears some had suspected not to be the case.

On the 11th, in a letter to Lady Hamilton, an evidence of his superstition creeps out:—

"May 11th, 1801.

"My dearest Friend,

"If I had stayed in Kioge Bay I should have been dead before this time, for what with ill health and the terrible disappointment of not going home, it would have overpowered me; but I trust that long before this time you will know that somebody is coming out to supersede me. I have wrote so strongly that they cannot avoid it. I have as much right to have my health taken care of as any other person in the fleet, and if they would make me Lord High Admiral of the Baltic I would not stay; but my dear Friend, you know enough of my attention to my duty that whilst I do hold the command every thing which is active shall go on, but being stopped fighting. I am sure that any other man can as well look about him as Nelson. I am now far on my way to Russia, where I shall be able to form a pretty decisive opinion as to the views and plans of the new Emperor. I have, my dear Friend, taken it into my head that within these few days your picture has turned much paler than it used to be; it has made me quite uneasy, I hope to God you have not been unwell, or any thing happened which could make you look differently on me. If it has, I care not how soon I leave this world of folly and nonsense; but why should I think so—innocent myself, I feel I deserve, and shall have a just return. Without friendship this life is but misery, and it is so difficult to find a true friend, that the search is almost needless; but if ever you do it ought to be cherished as an exotic plant. You will not forget to remember me most kindly to Sir William and the Duke. Apropos, Mr. Comyn has not yet joined, I suppose he is with Sir Edward Berry. He has several letters for me from you."

"May 12th, Gulph of Finland, off Pakerot
Lighthouse, 6 o'clock.

"My dearest Friend, here I am very near the latitude of 60° degrees North, the air like a fine January day; but my heart as warm towards you as the sincerest friendship can make it, and as if I were upon the Equator. You deserve every mark of kindness from me, and by the living God, you shall always experience it whilst I draw breath, which, notwithstanding the unkindness of some folks, I hope will be yet some years. I did not, my dear friend, come to the Baltic with a design of dying a NATURAL death. Who will thank me? *those* who care not one farthing for me. Our *friend* Troubridge has *felt* so little for my health that I have wrote him word I should never mention it again to him. By the 12th of June, or before, I hope to be in London, where I am fixed as to the plan of life I mean to pursue. It is to take a small neat house from six to ten miles from London, and there to remain till I can fix for ever or get to Bronté. I have never known happiness beyond moments, and I am fixed as fate to try if I cannot attain it after so many years of labour and anxiety. Forgive me tormenting you with my affairs, but I know you take a lively interest in all my affairs, and so do I every day pray for your complete felicity.

"May 13th. Here I am at Revel, as much to the surprise of the Russians as to most in the squadron. Expresses are gone to Petersburgh, and I have wrote to Count Pahlen the Prime Minister, and I dare say we shall be ordered a very friendly reception. I have ordered very fine beef and soft bread for our ships, but there is not a sign of vegetation. The Russian fleet sailed from hence on the 2nd to join the Cronstadt fleet at Caskna Gorku, where they are moored, forty-three sail of the line, but with twenty-five, if we were at war, I should not hesitate trying what stuff they were made of. In about a week I shall return from hence, and by the time I get down I hope a new Admiral will be arrived, when I shall proceed direct for England. To the Duke, Lord William, &c. say every thing. Troubridge has not been kind, but never mind. I have sent Galuchi, the child on board Foley, a present in your name. He is a fine boy but a pickle. Remember me most affectionately to all our friends, and to those I love most, say you what is proper. I will soon be in England."

Lieutenant-Colonel Stewart in his Narrative, states that Lord Nelson arrived in the Revel Roads on the 12th of May, and that he was disappointed in not finding the Russian fleet there, the breaking up of the ice having admitted of their departure for Cronstadt three days before. After some delay a salute was given and returned. Lord Nelson visited the Governor-General Sacken, on shore, and was received with military honours, and a welcome from the inhabitants. The Governor returned the Admiral's visit on the next day, accompanied by Count Pahlen's son, and many other officers, and Colonel Stewart observed that the Cossack officers gave infinitely more attention to what they saw than the Russians. These circumstances are confirmed by the details in the subjoined letter to Lady Hamilton:—

"St. George, May 15th, 1801.   Revel Bay.

"My dearest Friend,

"After seventeen days not out of my cabin, I was forced to row seven miles, to make the formal visit to the Governor-General, and head of the Admiralty here. It cost me about three hours; they wanted me to dine on shore; but if I had been ever so well I would not. It is a horrid nasty place, and nothing less than the arrival of the Emperor shall get me ashore again. As usual, I received all the compliments to which I have been used, and which have spoiled me. The crowd was, of course, all the town. This morning the Governor and Admiral will be on board the St. George, and to-morrow morning I shall get answers to my letters from Petersburgh. I have wrote a line, my dear Friend, by the post; but as the post is a month going, and my letter will assuredly be read, it is only a date to say where I am. I have wrote to Lord St. Vincent to say, I expect to find another Admiral when I return, or *probably* he will never see me again. I cannot, I will not stay here, that you may rely upon. Why should I, when my health and happiness can I hope be perfect by going to England?

"May 16th. Yesterday I had all the world on board, not

less than thirty officers and nobles of rank. Except to you, my own Friend, I should not mention it, 'tis so much like vanity; but hundreds come to look at Nelson, *that is him, that is him*, in short, 'tis the same as in Italy and Germany, and I now feel that a good name is better than riches, not amongst our great folks in England; but it has its fine feelings to an honest heart. All the Russians have taken it into their heads that I am like *Suwaroff, Le jeune Suwaroff.* This evening I expect the return of the courier from Petersburgh. I have increased my cough very much by going round the ship with the Russian officers and my trip on shore. I only hope the first land I next set my foot upon will be Old England, and the first house will assuredly be yours. As you will know when an Admiral is coming out to supersede me, or that permission is coming out for my return home, I hope to find you in London, for I have much to say to you."

The following relates also to this period and situation:—

### J. WOLLSTONECRAFT TO LORD NELSON.

"London, May 12th, 1801.

"My Lord,

"As your illness, when Sir Hyde Parker sailed, prevented my having the honour of seeing you, and being now fearful of intruding on your Lordship's time, I take the liberty of informing you that I passed a winter at Revel some years ago, and also of sending you what local knowledge of that place I was thereby enabled to acquire.

"The breadth of the Bay and the situation of the mole will admit of bomb vessels being placed sufficiently near to bombard the ships in the mole, and yet be themselves out of the reach of *point blank shot from all the batteries, viz.* those to the westward of the mole, those on the two small islands to the north north-west of it, and from any that may lately have been made (there were none some years ago) on the opposite side of the Bay and at the head of it.

"The mole is near a mile from the town, and is formed by a single wharf, which runs straight out towards the opposite side of the bay; this wharf is mounted with guns, and there is deep water on both sides close to it. The rest of the mole is perfectly open, and presents no obstacles or difficulties to prevent fire-ships sailing right in among the ships, which are ranged abreast of each other with their bowsprits over the wharf. Fire-ships attempting this service would be but little exposed, as the width of the bay will allow their keeping well to the eastward of the wharf until they are above it; the batteries, supposing any to exist, at the head of the bay and on the eastern side of it, the only ones which would then be able to fire at them, being at a great distance, could not prevent them, and the guns on the ramparts of the town could not be pointed at them when in the mole, and previous to their getting there they were too far off, without firing into their own ships, which from the manner they are placed in order to be in the deepest water, could only fire stern chases at fire-ships approaching them from the head of the bay.

"Supposing your Lordship might wish to cut the ships out of the mole, permit me to say, it appears to me that if the guns on the wharf were silenced, which might be facilitated by ships flanking them from the eastward and southward, in which situation they would only be exposed to the distant fire of the batteries at the head of the bay, and on the eastern side of it, men might be landed on the wharf and from *thence* board the ships and burn them, or get them out if the wind was favourable; for the guns which could be brought to bear on them from the town are but few, and at a considerable distance, and the batteries in the different parts of the bay are still farther off, and a ship placed *close to that part of the wharf which joins the shore* might prevent any fresh troops from coming on the wharf, to oppose the landing or to assist the enemy's ships. Should your Lordship be already acquainted with the above particulars, I beg you will have the goodness to excuse my troubling you with them, which I have only done because I have heard different opinions given to Sir Hyde Parker respecting the practicability of attacking, with success, ships at Revel.

"I have the honour to be your Lordship's

"Most obedient humble servant,

"J. WOLLSTONECRAFT."

Upon his arrival in the Bay of Revel, he made application for pilots to come on board, and give the British ships a safe anchorage, and he immediately received the following reply:—

ADMIRAL SPIRIDOW TO LORD NELSON.

"Revel, $\frac{30 \text{ April,}}{12 \text{ May,}}$ 1801.

"Sir,

"Agreeably to your Excellency's wish, I send two pilots who will point out a good place for anchorage in the Bay of Revel. I have the honour to be, with great consideration, your very humble and very obedient servant,

"SPIRIDOW.

"Right Hon. Lord Viscount Nelson, &c. &c."

He also applied to obtain fresh meat and vegetables, which was thus responded to:—

GOVERNOR OF REVEL'S DISPATCH TO LORD NELSON.

"May 12th. (Received 13th do. off Revel.)

"Sir,

"In reply to the letter with which your Excellency has honoured me, I have the honour to inform you that an unarmed sloop may come to Revel for the purchasing of provisions when you think proper; but that his Britannic Majesty's squadron, commanded by you, must not approach our shores within range of cannon shot, until orders have been received respecting it by General the Baron d'Often Sacken.

"Your Excellency's dispatches were forwarded immediately to St. Petersburgh.

"I have the honour to be, with the greatest consideration and profound respect,

"Your Excellency's very humble,

"And very obedient servant,

"A. BALASCHOFF,

"Military Governor of Revel.

"Right Hon. Lord Nelson."

On the 9th of May, Lord Nelson acquainted Rear-Admiral Totty that he was desirous of keeping his squadron strong enough to master the Swedes, should they put to sea, and gave him directions to that effect as well as to the obtaining of provisions. The following is from Rear-Admiral Totty:—

"*Zealous*, off Bornholm, the 15th May, 1801."

"My Lord,

"I have the honour to acquaint your Lordship, that I passed over the Grounds with the squadron under my orders, on the evening of the 13th instant, and I joined Captain Murray upon his rendezvous off the north-east end of Bornholm last night; and agreeably to your Lordship's directions I have given orders to Captain Murray to take the ships and vessels named in the margin under his orders, and proceed with all possible dispatch towards the Gulf of Finland, and endeavour to join your Lordship, agreeably to the best information he can obtain respecting your situation.

"I have sent some of the small fast sailing vessels with Captain Murray, as I think they may be useful to your Lordship. I have received a copy of the orders which your Lordship gave to Captain Murray for the government of the squadron stationed off Bornholm, and your Lordship may rest assured that I shall strictly regulate my conduct thereby.

"So soon as the *Dart* returns from Dantzick, and I receive any information of the terms upon which fresh beef can be supplied for the use of the squadron, if the price does not exceed the sum your Lordship has stipulated, I shall send the *Alkmaar* thither for a cargo of bullocks; and as I find many of the squadron are short of bread, I shall therefore give directions to the ships which came with me to go to two-thirds allowance of that article, as I find Captain Murray gave similar directions to the squadron left under his orders. As it was necessary to keep the ships as light as possible, in order to pass over the Grounds, they could not take any supply of water in Copenhagen Road, but I understand they may readily be watered at Bornholm.

"The *Zealous* and *Powerful* have each of them eight guns in their holds, with a proportion of ammunition for the use of the gun-vessels under your Lordship's command. Fourteen of the guns are eighteen pounders, the other two twenty-four's.

"Having so lately transmitted to your Lordship the state and condition of the ships and vessels under my orders, and as Captain Murray will deliver those of the ships and vessels that were stationed off Bornholm, I do not trouble your Lordship at present upon that head.

"I have the honour to be, with the highest respect,
"My Lord,
"Your Lordship's most obedient and humble servant,
"THOMAS TOTTY.

"P.S.—Since writing the above, the Alecto fire-ship, Captain O'Brien,[1] has joined me from Leith. He brings no intelligence. Captain Inman has also just been with me, and he gives a sad account of the wants of the gun vessels, &c. under his orders; many of them are in want of fuel, and cannot purchase any, as their bills are not negotiable.
"T. T."

Lord Nelson remained in Revel Roads until the 17th. On the 16th he received the following from Admiral Spiridow:—

"Revel, May 16, 1801.
"My Lord,
"Your Excellency's letter to Count Pahlen shall be forwarded immediately, and the lugger Skylark shall receive from me all the assistance and attention in my power, whilst she remains in the port of Revel.

"Accept, my Lord, our best wishes for the accomplishment of your objects, to the real merits of which we can render justice, as they are not opposed to Russia. You carry with you our regrets that circumstances prevent our further cultivation of your acquaintance. I write in the name of the civil and military Governors as well as my own. I fail in expressing the sentiments of esteem with which you have inspired me.

"I have the honour to be, with great consideration,
"Your Excellency's very humble,
"And very obedient servant,
"SPIRIDOW."

[1] Captain Edward O'Brien attained the rank of Rear-Admiral, and died in December, 1808.

On the 15th and 17th Lord Nelson wrote to Lady Hamilton:—

"St. George, Revel Bay, May 15th, 1801.

"My dearest Friend,

"The Harpy brig sails to-morrow for England. You will not receive this line for a fortnight after her arrival. I cannot say a word on politics. I expect to find a new Admiral on my return, which will be in a very few days.

"Yours, &c.

"NELSON AND BRONTÉ.

"Most probably you will never receive this letter. I have three wrote for you now lying by me. Finish of eight lines to Lord St. Vincent:—'I expect to find a new Admiral when I return off Bornholm, or most probably you will never see again

" ' Your affectionate,

" ' N. & B.' "

"St. George, May 17th, 1801. 7 o'clock in the Evening.
Last letter.

"My dearest Friend,

"I sailed from Revel this morning, and feel I am now steering for England for the recovery of my health. I expect to be there a few days after this letter; for if the Admiralty have any bowels of compassion, an Admiral must have long since sailed to supersede me. I have wrote a very strong letter to the Board in case none is sailed. I shall keep by Rostock and Lubeck in case I am to go by land; it is only one day's journey to Hamburgh. This day I reckon, if Sir Hyde Parker had not been ordered home, I should have arrived perhaps in London. What a thought! but the time *shall* soon come in spite of all the world, and all my enemies, damn them. I cannot obey the Scriptures and bless them.

"I am rather inclined to believe that the Emperor of Russia had some fears for his fleet of forty-three sail of the line, for he seemed very anxious to get rid of my small squadron. I have much to tell you—the boat is waiting—night coming on. Adieu.

"Yours, &c.

"NELSON AND BRONTÉ."

He quitted Revel in consequence of a letter he received from Count Pahlen, who, on the part of the Emperor, expressed his surprise that he should, professing pacific dispositions, have brought his fleet into Revel Bay. Colonel Stewart says, Lord Nelson received this letter about 3 P.M. on the 16th of May, and that it was accompanied by a letter from General Sacken, expressing a wish that the British fleet should retire from the anchorage of Revel. Lord Nelson received it a few minutes before dinner time; he appeared to be a good deal agitated by it, but said little, and did not return an immediate reply. During dinner, however, he quitted the table, and in less than a quarter of an hour sent for his Secretary to peruse a letter which, in that short absence, he had composed. The signal for preparing to weigh was immediately made; the answer was sent on shore, and although contracts had been entered into for fresh provisions, &c. for the fleet, his Lordship would not admit of the least delay, but caused it to weigh, and to stand as far to sea as was safe for that evening. In his reply to Count Pahlen, Lord Nelson says, that his intention was to pay a very particular respect to his Imperial Majesty, and that he had submitted it to his pleasure which port he would wish him to come to, Revel or Cronstadt, and he added: "Your Excellency will have the goodness to observe to the Emperor, that I did not even enter the outer Bay of Revel, without the consent of their Excellencies the Governor and Admiral. My conduct, I feel, is so entirely different to what your Excellency has expressed in your letter, that I have only to regret, that my desire to pay a mark of attention to his Imperial Majesty has been so entirely misunderstood. That being the case, I shall sail immediately into the Baltic."[1] Nelson repeatedly affirmed, that had the Russian fleet been at Revel, he should not have received such a reply. The officers there received him with great kindness, and were equally surprised with himself at the nature of the communication he had received. The fleet in the Baltic at this time consisted of twenty-two sail of the line and forty-six frigates, bombs, fireships and gun-vessels. In the whole fleet there

---

[1] Letter Book. Dispatches and Letters, Vol. iv. p. 373.

was not a man in the hospital ship, and to use Nelson's own words, "A finer fleet never graced the ocean." Sir Hyde Parker had previously to Nelson's taking the chief command in the Baltic, dispatched Captain Fremantle upon a mission to Petersburgh. Count Panin wrote to Lord Nelson by Admiral Tchitchagoff, and expressed the desire of the Emperor of Russia to return to amicable relations with England. He also addressed the following to Admiral Sir Hyde Parker:—

### COUNT PANIN TO ADMIRAL SIR HYDE PARKER.

"Charged by the Emperor my master to receive your Excellency's communications, I am also authorised to reply to the letter addressed on the 26th current to Count Pahlen, and I feel greatly honoured by a commission so flattering to me, of being made the medium of the first conciliatory proposals which may lead to a reconciliation so desirable in all respects, and so needful to the general welfare. The Emperor has already made his intentions known to the Court of London, upon the different points which may become claims on him, such as the release of British subjects and the raising the embargo on British ships, but as your Excellency could not yet be informed from your Court of the explanations given to it in those respects by Count Woronzoff, his Imperial Majesty has permitted me to communicate to you, Sir, that he is ready to satisfy every just demand of your Court, as soon as he shall learn, by the reply which he expects from London, that his Britannic Majesty shares in his sincere wish for the re-establishment of peace, and that the compliance of his Imperial Majesty shall meet with a just return both towards him and towards his Allies, which he has the more reason to anticipate, as one of the first acts of his reign has been to put a stop to the detention of English sailors, and to suspend the sale of the confiscated property of British merchants. The spirit of justice and moderation which your Excellency has exhibited unequivocally in causing hostilities against the flag of the three Courts to be suspended, convinces me that you will perceive the fidelity of my august master's intentions by this declaration, and likewise an additional reason to continue the suspension of arms in the waters of the Baltic Sea, and so to give the Cabinets of St. Petersburgh and of London the opportunity of terminating by negotiation the unfortunate differences which have troubled the peace of the North of Europe. His Imperial Majesty wishes to receive a positive assurance of the prolongation of this armistice, and expects, Sir, to find it in your reply to this letter. I send it, as requested by your Excellency, by Captain Fremantle, and I introduce to him at the same time Vice-Admiral Tchitchagoff, who is charged by the Emperor to receive the ultimate explanations you may judge proper to transmit to me. With sentiments of the highest consideration I have the honour to be, Sir,

"Your Excellency's
"Very humble and very obedient servant,
"PANIN.

"St. Petersburgh, 29 April, o. s. 1801.

"P.S. At the moment of sending this despatch to Captain Fremantle, a British Cabinet courier has brought us a letter from Lord Hawkesbury, of which a copy is subjoined. Its contents announce a disposition on the part of your august Master perfectly in accordance with that which animates his Imperial Majesty, for the prompt re-establishment of good harmony. The explanations entered into might now, in some degree, be considered superfluous; but the Emperor, wishing to give your Excellency a proof of his confidence, has ordered me to forward this dispatch, notwithstanding the subsequent communications, which besides can only confirm you, Sir, in your pacific intentions.

"Ut in litteris.

"St. Petersburgh, 29 April, o. s. 1801."

LORD HAWKESBURY TO COUNT PAHLEN, APRIL 17TH, 1801.

"Monsieur le Comte,

"I received the letter your Excellency did me the honour to address to me by the hands of M. Smirnove, in which you announce the melancholy news of the death of the Emperor Paul I. and the happy accession of his august son to the Imperial throne. I am sensible in the highest degree of your Excellency's attention, and have hastened to place before the King my Master, the letter of his Imperial Majesty the

Emperor Alexander. I congratulate you, Count, on the accession of a Prince whose virtues and great qualities are so well known, and feel the value of an event so important, not merely to his own subjects, but to all Europe. I am commanded by the King to acquaint you that his Majesty has dispatched orders to the Commander of his fleet to suspend all hostile operations against Russia, and at the same time to inform you that his Majesty will send immediately a Minister to the Court of St. Petersburgh, who will be charged to express to his Imperial Majesty the warm interest he takes in his succession to the Empire, and who will be furnished with full powers to discuss and arrange the unfortunate differences which have arisen between the two Crowns, in order to re-establish the ancient and intimate connexion which subsisted between them, the suspension of which has caused the King great sorrow. I seize this occasion to express to you, Count, the great satisfaction I experience in witnessing the renewal of accustomed communications between England and Russia, and to offer you the respect and high consideration with which I have the honour to be, &c. &c."

The following declaration relates to this negotiation:—

*Declaration of Vice-Admiral Tchitchagoff to Lord Nelson, Duke of Bronté, Commander-in-chief of his Britannic Majesty's Naval forces in the Baltic.*

"Charged by the Emperor, my august Master, to enter into explanations with the Commander-in-chief of his Britannic Majesty's Naval forces upon some points relative to the reconciliation of the two Powers, I declare, that his Imperial Majesty being chiefly animated by the principles of honour, moderation, and disinterestedness, desires to yield to, and even to facilitate every measure that may tend to terminate the unfortunate differences which have arisen between the Powers of the North of Europe and England, and that his wish is for the re-establishment of the ancient friendship existing between Russia and England.

"Given on board the St. George,
 "His Britannic Majesty's ship,
"the $\frac{8}{20}\frac{\text{o.s.}}{\text{n.s.}}$ May, 1801.
 " Paul de Tchitchagoff."

Lord Nelson transmitted his dispatches to the Admiralty through Sir James Crawfurd, as appears from the following:

SIR JAMES CRAWFURD TO LORD NELSON.

"Hamburgh, 19th May, 1801.

"My Lord,

"I had the honour to receive, by the last post from Copenhagen, your Lordship's letter of the 8th instant, accompanying your dispatches to Mr. Nepean, and various private letters which I forwarded to England by the first post. Though it is perhaps rather out of time, I cannot but seize this opportunity, the first which I have had, of congratulating your Lordship on the great and glorious event of the second of April. It is my most sincere prayer that you may long continue to adorn that country whose name, already the first in the world, you have so greatly exalted. I desire nothing so much as to have an opportunity of paying you my court in person, an honour which I hope you will allow me whenever an opportunity may present itself. In the mean time I beg leave to assure your Lordship of the great respect with which I am, my Lord, your most obedient and very humble servant,

"JAMES CRAWFURD."

From the Secretary of the Admiralty Lord Nelson received the following:—

"Admiralty Office, May 31st, 1801.

"My Lord,

"I received by the Hamburgh mail, through Sir James Crawfurd, your Lordship's letter of the 7th instant, acquainting me, for the information of my Lords Commissioners of the Admiralty, of the communication you had had with the Swedish Admiral, and with the determination you had formed of shewing yourself with a part of the fleet under your command in the Gulf of Finland, leaving Captain Murray with the remainder off the island of Bornholm. I also received on the 29th instant by the Harpy your Lordship's three letters of the 17th, one inclosing a copy of the correspondence which had passed with his Excellency Count Pahlen and the Russian Governor and Admiral at Revel, the other giving information of your having left the bay of Revel, in order to rejoin the squadron off Bornholm, and of the quantity of bread remaining on board the fleet; I lost no time in laying those letters before their Lordships, and I have received their commands to acquaint you that they cannot but feel some regret that your endeavours to mark your respect for his Imperial Majesty should not have been attended with success, and to desire you will transmit to me a copy of your letter to the Swedish Admiral, to which you have referred in your first mentioned letter. I have their Lordships' further commands to acquaint your Lordship that vessels are now loaded, and will proceed into the Baltic immediately with a supply of ten weeks provisions for the fleet, in order that your Lordship may send such instructions to the Officer who may be entrusted with the protection of these vessels as may be necessary for his guidance in respect to his junction with you. I have the honour to be, my Lord,

"Your Lordship's most obedient humble servant,
"Evan Nepean."

On the 20th of May Lord Nelson fell in with Lord St. Helens in the Latona on his way to Russia, having been appointed Ambassador to the Court of St. Petersburgh. He had three hours conversation with him. On the preceding day Lord St. Helens had left copies of his dispatches for Lord Nelson, as appears from the following letter:—

"Latona, off Bornholm, May 19, 1801.

"My Lord,
"Though I most sincerely hope and trust that I shall have the satisfaction of meeting your Lordship before I reach St. Petersburgh, I think it advisable to leave with Admiral Totty the inclosed duplicates of the dispatches which I am to deliver to your Lordship from the Lords Commissioners of the Admiralty.

"Admiral Totty has obligingly consented to allow the Courier cutter to accompany me to Cronstadt; and I shall not fail to dispatch her to your Lordship as soon as I shall be enabled to furnish you with any interesting intelligence.

"I have the honour to be, with great truth and respect,
"My Lord,
"Your Lordship's most faithful and obedient servant,
"St. Helens.

"Right Honourable Lord Nelson,
&c. &c. &c."

"Latona, at sea, 21st May, 1801.

"My dear Lord,

"I return your Lordship, with my very sincerest thanks, the different papers that you have had the goodness to confide to me. I have taken copies of most of them, but have not sent any to the Secretary of State, presuming that your Lordship will forward the whole to the Lords Commissioners of the Admiralty with your next dispatches. Those, which I now inclose to you for Lord Hawkesbury, contain nothing of a very pressing nature; but I could wish that they may be sent as soon as convenient, as his Majesty's Ministers will naturally be well pleased to hear that I am advanced so far on my voyage to St. Petersburgh.

"I hope to re-dispatch the Courier cutter to your Lordship very soon with some satisfactory intelligence. In the mean time, pray believe me ever with the sincerest attachment and respect, and most cordial wishes for your speedy recovery,

"My dear Lord,
"Your most faithful and obedient servant,
"St. Helens."

The following letters were addressed by his Royal Highness the Duke of Clarence to Lord Nelson:—

"Bushy House, May 27th, 1801.

"Dear Nelson,

"I am to acknowledge yours of the 27th of April, and shall say nothing at present upon the recall of Sir Hyde Parker, but shall defer that and many other points till we meet. Knowing, as you do, my attachment to you, it cannot but be to me a matter of satisfaction that you succeed to the command of the fleet. I hope you will give them enough to do, and keep them in good discipline.

"I rejoice you feel satisfied with what I said in the House of Lords; it was, believe me, but your due, and I shall be happy to be able to say very shortly a great deal more in honour of the Hero of the Nile and of Copenhagen. Assure Sir Thomas Graves it afforded me great pleasure to inform the country of his services, and I am happy he is pleased with me.

"My best wishes attend you publicly and privately, and ever believe me to be,

"Dear Nelson,
"Yours sincerely,
"WILLIAM H."

"Bushy House, May 31st, 1801.

"Dear Nelson,

"I am to acknowledge yours of the 10th and 17th instant, and most cordially agree with you at the improper recall of Sir Hyde Parker. I really know nothing, and have not yet even seen him; but this I am certain of, that a certain person *is not fit* for where he now is. I believe the Armistice with Denmark, and the correspondence with Russia and Sweden, has given offence to our Ministry, in my opinion without any reason. I always considered the fleet being sent to the Baltic, in the situation this country was at that time, a very dangerous measure, and might have been very fatal. Your representation of the North is as I have considered it: and really, after eight years of expensive war, it seems strange for Government to wish to increase our enemies. I see no chance of peace with France, and am therefore the more anxious to have tranquillity restored where you are. I take the contrary sentiments in Ministers here to have recalled Sir Hyde Parker.

"I am truly concerned you complain of your health, and sincerely hope to see you very shortly in this country, not to drink asses milk, but to enjoy the company of your friends, amongst whom I hope you number him who was, is, and ever will be,

"Dear Nelson,
"Yours sincerely,
"WILLIAM H."

## CHAPTER III.

### 1801.

WHILST in the Baltic Lord Nelson heard of the death of his elder brother, Maurice Nelson, Esq., of the Navy Office, who died on the 24th of April, after a few days illness of a brain fever, leaving Lord Nelson his executor, who, upon receiving intelligence of his death, immediately wrote to Mr. Davison to do " every thing which is right for his poor blind wife." He was ignorant of his brother's circumstances, or as to the manner in which he had provided for her, for she was not his wife. Her name was Ford; she had lived with him during many years, lost her sight, and become a cripple. Nelson felt that she was truly an object of compassion, and that was enough to direct him to take every care of her. He desires Mr. Davison to see that she has a proper and ample subsistence, and declares his willingness, if it be required, to make it up. Alluding to his deceased brother, he says, " It is the only true regard I can pay to his memory. He was always good and kind to me." The will printed below[1] is a

---

[1] " As the term of this life is at all times uncertain, and being at this time of sound mind and memory, and judging it unnecessary to employ an Attorney to make this my last Will and Testament, which I shall sign at the bottom of every page, should I have occasion to write more than one. Item, I give and bequeath the interest of all moneys whatever that I have now in the Funds or may hereafter have, together with all monies that may be due to me at the time of my decease from any person or persons, to Mrs. Susannah Ford (alias Nelson), with whom I have lived in the habits of the utmost friendship for many years, for the term of her natural life, which she is to enjoy without molestation from any one; and when it shall please God she shall depart this life, then my will is, that the sum of five hundred pounds, five per cents., be given to my brother Horatio Nelson, a Captain in the Royal Navy, as also the sum of five hundred pounds each to my two nieces, Susannah and Catharine Bolton, daughters of my sister, Susannah Bolton; but, if it should so happen that the aforesaid Mrs. Susannah Ford, alias Nelson, should die before my said nieces should arrive at the age of twenty-one years, then and in that case, I do request of my brother, Horatio Nelson, Esq. to take the said sums of

proof of the great affection Maurice Nelson entertained for his brother Horatio. William Nelson, it will be observed, is not mentioned in it.

On the 23rd of May Lord Nelson wrote to the widow thus:—

"St. George, May 23, 1801.

"My dear Mrs. Nelson,

"You are, and ever shall be, considered by me as the honoured widow of my dear brother; and before I knew in what circumstances he had left you I had desired our good friend, Mr. Davison, to take care of you in every manner which could make you comfortable; and I can assure you that I consider myself as only a faithful steward, and that if any more income is wanted than the interest of my brother's little fortune, that I shall have great pleasure in supplying it, for he was too generous to be rich.

"And ever believe me,

"Your truly affectionate brother,

"NELSON AND BRONTÉ.

"Our excellent friend, Lady Hamilton, will be the interpreter of my sentiments, for she is as good as an angel."

He wrote also to Lady Hamilton:—

"St. George, off Rostock, May 24th, 1801.

"My dearest Friend,

"Yesterday, I joined Admiral Totty, where I found little Parker with your dear, kind, friendly letters. How can I

---

five hundred pounds above given to my nieces, Susannah and Catharine Bolton, in trust for them until they shall attain the age of twenty-one years, or until they are married, which I request may be left at his discretion: but if both, or either of my said nieces should die before they attain the age of twenty-one years, then and in that case I request of my brother, Horatio Nelson, to accept of the said legacies I have left them, as well as all other moneys I may die possessed of, for his sole use and benefit: and I likewise request that my said brother will have the goodness to see the intention of this my last Will and Testament fulfilled. In witness whereof I have hereunto set my hand, as well to this as to the foregoing page, this sixteenth day of July, in the year of our Lord one thousand seven hundred and ninety-five.

"MAURICE NELSON."

"Witness the above being interlined,

"ROBERT DAVIES.
"C. N. FORBES."

sufficiently thank you for all your goodness and kindness to me, a forlorn outcast, except in your generous soul. My health I have represented to the Admiralty in such terms that I have no doubt but an Admiral has sailed to take my place. The Harpy has carried a stronger letter than any of the former. This vessel states that I do not know that I shall go to sea again, as my health requires the shore, and gentle exercise, and so it does, and really if the Admiralty had allowed me to go home, and in the event of hostilities being renewed in the Baltic, I might perhaps, in that case, have been able to command the fleet, but the Baltic folks will never fight me if it is to be avoided. In my humble opinion, we shall have peace with the Northern Powers, if we are *just* in our desires. Will you have the goodness to carry the inclosed after you have sealed it to Mrs. Maurice Nelson, and your own dear generous heart will say every kind thing for me. She shall be fixed where she pleases, and with every comfort in this world, and ever be considered as my honoured sister-in-law. I feel my dear brother's confidence, and she shall feel he has not mistaken me. Tell Mrs. William Nelson how much I esteem her for all her kindness, and that I shall never forget her complying with my request and staying with you, although I hope it has been truly pleasant to herself.

"Ever yours truly,
"NELSON AND BRONTÉ."

He gave to his brother's widow an annuity of £100. *per annum*, which she received until his death, and she was afterwards assisted by Lady Hamilton. She died about 1810 or 1811.

To the Earl of St. Vincent on the 24th he wrote, "The death of my dear brother, which I received only yesterday, has naturally affected me a good deal; and if I do not get some repose very soon, another will go—six sons are gone out of eight; but I hope yet to see you, and to cheer up once more."[1]

On the twenty-fourth he reached Rostock, and remained there until June 1st. Colonel Stewart draws a picture of Nelson's mode of life, whilst with his fleet. After alluding

[1] Clarke and McArthur, Vol. ii. p. 286.

to his manner of keeping it alert, of supplying it with proper provisions, preserving the health of all, economising its resources, &c. he says, "His hour of rising was four or five o'clock, and of going to rest about ten; breakfast was never later than six, and generally nearer to five o'clock. A Midshipman or two were always of the party; and I have known him send during the middle watch, to invite the little fellows to breakfast with him, when relieved. At table with them he would enter into their boyish jokes, and be the most youthful of the party. At dinner he invariably had every officer of his ship, in their turn, and was both a polite and hospitable host. The whole ordinary business of the fleet was invariably dispatched, as it had been by the Earl of St. Vincent, before eight o'clock. The great command of time which Lord Nelson thus gave himself, and the alertness which this example imparted throughout the fleet, can only be understood by those who witnessed it, or who know the value of early hours."

Lord Nelson despatched the Speedwell on the morning of the 25th. The following letter must therefore have been written on the 26th :—

"St. George, Bay of Rostock.

"My dearest Friend,

"Although I wrote you late last night by the Speedwell all my proceedings to that time, I yet should think myself a great beast if I was to omit an opportunity of writing to you a line by way of Hamburgh, where I am sending off an express to Sir James Crawfurd. I wrote to the Admiralty yesterday that I did not think I should be able to write any more letters to them, for the stooping so many hours hurts me very much. I trust yet to being in London before June 12th. If the new Admiral would arrive, I should certainly sail in two hours. I have directed the London to be the show ship, for I will have no visitors here that I can help. It is said that the Duke or Prince of Mecklenburg intends to come here to see the fleet, but nothing, you may rely, shall force me to go on shore. The hock I ordered to be sent by the waggon. The Harpy will arrive, I hope, to-morrow. The Speedwell will have a good passage. I have ten millions of things to say to you, and I long so to let all out. If Ministers had really thought highly of me they should have given me the command in February, not in May, when I can do no good. I am sure you will comfort poor blind Mrs. Nelson. Whatever you do, I will confirm; and there is an old black servant, James Price, as good a man as ever lived, he shall be taken care of, and have a corner in my house as long as he lives. My uncle left him £20. a-year.

" Ever yours,
" NELSON AND BRONTÉ.

" This day comes on my great cause against the Earl. May the *just* gain it. I am glad to hear of your determination not to leave London 'till my arrival."

I have previously alluded to the misconception of the Emperor of Russia as to the visit of Nelson in the Revel Roads. On the 26th a Russian lugger brought a reply to the letter of Nelson to Count Pahlen upon his departure. It apologized for the mistake, and expressed an anxious desire for the restoration of peace, and gave an invitation to Nelson to Petersburgh in any way most agreeable to himself. In his reply to this invitation he says, " His Imperial Majesty's justice has filled the idea I had formed of his excellent heart and head; and I am sure the handsome manner in which the embargo has been taken off the British shipping will give the greatest pleasure to my good and gracious Sovereign." He added, " I am truly sensible of the great honour done me by the invitation of his Imperial Majesty, and at a future time I hope to have the pleasure of presenting my humble duty. I have now only to pray, that a permanent (which must be honourable) peace may be established between our gracious Sovereigns, and that our august Masters reigns may be blessed with every happiness which this world can afford."[1] When the lugger departed with the reply she fired a salute, upon which Colonel Stewart says Lord Nelson observed to his Secretary, upon his return from the shore, " Did you hear that little fellow salute? Well,

[1] Letter Book. Dispatches and Letters, Vol. iv. p. 393.

now there is peace with Russia, depend upon it: our jaunt to Revel was not so bad after all."

The following was to Lady Hamilton:—

"St. George, Rostock, May 27th, 1801.

"My dearest Friend,

"A Russian lugger has this moment brought me a letter from the Russian Minister announcing that the Emperor, to mark the effect of my letter of the 16th of May, had instantly taken off the embargo from the English shipping in all the ports of Russia. This, my dear Friend, is such a strong proof of peace in the Baltic that this fleet must be home in a very short time; but I trust that another Admiral is arrived, or nearly so, by this time, when I shall set off in two hours. All the world is come to Rostock to see me, and are much disappointed at the finding that I do not either go on shore, or permit them to come on board the St. George. No, never, I have said so, and would not break my word for all the world. The London is the show ship. The General of the troops sent off to desire to make me a visit; my answer was, that I had no right to expect that honour, as I was unable to return his visit. However, yesterday, the old General and three Aides-de-camp came, walked over the ship, such a one as they had never seen, and went on shore again. I have announced to the Duke of Mecklenburgh the impossibility of my going on shore, therefore, he may come or not, as he pleases, for nothing shall make me go on shore unless to set off for England, if the Admiralty are unkind enough to refuse me a ship-of-war to carry me home, as the late Board did—but never mind.

"Yours ever,

"NELSON AND BRONTÉ.

"Best regards to Sir William, the Duke, Mr. Beckford, and all our friends. I have just had a deputation of the Senate to invite me on shore, but *No*."

On the 1st of June Lord Nelson was visited by the Duke of Mecklenburgh Strelitz, the brother of Queen Charlotte.

To Lady Hamilton he writes:—

"St. George, Rostock, June 1st, 1801.

"My dearest Friend,

"I was in hopes my successor would have been arrived long before this time, and why he is not I cannot imagine, unless it is wished to kill me; for a pistol put to my head would be charity to keeping me here dying a lingering death. I feel the cruelty of the measure, for everybody knows my readiness to serve when I am able, and there is anything to be done, but in the Baltic there can be nothing, and in fourteen days I believe we shall not have a ship in the Baltic, for all will be peace. May God send me safe amongst my friends, who will nurse and cherish me. I am going to Kioge Bay, there to wait my successor's arrival, for he cannot be many hours. Two days ago I had sailed from this place for Kioge Bay, when, being obliged to anchor with a fine wind, I received a letter from his Highness the Duke of Mecklenburg Strelitz, brother to the Queen, saying that he was arrived at Rostock to see me, and desired I would appoint the time for his coming on board the St. George. I was therefore obliged to return to this anchorage, and wrote, expressing my sorrow that my ill health would not allow of the possibility of my going on shore to wait upon him. Yesterday was a bad day, to-day fine, and I hope the old gentleman will come off, sixty-one years of age, and the moment he is gone the anchor shall be at the bows. Not all the princes in Europe should make me go on shore. I have said it, and that is sufficient. My word is my bond. There is one comfort, my dearest friend, they cannot keep this fleet when it comes peace, which will take place in ten days at farthest. I do not write all I could, as my letter goes by way of Hamburgh, and will most probably be read.

"Believe me ever yours,
"NELSON AND BRONTÉ.

"Best regards to Sir William. Hardy, Parker, Stewart, all desire their respects."

"St. George, June 1st, 1801, 8 A.M.

"My dearest Friend,

"I have been annoyed to death for an hour this day. The Duke of Mecklenburgh, with his whole Court, men, women, and children, to the amount of one hundred, I am told, came on board at two o'clock, but I got rid of them before three. He is a respectable venerable man, made ten thousand apologies for the liberty he had taken in bringing so many persons, for he knew that I had forbid it; to which I could only reply that *he commanded;* and having given him two salutes of the whole fleet of twenty-one guns each, he went off quite happy. He admired your picture most exceedingly, but who does not? At daylight I sail for Kioge to wait the arrival of the new Admiral.

" Ever yours,
"Nelson and Bronté."

On the 4th Lord Nelson arrived in Kioge Bay, and wrote to Captain Ball, the Commander of the Navy at Gibraltar, pitying the poor Maltese for losing one whose counsel they anxiously sought, and readily attended to. The apparent disorder of Nelson's heart gave rise to a fear of consumption. He says: " As I know you have always been kind to me, I know you will be sorry to hear that I have been even at *death's* door, apparently in a consumption. I am now rallied a little, but the disorder is in itself so flattering, that I know not whether I am really better, and no one will tell me, but all in the fleet are so truly kind to me, that I should be a wretch not to *cheer up.* Foley has put me under a regimen of milk, at four in the morning; Murray has given me lozenges, and all have proved their desire to keep my mind easy, for I hear of no complaints, or other wishes than to have me with them."[1]

On the 5th and 8th he wrote to Lady Hamilton :—

" St. George, Kioge Bay, June 5th, 1801.

" My dearest Friend,

" Little potatoe Harris has this moment given me your letter. I can only assure you that he brought the best recommendation in Europe, for if he had brought letters from all the Kings and Queens, &c. &c. in Europe, they would have all sunk as they ought before the orders of my guardian angel. When I consider how my saint Emma has

---

[1] Letter Book. Dispatches and Letters, Vol. iv. p. 401.

protected me, I am always full of gratitude. However, my devotion ended, as the boy cannot live upon prayers, I have asked him to dinner, and Hardy has put him in a mess, and you may rely on my care of him whilst I remain, which I trust will not be many days. Hardy says our youngsters amount to thirty-five, and none of them can now be shot at in the Baltic, if Lord St. Helens manages well. Apropos, you know him, did you dine with him? He seems a very mild, good man, but all our diplomatic men are so slow. His Lordship told me that he hoped in a month he should be able to tell me something decisive. Now, what can take two hours I cannot even guess, but Ministers must do something for their diamond boxes. I gained the unconditional release of our ships, which neither Ministers nor Sir Hyde Parker [could accomplish], by showing my fleet. Then they became alarmed, begged I would go away, or it would be considered as warlike. On my complying, it pleased the Emperor and his Ministers so much, that the whole of the British shipping were given up in the following words: 'Je ne saurais donner à votre Excellence un témoignage plus éclatant de la confiance que l'Empereur mon maître lui accorda qu'en lui annonçant l'effet qu'a produit sa lettre de 16 de ce mois. Sa Majesté Impériale a ordonné sur le champ la lever de l'Embargo mis sur les Navires Anglais.' I must stop, for old Mr. Sheppard, Purser of the Vanguard, is just come on board to dine with me. I never forget our old friends, and Mr. S. is really a good old man, but who is obliged to go to sea from the extravagance of his children. Old Sheppard has made his bow to your picture: so I made Harris, and every one I make do the same, that has the pleasure of knowing Santa Emma. I am anxious in the extreme at not getting letters from England, nor any notice of the speedy arrival of an Admiral.

"Ever yours,

"NELSON AND BRONTÉ.

"Best regards to Sir William, the Duke, Lord William, Mr. Beckford and all friends. Hardy and Parker desire their regards."

"St. George, June 8th, 1801.

"My dearest Friend,

"I may now tell you that I have been since April 15th rapidly in a decline, but am now, thank God, I firmly believe, past all danger. On the 15th of April I rowed five hours in a bitter cold night, in a boat, as I fancied Sir Hyde Parker was going after the Swedish fleet. A cold struck me to the heart. On the 27th I had one of my terrible spasms or heart-stroke, which had near carried me off, and the severe disappointment of being kept in a situation where there can be nothing to do before August, almost killed me. From that time to the end of May I brought up what every one thought was my lungs, and I was emaciated more than you can conceive; but Parker came, and brought me all your truly affectionate letters, in particular that of May 5th; it roused me, made me reflect that I had still one dear friend who would not desert me although *all* the world might. It gave a turn to my disorder. I have been mending ever since, firmly relying on your goodness, and am perhaps as well this day as ever I was in my life. I am in momentary expectation of the arrival of an Admiral, for I must not remain here. Probably I have lost my cause against Earl St. Vincent by it; indeed, after the letters I have wrote, unless the Admiralty have a desire to see me dead, they cannot allow me to remain; but God Almighty has protected me, in spite of all the little great men. It is this day thirty-four days since I have had a scrap of a pen from England, so little do the Admiralty think of us. Merchant ships from London bring papers of the 23rd of May, but the Admiralty not a line. Don't you recollect how I got scolded because I sent letters to them only three ways, and a fourth offered—it happened at Palermo,[1] when I was slaving—and for which the present First Lord of the Admiralty is trying to rob me of my honourable right; but if I am poor by such unjust means, what I have will wear well, for it is honestly got at the expense of my *blood*; therefore, never mind them, my happiness, thank God, does not rest either on their smiles or frowns. I keep a fast-sailing brig ready to carry me off the

---

[1] See Vol. i. page 298, *ante.*

moment my successor arrives. May the heavens bless and preserve you, my only true friend. I rejoice that Mrs. W. Nelson is still with you. I am sure of your goodness to poor blind Mrs. Nelson; whatever you promise her I will most punctually perform. Best regards to all friends.

"Ever yours,
"NELSON AND BRONTÉ."

Colonel Stewart had been dispatched to Copenhagen, and wrote to Lord Nelson as follows:—

"Copenhagen, June 8th.

"My dear Lord,

"I came here yesterday by water from Kioge through the Amack Channel, which is of an infinitely more intricate description than I had formed to myself an idea of. The greater part of the Strait, which begins across from Draco to the main, is so very shallow, as to admit of no vessels of any burden or draft of water above six feet in general, and the shallowest reef begins and seems to go right across at least four miles from this town. Yesterday being Sunday, no Ministers were in town, nor have I yet been able to find either Mr. Lizakowitz or Mr. Walterstorff at home, being not returned from the country. I had, however, occasion to have much explanation with the Governor, the Prince of Wurtemberg, relative to a very cavalier manner in which they sent on board the schooner again one or two of the sailors who had only landed with the St. George's officers' clothes, and to the circumstance of every officer being obliged to be attended by a Danish serjeant, if walking the streets. The Prince put everything on the best intentioned footing which I believe he could, but I could not bring matters to much understanding about the unpleasant mode in which our officers were followed by what they call 'military attention,' until Lindholm went to the Prince about it this morning, who has, I find, given directions that every such symptom of jealousy should cease in future.

"I have had fifty reports and informations about the hostility of the Danes towards us, the preparations for future offence, as well as defence, their breach of the armistice by repair and refit of their ships, &c. and have reason to think, from what could be gathered from a good deal of conversation with Lindholm this morning, that the sum total is, the whole nation is enraged at the loss of their colonies, and are certainly carrying on every preparation in their power, as far as relates to land operations, which Lindholm will, I think, explain to your Lordship as a measure of general preparation against the worst which may come on *all* sides. As he intends to be on board the St. George to-morrow, I need scarcely trouble you, my Lord, with the substance of our conversation this day, and will only observe, that he seems to feel equally confident of a peace as we do, but cannot help expressing the ill-humoured grace with which it will *now* be received, since the loss (which they pretend to call *unexpected*) of their colonies. To that event, rather than to new instructions supposed to have been conveyed from Petersburgh in the Russian brig, is, I believe, to be attributed the hostile feature which every thing has borne within these last ten days. I taxed Mr. L. pretty roundly with the circumstance of the refit of their ships, which you will find he will positively deny: I think, however, I shall ascertan before I leave this. As to appearances, they are the same to my eye as when here before; but I have scarcely had a view. I have been contending hard with the old lady of the hotel here to let me send by this conveyance the last three English papers, but she will not let them leave the club room. I however perceive no news in them, and no confirmation of the Guadaloupe surrender. Mr. Lindholm has informed me that by the Hamburgh mail, which is just arrived, the French are retaking possession of Ehrenbreitstein, and marching 50,000 men into Germany—that the King of Prussia is receding from Hanover—that 10,000 French have been shipped from Ancona into Turkey—and that we are in possession of Rosetta, the Grand Vizir's *advance* being within three days march of that place.

"Mr. Balfour promises to send this safe off, and also his newspapers the moment he receives them. I shall proceed to join you, my dear Lord, to-morrow night, if the *Blanchisseuse* be expeditious, if not at least on Wednesday morning, and shall do so with even more pleasure than I always must feel to join you, on this occasion, as the ill-natured and jealous eye, with which we English are now viewed here, is not very tempting to a longer residence among the Danes than is necessary. I have the honour to be, with the greatest respect and gratitude,

"Your Lordship's most faithful servant,
"WM. STEWART.

"My head is so annoying with the continuation of my cold, that I fear I have been penning sadly confused stuff."

The following to Lady Hamilton relates to the feeling of the Danes in regard to their West India islands:—

"St. George, June 10th, 1801, Kioge Bay.

"My dearest Friend,

"It is now thirty-six days since I received the scrap of a pen from England, although the wind has blown fair these four days. What it means is beyond my comprehension. We have newspapers to the 25th by which I see no movements of a new Admiral. *I duly appreciate* the kindness of the Admiralty, and nothing I believe but God's protection has saved my life, and thank God, but not them, I am perfectly recovered, and as far as relates to health, I don't think I ever was stronger or in better health. It is odd, but after severe illness I feel much better. I continue my warm milk every morning at four o'clock. In ten days the fleet must be ordered home, for no power in the Baltic will fight us this year. I shall not forget all these things. Yesterday I had the Prince Royal's Adjutant on board to dinner, with a civil message from the Prince. The Danes have a great confidence in my opinion, and we had much confidential conversation, *therefore* you may rely that Denmark *fights* no more against me, but I find the whole country is in a ferment at the unusual and hard capitulation forced upon their West India islands, and so I think them, such as even the French under monarchy never imposed when they took our islands last war.

"*June 11th.* This day twenty-two years I was made a Post Captain by Sir Peter Parker,[1] as good a man as ever lived.

[1] See Vol. i. p. 7, note.

If you meet him again, say that I shall drink his health in a bumper this day, for I do not forget that I owe my present exalted rank to his partiality, although I feel, if I had even been in an humbler sphere, that Nelson would have been Nelson still. My eyes are almost stretched out looking at that point of land where ships come from England, but alas! not a thing to be seen. I begin to be very uneasy. Little Harris has begged that he may have a full dress suit of uniform, which I have promised him when we get to England. If he is kept in order he will be a good young man, and with thirty-five there is no great danger of his being spoilt, but he is too much for his age. When will any thing arrive? May she bring me as kind affectionate letters as the last, and I shall bear till our arrival, which cannot be many days."

Captain Ball wrote to Lord Nelson to congratulate him on his victory:—

"Alexander at sea, 10th June, 1801.

"My dear Lord,

"Never did I feel a more joyful and happy moment, than when I heard of your Lordship's most glorious victory over the Danes. You may now claim the fairest title to Cæsar's motto, 'Veni, vidi,' &c. and this last brilliant occasion has proved to the world, that you possess the abilities of a statesman as well as the qualities of a great hero. May God preserve your Lordship's health to the end of a long life, that you may enjoy your great fame and well-earned laurels.

"Mrs. Ball has sent me a copy of your Lordship's letter to her respecting me, for which I can only offer the sentiments of the most grateful heart. It is truly flattering to me that your Lordship should be exerting every friendly effort to serve me at a time that you must be so fully occupied. Your Lordship has endeavoured to get me established at Malta; but I believe it would be much easier for you to gain another signal victory, than in this one instance, to conquer the jobbing system, although the Ministers are called to act patriotically by the unanimous voice of ninety thousand people, who have only asked this one favour of our Government, the refusal of which will not be forgiven; as the Maltese perceive that they are treated as a conquered people. When

Sir R. Abercromby paid a second visit to Malta, where he staid a month, it was his intention to have sent me on board of my ship, but the Bishop at the head of the clergy, and all the corporate bodies waited on him to express their gratitude to me, and solicit that I might not be removed, which Sir Ralph found was the effect of real attachment; and as he risked losing the island by removing me, he requested me to remain some time longer. The Maltese were so oppressed by General Pigot's government, that they had planned an insurrection, which would have broken out but for the assurances I gave them that their grievances would soon be redressed. I inclose an extract of a letter from Mr. Paget to Lord Grenville, and an extract from Sir Ralph's letter to me.[1]

"General Pigot was second in command of the army under Sir R. Abercromby, and was landed at Malta to make way for General Hutchinson to be second, who was a great favorite. A General Officer told a friend of mine that he might perceive Sir Ralph's opinion of the improbability of Malta surrendering by his giving the command to Pigot, who had orders to act *only* on the defensive, and it was agreed on between Lord Keith and Sir Ralph to withdraw our forces from Malta the first week in October, and it would have been done before, but from my sanguine report. Luckily for the credit of our country, it surrendered in September; the blockade of Malta has certainly contributed to strengthen the high opinion foreigners entertain of our naval abilities and wonderful perseverance. I expect Hallowell at Malta soon by whom I shall write more fully. I am very happy to hear that the worthy Sir William and my dear sister Hamilton are well. I beg my best respects to them.

"Troubridge has proved himself my warm friend, he has endeavoured to get me established at Malta, and has spoken in his strong language very fully his sentiments. Ministers may be sorry, when it is too late, at not having complied with the wishes of the Maltese. Adieu, my dear Lord, may God continue to protect you, and increase your prosperity, is the fervent prayer of

"Your Lordship's obliged and devoted,
"ALEXANDER JOHN BALL."

[1] These are wanting.

The following is from the Danish Adjutant-General, Lindholm:—

> "His Britannic Majesty's brig the Kite,
> June the 10th, 1801, at noon.
>
> "My Lord,
>
> "I have this moment received a letter from his Royal Highness the Crown Prince, who has given me orders to communicate to your Lordship that on the evening of the 8th, some English officers were on shore at Copenhagen, from his Majesty's schooner the Eling, and that some dispute had arisen between them and the populace of that city, but fortunately being near the guard, the officers thereof interfered immediately, and prevented any injury being done. The irritation of the people must be occasioned by the capture of our West India possessions, and from their idea that the capitulation is severer than they could have expected, considering the nature of the dispute between the two countries, for until that news arrived Sir Thomas Williams, Captain Devonshire, and other officers were on shore, did me the honour to call on me, and walked about the city entirely unmolested, and as a proof that his Royal Highness has endeavoured to prevent any disrespect being paid to the British officers since that time he had ordered that a non-commissioned officer should attend them to interfere in case of need. It gives his Royal Highness pain that this circumstance should have happened, and he certainly will prevent any repetition thereof as much as lays in his power; but his Royal Highness thinks the surest and most effectual manner of preventing it, in the present moment of the displeasure of the people, is, that the British officers should not go on shore at that city until the so much wished for happy reconciliation is settled between the two Courts. I beg your Lordship will excuse my not stating to you personally what I have the honour of writing, for in attempting to land last night at Kioge, it was so dark we could not find the harbour, and after being three hours in the boat we returned very wet to the Kite. I am awaiting the abatement of the wind to go on shore to shift myself, and if the weather is moderate I will certainly wait on your Lordship to-morrow; but if on

the contrary it should be stormy, I pray your Lordship will have the kindness to send a small vessel as near the harbour of Kioge as is safe, in order to facilitate my wish of waiting on your Lordship as early as possible.

"Your Lordship's kind reception of me yesterday, and the great attention and civility I experienced while on board the St. George, made that day one of the pleasantest of my life; but all the joy that arose in consequence thereof is damped by this very disagreeable and unpleasant communication which falls to my lot to be the conveyer of to your Lordship, as I assure your Lordship it is my private hope and I am sure it is also that of his Royal Highness, that this unpleasant accident may not be the cause of any coolness or alteration in the harmony that has subsisted since the conclusion of the armistice. With sentiments of the most unfeigned regard, I have the honour to subscribe myself, my Lord,

"Your Lordship's most obedient, and most
"Humble servant,
"H. LINDHOLM.

"The Right Honourable Lord Viscount Nelson,
&c. &c. &c."

Nelson, always alert, immediately wrote to express his hope that if any serious insult had been offered by any persons to British officers, they would be brought to punishment.

Adjutant-General Lindholm writes:—

"Kioge, June 11th, 1801.

"My Lord,

"I beg your Lordship will excuse me for not having the honour to wait on you to-day, as I am very unwell, and wish to go to Copenhagen as soon as possible. I hear that a Midshipman from the Eling is the cause of a little trouble which was of no consequence. I was almost sure that our populace has not been the aggressor, but I will not accuse any man. I hope and I wish that no animosity will exist between two nations who have been friends in many centuries.

"Permit me, my Lord, to ask if one of our frigates who is

arrived in Norway from the Mediterranean can return to Copenhagen?

"I have the honour to remain, with the highest esteem,
"My Lord,
"Your Lordship's
"Most obedient and most humble servant,
"H. LINDHOLM.

"Right Honourable Lord Viscount Nelson,
Commander-in-chief, &c. &c."

"Kioge, June 11th, 1801.

"My Lord,

"I have this moment had the honour to receive your Lordship's letter, brought me by an officer of the Kite. I am very sorry that I cannot, so much I desired, wait on your Lordship, as I am sick, and am going to Copenhagen this evening.

"Your Lordship may be assured that our Government certainly will punish any man who dared give the least insult to any British subject, and certainly that will never be the case; but I am afraid that perhaps some young men will not always be so cautious as they should.

"I beg once more that your Lordship will excuse me for not coming. I hope I shall soon have the honour to wait on your Lordship. I am, with sentiments of high esteem and respect, my Lord,
' Your Lordship's most obedient, and
"Most humble servant,
"H. LINDHOLM.

"Right Honourable Lord Viscount Nelson,
&c. &c. &c."

To this, Nelson replied, "Respecting my permitting a Danish frigate to pass from Norway to Copenhagen, I beg leave to inform his Royal Highness, that I have no power whatever to grant such permission. On the contrary, the Government of Denmark having refused to allow of Norway being included in the armistice, I believe that there would be no impropriety in any English man-of-war attacking them in the ports of Norway, much less if they put to sea, as Denmark has refused the temporary neutrality for that kingdom; but I have no doubt the British Government will do every thing of that nature, which his Royal Highness may think proper to *ask*."

Lord Nelson directed Captain Sutton[1] on the 11th to cruise between the Koll and Zealand to intercept Danish vessels laden with warlike stores, &c. I find a copy of this letter as follows:—

"St. George, Kioge Bay, June 11th, 1801.

" Sir,

"Having received information that a ship is bound from Copenhagen to Norway, loaded with cannon, and also that some other vessels are about sailing from Copenhagen, loaded with naval stores, contrary to the terms and spirit of not only the armistice, but also to the kindness of Sir Hyde Parker and the British Government, who allowed provisions to pass from Denmark into Norway; I therefore desire that you will proceed through the Belt, and cruise between the Koll and the Island of Zealand, and endeavour to intercept the ship and vessels above described, as also all other vessels which may be bound from Copenhagen or other parts of the Danish dominions to Norway, Iceland, Faro, or Greenland, loaded with warlike stores or naval stores; and you will send such ships as you may seize, of the above description, to England, and as there is a squadron of Danish ships of war

---

[1] Sir John Sutton attained the rank of Post Captain in 1782, and in 1793 was appointed to the Romulus of 36 guns, in which he proceeded to the Mediterranean, and afterwards commanded the Egmont of 74 guns. He was in the action in Gourjean Bay in 1795 with Sir Davidge Gould, and also off the Hières islands under Vice-Admiral Hotham. In 1796 he headed a party of boats belonging to a squadron sent to Tunis by Vice-Admiral Waldegrave, made an attack on some French vessels, and captured the Nemesis of 28 guns, the Sardine of 22 guns, and two other armed vessels. He served with Nelson at the evacuation of Corsica, and assisted in transporting the valuable public stores and other property to Porto Ferrajo. He was an able officer on the 14th of February 1797, off Cape St. Vincent, and received a gold medal on this occasion. He afterwards served in the Channel fleet, had the command of the Superb, of 74 guns, and in 1801 was made Captain of the Fleet, under the Honourable W. Cornwallis. In 1804 he was made a Rear-Admiral, and appointed to the harbour duty at Plymouth. In this he continued until 1809, when he was made a Vice-Admiral, and appointed Commander-in-chief on the Halifax station. He was made K.C.B. on January 2, 1815, became a full Admiral in 1819, and died at Ramsgate, an Admiral of the White, August 8, 1825, at the age of 67 years.

in Norway, who may wish to get to Copenhagen, it is my direction that you do your utmost in endeavouring to prevent their coming to Copenhagen; but you are to acquaint the Commander of your orders, and if he consents to remain with you till you receive directions from me or any other, your superior officer, for your conduct; in that case you are to allow him, or them, to keep their colours flying; but if they refuse your reasonable request, it is my direction, that you use your utmost endeavours to take possession of him or them, and acquaint me, or the Secretary of the Admiralty, as the case may require, of your proceedings.

"I am, Sir, your most obedient servant,

"NELSON AND BRONTÉ.

"Samuel Sutton, Esq.
Captain of H.M. Ship Amazon."

Nelson was exceedingly dissatisfied with the conduct of the Danes. He considered the conditions of his armistice disregarded. "Ships (he says) have been masted, guns taken on board, floating batteries prepared; in short every thing is doing, as my reporters say, in defiance of the treaty, except hauling out, and completing their rigging."[1] And to Earl

---

[1] To Evan Nepean, Esq. Dispatches and Letters, Vol. iv. p. 411. The evidence upon which Nelson makes these complaints, was afforded by the following report obtained by the Hon. Colonel Stewart, which I find among the Nelson Papers:—

"*Note of Ships of War now in the Harbour of Copenhagen.*

"Ten sail of the line, two thereof new ships of eighty guns, viz. the Neptunas and Waldemar. These ships are in the same state as before the action of the 2nd of April—having their guns on board, lower rigging set up, and topmasts ready to send up—are supposed to be the best ships in the navy, and have lately undergone a thorough repairing.

"Two sloops of war of 20 to 24 guns, new ships, the same as above.

"One new line of battle ship of 80 guns—took in her lower masts and bowsprit last week.

"One ship of 80 guns fitting out with all expedition, may be ready to take in her masts in the course of a fortnight.

"Three old ships of 60 to 70 guns, supposed to be fitting out for block ships, such as command the entrance of the Channel, or what is termed the Northern line of defence.

"One line-of-battle ship at present in dock.

"One frigate of 36 guns fitting out.

"Three cut down frigates, supposed to be intended for block ships or floating batteries.

St. Vincent on the 14th he writes: "I see every thing which is dirty and mean going on, and the Prince Royal at the head of it; but your astonishment will cease when I assure you that a French Republican officer, in his uniform, feathers, &c. is always with his Royal Highness. The measure is so indelicate towards England, that you will not be surprised, if every thing, which is sacred amongst nations of honour, should be broken. The Armistice, except their ships being absolutely hauled out, has been totally disregarded."[1]

His health improved greatly, and he wrote to Rear-Admiral Totty, and to Mr. Davison of its re-establishment. To the latter he says, "That great and good Being, who has so often taken care of me, has still protected me, and I am recovered contrary, I am sure, to the expectation of myself, and every one in this fleet: and within these last four days, am got stronger and better than I almost ever felt myself." He adds: "All my friends in the fleet have been more than kind to me. If I had not been so ill, I should, perhaps, not have believed how much I am respected, I may almost say beloved, in the fleet. Even Admiral Totty, an entire stranger to me, writes me,—'Your Lordship talks of going to England. I hope in God you will not stir from the Baltic until every thing is settled, and you take us all with you.'" Lord Nelson also alludes in this letter to " poor Mrs. Nelson:" "I am sure you

" One floating battery of 24 guns, saved on the 2nd of April.
" One polacre of 24 guns—formerly the guard-ship.
" All the gun-boats saved on the 2nd of April have their sails bent, and seemingly ready for sea.

"*Copenhagen, y<sup>e</sup> 8th June*, 1801."

"*Ships of War laying in the Inner Roads.*"

" Two ships of the line completely rigged and sails bent.
" One frigate do.
" Three brig cutters.
" Two line-of-battle block ships, and one 24-gun battery, a bomb, forming the Northern line of defence.
" The new ship formerly mentioned has got in some of her lower-deck guns this forenoon, and has men on board to rig her out with all expedition.
" Two of the cut down frigates have each twenty carpenters on board, and the other eighty-gun ship upwards of fifty, they work extra hours.

"*Wednesday, 2 o'clock.*"

[1] Letters and Dispatches, Vol. iv. p. 412.

have done every thing which is proper and kind for poor Mrs. Nelson: be liberal, and let her want for no comfort. I never wanted to make money of any one. The dead cannot do any more kindness than to repose a confidence in the living. Never shall poor Maurice, can he know what is going on, be sorry for his goodness to me."

TO LADY HAMILTON.

"St. George, Kioge Bay, June 12th, 1801."

"My dearest Friend,

"I am writing a last line as the Pylades is getting under sail, and in the moment a cutter is reported to be in sight. I am all now anxiety, therefore cannot get on, so you must excuse my short letter of this day, but since I wrote yesterday not a piece of news nor a boat has been on board. Let me have good, good news, it cannot be too good. Yes, then it would distract me with happiness—if bad from you it would so grieve me that I should become melancholy. Thirty-seven days, not a scrap of a pen. Bear me up.

"Ever your faithful,
"NELSON AND BRONTÉ."

"My dearest Friend,

"I am overjoyed. I shall be better and happier than ever, and be as soon in England as possible. I have sent off four letters this day, two by Troubridge, and two by Davison—this makes five.

"Ever yours,
"NELSON AND BRONTÉ."

"11 *at night.*

"*June* 12*th.* Have only read the Admiral's letter, and that Admiral Pole is coming. Will write to-morrow if I keep my senses."

His anxiety to be relieved was now met by the appointment of Admiral (afterwards Sir Charles Morice) Pole,[1] an

---

[1] Sir Charles Morice Pole, Bart. was descended from the Poles of Shute in Devonshire, and born January 18, 1757. He was educated at the Royal Naval

early friend of Nelson's. He invested Rear-Admiral Graves[1] with the Order of the Bath agreeably to the commands of

College at Portsmouth, sailed as a Midshipman with Captain Locker in the Thames frigate in 1772, and afterwards accompanied Sir Edward Hughes to the East Indies, where he was made Lieutenant of the Seahorse, when he formed acquaintance with Nelson. On the surrender of Pondicherry in 1778 he was made a Commander, and on March 22, 1779, a Post Captain. He was in the following year appointed to the Hussar of 28 guns, which, by the unskilfulness of a pilot, was lost in North America. He conveyed Vice-Admiral Arbuthnot's dispatches to England, and was then appointed to the Success of 32 guns, in which, in 1782, he fought a severe action with, and took the Santa Catalina of 34 guns, the largest frigate at that time in the Spanish service. Upon the establishment of peace in 1783 he was appointed to a guard-ship, and in 1790 to the Melampus, then to the Illustrious, and was made a Groom of the Bedchamber to his Royal Highness the Duke of Clarence. Upon the breaking out of the Revolutionary war, Sir Charles Pole was appointed to the Colossus, and accompanied Vice-Admiral Hotham to the Mediterranean. Upon his return to England in 1793 he was made a Rear-Admiral, served in the Channel Fleet, went to the West Indies under Sir Hugh Christian, displayed great activity and ability, and upon his return was made First Captain of the Grand Fleet, under the command of Lord Bridport. In 1799 he was moved into the Royal George, joined Rear-Admiral Berkeley's squadron, and engaged five Spanish line-of-battle ships. He was afterwards named Commander-in-chief and Governor of Newfoundland, whither he proceeded in the Agincourt of 64 guns, but was recalled to take Lord Nelson's place in the Baltic in 1801, having on the 1st of January of this year attained the rank of Vice-Admiral. Having seen an end to the Northern Confederacy, he was engaged off Cadiz, and was for his services raised to the dignity of a Baronet, September 12, 1801. He represented the Borough of Newark-upon-Trent in Parliament in 1802, took an active part in the discussion of Naval matters in the House of Commons, and was made Chairman of a Board to inquire into certain Naval abuses, after which, in 1806, he was made one of the Lords of the Admiralty, but retired upon a change of Administration in October of this year. At the general promotion after the Battle of Trafalgar, Sir Charles Pole was made a full Admiral and received the honour of G.C.B. He died an Admiral of the White at his seat, Wolverton Park, Hants, June 10, 1813.

[1] Sir Thomas Graves was the son of a Clergyman, who settled in the north of Ireland, and nephew to Admiral Samuel Graves, through whose interest he was introduced into the navy, prior to the American war. He was selected by Lord Mulgrave to accompany the expedition to the North Pole. With Commodore Hotham he was engaged in many services of great peril and difficulty, and uniformly displayed the greatest gallantry. Upon the breaking out of hostilities with France, he was sent to the West Indies, and afterwards appointed to the Bedford, 74 guns, and served in America under his relation, Rear-Admiral Thomas Graves, afterwards Lord Graves, who was Commander-in-chief in North America. He was subsequently engaged in the encounter with the Comte de Grasse, in 1782, and then in a desperate contest with La Sybille, French frigate. In 1801 he was raised to the rank of Rear-Admiral of the White, and proceeded to the Baltic with Sir Hyde Parker At the attack on Copenhagen he was second in command under Lord

George III. as a mark of distinction for his conduct at Copenhagen, and according to Colonel Stewart this ceremony was performed in a very distinguished manner. Nelson laid the sword across the Admiral's shoulder, in the name of his Sovereign, and addressed him in a dignified and animated speech: " Never (says Colonel Stewart) was Knight more honourably invested." The same excellent authority also acquaints us that Nelson's departure from the fleet was matter of deep regret to all, and that there was a complete depression of spirits on the occasion.

Nelson was much gratified by the manner in which his return to England was granted, as the letter from Mr. Nepean communicating the same was accompanied with the following expressions: " I have their Lordships' further commands to acquaint your Lordship, that your services in the Baltic have met their entire approbation, and to assure you that they feel the greatest concern that the state of your health should render it necessary you should quit the command, by which your country must be deprived (though it is hoped only for a short time) of the advantage of your Lordship's talents and experience, which have been so conspicuous on all occasions."

Lord Nelson alludes to the investiture and the levee in the following letter to Lady Hamilton :—

"June 13th, 1801.

" My dearest Friend,

" I was so overcome yesterday with the good and happy news that came about my going home, that I believe I was in truth scarcely myself. The thoughts of going do me good, yet all night I was so restless that I could not sleep. It is nearly calm, therefore Admiral Pole cannot get on. I wish I had a rope fast to him, I believe I should pull myself to pieces, but I will have a little more patience; but my nails are so long,

---

Nelson, who has spoken nobly of the services of his friend. The Order of the Bath was bestowed on him, and Nelson deputed to invest him with it, as will be seen by Nelson's letters on this occasion. He was made Rear-Admiral of the Red in 1804, and afterwards commanded in the Home or Channel fleet. In 1805 he was made Vice-Admiral, and obliged to return home from ill health. He attained the rank of Vice-Admiral of the Blue, and died at his seat, Woodbine Cottage, near Honiton, March 29, 1814.

not cut since February, that I am afraid of their breaking, but I should have thought it treason to have cut them, as long as there was a possibility of my returning for my old dear friend to do the job for me. How is Sir William—better? I shall do as you please about going into the country, but in the party to Wales there will be Mr. Greville, who I am sure will be a stop to many of our conversations, for we are used to speak our minds freely of Kings and beggars, and not fear being betrayed. Do you think of all this against my arrival.

"*June* 14*th*. Looking out very sharp for Admiral Pole. If he was not to come I believe it would kill me. I am ready to start the moment I have talked with him one hour. This day I am going to invest Sir Thomas Graves with the ensigns of the Order of the Bath. He will be knighted with the sword given me by the Captains of the Nile. Your green chair is to represent the throne, placed under a canopy, made of the Royal standard, and elevated. Your blue satin pillow is to carry the ribbon, star, and commission, and Hardy has trimmed out the quarter-deck in his usual style of elegance.

"*Sunday evening, June* 14*th*, 9 *o'clock.* Our parade is over, I have acted as King as well as I could. I have letters from Tyson of April 12th, he seems, poor fellow, very unhappy about his wife. The wind is fair for Admiral Pole, he must be here to-morrow, and I shall sail next day.

"Ever yours,
"Nelson and Bronté."

"*June* 15*th*. The wind is fair for Admiral Pole; he must arrive in the course of the day. How slow he moves—at least in my idea. I shall move faster homewards. Best regards to all our friends. My brother scolds me because I do not write to him. If he knew as you do what I have [to do] for near 80 sail of pendants he would not think so, but he has no patience, and now thinks that what would have satisfied him before, and which he has neither got, or is likely to get, is not worth his acceptance. Best regards to Mrs. Nelson."

Captain Parker also wrote to Lady Hamilton:—

"H. M. Ship, St. George, Kioge Bay,
June 14, 1801.

"My Lady,

"You are so very kind in every instance to me, and have been so continually my friend, that I should be most ungrateful was I not to acknowledge so many and repeated favours and attentions. I feel most particularly gratified at the receipt of your friendly epistle inclosed to my most valuable friend for me, and am happy beyond measure to tell you he has most perfectly recovered his late indisposition, which I assure you was such as to excite no little alarm in my breast, when I first saw him; but, thank God, the change of scene, added to the hopes he had of constantly receiving orders to go home from his own request, buoyed him up against the indisposition he laboured under, and the fresh and certain intelligence of another Admiral quitting England to take this command has altered him to every thing we can wish. He can, thank God, now eat and drink, laugh and joke, and in short, I never before saw him in such spirits. He purposes allowing me the honour of going home with him, and you can, I am sure, knowing the affectionate esteem I have for him, well conceive how peculiarly happy such attentions from him must make me.

"I got your letter by the Phœnix last night; she left England on the 5th, at which time Admiral Pole was at Yarmouth waiting for the Æolus's arrival to bring him out, and as the winds have been fair since that time, we are in hourly expectation of seeing him. The great and good Lord Nelson is anxious for the moment, and has so judiciously arranged all his papers that I do not think he will be six hours in preparing to quit the St. George. The great regret all the officers feel at losing their noble patron is distressing to witness. Hardy, who begs me not to forget him to you, remains with Admiral Pole, and I feel not a little interested, and indeed enthusiastic at accompanying the hero of Aboukir and Copenhagen to England. I hope my sister feels as much obliged to you as I do, and that she has not forgotten to acknowledge with respect and gratitude your mark of kindness. I have given her a strict order to wear it and reverence the man whose conduct claims such general admiration. I am glad to hear the beautiful Horatia is so well, and shall not easily forget your proposal, which I leave you to make to the Admiral. This day we have had grand doings on board—Lord Nelson, by the command of the King, has invested Sir Thomas Graves with the Knighthood of the Bath, and in the most handsome style, all the Captains of the fleet, full-dressed, present, under the Royal Standard, a grand guard, and a salute of twenty-one guns. I had the honour to carry the sword of the Nile with which Sir Thomas was knighted. At the close of this august ceremony Lord Nelson, with his usual goodness and ability, made one of the most appropriate and elegant speeches I ever heard; it pleased and awed everybody, and expressed how amply rewarded all glorious actions were by our Sovereign and our country. My best respects to Sir William, and Mrs. Nelson, nor do I forget Horatia, and with great esteem I remain, your Ladyship's most grateful servant,

"E. T. PARKER.

"You will soon see Lord Nelson in London. He says he will not let much grass grow under his feet after he lands until he sees you."

Another of Nelson's favourite Captains, who had heard that Sir William Hamilton was to be the Governor of Malta, wrote to congratulate her Ladyship :—

"Minotaur, off Alexandria,
June 15th, 1801.

"Dear Lady Hamilton,

"Although a considerable time has passed since I had the honour of taking my leave at Leghorn, believe me, I have not been backward in my inquiries after your health and Sir William's, and I have very often thought of writing; but this country has been so dull since you left it, that nothing but misfortunes and scenes of misery have taken place, and the many comforts we used to enjoy at the different places, are now vanished, and I am sorry to say, the French, with all their villainy, have taken possession.

"I shall ever acknowledge the many kind attentions

shewn me by you and Sir William, and I often, very often, regret the change that has taken place, and most sincerely hope the new appointment of Sir William Hamilton will answer his expectation, and which I most sincerely congratulate you both upon. The Governorship of Malta, which we are informed for certain is given to Sir William, may he live many years to enjoy it, and you to partake of every comfort. No doubt by the time he comes out, we shall have peace, and with a little of your good management, things may be brought round in this country, to make it pleasant once more.

"Our valuable friend, Lord Nelson, has been adding new laurels; may he live long to enjoy them. I have to lament my not going home, when I might have stood a chance to have been one of his party: I like no better company, I assure you. I hope if this country is to fall, that it will be soon, then no doubt it will be Minotaur's turn to go to Old England, when I shall have the pleasure and satisfaction of paying my respects to you and all my friends. I beg my kind remembrance to Sir William and Lord Nelson, when you see him. Miss Knight I had a line from some time since. My best wishes to her and Mrs. Cadogan. If I can be of any service to you or Sir William, in this part of the world, you have only to command me, and believe me with great truth, and every sincere wish, your much obliged and obedient humble servant,

"THOMAS LOUIS.

"P. S. Part of our army with Turks, &c. are near Cairo. *I wish they were in it.*"

Lord Nelson quitted the Baltic on the 19th, and sailed in the Kite brig for England, being unwilling to deprive the fleet of a large vessel. He was at this time in correspondence with the Prince Castelcicala relative to the affairs of Naples, and received the following from his Highness:—

"My noble and respected Friend,

"I received your obliging and very interesting letter yesterday. Accept, my dear Lord, my earnest thanks for the interest you shew for the welfare of the Two Sicilies, in this important event, a peace; an interest worthy of you who saved those kingdoms. We are under great obligations to England. My sentiments, my dear friend, towards the cursed French, remain unaltered, and I shall ever hate them, but in my opinion, the state of things in Europe cannot remain very long as it is; time will shew, but the prospect is not cheering. I wrote yesterday to our good King and Queen. Nothing can possibly more gratify my patrons than the affectionate expressions of your Excellency's sentiments towards them in your letter to me, to which they are so greatly indebted, and of which I am also so gratefully sensible. I have written again to Sir John Acton what you wrote to me for him. I ardently wish for your return to London, my dear friend, that I may have the pleasure of seeing you and talking with you; the moment I learn you have returned I shall hasten to you. My wife presents her kind regards and compliments to you, as well as all my little family. Ever faithful in my attachment and admiration of your incomparable virtues, my Lord, until my last breath I shall respect, and with the greatest gratitude, veneration, and esteem, remain,

"Your Excellency's obliged, faithful,
"and affectionate friend,
"CASTELCICALA.

"To his Excellency the Duke of Bronté,
Lord Viscount Nelson."

The Queen of Naples directed the following to Lady Hamilton :—

"Vienna, February 11, 1801.

"My dear Lady,

"I received your letter of the month of November by the courier sent by the good Prince de Castelcicala. I much wish to have further news from you, and to know how the Chevalier is, and if he thinks of returning to the genial climate of Italy, and tell me how you also find yourself situated, whether you are comfortable, for I am interested in everything that concerns such friends as you are, and I trust, ever will be. I say nothing of our troubles, the public papers have made you acquainted with them. The state of this monarchy is so reduced that the natives and their families are shocked by it. The general quarters of the army is at Schönbrun, and the insurrectionary Hungarians are one half in Luxembourg, the other still in Hungary. We were on the point of starting at Christmas, my people and baggage were already at Brun. Now I tremble for Italy, for the scoundrel Le Brun will not agree to an armistice, and I apprehend if he does he will not include us in it. The King, the Prince, and Princess, are all well, their two children have had the small-pox naturally, and very favourably, and are already quite recovered. All was quiet in our two kingdoms. I live very retired here. Harmony is in some degree established in our family. I shall hold the Empress's child at the baptismal font, and she will hold Louisa's. I do not go out at all now, for I have a violent cold, which torments me very much. St. Marco Corigliano is here. Luchesi also arrived last night. In the general alarm and departure at Christmas I sent poor D° Carolina and her family to Trieste. Adieu, my dear Lady, send me word how you feel, if you are happy, what your prospects are; all that concerns you interests me. Belmont has left Russia in very bad health; he could not stop there, all their proceedings were insupportable to him. He travels slowly by way of Germany, and will perhaps be at the marriage of his brother with the Princess of Courland, which takes place this month in Saxony. Adieu, my compliments to the Chevalier, and to the valorous and dear Lord Nelson, the hero of the Nile. How often I think of him. Adieu, my dear Lady, I hope some day to see you again, and rely on my constant friendship, which will cease only with the life of your tender and sincere friend,

"CHARLOTTE.

"All my dear children make their compliments to you; they are all well, thank God, but our misfortunes leave me no hope of establishing them. Adieu, again adieu."

"March 31, 1801.

"My dear Lady,
"Your letter has quite distressed me, for I see you are neither

so happy nor as satisfied as my sincere and grateful heart, and true friendship for you, would desire you to be, but these are bad times, and there is nothing but suffering. I have been ill again, I cannot quite recover, but, thank God, I am able to move about. My dear daughters are quite well, thank Heaven, and form my only consolation, though mingled with sorrow too, seeing, as I do, that there is no establishment for them, and thinking, if I die, what they may be subjected to; this often makes me regret escaping the tempest of the 23rd of December, when, engulphed in the waters, none with me, I should never have known so many horrors and such ingratitude; the entry of the French into the kingdom, and the horrible peace forced upon us, which brought me to the brink of death, and now, though I am partially restored to health, I fear it will not be durable, with my spirits so tired. Leopold has been very ill, and has been obliged to lose blood for the first time. I hope to go into the country soon, that will give me great pleasure, for plants and trees are not ungrateful. Adieu, my dear Lady, I hope we shall meet again. Rely on my constant friendship and gratitude; make my compliments to the Chevalier, let me often hear from you, and believe me ever your sincere

"CAROLINA."

Soon after his arrival in London, Lord Nelson wrote to the Hon. Henry Addington (July 8th), in which he says: "Prince Castelcicala has been so pressing that I should bear my testimony to you of the fidelity of the King of the Two Sicilies, and his fear that the loss of the island of Sicily may be the consequence of the want of assistance from this country; that it has struck me forcibly that the former plan of the French is still likely to be carried into effect, either by treaty or by force. I dare say that plan is much better known to you than to me, although having for a length of time seen the correspondence both public and private, from all the Neapolitan Ministers to their Government, and to the Queen of Naples, I am perfectly acquainted with the views of the several Powers. The plan of the French Directory was, not to have an army of French in Italy on a peace, but to make all the Powers of Italy dependent upon them; in order to do this, Corsica was to be taken from *us*, Elba, Sardinia, Sicily, if possible, Malta, Corfu, and those could be easily kept, and would awe their enemies in Italy (if any turned against them), and support their friends, and cut our trade both with Italy and Turkey to pieces; indeed, we could have none. From Castelcicala's conversation, I think that either by a forced treaty with the King of Naples, or by force of arms, these people will attempt, and even are attempting, the getting Sicily, which will be a very severe stroke upon us."[1]

It was on the 1st of July that Lord Nelson landed at Yarmouth, and the first act he performed was to visit the wounded at Copenhagen in hospital at this place; after which he departed for London, being escorted by the Volunteer Cavalry as far as Lowestoffe, a distance of eleven miles. Another act of kindness signalized his arrival; the following was directed to Mrs. Maurice Nelson:—

"My dear Mrs. Nelson,

"I beg that you will stay at Laleham, with horse, wiskey, and keep every convenience there to make your stay comfortable, and by Michaelmas you can determine as to the mode and manner of your future residence. Nothing, be assured, shall be wanting on my part to make your life as comfortable and cheerful as possible, for believe me, with every respect and regard, your affectionate friend,

"NELSON AND BRONTÉ.

"I send a hundred pounds, which you will accept from me.
"July 2nd, 1801."

Sir John Orde now courted communication with Lord Nelson, but failing to meet with him at his hotel, wrote the following letters:—

"Gloucester Place,
July 6th, 1801.

"My dear Lord,
"I yesterday called ineffectually at Lothians, to offer you

[1] From an Autograph in the Sidmouth Papers.

personally my sincere congratulations on the many recent marks of distinction which your eminent services have obtained. An act of attention due from me as a member of the community you have so much benefited; as an officer in that service you have contributed so highly to distinguish; and one greatly interested in your welfare. I felt true satisfaction in acquitting myself of it, by the first opportunity that presented since our meeting at Gibraltar.

"I wished also to offer for your perusal a copy of the Correspondence which passed between me, the Board of Admiralty, Lord Spencer, and Lord St. Vincent, on a subject where your name is implicated, and to add my verbal assurances to its ample testimony, that though I complained, as I must still do, of the preference given your Lordship over me, yet that I did so, merely in consequence of my *seniority*, and some peculiarities in my situation, and without the slightest intention of derogating from your great sufficiency, which I shall ever feel true satisfaction in acknowledging.

"This Correspondence also indisputably shews the ground of my subsequent difference with Lord St. Vincent, and the cause of my return to England, were totally unconnected with your Lordship's nomination above alluded to, as in it Lord St. Vincent assures Sir William Parker and myself he had no concern in your Lordship's nomination, which he styles a hard measure, calling for remonstrance on our part. But there seems a propriety in thus expressly assuring your Lordship I was not so influenced by it, as I am aware most uncommon and malicious efforts have been employed to circulate and establish a contrary opinion.

"My fear of occasioning some difference of sentiment in the Mediterranean fleet whilst Lord St. Vincent was with it, prevented my sending your Lordship a copy of this Correspondence when first prepared, as I otherwise should have done, to obviate every appearance of concealment; which I hope was in some measure effected by my having the honour of presenting one to Lady Nelson and your Father for perusal, who might communicate to your Lordship any part of its contents they thought expedient.

"As I shall leave town on Thursday morning, I fear I shall

not have the pleasure of seeing you before my return; I will therefore now mention my regret at your having found it needful to put the agency of the Flag share of the Nile Prize Money in other hands than those of our approved and very worthy agent, Mr. Purvis, as the change has already occasioned some difficulties to the parties, and may eventually, from some mistakes, be a means of preventing his getting a Commission on it, unless your Lordship interferes in his behalf; though his doing so is, I believe, desired by a great majority, perhaps the whole of the flag-officers with whom, I conceive, the appointment of an agent rests.

"I have the honour to be, with great condescension and regard,
    "My dear Lord,
  "Your most obedient humble servant,
        "J. ORDE.

"The Right Honourable
 Viscount Nelson, K.B."

         "Hackwood, July 13th, 1801."

"My dear Lord,

"As I found some difficulty in reading your letter sent by Captain Parker, not being accustomed to your writing, I would not detain him for my answer, and since perusing its contents, I have thought it prudent before making my reply, to allow you time to satisfy yourself from the correspondence put into your hands, as I reasonably thought you might have done from my letter of the 6th instant, that I have been very far from saying anything in it against you.

"Ambition is a sentiment natural to the breast of every good officer, and equally urges him to push by every honourable means, at opportunities for distinction, and to complain when such occasions appear unfairly withheld from him—liberties, the exercise of which, ought not to be repined at by the fortunate candidate, nor to be readily given up by the unsuccessful. We all perhaps have aimed at chief command, and might, without blame, have employed our friends to assist in obtaining it. That I have some who are both able and willing to second my views, I am proud to say, but I could protest to you, I never solicited their interference with the Admiralty on my behalf since promoted to the rank of an Admiral.

"No idle apprehensions of exposing to the knowledge of our enemies the defects in our naval discipline, and in the character of some of our highest sea officers (circumstances of great public notoriety), would have prevented my publishing the correspondence in question immediately on my being refused the Court-Martial I demanded. Considerations of a very different nature have hitherto restrained my exercise of this necessary act of justice to myself, and the service, such as I trust, however, will now soon be removed, and leave me at liberty to adopt such measures as in my judgment events shall make needful.

"I did not mention Purvis to your Lordship in view to discuss his general claim to your favour, or the propriety of his conduct in any transactions between you. I did so in justice to his character as a very honest honourable agent, and in support of the consistency and propriety of my own conduct in not abandoning such a man, who your Lordship will recollect, was in possession of this appointment, when I conceive my right to continue him in it is equal to your power of taking it from him. I should not wonder if subordinate officers detached from a fleet when so fortunate as to make some prizes might wish to appoint a sole agent to dispose of them, although I never remember hearing of any such instance; and I am ready to allow they might *on soliciting* expect an acquiescence with their views from all parties concerned *when perfectly disengaged;* but I must own I feel distressed and astonished to find your Lordship expecting such a sacrifice on the part of your brother Admirals interested in the Nile prize-money, in favour of a man unknown to most of them, and little acquainted with the nature of the employment, when it was not solicited on your part, nor to be effected but at the expense of a man who had every claim to the continuance of their support and confidence: much more still am I astonished to find your Lordship not only expecting from them such an abandonment of a faithful servant, but seemingly dissatisfied with your brother Admirals for starting any objections to your persevering in the appointment of a man as their agent whom they are uninterested about.

"I am, my dear Lord,
"Your most obedient and humble servant,
"J. ORDE.

"Right Honourable Viscount Nelson, K.B.
&c. &c. &c."

### LORD NELSON TO SIR JOHN ORDE.

"My dear Sir John,

"I return your pamphlet, with many thanks for the perusal. I cannot but see clearly the cause of Lord St. Vincent's differences latterly with you—they evidently took their rise from my being sent up the Mediterranean. The order you gave out at Gibraltar in contradiction to the Commander-in-chief, from the slow approach of the Princess Royal, which hurt your feelings, and from the entirely very wrong conduct of Captain Draper and Colonel Desborough relative to the marine. I can now assure you on my word of honour, that neither Earl St. Vincent nor Lord Spencer were the original cause of my being sent to the Mediterranean. The arrangement was made in April 1797, a year before I was sent. It is plain that neither the First Lord of the Admiralty, nor the Commander-in-chief, thought it right to tell you the causes which naturally sent me in particular into the Mediterranean; and I verily believe, that if Admirals, with flags of the main, had been in the same situation as yourself, that I should have been equally employed in the Mediterranean. I own myself sorry that the pamphlet was ever printed, and am glad that you saw the propriety of calling them in; for if answers had appeared by anonymous writers, you would have had to contend with a shadow. Excuse my observations on your book, and believe me,

"&c. &c. &c.,
"NELSON AND BRONTÉ."

### SIR JOHN ORDE TO LORD NELSON.

"Hackwood Park, July 16th, 1801.

"My dear Lord,

"I did not receive your letter of the 11th until I had despatched mine of the 13th instant.

"Although, I confess, I cannot help expressing concern at some of your Lordship's remarks on the correspondence sent for your perusal, which differs so very materially from all I had hitherto received from other quarters, yet as they appear in the shape of a statement, of what you consider to be the causes of the difference between Lord St. Vincent and myself; and as they are, in fact, most of them new and extraordinary, I feel some degree of satisfaction from your communication of them: because I trust you will allow me to indulge a hope of such further explanations as may perhaps lead to the unravelling a mystery I have hitherto found inexplicable. I must own, that from those I am induced to suspect that some representations, very opposite from facts, have been circulated, and reached your Lordship, making an impression on your mind, which I should be very anxious to remove. And for this purpose I must beg to trouble you with such observations as occur to me, from your ideas, as they appear at present from your letter, which I wish you to consider as a sort of inquiry, whether I am right in regard to the points I suppose you allude to, and as a request for your fuller information where you may find me wrong in my conjectures, and my consequent explanations. But before I begin, I must state my surprise at your Lordship omitting to notice some of the reasons assigned in my correspondence, as causes of our difference, which I cannot conceive as an officer possessing a high sense of honour, you could deem too insignificant to be urged by me.

"Among the reasons supposed by your Lordship to have occasioned the difference in question, you mention, 'The order I gave out at Gibraltar in contradiction to the Commander-in-chief.' What order this alludes to I have no conception; for until I received your letter I never understood such a fact had been imputed to me. When about to leave Lord St. Vincent for Gibraltar, I waited on him, and in the most respectful manner, as I am certain his Lordship will bear me witness, requested his verbal explanations on the instructions he had sent for my future guidance, in order that I might be more certain (on this my intended first separation from his Lordship to be in port) fully to act in all things up to his plans and regulations, telling his Lordship that none of my own should interfere with his, aware, as I was, of the mischiefs that had accrued in the fleet from such imprudent variance. His Lordship very readily complied with my wish. I went to Gibraltar; and whilst there, I solemnly declare it was my first and only study how best to obey his orders, and faithfully second his views in every instance. On my rejoining his Lordship off Cadiz, I waited upon him with copies of my journal, and of every order and memorandum I had issued, whilst absent from his flag, and most pressingly requested him to peruse them; saying, that though I conceived I had most strictly conformed to his instructions as explained by himself to me, yet it was possible I might have erred unintentionally, and in such case I should desire to be set right. His Lordship declined looking at them, and with great politeness assured me, in the most unequivocal terms, he was fully satisfied with my conduct at Gibraltar, as he had been on every other occasion.

"As a third reason you mention, 'the slow approach of the Princess Royal which hurt my feelings.' What I am to understand from this I am at a loss to judge. The Princess Royal approaching the fleet off Cadiz, had every sail set, which I judged useful to accelerate her junction with it. On a signal being discovered, and, after some time clearly made out from the Ville de Paris to the Princess Royal to make more sail, and reported to me, I directed Captain Draper to obey it instantly in the fullest extent, which I have no doubt he did in an officer-like manner.

"The next reason you mention, 'The certainly very wrong conduct of Captain Draper and Colonel Desborough about the marine.' How far the conduct of Captain Draper and Colonel Desborough about the marine, which your Lordship decides to be wrong (from what evidence I know not), was really so, I will not presume to say, the matter never having been submitted to my judgment. But, admitting they were to blame, what is that to me? My memorandum, ordering the discharge of a marine from several ships, into Captain Hardy's brig, will shew I complied most strictly with Lord St. Vincent's orders on that head; and as Captain Hardy made no representation to me afterwards on the business, how was I to know it had not been fully observed? Besides, had Lord St. Vincent thought my conduct exceptionable in any of these instances, would he have approved of it as he had done? or would he have omitted mentioning his objections to me, had any occurred to make the impression on his mind you seem to suggest? To judge the contrary, would in my opinion be a reflection on Lord St. Vincent, both as an officer and as a gentleman.

"Lord St. Vincent indeed wrote to me a very extraordinary letter on the business of the marine, but that he afterwards declared, with apologies, to have been in mistake for Colonel Desborough; but not, as you will have seen, until he had had my answer to this letter two or three days in his possession without opening it. His Lordship afterwards refused to allow this answer, still unopened, to be entered in his letter book, telling me, incorrectly as I have since found, that Mr. Purvis has assured him his letter to me had not been so entered: a conduct, if not calculated to disgust every officer of common feeling, certainly not conciliatory, or like to prevent a difference.

"With respect to the point of your being sent up the Mediterranean, which I observe you place as the first cause of difference, I really think it more than unnecessary to trouble you with a repetition of that representation upon it, which you will have already read in my correspondence; but I cannot help expressing my disappointment and mortification at finding my assurances of its not being a ground of my subsequent differences with Lord St. Vincent (although I allow it hurt my feelings), still fail to produce the effects on your Lordship's mind, I had reasonably looked for. After Lord St. Vincent's positive denial to Sir William Parker and myself, of having any concern in your Lordship's nomination, and his expressing his disapprobation of it, saying it was a hard measure calling for remonstrance on our parts, I must have had a worse opinion of his Lordship than I had to have doubted his veracity; and have been more unreasonable than I trust I have hitherto approved myself to differ with him on such a business.

"Your Lordship is good enough to 'give me your word of honour, that neither Lord Spencer, nor Lord St. Vincent, were the original cause of your being sent into the Mediterranean; that the arrangement was made in 1797, a year before you were sent.' Strange circumstance certainly (Lord Spencer being at that time at the head of the Admiralty, and Lord St. Vincent of the Mediterranean fleet), as the French had not begun their preparations for the invasion of Egypt, and such as I could have little idea of. For your Lordship must recollect the conversation we had together on the subject at Gibraltar, when you told me, Lord St. Vincent had mentioned to you, that I wished to be sent on detached service; and when you gave it me as your opinion, that I should be sent after you up the Mediterranean, by Lord St. Vincent, should he find it expedient to augment your small squadron to ten or twelve ships of the line. Besides, the last conversation I held with Lord Spencer previous to my leaving England, and those I had had with Lord St. Vincent on my first joining him, both events subsequent to the month of April, 1797, were calculated to convey to me a very different idea of the importance of the service I was destined to be employed on.

"But, to take the matter as your Lordship puts it, why the laboured concealment of such a fact on the part of Lord Spencer, and Lord St. Vincent, which you notice on the part of Sir William Parker and myself? Why endeavour to deceive us, when the simple communication of such particular motives, as you allude to, might have served to assuage our wounded feelings, and to satisfy us we ought, on such extraordinary grounds, to be reconciled to the measure? Surely, my dear Lord, I must have mistaken your character, or you do not think such communication would have been too great a sacrifice to the reputation, or even the prejudices of old officers! Surely some little attention to officers, placed in so unfortunate a predicament, was not too much to expect from the liberality, or even the justice of their country! But after all, in this case, as in every other arising out of my correspondence, I am far from wishing to bias the opinion of any sea officer, however low in rank, much less that of your Lordship; every officer of liberality will judge for himself, without condemning his neighbour, who may happen to differ from him in point of sentiment.

"My last letter would have conveyed to you my sentiments and resolutions respecting the publication of my correspondence. Be assured I have not recalled *a copy* of those I gave out, but in view to increase the circulation of them. I am not so undecided in my measures as to be deterred from the execution of any plan I deem necessary to the support of my own character, or the good of the corps to which I belong, by silly apprehension of the malicious workings of anonymous writers, whose impudent efforts I should ever disregard.

"I am, my dear Lord,
"Your most obedient humble servant,
"J. Orde.

"To the Right Hon. Viscount Nelson, &c. &c."

"Warwick, August 1st.

"My dear Lord,

"I had purposely avoided every appearance of soliciting the opinion upon my pamphlet of any naval officer to whom I addressed it. But I felt much gratified by the voluntary offer of your Lordship, with your supposed reasons of the cause of my difference with Lord St. Vincent (although the former was not exactly conformable to what I might have expected), as they afforded me some prospect of discovering the grounds of that inexplicable business, and of counteracting the effects of any misrepresentation from whatever quarter or misconception concerning it made on your Lordship's mind.

"The information your Lordship has been pleased to convey to me, by your explanations on these heads, gives me perfect satisfaction, except in as far as I have cause to lament some appearance of a difference in judgment between you and I in points of discipline, which I consider material.

"Admitting for an instant, in its fullest extent, the only pretext your Lordship seems to urge as a ground for Lord St. Vincent's extraordinary treatment of me, that I had issued an order at Gibraltar on the trifling subject of round hats, in contradiction to the one given by the Commander-in-chief, as it is not pretended I did so, knowing it to be the case, or with any view of opposing his regulations, which it was notorious I ever promoted, it would not, I conceive, be deemed by the strictest officer, a ground for the persecution I have met with; or for any other step than a fuller communication from the Commander-in-chief, of his wishes on that subject, which I had ever solicited upon all, but which, from his Lordship's silence, after general declaration of satisfaction, he should not be supposed to have judged more needful upon this than any other occasion. But the simple fact is, that I know of no instructions given by Lord St. Vincent on the subject; and finding that the officers under my orders suffered extremely in their sight, from the excessive glare and reflected heat of the Rock, insomuch that they were generally compelled to wear round hats; and as General O'Hara had, by order, permitted the officers of the garrison to do, I judged it better, and more conformable with the general system of discipline adopted by Lord St. Vincent, generally to authorise the practice in a military form by a public order, than to be a daily witness of officers wearing an uniform differing from that established, and thereby forfeiting, in some sort, their just pretensions to military compliments from the guards and sentinels of the garrison.

" With respect to the effect which Captain Hardy's statement seemed strongly to have produced on your Lordship's mind, I think it impossible to apprehend any further bad impressions of that nature, after the full explanations I have now given upon the subject of the marine. With respect to the command of the Mediterranean, I certainly ever thought that Sir William Parker was best entitled to command the squadron sent upon that service in May, 1798: and I only adverted to myself, as your Lordship had mentioned me, and to remind you of the conversation that passed between us on the subject. I cannot, however, cease to think that the injustice done to Sir William Parker, under whom I should have been zealous to serve upon that occasion, did not put me out of the fair line of next immediate preference, and should not now make me reconciled to the secondary injury done to myself, and of which I assuredly complain, without an idea of thereby detracting from your acknowledged sufficiency.

" I have the honour to be,
 " With great consideration and regard,
  " My dear Lord,
  " Your most faithful humble servant,
   " J. ORDE.

" To the Right Hon. Viscount Nelson, K.B. &c. &c. &c."

In London Nelson took up his residence at Sir William Hamilton's in Piccadilly, where a party, consisting of the Rev. Dr. and Mrs. Nelson, with their son and daughter, were assembled to meet him, and they, together with Captain Parker, went to Box Hill for a change of air for a few days, and then to Bush Inn at Staines, where Sir William Hamilton could indulge his taste for angling. The following lines were addressed to Lady Hamilton by Lord William Gordon at this time. Her Ladyship has prefaced the original by the following observations:—

"When our glorious Nelson came home ill, and worn out with fatigue, after the glorious 2nd of April, we thought it right to let him change the air and often. We therefore went for three or four days at a time to different places, one of which was to the Bush at Staines, a delightful place, well situated, and a good garden on the Thames. Sir William was fond of fishing, and Lady Hamilton wrote to the Duke of Queensberry and to Lord William Gordon an account of their occupations, which brought the following verses from Lord William. The company at Staines consisted of Sir William and Lady Hamilton, the gallant Nelson, Rev. Dr. and Mrs. Nelson, Miss Nelson, and the brave little Parker who afterwards lost his life in that bold, excellent, and vigorous attack at Boulogne, where such unexampled bravery was shewn by our brave Nelson's followers."

"So kind a letter, from fair Emma's hands,
Our deep regret, and warmest thanks, commands.
Ah! Lady, could we both, with happier you,
Now form a part of gallant Nelson's crew,
Six sable, foaming coursers, long ere night,
Had brought us, willing, to—the Bush —Tom White,
There to have witnessed Father Thames's pride,
While Anthony, by Cleopatra's side—
While you, I mean, and Henry,[1]—in a wherry,
Are, cheek by jole, afloat there, making merry;
But sickness, and old age, resist the will,
And keep us bound in Piccadilly still.
Yet since, nor sickness, nor old age, can bind
The frequent—friendly wishes of the mind,
We send them, *fresh and fresh*, by every wind.

Though, to say truth, I should not, vastly, like,
To trust my dinner to an uncaught pike,

---

[1] Lord Viscount Nelson.

At five, at Staines, I gladly would take post,
Close to the Cavallero,—and a roast,
And should he, talking, better like, than eating,
Lend him an ear, while mouth was stowing meat in;
And, on his water pranks, while he was dwelling,
Of bites confirm'd and doubtful nibbles telling,
I still would listen, (though I thought it dull)
Till he was out of breath, and I chokefull.
Or, if it were his fancy, to regale
My ears, with some long, subterraneous tale,
Still would I listen, at the same time, picking,
A little morsel of Staines ham and chicken,
But should he boast of Herculaneum jugs,
Damme! I'd beat him, with White's pewter mugs.

The little, reverend Mistress Nelson[1] next,
Shall be our Muse's very welcome text;
And, should the verse of praise be longer far,
Than any of her husband's[2] sermons are,
It will be better listen'd to, I'm sure,
And, what is more,—believed, by all his cure.

Next to her baby[3]—with her cheeks of rose,
Her teeth of ivory—and eyes of sloes!
Ah! henceforth, never, may she unmov'd look
On the poor worm,—that writhes upon the hook!
Nor seek, with cruel guile, and barbed steel
The guileless victims of a murderous meal!
But, recollecting still, the tortur'd fish,
Heave a young sigh, and shun the proffer'd dish,
With glistening eyes, confess the morning's guilt,
And shed atonement, for the blood she spilt.

Not so—the Parson! on it let him fall,
And, like a famish'd otter, swallow all.
Nor for the gudgeon's sufferings, care a groat,
Unless some bone stick in his own damn'd throat.
Now, here, perhaps, it may not, (by the way),
Be much amiss, a word or two, to say
Of this same Pastor, who, to every claim,
Of individual merit, adds a name;
A name! which shall remain, to latest time,
In every nation, and in every clime,
Rever'd and honour'd! long as Nile shall flow,
Long, as the changeful winds of Heaven shall blow,

---

[1] Afterwards the Countess Nelson.
[2] Rev. William, afterwards Earl Nelson.
[3] Miss Charlotte Nelson, now Lady Bridport.

Long, as our ships, to northern seas, shall steer,
Or naval glory, be, to Britons, dear!
But, stop, my Muse! avast! there, if you please,
Or damme! you'll run longer than all these!
Though, when you've got brave Nelson on your back,
You'd prove yourself a curs'd unworthy hack,
If you should spurring want, or tire—or jade,
'Ere, round the world, a journey you had made;
Though, for that job, he has a nag more steady,
For Fame has carried him twice round already.

But, to return to this same worthy Vicar,
Who loves, you say, good eating and good liquor,
Know, Lady, that it is our earnest wish,
That we, ere long, may greet him—Lord Archbish:
For this, no common pains, or I'm mistaken,
Our best of friends, the Duke,[1] hath lately taken,
And, if a mitre fall not on his head!
Justice and gratitude are gone to bed!

Of Norfolk Sally, you have nothing said,
Though she be such a pretty, black-eyed maid!
But, Lady, lest the Rector go astray,
Read the Commandments to him, thrice, each day;
Once,—after breakfast—and once, after dinner,
Lest, after full meals, he become a sinner,
Thirdly and lastly, ere he go to bed,
Lest sinful thoughts or strange dreams fill his head.

Nor, by our Muse, shall Allen[2] be forgot,
Who, for himself, nor bullets fear'd, nor shot,
But for the Guardian Angel[3] of his master,
Knowing, full well, the Doctor had no plaster,
He wisely, as a lady, and a stranger,
Took her below, and plac'd her out of danger.

Let not, poor Quasheebaw,[4] fair Lady, think,
Because her skin is blacker than this ink,
That, from the Muse, no sable praise is due,
To one so faithful, so attached, and true!
Though in her cheek, there bloom no blushing rose,
Our Muse, nor colour, nor distinction knows,
Save of the heart!—and Quasheebaw's I know,
Is pure, and spotless, as a one night's snow!

---

[1] Nelson, Duke of Bronté.

[2] Tom Allen, Nelson's servant.

[3] The portrait of Lady Hamilton, so called by Nelson, framed and glazed, and hung up in Nelson's cabin. It was taken down upon entering into battle, lest it should sustain injury.

[4] A black servant.

> For thee! and Henry, silent are our lays!
> Thy beauty, and his valour mock all praise.
> Yet haply, shall these verses serve to prove,
> How much, and oft, we think of those we love."

Mrs. Maurice Nelson, the widow of Lord Nelson's brother, resided at Laleham, two miles distant from Staines. She was completely blind, and Nelson took the opportunity of visiting her, and condoling with her, while at the Bush, and made up the pittance bequeathed to her by his brother to the amount of a regular annuity of £200. *per annum*, besides providing for her immediate exigencies. Although Lord Nelson had made many attempts to get his brother promoted, he did not live to be even a principal clerk in the Navy Office more than four months.

The following is from Major-General Count Walterstorff, Chamberlain to his Danish Majesty:—

"Copenhagen, July 13th, 1801."

" My Lord,

" I learn by the newspapers with great pleasure your Lordship's safe arrival in England, and that your health is so far re-established as to have permitted your Lordship to take again your seat in the House of Lords. We were in hopes that your Lordship would have favoured Copenhagen with a visit, previous to your sailing for England, and I anticipated the satisfaction of finding an opportunity to return my best and respectful thanks to your Lordship for your very kind letter to me of the 16th June, and for the distinguished favour you have conferred on my son, by sending him your picture in a very good print, a sketch of your life, and the medal struck in memory of your Lordship's victory of the Nile. The advice to my son, which accompanied that present, from your Lordship's hand, is what my son will, I hope, when six or eight years older, put a still greater value on, and what will make a deep impression on his mind.

" It must give every friend of England and Denmark equally pleasure to see peace and harmony restored between the former Power and those of the North, though, as a Dane, I confess I could wish that my country had been led back to its former connexion with Great Britain in a more gentle manner, and less by the sudden impulsion (if I may be permitted that expression) of another Power. It is, however, always a great consolation to know, that we shall enjoy peace, and that short and unfortunate as the war has been for Denmark, it has not shewn the character of the Danes in an unfavourable light.

"I wish very much I could make a trip to England for the sake of my health, and spend next winter at Bath. It would naturally make me still more happy to go there in a diplomatic character, and I flatter myself my conduct would be such as to entitle me to the esteem and confidence of his Britannic Majesty's Ministers; but I suppose that Count Wedel, who before the late unfortunate quarrel between our two Governments, was Envoy-extraordinary from our Court, will do his utmost endeavours to get re-appointed. I cannot, however, give up the hopes of paying my respects to your Lordship in England, and of renewing to your Lordship the assurance of the high regard I feel for your personal, as well as for your public character, and of the sincere and respectful attachment with which I have the honour to be,

"My Lord,
"Your Lordship's
"Most obedient and most humble servant,
"ERNEST FREDERICK WALTERSTORFF."

In a previous letter of the 15th of June the Count remarked, "Whoever may be the respective Ministers who shall sign the Peace, I shall always consider your Lordship as the Pacificator of the North, and I am sure that your heart will be as much flattered by that title as by any other which your grateful country has bestowed upon you."[1]

In July Lord Nelson made application to have the Barony of Nelson extended. The King graciously acquiesced, and to prevent the extinction of the Barony from failure of heirs male on his own part, on the 18th of August a new Barony, called Nelson of the Nile and of Hilborough in the county of Norfolk, was granted. This was limited in default of male issue of his Lady to his father, and the male issue of his

---

[1] From an autograph in the possession of the Right Honourable John Wilson Croker, printed in the Dispatches and Letters, Vol. iv. p. 417.

body, failing which, it was to extend to the heirs male of the bodies of his sisters Mrs. Bolton[1] and Mrs. Matcham respectively. Agreeably to his wish, expressed in his application to the First Lord of the Treasury, his foreign orders, which he regarded as honourably obtained and approved by the King's Sign Manual, were described in the Patent, which also declares that any successor to the Barony so created shall use the surname of Nelson only. The Rev. William Nelson alludes to this patent in a letter to Lady Hamilton :—

"Hilborough, August 6th, 1801.

"My dear Lady Hamilton,

"You can easily conceive what joy your letter gave me this morning; thank God, our great, glorious, and invincible friend is safe. I was at Swaffham when I received it, and read the Gazette honours to my father. He made but little observation upon it, only said he liked him as well *plain Horace* as with all these high-sounding titles; that may be true, but still I could have wished him to have appeared pleased with the prospect of his family honours descending to his posterity, and I could not help remarking to him, that we ought not to be like the selfish man who is reported to have said, 'Why should I care for *posterity*, for posterity never cared for me.' Mrs. Bolton made no remarks, nor seemed in the least elated or pleased; indeed, to say the truth, there appears a *gloom* about them all, for what reason I can't devise, unless they are uneasy. They did not deserve to have a *chance*, and I wish it had gone to *Charlotte* and her heirs *male*, but I hope to God it will be a long time before it leaves the TRUE *Nelson* line, and that the young *Baron*[2] and Duke (who is now writing by my side) will raise up posterity, and cut all the others out. The clergy are all busy here calling meetings of their parishes for the defence of the country and coast, and cannot stir from home at present, but I hope our great hero's doings will set us all at ease. When you write, give my love to him, and express all my gratitude to him for what he has already done for me and mine; I only now hope for a good Deanery for myself. Believe me your affectionate friend,

"WM. NELSON."

---

[1] The present Earl Nelson is the grandson of this lady.
[2] Afterwards Viscount Trafalgar. He died at the age of 19 years.

The following letter I presume relates to the difference of opinion entertained upon the conduct of Sir Hyde Parker:—

"Sir,

"You must be sensible that I cannot continue to correspond with an anonymous correspondent. I am convinced that the partiality of my countrymen, with some very few exceptions, have far overrated my abilities, and I wish that placing my talents on its proper level may be useful to my late Commander-in-chief, but I do not believe that a wish to detract from me will be consonant to his wishes. I am such as I am, neither better nor worse, from either the partiality of my friends, or the envy of my enemies.

"I am, Sir, &c.

"NELSON AND BRONTÉ.

"July 24th, 1801."

In a letter to his friend Mr. Davison on the 15th of June, he writes: "Secret.—They are not Sir Hyde Parker's real friends who wish for an inquiry. His friends in the fleet wish every thing of this fleet to be forgot, for we all respect and love Sir Hyde; but the dearer his friends, the more uneasy they have been at his *idleness*, for that is the truth—no criminality. I believe Sir Hyde Parker to be as good a subject as his Majesty has."[1]

[1] Dispatches and Letters, Vol. iv. p. 416.

## CHAPTER IV.

### 1801.

DURING the summer of 1801, reports of the intended invasion of England by France were very general. The conquests achieved from the Red Sea to the Baltic had not only humbled the pride of Buonaparte, but excited him to feelings of the bitterest animosity and revenge. Camps were formed opposite to the British coast: one at Ostend, a second between Gravelines and Dunkirk, and a third at Boulogne. Added to these martial demonstrations, great activity prevailed along the Dutch and Flemish shores, as well as on the part of France, whose naval force combined with that of Spain, now amounted to a fleet of no less than fifty-two ships of the line, lying in the harbour of Brest.

The people of England generally entertained very little apprehension with regard to the accomplishment of the threatened invasion, yet those who were in power, and moving in the best informed circles, were certainly not at all indifferent to the matter. Lord Nelson and others high in the Naval service of the country, participated in this alarm, and from a letter addressed by Mr. Windham to Lord Eldon, and published in Mr. Twiss's Life[1] of the Chancellor, he seems to have entertained serious apprehensions as to the possibility of its accomplishment, and under these impressions no precautions were omitted to be taken for the safety of the country. The spirit of patriotism combined with military ardour, and the general heroism of the British nation displayed in so remarkable a manner on this occasion, served doubtless to repress any feelings of terror that might otherwise have prevailed, and a great and just confidence was placed in the national courage and resources of the country. Lord Pelham, then one of the Secretaries of State, issued a circular at the end of July to the Lord Lieutenants of counties, communicating

[1] Vol. i. p 391.

to them, "that the naval and military preparations, carried on in the ports and on the coasts of France and Holland, had of late been pursued with increasing activity; and signifying his Majesty's earnest wish that the several corps of volunteer cavalry and infantry throughout the kingdom, might be kept in a state of immediate service." The extent of and alacrity with which this summons was obeyed, was a glorious exhibition of British patriotism. The whole country answered to the call, and constituted a body not only adequate to all the purposes of defence, but one capable of exhibiting and exercising the utmost defiance. The whole coast was effectually guarded, and a chain of vessels stretched across the extent of the Channel. The preparations at Boulogne by the French were of a formidable description: a large army being there assembled, and a flotilla collected. To this point, therefore, attention was particularly directed; and for the arrangements necessary to be made on this occasion, Lord Nelson was consulted, and appointed to the command of a force consisting of frigates, brigs, and other smaller vessels, between Orfordness and Beachy Head. Admiral Lutwidge had at this time the command in the Downs: but Nelson's was to be confined to the specific object of watching the enemy on different parts of the coast in the Channel, and of making defence against any attack that might be contemplated. The following were the instructions received by Lord Nelson on this occasion:—

"By the Commissioners for executing the Office of Lord High Admiral of the United Kingdom of Great Britain and Ireland, &c.

"Whereas intelligence has been received that considerable preparations are making by the enemy on different parts of the coast between Dieppe and Ostend, and that a great number of boats and other craft, calculated for the reception of troops, have been collected, particularly at Boulogne and Calais, for the purpose of making a descent on some part of this country; and whereas by our Commission bearing date the 24th instant, we have appointed your Lordship Commander-in-chief of a squadron of his Majesty's ships to be employed on a particular service, intending to place under your orders the ships of war and craft described in the inclosed list, and such others as may hereafter be sent to you, to be employed in the defence of the mouths of the Thames and Medway, and all that part of the coasts of Sussex, Kent and Essex comprised between Beachy Head and Orfordness; your Lordship is hereby required and directed to proceed without delay to the Nore, and hoisting your flag on board either of the said ships or vessels that you may find there, carry these our orders, and such farther orders and instructions as we may judge it necessary to give you, into execution.

"On your arrival at the Nore, you will communicate with Vice-Admiral Græme,[1] and inform yourself from him of the arrangements he has already made, and the various orders and instructions which have been given by him to the several Captains and Commanders of the ships and vessels appointed for this particular service, and having gained such information as you may be able, you are to lose no time in satisfying yourself how far the officers so employed are conducting themselves in obedience to those instructions, and whether the ships and vessels are in all respects fitted, stored, and manned for the performance of the service for which they are designed.

"And whereas the Corporation of Trinity House has placed a proper number of vessels at the buoys and beacons in the Channels leading to the Thames and Medway for the purpose of sinking or destroying them, in the event of the approach of the enemy, and one of its officers to superintend and direct the proceedings of the persons employed on that service; your Lordship is to arrange such a plan with the officer so employed as may in your opinion be most effectual for that purpose, and in the event of his finding it necessary to cut away and sink the beacons and buoys, to place such craft on

---

[1] This officer distinguished himself when Captain of the Preston in Sir Hyde Parker's action with the Dutch squadron off the Dogger Bank, in 1781, on which occasion he lost an arm. He lived to attain the rank of Admiral of the Red, and died in 1818.

the shoals as may be requisite for securing to us the advantage of the navigation.

"And whereas it is judged expedient that some of the ships and vessels under your Lordship's command should be placed in the different channels for the purpose of more effectually obstructing the passage of the enemy into the Thames or Medway, your Lordship is to consider of the stations the best adapted to that purpose, and so station any of the ships and vessels under your command that may be best calculated for that purpose in such channels, giving their Commander the necessary instructions for the regulation of their conduct under the different circumstances that may arise; and in order the more fully to explain our ideas to your Lordship on this head, we annex a chart, shewing the disposition made of the force employed for the same purpose in the year 1798, with copies of instructions given to the Commanders of some of the ships and vesssls so employed, and though we conceive the plan then settled generally to be well deserving your attentive consideration, we do not confine your Lordship to a similar disposition, intending, that you shall, after you have made yourself completely master of the subject at the spot, and taken the opinion of such persons as you may think it necessary to consult, adopt such plan as, upon a full consideration of all the circumstances, you may judge to be most advantageous for the public service.

"When your Lordship shall have made your arrangements for defending the passages of the Thames and Medway, and also made a disposition as may appear necessary for the protection of those parts of the coast of Essex and Suffolk within the limits of your command, you will proceed to the Downs, and make such a disposition of the force intended to be actively employed as you may judge most advisable for blocking up or destroying, if practicable, the enemy's vessels and craft in the ports wherein they may be assembled, or if they should be able to put to sea, for destroying them: in the former case your Lordship will have the advantage of no less than seven bomb vessels, which will be prepared in all respects for service with all possible expedition, but which ought not to be brought into action until, after visiting the coast of France, your Lordship shall be satisfied that they can be employed with effect: in the latter case it must be obvious to your Lordship that by attempting to capture the numerous vessels and craft of the enemy, the object will be totally defeated, and therefore some expedient must be found if they cannot be destroyed, of effectually disabling them, and rendering them incapable, by depriving them of the means of pursuing any direction, they would be likely to take even for the purposes of reaching the nearest shore.

"We have ordered the Amazon to be prepared for the reception of your Lordship's flag the moment she shall arrive at the Nore, but before she can be ready for that purpose, or indeed at any time hereafter, your Lordship will feel yourself at full liberty to hoist it on board any other ship or vessel of your squadron, and proceed from time to time to those parts either of the coast or of this country within the limits of your station as you may judge most convenient to enable your Lordship to execute the important service entrusted to your care.

"And whereas Admiral Dickson has ordered his Majesty's ship Ruby to be placed in Hosely Bay for the purpose of defending that part of the coast, your Lordship is at liberty to send any orders or instructions to her Commander that you may judge necessary, until we shall be able to make such an addition to your force as to enable you to station a proper ship in that bay in her stead.

"When your Lordship shall have arranged the whole of your plan, you are to transmit a copy thereof to our Secretary for our information, and acquaint us, through him, from time to time of your proceedings, and of all occurrences which may take place that may be worthy of our knowledge.

"Given under our hands the 26th July, 1801.

"St. Vincent.
"T. Troubridge.
"J. Markham.

" To the Right Hon. Lord Viscount Nelson, K.B.
   Vice-Admiral of the Blue, &c. &c. &c.

" By command of their Lordships.

"Evan Nepean."

Lord Nelson hoisted his flag aboard the frigate L'Unité at Sheerness on the 27th of July, and on that day wrote to Lady Hamilton:—

"Sheerness, July 27th, 1801.

"My dearest Emma,

"My flag is flying on board the Unité frigate. She will probably go to the Nore to-morrow, as the wind is easterly. It is lucky I followed my plan of coming by land instead of water, for it would have taken me two days. If I have any ship fit to sail with me on Wednesday, certainly I shall go either for Margate or towards Hosely Bay. Coffin does not return till Wednesday, therefore Parker and myself are alone, and we have enough to do. To-day I dine with Admiral Græme, who has also lost his right arm, and as the Commander of the Troops has lost his leg, I expect we shall be caricatured as the *lame* defenders of England.

"Remember me affectionately to my charge, to my father, brother, &c. Say all that is proper to them, and also to the good Duke, and Lord William, and ever believe me,

"Yours affectionately,
"NELSON AND BRONTÉ.

"A little tired."

Many officers were anxious to be with Lord Nelson on this service. To Lady Hamilton he writes:—

"July 28th, 1801.

"My dearest Emma,

"Ten thousand thanks for your affectionate letter. At this moment I could do nothing with volunteer Captains, having no post to give them. Should the enemy really approach, the country must have their services, and I should be glad to have on that occasion our friend Bowen. I have many offers on that head, but Bowen may rely, if any come to me, that he shall. My time is so fully employed, that I am not able to get off my chair. I can only say, that I am as ever,

"Yours,
"NELSON AND BRONTÉ.

"I dine at the Admiral's, who seems a good man. It blows hard. If the Dutch mean to put to sea, this is their time. How vexed I am at the Spaniards being able with impunity to come before Gibraltar, and to protect the French ships. Parker desires his compliments, and shall expect your letter to-morrow."

"July 29th, 1801.

" My dearest Emma,

" Your letter of yesterday naturally called forth all those finer feelings of the sort which none but those who regard each other as you and I do can conceive, although I am not able to write so well, and so forcibly mark my feelings as you can. Not one moment I have to myself, and my business is endless. At noon I set off for Faversham to arrange the Sea Fencibles on that part of the coast; at nine o'clock I expect to be at Deal to arrange with Admiral Lutwidge various matters; and to-morrow evening, or next day morning, to sail for the coast of France, that I may judge from my own eye, and not from those of others. Be where I may, you are always present to my thoughts—not another thing, except the duty I owe to my country, ever interferes with you.

" Yours,
" NELSON AND BRONTÉ.

" In about five days I hope to be again upon some part of the English coast. You shall hear from me every day if possible. I have not rose from my chair since seven this morning. A post chaise is at the door. Best regards to my father, brother, Mrs. Nelson, the Duke of Queensberry, Lord William Gordon, &c."

"Deal, July 30th, 1801.

" My dearest Emma,

" Having finished all my business at Sheerness yesterday at one o'clock, I set off for Deal, calling on my way at Faversham, in order to examine into the state of our Sea Fencibles at that place, and on that part of the coast I found that reception which I have been so used to, and it seemed the general opinion, that if I was authorised to say to the seamen on that coast that it was necessary for them to embark on board our floating batteries, that they would go on the assurance, that when the danger was passed, they should be landed at their homes again, for the expression was that they never believed the thing serious until I was appointed to this command. However, unless the matter comes closer, I hope the Admiralty will not make me speechifyer ;[1] but the fact is, the men are afraid of being tricked. At nine o'clock I got to Admiral Lutwidge, not having tasted a morsel since seven in the morning. At ten we supped. The Admiral and his wife, Parker, myself, and Captain Bazeley.[2] My flag was hoisted this morning in the Leyden, 64, which ship, if the surf will allow me, I shall be on board of to-morrow morning. I have no bed, but that does not matter, although I shall doubtless have much envy against me, yet I wish to shew good people that they have not mistaken their man. This service must soon be over, I have sent for the Medusa frigate, in which ship I mean to go over to the coast of France; it is William Cathcart's[3]

---

[1] In his letter to Earl St. Vincent (July 30) he says, that he had desired a Mr. Salisbury to meet him, as he was a person of respectability, rich, (got it by fair trade) and of great influence amongst the seafaring men on that part of the coast, particularly about Whitstable. " I made him (says he) sensible of the necessity of our ships, which were to be stationed off the sand-heads being manned. He thought, if the Admiralty, through me, gave the men assurances that they should be returned to their homes, when the danger of the invasion was passed, that the sea folk would go; but that they were always afraid of some trick; this service, my dear Lord, above all others, would be terrible for me: to get up and harangue like a recruiting sergeant! I do not think I could get through it; but as I am come forth, I feel that I ought to do this disagreeable service as well as any other if judged necessary."—Clarke and McArthur, Vol. ii. p. 294.

[2] Captain John Bazeley was the son of Admiral John Bazeley, who had seen a great variety of service under Sir Edward Hughes, Sir Hugh Palliser, Admiral Keppel, Lord Rodney, Lord Howe, and Lord Hotham. His son, mentioned above, was in Lord Howe's action of the 1st of June, 1794, being at that time Third Lieutenant of the Royal George. He served in 1795 under Lord Bridport, and carried the flag of Rear-Admiral Harvey in the action off L'Orient as Captain of the Prince of Wales, of 98 guns, and was afterwards appointed to the Hind, and stationed in the Channel. In 1797 he joined Admiral Peyton in the Overyssel of 64 guns, and was at the capture of the Dutch Fleet in the Texel in 1799. He continued in this ship until the Peace of Amiens, and was appointed to the command of the Sea Fencibles from the mouth of the Humber to the river Ouse. He was made a Post Captain in 1794, and superannuated as Rear-Admiral, July 18, 1814. He was placed on the Active List a Vice-Admiral of the Blue, July 5, 1827, and died March 21, 1828.

[3] The Hon. Captain William Cathcart, eldest son of Lord, afterwards General Earl Cathcart, died of the yellow fever at Jamaica, June 4th, 1801, when in command of the Clarinde, being then only twenty-two years of age.

ship you know. Captain Gore[1] of the Amazon, is not yet arrived in England. Reports are so vague, that it is difficult to say whence this host of thieves is to pour forth. Your letters are gone to Sheerness, and I shall be deprived of the pleasure of receiving them till to-morrow.

"Yours,

"NELSON AND BRONTÉ.

"When you write to Sir William[2] say every thing which is kind, also to my father, Mrs. Nelson, the Duke, Lord William Gordon, who I shall always esteem amongst my truest friends. Pray have you heard of any house from Mr. Christie? I am very anxious to have a home where my friends might be made welcome. Coffin charged me to say how sorry he should be to lose your good opinion, and that he never failed calling."

Captain Parker describes to Lady Hamilton the manner in

---

[1] Captain John Gore was the son of Major Gore, many years Governor of the Tower of London, and a brother of Brigadier-General Gore, who nobly fell at Bergen-op-Zoom in 1814. He was made Lieutenant in 1789 on board the Victory with Lord Hood, and was at the taking of Toulon in 1793. He was also at the taking of Bastia. Engaged in a variety of services, but of no great importance, he was made a Post Captain in 1794, and was appointed to Le Censeur of 74 guns. In conveying a convoy home, he fell in with a French squadron under Admiral Richery, of six ships of the line, besides frigates, and was compelled to surrender after sustaining a very severe fire. He regained his liberty in 1796, and was appointed to the Triton of 32 guns, in which he cruised against the French privateers. In October, 1799, he was at the capture of the Santa Brigida from Vera Cruz, bound to Old Spain, and received as his share of prize-money, on this occasion, upwards of £40,000. sterling. In 1801 he was appointed to the Medusa, under the orders of Lord Nelson. In 1803 ne was again employed, and sent to the Mediterranean. On the 5th October, 1804, he shared in another capture of three Spanish frigates laden with specie and valuable merchandize, and in November took another vessel laden with quicksilver. He received the honour of Knighthood in February, 1805, and took the Marquis of Cornwallis to India, and had the melancholy task of bringing home the remains of this nobleman in the Medusa, which made the extraordinary passage of 13,831 miles in 84 days. In 1806 he was appointed to the Revenge, of 74 guns, and subsequently commanded the Tonnant of 80 guns, having been engaged in treating with the Spanish Commissioners at Cadiz in 1808. He was made a Rear-Admiral, December 4, 1813, and sent to the Mediterranean. In 1815 he was made K.C.B. and appointed Commander-in-chief in the Medway. He died August 21, 1836, having attained the rank of Vice-Admiral of the Red.

[2] Sir William was at this time on a tour.

which Lord Nelson was received, and the activity of his proceedings upon his arrival, in the following letter:—

"Deal, July 30, 1801.

"My Lady,

"I hope Lord Nelson has told you how busily I have been engaged; if not, you must believe me when I say nothing could have prevented my acknowledging the receipt of your very kind and affectionate letter before. He is, thank God, extremely well, and in good health. We got down to Sheerness very quick and well, and were received by the acclamations of the people, who looked with wild but most affectionate amazement at him, who was once more going to step forward in defence of his country. He is the cleverest and quickest man, and the most zealous in the world. In the short time we were at Sheerness, he regulated and gave orders for thirty of the ships under his command, made every one pleased, filled them with emulation, and set them all on the *qui vive*. How, what, I feel when I reflect how warmly I am attached to so great and noble a patron; but I fear I am a little envied.

"We arrived at Deal last night, and this morning the flag was hoisted on board the Leyden, but it is to be removed to the Medusa, and she is now in sight coming in. I believe we shall then take a peep at them on the coast of France, and see what can be done.

"Not a word of little Horatia. You don't mean to mention her for sixteen years I suppose.

"Pray send him cream cheese, and whatever you can get you think he likes, and *I will cut it up*.[1] I hope you will write to me often, as nothing can flatter or please me more, and believe me, my Lady, your ever obliged and grateful servant,

"E. T. PARKER.

"Remembrances to Mrs. Nelson and Charlotte."

---

[1] Extract of a letter from Lord Nelson to Lady Hamilton:—"Parker sits next me to cut my meat when I want it done."

TO LADY HAMILTON.

"Deal, July 31, 1801.

"My dearest Emma,

"My time is truly fully taken up, and my head aches before night comes. I got to bed, last night, at half-past nine; but the hour was so unusual, that I heard the clock strike one. At this moment, I see no prospect of my getting to London; but, very soon, the business of my command will become so simple, that a child may direct it. What rascals your post-chaise-people must be! They have been paid every thing. Captain Parker has one receipt for seven pounds odd, and I am sure that every thing is paid; therefore do not pay a farthing. The cart-chaise I paid at Dartford. Give ten thousand kisses to my dear Horatia. I did not get your newspapers; therefore, do not know what promise you allude to: but this I know, I have *none* made to me. The extension of the patent of peerage is going on; but the wording of my brother's note, they have wrote for a meaning to. The patent must be a new creation. First, to my father, if he outlives me; then to William and his sons; then to Mrs. Bolton, and her sons; and Mrs. Matcham, and hers. Farther than that I care not; it is far enough.

"NELSON AND BRONTÉ.

"I have failed for poor Madame Brueys. Buonaparte's wife is one of Martinique, and some plan is supposed to be carried on."[1]

At this time Nelson received the following compliment from the Committee of Lloyds :—

"Lloyd's, July 30th, 1801.

"My Lord,

"Fortunately I have had an opportunity of getting acquainted with the manner that your Lordship acquired your last very severe illness, the consequences of which might have been so fatal to the country in the loss of so very valuable a life as that of your Lordship. I informed the Committee for the sufferers of the glorious action at Copenhagen the particulars, and they have directed me to inform you that they

[1] Collection of Letters, Vol. i. p. 43.

have voted five hundred pounds to be laid out in plate, in such a manner as you will please to direct, as a small token of their gratitude for the extraordinary exertions of your Lordship in that ever-memorable victory.

" I am, my Lord,
" With the utmost respect,
" Your most obedient humble servant,
" JOHN JULIUS ANGERSTEIN.

" Lord Viscount Nelson, and
Duke of Bronté, K.B.
&c. &c. &c.

" P. S. The Committee have voted £60 *per annum* Long Annuities to Mrs. Mosse[1] and her children, and £500 to Sir T. B. Thompson."[2]

The 1st of August must, of necessity, as the Anniversary of the Battle of the Nile, have been a day dear to Nelson's remembrance. He wrote to Lady Hamilton thus:—

" Medusa at sea, between Calais and Boulogne,
August 1, 1801.

" When I reflect, my dearest Emma, that for these last two years on this day we have been together, the thoughts, and so many things rush into my mind, that I am really this day very low indeed, even Parker could not help noticing it, by saying, 'on this day you should be cheerful,' but who can tell what passes in my mind—yes, you can, for I believe you are feeling as I do. When I was in the bustle, perhaps I did not feel so strongly our separation, or whether being at sea makes it appear more terrible, for terrible it is. My heart is ready to flow out of my eyes; but we must call fortitude to our aid. I did not intend to have sailed until this morning, but at ten last night we had intelligence that the enemy were come out of Boulogne. I put to sea of course, but as yet have not been able to get off Boulogne. I send you one receipt for money paid Mr. Dean, and although I have no receipts for the other journey, you may rely that by James, Captain Parker says, they were each paid before I ever took a chaise a second time. It only shews what rascality there is moving—always get a receipt, and every now and

---

[1] The widow of Captain Mosse, who fell in action on the 2nd of April.
[2] This officer lost a leg on the same occasion.

then a receipt in full, or one day or other you will be ruined. Consider how you are at the mercy of all your servants.

"*August 2nd.* I am going this morning to take a look at Boulogne, and shall then send over a cutter with this letter. Many of the officers here think that the enemy are afraid we have some design of invading their coast, for they are erecting many new batteries on this part of their coast. Be that as it may, in a very short time we shall be so well prepared, that our sea officers wish they may come forth. I have not had a letter from you since Wednesday—I only mention this to shew you, that although we may write every day, yet they cannot always be as regularly received. I am not unwell, but I am very low. I can only account for it by my absence from all I hold dear in this world. Captain Gore is very good and kind to me, and your nephew Cathcart bears a very high character as a seaman and an officer, although he certainly does not possess the graces. To Mrs. Nelson say every thing which is kind, and to the Duke and Lord William.

"Yours,
"NELSON AND BRONTÉ."

And on the 3rd off Boulogne :—

"Off Boulogne, August 3rd, 1801.

"My dear Emma,

"The wind is too far to the northward to allow our bombs to go on the coast this morning, or some of the rascals should repent their vapouring nonsense. I believe my head will be turned with writing so much as I am forced to do. You may assure our friends that between Dieppe and Dunkirk I will insure them from any invasion for the present. The French had better be damned than to allow us to catch them three miles from their own ports. Your dear letters of the 1st I received at eight o'clock last night. Best regards to all our friends.

"Yours,
"NELSON AND BRONTÉ."

He now resolved on making an attack upon the enemy, and at break of day, on the 4th, began to throw bombs and shells into Boulogne harbour. Ten vessels were by these means disabled, and five sunk. Nelson upon this, though undecisive effect, remarked that it would "serve to convince the enemy that they could not come out of their harbours with impunity."

"Medusa, off Boulogne, August 4th, 1801."

"My dearest Emma,

"Boulogne is evidently not a pleasant place this morning. Three of their floating batteries are sunk; what damage has been done to the others, and the vessels inside the pier, I cannot say, but I hope and believe that some hundreds of French are gone to hell this morning; for if they are dead assuredly they are gone there. In fire or out of fire I am,

"Yours,

"NELSON AND BRONTÉ.

"Tell the Duke and Lord William that the embarkation of the French army *will not* take place at Boulogne. Beyond this I cannot say. In my visits to the bombs in my barge, my friends think the French have been very attentive to me, for they did nothing but fire at the boat and the different vessels I was in, but God is good."

"Medusa, off Calais, 7 o'clock, August 4th, 1801."

"My dearest Emma,

"Your kind and affectionate letters up to yesterday are all received. Ten times ten thousand thanks for them, and for your tender care of my dear little charge Horatia. I love her the more dearly, as she is in the upper part of her face so like her dear good mother, who I love, and always shall with the truest affection. I am on my way to Ostend and Flushing, and shall probably be off Margate on Friday. Captain Gore is very kind and good to me, for I must be a great plague to him. I have to thank him even for a bed. I have only one moment to write this, as Admiral Lutwidge sent his own boat with my letters of this day's post. Best regards to Mrs. Nelson, kind love to Horatia, and believe me,

"Yours,

"NELSON AND BRONTÉ.

"This goes through my kind friend, Admiral Lutwidge. I wrote to you to-day through Troubridge."

"Medusa, August 5th, 1801."

"My dearest Emma,

"There is not in this world a thing that I would not do to please my dearest friend, but you must not take things amiss that never were intended. I know not that I wrote to my father more news than to you; in fact, I know not my own movements, they are as uncertain as the wind. I can always tell you where *I am* when I write, but at what spot where letters may find me is impossible. I intend going towards Flushing, from thence towards Margate, Hosely, or Harwich; but if I was to die for it, I cannot tell which. I really wish you would buy the house at Turnham Green. I have £3000, which I can pay in a moment, and the other I can get without much difficulty. It is, my dear friend, extraordinary, but true, that the man who is pushed forward to defend his country, has not from that country a place to lay his head in; but never mind, happy, truly happy, in the estimation of such friends as you, I care for nothing. How great has been Sir James Samaurez's success!![1] From my heart I rejoice. The Spaniards will never surely go to sea again. My command is only against small craft, therefore small must be my services in the taking and destroying way, but you know I will not be inactive. I hope soon to be able to get to London for a day or two, at least I will try. Make my best regards to Mrs. Nelson, the Duke, and Lord William.

"Ever yours,
"NELSON AND BRONTÉ."

"Medusa, back of the Goodwin Sands,
August 6th, 1801."

"My dearest Emma,

"The wind being easterly, and the Sea Fencibles not being so forward as I could wish them, I have deferred my visit to Flushing until they are embarked, and our floating batteries placed in the places assigned them. All your dear kind letters received yesterday made me much better, for I was not quite so well as when in London. I could not drink Champagne, a sure sign that all is not right; but indeed I

---

[1] His celebrated victory off Algeziras.

am not to call ill, but sometimes the exertion of my mind is beyond the strength of my body. I hope you will be able to get the house at Turnham Green, either to hire or buy. Shall I desire my lawyer to call and talk to you, if you think it will suit me, and he shall hire or purchase it, Messrs. Booth and Haslewood, No. 4, Craven Street, Strand. I really want a house. I am grieved to hear you complain.— Keep well, get well, for the sake of all your friends, and for the sake of none more than

"Yours,
"NELSON AND BRONTÉ.

"The Guardian Angels, although lying by in their cases, are not hung up in this ship. Best regards to Mrs. Nelson, the Duke, and Lord William."

Of the proceedings off Boulogne (which certainly were not deserving or rather demanding the service of an officer of the rank and importance of Nelson) he writes on the 5th to his Royal Highness the Duke of Clarence: "The whole of this business is of no farther moment than to shew the enemy, that, with impunity, they cannot come outside their ports." The operations of the 4th were noticed by Nelson in laudable terms: "Lord Nelson has reason to be very much satisfied with the Captains of the bombs, for their placing of the vessels yesterday. It was impossible that they could have been better situated; and the artillery officers have shewn great skill in entirely disabling ten of the armed vessels out of twenty-four opposed to them, and many others Lord Nelson believes are much damaged."[1]

On the 6th he directed the following to Captains Shield,[1] Hamilton,[2] Schomberg,[3] and Edge[4]:—

[1] To the Squadron. See Naval Chronicle, Vol. vi. p. 160.
[1] Captain William Shield acquired a notoriety from an action brought against him, and tried before Lord Chief Justice Loughborough in the Court of Common Pleas, in 1792, in which Mr. Leonard, the plaintiff, complained of an assault and violence offered to him in consequence of the disobeyance of an order of Captain Shield, at that time Lieutenant of the Saturn of 74 guns. The usage of the service was proved, and the thirty-sixth naval article of war authorized Lieutenant Shield in the measure he had adopted, and the jury gave a verdict in his favour accordingly. The Court, moreover, finding that a spirit contrary to the maintenance of good discipline prevailed among the Midshipmen of the

"Medusa, August 6th, 1801.

"As there can be no doubt of the intention of the French to attempt the invasion of our country, and as I trust, and

London and Edgar, submitted to the Admiralty the propriety of trying Mr. Moore of the London, for the same, as a necessary means of preserving good order, and preventing improper combinations. The trial took place, and Mr. Moore was sentenced to one month's imprisonment in the Marshalsea. Mr. Shield was promoted to the rank of Commander, in La Sincère of 20 guns, one of the Toulon prizes, and he afterwards commanded the Berwick, and also the Windsor Castle. He was made a Post Captain in 1794. In 1795 he commanded the Audacious, and was present at the destruction of L'Alcide off Frejus, July 13th, 1795. He was then employed in the Southampton under Lord Nelson's orders, harassed the enemy on the coast of Genoa, and co-operated with the Austrian army encamped at Sarone. After this service he was appointed to L'Unité in the North Sea, was with Nelson off Boulogne, and in 1805 commanded the Illustrious, of 74 guns, on the coast of Spain. In 1807 he was made Naval Commissioner at Malta, then appointed to superintend the payment of ships afloat at Portsmouth, thence transferred as Commissioner of the Cape of Good Hope, after which he was placed at the Navy Board. In 1814 he was made Deputy Comptroller of the Navy, and in the following year Resident Commissioner at Plymouth. He retired as Rear-Admiral, January 9, 1829; was placed on the Active List, as Admiral of the White, November 12, 1840; and died June 25, 1842.

[2] Sir Charles Hamilton, Bart. is lineally descended from the Earl of Mallent, in Normandy, whose nephew is celebrated in history for the part he took at the Battle of Hastings. The Captain above mentioned is the son of Sir John Hamilton, Bart. who acquired his Baronetcy for his conduct during the siege of Quebec, where he commanded the Lizard frigate, and was born August 25, 1767. He served as a Midshipman with his father, on board the Hector in 1776, and afterwards studied at the Royal Naval Academy at Portsmouth. He was made Lieutenant of the Tobago on the Jamaica station. He was made a Post Captain November 22, 1790, having previously been elected M.P. for St. Germains in Cornwall. He afterwards represented Honiton in Devonshire, and Dungannon in the County of Tyrone. Upon the commencement of the Revolutionary War in 1793 he was appointed to the Dido of 28 guns, and cruised off Norway, and then with Lord Hood at Corsica. Upon his return to England in 1794 he was appointed to the Melpomene, and remained in the command of that vessel upwards of seven years. He was engaged under Admiral Mitchell in the expedition against the Helder, at the blockade of Amsterdam. In 1800 he had the chief command on the coast of Africa, and took possession of Porto Praya. In the Ruby he commanded the Sea Fencibles at Harwich. In 1802 he acted as Commissioner at Antigua in the West Indies, and in the following year commanded the Illustrious of 74 guns, in the Channel fleet. In 1809 he obtained a Colonelcy of the Marines; in 1810 was made a Rear-Admiral, and Commander-in-chief in the Thames, and in 1814 was advanced to the rank of Vice-Admiral. In 1818 he was made Commander-in-chief and Governor of Newfoundland, and returned to England in 1822. He is the present senior Admiral of the Red, and K.C.B.

[3] Captain Isaac Schomberg was made a Post Captain, November 22, 1790. He was in Lord Rodney's action in 1782, and commanded the Culloden in

am confident, that if our sea-faring men do their duty, that either the enemy will give over the folly of the measure, or, if they persist in it, that not one Frenchman will be allowed to set his foot on British soil; it is, therefore, necessary that all good men should come forward on this momentous occasion to oppose the enemy, and, more particularly, the Sea Fencibles, who have voluntarily enrolled themselves to defend their country afloat, which is the true place where Britain ought to be defended, that the horrors of war may not reach the peaceful abodes of our families. And as the Lords Commissioners of the Admiralty have been pleased to appoint me to command the sea defence of Great Britain, within the limits of your district, it is my duty to request that you will have the goodness to acquaint all the Sea Fencibles under your command, and all other sea-faring men and fishermen, that their services are absolutely required at this moment on board the ships and vessels particularly appointed to defend that part of the coast where the enemy mean to attempt a landing, if unopposed.

"I am authorized to assure the Fencibles, and other sea-faring men who may come forward on this occasion, that they shall not be sent off the coast of the kingdom, shall be kept as near their own houses as the nature of the service will admit, and that the moment the alarm of the threatened invasion is over, that every man shall be returned to their own homes; and also, that during their continuance on board ship, that as much attention as is possible shall be paid to their reasonable wants. And I flatter myself, that at a moment when all the volunteer corps in the kingdom are

Lord Howe's action of the 1st of June, 1794. He was appointed to the Command of the Sea Fencibles at Hastings. He was afterwards made a Deputy Comptroller of the Navy, which he resigned, and had a seat given to him at the Navy Board. He published the Naval Chronology, an useful work. He died at his house in Cadogan Place, January 20, 1813.

⁴ Captain William Edge, a Captain of the Royal Hospital at Greenwich, to which he was appointed in 1809; was made a Commander in the Alert, a French brig taken at Toulon and fitted as a fire-vessel. He honourably distinguished himself in this dangerous service under Sir Sidney Smith upon the evacuation of Toulon. He was afterwards appointed to the Vulcan fire-ship, and thence removed to the Prince George of 98 guns, in which he was present at the attack on the French fleet off L'Orient in 1795. On the 29th of June, 1795, he was made a Post Captain, and appointed to the Sea Fencibles between Harwich and Yarmouth, and thus came under Lord Nelson's command.

come forward to defend our land, that the seamen of **Great Britain** will not be slow to defend our own proper element, and maintain as pure as our glorious ancestors have transmitted it to us, our undoubted right to the Sovereignty of the Narrow Seas, on which no Frenchman has yet *dared* to sail with impunity. Our country looks to its Sea Defence, and let it not be disappointed.

"I shall send cutters to bring the Sea Fencibles, and other sea-faring men to me, in order that I may dispose of them in the way most proper for the defence of our King and Country, and, at the same time, in the most commodious way to the men themselves.

"NELSON."

To Lady Hamilton he writes :—

"Medusa, Margate Roads,
August 7th, 1801.

"My dear Emma,

"I arrived here yesterday evening, and received your kind letters from the Downs of the 5th. I am vexed such a racket should be made of these trifling things—consider, that when I do my utmost they are boats of fifty or sixty tons; but I ever have done my best. I grieve, my dear Emma, to hear you are unwell. Would I could do anything to comfort you; try and get well. We shall all meet at Naples or Sicily one of these days. I thank Castelcicala for his affectionate note, and send him an answer. To-morrow morning I go over to Hosely Bay or Harwich, to see what is to be done with the Sea Fencibles on that coast. I have given directions to Captain Gore (or rather requested) not to let any body come into the ship but who had business with me, for the Medusa would be full from morning till [night]. Fifty boats, I am told, are rowing about her this moment, to have a look at the one-armed man. I hope Reverend Sir will be satisfied with the new patent, as it is taken from Hilborough on purpose to please him, and if I leave none, he must breed stock from his own place. A letter to-morrow will find me at either Hosely or Harwich, perhaps Troubridge will send it for you. With my best regards to Mrs. Nelson, and the Duke, and Lord William, believe me,

"Ever yours,

"NELSON AND BRONTÉ.

"Captain Gore is very good to me, for I must be a great plague to him. Parker is very well, and much to do. I delivered your message to Allen. He says he has no fear for his wife whilst she is with you."

"Medusa, August 7th, 1801.

"My dear Emma,

"Pray send good Castelcicala's letter. My mind is not so perfectly at ease as I wish it, but I hope by your next letters I shall be made better. To our friends say every thing which is kind.

"Ever yours,
"NELSON AND BRONTÉ."

The following is the Prince Castelcicala's reply to the letter above alluded to :—

"London, August 8th, 1801.

"My noble and revered Friend.

"I received your obliging and friendly reply, and perceive the goodness of heart of the incomparable friend and hero, whose modesty renders him superior to all others with whom I am acquainted. There cannot be another Nelson in the world. I shall inform the King and Queen of what you have written to me respecting them with so much solicitude. My patrons owe you so many, and such great obligations; they love and venerate you so perfectly, that they experience the highest gratification in your triumphs, and in being constantly remembered by you. I hope you will soon bring your enemies here to reason, and that then you will be able to proceed to save the Sicilies a second time. I beg you to accept my unbounded thanks for what your goodness induces you to write to me. Permit me, my dear and worthy Lord, to solicit care and attention to yourself, to avoid exposing a person precious to all the world, to your country, to the Two Sicilies, to your affectionate friends, amongst whom I beg you to believe me the warmest, for none can put a higher value on your friendship, and the opinion you deign to entertain of me; believe me until my latest breath, penetrated with enthusiasm and respect, with gratitude and friendship,

"Your grateful, respectful,

"and obsequiously attached,

"Castelcicala.

"My wife begs to present her best compliments to you."

"To his Excellency,
Lord Nelson, Duke of Bronté."

From Margate Roads Lord Nelson wrote to Earl St. Vincent respecting the Sea Fencibles, and received the following reply:—

"My dear Lord,

"I have to thank your Lordship for the continuance of your correspondence, touching the arrangement and disposition you have made of the Sea Fencibles, the whole of which will be left to your judgment, as it is fitting it should, from the unbounded confidence we repose in you. I am very sorry they do not turn out in greater numbers; it is understood here that they entered into a written engagement, which is supposed to be in the hands of the Captains, and we conclude has been communicated to you.

"The public mind is so very much tranquillized by your being at your post, it is extremely desirable that you should continue there; in this opinion, all his Majesty's servants, with Sir Thomas Troubridge, agree; and happy as I should be to see you, let me entreat your Lordship to persevere in the measures you are so advantageously employed in, and give up, at least for the present, your intention of returning to town, which would have the worst possible effects at this critical conjuncture. I will explain further when we meet. De Ruyter was intended to be placed under your command, and orders will be sent for that purpose; heartily hoping you are recovered from the fatigue you have undergone, believe me to be,

"Most affectionately yours,

"St. Vincent.

"Admiralty, August 8th, 1801."

Off Yarmouth on the 9th Nelson wrote to Lady Hamilton:—
"*Medusa*, Harwich, August 9th, 1801."

"My dearest Emma,

"I find from Lord St. Vincent that even my quitting my post at this moment would create an alarm, therefore I must give it up; but, my dear friend, the time will come when I am more at liberty. I hope that you and Sir William will come and see me when I can get a little more stationary, for at present I am running to every port. To-morrow I intend to go to the Nore, and from thence to Margate, perhaps the Downs, or over the water, not to fight, I have no such thing at this moment in my head. Times are when it is necessary to run risks: I do not mean myself, for I should be very sorry to place any one where I would not wish to be myself; but my flotilla must not be wantonly thrown away, I reserve them for proper occasions. I wish, my dear Emma, that my name was never mentioned by the newspapers; it may create poor Nelson enemies, not that I care, only that I hate to be praised except by you. My conduct at this time of service, is not to be altered by either praise, puffs, or censure. I do my best, and admit that I have only zeal to bear me through it. Thank our excellent friend, Lord William, for his new song—the last seems always the best. How is the Duke? I saw Sir Edward Berry last night: he inquired after you kindly. We only got the Medusa into Harwich at noon. I have been in a cutter since six o'clock; apropos, I have seen Captain Dean, late of the King George packet. You may remember the other cutter which conveyed us over; she was dismasted on the Sunday, and very near sinking. We had a good escape. Make my best regards to Mrs. Nelson, and believe me,

"Yours, &c.

"NELSON AND BRONTÉ.

"I passed close to our Baltic friends yesterday; sent a boat aboard the St. George, got a letter from Hardy, a nod from George Murray, &c. &c."

"*Medusa*, Harwich, August 10th, 1801."

"My dearest Emma,

"Your letter from Margate I received last night, and those from the Downs yesterday morning. Although I cannot get to London yet, I hope that the business of the house will go on. I should think the purchase would be the best, then I should collect all my little matters together. Having arranged all my business here, at noon I am going to the Nore. I may be there two days, but it is impossible to say. I wish I could fix any time or place where I could have the happinesss of meeting you, but in my vagabond state I fear it is impossible. I think I could have come to London for a day, to arrange about the house, without any injury to the King's service; but patience, my dear Emma, and be assured I am,

" Yours, &c.<br>
" NELSON AND BRONTÉ.

" Best regards to the Duke, Lord William, Mrs. Nelson, and all our real friends."

" Sheerness, August 11th, 1801.

" My dearest Emma,

" I came from Harwich yesterday noon; not having set my foot on shore, although the volunteers, &c. were drawn up to receive me, and the people ready to draw the carriage. Parker had very near got all the honours.

" I came on shore; for my business lays with the Admiral, who lives in a ship hauled on shore, and the Commissioner. Slept at Coffin's: and having done all that I can, am off for the Downs, to-day if possible.

" As far as September 14th I am at the Admiralty's disposal, but, if Mr. Buonaparte does not choose to send his miscreants before that time, my health will not bear me through equinoctial gales. I wish that Sir William was returned; I would try and persuade him to come to either Deal, Dover, or Margate; for, thus cut off from the society of my dearest friends, 'tis but a life of sorrow and sadness, but *patienza per forza!*

" I hope you will get the house. If I buy, no person can say, this shall or shall not be altered; and you shall have the whole arrangement. Remember me most kindly to Mrs. Nelson, the Duke, Lord William. Write to me to the Downs.

" NELSON AND BRONTÉ.

"The Mayor and Corporation of Sandwich, when they came on board to present me with the Freedom of that ancient town, requested me to dine with them, I put them off for the moment, but they would not be let off. Therefore, this business, *dreadful* to me, stands over, I shall be attacked again when I get to the Downs. But I will not dine there, without you say approve; nor perhaps then, if I can get off. Oh! how I hate to be stared at."[1]

Off Margate Nelson wrote to the Premier: " In my command, I can tell you with truth, that I find much zeal and good humour; and should Mr. Buonaparte put himself in our way, I believe he will wish himself *even in Corsica*. I only hope, if he means to come, that it will be before the 14th of September, for my stamina is but ill suited for equinoctial gales and cold weather." On the 12th he wrote to Lady Hamilton:—

"August 12th, 1801.

"My dearest Emma,

"You must know me well enough that even when I cannot fully repay an obligation, yet I always wish to do something which may at least mark my gratitude, so is my situation with Captain Gore. I therefore wish you to order for me a piece of plate, value £50, in order that I may leave it as a memento that I am not insensible of his kindness to me. He is very rich, therefore, I must take care not to offend. He has every thing except a silver urn or tea-kettle and lamp, I think the latter a useful piece of plate, and will come to about the sum. I propose to have wrote on the kettle, 'From Vice-Admiral Viscount Nelson, Duke of Bronté, to Captain John Gore, of His Majesty's ship Medusa, in gratitude for the many acts of kindness shewn him when on board the Medusa in August, 1801;' and let it be done as soon as possible, as I expect about next Tuesday to leave this ship and go into the Amazon. Have it directed for me at Deal, and a bill sent with it; but if, my dear Emma, you think anything else more suitable of the same value, be so good as to order it.

[1] Collection of Letters, Vol. i. p. 47.

"That beast, Allen,[1] has left behind, or lost all my papers, but I have sent him after them, and he is such a notorious liar, that he never says truth—no, such is his delight in lying that even to do himself good he cannot resist the pleasure he has in telling a lie, for I asked him in the boat for my red case, as I did not see it. His answer was, 'Sir, I put it in the stern locker.' I then desired him to take particular care in handing the case up the side, when he knew perfectly well that he had not put it in the boat, and as all my things were brought by him from Coffin's house to the landing-place I never expect to see it more. There is £200 in it, and all my papers. *Huzza! Huzza!* What a beast he is, but I trust more to other people's honesty than his cleverness. He will one day ruin me by his ignorance, obstinacy, and lies.

"I am pushing for the Downs, but whether I can stay one day or two is impossible to say, but it shall not be long before we meet. As for going out of the kingdom without seeing you, nothing shall prevent me; I would sooner give up my command. We are just off Margate, and I think one of my vessels may save post. I send it under cover to Sir Thomas Troubridge.

"Ever yours,
"NELSON AND BRONTÉ."

On the 13th, he wrote many letters: two to Lady Hamilton, one to Earl St. Vincent, another to Mr. Nepean, and one also to Mr. Davison.

"Medusa, Downs, August 13th, 1801.

"My dearest Emma,

"I have received all your truly kind and affectionate letters, and you may rely it is not my fault that I cannot get to London to see you and Mrs. Nelson; but I believe it is all the plan of Troubridge, but I have wrote both him and the Earl my mind. But 'Cheer up, fair Emma,' cheer up, then I shall be better to hear you are so, for I would not give a farthing for friendship that could be in good health when the friend of my heart is sick. I have had a fever all night, and am

---

[1] His old servant.

not much better this morning. I am going to-morrow morning over to the French coast, therefore you may be one day without hearing from me; but I assure you, my dear friend, that *I* am going into no danger. The services on this coast are not necessary for the personal exertions of a Vice-Admiral, therefore, I hope that will make your dear good friendly heart easy, you would naturally hate me if I kept back when I ought to go forward—never fear, that shall not be said of me. I find both at Harwich and Margate that they are disappointed at my not going on shore; the whole gentry of the country came to see me just as I came away, but a Sir George Murray, a very loyal gentleman, related to Princess Augusta,[1] came near Margate in a Custom House cutter to see me. I was in hopes to have seen Lord William. Respecting Banti's son I will ask Captain Gore to take him, and I should hope he would not refuse me, or I will take him into the Amazon, and fix him with Captain Sutton, and under Robert Walpole's eye, who is Lieutenant of her. Get the lad ready and send him to me. Whatever I can do you may command, for yours are acts of kindness. Look out for a house for me (to buy, if you like it), but have a dry situation.

"Yours,
"NELSON AND BRONTÉ.

"I have received, I believe, every letter and paper. Never ask the question, do they bore me? All others do most damnably. Yesterday I received more than one hundred. Pray write me everything and of everybody—all you say must be most interesting to your,

"NELSON AND BRONTÉ.

"Allen is returned with my case."

"Downs, August 13th, 1801.

"My dearest Emma,
"Your letters to-day make me happy. Thank Mrs. Nelson for the perusal of Mrs. White's letter. She is a woman

---

[1] Lady Augusta Murray, who was married to His Royal Highness the Duke of Sussex.

of sense. I send you a letter from Mrs. Cannon. I suppose I must give her the money. What can I do, but it must be as you please. Keep it secret, I will send an order by return of post, if you choose, and you shall write her a kind letter. My head is split.

"Ever yours,
"NELSON AND BRONTÉ.

"Send me a translation of the Queen's letter. Must I write? I shall write to General Jerningham."

To Earl St. Vincent he sent the Reports of the Sea Fencibles Captains, and asks, "Where, my dear Lord, is our invasion to come from? The *time* is gone; owing to the precautions of Government, it cannot happen at this moment, and I hope that we shall always be as much on the alert as our enemies." He then goes on to the consideration of an attack: "Flushing (says he), is my grand object; but so many obstacles are in the way, and the risk is so great of the loss of some vessels, that, under all circumstances, I could hardly venture without a consultation with you, and an arranged plan, with the Board's orders."[1]

The Rev. William Nelson never let slip an opportunity of soliciting preferment. He applied in every quarter to promote his object. The following was addressed by him to Lady Hamilton:—

"Hilborough, August 13th, 1801.

"My dear Lady,

"If London, the capital and metropolis of this great empire, which is herself able, single and alone, to keep the rascally French villains at bay, cannot afford a subject for a letter, 'tis no wonder that such an obscure village as this cannot. Indeed, the truth is, there is but one object, both here and there, that engrosses our whole thoughts and soul, and him we can for ever dwell upon. Pray God continue to protect and preserve him. The greatest comfort we have in the country is in the abundant crops of all kinds of corn we are now blessed with, and the extreme fine weather to get in the

---

[1] Clarke and McArthur, Vol. ii. p. 298.

harvest. I think things must be cheaper very soon; hops are so plentiful, that what was sold last year for £16, are now offered only at £5, and of best quality, so that your friend, Tim Brown, must let us have some of his best *brown stout* considerably cheaper.

"I was told yesterday by a person who lately came from *Exeter*, that Dr. Harward, the Dean, is eighty years old, and is lately grown very infirm. If a vacancy should happen there, it would be a most desirable thing if Mr. Addington would make me Dean of Exeter, 'tis about seven or eight hundred pounds a-year, and a good house and pleasant town and country, nothing could scarce be better of the sort, and is one of the things I desired my brother to mention to him, only you know Mr. Addington *at that time* could not be pinned down to anything. But *now* we have secured the Peerage, we have only *one* thing to ask, and that is, my promotion in the Church, handsomely and honourably, such as becomes Lord Nelson's brother and heir apparent to the title. No put off with small beggarly stalls. Mr. Addington must be kept steady to that point. I am sure *Nelson* is doing everything for him. But a word is enough for your good sensible heart, so I remain,

"Your most affectionate and obliged friend,

"WILLIAM NELSON."

Lord Nelson was far from well during this service. He writes :—

"Medusa, at sea, August 14th, 1801.

"My dearest Emma,

"The fever which I had seems fallen in my head, which is much swelled, and my poor teeth pain me very much. I fear my letter will not be in time for the post to-day, and to-morrow likewise, the winds and tides fall out so cross that the vessels cannot get over the same day, therefore, do not expect one; you know I will write and send over if it is possible, but we cannot command the winds and the waves. Do not be uneasy about me, as I told you yesterday there is at this moment no service for a Vice-Admiral; but, my dear Emma, your good heart fancies danger for your friend, and a more true-hearted one does not exist than

"Your faithful,
"NELSON AND BRONTÉ.

"I am obliged to send off the cutter, and have not a moment. The cheese arrived safe and excellent. Send to some good wine merchant for three dozen of the best champagne, and order to the Downs by waggon, directed on board the Amazon, or I shall have nothing to give you, and that would be shameful in me who receive all good things from you."

Contemplating the intended attack, Lord Nelson writes thus :—

"Medusa, off Boulogne, August 15th, 1801.

"My dearest Emma,

"From my heart I wish you could find me out a good comfortable house, I should hope to be able to purchase it. At this moment I can only command £3000; as to asking Sir William, I could not do it, I would sooner beg. Is the house at Chiswick furnished? if not, you may fairly calculate at £2000 for furniture, but if I can pay, as you say, by little and little, we could accomplish it. Be careful how you trust Mr. ——— ; all must be settled by a lawyer. It is better to pay £100, than to be involved in law. I am very anxious for a house, and I have nobody to do any business for me but you, my dear friend. If Davison was in town, I would get him to look about, and settle all the law business for me; but as to a house, you are an excellent judge, only do not have it too large, for the establishment of a large house would be ruinous. As you may believe, my dear Emma, my mind feels at what is going forward this night; it is one thing to order and arrange an attack, and another to execute it; but I assure you I have taken much more precaution for others, than if I was to go myself—then my mind would be perfectly at ease, for after they have fired their guns, if one half the French do not jump overboard and swim on shore, I will venture to be hanged, and our folks have only to go on, never think of retreating. This will not go away till to-morrow. Many poor fellows may exclaim, *Would it were bed-time, and all were well;* but if our people behave as I expect, our loss cannot be much. My fingers itch to be at them. What place would you like to come to, Margate or Deal? Dover, I fear, would be inconvenient; Hosely Bay would be also the same. As for having the pleasure of seeing you, that I am determined upon. I am fagging here, and perhaps shall only get abuse for my pains to be half ruined in my little fortune, but rich or poor, believe me,

" Ever yours,
" NELSON AND BRONTÉ."

On this day he drew up the plan of attack on the enemy's flotilla at Boulogne, and dispatched memoranda for the ships. The first division was to be under the command of Captain Somerville,[1] the second under Captain Parker,[2] the third under Captain Cotgrave,[3] and the fourth under Captain Jones.[4] There was also a division of howitzer-boats under Captain Conn.[5] Each division was to be subdivided into two, and to be made fast to one another as close as possible. The utmost silence was to be preserved, and the oars were to be muffled. The boats were to be manned at half past ten, and at eleven they were to sail, upon a signal of six lanterns hung over the guns of the Medusa, Nelson's vessel.[6] The

---

[1] Captain Philip Somerville was a Post Captain of April 29, 1802.

[2] Captain Edward Thornborough Parker.

[3] Captain Isaac Cotgrave was made a Post Captain in 1802. He was upwards of fifty years in the service, and many years Agent for French prisoners at Plymouth, where he died in 1814.

[4] Captain Richard Jones was a Lieutenant on board the Defence at the Battle of the Nile, and was made a Commander upon that victory. After commanding the Diligence sloop-of-war, he was appointed to the Sea Fencibles in the Chepstow district. He was made a Post Captain, April 29, 1802, and died December 11, 1829.

[5] Captain John Conn was a Post Captain in 1802. He commanded the Dreadnought at the Battle of Trafalgar, and was afterwards appointed to the Swiftsure, from which vessel, whilst in chase off the Bermuda Islands on the 4th of May, 1810, he fell overboard and was drowned.

[6] See Appendix No. 1, for the rough draft of the Plan of attack. The alterations in the wording of it are very few, and the whole marks the genius of Nelson for the service, displaying an attention to the minutest details.

watchword was NELSON, and the answer BRONTÉ. The attack was unsuccessful. The flotilla could not be brought out of the mouth of the harbour. Great bravery was displayed by the officers and men employed, and the loss was severe. The flotilla, brigs, and flats, were moored by the bottom to the shore, and to each other by chains, and our force was severely injured by the firing of musketry from the shore. In this attack, Captain Parker, one of Nelson's greatest favourites, received a shot in the thigh, shattering it. He was saved from being killed or taken prisoner, by the Honourable Mr. Cathcart, for every man in Parker's boat was either killed or wounded, and his boat had drifted alongside a flat full of men. Parker's condition excited Nelson's deepest commiseration—he truly loved him. In his account to Mr. Nepean, at the Admiralty, he says:—" Amongst the many gallant men wounded, I have, with the deepest regret, to place the name of my gallant, good friend and able assistant, Captain Edward T. Parker, also my Flag Lieutenant Frederick Langford,[1] who has served with me many years; they were wounded in attempting to board the French Commodore." The following letters will shew the deep interest he took in the fate of his friend and aide-de-camp:—

" Medusa, August 16th, 1801.

" My dearest Emma,

" You will be sorry to hear that dear little Parker is wounded, but the doctors assure me he will do well. Langford has his leg shot through, but will do. The damned French had their vessels chained from the bottoms to the shore, and also to each other; therefore, although several of them were taken, yet they could not be brought off. They will not unchain them for us to catch them at sea. The enemy have lost many men, so have we, about 100 killed and wounded. Nobody acquitted themselves in every respect better than Cathcart; he saved Parker from being a prisoner. Parker shewed the most determined courage; so did Langford.

---

[1] Lieutenant Frederick Langford died at Jamaica in 1815, being then in command of the Cydnus. He was made a Commander in 1801, but was not posted until 1806.

You will believe how I am suffering, and not well into the bargain. Troubridge has wrote me such letters, that I do not know if I shall ever write to him again. It is all his doing, my not coming to London. I shall be two days in the Downs, but it is just at Sir William's arrival. How I envy him the sight of your blessed face! and probably I shall be gone before you can come. I have no friend but one, as I wrote Troubridge; that is you, good, dear, disinterested Emma. I am agitated, but believe me,

" Yours,

" NELSON AND BRONTÉ.

"This letter will be opened to a certainty, to hear news from Boulogne."

" Medusa, Downs, August 17th, 1801.

" My dearest Emma,

" Your kind letter of Saturday I received last night, and I regret that I cannot find a house and a little piece of ground, for if I go on much longer with my present command, I must be ruined. I think your perseverance and management will at last get me a home. I am now likely to be here till Thursday. I wish Sir William had been either at home or not coming. Perhaps you, my excellent friend, and Mrs. Nelson, might have come down to Deal; how happy you would have made me, but I hope to get in again somewhere after this next trip, and by that time Sir William will have arranged his affairs in London. As for Troubridge, never send a letter through him. I shall never write to him again unless his letters are done away. I am no longer useful, and we know, 'No longer pipe, no longer dance.' The Admiralty are beasts for their pains; it was only depriving me of one day's comfort and happiness, for which they have my hearty prayers. Parker will do well, I hope, but he must be kept very quiet; his thigh is broken in three places, but as he has youth, the doctors hope it will unite; it is the only chance he has. Langford is suffering very much. I have sent and taken lodgings for them both, and I trust they will get well as fast as I wish them. Now we shall see whether the

Admiralty will again neglect me, or whether officers and men who serve under me are to be neglected. We all dine at the Admiral's to day, and sleep on shore, contrary to my inclination; but Captain Gore has requested it, that the ship may be cleaned and purified, for the wounds smell very bad, and they cannot begin to wash till Parker and Langford are removed out of the cabin. To-morrow morning I will be on board again. Mr. Pitt is coming to Walmer Castle. If he asks me to dinner, I shall go to Sandwich; at present I shall not think of it. What pleasure can I derive from it? Remember me to Sir William. I wish you were here.

"Ever yours,
"NELSON AND BRONTÉ.

"To Mrs. Nelson, the Duke, and Lord William, say every thing which is kind. How can the Duke think you would take his house? Never."

Parker wrote to Lady Hamilton:—

"Deal, August 18th, 1801.

"My Lady,

"Your letter has made such strong impressions on me, that I hardly know how my feelings allow me to answer, but still I must, as long as nature allows me to hold a pen. To call me a *Nelsonite* is more to me than making me a Duke: oh God, how is it possible for me ever to be sufficiently thankful for all his attentions! He is now attending me with the most parental kindness, comes to me at six in the morning and ten at night; both late and early his kindness is alike. God bless him and preserve him. I would lose a dozen limbs to serve him. Thank Mrs. Nelson for me. Excuse me, for I am tired, and believe me,

"Your most grateful servant,
"E. T. PARKER."

In communicating the approval of the zeal and courage of the squadron by the Lords of the Admiralty, Nelson assures them, "that the enemy will not have long reason to boast of their security; for he trusts ere long to assist them in person in a way which will completely annihilate the whole of them. Lord Nelson is convinced, that if it had been possible for man to have brought the enemy's flotilla out, the men that were employed to do so would have accomplished it. The moment the enemy have the audacity to cast off the chains which fix their vessels to the ground, that moment Lord Nelson is well persuaded they will be conducted by his brave followers to a British port, or sent to the bottom." He burned with anxiety for an attack in which he might personally partake. He was desirous of attacking the enemy at Flushing; he even contemplated a bombardment of Calais. To Earl St. Vincent he says, "I own I shall never bring myself again to allow any attack to go forward, where I am not personally concerned; my mind suffers much more than if I had a leg shot off in this late business. I am writing between poor Parker and Langford; therefore I must beg great indulgences, only believe that I will do my utmost."[1]

This service was considered by many as of too petty a description for an officer of Lord Nelson's rank and character to be employed upon; but it was undertaken at the request of the Hon. Mr. Addington, to satisfy the British people, and subdue the alarm entertained by many at Buonaparte's threats of invasion. Nelson was not a man to cavil at a service when an opportunity offered by which he could benefit his country. Although his attack on the Boulogne flotilla was unsuccessful in its object, it failed not to demonstrate the utter futility of all attempts at invasion. M. Thiers says, that the confidence of the English in the enterprising genius of Nelson, was greatly diminished by the failure of his attack! "La confiance des Anglais dans le génie entreprenant de Nelson était fort diminuée."[2] The best refutation of this is to be found in his subsequent career, and the unbounded attachment and admiration entertained for him by the whole British nation.

[1] Clarke and McArthur, Vol. ii. p. 301.
[2] Hist. du Consulat. tom. iii. liv. xi. p. 175.

On the 18th he wrote to Lady Hamilton:—

"Deal, August 18th, 1801.

"My dearest Emma,

"I have this morning been attending the funeral of two young Midshipmen: a Mr. Gore, cousin of Captain Gore, and a Mr. Bristow.[1] One nineteen, the other seventeen years of age. Last night I was all the evening in the hospital, seeing that all was done for the comfort of the poor fellows. I am going on board, for nothing shall keep me living on shore without you were here. I shall come in the morning to see Parker, and go on board again directly. I shall be glad to see Oliver: I hope he will keep his tongue quiet about the tea-kettle, for I shall not give it till I leave the Medusa. You ask me what Troubridge wrote me? There was not a syllable about you in it. It was about my not coming to London, at the importance of which I laughed: and then he said, he should never venture another opinion. On which I said, 'Then I shall never give you one.' This day he has wrote a kind letter, and all is over.

"I have, however, wrote him in my letter of this day as follows, *viz.*:—'*And I am this moment, as firmly of opinion as ever, that Lord St. Vincent, and yourself, should have allowed of my coming to town, for my own affairs; for every one knows I left it without a thought for myself.*' But this business cannot last long, and I hope we shall have peace; and I rather incline to that opinion.

"I hope, my dear Emma, you will be able to find a house suited for my comfort. I am sure of being happy by your arrangements. I have wrote a line to Troubridge about Darby. Parker will write you a line of thanks if he is able. I trust in God he will yet do well! You ask me, my dear friend, if I am going on more expeditions? And even if I was

---

[1] These two poor fellows were Midshipmen in the Medusa. Mr. Gore was a son of Lieut.-Colonel Gore, and only in his 16th year. In attempting to board the enemy he was wounded by no less than five musket balls. They were buried at Deal in one grave, Lord Nelson and eight Captains of the Navy attending the funeral. His Lordship's sensibility was freely expressed on this occasion by a flow of tears. A file of marines preceded the bodies, and three volleys were fired over the place of their interment.

to forfeit your friendship, which is dearer to me than all the world, I can tell you nothing. For, I go out; if I see the enemy, and can get at them, it is my duty, and you would naturally hate me if I kept back one moment.

"I long to pay them for their tricks the other day, the debt of a drubbing, which surely I will pay: but *when, where, or how*, it is impossible, your own good sense must tell you, for me or mortal man to say.

"I shall act not in a rash or hasty manner, that you may rely, and on which I give you my word of honour. Just going off.

"Ever your faithful,
"NELSON AND BRONTÉ."[1]

And on the 19th:—

"Deal, August 19th, 1801."

"My dearest Emma,

"Oliver came on board about two o'clock this morning with young Banti, who you may be assured I will take every possible care of. I have all your truly kind and affectionate letters by Oliver, and also those by the post to-day. You may rely, that as soon as I can with honour get clear of this business, I shall resign it with pleasure; but if I was to give it up at this moment, you would hate me. The whole history must be over by the 14th of September, if not, I will certainly think of giving the command up; but as I have had all the fag, and what is to come must be playful compared to what has passed, I may as well have the credit of finishing this business. I think it very probable I shall never personally be engaged, therefore, my dear Emma, do not let your disinterested friendship make you uneasy. How often have I heard *you* say, that you would not quit the deck if you came near a Frenchman. Would you have your attached friend do less than you purpose for yourself? That I am sure you would not. In these bombardments there is no risk for my rank, therefore I pray be quiet. I have wrote Sir William a letter, which you will see; he was so good as to write me one from Milford on the 12th, by a Revenue cutter, which arrived

[1] Collection of Letters, Vol. ii. p. 48.

this morning. I had a note from Mr. Trevor;[1] he is at Ramsgate; he was sailing about with Mrs. T., but did not, he says, come near the ship, as he heard I had been *unfortunate*. I write a line to Mrs. Nelson. I am sure she will not leave you. I will entreat it of her. I am sure the kettle is all right, and as it should be; I shall leave it packed with a letter to-morrow. I expect the Amazon; but all my movements are uncertain; but this is the most likely place to find me. The Three Kings I am told is the best house (it stands on the beach), if the noise of the constant surf does not disturb you. Dear Parker is much better. I am sure he will be much gratified with your uniform kindness. When I left him to go on board yesterday, for I would not stay on shore, he got hold of my hand, and said he could not bear me to leave him, and cried like a child. However, I promised to come on shore this morning to see him, and nothing else could have got me out of the ship, for this beach is very uncomfortable to land upon. Oliver will tell you that I have been to the hospital to see my poor fellows, and altogether it has almost upset me, therefore I have not wrote so much as I should. Forgive me, and believe me,

"Yours,

"NELSON AND BRONTÉ.

"Your interest with Sir William is requested to come and see a poor forlorn sailor."

"Medusa, Downs, August 20th, 1801.

"My dearest Friend,

"I approve of the house at Merton; and as the Admiralty are so cruel (no, I never asked the Board of Admiralty), as Troubridge and the Earl are so cruel as to object to my coming to London to manage my own matters, I must beg and entreat of you to work hard for me. Messrs. Booth and Haslewood will manage all the law business. I have £3000. ready to pay to-morrow, and I can certainly get more in a

---

[1] John Trevor Hampden, third Viscount Hampden, born February 24, 1748-9. was in 1780 Minister Plenipotentiary to the Diet of Raleston; and in 1783, to the Court of Sardinia. He succeeded to the title upon the death of his brother, and with him the title has become extinct.

little time if the people will have patience, therefore pray, dear Emma, look to it for me. I shall approve your taste. How often have I, laughing, said I would give you £500. to furnish a house for me—you promised me, and now I claim it; and I trust to your own dear good heart for the fulfilment of it. I wrote Sir Thomas Troubridge that I had but one real friend; his answer was, that he knew I had a hundred, but I do not believe the ninety-nine. It is calm, and our men are not arrived, therefore cannot go to sea this day. How happy I shall be to see you, Sir William, and Mrs. Nelson here, and how dear Parker will be delighted. He is much better to-day. I went on shore one minute to see him, and returned instantly on board. Captain Gore told me that Mr. and Mrs. Trevor had been alongside, inquiring for me; that he had asked them to dinner, and that they would call again, so alongside they came. Captain Gore told them he was afraid he had done wrong, for that I was very busy; upon this Mr. Trevor came into the cabin, and begged pardon, but asked for Mrs. Trevor and two ladies to come in. My answer was, for being acquaintances of yours, Yes, if they wished to see the ship; but that I really could not allow them to stay dinner, for that every moment of my time was taken up. I did not go upon deck to receive them. They stayed ten minutes, inquired after you and Sir William, hoped you would come down and stay at Ramsgate, and away they went, making many apologies. I told him no other person should have come in, but for old acquaintance sake I could not refuse him. The other ladies were a Lady Somebody, and a Mrs. Somebody. I neither know or care for their names. Make my kindest regards to Sir William, Mrs. Nelson, the Duke, and Lord William. I think if you will take the trouble for my house you will have country employment enough without going to Richmond, where you never can do as you please.

"Ever yours,
"NELSON AND BRONTÉ."

About this time, Captain, now Sir Alexander John Ball, Bart., wrote to Lord Nelson :—

"Minorca, August 17th, 1801.

"My dear Lord,

"Our friend Hallowell, who has had the misfortune to be captured by Gantheaume's squadron, is arrived here, and will proceed immediately to England, where on his arrival he will pay his respects to your Lordship, and communicate the many interesting naval and military operations which have been transacted since you left us, and he will assure you of the ardent wish of the navy to see your Lordship command once more in these seas.

"I inclose a copy of a letter from Lord Hobart (Secretary for Foreign affairs),[1] expressing his Majesty's approbation of my conduct at Malta, and that he is pleased to give me a thousand pounds for my loss of prize money. Had I not landed at Malta, your Lordship would have given me the same friendly protection and advantage which you gave to

---

[1] "Downing Street, May 15th, 1801.

"Sir,

"I have to acknowledge your several letters to Mr. Dundas, of the dates mentioned in the margin, and to express the great satisfaction which his Majesty's confidential servants have received from the valuable and interesting communications they contain respecting the revenues and interior situation of the island of Malta.

"I am particularly commanded by his Majesty to convey to you his entire approbation of your conduct during the time you exercised the Administration of the Island, as a testimony of which, it is with very sincere pleasure that I have to inform you his Majesty has been graciously pleased to confer upon you the dignity of a Baronet of the United Kingdom of Great Britain and Ireland.

"With respect to the loss of Prize Money which you have sustained, by ceasing the command of the Alexander, you will, I am sure, on reflection, be aware of the great inconvenience that would arise from entertaining so delicate a question, by the numberless applications of different cases to which it might give rise. His Majesty, however, on a consideration of the peculiar circumstances of your situation, has been pleased to give directions that the sum of one thousand pounds shall be paid to you from the revenues of Malta; and you may rest assured that you will be included in the distribution of the proceeds arising from the shipping, ordnance and stores captured in the ports and fortresses on the surrender of the island to his Majesty's arms. Whenever that distribution shall be made, the claims of the Neapolitan and of the Maltese troops appear to me equally entitled to attention, and I shall not fail to recommend them to his Majesty's favourable consideration.

"I am, Sir,
"Your most obedient humble servant,
"Hobart."

"To Captain Ball."

the other Captains, who made from eight to sixteen thousand pounds, while I was at Malta; had I remained in the Alexander I should have received three thousand pounds for the captures made before Malta. With respect to precedent, Governor Phillip receives £500. a year for his services at Botany Bay. Lord Minto has a handsome pension. I certainly do not put my services in competition with those of Sir Sidney Smith; but when these gentlemen receive such handsome rewards, and I only get one thousand pounds to make up for the loss of several thousand pounds, I must think that his Majesty's Ministers do not know the difficulties I have had to encounter. They have appointed a Mr. Cameron Civil Commissioner of Malta, and the line is distinctly drawn between the civil and military departments. This gentleman has never been in a public situation; he is in distressed circumstances from a mercantile house, in which either he or his father was concerned, having failed. He married a sister of Lord Errol's, whose interest procured him this situation. The Maltese are astonished at this arrangement, and that so little deference is paid to their wishes, and the great injustice done me; particularly after Mr. Dundas's declaration in his letter to General Pigot, an extract[1] of which I inclose herewith. If Government suppose that the Commissionership is a recompense, I shall regret having applied for it. I have written for leave to go to England, in the hope that I shall, with the assistance of my friends, obtain at least a full indemnification for my losses. Tyson[2] is still at Malta.

[1] *Extract of a Letter from the Right Hon. Henry Dundas, November* 17, 1800, *to Major-General Pigot.*

"'The judgment and zeal with which Captain Ball, of the Royal Navy, conducted the affairs of the island, during the whole of the blockade, and the esteem and confidence which have been so justly and frequently shewn him by the inhabitants, render him in every respect a most fit person for you to consult and advise with as long as the duties of his profession may allow him to remain on the island; and I cannot more fully explain to you how much weight is due to his opinions and suggestions on the subject, than by informing you that his Majesty feels so forcibly how very materially his indefatigable services, and superior abilities have contributed to rescue Malta from the French, that it is a matter of regret to his Majesty, that the nature of the command and government being purely military, at least for the remainder of the war, precludes Captain Ball from retaining a situation adequate to his rank, and just expectations in this island."

[2] Lord Nelson's Secretary.

I shall join him in a few days, and then proceed to Gibraltar. I wrote to your Lordship about him several months since. I am under great obligations to him for the assistance he has given me, which I fear has prevented his joining your Lordship, by which he will be a great sufferer. I believe he has never received a line from your Lordship since your arrival in England. Adieu, my dear Lord. My very best respects to my worthy and good friends, Sir William and Lady Hamilton. With the greatest respect, I have the honour to remain,

"Your most obliged and devoted,

"ALEXANDER JOHN BALL."

Merton was now an object of attention, and was ultimately purchased by Nelson. To Lady Hamilton he writes:—

"August 20th, 1801.

"My dear Friend,

"I am very much flattered by Mr. Greville's kindness, and the great honour he has done me, but independent of that, I admire his description of the rising prosperity of Milford,[1] and the rising of its industrious inhabitants, which will make proprietor and tenant rich in time, and not like many fools be like the boy with the *golden egg*. I hope Græffer is going on so at Bronté; I am sure I take nothing from that estate. I entreat, my good friend, manage the affair of the house for me, and believe me, yours,

"NELSON AND BRONTÉ.

"Furniture and all fixtures must be bought."

The Rev. W. Nelson wrote to Lady Hamilton:—

"Burnham, August 20th, 1801.

"Your letters, my dear Madam, though they make us easy about my dear brother, yet make me very uncomfortable about poor Parker; I hope to God his limb may be set again, so that he may be able in time to return to his duty, for it will be a wretched thing for so young a man to be set aside so early in life; but God's will be done. I am glad Oliver is gone down to Deal, it will be a comfort to my brother. I shall be happy when he has done with these boat expeditions;

[1] Sir William Hamilton had much property here.

you see, nothing can be done with these rascals, they are too knowing: they well know nothing but iron chains will keep their vessels in their own ports when Nelson commands. Give my love to him when you write, and tell him I don't write to him myself, as he has so much to do, but my regard and love and *gratitude* to him is, and *always will* be, *unalterable*. You say I was silly I did not press for the entail of the peerage on Charlotte and her heirs male, as my brother was half inclined; had I known as much, I would have done it, for I agree perfectly with you, they don't value the thing as they ought; they are a little tickled with it at first, and that is all. However, if he is made an *Earl*, then will be the time, and I will get you to try to have it settled on me and my *heirs male*, and failure of them, on my *daughter* and *her* heirs *male*, that will do the business at once.

" I get on very well; the old gentleman is pretty well, and seems anxious about my brother's safety. He desires his compliments to you, and says you promised to write to him if any thing particular occurred. I shall be glad to know when Sir William returns, on your account as well as my own, that you may send my dear jewel to me, for I shall be quite alone. I shall be home on Saturday, and expect to find letters.

" Yours most faithfully and affectionately,
" WM. NELSON."

The Hon. Col. Stewart's practice at Copenhagen with Nelson, seems from the following letter, to have inspired him with the desire of having been present at the unsuccessful attempt upon the French flotilla at Boulogne :—

" Weymouth Camp, August 21st, 1801.

" My dear Lord,
" The anxiety and interest with which I have entered into the spirit of your Lordship's late gallant attempt against the Boulogne fleet, must apologize for my intruding this letter upon time more seriously occupied than even the perusal of it can perhaps afford. I know not how it is, but some how or other, I do not feel comfortable at the not having requested your Lordship more particularly to have taken me with you,

on the late occasion, although out of my line immediately, and liable to have created jealousy had I been honoured with any thing like a considerable share of friendship; be it as it may, I cannot read your Lordship's letter, accompanied by our dear Parker's, without tears coming in my eyes, and wishing that I might at least have borne some share in the danger which surrounded that gallant young friend of your Lordship's on the late occasion. How true is it, that fortune is a capricious dame, and favours our attempts in this world only when she pleaseth. Those only who understand where to attach glory to the attempt and to enterprise, and *not to success*, can fully feel all that they ought to feel, or enter into the grandeur of the action which last Saturday night took place. How strongly does that admirable line in the tragedy of Cato come to our minds, when he says,

' 'Tis not in mortals to command success,
But we'll do more, Sempronius; we'll deserve it.'

"After having been on this occasion not so fortunate as to have been of any use under your command, if chance or situation can still, my dear Lord, bring me in any manner, with or without *my willing fellows*, into play, where you lead I shall be made one of the happiest of soldiers, for much as I before wished to accompany your Lordship, more anxious do I feel now than ever, since the Goddess of Fortune has seemed to shew an inclination to be ill-natured, and to dare us to still harder trials. I am an individual, who from my situation in life, and from my turn of feelings upon certain subjects, feel not perhaps more desirous to preserve myself beyond this war than many of my contemporary officers. Without being tired of the world, I, perhaps, attach not that idea of value to it which is so much felt, and am of that turn of mind which induces a man sometimes to look forward to a long dull and lingering decline, as in the main less enviable than a more rapid exit from this world, tinged with a moderate degree of honour.

"I am doing my utmost to bring my young regiment here into a state worthy of being called upon by your Lordship, wherever their services may be useful. My Baltic party has at length joined me, and with heartfelt sincerity, (my friend

Beckwith at their head), submit their hopes of remembrance to you. With the same feeling, I beg leave to subscribe myself, my dear Lord,

"One of your very faithful and humble servants,
"W. STEWART."

Captain Parker again wrote to Lady Hamilton :—

"Deal, August 21st, 1801.

"My Lady,
"How much I feel for your goodness to me. I am as well as the nature of my wounds will allow, and eat and drink all the Doctors will let me. I have strong hopes from what my dear Lord says, that I shall see you all down on his return. What a joy that will be. I dare say I shall be half well by that time. Langford is much obliged to you; he is upon the mending hand, and I hope will soon be well. Companions in misfortune are not desirable. I was afraid my friend, my nurse, my attendant, my patron, my protector, nay, him whom the world cannot find words sufficient to praise, would have sailed; but he is not yet gone. Remember me most affectionately to Sir William, with every thing you can say kind and grateful to Mrs. Nelson, and believe me your Ladyship's grateful and obedient servant,

"EDWARD T. PARKER.

"Thank you for your plan about the letters. I wish the newspapers did not say so much; they are too lavish a great deal, they do nothing but cut and shoot, and everything that is dreadful."

And Nelson :—

"Medusa, August 22nd, 1801.

"My dear Emma,
"I shall try and get this letter through Troubridge, but one day he is angry and another pleased, that, to say the truth, I do not wish to trouble any of them. I have been sea-sick these last two days, and I should die to stay here one quarter of the winter. God knows whether those fellows will try and come over, I can hardly think they are fools enough. You may rely, my dearest friend, that I will run no unnecessary risk, therefore let your friendly mind be at ease. Would

to God it were peace, and then I would go to Sicily, and be happy. I cannot get on shore and afloat again, the surf is so great, and yet I could have wished to have seen Parker, but nothing but necessity should have made me remain on shore, and if I was to go I could not get off. I expect the Amazon to-day, and shall get on board her, but in a very wretched state, for I have nothing in reality fit to keep a table, and to begin and lay out £500. is what I cannot afford, therefore in every respect I shall be very miserable. I know not why, but to-day I am ready to burst into tears. Pray God your friendly letters may arrive and comfort me. I am sure I get not one *scrap* of comfort from any other quarter. Banti seems stout, and will, I dare say, do very well. He is not sea-sick, which I am—that is very odd, and I am damned sick of the sea. This moment I have your letters, and although I rejoice from my heart that you are coming, yet I am fearful I shall not be here by Wednesday night, but I hope on Thursday, or Friday at farthest. The three rooms next the sea are all sitting-rooms, with a gallery before them next the sea. I will desire two of the rooms, if possible, for I believe, except a dark sitting room, they are the only rooms in the house, and I will desire good bed-chambers to be kept for you at an inn. You cannot take rooms without being in the house, for it is the eating and drinking that is charged, and not the rooms, but I am sure the house will give you accommodation, and I will send to say so this day. I will lose no time in returning, for the meeting of you and Sir William and Mrs. Nelson will be the day of my life, being yours,

"Nelson and Bronté.

"I send this under cover to Nepean. Your letters for Parker had better be directed for me at Captain Parker's, but explain this to him; but the postage is nothing, therefore direct to him; the cost is nothing, for I should not like my letters to be opened, therefore do away to him the direction you sent to-day. I hear he is much better to-day; he will rejoice to see you. Remember me kindly to Sir William and Mrs. Nelson. I am glad she is coming down with you, but I fancy you will hate the town of Deal, at least I do at this moment, but I shall think it Paradise when my dear only friends come to it. Pray get the house and furniture. I have sent to pay Mr. Salter,¹ but I have not got the other bills.

"Medusa, Downs, August 23rd, 1801.
Six in the morning.

"My dearest Emma.

"I am ready to run mad, I have been at this horrid place one whole week, and now on the approach of my dearest friends am forced to go to sea and am fearful that I cannot be here by Wednesday night, or before Thursday or Friday at soonest, and I am more fearful that you will hate Deal and be as tired of it as I am without you. If you were here we would drive to Dover Castle and Ramsgate if you pleased. Poor little Parker cannot occupy much of your time, and Sir William may be so tired as to shorten his visit when I arrive, therefore had it not better be Friday, by which I hope to be able to get back, but for two or three days, when we are once afloat you know no one can answer, witness our voyage to and from Malta. We are just getting under sail. May God bless you and believe me,

"Your most faithful,
"NELSON AND BRONTÉ.

"If you are here before my arrival, and choose to be known to Admiral Lutwidge, he is as good a man as ever lived. I know very little of her; she is a very good woman, but her figure is extraordinary. Oh that I could stay. How I hate going to sea. The rooms are taken, and the master of the inn sends me word everything shall be done. I shall send a cutter in two days."

"Medusa at sea, August 24th, 1801.

"My dearest Emma,

"So little is newspaper information to be depended upon, that on Thursday although with a + I was not a quarter of an hour on shore. I went to Parker, from him to the Admiral, from the Admiral to Parker, did not stay five minutes, was very low, did not call upon any of the wounded,

---

¹ The respected Silversmith in the Strand, well known to all Naval Officers.

nor at the Three Kings, got into the boat, and have not since been out of the Medusa. If I had staid ashore, I should not have had Trevor on board. The information I have received about Flushing is not correct, and I cannot get at the Dutch; therefore, I shall be in the Downs I trust on Wednesday evening, ready and happy to receive you. Whatever Sir Thomas Troubridge may say, I feel I have no real friends out of your house. How I am praying for the wind to carry me and to bring me to your sight. I am tired at not being able to get at the damned rascals; but they are preparing against me in every quarter, therefore they cannot be preparing for an invasion. I agree with you, fight them if they come out, so I will and reserve myself for it. I believe the enemy attaches much more importance to my life than our folks, the former look up to me with awe and dread, the latter fix not such real importance to my existence. I send this under cover to Parker in case you are not come, that he may send it to London. I am making some arrangements and shall be across directly. With my kindest regards to Sir William believe me,

"Yours,
"NELSON AND BRONTÉ."

"Medusa, Downs, August 31, 1801.

"My dear Emma,

"Sir William is arrived, and well; remember me kindly to him, I should have had the pleasure of seeing him, but for *one of my lords and masters*, TROUBRIDGE; therefore, I am sure, neither you nor Sir William will feel obliged to him.

"The weather is very bad, and I am very sea-sick. I cannot answer your letter, probably; but I am writing a line, to get on shore if possible: indeed, I hardly expect that your letter can get afloat.

"I entreat you, my dear friend, to work hard for me, and get the house and furniture; and I will be so happy to lend it to you and Sir William!

"Therefore, if you were to take the Duke's (Queensberry's) house, *a cake house*, open to everybody he pleases, you had better have a booth at once; you never could rest one moment quiet. Why did not the Duke assist Sir William, when he wanted his assistance? why not have saved you from the distress, which Sir William must every day feel, in knowing that his excellent wife sold her jewels to get a house for him; whilst his own relations, great as they are in the foolish world's eye, would have left a man of his respectability and age, to have lodged in the street. Did the Duke or any of them, give him a house then? Forgive me! you know if anything sticks in my throat, it must out. Sir William owes his life to you; which, I believe, he will never forget.

"To return to the house. The furniture must be bought with it, and the sooner it is done, the better I shall like it. Oh! how bad the weather is! The devils here wanted to plague my soul out, yesterday, just after dinner. The Countess M., Lady this, that, and t'other, came alongside, a Mr. Lubbock with them—to desire they might come in. I sent word, I was so busy that no person could be admitted, as my time was employed in the King's service. Then they sent their names, which I cared not for, and sent Captain Gore, to say it was impossible; and, that if they wanted to see a ship, they had better go to the Overyssel (a sixty-four in the Downs). They said, no, they wanted to see me, however, I was stout, and will not be shewn about like a *beast!* and away they went.

"I believe Captain Gore wishes me out of his ship; for the *ladies* admire him, I am told, very much: but, however, no Captain could be kinder to me than he is. These ladies, he told me afterwards, were his relations.

"I have just got your letters; many thanks for them! You do not say in the end, Sir William is arrived. I am glad that you approve. You may rely, my dear friend, that I will not run any unnecessary risk! No more boat work, I promise you; but ever your attached and faithful,

"NELSON AND BRONTÉ.

"To the Duke and Lord William, say everything which is kind; and to Mrs Nelson. I am so dreadfully sea-sick, that I cannot hold up my head."[1]

Lord Nelson's father's anxiety became great on his account, and he wrote the following to Lady Hamilton:—

---

[1] Collection of Letters, Vol. i. p. 57.

"Madam,

"I heartily congratulate you upon Sir W. Hamilton's return from his late excursion, which I hope has firmly established his health. As your Ladyship flattered me with the favour of a letter from you, whenever any event respecting my dear son called forth our immediate notice, I have been in hope that you might tell me something more than public papers. His situation is more than usually dangerous, and I do feel much on that account, perhaps you may have seen him, certainly you know more of his health and movements than come to my ear. Anxiety is a continual smart. I am, Madam, with best compliments to Sir William.

"Your obliged and obedient servant,
"EDMUND NELSON.

"Love to my much esteemed daughter-in-law, Mrs. Nelson."

The parental anxiety of the Rev. Edmund Nelson also appears in the following letter to Lady Hamilton, who wrote to the venerable man:—

"Madam,

"I am much favoured by your polite letter, and the very friendly regard with which Sir W. Hamilton and yourself always mention my dear son; who is, certainly, a worthy, good, brave man, parental partiality *apart*. But I myself am by no means satisfied with his present situation; as to its importance, its safety, or its merited rewards. It is his to sow, but others to reap the yellow harvest, all things, I trust, however, will work together for good. Captain Parker's misfortune, I see in every point of view, with a friendly concern. Langford will quickly be upon his legs.

"Though the amusements of a dirty sea-port are not the most refined, good health, and domestic cheerfulness, will be a happy substitute. I beg the whole party to accept this my remembrance, and assurance of my regard, respect and love, and am, Madam,

"Your most humble servant,
"EDMUND NELSON."[1]

Nelson was visited by Sir William and Lady Hamilton,

[1] Collection of Letters, Vol. i. p. 190.

and Mrs. Nelson, (wife of the Rev. William Nelson) towards the end of August. He was then very anxious about obtaining Merton, the price of which was to be £9000, but he was doubtful of his ability to purchase it. The Bronté estate was threatened by a considerable charge upon it, and Lord Nelson's agent, Mr. John Græffer, addressed the following to Sir John Acton, Bart.

"Bronté, September 3rd, 1801.

"Sir,

"Your Excellency's attachment towards the welfare of my Lord Nelson, Duke of Bronté, has emboldened me to transmit the inclosed memorial, craving, in the name of his Lordship, your Excellency's assistance to ease the demand, so that the same may not become too great a burthen for my Lord Nelson to support. Permit me to have the honour to be, Sir,

"Your Excellency's
"Most obedient and most devoted,
"Humble servant,
"JOHN GRÆFFER.

"His Excellency General Sir John Acton, Bart.
Palermo."

SIR JOHN ACTON'S REPLY.

"Sir,

"I have received your letter of the 4th instant, and what therein you have thought proper to acquaint me of, in regard to Bronté, is certainly much deserving of attention. I shall ever be ready to promote whatever may be useful to our worthy and most excellent Lord Nelson. I have taken his Majesty's order, and the *Conservatore* Tomasi shall settle and fix the military service in the proper rule, directed to avoid certainly that our good Admiral should not be under conditions more grievous than any other Baron in Sicily. I am going to Naples, but confide that every care in my absence shall be taken to favour the just demands in Lord Nelson's name. I remain constantly, Sir,

"Your most obedient and most humble servant,
"J. ACTON.

"Palermo, September 15th, 1801."

"The memorial transmitted to General Acton was a demand on your Lordship for military service; to be better understood, a quota of horses for the King's military use, maintained at your expense, the number proportioned according to the annual income of the estate, which would have been no less than twenty fixed for ever on the Bronté estate. But General Acton interesting himself in behalf of your Lordship, the number, from what I can learn, is to be fixed either at two or three horses.

"J. G."

The attachment of Nelson's officers to his person, their desire to give him intelligence, and anxiety to be again with him, are shewn in the following:—

"H. M. S. Kent, Aboukir Bay,
4th September, 1801.

"My Lord,

"Presuming on your Lordship's attention to those who formerly have had the honour of serving with you, I am encouraged to trouble you on the present occasion. The surrender of Alexandria, and the entire conquest of the country by the exertions of our army and navy, will, I doubt not, afford your Lordship very great satisfaction.

"It has been my good fortune to render to a detachment of our army under Major-General Coote, a piece of service that has called forth the acknowledgments of the General, and has met with the approbation of Lord Keith and Sir Richard Bickerton; to the latter, and to the Honourable Captain Cochrane,[1] I am under great obligations for the very

---

[1] The Hon. Sir Alexander Forrester Inglis Cochrane was born April 23, 1758, entered the Navy early, and having, in 1778, attained the rank of Lieutenant, was made signal officer to Sir George Rodney in his action with the Count de Guichen in 1780, on which occasion he was wounded. In 1782 he was made a Post Captain, and served on the American station. In 1795 in the command of the Thetis, he took La Prévoyante frigate with stores for France. He captured many American privateers, and in 1800 served with Lord Keith in the Mediterranean, and on the coast of Egypt. In 1803 he was made a Rear-Admiral. He joined Lord Nelson in 1805 in his pursuit of the French Fleet, and in 1806 was with Admiral Sir John T. Duckworth in the West Indies. In the Northumberland he was engaged in the action with the squadron that had sailed from Brest, and had a miraculous escape, his hat being carried away by a grape shot early in the battle. The Corporation of London voted him the Freedom of the City on

handsome manner they were pleased to represent my services to the Commander-in-chief, but excepting the zeal by which I was animated, I am sensible they were over-rated. The copies of the letters which passed on the occasion, I have the honour to inclose, for your Lordship's perusal, they will inform you of the nature and extent of the service I have had the good fortune to perform. It may be proper to observe that the survey and offer to lead his Majesty's ships into a harbour very little known, was a voluntary act of my own, the survey of the channels being at the time a service I was not employed on, or had any connection with.

"Our boats had been driven from the survey of the middle channel by the enemy, and the Arab Pilot had refused to conduct the ships through any other, when it occurred to me, that as the enemy's attention seemed to be directed against the survey of the middle and eastern channels only, the western might be examined without being materially annoyed by the guns of Marabou. I was resolved to try, and was lucky enough to succeed in the attempt, and in consequence had the satisfaction to lead the squadron under the order of Captain Cochrane, through the shoals to a safe anchorage in the harbour of Alexandria. By transmitting this account to your Lordship I hope to obtain your approbation of my conduct, as it was under your auspices I entered his Majesty's service, and under whose command I have principally served. I cannot but look forward to a time when I may again have

---

this occasion, and a sword of 100 guineas value; the Patriotic Fund a vase valued at £300., and March 29, 1806, he was made a Knight of the Bath. The inhabitants of Barbadoes voted him a piece of plate of the value of £500. sterling. In 1807 he was appointed to the Belleisle, of 74 guns, and took possession of the Danish islands of St. Thomas, St. John, and St. Croix, also co-operated with Lieutenant-General Beckwith to take possession of Martinique. In 1809 he was advanced to the rank of Vice-Admiral, and assisted in the reduction of Guadaloupe, and the Dutch islands of St. Martin, St. Eustatia and Saba. He was made Governor and Commander-in-chief of Guadaloupe in 1810, and in 1813 commanded the fleet on the coast of North America, and distinguished himself by his great activity in this service. He returned to England in 1815, and in 1819 became full Admiral, hoisting his flag on board the Impregnable, of 98 guns, as Commander-in-chief at Plymouth, February 1, 1821. He died January 26, 1832, Admiral of the White, and G.C.B.

the honour of serving with you.  Wishing you the continuance of your health, I have the honour to be, my Lord,

"Your Lordship's most obedient faithful servant,

"THOMAS WITHERS."[1]

"Success (as Sir Thomas Suckling writes) is a rare paint; it hides all manner of ugliness;" so the want of it excites discussion and censure.  A Mr. Hill, it appears, ventured to criticise Lord Nelson's conduct in the attack upon the flotilla off Boulogne, and sent to him a paper entitled, "Remarks by a seaman on the attack at Boulogne," which contained severe strictures on Lord Nelson's official dispatch.  To this was appended a note to say, "should Lord Nelson wish the inclosed not to be inserted in the newspapers, he will please to *inclose, by return of post, a Bank note of* £100. to Mr. Hill, to be left at the Post Office, till called for, London."  Lord Nelson transmitted it to the Secretary of the Admiralty, saying, "If their Lordships think it proper to save me from such letters, they will be pleased to send proper people to take up whoever comes for Mr. Hill's letter.  I have franked it with the following direction :—

"Mr. Hill,

"To be left at the Post Office till called for."[2]

To Mr. Hill he wrote as follows :—

"Amazon, Downs, 6th September, 1801.

"Mr. Hill,

"Very likely I am unfit for my present command, and whenever Government change me, I hope they will find no difficulty in selecting an officer of greater abilities; but you will, I trust, be punished for threatening my character.  But I have not been brought up in the school of fear, and, therefore, care not what you do.  I defy you and your malice.

"NELSON AND BRONTE."[3]

---

[1] This officer died a Post Captain.  His exertions as Agent of Transports at Alexandria were highly eulogised by Major-General Fraser in his Dispatch to General Fox on the surrender of the town and fortress on the 20th March, 1807.

[2] In the possession of the Right Hon. J. W. Croker.

[3] Letter Book.

Mr. Hill was too cunning however to be taken. A porter sent to the Post Office for the answer, was taken up, but he either did not or would not know his employer. The confidence in Lord Nelson's zeal and ability entertained at the Admiralty, was in no degree abated by the discomfiture off Boulogne, as is seen by the following letters:—

"Confidential. Admiralty, 9th September, 1811.

"My dear Lord,

"A plan has been in contemplation for attempting the destruction of the Dutch squadron at Helvoet, and some communications have taken place with Admiral Dickson on the subject. The person whose opinions have been taken is Captain Campbell[1] of the Ariadne, who, I understand, is an intelligent, enterprising man, and not likely to take up the subject lightly, being very well acquainted with the port of Helvoet.

"The inclosed paper contains Admiral Dickson, or rather Captain Campbell's idea of the nature and extent of the force to be employed on this enterprise. It is wished that your Lordship would consider the subject in all its points, and if you think the plan to be practicable, there will be no difficulty in sending Captain Campbell to you. If it should be agreed to undertake it, your Lordship must leave it to Lord St. Vincent to make some arrangement with Admiral Dickson for placing it under your Lordship's direction. I cannot send your Lordship the plan of Helvoet to-day, but you shall have a very good one to-morrow.

"Believe me to be,
"My dear Lord,
"Very truly and sincerely yours,
"EVAN NEPEAN.

[1] Captain Patrick Campbell, K.C.B. died a Vice-Admiral of the Blue, Aug. 13, 1841. He was with Captain Inman in the attack upon the French squadron in Dunkirk harbour, in which he took La Desirée, for which he was promoted and made Post Captain of the Ariadne. In 1805 he commanded the Doris, which struck upon a sunken rock in his progress to Quiberoon Bay, and was ultimately so disabled as to be burnt. He had also a narrow escape at Rochfort, and most laudably exerted himself to save the life of his Commander, Captain Jervis, who, however, was unfortunately drowned from the upsetting of his boat. In 1815 he commanded L'Unité, was stationed off Corfu, and afterwards moved into the Leviathan on the Mediterranean station. He was made C.B. in June 1815.

"Markham tells me that he thinks you have already a copy of the chart of Helvoet."

"My dear Lord,

"Until your Lordship has had a conference with Captain Campbell, we are not disposed to come to a final determination on the design against the port in question, and as we have observed more than common caution, I trust it will not be let out. The preparations being made under your direction, is the only mode we can employ to mask it. Happy should I be to place the whole of our offensive and defensive war under your auspices, but you are well aware of the difficulties on that head.

"Your's most affectionately,
"St. Vincent.

"Admiralty, 14th September, 1801."

Lord Nelson approved the idea and the spirit of Captain Campbell. In a letter to Earl St. Vincent he says, "The attempt is worthy of an English Admiral. It is one of those judicious enterprises in which we hazard only a few boats, and may destroy an enemy's squadron."

To the Earl of Eldon Lord Nelson made application for a living for the Rev. Mr. Comyn, his Chaplain. The following was the Chancellor's reply:—

"My Lord,

"I am honoured with your Lordship's letter; I can't agree with your Lordship's observation that you have no claim on Lord Loughborough or on me, because I don't know the individual in this country, upon whom your Lordship may not be said to have a claim. The living you mention I cannot promise your Lordship, because I have made it a rule, from which I have never departed, not to promise a living not yet vacant. I am scrupulous upon this point, because a Chancellor is but a being of a day, and I think he can't with propriety promise what it may not belong to him to give; and he has no right to embarrass his successor with the hardships which belong to the situation of those whose expectations are crossed by the accidents which remove Chancellors from their offices. But I shall not forget that I have received your Lordship's letter upon this subject, and I hope I shall not be wanting in the attention which is due to your wishes at any time. I remain, my Lord, with the greatest possible respect,

"Your obedient humble servant,
"ELDON.

"16th September, 1801.

"P.S. I am the more unwilling, my Lord, to make a promise upon the subject of a living, though I hope I shall not be less anxious to attend to your wishes, because in the five months in which I have been Chancellor, I have hardly had three vacancies of most trifling livings to answer many hundred applications."

In the life of the Earl of Eldon, by Horace Twiss, Esq.[1] is Lord Nelson's response to the preceding letter:—

"Amazon, September 17th, 1801.

"My Lord,
"I feel very much obliged by your open and very handsome answer to my request, which so exactly accords with what my friend Davison told me of your Lordship's character; and allow me to consider myself, in every respect, your most obliged,

"NELSON AND BRONTÉ."

Sir William and Lady Hamilton remained with Nelson until the 20th September. On this day he wrote to Lady Hamilton:—

"Amazon, Sept. 20th, 1801.

"My dearest Emma,
"Although I ought to feel grateful for Sir William, you, and Mrs. Nelson's goodness in coming to see a poor forlorn creature at Deal, yet I feel at this moment only the pain of your leaving me, to which is added, the miserable situation of our dear excellent little Parker. Dr. Baird[2] is in great distress

---

[1] Vol. i. p. 390.
[2] Physician in the Royal Navy. He died July 17, 1843.

about him, and it can hardly be said that he lives at this moment, and before night will probably be out of this world, and if real worth and honour have a claim to Divine favour, surely he stands a fair chance of happiness in that which is to come. I will not say what I feel because I know that your feelings are similar. We might have comforted each other, but the Fates have denied us that comfort. Sir William's business forces him to London, and mine irresistibly forces me to remain on this miserable spot. I got on board at seven o'clock, and found what a difference! I must not think of it. My sailing to-morrow depends on poor Parker. If he dies he shall be buried as becomes so brave and good an officer. Mr. Wallis is just come on board; he says, there are no hopes. I am sick to death, but

"Ever yours,
"NELSON AND BRONTÉ.

"I send you Mr. Haslewood's letter about the furniture. Do what you think best, I shall be content. We must not sink under the will of Providence. The valuation had better be, probably, by Mr. Haslewood's man—it can make no difference to Mr. Dods; but do as you please, and see it right."

His mind had endured much suffering on Parker's account. In his letters of this period to Earl St. Vincent, Mr. Davison, and others, his case and condition is never omitted to be noticed. He wrote also to Dr. Baird, (whose kindness and ability made a great impression upon Nelson), on the 20th: "Your kind letter has given me hopes of my dear Parker; he is my child, for I found him in distress. I am prepared for the worst, although I still hope. Pray tell me as often as you can. Would I could be useful, I would come on shore and nurse him; I rely on your abilities, and if his life is to be spared, that you, under the blessing of God, are fully equal to be the instrument. Say everything which is kind for me to Mrs. Parker, and if my Parker remembers me, say, 'God bless him;' and do you believe me,

"Your most obliged and faithful friend,
"NELSON AND BRONTÉ.

"I have been in real misery. Hawkins[1] will come off night or day."[2]

To Lady Hamilton he writes:—

"Amazon, Sept. 21st, 1801.

"My dear Emma,

"My letter from Dr. Baird last evening, and from the Assistant-Surgeon at four this morning, again revive my hopes of our dear little Parker. He is free from fever, and his stomach got rid of the sickness. He can speak, therefore I hope the blood is forming again, and if the ligature can hold fast he may yet do well. Pray God he may, in which I know you and all with you most heartily join; but I dare not be too sanguine. We have a good deal of swell, and it blows strong, so that I cannot go under Dungeness, indeed, I know of no use I am, either there or here. We can do nothing in future but lay at anchor and wait events. I have wrote Lord St. Vincent strongly on the subject this day. A gale of wind is brewing, and I think our communication with the shore will be cut off. The moon is also eclipsed to-morrow. Would to God I was on shore at the farm. I have sent to Mr. Dods to carry you a list of my things at his house, and to receive your orders what is to go to the farm. I have not yet any answer from the Admiralty on the subject of my last letter. Make my best regards to Sir William, Mrs. Nelson, Mrs. Cadogan, &c. &c. To the Duke, and all friends of ours, and believe me ever

"Yours,

"NELSON AND BRONTÉ.

"Yesterday, if I could have enjoyed the sight, passed through the Downs 100 sail of West Indiamen. If Sir William had accepted Mrs. Lutwidge's bribe of the ginger, I suppose he would now have got it, for Captain Beresford is

---

[1] Captain Richard Hawkins was born at Saltash in 1768, and was present in the Windsor Castle in 1793 at the evacuation of Toulon. He distinguished himself at Hières Bay, and served as First Lieutenant of the Theseus at the Battle of the Nile, at which he was wounded. He afterwards commanded the Galzo, and was made Post Captain in 1802. Five years afterwards he was in the command of La Minerva, and continued in her until 1814. He died in 1826.

[2] From the Athenæum. Dispatches and Letters, Vol. iv. p. 491.

arrived. I send you verbatim a postscript of Admiral Lutwidge's letter: viz. 'Remember us to your friends who have just left you, when you write, with the sincere regret we felt in parting with them.' I shall keep my letter open to the last moment.

"*Noon.* I have this moment your kind line from Rochester. I grieve at your accident. I am obliged to send my letters now, for I doubt if a boat can go at three o'clock."

"Amazon, Sept. 22nd, 1801.

"My dear Emma,

"It blows so fresh to-day that I almost doubt whether a boat will be able to get on shore with our letters, therefore, if you ever miss receiving letters, you may be sure that it is either from bad weather, or that I am gone out of the Downs. I shall write you every day if it is possible, and you may always be assured that if you do not get a letter from me, that no person in London does. At six this morning, I received a letter from Dr. Baird, saying, dear Parker had a bad night, and he was afraid for him, he was so very weak, therefore, we must not flatter ourselves, but hope the best. I am more than half sea-sick. I can tell you no news, for we can at present hold no communication; the surf is very high on the beach. I shall try if it is possible at three o'clock, but I do not expect your letters off to-day although I am most anxious to hear of your safe arrival in town, with all the news. Your letters are always so interesting that I feel the greatest disappointment when I do not receive them. Have you seen Troubridge? I dare say he came the moment you arrived. I hope you have seen Mr. Haslewood and Mr. Dods, and that you will be able to get to Merton long before the 10th of October, before which I hope the Admiralty will remove me from my command; much longer than that, I assure you, I will not stay. I leave the letter open in hopes I may get a communication with the shore. Charles is very well, is a very good boy. So is Banti; but the latter is initiated into the vices of London, I fancy, at least, he loves to spend money. Make my best regards to all your party, and believe me,

"Yours,

"NELSON AND BRONTÉ.

"What a difference to when you was here. A boat that sells things to the people is the only boat that has come to us since six this morning. He says, he will get on shore, therefore, I send my letters. Captain Sutton desires his best compliments. I am very sick."

The following is from Mrs. Lutwidge, wife of the Admiral, to Lady Hamilton :—

"Deal, September 23rd.

"Here I am, my dear Lady Hamilton, pen in hand, to write to you, and so charming is the task, that pleasure, in her gayest attire, should not for one moment induce me to relinquish an employment which nothing (but the idea of affording the fair Emma amusement) can render more delightful. Your welcome epistle I found upon the table this morning, and it had the good effects of a cordial without the bad, for it raised my spirits without intoxicating me. I am, indeed, infinitely indebted to your Ladyship for bestowing this kind mark of attention upon me, which really was in some measure necessary to enable us to support the pain occasioned by your absence. It appears to me that all the agreeables, like birds of passage, take their flight, and *ce n'est que les ennuyeux nous restent*. We have not seen Lord Nelson since you left us, for how is it possible he could remain on shore when his amiable friends were no longer to be found there. Report says, his Lordship and squadron are getting under weigh, and if my correspondence in his absence can be of any use to your Ladyship, you may command it, and though I cannot boast of affording much amusement I can assure you of a sincere zeal in your service. I am truly sorry I cannot give a favourable account of poor dear Captain Parker; he had a most wretched night, but though considerably better at present, there is much more reason for apprehension than hope; we are all anxiety on his account, and should be most truly happy to have it in our power to announce his amendment to your Ladyship. Tell Sir William, with my best regards, that had he waited one day longer, I would have had an opportunity of presenting him with the ginger, as Captain Beresford and two hundred sail of ships arrived on Sunday. However, the ginger is safe in the closet, whence it shall be conveyed to Piccadilly by the first safe opportunity, only that I should have been much more happy in presenting it myself. Adieu, my dear Lady Hamilton; forgive this sad scrawl, which has been written amidst a thousand interruptions. My Admiral desires I'll say every thing kind and affectionate for him to yourself and Sir William; he also desires I will speak our regrets at your absence, but this I find impossible, for were I to fill a whole quire of paper, I could not tell you half of what I feel; however, we both live in the hopes of meeting soon, when I hope to assure your Ladyship by word of mouth, how very sincerely I am your affectionate friend,

"C. LUTWIDGE.

"My Admiral desires to unite in best regards to Mrs. Nelson, Sir William, and your social circle."

Lord Nelson's correspondence with Lady Hamilton is continued :—

"September 21st, 1801. Quarter past ten o'clock.

"I send you Dr. Baird's comfortable note, this moment received. You will find Parker is treated like an infant. Poor fellow! I trust he will get well, and take possession of his room at the farm.

"N. & B."

"Amazon, September 23rd, 1801.

"My dear Emma,

"I received your kind letters last evening, and in many parts they pleased and made me sad; so life is chequered, and if the good predominates, then we are called happy. I trust the farm will make you more so than a dull London life. Make what use you please of it; it is as much yours as if you bought it. Whatever you do about it will be right and proper; make it the interest of the man who is there to take care I am not cheated more than comes to my share, and he will do it; *poco, poco*, we can get rid of bad furniture, and buy others: all will probably go to Bronté one of these days. I shall certainly go there whenever we get peace. I have had odd letters from Troubridge about what Captain Bedford[1] told me of the conversation about officers. Whether it is intended to quarrel, and get rid of me, I am not clear, but do not take any notice if you see him, which I dare say you will, for he likes to come to you. Remember me kindly to Mr. Este.[2] I hope we shall have peace.

"Ever yours, faithfully,
"NELSON AND BRONTÉ."

"Amazon, September 23rd, 1801."

"My dear Emma,

"I send Dr. Baird's note, just received; it will comfort you. Captain Bedford says he is thought better since the report.

"Ever yours,
"NELSON AND BRONTÉ.

"If he lives till Thursday night I have great hopes."

"Amazon, September 24th, 1801."

"My dear Emma,

"This morning's report of Parker is very favourable indeed, and if he goes on well this day I think he will recover. I should have gone out of the Downs to look about me this morning, but I wish to leave Parker in a fair way. Sutton is gone on shore to make inquiries, and if Dr. Baird will allow me to see him for a few minutes, I intend to go on shore to assure him that I love him, and shall only be gone a few days, or he might think that I neglected him; therefore,

---

[1] Captain William Bedford served as a Lieutenant during the Russian Armament, in the Edgar of 74 guns, and afterwards in the Formidable. He was appointed to the Queen of 98 guns, bearing the flag of Sir Alan Gardner in the Channel fleet, and was in Lord Howe's action in 1794, and made a Post Captain, August 15. He was in the attack off L'Orient, and afterwards went into the Royal Sovereign of 110 guns. He remained in this vessel until the Admiral struck his flag, being appointed Commander-in-chief on the coast of Ireland. He commanded the Leyden, 68 guns, in the North Sea, and was then with Nelson off Boulogne. In 1803 he commanded the Thunderer of 74 guns, and took the Venus, a French privateer. In 1805 he commanded the Hibernia, and afterwards the Caledonia. He was raised to the rank of Rear-Admiral, August 12, 1812, and joined the North fleet under Sir William Young. He was made a Vice-Admiral, July 19, 1821, and died in October, 1827

[2] Rev. Mr. Este, author of "My own Life," Lond. 1787, 8vo., and "A Journey in the year 1793, through Flanders, Brabant, and Germany, to Switzerland," Lond. 1795, 8vo.

my present intention is to sail in the morning at daylight; therefore you will not probably get a letter on Saturday, but you shall if I can, but do not expect it. I would give the universe was I quit of my present command, and in October, one way or other, I will get clear of it. The wind is now freshening, and I do not think I shall be able to land, but I will write him a line. Dr. Baird is very unwell, and I should not be surprised if he is seriously ill from his attention to the wounded under his care. Whether I can afford it or not, you must have made for me a silver cup, gilt inside, price about thirty guineas, with an inscription, "As a mark of esteem to Doctor Andrew Baird, for his humane attention to the gallant officers and men who were wounded at Boulogne, August 16th, 1801, from their Commander-in-chief, Vice-Admiral Lord Viscount Nelson, Duke of Bronté, &c. &c. &c." What do you think of this? Will you order it? I must find money to pay for it. Never mind the newspapers, they cannot say we are saving of our money. We give it where it is wanted. Even Troubridge writes me, he wished you had stayed at Deal. What can you do in London? I have already got cold, but I hope it will go off; I long to hear the result of your visit to Merton. I hope Mr. Greaves will give up sooner than the 10th. Mr. Dods will do anything for you, and have them removed to Merton as soon as you can: I long to see you at work. I hope Mrs. Nelson will stay with you as long as possible. Make my best regards to Sir William. I hope he has had plenty of sport. To Mrs. Nelson say every thing which is kind, to the Duke, &c. &c. and be assured I am

"Yours,

"NELSON AND BRONTÉ.

"All the Captains regret your absence. Charles is a very good boy, and so is Banti: Captain Sutton is very kind to them."

"Two o'clock (September 24th).

"Allen has given the inclosed for his wife. Captain Sutton is this moment come from the shore. Parker's stump has been dressed, looks very well; he has taken port wine, has eat, and is asleep. I have now great hopes. A gale of wind I believe is coming on.

"Ever yours,
"NELSON AND BRONTÉ.

"I am very low—bad weather."

"Amazon, off Folkstone, September 25th, 1801.

"My dearest Emma,

"I got under sail this morning at daylight, intending to return to the Downs on Sunday or Monday, but receiving a note from Dr. Baird of our dear Parker's being worse, and requesting me to stay a day or two longer, and as it is calm, so that I can neither get to the coast of France or to Dungeness, I am returning to the Downs. My heart, I assure you, is very low; last night I had flattered myself, I now have no hopes. I dare say Dr. Baird will write you a line, but we must bear up against these misfortunes. I have not had your letters to-day; they are my only comfort. Yesterday the Calais flat boats, &c. came out. Captain Russel[1] chased them in again, but they can join at any time, as the season approaches when we cannot go on their coast. You must, my dear friend, forgive me, for I cannot write any thing worth your reading, except that I am at all times, situations, and places,

"Yours,
"NELSON AND BRONTÉ"

On the 26th he again wrote to Dr. Baird: "Although the contents of your letter were not unexpected, yet I am sure you will judge of my feelings—I feel all has been done which was possible: God's will be done. I beg that his hair may be cut off and given to me; it shall remain and be buried with me. What must the poor father feel when he is gone! I shall request Captains Sutton and Bedford to arrange the funeral, and I wish you to ask Admiral Lutwidge to announce it by telegraph to the Admiralty; the Board ought to direct

---

[1] Of the Gier, he was Post Captain in 1802, commanded the Sea Fencibles in Argyleshire, and died on half-pay in 1813.

every honour to be paid to the memory of such an excellent gallant officer."

To Lady Hamilton on the 27th:—

"My dearest Emma,

"I had intended to have gone on shore this morning, to have seen dear Parker, but the accounts of him are so very bad, that the sight of his misery poor fellow would have so much affected me, and if he had been in his senses must have given him pain, that I have given up the idea, unless he feels better and expresses a wish to see me, then dear fellow I should be too happy to go. I slept not a wink all night, and am to-day very low and miserable. Captain Sutton is gone to see how he is, and should he express a desire to see me, I will go whatever I may suffer from it, but he will soon be at a place of rest, free from all the folly of this world.

Sutton is returned. Dear Parker left this world for a better at 9 o'clock; I believe we ought to thank God. He suffered much, and can suffer no more. I have no one to comfort me. I shall try and keep up, and I beg you will. We can now do no good. I shall leave the Downs as soon as the funeral is over.

"Your management of my affairs at Merton, are like whatever else you undertake, excellent. I shall write this day to Mr. Haslewood to order £1000. to be paid for the furniture, and what you bargained for. Mrs. Nelson's quarter is to commence October the 1st. If Davison has left no directions I must pay it. I know not who else to desire. Would to God I was with you, then I might cheer up a little. I have wrote to Mr. Haslewood and desired him to call on you at noon. You will see my letter, it is more regular for me to desire my agents to pay Mr. Greaves, I can do it by Tuesday's post, but these lawyers know how to take a regular receipt, which we do not. Remember me most kindly to Mrs. Cadogan, Oliver, &c. Sir William gone to Newmarket! well wonders will never cease. Believe me,

"Ever yours,
"NELSON AND BRONTÉ.

"My heart is almost broke, and I see I have wrote nonsense, I know not what I am doing. Send down Dr.

Baird's cup as soon as you can. I shall not write or say any thing about it."

On the same day to Mr. Davison Lord Nelson writes: "My dear Parker left this world for a better at nine o'clock this morning. It was, they tell me, a happy release; but I cannot bring myself to say I am glad he is gone; it would be a lie, for I am grieved almost to death."

To Earl St. Vincent also: "The scene, my Lord, with our dear Parker, is closed for ever; and I am sure your good heart will participate in our grief, both as a public and private loss; not a creature living was ever more deserving of our affections. Every action of his life, from Sir John Orde to the moment of his death, shewed innocence, joined to a firm mind in keeping the road of honour, however it might appear incompatible with his interest: his conduct in Orde's business won my regard. When he was abandoned by the world, your heart had begun to yearn towards him—how well he has deserved my love and affection his actions have shewn. His father, in his advanced age, looked forward for assistance to this good son. Pensions, I know, have sometimes been granted to the parents of those who have lost their lives in the service of their King and country. All will agree none fell more nobly than dear Parker; and none ever resigned their life into the hands of their Creator with more resignation to the Divine will than our Parker. I trust much to your friendship to recommend his father's case to the kind consideration of the King. I fear his loss has made a wound in my heart, which time will scarcely heal. But God is good and we must all die."[1]

To Dr. Baird Nelson wrote: "I should be a wretch if I did not feel sensible of all your kindness to my dear Parker; we have the melancholy consolation to think that every thing was done which professional skill and the kindest friendship could dictate. God's will be done; but if I was to say I was content, I should lie—but I shall endeavour to submit with all the fortitude I am able."

And to Mr. Nepean he officially writes: "Captain E. T. Parker having died in consequence of the wounds he received on the 16th of last month, I have given directions for his

---

[1] Clarke and McArthur, Vol. ii. p. 203.

being buried this day with all the honours and respect due to so meritorious and gallant an officer; and I have to request that their Lordships will be pleased to direct the Sick and Hurt Board to defray all the expenses of his lodgings, &c. on shore, and also of his funeral."

To Lady Hamilton:—

"Amazon, September 28th, 1801.

"My dearest Emma,

"We are going this noon to pay our last sad duties to dear good Parker. I wish it was over for all our sakes, then we must endeavour to cheer up, and although we cannot forget our Parker, yet we shall have the comfortable reflection how we loved him, and how deserving he was of our love. I am afraid his father is but in very indifferent circumstances; but I doubt if the Admiralty will assist him, however, they shall be tried. I hope the Admiralty will direct all the expenses of the lodgings, funeral, &c. to be paid—if not, it will fall very heavy upon me. Pray write me when I am to direct my letters to Merton. Is it a post town, or are the letters sent from the General Post Office? I wish I could see the place, but I fear that is impossible at present. I entreat I may never hear about the expenses again. If you live in Piccadilly or Merton it makes no difference, and if I was to live at Merton I must keep a table, and nothing can cost me one-sixth part which it does at present, for this I cannot stand, however *honourable* it may be. God bless you and believe me,

"Yours,

"NELSON AND BRONTÉ.

"If the wind is to the westward, I shall go to Dungeness, but you must not, by Gore's account, which I send, be surprised at not hearing from me regularly, but you know I always shall write and send when it is possible. I only send this that your dear friendly mind should be easy.

"*Half past one.*—Thank God the dreadful scene is past. I scarcely know how I got over it. I could not suffer much more and be alive. God forbid I should ever be called upon to say or see as much again. Your affectionate letters are just come, they are a great comfort. The worst, thank God, is past. I must have plate, &c. at Davison's, and I agree with you, that nothing but what is mine should be there, and that Sir William should always be my guest. I told you so long ago. I will find out what spoons, &c. I have, and send you a list to-morrow, but to-day I am done for, but ever

"Yours,
"NELSON AND BRONTÉ.

"I will write to my Father to-morrow."

Captain Parker's funeral took place at Deal on the 27th, and was conducted as Nelson had determined, with all the honours due to his rank and distinguished character. His Lordship attended as chief mourner, and was accompanied by Admiral Lutwidge, Lord George Cavendish, and several officers of the Army and Navy. The ships in the Downs had pendants half-mast high and the yards reversed. Minute guns were fired from the Amazon and shore alternately at noon.[1]

To Lady Hamilton Nelson writes:—

"Amazon, September 29th, 1801.

"My dearest Emma,

"I send by the coach a little parcel containing the keys of the plate chest and the case of the tea urn, and there is a case of Colebrook Dale breakfast set, and some other things. Mr. Dods had better go to the house, for he is Davison's man. Will you have your picture carried to Merton? I should wish it, and mine of the Battle of the Nile. I think you had better *not* have Sir William's books, or any thing but what is my own. I have sent in the parcel by the coach this day, two salt-cellars, and two ladles, which will make four of each, as two are in the chest. You will also find spoons and forks sufficient for the present. If sheets are wanting for the beds, will you order some and let me have the bill. I also think that not a servant of Sir William's, I mean the cook, should be in the house, but I leave this and all other matters to your good management. Would to God I could come and take up my abode there, and if such a thing should happen that I go abroad, I can under my hand lend you the house that no person can molest you, not that I have at

[1] Naval Chronicle, Vol. vi. p. 340.

present any idea of going anywhere but to Merton. Do you take black James? Do as you please. I have no desire one way or the other. Our dear Parker's circumstances are a little out of order, but I have undertaken to settle them if the creditors will give me time, for the poor father is worse than nothing. I have given him money to buy mourning and to pay his passage home again. I trust in God that he will never let me want, for I find no man who starts up to assist me. I can with a quiet conscience when all is gone, live upon bread and cheese. Never mind so long as I have your friendship warm from the heart. I have got some of dear Parker's hair, which I value more than if he had left me a bulse of diamonds. I have sent it in the little box, keep some of it for poor Nelson.

"*Noon.* Blows strong. I have just received your kind letters, they indeed comfort me, and I hope we shall live to see many, many happy years.

"Ever yours,
"NELSON AND BRONTÉ."

Sir William Hamilton, who was on a visit to his relative the Earl of Warwick at this time, wrote the following to Lady Hamilton upon receiving intelligence of the death of Parker:—

"Wednesday, September 29th.

"I was not, my dear Emma, the least surprised by the account I received from you of the brave young Parker's death. What comfort can I give you in a case where there is no remedy? We must cherish his memory, and ever do him justice when we speak of the glorious attempt he made at Boulogne, and the exemplary courage and patience with which he bore his misfortune, and of which you and I were eye-witnesses. I am sorry he died hard; youth will struggle with death, but perhaps he might not feel so much as he appeared to do in the convulsion of death. I flatter myself that Lord Nelson after he has done everything he can do to shew his respect for his departed friend, will console himself; but I am sorry we are not with him at this cruel moment. The accident of the clock in the Nelson room was really singular, but I hope that you and I think pretty nearly alike as to such sort of accidents.

"WILLIAM HAMILTON."

To Lady Hamilton Nelson writes:—

"Amazon, September 30th, 1801.

"My dearest Emma,

"I well know by my own feelings that you would think of my birth-day with a degree of pleasure and pain. I am sensible of all your goodness. Respecting the farm and all the frugality necessary for the present to be attached to it, I know your good sense will do precisely what is right. I only entreat again that everything even to a *book* and a cook at Merton may be mine. The house should be insured for three or four thousand pounds, including the furniture, that all may not be lost in case of fire. The Admiralty have refused to bury Captain Parker. He might have stunk above ground, or been thrown in a ditch; the expense of that and lodgings, &c. has cost me near £200, and I have taken, poor fellow, all his debts on myself, if the creditors will give me a little time to find the money. Dr. Baird has been very, very good indeed. I wish the cup had arrived, for I have taken leave of him with only thanks much against my inclination. You are very good, my dear Emma, about poor Parker's father. If he calls you will of course see him, but he is a very different person from his son. He has £72. more in his pocket than when he came to Deal. I wish for his own sake that his conduct had been more open and generous like mine to him, but never mind.

"As I shall go under Dungeness to-morrow for three or or four days, I went on shore at nine to call on the Admiral (Lutwidge), and to thank him and her for their attentions to dear Parker, and I presented your regards, &c. I called on poor Langford, who has got full possession of your chaise. He removed from the other lodgings to where Captain Bedford's officers are—much more airy. Dr. Baird is in great wrath with the methodist.—He gave her six guineas as a present from me, and she was not satisfied. I shall endeavour, in a very little time, to get a few days leave of absence, if not, to get rid of my command. The business of G. is over, it is gone to Dickson. I wish I could with propriety have undertaken it, it could not fail, if well managed, and it would have made me an Earl. You asked me did I see Parker after he was dead? I believe if I had it would have killed me. I intend Flaxman to prepare a little monument, about fifty pounds, for him, on a column or pyramid. I shall use Sir William's or your taste on the occasion. I cannot afford one, or it should be handsomer, but the will must be taken. Remember me kindly to Mrs. Cadogan, Oliver, and all friends. Langford desires me to say everything which is kind. To the Duke say all that is kind, and ever believe me,

"Yours,
"NELSON AND BRONTÉ."

Nelson, from the day of Parker's death, and for a considerable time after that event, sealed his letters with black wax.

Mr. Græffer forwarded Lord Nelson some intelligence respecting the state of his Duchy of Bronté.

"Bronté, 26th September, 1801.

"My Lord,
"The letter dated London, July the 5th, your Lordship was pleased to honour me with, I received under cover from General Acton, accompanied by one of his Excellency's own hand-writing, whereof inclosed I have sent a copy, to shew your Lordship the attachment the General has for your welfare. Your letter, my Lord, has not only quieted my mind of the fear that none of my letters had reached London, but it has given both myself and Mrs. Græffer the most heartfelt pleasure and satisfaction to hear of your Lordship's health, after, not only dispersing the Northern cloud that hung so heavy over Great Britain, but also to change the affairs of the whole of Europe a second time, to the interest and welfare of a country which every unbiassed man must and ought to love and adore. My Lord, I feel proud to have the honour of being thought worthy by your Lordship to take upon me the principal management of the Duchy of Bronté. I shall always think it a glory to sacrifice both health and life for your advantage; I flatter myself, that in a very few years, your Lordship will find that my time has not been foolishly employed in the improvement of your estate. It is true, my Lord, and I own it, I am not the man that can augment the income of your estate from six thousand ounces to thirty

thousand pounds sterling, either through economical or political means; of the first, I have not acrostatical knowledge sufficient to build castles in the air, and the second I detest abominably.

"Mr. and Mrs. Leckie and sister have made a stay with us above three weeks. Mr. Leckie took an eight days political excursion; he had a great inclination to purchase a woody mountainous estate, not many miles from Bronté, have since heard the owner will not sell it, better for Mr. Leckie, although he does not think so; I am sorry for his thoughts. The farming utensils and cask with seeds are not as yet arrived; Mr. Noble, who had some interest in the ship, informed me, that the ship had put in at Mahon, and discharged her cargo there, on account of the peace between France and Naples. I have written to Mr. Noble, and begged of him to do his utmost to get these packages forwarded: I am very anxious about them, particularly the seeds, as the season is already far advanced for sowing. I hope your Lordship's repose from public employments will not be long first, and your glorious and ever-memorable actions hasten a general peace. We are very happy to hear of your intended unexpected visit, together with good company, and to have the honour to kiss that hand which has written the confirmation of this promise; *this is as true as the Gospel.*

"I hope we shall see your Lordship and company come as gentle shepherds and shepherdesses, and peaceable ploughmen, rural amusement alone can be the diversion here. I am very happy of the determination to stay some time with us at Bronté. If those gentlemen that have a desire to come out to settle here with an intent to acquire a fortune by farming, they are mistaken; but if they are desirous to cultivate and improve a small farm by way of amusement, they may live thereon comfortably without lessening their annual income, and this they must not altogether expect the first two years; they are to study both soil and climate. Your Lordship will please to give me leave to say without reserve several difficulties will arise before a small English family of a decent income can be fixed or situated comfortably on your Lordship's estate, or to say more, on any other in Sicily;

there is not a house on the farms (a very few excepted), for a decent English family to live in; they are, for the most part, hovels, it is therefore necessary to build, either by the landlord or the new settler. The farmer in Sicily lives in the town, and so do all the ploughmen and other husbandry workmen, although many of the farms are above six miles distant from the town. This accursed custom, detrimental as it is to the advantage of agriculture, yet does not meet with any reproach. The farmer (except a few industrious ones), lounges half the day about the market-place, and the labourer, if the wind blows a little fresh on the Monday morning, is furled up, and does not venture to leave the town to go to work, but stands in the street to listen to a cock-and-bull story; when he moves he is half tired before he arrives at his work: this is another difficulty for a new settler, particularly for an English constitution, not easily to digest. Nothing would give me more pleasure than to have about four or five English agricultural families about us, I foresee it would in a short time change this most odious and ignorant system of Sicilian agriculture.

"It is in your power at present, my Lord, to do that for Sicily as a great promoter of agriculture, what you have done for this island as a great warrior. I shall not trouble your Lordship any longer at present, because your great national employment giveth you little time to attend to private affairs. But I hope your repose is not very distant, as I understand there is great hopes of a peace with France. I shall, in my next letter, my Lord, send you my observations and thoughts of a remedy for the husbandry of this country. Your Lordship may perhaps have an opportunity to converse with Arthur Young, Esq. on this subject. Mrs. Græffer joins me in duty to your Lordship, and I have the honour to be, my Lord,

"Your Lordship's
"Most obedient, and most devoted humble servant,
"JOHN GRÆFFER.

"The Right Hon. Lord Nelson,
    Duke of Bronté in Sicily,
        London."

In October the correspondence with Lady Hamilton continues:—

"Amazon, October 1st, 1801.

"My dearest Emma,

"From various causes it is as well for me to leave the Downs for a few days to change the scene a little, and also it is right to look a little at my squadron under Dungeness. I left the Downs at day-light, and am now writing off Folkestone. I shall have Hardy to dine which will be a pleasure to me, for he is a good man. Captain Sutton has just been giving me such instances of want of feeling in Mr. Parker, that I am quite disgusted with him; he is a dirty dog. How unlike his worthy son! but I have done with him. I shall send this letter on shore to New Romney, but I think you had better, after a day or two, direct your letters to Deal, for longer than three or four days I shall not remain here. At this moment I fancy you setting forth to take possession of your little estate, for this very day I shall make a codicil to my will, leaving it in trust for your use, and to be at your disposal until you wish me to leave it to my *nearest and dearest relation*.[1] We die not one moment the sooner by doing those acts, and if I die, my property may as well go to those I tenderly regard, as to those who hate me; but I trust to live many years with those who love me. I send you a very handsome letter from Lord George Cavendish.[2] I must return his visit when I get back to Deal, but shall not dine there or anywhere else. I hope soon to be done with this command. I am yet of opinion it will be Peace before this month is out. Pray God send it calm, and we shall hardly save post as it goes out at one o'clock. The French have all gone into Boulogne, but probably they will be out to-day. Dr. Baird has been very attentive and good to me, and he gave your good things to Langford.

"Ever yours,
"NELSON AND BRONTÉ."

---

[1] An evident allusion to Horatia.
[2] He attended the funeral of Captain Parker with Lord Nelson.

"Amazon, Dungeness, October 2nd, 1801.

"My dearest Emma,

"I am sorry the lawyers should have been the cause of keeping you one moment from Merton, and I hope you will for ever love Merton—since nothing shall be wanting on my part. From me you shall have every thing you want. I trust, my dear friend, to your economy, for I have need of it. To you I may say, my soul is too big for my purse, but I do earnestly request that all may be mine in the house, even to a pair of sheets, towels, &c. You are right, my dear Emma, to pay your debts—to be in debt is to be in misery, and poor tradespeople cannot afford to lay out of their money. I beg you will not go too much on the water, for the boat may upset, or you may catch an autumnal cold which cannot be shook off all the winter. Wrap yourself up warm when you go out of the house, and for God's sake wear more clothes when winter approaches, or you will have the rheumatism. I hope you are this moment fixed—damn the lawyers. If black James has no particular desire to come, I can have none to have him, he must be a dead expense. You will do what is right, and I shall be happy in leaving every thing to your management. I don't wonder Sir William is tired of Warwick Castle. How could he expect to find anything equal to what he left—he might as well have searched for the Philosopher's Stone. Poor Mrs. Nelson, I pity her. She never was so happy in her life, but the little woman will try and be with you again very soon, and she will succeed. Tell me how I can do anything for you at this distance. You command me. I obey you with the greatest pleasure. Your letters for the next two or three days, may be directed for me here, but after that to Deal. I have had dear Hardy on board all the morning, he is a good man and attached to me; indeed, so is Bedford, Sutton, Gore, and others, but these from no interested motive. Make my best regards to Sir William when you write; and to Mrs. Cadogan, say every kind thing.

"Yours,
"NELSON AND BRONTÉ."

Mr. Davison wrote a letter of condolence to Lord Nelson, on the death of Captain Parker:—

"Swarland House, 3rd October, 1801.

"My dear Friend,

"It is very often and justly observed, how serious a misfortune it is to outlive those to whom we have formed an attachment. The loss of poor dear Parker, I feel most sensibly, having seen such proofs of the rectitude of his mind—the goodness of his heart—the high sense of honour he possessed—all combined to rivet and cement a friendship, I had fondly hoped would have been of long duration. If there be a better world, which we are taught to believe there is, he must be gone there to enjoy it, and possibly to be relieved of troubles in this, had he survived, as to have involved him in misery. Dear fellow—a more sincerely attached friend you never had, his whole study and delight was how best to secure your approbation of his conduct.

"I heartily wish you were relieved of your present command, though however honourable it may be, must, if it be continued for any length of time, wear you down with fatigue and incessant anxiety. It will make me very happy when the post bears me a letter of your being superseded.

"I have been in Scotland with my sister, trying all in my power to support her under the most afflicting calamity, nearly proving fatal to herself.

"If you have settled for the house in Surrey you write me about, I am sure you must be in want of money to pay for it, and lest that should be the case, I have written to my Bankers, Messrs. Vere, Lucadou, and Co., to honour whatever bills you may draw on them, with orders to those gentlemen to charge the same to my account. You may draw at sight on them whenever you please. In my absence this will be the easiest mode for you making your payments. We are all well here, and all unite in constant prayer for your happiness. God ever bless and protect you, my dear friend's affectionate

"ALEXANDER DAVISON."

To this he replied: "Your kind letter has truly affected me. Can your offer be real? Can Davison be uncorrupted by the depravity of the world? I almost doubt what I read; I will answer, my dear friend, you are the only person living who would make such an offer. When you come to town you shall know all my pecuniary affairs, and if in arranging them I should want your kind assistance, I will accept it with many thanks. In my present purchase I have managed tolerably well."[1]

### TO LADY HAMILTON.

"Amazon, Dungeness, October 3rd, 1801.

"My dearest Emma,

"Your kind letters of Wednesday night and Thursday morning I have just received, and I should be too happy to come up for a day or two, but that will not satisfy me, and only fill my heart with grief at separating. Very soon I must give in, for the cold weather I could not bear; besides, to say the truth, I am one of those who really believe we are on the eve of peace. As mine can be only guess from various circumstances, do not give it as my opinion. I think we are almost signing. You may ask, do you know any good reason for this joyful idea? I can answer, *No*, but my mind tells me it must be. I shall long to have the picture of the little one[2] —you will send it to me; but very soon I shall see the original, and then I shall be happy. Do not think I am seriously unwell, but I am naturally very low. What have I to raise my spirits? Nothing. The loss of my friend, the loss of Parker. The Surgeon recommends me to walk on shore, but that I cannot do, we lay so far off, and surf, and what is to become of my business—but it cannot last long. What you want with all the Heraldry I know not—they are devils for running up a bill. I shall not agree to Sir William's keeping house whenever I come, that is impossible. I hope Mr. Haslewood has done every thing to get you into the possession, and for the rest and management I give all up to you. I have had a letter from Lieutenant Turner—he has got the gout, and desires his kind regards. I have had rather a begging letter from Norwich, but I cannot at present do any thing, for I have nothing; for heaven's sake never do you talk of having spent any money for me. I am sure you

[1] Dispatches and Letters, Vol. iv. p. 412.
[2] Horatia.

never have to my knowledge, and my obligations to you can never be repaid.

"Ever yours,
"NELSON AND BRONTÉ.

"Make my kind regards where proper. Captains Sutton, Bedford, and Gore, all inquire after you. Are there any images standing in the grounds? Gore says there are. If so you will take them away—they look very bad. *Patienza.* Pray is our Belmonte dead at Baden? Tell me."

The preliminaries of Peace were now entered upon, and Lord Nelson wrote to Lady Hamilton:—

"Just anchored, October 4th, nine o'clock.

"My dear Emma,
"You are right, *no* champagne till we can crack a bottle together. Your letter with the papers I suppose are gone to Romney. I shall have them in the evening.
"Yours,
"NELSON AND BRONTÉ.

"Send to Castelcicala that from my heart I congratulate him, and beg to present my duty to his and mine august Sovereign. The Lutwidges' have sent off congratulations for you, and I always send your regards and respects."

"Amazon, off Folkestone, October 4th, 1801.

"My dearest Emma,
"Although preliminary articles are signed, yet I do not find that such lengths are gone towards peace as to point out a time when hostilities shall cease, and I am directed to be particularly vigilant, and the Earl says the country has received so many proofs of my zeal in its service as leaves no doubt of my remaining at the head of the squadron until peace is proclaimed.

"I was in hopes that at least all my feeble services might be dispensed with. This has fretted me a good deal, for they would perhaps gladly get rid of my claim, at least for poor

Langford. I have wrote to the Earl, saying that I was in hopes my humble services were no longer wanted, but at least I hoped that I might have four or five days leave of absence, for that I wanted rest, and could not stay in the Channel when the cold weather set in. I shall try the effect of this letter, and although my whole soul is devoted to get rid of this command, yet I do not blame the Earl for wishing to keep me here a little longer. It is probable disturbances may break out in these squadrons when I am gone; I am of some consequence. If I can I should like to come on shore good friends with the Administration, or my brother will stand no chance, probably he does not much at present. I have wrote congratulations to Mr. Addington, but if Ministers can shake off those who have a claim on them, they are glad of the opportunity. If I am forced into this measure for a month, you and Sir William might come down, and I would hire a house, and have our own things on shore, and not cost one-eighth part of the other cheating fellow's expense. I hear he has been fool enough to say as nobody goes twice to his house, he takes care to make them pay enough the first time. What a fool, but he did not know, if it had been fifty times as much I should have paid it with pleasure for the happiness of my Emma's company. I think I shall get off this staying here, but I hope you will agree with me that a little management may not be amiss. Sir Charles Pole has sent the two pipes of sherry. I have wrote to Portsmouth this day to have them sent to Merton, therefore the wine cellar must be prepared.

"It is impossible to get on board in a dark night, heavy surf, &c. therefore I shall stay on board altogether, unless it is a very fine day, which is not to be expected. The surf seldom is little at this season. Make my best regards to Mrs. Cadogan, and all friends, and believe me,

"Yours,

"NELSON AND BRONTÉ.

"To the Duke, Sir William, &c. say every thing which is proper. Yawkins[1] desires to be remembered."

---

[1] Master of the King George hired cutter.

"Amazon, October 5th, 1801.

"My dearest Emma,

"Give the inclosed to Allen's wife. I have been expecting the pleasure of hearing from you by the coach, and when the tide turns, I shall send on shore and examine the coach office. Your kind letters are my only consolation.

"Yours,
"NELSON AND BRONTÉ.

"When does Sir William return? Say every thing which is kind to Mrs. Cadogan, &c."

"Amazon, October 5th, 1801.

"My dearest Emma,

"The weather is getting so very bad, that I doubt whether the letters can be got on shore. I am half sea-sick and much vexed, but still if the Admiralty would send me leave by telegraph, it should go hard but I would get on shore at Ramsgate, or some where. Nothing should keep me; it is hard to be kept here, but I should be sorry to quarrel the last few days. Admiral Lutwidge has offered to dine at three o'clock, but if I dined it would be almost impossible to get afloat, and all my wish is to get a-shore for good, as the folks say.

"Thank God it is peace—may the heavens bless us. Say every thing kind to Charlotte—hers is a nice innocent letter, and to Mrs. Nelson, and my brother, you know what to say. As to Mr. Addington's giving him any thing, I do not venture to believe he ever will. I never had a kind thing done for me yet. As the Order of Malta will be restored, I suppose now you and Ball will have permission to wear the order, however, you shall abroad. I am vexed that you are so much troubled to get into the house—I wish we were all in it. I shall only come to town on particular business, or to give a vote on some interesting question, and that in order to get something for my brother. I have not yet wrote to my father, but I shall to-day. It rains dreadfully. Pray take care and do not catch cold. You have not told me if you have seen Troubridge. Hallowell will call of course, or he will behave very ill. Mr. Turner desires his thanks for your kind inquiries (for I always say those things for you, as I am sure you do for me), and he will certainly come and see you when he comes to London. Believe me,

"Ever yours,
"NELSON AND BRONTÉ.

"Your kind letter just arrived—it has quite cheered me up. May the heavens bless you. I always send your remembrances to Admiral and Mrs. Lutwidge. We must think about Charles and Banti. Charles says he should like to get into a public office, but I shall do every thing you wish me for him. Pray God I may soon see you."

"2 o'clock, just going on shore.

"My dearest Emma,

"I did not pay Mr. B. for the drawing of the San Josef, £10. is the price. Pay him out of the £300. Have you bought any cows. I wish you were got in, and I with you. It is dreadfully cold to-day. Good Admiralty, let me get on shore. I have settled with Lutwidge for them to forgive my dining with them. How the lawyers torment you.

"Yours,
"NELSON AND BRONTÉ.

"I have just got a letter from a Surgeon in the Navy, begging for money. If I do not get away very soon, I shall be ruined."

"Amazon, Oct. 6th, 1801.

"My dear Emma,

"To my astonishment, Captain Sutton, of the Romulus, sent me word last night that he was arrived, and ordered to hoist a broad pendant aboard the Isis, and he came on board this morning at seven. It being a very fine beach, I went on shore with him and Bedford, to call on Admiral Lutwidge for the first time since my return from Dungeness, and for the second time since your departure. I expected, I own, and had prepared Allen, &c. with my trunk, and directed Mr. Wallis to make out the necessary orders, to leave with Sutton, when in came the letters, and one from Troubridge, of which I send you an extract, 'The Earl desires me to beg of you to remain until the time for hostilities ceasing in the Channel is fixed, and then, if you wish it, you can have leave of absence, I think, without striking your flag, if that is your wish; in short, everything that can be done to meet your wishes will, but pray remain for the few days. The ratification is expected to-morrow, and the time for hostilities ceasing will be settled directly, and in the Channel very soon indeed.' Under all these desires, I cannot help staying—fourteen days at the outside—but by complying I hope to get rid of it long before that time.

"I have had a letter of thanks from Parker's uncle at Durham. I shall be glad the cup is coming. Dr. Baird dines on board to-day. What a curious letter of Mrs. Nelson's and my brother's. How I regret this fortnight, at all events Sutton's being here will be ready for me to start when the Board will give me leave, or otherwise I want no assistance. I shall perhaps go to Dungeness, where we lay, five or six miles from the shore. As for ——, he is a fool, and I dare say we need not carry that article to Bronté. Mr. Scott,[1] who writes Italian and all languages, and is a very clever man, would be truly useful, and wants to go, but more of this when we meet, which, pray God, may be soon. I shall come straight to Merton.

"N. & B."

"Amazon, Oct. 6th, 1801.

"My dearest Friend,

"I have just got your letter of yesterday, and am very angry with Mr. Haslewood for not having got you into possession of Merton, for I was in hopes you would have arranged everything before Sir William came home. I shall write Mr. Haslewood to-day on the subject. The Peace seems to make no impression of joy on our seamen, rather the contrary, they appear to reflect that they will go from plenty to poverty. We must take care not to be beset by them at Merton, for every beggar will find out your soft heart, and get into your house. Lord George Cavendish has just been on board to

[1] See Appendix, No. II.

make me a visit before he leaves Walmer to-morrow. If the weather is moderate, I shall return his visit and call on Billy Pitt, as they say he is expected to-day. I intend to land at Walmer Castle. But for this visit I should not have gone ashore till all was finished. Make my best regards to Sir William. I hope he will be able in bad weather to catch fish in the water you so beautifully describe. You must take care what kind of fish you put into the water, for Sir William will tell you one sort destroys the other. Commodore Sutton has been on board all the morning, but dines with Admiral Lutwidge. You will see amongst my things return the round table and the wardrobe—extraordinary that they should return again into your possession. You are to be, recollect, Lady Paramount of all the territories and waters of Merton, and we are all to be your guests, and to obey all lawful commands What have you done about the turnip field, duck field, &c.? Am I to have them? I wish I could get up for four or five days. I would have roused the lawyers about. The Isis is just coming in—Sutton's broad pendant is to be in her. Yawkins has just been on board, and I delivered your compliments as directed. He always inquires after you and Sir William, and he desires me to say that he wishes Sir William was now here, for there were never so many fish in the Downs. The beach for two days has been remarkably smooth—not a curl on the shore. I shall send to Mr. Turner: you will win his heart by your goodness. Your going away made a blank in our squadron. Dr. Baird is very much affected at receiving the cup; it made him really ill, so that he could not come to dinner, but he deserved it for his humanity. Lord St Vincent, never, I dare say, gave him a sixpence. Best regards to Sir William, Mrs. Cadogan, and all our friends,

"Yours,
"NELSON AND BRONTÉ."

Dr. Baird, who was specially sent down by the Earl of St. Vincent to attend the wounded at the attack of the Boulogne flotilla, acknowledged the receipt of Lord Nelson's present of a silver vase, through Lady Hamilton, in the following letter:—

"Deal, 7th October, 1801.

" Madam,

" I had the honour of receiving your Ladyship's letter yesterday, and with it the Duke of Bronté's token of approbation: so flattering a testimony of his Lordship's esteem has affected me most sensibly, and made such an impression on my heart as no time can erase; for indeed, his attention to me has ever been very kind. I beg your Ladyship to accept my warm acknowledgments for the share you have taken, and request you will be so good as to present my respects to Sir William Hamilton. Mr. Langford reclines on your Ladyship's sofa, the comfort of which he enjoys much. His general health is much improved, he is totally without pain, and his wounds look well, and if there be no further exfoliation, we may soon look forward to all being well, but in this, I must not pronounce hastily, for when exfoliation of bone has taken place, it is difficult to foresee when it will end. I can, however, assure your Ladyship, in general terms, that everything has a very favourable appearance. I do not know anything he wants. I thought the basket you sent for poor Parker, and which came too late, should go by descent to Langford, and he had it. I do not mean to prevent your Ladyship indulging in your usual benevolence in sending him any little nice things you may wish, for I really do not know anything that can do him harm at present.

" I mean to send his Lordship's present into the different surgical wards in the hospital, that the wounded may see how much their Commander-in-chief has been interested about their well-doing.

" I have the honour to be,
" Madam,
" Your Ladyship's very obliged humble servant,
" ANDREW BAIRD."

## CHAPTER V.

### 1801.

Upon the return of peace, Nelson received the following letter from his father:—

"Burnham, Oct. 8th, 1801.

"My dear Horatio,

"Upon the happy return of peace, I may, with a little variation, address you in the words of an Apostle, and say, You have fought a good fight. You have finished your military career with glory and honour; henceforth there is laid up for you much happiness, subject, indeed, in this present time to uncertainty, but in a future state immutable and incorruptible.

"As a public character, I could be acquainted only with what was made public respecting you. Now, in a private station possibly you may tell me where it is likely your general place of residence may be, so that sometimes we may have mutual happiness in each other, notwithstanding the severe reproaches I feel from an anonymous letter for my conduct to you, which is such, it seems, as will totally separate us. This is unexpected indeed. Most likely the winter may be too cold for me to continue here, and I mean to spend it between Bath and London. If Lady Nelson is in a hired house and by herself, gratitude requires that I should sometimes be with her, if it is likely to be of any comfort to her. Everywhere age, and my many infirmities, are very troublesome, and require every mark of respect. At present, I am in the Parsonage; it is warm and comfortable. I am quite by myself, except the gentleman who takes care of the churches. He is a worthy, sensible, sober man, and as far as rests with him, makes me very happy. I cannot do any public duty, nor even walk to the next house. But, my dearest son, here is still room enough to give you a warm, a joyful and affectionate reception, if you could find an inclination to look once more at me in Burnham Parsonage. I pray God to continue his blessings in all stations, places, and undertakings.

"EDMUND NELSON."

Lord Nelson's memorandum for reply to this letter is as follows:—

"I think of writing my poor old father to this effect—that I shall live at Merton with Sir William and Lady Hamilton—that a warm room for him and a cheerful society will always be there happy to receive him—that nothing in *my conduct* could ever cause a separation of a moment between me and him, for that I had all the respect and love which a son could bear towards a good father—that going to Burnham was impossible, as my duty, even if I was inclined, would not permit it—that as to anonymous letters, they made no impression where they did not fit, and that I should ever conduct myself towards him as his dutiful son.

"N. & B."

To Lady Hamilton, communicating the above, he writes: "Tell me, my friend, do you approve? If he remains at Burnham he will die, and I am sure he will not stay in Somerset Street, (Lady Nelson's residence). Pray let him come to your care at Merton. Your kindness will keep him alive, for you have a kind soul."

Lord Nelson's letters to Lady Hamilton continue:—

"Amazon, Oct. 8, 1801.

"My dearest Friend,

"I do not expect, although I am writing, that any boat can communicate with us to-day.

"What can be the use of keeping me here; for, I can know nothing such weather; and, what a change since yesterday! It came on, in one hour, from the water, like a mill-pond, to such a sea as to make me very unwell. If I had gone to make my visit, I could not have got off again. I rejoice that I did not go. Until I leave the station, I have no desire to go on shore; for Deal was always my abhorrence.

"That Parker is a swindler. Langford owed our dear Parker twenty-five pounds, of which there was no account; but Langford desired his agents to pay Mr. Parker. Langford requested, that he would wait two or three months, as it would be more convenient to him, to which the other agreed— 'Aye, as long as you please.' He got one pound, eleven shillings and sixpence, from Samuel, by casting his account wrong. The first thing he does is to desire Langford's agents to pay £34. for Langford, nine pounds more than the debt. He is worse than a public thief. His conduct to me was, absolutely, the worst species of thieving; for, it was under false pretences. He sent Dr. Baird on board to me, to say that, in London, his pocket-book was stole, in which was twenty pounds; and begged my assistance to get him home; and that he had not a farthing to buy mourning for his dear son. At this time, he had £47. in his pocket, besides what he had sold of his son's. He has behaved so unlike a gentleman, but very like a blackguard, to both Captain Sutton, Bedford, and Hardy. I am now clear that he never lost one farthing, and that the whole is a swindling trick. So you see, my dear friend, how good nature is imposed upon. I am so vexed that he should have belonged to our dear Parker! I have now done with the wretch, for ever. I hope he has got nothing from you; and, if you have promised him anything, *do not send it.*

"NELSON AND BRONTÉ."[1]

"Amazon, October 8th, 1801. Half-past seven.

"My dearest Friend,

"I send on shore one line by the boat which goes for our letters, to tell you not to be surprised if you get no other letter to-morrow, for it now blows very hard, and every appearance of an increasing gale. How I am praying for the Admiralty. Last night I had one of the attacks on my heart, which some day will do me up; but it is entirely gone off. I know it has been brought on by fretting at being kept here doing nothing. I shall write late, and if possible get it

[1] Collection of Letters, Vol. i. p. 67.

on shore, but you must not expect. Make my best regards to Sir William, and believe me,

"Yours,

"NELSON AND BRONTÉ."

"Amazon, October 9th, 1801.

"My dearest Friend,

"How provoked I am at the slowness of that damned rascal Buonaparte, in ratifying the Treaty. I hope he will, for if we are involved in a war again, our fools, who rejoiced that the French could not come to eat them up, will frighten themselves to death, and our country become an easy prey. There is no person in the world rejoices more in the peace than I do, but I would burst sooner than let a damned Frenchman know it. Let them rejoice that the English rod (its navy) is taken from them; the rod that has flogged, and would continue to flog them from one end of the world to the other. We have made peace with the French despotism, and we will, I hope, adhere to it whilst the French continue in due bounds; but whenever they overstep that, and usurp a power which would degrade Europe, then I trust we shall join Europe in crushing her ambition; then I would with pleasure go forth and risk my life for to pull down the overgrown detestable power of France. The country has so foolishly called out for peace, that I almost wonder we had not to make sacrifices. It has been the cowardice and treachery of Europe that has elevated France, and certainly not her own courage or abilities. But, I long to get on shore, and why am I troubling either you or myself with all this stuff. From my heart I wish I was at Merton, and you shewing me the place and your intended improvements, for I have the very highest opinion of your taste and economy. I have not had an opportunity of sending Mr. Turner your kind message, and probably he has got the trumpet before this time; but you are good and thoughtful to every body. I am going to send Sutton under Dungeness to watch the fellows that they do not pick up any of our trade for the few days that remain. Letters just come off. Lutwidge has sent me word that the vessel with the ratification arrived at eight this morning. Mrs. Lutwidge has sent me partridges and a pine-apple, and always inquires for you and Sir William. Troubridge writes me, that I may rest assured *we* will not keep you longer than I have before stated, that is, I suppose, fourteen days; and he hopes the exercise ashore will quite restore me. Now, I never will go on shore but only *per force*. I hate Deal, and from my heart wish I was out of sight of it. Remember me kindly to Sir William, the Duke, and all our friends, and none but real friends shall come to Merton; but you are to manage every thing.

" Yours,

" NELSON AND BRONTÉ.

" The wine from Portsmouth is on its journey. Is there a good wine cellar? I have a good deal at Davison's. We will eat plain, but will have good wine, good fires, and a hearty welcome for our friends, but none of the great shall enter our peaceful abode. I hate them all. I have had a real kind letter from Davison, such a one as is scarce in these degenerate times. God bless you."

"Amazon, October 11th, 1801.

" My dearest Friend,

" I ought, and do beg you 10,000 pardons for not having sent the memorandums for Davison's house, but I was really so unwell that I could not. Would to God I was liberated, for cooped up on board ship, with my head for ever leaning over paper, has almost blinded me, and it is impossible to be sure of a beach for one hour together. Captains Bedford and Sutton say they will not go any more unless it is perfect calm, for they got wet with all their care and activity, and yet I ought to return Lord George Cavendish's visit, and I see Billy Pitt has arrived, as the colours are hoisted. I will see him before I leave the station; he may perhaps be useful to me one day or other. We have now cold fogs, and you cannot conceive how truly uncomfortable I am. A Bay Master and Commander is just come, made Post—never performed a jot of service, whilst dear Parker, Somerville, Langford, and others, smarting and dying of their gallant wounds, cannot get a step. You cannot conceive how full every body's mouth is. As to Merton, you are the whole and sole commander. I wish naturally that every thing in the place should be mine; but as to living, we will settle that matter very easily. I only wish I was with you. I agree with you —no *great* folks; they are a public nuisance. How odd that the King has had no levée. I hope he is well, but should almost fear it. I have had a very affectionate letter from Colonel Stewart, on the death of dear Parker. He desires something as a remembrance of him. I have secured a book and a chart. The newspapers are not come. I am out of patience—a damned rascally Frenchman to be drawn by Englishmen! I blush for the degraded state of my country. I hope never more to be dragged by such a degenerate set of people. Would our ancestors have done it? So, the villains would have drawn Buonaparte if he had been able to get to London to cut off the King's head, and yet all our Royal Family will employ Frenchmen. Thanks to the navy, they could not. *Eleven o'clock.* Your letters are just come, but now we cannot get newspapers; they cannot come the same day to and from Merton. Soon, very soon, I hope to be with you, for there can be no use in keeping me here. Sutton, Bedford, &c. all inquire after you. Old Yawkins I always give your and Sir William's remembrance to.

"Ever yours,
"NELSON AND BRONTÉ.

"The Bay will come of course, and stupid De Graves' men, but not my steward; he is too fine for me. Our navy is all blank at the peace. If you see the Duke, say every kind thing. Best regards to Mrs. Cadogan, Oliver, &c."

"Amazon, ten o'clock, October 12, 1801.

"My dearest Friend,

"This being a very fine morning, and smooth beach, I went with Sutton and Bedford, and landed at Walmer, but found Billy fast asleep; so left my card; walked the same road that we came, when the carriage could not come with us that night; and all rushed into my mind, and brought tears into my eyes. Called at the barracks on Lord George (Cavendish), but he is gone to London. From thence to the Admiral's; found him up; and waiting half an hour to see Mrs. Lutwidge, who entreated me to stay dinner, came directly on board. I did not even call to see poor Langford, who has been worse these few days past, and God knows when he will be well. I am afraid it will be a long time, for several pieces of bone have lately come away, and more to come.

"But Troubridge has so completely prevented my ever mentioning any body's service, that I am become a cypher, and he has gained a victory over Nelson's spirit. I am kept here; for what, he may be able to tell, I cannot; but long it cannot, shall not, be. Sutton and Bedford are gone a tour, till dinner-time; but nothing shall make me, but almost force, go out of the ship again till I have done, and the Admiralty, in charity, will be pleased to release me. I am, in truth, not over well.

"Just as I was coming off I received your packet, and thank you from my heart for all your kindness. What can Reverend Sir want to be made a Doctor for? He will be laughed at for his pains. I thank you for the King's letters. I shall write a kind line to Castelcicala, and answer the King's very soon, and write to Acton, for he can make Bronté every thing to me, if he pleases. I dare say I did wrong never to write to him, but as he treated Sir William unkindly, I never could bring myself to it.

"I wish you had translated the King's and Acton's letters, Banti cannot.

"Ever yours,
"NELSON AND BRONTÉ."[1]

"Amazon, October 13th, 1801.

"My dearest Friend,

"Sutton and Bedford would fain persuade me, that by the post to-day the Admiralty will give me leave to go on shore. I own I do not believe it, or I should not begin this letter, for I should certainly be at Merton to-morrow at breakfast; but they have no desire to gratify me. Thank God there is no more than nine days to the cessation of hostilities, after that they can have no pretence. My complaint is a little better, and you cannot think how vexed I am to be unwell at a time when I desire to come on shore, and to enjoy a

[1] Collection of Letters, Vol. i. p. 73.

good share of health; but at this season, and in this place, it is impossible that I can be free from colds. The wind is set in very raw from the westward. Mr. Turner came and dined with me yesterday, and brought the trumpet with him, and he has charged me to say how much he feels obliged by your kind remembrance of him. This is the first time for five years he has been on board.

"*Eleven o'clock.* The letters are arrived, and Troubridge tells me not to think of leaving my station, so here I shall stay, miserable, shut up, for I will not stir out of the ship. I told Dr. Baird yesterday, that I was determined never to mention to Troubridge's unfeeling heart whether I was sick or well. I wish to my heart I could get to Merton: I had rather be sick there than well here; but in truth, I am so disgusted, that this day I care but little what becomes of me.

"I have this day received a curious letter from the Order of Joachim,[1] in Germany, desiring to elect me Knight Grand Commander thereof. I shall send it to Mr. Addington, that he may give me his opinion, and obtain, if proper, the King's approbation:—this is very curious. Dr. Baird is just come on board. Although I am not confined to my bed, I should be much better out of a frigate's cold cabin; but never mind, my dear friend, I see and feel all kindnesses and unkindnesses towards me. Make my kindest regards to Sir William, Mrs. Cadogan, and all friends, and believe me yours,

"NELSON AND BRONTÉ.

"Mr. Pitt has just been on board, and he thinks it is very hard to keep me now all is over. He asked me to dine at Walmer, but I refused. I will dine no where till I dine with you and Sir William.

"Yours,

"N. B.

"Sutton and Bedford desire their respects. If I am cross you must forgive me. I have reason to be so by *great* Troubridge."

"Amazon, October 14th, 1801.

"My dearest Friend,

"To-morrow week all is over—no thanks to Sir Thomas. I believe the fault is all his, and he ought to have recollected

[1] See Appendix, No. III.

that I got him the medal of the Nile. Who upheld him when he would have sunk under grief and mortification? Who placed him in such a situation in the Kingdom of Naples, that he got by my public letters, *titles, the Colonelcy of Marines, diamond boxes,* from the King of Naples, 1000 ounces in money, for *no* expenses that I know of? Who got him £500. a year from the King of Naples? and however much he may abuse him, his pension will be regularly paid. Who brought his character into notice? Look at my public letters. *Nelson,* that Nelson that he now *Lords* it over. So much for gratitude. I forgive him, but, by God, I shall not forget it. He enjoys shewing his power over me. Never mind; altogether it will shorten my days. The day is very bad—blows, rains, and a great sea. My complaint has returned from absolutely fretting; and was it not for the kindness of all about me, they, damn them, would have done me up long ago. I am anxiously waiting for your letters; they are my only comfort, for they are the only friendly ones I receive. Poor Captain Somerville is on board; himself, wife, and family, make twenty, without a servant, and has only £100. a year to maintain them. He has been begging me to intercede with the Admiralty again; but I have been so *rebuffed,* that my spirits are gone, and the *great* Troubridge has what we call *cowed* the spirits of Nelson; but I shall never forget it. He told me if I asked any thing more that I should get nothing, I suppose alluding to poor Langford. No wonder I am not well.

"*Noon.* Your kind letters are just come, and have given me great comfort. Pray tell Sir William that if I can I will write to him this day, but certainly to-morrow. I have much to do from Admiralty orders, letters, &c. I rejoice at your occupation. Live pretty, and keep a pig. Have you done any thing about the turnip field? Say every thing that is kind for me to Sir William, Mrs. Cadogan, &c. I have delivered your message to Sutton and Bedford. You may rely on a visit.

"Ever yours,
"Nelson and Bronté.

" Half sea sick. I thank you for Rev. Doctor's letter, and

Mrs. Nelson's. Her going to Swaffham is mentioned seven times, and in the postscript. It puts me in mind of the directions for the *Cardinal*. I have laughed, but she is a good wife for him, or he would have been ruined long ago. His being a Doctor is nonsense; but I must write to-morrow and congratulate him, or else the fat will be in the fire.

" Ever yours,<br>
" N. & B.

"To the Duke say every thing. I have wrote to Sir William at Merton; it goes on shore with this."

On the 14th Lord Nelson wrote to the Admiralty for leave to go ashore. This letter has been printed from the original in the Admiralty.[1] The original draft now before me makes an allusion to "revenue vessels, &c. which were added to the vessels formerly under the command of," which he afterwards ran his pen through, and it stands thus :—

"Amazon, Downs, October 14th, 1801.

" Sir,

" Their Lordships' appointment for my particular service being now done away by the preliminary articles of peace, viz. to prevent the invasion of this country, which service I have not only, by their Lordships' appointing so large a force to serve under my command, been enabled effectually to perform, but also to be able to acquaint you that not one boat belonging to this country has been captured by the enemy; and as my state of health requires repose on shore, I have, therefore, to request that their Lordships will, when they think the service will admit of it, allow me permission to go on shore."

On the following day he received orders for the cessation of hostilities against the French Republic, and a copy of the preliminary articles of peace between his Majesty and the Republic. On the 15th he wrote to Lady Hamilton, and was again ill :—

---

[1] Dispatches and Letters, Vol. iv. p. 511.

"Amazon, October 15th, 1801.

"My dearest Friend,

"The Admiralty will not give me leave till the 22nd; and then, only ten days. What a set of beasts! My cold is now got into my head; and I have such dreadful pains in my teeth, I cannot hold up my head: but none of them cares a d——n for me or my sufferings; therefore, you see, I cannot discharge my steward. And yet, I think, upon consideration, that I will send up my things, and take my chance as to their sending me down again. What do you think? At all events, everything except my bed. I have table spoons, forks, every thing; at least, I shall have, soon, two hundred pounds worth.

"Admiral Lutwidge is going to Portsmouth. Sir W. Parker is going to be tried for something. Make my kindest respects to Sir William, and believe me,

"Yours, &c. &c.
"NELSON AND BRONTÉ."[1]

"Amazon, October 15th, 1801.

"My dearest Friend,

"I have wrote by the way of London, but as your letter came regular, mine may go most likely. The Admiralty will not let me move till after the 22nd, and I have got a dreadful cold. I send you a letter for my father; when read, send to London, to be put in the post. I could not say less; I hope you will approve. Forgive my short letter, but the toothache torments me to pieces.

"Ever yours,
"NELSON AND BRONTÉ.

"Sutton and Bedford desire their best respects, and will certainly come and eat your brown bread and butter."

"Amazon, October 16th, 1801.

"My dearest Friend,

"It being a very fine morning, and the beach smooth, I went to call on Admiral Lutwidge, and returned on board before ten o'clock. Mrs. Lutwidge is delighted with your present. Sutton, &c. were called forth to admire it. She

[1] Collection of Letters, Vol. i. p. 76.

joins in abusing the Admiralty. She pressed me very much to dine with them at three o'clock; but I told her, I would not dine with the angel Gabriel, to be dragged through a night surf! Her answer was, that she hoped soon I should dine with an angel, for she was sure you were one. You are so good, so kind, to every body; old, young, rich, or poor, it is the same thing!

"I called on poor Langford; who has a long time to look forward to, for getting well; he told me your goodness, in writing him a line: and I called upon Dr. Baird; he disapproves of rhubarb, and has prescribed magnesia and peppermint;[1] and I called on Mr. Lawrence. So you see, I did much business in one hour I was on shore.

"The moment I got your letters, off I came, and have read them with real pleasure. They have made me much better, I think; at least, I feel so. I admire the pigs and poultry. Sheep are certainly most beneficial to eat off the grass. Do *you* get paid for them; and take care that they are kept on the premises all night, for that is the time they do good to the land. They should be folded. Is your head-man a good person, and true to our interest? I intend to have a farming book. I am glad to hear you get fish; not very good ones, I fancy.

"It is, I thank God, only six days before I shall be with you, and be shewn all the beauties of Merton. I shall like it, leaves or no leaves.

"No person there can take amiss our not visiting. The answer from me will always be very civil thanks, but that I wish to live retired. We shall have our sea friends; and I know, Sir William thinks they are the best.

"I have a letter from Mr. Trevor, begging me to recommend a youngster for him; but none before your Charles.[2] Banti, I suppose, must return; but, at present, we know not what ships are to be kept in commission. I have a letter from a female relation of mine. She has had three husbands; and he, Mr. S. three wives. Her brother, a Nelson, I have been trying, ever since I have been in England, to get pro-

---

[1] The irritability of Nelson had at this time occasioned derangement of his bowels.

[2] Lady Hamilton's nephew, Charles Connor.

moted. The last and present Admiralty promised. I never saw the man; he is in a ship in the North Seas, forty-five years of age.

"I have a letter from Troubridge, recommending me to wear flannel shirts. Does he care for me? *No;* but never mind. They shall work hard, to get me back again.

"Remember me kindly to Sir William, &c. &c.

"NELSON AND BRONTÉ.

"Do you ever see Castelcicala? He is a good man, and faithful to his master and mistress."[1]

"Amazon, October 16th, 1801.

"My dearest Friend,

"I have a letter from Reverend Doctor; he is as big as if he was a bishop; and one from the Bedel of the University, to say how well he preached. I hope you ordered something good for him, for these big wigs love eating and drinking.

"N. & B."[2]

"Amazon, October 17th, 1801.

"My dear Friend,

"Although my complaint has no danger attending it, yet it resists the medicines which Dr. Baird has prescribed; and I fancy, it has pulled me down very much. The cold has settled in my bowels, I wish the Admiralty had my complaint: but they have no bowels; at least for me. I had a very indifferent night, but your and Sir William's kind letters have made me feel better. I send you a letter from Lord Pelham; I shall certainly attend, and let them see that I may be useful in council as I have been in the field. We must submit; and perhaps, the Admiralty does this by me, to prevent another application. You may rely, that I shall be with you by dinner on Friday, at half past three or four at farthest. I pray that I may not be annoyed, on my arrival; it is retirement with my friends, that I wish for. Thank Sir William kindly for his letter; and the inclosure, which I return. Sutton is much pleased with your letter; and, with Bedford, will certainly make you a visit. They are both truly good and kind to me. Our weather has been cold these two days,

[1] Collection of Letters, Vol. i. p. 81.   [2] Ibid. p. 83.

but not bad. I have got a fire in the cabin; and, I hope my complaint will go off.

"May heaven bless you! I send this through Troubridge, direct in Piccadilly. I shall, you may rely, admire the pigstye, ducks, fowls, &c. for everything you do, I look upon as perfect. Dr. Baird has been aboard to see me. He thinks I shall be better; and that a few days on shore will set me up again.

"Make my kind remembrances to Sir William, the Duke, and all friends; and believe me, ever, your most affectionate
"NELSON AND BRONTÉ."[1]

Nelson was eager for the interest of those officers who had served with him, and he accordingly applied to Earl St. Vincent, who gave the following answer:—

"My dear Lord,

"Your Lordship may rest assured that the interest you have taken in Captain Somerville's fortunes has not been lost upon me. I have made inquiry for the passing certificate of his son, but neither it nor his appointment appear.

"Captain Tobin[2] has been a little in disrepute with the

---

[1] Collection of Letters, Vol. i. p. 84.

[2] Captain George Tobin entered the Navy in 1780, accompanied Sir George Rodney to the West Indies, and was in the actions of April 9th and 12th, 1782. After a variety of service, he learnt that Lord Nelson, whose wife was related to Captain Tobin's mother, had retained for him the Third Lieutenancy of the Agamemnon; but not then contemplating the eminence to which his Lordship would arise, he congratulated himself upon being Second Lieutenant to the Hon. Sir A. Cochrane, of the Thetis. After the Battle of the Nile his efforts to be with Lord Nelson were unsuccessful, and he was paid off at Plymouth in October, 1801. He was made a Post Captain in 1802, and was in the Northumberland, with his former Captain as Rear-Admiral. In 1805 he was on the Leeward Island station, and in the following year had a homeward-bound convoy. He was then on the Irish station, afterwards escorted a West India fleet of merchant-men, and was engaged by the Honourable East India Company to bring home the trade collected at St. Helena. He was now employed on the Irish station, and in the Channel, and in the Bay of Biscay, where he succeeded in making several captures. He was with Sir George Collier at the siege of St. Sebastian. He captured La Trave, a large French frigate, and in the Andromache, with Rear-Admiral Penrose, forced the passage of the Gironde. His vessel formed part of the assembled fleet at Spithead during the visit of the Allied Sovereigns in 1814, at the expiration of which year she was paid off. He died Rear-Admiral of the White and C.B., April 10, 1838.

Board, on account of his pertinacity about refitting, a very contagious disease in frigates and sloops, extremely difficult to eradicate; I apprehend his health to be delicate. Encompassed as I am by applications and presumptuous claims, I have nothing for it but to act upon the defensive, as your Lordship will be compelled to do, whenever you are placed in the situation I at present fill.

" Yours, most affectionately,
" ST. VINCENT.

" Admiralty, October 15th, 1801."

On the 16th Sir William Hamilton wrote Lord Nelson from Merton:—

"Merton, October 16th, 1801.

" My dear Lord,

" We have now inhabited your Lordship's premises some days, and I can now speak with some certainty. I have lived with our dear Emma several years. I know her merit, have a great opinion of the head and heart that God Almighty has been pleased to give her, but a seaman alone could have given a fine woman full power to choose and fit up a residence for him without seeing it himself. You are in *luck*, for in my conscience, I verily believe that a place so suitable to your views could not have been found, and at so cheap a rate; for if you stay away three days longer, I do not think you can have any wish but you will find it completed here; and then the bargain was fortunately struck three days before an idea of peace got abroad. Now every estate in this neighbourhood has increased in value, and you might get a thousand pounds to-morrow for your bargain. The proximity to the Capital, and the perfect retirement of this place are for your Lordship two points beyond estimation; but the house is so comfortable, the furniture clean and good, and I never saw so many conveniences united in so small a compass. You have nothing but to come and enjoy it immediately, and you have a good mile of pleasant dry walk around your own farm. It would make you laugh to see Emma and her mother fitting up pigstyes and hencoops, and already the canal is enlivened with ducks, and the cock is strutting with his hens about the walks. Your Lordship's plan as to stocking the canal with fish is exactly mine, and I will answer for it that in a few months you may command a good dish of fish at a moment's warning. Every fish of any size has been taken away, even after the bargain was made; for there are many *Troubridges* in this world, but *Nelsons* are rare. I think it quite impossible that *they* can keep you at Deal more than three or four days longer. It would be *ridiculous*. This neighbourhood are anxiously expecting your Lordship's arrival, and you cannot be off of some particular attentions that will be shewn you, and which all the world know that you have merited above all others. I inclose a letter which I have just received from Count Dillon O'Kelly, who supped with us at Coblentzall's at Prague. See how your merit is estimated on the Continent, and shame be it that so little justice is done you at home. Be so good as to bring or return the letter, as I must answer it. Adieu, my dear Lord, and most sincere friend I have in this world.

"Yours,

"WILLIAM HAMILTON."

Nelson continued his correspondence with Lady Hamilton, until his return to London on the 22nd:—

"Amazon, October 18th, 1801.

"My dearest Friend,

"I am to-day much better than I have been for several days past, and I believe my cold has taken a favourable turn, and I trust to being perfectly stout and strong before Friday. No thanks to the Admiralty. We have had, and it still blows a very heavy gale of wind from yesterday five o'clock. I doubt whether any boat will be able to get to us to-day with your letters, and less do I believe that mine will get on shore, for the wind blows partly from the land. I could not write all my thoughts through the Admiralty, for I should not be surprised if now and then, for curiosity's sake, they wish to know our truly innocent correspondence. I think it probable that I shall be obliged, for a week perhaps, to return to Deal, for I find, and there they are right, to put by all superfluous expenses, and only to keep what I call clean men-of-war in commission till the definitive Treaty is signed. What has been done already in the Naval department will reduce our expenses £150,000 a month. We shall make a better treaty with arms in our hands. I am very angry at the great rejoicings of the military, and, in some ports, of our naval men, at peace. Let the rejoicings be proper to our several stations—the manufacturer, because he will have more markets for his goods—but seamen and soldiers ought to say, 'Well, as it is peace, we lay down our arms; and are ready again to take them up, if the French are insolent.' There is a manly rejoicing, and a foolish one; we seem to have taken the latter, and the damned French will think it proceeds from fear. I hope to manage so that I shall get something for my brother; for myself it is out of the question; they can give me nothing as a pension at this time, but good things may fall. I shall talk and be much with Mr. Addington, if he wishes it. If not, I can have no desire to go to the House, and give myself trouble. Lord St. Vincent says two days ago, 'When you, my dear Lord, *hold* my place, you will be obliged, as I am, to act on the defensive against such presumptuous claims.'

"I am in hopes the weather will moderate after twelve o'clock, for you will fancy I am ill, but recollect in the winter it is often a week, has been fourteen days, without any communication with the shore. I received all your letters yesterday, but you need not direct them to the care of Admiral Lutwidge. Wednesday will be your last day of writing. Have you thought of the turnip field? can we get it? We will, if possible, and in any reason of price. I finish my letter, that, if it is possible, it may get on shore, but I have no expectation at present. Make my kindest regards to Sir William, Mrs. Cadogan, the Duke when you see him, and all our friends. I am certainly in luck not to be ordered to these court-martials; they will altogether take a fortnight at least.

"Ever yours,
"NELSON AND BRONTÉ.

"What a gale! does it blow with you?"

"Amazon, October 19th, 1801."

"My dearest Friend,

"What a gale we have had! But Admiral Lutwidge's boat came off; and as your letter was wrote, it got on shore; at least, I hope so, for the boat seemed absolutely swallowed up in the sea. None of our boats could have kept above water a moment; therefore, I could not answer all the truly friendly things you told me in your letters, for they were not opened before the boat was gone.

"They (the Lutwidges) dine with Billy Pitt to-day; or, rather, with Mr. Long; for Pitt does not keep house, in appearance, although he asked me to come and see him; and that I shall do, out of respect to a great man, although he never did anything for me or my relations.

"I must leave my cot here, till my discharge, when it shall come to the farm, as cots are the best things in the world for our sea friends. Why not have the pictures from Davison's, and those from Dodd's, especially my father's and Davison's? *Apropos*, Sir William has not sat, I fear, to Beechey. I want a half length, the size of my father's and Davison's. The weather to-day is tolerable, but I do not think I could well get on shore; but Thursday, I hope, will be a fine day. I shall call on Mr. Pitt, make my visit at the hospital, and get off very early on Friday morning. My cold is still very troublesome, I cannot get my bowels in order. In the night I had not a little fever. But never mind; the Admiralty will not always be there. Every one has his day.

"Ever yours,
"NELSON AND BRONTÉ."[1]

On the 20th he received another letter from Earl St. Vincent.

"My dear Lord,

"Many thanks for your hints about the block ships, which are approved by the Board, and will be acted upon; directions have been given to the Navy Board to dispose of all the gun-vessels out of repair; the twenty last built are efficient, and will be useful in peace.

---

[1] Collection of Letters, Vol. i. p. 94.

"Captain Thomson had justice done him, the moment I was apprized of his merits, and a notification was sent to him some time ago. I wish I could provide for Mr. Priestly with the same facility; the great number of Pursers out of employment by the loss and sale of small ships, calls for all the vacancies which occur, and it is so beggarly and ruinous an office, that I fear very many of those who fill it will be thrown into prison at the winding up; it is no easy matter for any of them to find security when they do get warrants.

"I heartily hope a little rest will soon set you up, but until the definitive Treaty is signed, your Lordship must continue in pay, although we may not have occasion to require your personal services at the head of the squadron under your orders.

"Remember me kindly to all those whom we mutually esteem within your reach, and believe me to be,
"My dear Lord,
"Yours most affectionately,
"ST. VINCENT.

"Admiralty, 20th October, 1801.

"Your Lordship acted with great judgment in releasing the French coaster.
"ST. VT."

To Lady Hamilton on the 20th, Nelson writes:—

"Amazon, October 20, 1801.

"My dearest Friend,

"How could you think for a moment, that I would be a time-server to any Minister on earth! and if you had studied my letter a little closer, you would have seen that my intention was, to shew them that I could be as useful in the cabinet as in the field. My idea is, to let them see that my attendance is worth soliciting. For myself, I can have nothing, but for my brother something may be done.

"Living with Mr. Addington a good deal: never, in your sense of the word, shall I do it. What, leave my dearest friends, to dine with a Minister? Damn me if I do, beyond what you yourself shall judge to be necessary! Perhaps it may be once; and once with the Earl, but that you shall judge for me.

"If I give up all intercourse, you know enough of Courts, that they will do nothing: make yourself of consequence to them, and they will do what you wish in reason; and, out of reason, I never should ask them. It must be a great bore to me to go to the House, I shall tell Mr. Addington, that I go on the 29th to please him, and not to please myself; but more on this subject when we meet.

"Dr. Baird is laid up with the rheumatism; he will now believe that the cold may affect me. This is the coldest place in England most assuredly. Troubridge writes me, that as the weather is set in fine again, he hopes I shall get walks on shore. He is, I suppose, laughing at me; but, never mind. I agree with you in wishing Sir William had a horse. Why don't you send to the Duke for a pony for him?

"I am just parting with four of my ships. Captains Conn, Rowley,[1] Martin, and Whitter—who are proceeding to the Nore on their way to be paid off. The surf is still so great on the beach, that I could not land dry, if it was necessary to-day; but I hope it will be smooth on Thursday: if not, I must go in a boat to Dover, and come from thence to Deal. Sutton says, he will get the Amazon under sail, and carry me down; for, that I shall not take cold: Bedford goes with a squadron to Margate, so that all our party will be broke up. I am sure, to many of them I feel truly obliged.

"NELSON AND BRONTÉ."[2]

"Amazon, October 20th, 1801.

"My dearest Friend,

"Only two days more, the Admiralty could with any conscience keep me here; not that I think they have had any

---

[1] This officer appears to have been Samuel Campbell Rowley, who was a brother of Rear-Admiral Sir Josias Rowley, Bart., and made a Commander April 6, 1799 He served in the Terror bomb at the attack on Copenhagen, April 2, 1801, returned to England and was made a Post Captain, April 29, 1802. He commanded the Laurel frigate, which, at the commencement of 1812, was wrecked from striking on a rock called the Govivas, when proceeding through the Teigneuse passage in company with the Rota and Rhin. On the wreck he was exposed to a very severe fire most inhumanly directed from the French batteries and fieldpieces, until every officer, man and boy were removed in the boats sent to their relief. He afterwards commanded the Impregnable, of 104 guns, and was on the Mediterranean station.

[2] Collection of Letters, Vol. i. p. 99.

conscience. I dare say Master Troubridge is grown fat. I know I am grown lean, with my complaint, which but for their indifference about my health, would never have happened; or at least, I should have got well long ago, in a warm room, with a good fire and sincere friends. I believe, I leave this little squadron with sincere regret, and with the good wishes of every creature in it.

"How I should laugh to see you, my dear friend, rowing in a boat; the beautiful Emma rowing a one-armed Admiral in a boat! it will certainly be caricatured! Well done, farmer's wife! I'll bet your turkey against Mrs. Nelson's; but, Sir William and I will decide. Hardy says, you may be sure of him; and that he has not lost his appetite. You will make us rich, with your economy. I did not think, tell Sir William, that impudence had got such deep root in Wales. I send you the letter, as a curiosity; and to have the impudence to recommend a Midshipman! It is not long ago, a person from Yorkshire desired me to lend him three hundred pounds, as he was going to set up a school! Are these people mad; or do they take me for quite a fool? However, I have wisdom enough to laugh at their folly; and to be, myself, your most obliged and faithful friend,

"NELSON AND BRONTÉ."[1]

"Amazon, October 21st, 1801.

"My dearest Friend,

"It blows strong from the westward, and is a very dirty day, with a good deal of surf on the beach, but Hardy and Sutton recommend my going on shore this morning, as they believe it may blow a heavy gale to-morrow. But what comfort could I have had, for two whole days at Deal! I hope the morning will be fine, but I have ordered a Deal boat, as they understand the beach better than ours; and if I cannot land here, I shall go to Ramsgate Pier, and come to Deal in a carriage. Has Mrs. Cadogan got my Peer's robe? for I must send for Mr. Webb, and have it altered to a Viscount's. Lord Hood wrote to me to-day, and he is to be one of my

[1] Collection of Letters, Vol. i. p. 103.

introducers. He wanted me to dine with him on the 24th, but I will be d——d if I dine from home that day, and it will be as likely we shall dine out on the 23rd. If you and Sir William wish me to dine with his brother, it must be the time of a very small party, for it would be worse than death to me, to dine in so large a party.

"I expect that all the animals will increase where you are, for I never expect that you will suffer any to be killed. I am glad Sir William has got the Duke's pony; riding will do him much good. I am sorry to tell you that Dr. Baird is so ill that I am told it is very probable he may never recover. This place is the devil's for dreadful colds: and I don't believe I shall get well all the winter; for both cough and bowels are still very much out of order. I am literally starving with cold, but my heart is warm.

"Yours, &c.

"N. & B."[1]

On the 22nd Nelson first visited Merton, and on the 29th took his seat in the House of Lords, upon being created a Viscount. He was introduced by Viscounts Sidney and Hood. On the following day he seconded Earl St. Vincent's motion of Thanks to Rear-Admiral Sir James Saumarez, for his action with the combined fleet off Algeziras, in the month of July. He entered into the details of the action, and lauded the conduct and skill of the Commander. In this speech he ingeniously complimented Lords Hood and St. Vincent as forming the school in which Sir James Saumarez had been educated, and elicited the warm approbation of the Peers assembled. On the 3rd of November he again spoke in the House, and defended the preliminaries of peace. He considered Minorca as an island of little value to us, and he also held Malta of no consequence to this country. He yet conceived it to be an object of importance to rescue it from the French. He estimated 7000 soldiers to be necessary to man the fortifications, and expressed his admiration of the extent and convenience of the harbours. He spoke of the Cape of Good Hope as a tavern to be called at, and thereby often to delay

[1] Collection of Letters, Vol. i. p. 107.

a voyage from India. When the Dutch possessed it, you could buy a cabbage for two-pence, but since it had come into our hands, we were obliged to pay a shilling. It could only be maintained at an enormous expense, and produced little that made it worth holding. Lord Nelson finished his address by declaring his approbation of the preliminaries as honourable and advantageous to the country.

Lord Nelson also spoke on the 12th, upon a motion of Thanks to Lord Keith and the Officers under his command for their services in Egypt.

On the following day he spoke in the Debate on the Convention with Russia. He gave his approval of it, and contended that it had put an end to the principle endeavoured to be enforced by the armed neutrality in 1780, and by the late combination of the Northern Powers, that *free ships made free goods*, a proposition he looked upon as monstrous in itself, and contrary to the law of nations, as well as injurious to the maritime rights of this country. The rashness and violence of the Emperor Paul, he considered, had formed the confederacy against us to support and enforce that proposition; but the moderation and temper of his successor Alexander had consented to give it up and renounce it. He approved of the article restricting the right of search of ships under the convoy of a neutral flag-ship of war to our navy, only during hostilities, and stated what would have been his own conduct if he had met with such convoy, declaring that he should have endeavoured to discharge his duty with all possible civility to the Captain of the neutral frigate, should have inspected his papers, and if, from the information of any seaman, he was led to entertain a suspicion that the papers were fraudulent or fabricated, and that the convoy did contain what was contraband or illicit, he should in that case have insisted on a search, and if he found any contraband articles on board, he should have detained such ship or ships.

The following letter from his father must have been acceptable to him:—

"Hilborough, November 2nd.

"My dear Horatio,

"I have to acknowledge many kind and polite invitations from yourself and Lady Hamilton to visit Merton, which it is my intention to accept before my winter residence commences at Bath. My journey to London is very slow, not only from infirmities, but by necessary and pleasing visits with my children, whose kindnesses are a *cordial for age* such as few parents can boast of. After finishing some necessary business in town, if convenient to your family, I shall, with the highest gratification a fond parent can receive, pass a time with you. I am, with all proper regards to the family at Merton,

"Yours most affectionately,
"EDMUND NELSON."

Hercules Ross, Esq. whom he had known at Jamaica in 1779 and 1780, and from whom he had received great attention, solicited Lord Nelson to become godfather to his child. He readily assented, and the boy was named Horatio. In his reply to this request, Nelson writes: "Whatever call the public duty has to my services, yet I must not altogether forget the duty of private friendship. You do not think me capable of forgetting when your house, carriages, and purse were open to me; and to your kindness, probably, I owe my life, for Green Bay had very often its jaws open to receive me. But as money never was my object, so I am not much richer than when you knew me, except by my pension. No! the *two* Parkers have had the sweets of Jamaica, but I would not change with them. I pray God we may have peace, when it can be had with honour; but I fear that the scoundrel Buonaparte wants to humble us, as he has done the rest of Europe —to degrade us in our own eyes, by making us give up all our conquests, as proof of our sincerity for making a peace, and then he will condescend to treat with us. He be d—d, and there I leave him."[1]

This letter is acknowledged by the following:—

"My dear Friend,
"So many important events have crowded into the last six weeks, that I thought it better for a time to delay intruding my grateful acknowledgment of your kind letter from the Downs, of the 12th September. Be pleased now to accept

[1] From an autograph in the possession of Horatio Ross, Esq. printed in Dispatches and Letters, Vol. iv. p. 488.

my best thanks and high sense of the honour done me, by your Lordship's remembrance of our early friendship, your good wishes for my son, and the affectionate sentiments of regard so warmly expressed. It shall be carefully preserved as a record, a valuable one, for your godson, to hereafter shew why and wherefore he was named Horatio. On the 27th of last month the baptismal ceremony was performed; Sir John Wedderburn had the honour of representing your Lordship, Lady Northesk (Lord St. Vincent's niece), and Lady Jane Stuart, daughter of the Earl of Leven, were godmothers.

"I am particularly instructed by the partial mother, to assure your Lordship, that our young Horatio is one of the finest children imaginable, and likewise to request that you will be so good as to express our just sense of Sir William and Lady Hamilton's compliments.

"I shall not attempt to congratulate your Lordship on the peace, such a diversity of opinion prevails; at the same time, I confess my firm belief that it is the best our Ministry could make. An enormous sum has been expended, but in fact, I know no better way in which money can be spent than for the safety of our country and the preservation of our honour. Speaking of money, I note what you say about the two Parkers, and I wonder what has become of our old friend Sir Peter. The other day, tumbling over some old papers, I fell in with a letter of yours of the 12th of June, 1780, from Lady Parker's Mountain, it will amuse you one day or other, when we shall have the happiness of meeting here. By the newspapers, I remarked you lately in the House of Peers, thence I conclude in good health, otherwise your Lordship would prefer the country. Nothing can give me higher pleasure than learning that you enjoy that blessing.

"We have some thoughts of a trip to London in the spring, as a jaunt of variety to our eldest daughter in her 15th year; I shall then hope to have the happiness of shaking my noble friend by the hand. May the Almighty bless and preserve him, says his faithful and affectionate

"H. Ross.

"Rossie Castle, North Britain,
  7th November, 1801.

"I must not forget your remembrance of the Nurse.

What! couldn't you trust that pecuniary matter to your old Agent?"

Lord Nelson was gratified by a letter from Lord Elgin:—

"Constantinople, November 24th, 1801.

"My dear Lord,

"In forwarding to your Lordship the accompanying letter from the Porte, and the remaining insignia of the Order of the Crescent, it is but justice to add, that they have a very peculiar degree of pleasure in recollecting your services, and their infinite obligations to you. Your naming the *Order of the Crescent*, in your Convention at Copenhagen, suggested to them the idea of extending that decoration on the occasion of the conquest, of which you had laid so solid a basis, and really one of their principal inducements in it, was the opportunity it afforded them of saying once more, how proud they are of being connected with you.

"They have followed your glories in the North with infinite satisfaction; indeed, I say a great deal when I can assure you, the interest in you is as alive here as it ever was. I rejoice in every incident that brings me to your Lordship's recollection, and enables me to express the respect and sincere regard with which I have the honour to be,

"Your faithful humble servant,

"ELGIN."

The Rev. Edmund Nelson visited his son at Merton, and upon his return to Bath, wrote as follows on the 5th, 13th, and 19th:—

[Bath, December 5th, 1801.]

"My dear Horatio,

"The affectionate and kind manner in which you received and entertained me at Merton, must have excited all those parental feelings which none but fond parents know; and having seen you safe through the perils which infancy, childhood, and even the early years of manhood are exposed to, how must I now rejoice to see so few impediments to as much felicity as falls to the share of mortals. What you possess, my good son, take care of—what you may still want, consult your own good sense in what way it can be attained.

Strive for honours and riches that will not fade, but will profit in time of need. Excuse my anxiety for what I esteem your real good.

"My journey here was cold, yet safe—arrived last night; met with a kind and warm reception from your good sister and her indulgent husband. Am now going to a warm lodging, No. 10, New King Street. Though tired with scrawling, yet must add my best thanks to Sir William and Lady Hamilton for their very many civilities to me. Your sister and Mr. M.'s best regards as ever with you.

"Affectionately,<br>"E. NELSON.

"December, Friday."

"My dear Horatio,

"The little addition you are likely to make to your landed property will, I hope, bring some further pleasure and domestic comfort, such as the real comfort of a private and independent life must consist of, and every event which you are so good as to communicate to me, which is likely to increase your happiness, adds a prop to my declining life, and the little incidents, even of indifference, which Lady Hamilton politely communicates to me, are at all times very acceptable. Your sister's daily care in watching my infirmities, and rendering them as easy as in her power, I feel with delight. She is, as usual, cheerful, often regretting not having been able to see you, and even still she and Mr. M. [Matcham] meditate a visit to Merton for a day or two, to wait upon Lady Hamilton and yourself, if the weather is tolerably good, and she herself can prudently undertake such a journey five or six weeks hence, when the Bairns are all returned to their several academies. The box came safe, as did the plaid—very handsome. Lady Hamilton will accept my thanks for her care about it, to whom with Sir William present my respects, as also to the whole party.

"I am,<br>"My dear,<br>"Your affectionate Father,<br>"EDMUND NELSON.

"December 13th, 1801."

"By inclosing a letter now and then I would not infringe upon your privilege."

"My dear Horatio,

"From an old man you will accept the old fashioned language at the approaching happy season, which is, I wish you a merry Christmas and a happy new year.

"For multiplied favours Lady Hamilton has my respectful thanks.

"E. N."

The Rev. Edmund Nelson also wrote to Lady Hamilton:

"Madam,

"The intelligence you have troubled yourself to communicate to me, respecting the lad Cook, vexes me more than a little, as I am concerned that any act of mine should have given any the least anxiety, or for a moment interrupted the domestic quiet of my good son, who is every day so affectionately shewing marks of kindness to me; but the idleness of youth and their easiness of receiving bad examples are not to be guarded against. The lad's mother must also be very much grieved, and his brother is greatly disappointed by this rash act, who I think is too good a youth to have given any advice so contrary to their mutual interest. But I hope it will blow over without much blame on my recommendation, who would avoid whatever should hurt or bring expense upon so good and benevolent a mind.

"Even the severity of the season, which makes many a poor creature, such as myself, to shake, gives much pleasure to the skating parties, so that I hope all in their turns have their hours of enjoyment at a season when all the Christian world do celebrate with songs of praise the return of Christmas. Long may you all feel the happy influence of such an event *here*, and the inestimable benefit of it hereafter.

"EDMUND NELSON.

"December 21."

Apartments were prepared at Merton Place to receive the Rev. Edmund Nelson, after passing his winter at Bath, it being his intention (according to a statement made in Harrison's Life of Lord Nelson)[1] to return in May, and then to take up his residence entirely with his son, and Sir William and Lady Hamilton. His death in April, of course, prevented this being carried into effect. He had for many years been a great invalid, suffering from paralysis and asthma. He was not able for several hours after rising in the morning to hold any conversation, and was compelled to pass his winters at Bath.

About this time Lady Hamilton received the following from the Queen of Naples :—

"December 6th, 1801.

"My dear Lady,

"I take the opportunity of the departure of the courier, to write to you. You have, I know, shared in the sad misfortune which has befallen me in the loss of my dear and good daughter-in-law, which destroys the only happiness remaining to me, in a perfect union and domestic peace; this dear and good princess died like a saint. Her husband is in the most profound grief; my poor children do nothing but weep for a sister-in-law, who was a tender sister, and who at my death (to which my sorrows and troubles are hastening me) would have been a mother to them. I flatter myself that, though you do not write to me, and I think myself half forgotten, yet that you preserve so much recollection of me as to feel this cruel trial which is so much more painful now, a thousand untoward circumstances preventing my establishing my dear children, whom I must take back to Naples, where, without their sister and friend, they will probably remain for life. Let me hear how you are, and the Chevalier also—they say he has bought an estate near London. My compliments to the worthy, valorous Lord Nelson, to whom I shall feel grateful as long as I live, notwithstanding his speech in Parliament against the importance of maintaining a position in the Mediterranean, Malta, &c. has greatly distressed me; it is true, he only followed the bitter and unjust Lord Hawkesbury, even Pitt and many others, who have decided to leave Italy as a mere French dependent province,

[1] Vol. ii. page 379.

and the Mediterranean free for them, where they will find all the needful resources for the Levant, Egypt, &c. and all the commerce; but it is not for females to reason, we can only sigh and weep. My attachment to England has been perfect, entire, all our movements, misfortunes, losses and sufferings have shewn it, therefore I own this complete abandonment is cruel, and so much the more so as one must be silent even when laughed at, and asked if our Anglo-mania is cured. I grieve, and my tears suffocate me. My attachment may be unfortunate, but cannot be destroyed, and leads me to hope that England will not before ten years have to repent of this peace, now concluded with a nation whose activity, pugnacity, and good fortune, will make such efforts as will surprise and incommode her; but I am a woman, and have no right to talk about it, and must endeavour neither to think nor to trouble myself further with it. Tell me all that concerns you, for my heart is interested in it. I can say nothing to you at present of my intentions and movements, as they depend on the orders of the King, on the evacuation of the French, and the season. I think at the commencement of the spring of going to die at my post—if my children were established, their position certain, I should regard such an event as my deliverance from this prospect of further misfortunes, but until my children's condition is fixed (I do not say permanently secured, for no one could, in such times as these), I should wish to live to be serviceable to them, and then I would quit life without regret. Adieu, my dear lady, I have spoken to you with sincerity and frankness, as I have always been accustomed to do. I hope that your sentiments are not changed, mine are unchangeable, and believe me for life, your very sincere and grateful friend,

"CHARLOTTE.

"A thousand compliments to the good Chevalier Hamilton, and the hero of the Nile, the valorous Nelson."

A letter to his agents, Messrs. Marsh, Page, and Creed, will shew that the demands upon Lord Nelson's purse had placed him rather in embarrassment, and that he had been obliged to dispose of the diamonds which had been at different times presented to him. Allusion to a valuation of these is made in a letter to A. Davison, Esq. December 18th, 1801, in which he says, "The valuation of the diamonds is, as far as I have been told, shameful; therefore, although I am naturally very anxious not to obtrude more on your goodness than necessity obliges me, yet I wish to talk to you on the subject of being *even* a little longer in your debt, taking care, which I hope I shall be able, to secure the payment to you: but more of this to-morrow."

The subjoined letter shews Nelson's anxiety to relieve his Secretary, Tyson, from whom he received the following letter:—

"Malta, 21st October, 1801.

"My Lord,

"I refer your Lordship to Sir Alexander Ball, Bart. the bearer of this, for all the particulars of my cursed detention in this country, and the difficulties I have had to encounter in the final settlement of my accounts, a thing beyond all calculation grievous to me, and hath very materially affected my health. I have been ill for near two months last past, of a slow fever, attended with boils, with which I have been covered from head to foot, and even to the finger ends, a more miserable wretch never crept on the face of the earth than I was for some time—disease added to disappointment in the adjustment of my affairs, have all added to make me extremely unhappy. However, I hope in a few days to take my departure with Captain Louis to Mahon and Gibraltar. I have yesterday received from Mr. Brown on your Lordship's account the sum of £767. 13s 5d sterling, which is all he *says that* is as yet payable, and if there is any payable at Mahon or Gibraltar, he will give me orders to receive it also. The utensils for Græffer at Bronté arrived a few days ago, and I got Captain Martin's and Captain Louis's launches to land them in the dockyard here. Mr. Lawson, the late Master of the Alexander, who is now the Master Attendant, has them in his care, but I have to mention to your Lordship that all the seeds which were stowed in one cask, were dropped overboard; we had them immediately opened and spread to dry, and I believe the most of them are yet good, except the flax seed, which seems to have been rotten before, by stowing it in a damp place. The villain that landed them at Mahon, although by license of the Court of Admiralty, ought not to have been paid his freight: there is a charge on those packages of 1144 dollars with the agio on them, and Mr. Lempriere has drawn on Noble for the sum, which I shall pay on your Lordship's account. Should Græffer send for those things or the seed, Noble will send them over; Captain Sayer brought them up from Mahon in the Ulysses troop-ship. I sail for Mahon, as I am told, in six days. God be thanked it is a peace, and that your Lordship will not have any more dangers to encounter, in small vessels particularly. We are not yet informed of the terms of peace, but expect them soon. Sir Alexander will tell you all the news of and about the Great Chief and his Secretary, and in the hope of seeing your Lordship in two months from this date, I have the honour to be, with the most sincere respect and esteem,

"My Lord,
"Your Lordship's
"Most obedient and most faithful servant,
"J. TYSON.

"I beg your Lordship to make my most respectful compliments to Sir William and Lady Hamilton."

To his Agents, Lord Nelson wrote thus:—

"Merton, December 29th, 1801."

"Most private, to be returned to me, as I consider this letter as a confidential communication to my friends.

"Mr. Tyson, my Secretary, and as good a man as ever lived, is arrived, and I have an account with him which makes me his debtor about £4000. There may be some set off, but I choose to consider that the sum, and I not only wish, but am fixed to pay him the day after he gets to London, therefore I wish to prepare this money for him. If I have money in the funds (and I think I have Indian Stock) it must directly be sold; this, with my arrears of pay, will, I hope, go far towards raising the money, and if it will not, I must trespass on your indulgence. I have the means to repay you in (even if I lose my cause with Lord St. Vincent) £5000. from the Alcmene prizes, and near £3000. from the Lima convoy, and even Merton, any part of which I shall with pleasure make over to secure you in any advance. I have sold diamonds to pay one person to whom I was indebted by his goodness in trusting me £3000. I TAKE NO SHAME TO BE POOR; never for myself have I spent sixpence, it has all gone to do honour for my country, and in a way which, whether the persons have deserved it or no, is for their consideration not for mine. I intended to have gone to town to-day, but I am not very well, and perhaps I have explained myself better in writing than by speaking, and give you time to reflect whether you can or not comply with my request."

Wounds received by Lord Nelson

His Eye in Corsica

His Belly off Cape St Vincent

His Arm at Teneriffe

His Head in Egypt

Tolerable for one War

LORD NELSON'S STATEMENT OF HIS WOUNDS.

*(MS in possession of the Author.)*

## CHAPTER VI.

### 1802—1803.

In the year 1802 we find Lord Nelson living at Merton, enjoying the society of Sir William and Lady Hamilton, who resided with him, and a select few of his friends.

It was at this time probably pondering over the proceedings during the war, that he marked down the following summary of the wounds he had received in the defence of his country: (See *Fac-simile*.)

> "*Wounds received by Lord Nelson.*
> "His eye in Corsica.[1]
> "His belly off Cape St. Vincent.[2]
> "His arm at Teneriffe.[3]
> "His head in Egypt.[4]
> "Tolerable for one war."

The Queen of Naples addressed Lord Nelson:—

"I received, my worthy Lord, your letter of the 24th of December, and was much affected by your expressions of attachment. I was very sorry that amongst other speeches in Parliament, my Lord, even yours was in favour of the plan of abandoning Malta to the domination of the masters of the world, to execute their sway without hindrance over us—this is very painful to me, and my frank and loyal sincerity compels me to say so. But I shall never forget what we owe to you. A lively and sincere gratitude towards you will accompany me to the grave. And I fervently hope that the opportunity may once more occur to enable me personally to tell you, that I am your sincere and grateful friend,
"CHARLOTTE.

"Vienna, the 5th February, 1802."

---

[1] At the siege of Calvi.
[2] He was struck by a splinter on the 14th of February, 1797, in Sir John Jervis's action.
[3] The unfortunate attempt on Santa Cruz.
[4] Scalp wound from a langridge shot at the Battle of the Nile.

Although away from his command between **Orfordness and Beachy Head**, Lord Nelson was only on leave, and did not strike his flag until the 10th of April. He made many applications to the Admiralty in favour of those who had served with him, but with very limited success, and he got some provided for by the aid of some of his officers who were continued in service.

In the previous year he had received a communication from Lord Elgin of the honour conferred upon him by the Grand Signior for the Battle of Copenhagen, and on the 30th of January he received the letters and ribbon of the Order. He forwarded the same to the Hon. Henry Addington with the following letter :—

"Merton, January 31st, 1802.

"My dear Sir,

"I have received yesterday from Lord Elgin the letters and ribbon sent herewith, and I have to request that you will have the goodness to lay them before the King, in order that I may know his Royal pleasure as to wearing the ribbon. This mark of regard from the Sultan has made a strong impression on my mind, as it appears that the Battle of Copenhagen has been the cause of this new decoration from the Porte. If his Majesty should, from regard to the Sultan or honour to me, intend to place the ribbon on me, I am ready to attend his commands, but I own, my dear Sir, that great as this honour would be, it would have its alloy, if I cannot wear the medal for the Battle of Copenhagen at the same time, the greatest and most honourable reward in the power of our Sovereign to bestow, as it marks the personal service of,

"My dear Sir,
"&c. &c. &c."[1]

Nelson was very much annoyed that no medals had been voted for the Battle of Copenhagen, which he designated, and always looked upon, as, under all its circumstances, the most hard fought battle, and the most complete victory that ever was fought and obtained by the Navy of this country.

[1] This letter is printed from Lord Nelson's autograph, and differs a little from that in the Dispatches and Letters, Vol. v. p. 3.

He had been led to expect, from a conversation he had with the First Lord of the Admiralty, that they were intended to be granted, and he did not hesitate to communicate the same to several of the officers who had been engaged in this honourable service. When, therefore, he received from Earl St. Vincent a letter which stated that he had never given encouragement to the expectation of receiving medals for the action of the 2nd of April, he was exceedingly astonished and mortified. On the 20th of November, 1801, he wrote a letter to the Lord Mayor of London, having seen that the thanks of the City had been voted to the army and navy, who brought the campaign in Egypt to an honourable conclusion. Nelson expressed his satisfaction at this vote so truly deserved, and after noticing the attention of the citizens to services in honour of the country, remarked, that there existed only one exception, namely, that of the action of the 2nd of April, 1801; "a day when the greatest dangers of navigation were overcome, and the Danish force, which they thought impregnable, totally taken or destroyed by the consummate skill of the commanders, and by the undaunted bravery of as gallant a band as ever defended the rights of this country." He appealed to the Lord Mayor, as the natural guardian of the characters of the officers of the navy, army, and marines who fought, and so profusely bled, under his command on that day. In no sea action during the war had so much British blood flowed for their King and country. He forwarded this letter to the Hon. Henry Addington, and solicited his opinion; but three days having elapsed without a reply, his impatient spirit could brook no further delay, and he sent off the letter. Mr. Addington, however, was averse to the communication, and was led to be so upon private as well as public grounds, and he expressed his willingness to state them to Lord Nelson at Downing Street. They were, it may be presumed, sufficiently convincing at this time, as Lord Nelson in consequence withdrew his letter.[1]

[1] The following is from the rough draft of this letter, found among the present collection of Lord Nelson's papers:—

"My Lord,

"I have seen in this day's papers that the City of London have voted their thanks to the brave Army and Navy who have so happily brought the campaign

To have services of so arduous and important a nature unacknowledged by the City, and so disregarded by the Government in refusing the medals, occasioned Nelson the greatest disappointment. He declared to Captain Foley that he never would wear his other medals until that for Copenhagen was granted, and he refused to dine with the Lord Mayor in his official capacity until justice was done to his companions in arms on the 2nd of April. He never ceased to urge these subjects even two years posterior to the action, and when Lord Melville had been placed at the head of the Admiralty. Nor did the officers, many years after his death, cease to put forth their claims to such a distinction. When his Royal Highness the Duke of Clarence was appointed Lord High Admiral in 1828, a memorial was presented to him, praying him to obtain for them the medals they felt they had so strong a claim to possess, and also the rank of Commander of the Bath, to which some of the officers conceived themselves entitled. Time, however, only served to render the matter more difficult, and it was never accom-

---

in Egypt to a glorious conclusion; and no thanks were certainly ever better deserved. From my own experience I have never failed seeing that the smallest services rendered by either Navy or Army to the country, have missed being noticed by the Great City of London, with one exception—I mean, my Lord, the glorious second of April, a day when the greatest dangers of navigation were overcome, and the Danish force, which they thought impregnable, totally taken or destroyed by the consummate skill of the Commanders, and by the undaunted bravery of as gallant a band as ever defended the rights of this country. For myself I can assure you that if I was only personally concerned, I should bear the stigma, first placed upon my brow, with humility; but, my Lord, I am the natural guardian of the characters of the officers of the navy, army, and marines who fought and so profusely bled under my command on that day. In no sea action this war has so much British blood flowed for their King and country. Again, my Lord, I beg leave to disclaim for myself more merit than naturally falls to a successful Commander; but when I am called upon to speak of the merits of the Captains of his Majesty's ships, and of the officers and men, whether seamen, marines, or soldiers, I that day had the happiness to command, I say, that never was the glory of this country upheld with more determined bravery than on that occasion, and if I may be allowed to give an opinion as a Legislator, then I say that more important service was never rendered to our King and country. It is my duty, my Lord, to prove to the brave fellows, my companions in dangers, that I have not failed at every proper place, to represent, as well as I am able, their bravery and their services. When I am honoured with your Lordship's answer, I shall communicate it to all the officers and men who served under my command on the 2nd of April last."

plished. The Lord High Admiral would not advise the King at that late period to issue the medals, and although the subject was again revived when William IV. ascended the throne, it was not attended with better success.

In the month of September, 1801, Lord Nelson received from Germany an Order of Knighthood—that of St. Joachim,[1] and he, in October, wrote to Mr. Addington to have his Majesty's opinion relative to accepting or refusing it. The following is the reply of the First Lord of the Treasury to this application, as well as to the Order of the Grand Signior, and to a solicitation to promote his brother in the Church:—

"Downing Street, February 19th, 1802."

"My dear Lord,

"Many considerations combine to make me particularly desirous of giving effect to your wishes in favour of your brother; and I can only repeat that I shall not miss an opportunity of doing so, of which I can avail myself consistently with claims and engagements which leave me no alternative.

"On Wednesday last, I communicated to his Majesty the wish entertained by the Grand Signior that you should wear the Insignia of the Order of the Crescent, and likewise that of the Order of St. Joachim, that you would accept the dignity of Knight Grand Commander thereof; and I have great satisfaction in assuring your Lordship of His Majesty's most gracious and entire acquiescence.

"With true regards,

"I am ever, my dear Lord,

"Your faithful and obedient servant,

"HENRY ADDINGTON."

The question of prize-money for Copenhagen was brought under Nelson's consideration by the following letter:—

---

[1] The letters relating to the Order of St. Joachim will be found in Appendix, No. III.

" Yarmouth, March 31st, 1802.

" My dear Lord,

" I have a letter from Sir Hyde Parker respecting some money which is to be paid on account of the Baltic expedition. He tells me that Lieutenant-Colonel Stewart, with the detachment of troops, was borne as supernumeraries on board the fleet; but, according to the regulation of Prize Laws, to share, they can only share in one class *officers* and *soldiers* together, not being part of the complement of the ship. We will allow being on the expedition joint with the fleet they then can only share if His Majesty should be pleased to direct a proportion agreeable to their different rank; in that case, it cannot affect the Admiral's right. Sir Hyde says, they mean to Memorial the King, and it is become a question whether it would not be better to allow them to share according to their several ranks, as he understands it has been the case, in most of similar kind, instead of keeping back the distribution of £30,000., he says, now in the hands of Mr. Davison, to be paid; there can be no objection, I should suppose; and had there been a Major-General sharing in the different classes, in that case, I rather think the Major-General Commander-in-chief of the army would have shared with the Commanders-in-chief, as at the Texel, and other places, *by the King's order ;* but Sir Hyde tells me, it has been suggested that Lieutenant-Colonel Stewart's proportion should be, with the Junior Flag Officers. We cannot allow, my dear Lord, a Lieutenant-Colonel in the Army to share with us, it never has been, and I hope we shall not be the first to make a precedent; I have no objection to making Colonel Stewart a compliment equal to what you think is right. Sir Thomas Young is with me, and begs me to say, he is ready, as well as myself, to do whatever you think is right.

" I am, my dear Lord,
" Yours faithfully,
" ARCHIBALD DICKSON.[1]

---

[1] Sir Archibald Dickson, Bart. was a brother of Admiral William Dickson. (See Note, Vol. 1. p. 438.) Sir Archibald was made a Post Captain in 1773, a Rear-Admiral in 1794, a Vice-Admiral in 1795, and an Admiral of the Blue Squadron in 1801. His Baronetcy was created July 13, 1802. He died in the early part of the year 1803.

"I long much to see you to ask your advice similar to what you are contending for respecting sharing of prize-money. You would see the opinion I gave to Booth; mine is a strong claim."

Nelson's opinion is given in the following Memorandum, found among Mr. Davison's papers:—

"From the very particular situation in which the Honourable Lieutenant-Colonel Stewart, with the troops under his command, were placed on board the fleet under the command of Sir Hyde Parker, for they certainly did not belong to any of the ships, therefore, they were borne as supernumeraries, and they cannot be considered merely as passengers, therefore, they must, in fairness, be considered as connected with the services of the fleet, and, as the situation is entirely new, and being truly sensible that the Army shared with us the toils and dangers of the expedition, we do, therefore, (as the Proclamation for the distribution of prize-money, nor any joint expedition, is in the smallest degree similar to the present), as a mark of our high sense of the services of the Honourable Colonel Stewart and the Army, agree to give up a proportion of the Admiral's one-eighth of prize-money, so as to make Colonel Stewart's share of prize-money equal to that of a Junior Flag-Officer; and we hereby authorize our Agent, Alexander Davison, Esq., to take from the one-eighth due to the class of Admirals such a sum as will make Colonel Stewart's share equal to a Junior Flag Officer; and we are of opinion, that the Field Officers of the 49th Regiment ought to share with the Captains of the Navy, and the other classes according to their rank with the Navy."[1]

His mind was very actively directed to improvements in the Navy. His observations on the culture of oak in the forest of Dean have been already printed;[2] and a proposal for building superior line-of-battle ships at a small expense to the nation was transmitted for his consideration by Lieutenant Layman.[3]

[1] Dispatches and Letters, Vol. v. p. 22.
[2] From an Autograph in the Sidmouth Papers in the Dispatches and Letters, Vol. v. p. 24.
[3] See Appendix, No. IV.

On the 24th of April, Lord Nelson was made acquainted by his brother-in-law with the serious illness, which terminated in the death of his venerable parent:—

"My dear Lord,

"Your good old father is very ill, and I have directions from Dr. Parry and Mr. Spry to say to you that he is certainly in great danger. Whatever orders you send me shall be executed. Believe me, my dear Lord,

"Yours affectionately,
"G. Matcham.

"April 24th, 1802."

The Rev. Edmund Nelson died at Bath on the 26th of April in the 79th year of his age. Sir Alexander Ball sent the following letter of condolence to Lady Hamilton:—

"Clifford Street, April 30th, 1802.

"My dear Lady Hamilton,

"I most sincerely condole with our dear friend Lord Nelson, on the death of his Father, an event which his mind has been prepared to receive by the advanced age and gradual dissolution of the Doctor.[1] I therefore hope that he will soon recover from the shock which this melancholy separation has occasioned, and I am very glad that he did not go to Bath, as it would have added considerable distress to his afflicted mind without answering any one good purpose. I shall visit Merton early next week; you have, no doubt, great reason at times to feel some of the indignity and contempt of a misanthrope, but a little reflection will make your mind rise superior to such petty neglects and ingratitude. I have to regret that I have never had the power to prove to you and Sir William how very much I feel your kindness and friendship to me on many occasions.

"I called yesterday on Sir Thomas Troubridge, and requested him to move Mr. Rhode to a ship building, and I named the Ocean—which could not be done, as the Admiralty have determined not to appoint Pursers to ships which are upon the stocks. I shall call upon Mr. Rhode to know in what manner I can be useful to him.

---

[1] The Rev. E. Nelson was not a Doctor of Divinity. His degree was that of Master of Arts.

"*Entre nous*, the Cabinet Ministers are of opinion that I am fitted for the station of Minister at Malta. Mr. Cameron is to be provided for, and an offer has been made to me *unsolicited* to go to Malta; but the salary is so inadequate to maintain that appointment, so as to render the services which will be expected of me, that I have refused to accept of it. Lord Hawkesbury has desired to talk to me on the subject early next week, and I am likewise to have a meeting with Lord Hobart. I am determined, however, not to accede to the terms they first proposed. Adieu, my dear sister, be assured of my unalterable regard. My best regards to Lord Nelson and Sir William, and believe me truly, your obliged and devoted,

"ALEXANDER JOHN BALL."

From a variety of letters entering into private matters and family affairs, it appears that the Rev. Edmund Nelson was buried on the 11th of May, at Burnham Thorpe, and that the Rev. William Nelson, D.D. conducted the melancholy duties. Lord Nelson was exceedingly ill at Merton at the time, and in one of the letters, his brother recommends him to consult Mr. Hawkins or Mr. Everard Home, as his case appeared to be a surgical one, and might be serious.

The Reverend Doctor was desirous of the living of Burnham Thorpe, and writes:—

"If Lord Walpole had a proper feeling for the family, or had a pride in the name of Nelson being related to him, he would give it me, and not barter it away to some electioneering purposes. The parishioners say enough about it, if their wishes would do; however, that is kind and flattering on their part, I can't say but the sight of the place brings many pleasant things to remembrance, but then, that is alloyed by the reflection of what I am here for, and perhaps for the *last time*, at least the last time one can call it home."

On the 6th of May the Rev. Dr. Nelson heard of the severe illness of the Dean of Exeter (Dr. Harward), and that he was talked of as his successor. He writes to his brother: "I wish it may be so. If you see Mr. Addington soon, you may offer my vote for the University of Cambridge, for Members of Parliament, and for the county of Norfolk to any candidates he may wish." The Dean died on the 15th of July, and Lord Nelson applied to Mr. Addington, but Dr. Nelson was not appointed. Exeter failing, in a short time he directed his views to Durham, as is shewn by the following letter to Lady Hamilton:—

"Dear Lady Hamilton,

"The Doctor says that he is very angry with you for not calling him *Doctor*, and for degrading the name and dignity; for a Doctor in Divinity of the ancient and learned University of Cambridge, is as much superior to a Doctor of Physic in any of your Scotch Universities (where they confer a diploma for two guineas on every *quack* who applies) as an arch-angel is to the arch-fiend.

"If the old Earl[1] should slip his cable, and be forced to resign, I hope our Great Defender will be able to get into his anchorage. He must try hard to get to windward of the Minister (in spite of the R—l Duke), speak often, and lay his plans accordingly, it will be a nice town house.

"We have sent half-a-dozen apple trees, which we hope will arrive safe at Merton on Thursday; some have been grafted *two*, some *three* years, and some only *last* spring, I would recommend them to be trained as *standards*, and of course not headed down; they don't do so well to be trained as Espaliers, your gardener will understand me. They are the true Norfolk Beefen, such as we have sent in the large hamper. I call them '*Lord Nelson's Norfolk Beefen.*'

"If the *Earl* is only going to the south of France for his health, I am afraid he will not resign, he will have leave of absence for the winter, and the other Lords of the Admiralty will do the business; any *three*, I think, are sufficient. Let us hear every thing that goes on, your letters are better than the newspapers, and we look for them with greater anxiety and receive them with greater pleasure. I see by the papers that there is a stall vacant at Durham, I suppose worth a thousand a year, in the gift of the Bishop (Barrington). I re-

---

[1] St. Vincent.

member some years ago, when the Duke of Portland was Prime Minister, he secured one for Dr. Poyntz, at Durham. There is another vacant at York (if not filled up), in the gift of the Archbishop, but I don't know the value, no very great sum I believe.

"I beg my compliments to Sir William and Mr. Greville when you see him, and love to my brother.

"And believe me,
"Yours very faithfully and affectionately,
"WILLIAM NELSON."

Sir Alexander Ball, who was sent to Malta, wrote Nelson from Portsmouth.

"Portsmouth, 14th June, 1802.

"My dear Lord,

"I regret extremely that I had it not in my power to pay your Lordship another visit before I left town. I had the pleasure of seeing Sir William Hamilton, who informed me of your having discovered the cause of your stomach and bowel complaint, which being removed, I hope to hear of your Lordship soon enjoying the most perfect health. When I was at Malta I was often much indisposed, and could not find the cause until I met with a medical book of Dr. Townsend, and found out my case so minutely described, that I immediately proved it to be a worm case, and soon recovered better health. I had before this read Buchan and many other medical books, without fancying any of the numerous complaints so fully detailed. The Penelope is having her people paid to-day, and we are to sail this evening. I shall write to your Lordship from Malta, and give every information I can collect of Bronté. I write this in great haste, and have only time to offer my sincere wishes to your Lordship and kind compliments to Sir William Hamilton, with my love to my dear *sister Emma.*

"Ever your Lordship's obliged and devoted,
"ALEXANDER JOHN BALL."

In the month of June, Lord Nelson resumed his correspondence with the Lord Mayor, upon observing a notice of motion in the Court of Common Council to vote **Thanks** to him for his conduct in taking the command of a force destined to prevent any designs the French might have of approaching the City of London. He entreated that such notice might be withdrawn, as the Battle of Copenhagen had not been approved by the City of London in the way they were in the habit of doing, and stated that he should feel mortified to receive their proposed Thanks for a service so inferior in its nature to that which remained unrecognized by them. In September he declined dining with the Lord Mayor, but offered to be his private guest on any day he would name after his Mayoralty, but not in his public capacity, as he had determined that until the City of London thought justly of his brave companions in arms on the 2nd of April, 1801, he as their Commander could not receive any attentions from the City of London. The following is printed from a rough draft among the Nelson Papers:—

"My Lord,

"A few days past, I saw in the newspapers a Motion had been made in a Court of Common Council to thank me for my conduct in taking the command of a force destined to prevent any designs our enemies might have of approaching the City of London; but which question stands over for some future Court. I have therefore, my Lord, to entreat that you will use your influence that no such question may be brought forward.

"There is not, my Lord, one individual in the world who appreciates the honour of having their conduct applauded by the City of London, higher than myself. I was desired, my Lord, to take the command in question when in a very indifferent state of health, as I was flattered with the opinion it would keep quiet the minds of all in London, and on and between the coast of Beachy Head and Orfordness. This would have been a sufficient reason for me to have laid down my life, much less suffering from ill health; and my Lord, his Majesty's Government gave me such a powerful force, that the gallant officers and men I had the honour to command almost regretted that the enemy did not make the attempt of invasion. Therefore, my Lord, you see I have no merit, I only did my duty with alacrity, which I shall always be ready to do when directed. But, my Lord, if any other reason was wanting to prevent the City of London from thanking me for only shewing an anxiety to step forth in time of danger, it is this:—that not four months before, I had the happiness of witnessing, under all its circumstances, the most hard fought battle and the most complete victory, as far as my reading goes, that ever was fought and obtained by the navy of this country—a battle in which the honour of the British flag was supported, and the just rights of our country defended. This battle had not, my Lord, the honour of being approved in the way in which the City of London has usually marked their approbation: therefore may I entreat that you will use your influence that no vote of approbation may be ever given to me for any services since the 2nd of April, for I should feel, when I reflected on the noble support I received that day from Sir Thomas Graves, the Captains, Officers, Seamen, Marines and Soldiers I had the honour to command, much mortified at any intended honour which would separate me from them, for whatever my demerits may be, I am bold to say they deserve every honour and favour which a grateful country can bestow. I entreat your Lordship's indulgence for thus expressing my feelings, and again request that the intended motion of Thanks may not be brought forward. I trust your Lordship will give me full credit for the high estimation in which I hold the City of London, and with what respect I am,

"Yours, &c. &c."

In 1801 it will be recollected Lord Nelson made application to the Lord Chancellor to promote the Rev. Mr. Comyn, Lord Nelson's Chaplain on board the Vanguard at the Battle of the Nile, and one of his Domestic Chaplains. From an autograph in the possession of Robert Cole, Esq., it appears that so far back as August 4th, 1799, when on board the Foudroyant in Naples Bay, Lord Nelson drank at supper to Mr. Comyn, with his good wishes for a good living. Lady Hamilton promised to write to Lord Loughborough, the Chancellor, and this letter was signed by Lord Nelson and Sir William Hamilton, to the latter of whom Lord Loughborough was well known. Lord Eldon's reply to the renewed application will be seen (page 180), and the following letter will shew the recollection he bore of the solicitation:—

"June 23rd, 1802.

"My Lord,

"I received the honour of your Lordship's letter, and I presume that the living which you state to be vacant is Bridgham, though your Lordship has not named it. Upon that supposition I state to your Lordship that I formerly refused to promise it, because I hold it contrary to my duty, to my station and my successors to make promises, which, as I may not be in office when they may require it to be made good, I may be unable to perform. This living I could certainly make use of to gratify strong personal wishes of my own, founded on strong claims which individuals have upon me to be attentive to their welfare. But I don't hesitate a moment to assure your Lordship, that I think public duty calls upon me to make use of the opportunity which public situation gives me, to accede to the wishes of a person to whom the country is so largely indebted as to your Lordship, and I shall give orders to my Secretary to prepare the necessary papers for presenting your friend to Bridgham. I am, with all possible respect,

"Your obedient humble servant,
"ELDON."

Lord Nelson, upon the receipt of this, sent an express off to the Rev. Mr. Comyn, with information of his appointment.

From General Walterstorff Lord Nelson received the following:—

"St. Croix, 30th June, 1802.

"My dear Lord

"I have had the happiness of receiving your Lordship's letter in answer to mine from Madeira, and you do me justice in thinking that the attachment I profess for you is as unalterable as it is sincere. I hope your Lordship has received a small box with liqueurs, which I did myself the honour of sending you from Martinique, per the ship the Union. But where this letter shall find you I really do not know. About three months ago, we expected your Lordship in the West Indies, and I was thinking of going to Martinique to pay you my respects there. The newspapers have since mentioned your having been appointed Commander-in-chief in the Mediterranean, I have not been able to find out if it be true or not; at all events I direct this letter to be left at the house of Sir William Hamilton.

"I have now finally settled my business with Mr. Swinburne, and have found that gentleman exactly as Lady Hamilton described him to me. We have, upon the whole, agreed very well, and have parted upon the most friendly terms. Only few claims have been referred to Ministerial discussion and decision, and the number of them should have been still less had not Mr. Swinburne sometimes suffered himself to be influenced by those whose interest it evidently was to defend, or to draw a veil over those numerous irregularities which have been committed here. Mr. Swinburne is certainly a good and very honest man, but sometimes rather weak.

"I long extremely, my dear Lord, to hear how your health has been this spring; I hope you have followed the advice and prescriptions of your friends, and exposed yourself as little as possible to cold and moist weather. But were it not that the public ought sometimes to be gratified with the sight of those who have been the saviours of their country, and that the presence of Lord Nelson must give an additional lustre to any festivity, I should have found fault with your Lordship's going to the Lord Mayor's feast. I am afraid that the French West India islands are as yet far from having their tranquillity secured; I cannot approve of the plan adopted by the Commander-in-chief at St. Domingo, and still less the measures adopted at Guadaloupe, where the new Government already finds itself too weak. The negroes at Martinico are ripe for an insurrection. General Rochambeau is the man who ought to have been sent to that island.

"It will hardly be in my power to leave the West Indies before the month of April next, but I anticipate already the agreeable moment when I shall again take your Lordship by the hand, and when I shall have the happiness of spending some days at Merton, where I hope to renew my respects to

Sir William and Lady Hamilton. I am, with the sincerest sentiments,

"My Lord,
"Your Lordship's
"Faithful, obedient and obliged servant,
"ERNEST FREDERICK WALTERSTORFF."

The Rev. Dr. Nelson went to Cambridge on occasion of an election of Members for the University. He thus writes to Lady Hamilton:—

"Christ Coll. July 6th, 1802.

"My dear Lady,
"Dr. Fisher is very much flattered by your kind and friendly expressions towards him, and desires his best respects. The election for the University took place yesterday, the whole was over in five minutes. Mr. Pitt and Lord Euston are re-elected. I had a bow this morning from Billy in the Senate House, so I made up to him, and said a word or two to him. I purpose leaving this place to-morrow morning, but I don't think I can possibly be at Merton before 5 o'clock, so don't wait for me, for if I could get there sooner I should not like the trouble of dressing and going out to dinner immediately; no doubt I shall find enough to dine upon at home; a beef-steak, or any thing will do for me. I am glad you think the jewel so well. Make my love to my brother, &c. &c. and believe me your most faithful, obliged, and affectionate friend,

"WILLIAM NELSON.

"P. S. The bells are now ringing for the re-election of the members for the *Town* of *Cambridge*."

Lord Nelson made a tour into Wales in the months of July and August, and was every where received with the liveliest joy and satisfaction.

The principal object of this tour was to view Milford Haven, and examine the improvements made by Mr. C. F. Greville upon his uncle's estate, under the powers of an Act of Parliament passed in 1790. Besides Lord Nelson, Sir William and Lady Hamilton, there were the Rev. Dr. Nelson, Mrs.

Nelson and their son. At Oxford they were joined by Mrs. Matcham, Lord Nelson's sister, her husband and son. Lord Nelson was presented with the Freedom of the City in a gold box, and the University conferred upon him the degree of Doctor of Laws, and also upon Sir William Hamilton. Lord Nelson's brother being already a Doctor of Divinity of Cambridge University, was admitted *ad eundem*—thus they were all complimented on this occasion. The party visited Blenheim; but were annoyed at not being received by the Duke of Marlborough, who was there at the time. Refreshments were sent to them, but were declined. This apparent neglect of civility and attention due to so distinguished a naval warrior, from the descendant of so renowned a military chief was attempted to be explained by the absence of the usual ceremonials of introductory etiquette, which the Duke's shy and retiring habits prevented him from putting aside on the occasion.

At Gloucester the bells were rung upon their arrival, the cathedral and other objects of interest were visited, and here separating from the Matchams, who left for Bath, Lord Nelson, Sir William and Lady Hamilton proceeded to Ross. Preferring the passage to Monmouth by the River Wye to that by land, a vast concourse of people attended them in boats, that which Nelson occupied being tastefully decorated with laurels. The shore was lined with spectators, guns fired, and other demonstrations of delight manifested. Nelson was made a Burgess of the Borough, and escorted into the town by the bands of the Monmouth and Brecon militia, playing "God save the King," and "Rule Britannia." Nelson visited his old friend Admiral Gell. At Brecon he was warmly greeted by the farmers, and at Milford, where preparations had been made, the reception was most enthusiastic. Here Sir William Hamilton visited his tenants, from whom he had been absent many years. The first of August was of course selected as a grand fête day; all the nobility and gentry round had been invited by Mr. Greville to do honour to Nelson, and to commemorate this visit and the victory of the Nile. An annual rowing match, fair day, and exhibition of cattle were established. At the dinner Lord Nelson was peculiarly happy, and delighted every one with the judicious observations he made upon the harbour at Milford, which with that at Trincomalee, he observed, were the two finest he had ever beheld.

Lord Nelson put up at the New Hotel during his stay in this place, and Sir William Hamilton left a fine whole length picture of his Lordship, which had been painted in 1799 by Leonardo Guzzardi of Palermo, to be preserved there for the gratification of the visitors. This portrait has been recently purchased by the Lords of the Admiralty, and now hangs up in the Council Room at the Admiralty, facing that of his late Majesty William IV.[1]

Lord Nelson visited Lord Cawdor, Lord Milford, Lord Kensington, Mr. Foley, the brother of his friend Captain Foley, and many others. At Haverfordwest he was drawn through the streets by the populace, and at Swansea he received the same attention from a body of exulting tars. Lord Nelson and Sir William Hamilton received the Freedom of this place. Returning to Monmouth he dined with the Mayor and Corporation, according to a promise he had made; thence he proceeded to Ross, where a triumphal arch had been erected for the hero to pass through, after which he went to Hereford, and received the Freedom of that city inclosed in a box, cut from the wood of the apple tree, the pride of that county. Nelson viewed the cathedral, and afterwards paid a visit to the Bishop, who was confined by illness to his room. He then departed for Downton Castle, near Ludlow, the seat of Richard Payne Knight, Esq. where he was received by similar marks of regard, and had conferred upon him the Freedom of the Borough of Ludlow. Thence he proceeded to Worcester, where he partook of a collation prepared by the Corporation, and was admitted a freeman of the city. He visited the China manufactory of Messrs. Chamberlain, the cathedral, &c. and then left for Birmingham, arriving there two hours before the time he was expected, to avoid tumult in so populous a place. He examined the principal manufactories of this town, saw medals struck to commemorate his visit, attended the theatre, where he was

---

[1] I have thankfully to acknowledge the kindness of their Lordsh'ps in granting me permission to engrave this portrait for the present biography of the celebrated Admiral.

received with the most heartfelt pride, and after the performance escorted to his hotel by an immense throng carrying hundreds of lighted torches. At Warwick and at Coventry similar honours awaited him. He then paid a visit to the Earl Spencer at Althorp, and returned to Merton on the 5th of September. The excitement attendant upon this journey tended to the perfect restoration of his health, and he could not fail to have been exquisitely delighted by the grateful and affectionate manner in which he had been every where received by all classes of society.

During his tour he made many inquiries respecting the growth of oak timber, and recorded notes upon the subject.

By the following letter Lord Nelson learnt of the death of his steward at Bronté.

"Naples, 21st August, 1802.

"My Lord,

"I take the liberty of accompanying a letter from Mrs. Græffer, which I am sorry to say conveys your Lordship the sorrowful tidings of the sudden death of poor Græffer. From my own feelings for the loss of so worthy a character, I can judge what distress it must give your Lordship, and more particularly Mrs. Græffer on so trying an occasion; but I have endeavoured to console her, and hope that as we must all be deprived of our nearest and best comforts, she will bear her loss with fortitude and resignation. Mrs. Græffer entreated I would apply to General Acton and press him to allow her to continue the administration of the estate until your Lordship's answer, but the General told me this afternoon that a proper person had been already named at the request of Cavalier Forcella, as a necessary step that your Lordship's interest might not be prejudiced, and which the General seemed to have much at heart. I presume Cavalier Forcella will have written to your Lordship every circumstance that has occurred. If it should be your Lordship's intention to send out a farmer from England, he must take with him all the implements he may want, as the former ones sent out were mostly lost or spoilt.

"The Revolutionary principles in Italy are nearly the same; no social order or steadiness in the Government are re-established, and consequently there can be no security given to individuals, which prevents many commercial people from fixing their residence in Italy. General Doyle is here, and General Fox is hourly expected—they have no orders as yet for evacuating Malta. The Queen returned here last Tuesday, and will shortly accompany the Prince and Princess to Barcelona; it is considered it would not be prudent for the King to quit the capital.

"Permit me to request your Lordship to present my best respects to Sir William and Lady Hamilton, and to Mrs. Cadogan, and I have the honour to be,
"My Lord,
"Your Lordship's most obedient and
"Most humble servant,
"ABRAHAM GIBBS.

"The Stately and Hydra are here, and the Medusa is at Civita Vecchia. The Greyhound, Captain Hoste, is going to the Levant. General Acton considers that nothing is forthcoming to the British officers for the reduction of Civita Vecchia and Rome, since those places have been given up again."

Lord Nelson wrote to Mr. Davison on the subject: "*How short-sighted we are!* I have lost Mr. Græffer, my Governor of Bronté: he died August 7. It embarrasses me a little, but I endeavour to make the best of things, and it may possibly turn out to my pecuniary advantage. I have his full account of my estate; rather more than £3000. a year nett, and increasing every year in value. General Acton has taken possession of every thing for me, and is behaving very friendly."[1]

From an old schoolfellow Lord Nelson received the following curious epistle:—

"My Lord,
"Dean Swift closes, or terminates, a letter to the great Earl of Peterborough, by telling that nobleman—'That he should be happy to have it in his power to shew one of his

---

[1] Dispatches and Letters, Vol. v. p. 30.

Lordship's to his Parishioners.' You, my Lord, have not suffered me to languish respecting *that point*. For these some months past I have had it in mind to shew to my acquaintance and friends a letter from you, and thereby to convince them I had once the pleasure of being your schoolfellow, and have now the honour to be considered by you as a friend. In truth, my Lord, we never were otherwise, though not intimate.

"Your Lordship, though in the second class, when I was in the first, was five years my junior, or four at least, and at that period of life such a difference, in point of age, is considerable. I well remember where you sat in the school-room. Your station was against the wall, between the parlour door and the chimney: the latter to your right. From 1769 to 1771 we were opposites. Nor do I forget that we were under the lash of Classic Jones, as arrant a Welshman as Rees-ap-Griffith, and as keen a flogger as merciless Busby, of birch-loving memory! Happy am I indeed, my Lord, to find, by your very kind letter, that *Hæc meminisse juvat!* According to an old sentimental toast, we imprecate the meeting an 'old friend with a new face:' consequently, how very pleasing it is to find *that* not to be the case, respecting an old schoolfellow! As a philosopher, I observe, my Lord, with great satisfaction, that your honours have not changed you. Reasonable men always behold those things through the proper medium. Titles and Peerages may honour Lord Barrington, or Lord Carrington, or Lord Lavington, or Lord Borringdon: Lord Nelson confers honour upon them by his acceptance. *I* regard my old schoolfellow as the saviour and deliverer of Europe in general, and of his country in particular: and in my eyes, those titles are superior to all others. Nevertheless, far be it from me to despise honours. That I never do, nor those who bestow them. But I often do those upon whom they are bestowed. Animated by these principles, and considering your Lordship as the hero of this age, I particularly suggested to my friend, the Baron d'Ednor, the idea of the Chapteral Order of Saint Joachim's requesting you to accept the dignity of Knight Grand Commander of that Order, according to a particular clause in the statutes of that body. This I mention without pretending to arrogate any merit to myself, since my advising such a measure could not have had any effect, unless the whole Chapter was unanimous. It was I likewise who advised M. Rühl, the Chancelist of that Order, to dedicate his learned history of all the Existing Orders of Knighthood to your Lordship, and procured him the assistance of one or two learned men, to facilitate the completion of that ingenious work, upon which he has bestowed indefatigable perseverance. In my last letter I observed to your Lordship, that like the Senator, who boasted that he possessed the Curule chair, on which Cæsar, the Dictator, sat when he was assassinated, and was married to Terentia, the widow of Cicero; so would it ever be my boast—that I was two years your schoolfellow; and so long the fellow student at the University with Mr. Pitt: I now, my Lord, beg leave to add, that were I ambitious of monumental fame, these two circumstances should form parts of my epitaph; but I should only imitate Sir Fulke Greville, (first Lord Brooke of Beauchamps Court, and a collateral ancestor of Sir William Hamilton's nephew, the present Earl of Warwick), whose epitaph is as follows:—

> ' Fulke Greville,
> Servant to Queen Elizabeth,
> Councellor to King James,
> And friend to Sir Philip Sidney,
> Trophœum Peccati.'

"I wish, my Lord, as well as this epitaph, I could send you the Dictator's curule chair, and a joint of the little finger of the Centagenary Terentia. What a treat it would be to Sir William Hamilton!!! I am sure he would prefer the chair to those of the Speakers of both Houses; and the tip of Terentia's little finger to that of any one woman, save Lady Hamilton! Respecting Mr. Rühl's work, I trust, my Lord, you will patronise it amongst your friends and acquaintance; since it is certain we have not so complete a compendium, on that subject, in our language. I think his accounts of the Orders of Saint Joachim, the Crescent, the Bath, and Saint Ferdinand are drawn up—*de main de maître* as old *Jemmy Moisson*, the French master at N. Walsham school, used to express himself. Pray, my Lord, are we to have a commercial treaty with the French or not? If we are, I wish your Lordship could procure me a place of Consul in some one of the ports of the *Republic*. I am sure, if you would ask for it, it would not be refused you. With the topography of the French nation, its resources, manufactures, commerce, exports and imports, I am perfectly well acquainted; having lived ten years, and upwards, in that country. As to the language, I know it as well as my own. Of the Italian and German I have a competent knowledge. With Mortimer's *Lex Mercatoria* I should be able to make my way. It is not that I want this to *live*. Thank God, no—but it would be some employment for me; and no bad thing when joined to *Captain's pay!* I could bear being under an obligation to you, my Lord, whom I venerate beyond expression: but I should be sorry to be so to many, and many of those whose names enjoy a *niche* in the red book. If you and Sir William Hamilton could compass this, I could manage to pay the official fees, and you would enable me to bless you every day for the additional comforts of life you procured me. Excuse my taking the liberty of inclosing to you this letter for Sir William Hamilton, and believe me with every kind wish for your health and felicity,

"My Lord,
"Your much obliged old friend,
"Levett Hanson.

"P. S. I suppose, my Lord, it is not necessary for me to observe to your Lordship, that twenty-five guineas are the usual *douceur* which is bestowed upon any one for a dedication when it is accepted: and as this honest man Rühl has nothing save a place of eighty pounds a year, and official fees; I think therefore, that in case you doubled that sum, (as he was charged with the whole of the correspondential business relative to your Lordship's promotion), that you will do no more than is proper. In case you think fit, my Lord, to make him this compliment, I will pay him that sum in your name, and will, when you permit me so to do, draw upon you for the same through the channel of Messrs. Hammersleys and Co. my Bankers, and will finally send you Mr. Rühl's receipt as my voucher. Since the month of June I have been at Hambro' to see several old acquaintances. You may, my Lord, send your answer under cover, or for me at Messrs. Thornton and Power's, who are my friends and bankers, as they are, I find, of all English travellers. Ever yours! I shall not fail to drink your Lordship's health to-day, nor so long as we live, to celebrate that and the Anniversaries of Aboukir and Copenhagen.

"Hamburgh, September 29th, 1802."

Mr. J. Hiley Addington of the Treasury alludes to the hearty reception given to Lord Nelson in his Welsh tour:—

"Langford Court, October 4th, 1802.

" My dear Lord,

" I was honoured with your letter just as I was stepping into my carriage on Friday morning, to wing my flight westward. You may be perfectly assured that I will do every thing in my power to give effect to your wishes in favour of Mr. Brent, as I am certain that my brother will be well disposed to do; and trust that it will not be long before some means may present themselves.

" It was matter of real regret to me that I had not the good fortune to be at home when you were so good as to call in Great George Street, when I should have been glad to have talked over with you your Welsh tour. We almost trod upon your heels. I heard with infinite satisfaction your reception in every part of the principality, which was highly creditable to the honest Cambrians, who know how to appreciate eminent services and superlative merit.

" With the most cordial esteem and respect,
" I am ever, my dear Lord,
" Yours very faithfully,
" J. HILEY ADDINGTON."

The Hon. Colonel Stewart had been unsuccessful in an attempt to get into Parliament. Lord Nelson had written to him on the occasion, and the following was the reply:—

" Shorne Cliffe Barracks, Sandgate,
October 10th, 1802.

" My dear Lord,

" I have the honour of having now at my elbow your Lordship's two letters of the 27th and 28th of last month, and should apologize for not having earlier answered the application in favour of Mr. Porter, did I not conceive that the last ten days' mode of occupation, marching, preparing my regiment for a march, and arranging it in very uncomfortable cantonments, will in some measure plead my excuse. Having earnestly solicited a removal of my young regiment from the iniquity of Chatham, we have been ordered into these barracks, and into the three forts which are in front of Hythe, and shall probably be stationed here for the ensuing winter, the country is excellent for the movement of Chasseurs, and the neighbourhood seems tranquil and good; very ill equipped barracks, and much dispersion of my corps is my only complaint, but as a soldier and a man I, as well as my neighbours, find the world much composed of contrarieties, ' *Et qu'il n'y a point de roses sans leurs épines.*'

"Your Lordship's letter of the 28th September contains many sentiments of kindness towards me, and my private concerns of a political nature, which I must ever feel grateful for; on the subject of my late unsuccessful canvas in Scotland, you are pleased to express yourself with a degree of interest which no merits of mine have called for, and the whole history of Parliamentary representation, (as it is carried on at least in that part of our island) has moreover blunted all my feelings so much, that I am not worthy to have an interest felt for me, whilst I am totally careless of the matter myself; for the six years that I represented the County of Wigton, I did my best to deserve well of it; it was apparently thought otherwise, and feeling tranquil in my own conscience upon the occasion, the present choice of that shire meets with my quiet acquiescence. I shall not be apt to try the seat again, feeling as I now do; but enough, my dear Lord, of personal concerns. Mr. Porter shall, upon the strength of your Lordship's recommendation, have my support and voice at the Magdalen. I have written to this purport to the clergyman of the Institution, Mr. Prince, who will inform me if any forms but that of my epistolary promise be necessary. I should like, if a leisure half hour bring the recollection of what I might like into your Lordship's memory; I should like, I was observing, to have your opinion upon the probable chance of long tranquillity to us all in this country, from the other side of the Channel.

"Some things which were in yesterday's newspaper, and the view of the Boulogne shore from my barrack window have together united, to make me think more than usual of this possibility, and when I have before me the spot where, little more than one twelvemonth ago, nearly the last gallant effort of our country was made under your guidance, and poor Parker fell, the thoughts of renewed hostilities run much in my mind. Heaven grant that there may be no necessity for such an event; but may Heaven also grant that we may not be so wanting in spirit as to await provocations and encroachments too long!

"Adieu, my dear Lord. May I request that my respects may be made to Sir William and Lady Hamilton, and that I may ever sign myself, with the greatest truth,

"Your Lordship's very faithful friend,
"And very humble servant,
"WM. STEWART.

"I hear nothing from our Agent about the Baltic prize-money being arranged."

From Jamaica, Lord Nelson received the following:—

"Kingston, Jamaica, Oct. 15th, 1802.

"My dear Lord,

"I am favoured with your Lordship's kind letter to me of 12th of July, informing me your Lordship had seen Mr. Pedly, who had informed your Lordship that I was still alive. I am also very happy to congratulate your Lordship that you are alive too, after the great number of perils, dangers, and battles, your Lordship has been engaged in, and I most sincerely hope and wish that your Lordship will live many, many more years to enjoy the honour your Lordship has so gloriously earned, and to experience the gratitude your Lordship is so well entitled to from a nation to whom your Lordship has been so great a bulwark and support. I am much afraid, and indeed know, that we unhappy Colonists will want the aid and assistance of any friend we have in the new Parliament, for Mr. Addington's speech on the 27th of May, seems to prognosticate to us nothing but evil; indeed, if there is not a totally new system adopted towards the Colonies to what has been followed and carried out for these many years past, they will become altogether useless to Britain, as they must be abandoned by the white inhabitants, for it will be impossible to carry on the culture of them, from the numberless impediments that are thrown in their way. Myself, and our whole country, must consider ourselves under the highest obligations to your Lordship for your intended support of us in the arduous trial that we expect will come on in the next Session of Parliament, and consider it will decide whether in future Britain shall have West India Colonies, or not, or whether eighty millions sterling, and the lives of all the white people in them are to be sacrificed or not. Ministers, before they are in too great a hurry, should contemplate the scene that St. Domingo just now presents. The first Colony that ever was in the world, covered with the vestiges of houses, and works burnt, and bushes growing where the most fertile crops were raised. Forty millions of property annihilated, 200,000 Negroes and Mulattoes, as well as 30,000 white people butchered, massacred, and murdered, in consequence of the dream of Liberty having been promulgated among them under the pretence of humanity. Of 25,000 military that have been sent there from Europe since the Peace, not 3000 alive. Those that are arriving are melting off as ice in a hot sun, and it will require 100,000 more troops to settle tranquillity in this island, and from eighty to one hundred millions sterling money to put it into the state it was in in 1787, and 700,000 Negroes to be imported from Africa. There is not a proprietor on the north side of the island that is restored to, or in the possession of, his former property, or who dares to go out to look at it. Four gallows were erected in each of the towns of that island, on which every Negro is hung without the least ceremony, or question asked, who is found in the streets after dusk, and it will be an utter impossibility ever to settle that island or Guadaloupe again so as to become useful Colonies to France, or any other European nation, until the whole present breed of Negroes on them is totally extirpated.

With all these matters staring him in his face, a British Minister is still paying attention to those men who have been by their writings, and going to France, encouraging the visionaries there to effect these things in their Colonies, and who are now endeavouring to scatter the same through the British ones, and who have as far blinded him as to keep still regimented and armed black troops in the islands, who will not fail, whenever opportunity offers, to aid and assist those of their colour to act the same part in our islands as has been done in St. Domingo and Guadaloupe, and they cannot plead ignorance, after what has happened at Dominica, where they murdered their white officers. I have thoughts, and do intend to go to England in the spring, and your Lordship may be assured that I shall do myself the honour to pay my respects to your Lordship wherever you are, and to return my grateful thanks for your Lordship's good intentions and wishes towards me and my native country, and I have the honour to be, with the greatest respect,

" My dear Lord,
" Your Lordship's most obedient humble servant,
"SIMON TAYLOR."

From Malta, Sir Alexander Ball wrote to Lady Hamilton :—

"Malta, 8th November, 1802.

" My dear sister Hamilton,

"I participated in the gratifying scene you and your good Sir William witnessed in the national testimonies of gratitude which our brave and good Nelson received in his journey to Wales. I desired all the paragraphs in the newspapers which mentioned it, to be marked for my perusal. I think his Lordship and Sir William must have been almost overpowered by such a load of caresses and kindness, and would feel relieved at the sight of Merton and the prospect of repose; as for your Ladyship, I believe you could *hip, hip, hip,* your Nelson when every other power was exhausted. I have introduced your relation to my son, who has carried him about the country, and delighted him much. Captain Capel is very kind to all his young gentlemen, and attends particularly to their improvement. I am glad to hear the Tysons are well, have the goodness to tell honest John that I have written to the Treasury, and represented his losses by undertaking the commission of purchasing corn for the Island of Malta. I shall write to him soon. Miss Charlotte Nelson, I dare say, is fully sensible of the great and very rare advantages she has in the tuition of so accomplished a patroness. Pray give me all the traits you know of the Prince of Pantelaria, who is the Neapolitan Minister here; he has a difficult task; he is afraid of offending the French Minister, and it is to be apprehended that this passion will operate more powerfully than love for the English—time will prove this.

"The Deputies often talk of the kind attention and hospitality with which they were honoured by your Ladyship, Sir William, and Lord Nelson. Our business here is a jumble, and it is difficult to say what will be finally arranged.

"Adieu, my dear sister, present my best respects to good Sir William, and believe me ever

"Your obliged brother and friend,
"ALEXANDER JOHN BALL."

Lord Nelson was anxious to have something done for his eye, as appears from the following letter to his Physician, Dr. Benjamin Moseley:—

"Merton, October 26th, 1802.

"My dear Sir,

"I shall be in town in a few days, and will endeavour to see you. I agree with you, that (if the operation is necessary) the sooner it is done the better; the probable risk is for your consideration; I cannot spare very well another eye.

"Ever yours, faithfully,
"NELSON AND BRONTÉ."

"To Dr. Moseley."

The military successes on land by France, and the naval glory of England established by her victories at sea, had rendered the contending nations unable to prosecute further the war with vigour. The French navy was not only reduced in number, but its spirit was completely disheartened. The force of the British navy had been augmented by captures and newly built vessels of war to a considerable extent. It is stated that at the time of the Peace of Amiens, we had nearly 800 war vessels of one description or other, ready to be arranged against an enemy. Two hundred and ninety-eight French vessels had been taken, and fifty-five ships destroyed. James, in his Naval History records, that in 1796, eighty-two ships were added to the British Navy, and in 1798, sixty-three; the former measuring 64,847 tons, and the latter 30,910. To the prizes obtained from the French, the Spanish and Dutch forces, taken and destroyed, are to be enumerated; and the loss sustained by the Danes in the attack on Copenhagen is also to be considered. Whilst the British navy held itself to be invincible by sea, France regarded herself as unconquerable by land; the former triumph had been achieved principally by the genius and valour of Nelson, the latter by the sagacity and vigour of Buonaparte.

The object of France in obtaining a recognition of the Republic on the part of England, the last of the powers to do so, was accomplished by the Peace of Amiens, which was entered into on the one side by that of his Majesty the King of Great Britain and Ireland, and on the other, by that of the French Republic, the King of Spain and the Indies, and the Batavian Republic. The preliminaries were agreed upon October 1, 1801, but the Treaty was not signed until March 27, 1802. There were but few sanguine enough to regard the Peace of Amiens as likely to enjoy any permanence, for even whilst the negotiations for the definitive treaty were in progress, a French fleet, with a large armament, departed from Brest to San Domingo, to recover that place from the revolted, or the free and independent negroes. This measure, which compelled England to maintain a force of thirty-five sail of the line in the West Indies, so directly undertaken, naturally excited distrust, and the naval and military forces of Great Britain were directed to remain unreduced for three months. Buonaparte's views with regard to Italy, as shewn in his transactions with the Cisalpine Republic at Lyons, increased the suspicions already entertained, and Mr. Addington obtained the sanction of the

House of Commons on the 3rd of March to a supply on the war establishment for sixty-one days more.

When the French landed under General Le Clerc at St. Domingo, they found every negro in the island hostile to them; which, added to the destructive nature of the climate, rendered the warfare one of the most perilous description. Early successes had given to the French a dangerous confidence, inspiring hopes of conquest that never were to be realized, and although Toussaint L'Ouverture, a black slave of considerable ability, and the leader of his race, decoyed by false promises of amnesty, honours, and the viceroyalty of the island was entrapped and sent a prisoner to France, loaded with chains, and confined in a loathsome dungeon, the opposition rendered by Henri Cristophe and others, supported by the bravery and revengeful feelings of the negroes, and above all, the mortality among the French troops from the yellow fever, proved so destructive, that the army was reduced down to a few hundreds. Under General Rochambeau, however, Le Clerc having fallen a victim to the fever, a reinforcement of 15,000 men arrived, but they fared little better than those by whom they had been preceded, and the war recommencing between France and England, neither more troops nor ships could be afforded to follow up so hazardous an enterprise. A capitulation was therefore entered into; Cape Français was evacuated, and the French under Rochambeau, together with a number of white families, who left the island fearing the revenge of the black population, departed. The fleet or convoy, together with the remaining troops, &c. fell into the power of the English, being captured by the British squadrons; Rochambeau was brought a prisoner to England, and not less than 8000 Frenchmen are reported to have been taken on this occasion.

The Irish exiles in France were at this time carrying on an active correspondence with their countrymen, and endeavouring to provoke insurrection and civil war. At Paris this movement was warmly cherished, and the exiles had pledged themselves to its success if provided with money, arms, artillery, and troops. The shores of England were also threatened with invasion, and Buonaparte, although fully alive to the difficulties and the chances against his success, yet in his interview with the British Minister, Lord Whitworth, did not hesitate to declare his determination to attempt it, should the war be renewed. This threat, however, failed to disturb the equanimity of our Ambassador. Buonaparte collected all the fugitive or disaffected Irish on the Continent, embodied them in what was called the Irish Legion, and contemplated effecting a universal civil war.

The speech from the Throne delivered November 16, 1802, clearly intimated the probability of a renewal of hostilities. His Majesty said: " In my intercourse with foreign powers I have been actuated by a sincere disposition for the maintenance of peace. It is nevertheless impossible for me to lose sight of that established and wise system of policy, by which the interests of other States are connected with our own; and I cannot therefore be indifferent to any material change in their relative condition and strength. My conduct will be invariably regulated by a due consideration of the actual situation of Europe, and by a watchful solicitude for the permanent welfare of my people. You will, I am persuaded, agree with me in thinking, that it is incumbent upon us to adopt those means of security which are best calculated to afford the prospect of preserving to my subjects the blessings of peace."

Lord Nelson seconded the address, moved in the House of Lords by Lord Arden, on the 23rd of November, and in doing so, emphatically declared, " I, my Lords, have in different countries, seen much of the miseries of war. I am, therefore, in my inmost soul, a man of peace. Yet I would not, for the sake of any peace, however fortunate, consent to sacrifice one jot of England's honour. Our honour is inseparably combined with our genuine interest. Hitherto there has been nothing greater known on the Continent than the faith, the untainted honour, the generous public sympathies, the high diplomatic influence, the commerce, the grandeur, the resistless power, the unconquerable valour of the British nation. Wherever I have served in foreign countries, I have witnessed these to be sentiments with which Britons were regarded. The advantages of such a reputation are not to be lightly brought into hazard. I, for one, rejoice that his Majesty has signified his intention to pay due regard to the connection between the interests of this country and the preservation of the liberties of Europe. It is satisfactory to know, that the preparations to maintain our dignity in peace, are not to be neglected. Those supplies which his Majesty shall for such purposes demand, his people will most earnestly grant. The nation is satisfied that the Government seeks in peace or war no interest separate from that of the people at large; and as the nation was pleased with that sincere spirit of peace with which the late treaty was negotiated, so, now that a restless and unjust ambition in those with whom we desired sincere amity has given a new alarm, the country will rather prompt the Government to assert its honour, than need to be roused to such measures of vigorous defence as the exigency of the times may require."

On a motion for the Army Estimates, the House of Commons readily acceded to the proposal of the Secretary of War, Mr. Charles Yorke, and in the course of the debate on this occasion, Mr. Sheridan observed that "the ambition of the ruler of France must now be principally directed against this country. Prussia was at his beck, Italy his vassal, Spain at his nod, Portugal at his foot, Holland in his grasp, and Turkey in his toils. What object then remained for his devouring ambition greater than, or equal to the conquest or destruction of England? This is the first vision that breaks on the French Consul through the gleam of the morning: this is his last prayer at night, to whatever deity he may address it, whether to Jupiter or Mahomet, to the Goddess of Battle or to the Goddess of Reason."

The whole country was in favour of war—the expense attending an armed truce was severely felt and disliked, and it was only to be lamented that through the stratagems and cunning of Buonaparte and his Minister Talleyrand, our ambassador, Lord Whitworth, could not sooner obtain his passport and quit the soil of France, as the delay served only to give time to France to recruit her strength and prepare for renewed hostilities.

On the 21st of December Lord Nelson spoke with great fervour in the House of Lords in favour of the Naval Commissioners' Bill; he gave his opinion that great abuses existed in the navy, and were most especially practised by the Prize Agents. He stated the difficulties of getting money out of the hands of the Agents, and frequently the impossibility of obtaining it at all. The Bill gave great powers, but they were necessary to correct the abuses complained of. He afterwards gave evidence before the Committee of Naval Inquiry.

Lord Nelson was always eager to serve his friends, either by advancing their interest, or contributing to their comfort. He had spoken in great praise of the Maltese asses, and undertook to obtain one for his old friend, Mr. Richard Bulkeley.[1]

---

[1] Mr. Bulkeley was with Lord Nelson at the attack on St. Juan, and as one of the very few who survived that disastrous affair was naturally much attached to him. They maintained an occasional correspondence, and Lord Nelson obtained admission into the Navy for one of Mr. Bulkeley's sons. The following is the letter, making request for this purpose, and also alludes to the present most able Hydrographer of the Admiralty, Rear-Admiral Sir Francis Beaufort, K.C.B.

"Chaceley, Tewksbury, 12th March, 1800.

"My dear Nelson,

"Your very kind letter of the 8th October reached me about six weeks ago, it came by the way of Cork. Accept my sincere thanks for the manner in which you received my recommendation of Mr. Beaufort. I trust and believe he will not prove a discredit to either of us. I have been twice in London within the last four weeks, both times I saw, as you may suppose, **Lady Nelson very often**, and your good old father, on whom the hand of time presses hard; he appears gradually to sink, and with Christian resignation to look forward to those blissful regions which are the ultimate abode of such men as him. God grant him an undisturbed journey, and the reward he merits. Lady Nelson's health appears much mended since last summer; she looks anxiously for your return, but as well as the rest of your friends, knows not how to flatter herself; reports have been so many and positive, that, at last, I expected to see you so soon as to determine me not to write, however, I find it is so uncertain, that I can withhold no longer, and the report of an expedition from home to the Mediterranean almost assures me that *you can't* come home for the present for the sake of the general cause. I wish from my heart that I may not see you till you have given *fresh cause* for *envy:* to be envied by the brave and deserving may be reconcileable, for from such men one expects liberality, but to be the envy of *blockheads* and *fellows*, who, if the opportunity presented itself, could not, and would not if they could, avail themselves of the precious moment, quite drives me mad. For one part of the many things said of you, you may have some reason to be vain, for it has begot you the prayers and praises of the fair sex, who all impatiently wait your return.

"In three or four weeks I hope to move to a house, which I have just purchased in Shropshire; my address, remember, when you write, will be Ludlow, Shropshire. You may recollect, one evening I called on you and Lady Nelson in Bond Street;

The following is an acknowledgment of the arrival of the animal:—

"Ludlow, Saturday, 8th January, 1803.

"My dear Nelson,

"I am very sincerely obliged to you for your letter of the 6th, giving me information of the arrival of the Maltese, for which I shall dispatch a messenger to-morrow, and I have by this day's post written a letter of thanks to Captain Maxwell, and have directed a person at Portsmouth to give a guinea to the man who took care of the ass on the passage, and to pay other charges. I look with impatience to the time when I shall get the animal into my stable. Sir A. Ball's account of him raises my hopes, and I expect a nonsuch.

"In your last letter, you told me that he cost thirty pounds, which I now send you an order for, and to which I have added five pounds, as I recollect my son's writing to me from on board the St. George, in the Baltic, to tell me that you had given him five pounds, and when I mentioned it to you at Merton, my boys were with me; you then shewed them your sword, that with what passed at the same time, and frequently hearing me speak of you, made such an impression on one of them, who is in his thirteenth year, that for two years past, he has been secretly indulging a fancy to go to sea : this, however, he cautiously kept to himself, believing I would not give my consent; however, within the last six weeks, he determined on *writing himself to you* to solicit your intercession with me. He actually wrote the letter, which I intercepted, and this made a discovery which surprised, and of course, led to a conversation, in which I found him so determined, that no arguments I was master of could move him from his purpose, and, at last, I have been forced to make him happy, by promising him that if he applies diligently to Mathematics, French, and Italian, till he is fourteen, he should then pursue his inclination, and by that time I trust in God peace will be restored, so that he will have quite an uphill game before him. However, as you have *bit* him, you must be his physician. I hope you may be back by the time *Pat* takes his seat in the Imperial Parliament, for it will be necessary some cool and determined hands should be in each House to keep my poor countrymen in order. I am endeavouring to be one of the Hundred in the Lower House, but I fear I have not much chance.

"Mrs. Bulkeley desires her best regards, and compliments to you, and I am,

"My dear friend,
"Very affectionately yours,
RICHARD BULKELEY."

Mr. Richard Bulkeley served as a Midshipman on board the Victory, and was at the Battle of Trafalgar, and wounded on that occasion. He was made a Lieutenant in 1806, and died in 1810.

you said, 'Hardy will settle it,' but when I paid him his advance to Dick, he took no notice of the money that you advanced; it therefore remained unpaid, and for that reason I have included it in the present draft. I have heard from one or two quarters that the Amphion is intended for the East Indies; it therefore occurs to me to suggest, what appears to me of some moment to Dick. Next month, he will have served three years, and I hope and believe that when he shall have served his time, he will be found perfectly qualified to be made; supposing him then to be in the East Indies at that period, and that the then Commander-in-chief should be a person of whom you may not like to ask a favour, and that the Captain of Dick's ship should not have weight with the Admiral, may he not miss his promotion? This reasoning you can easily enter into, and judge of its propriety better than I can. I am, therefore, particularly desirous of knowing your opinion, by which I shall be entirely guided. If you say, Let him go, I shall be satisfied; but should you prefer his being on the Home or Mediterranean station, I shall be equally pleased. Do, therefore, my dear friend, let me hear from you on the subject.

"Mrs. Bulkeley desires her best remembrance to you, and joins me in compliments to Sir William and Lady Hamilton.

"I am, my dear Nelson,
"Most affectionately and truly yours,
"RICHARD BULKELEY."

From Captain Louis:—

"Chilston, Newton Abbott, January 16th, 1803.

"My Lord,

"I have had the honour of receiving your Lordship's letter of the 11th instant, and that of my good friend Lady Hamilton, of the 13th. I can never sufficiently express my gratitude for the warmth in which you have interested yourself in my behalf; the recollection of your Lordship's letter will ever be highly gratifying to me; and though the result has not been favourable to our wishes, your Lordship's taking it up so kindly is so great a mark of your attachment to me, that it never can be erased from my memory, and considerably lessens the disappointment. How truly happy should I feel myself, my Lord, were it ever in my power, in the least degree, to be useful to your Lordship.

"My best respects to all at Merton; and I beg to remain,
"Your Lordship's faithful
"and grateful humble servant,
"Thomas Louis."

Rear-Admiral Duckworth wrote on the question of Prize-Money :—

"My Lord,
"The November and December packets having trod so close upon each other as to be here together, I have by the former to express my warmest thanks for your friendly letters of October 9th and November 28th, which drew forth my admiration at the glorious uncertainty of the law, even when all the combinations of it, turn them in common sense which way you will, must be operative in our favour; but if influence or power can cause the palladium of our liberty to be thus perverted, I shudder for our posterity. Yet, as I am convinced you will take every just care of our interest, let it turn as it will, I shall be satisfied in having endeavoured to protect the rights of our profession against what appears to me a most unjust and unprecedented claim; and from the arguments which appear in the paper, they dwell much upon the cause of the St. Ann with Admiral Murray, which, in my opinion, is quite irrelevant, as he was a Flag Officer, serving *alone*, and consequently, when not relieved, is like other Flag Officers coming from abroad, entitled to share till under other orders, or his flag struck. With respect to the Marquis de Niza, the law of reciprocity must prevent him from sharing for the capture of vessels of a nation with which he was in amity, and I shall think even for French, if the Portuguese colours were not in sight; but should common sense lose its force in these, we must have a claim upon the captures made by his squadron from the Tunisians, &c.

"I cannot but feel sensible of your Lordship's friendly sentiments of the public benefit by my continuance in this command, but I consider, whilst *a peace lasts,* an officer that has been above forty out of forty-four years servitude on board ship, and for these last ten years never had a moment to attend to his private affairs, or see a favourite daughter for six years, has a full claim to relief, and I trust we have a thousand as good as he to occupy the place; besides, if I was to stay till Buonaparte's ambition was satiated, or St. Domingo in a perfect state of tranquillity, I must have a longer tenure in this world than I expect. I therefore, my good Lord, cannot but be anxious to return, on which event I anticipate much pleasure in paying my respects at Merton, and personally assuring your Lordship that I have the honour to feel, with real regard,

" Your much obliged,
" and faithful humble servant,
" J. T. DUCKWORTH.

" P. S. I will beg your Lordship to say all that is kind and respectful to Sir William and Lady Hamilton, believing me ever yours,

" J. T. D.

" Leviathan, Jamaica, January 16, 1803."

And Captain Hardy :—

" Amphion, Portsmouth Harbour, January 20th, 1803.

" My Lord,

" The Amphion is to be paid off in a few days, and I shall be happy to take the youngsters your Lordship wrote to me about. Young Bulkeley continues to behave very well, and I have no doubt but he will make a very good officer. I have not the least idea what is to become of us, but shall always be proud to follow your Lordship, in whatever part of the world I may be in, should the country call for your Lordship's services again. I will trouble your Lordship to make my best compliments to Sir William, Lady Hamilton, and all friends at Merton. I have the honour to be, with the greatest respect,

" Your Lordship's obliged,
" very humble servant,
" T. M. HARDY."

In Lady Hamilton's handwriting, probably by the dictation of Nelson, I find the following letter, the autograph of which is in the Sidmouth Papers,[1] addressed to the Earl St. Vincent :—

"23, Piccadilly, January 28th, 1803.

"My dear Lord,

"As your indifferent state of health will, I fear, prevent your coming to town for some time, I write to your Lordship on a subject which we once entered upon, but which you desired to defer till the Dutch ships were paid for, when you would settle our Copenhagen business with Lord Hawkesbury. I am now, by desire of several Captains, asking your Lordship if any decision has taken place on this business. If you refer me to Lord Hawkesbury as the proper Minister for this business, or any other Minister, I shall address myself to him (or them); or if you think that a public letter to the Secretary of the Admiralty is the proper channel, I will write one to him. It is now two years since that battle was fought.

"I own myself exactly of the same opinion as when I wrote to you from the Baltic, that under all the peculiar circumstances of the case, *no war with Denmark*, therefore, no condemnation could take place; that it would be better to give a gratuity for our services; I said (I believe) £100,000. was as little as could be offered. You differed from me, but wrote me that you would recommend a large price to be given for the Holstein. You will, my dear Lord, see the situation I am placed in, and excuse my resorting to you to advise me in what channel I shall proceed, to bring our Copenhagen prize business to a close. With every kind wish for the re-establishment of your health, believe me yours,

"Most faithfully,

"NELSON AND BRONTÉ."

Another letter from Captain Hardy prefers a request for Mr. Danes :—

---

[1] Printed in the Dispatches and Letters, Vol. v. p. 41.

"Amphion, Portsmouth, February 2nd, 1803.

"My Lord,

"Mr. Daniel Danes, who was pilot on the Downs station under your Lordship's command (and a short time in the Isis) will be thankful if you can intercede with Mr. Pitt to get him a branch for that place. I am convinced that your Lordship has already asked so many favours, that you will not like to do it, and I shall not press it unless quite convenient. Thomas Ramsey has requested me to ask your Lordship if you received a letter from him lately, which he thinks (without cause, I suppose) has miscarried. I will trouble your Lordship to make my best compliments to Sir William and Lady Hamilton. I have the honour to be,

"Your Lordship's obliged humble servant,
"T. M. HARDY.

"Mr. Danes commanded a small lugger, I believe, under your Lordship's command."

Mr. Davison was very liberal in his offers of assistance to Lord Nelson:—

"Calais, February 3rd, 1803.

"My dear Friend,

"Long ere this I had settled my return to St. James's Square, after having reached Paris, spending a fortnight there, and setting off from thence in great good health for Bruxelles and Antwerp, my dear boy William[1] was taken extremely ill at Lisle, and it was with difficulty I could get him with safety on to this place. He has now been confined to his bed a fortnight, in a delirium, and only within these two days the fever has taken a favourable turn, and the physician considers him out of danger. You may well believe the vexation and concern this unfortunate circumstance occasions me. I shall hope the best, though the doctor tells me I must not expect to move from hence sooner than the 15th. What a prison—state of misery. If my absence occasions to you any pecuniary inconvenience, apply to my bankers, and shew to

[1] The William Davison was afterwards Lieutenant-Colonel William Davison, K.H.

them *this* side of my letter, and I authorise them to pay to your order five thousand pounds sterling. This possibly may supply your present wants. If an extension be necessary, command the purse of your ever

"Unalterably affectionate friend,
"ALEXANDER DAVISON."

Nelson acknowledged this letter on the 8th, and says, "Your kind offer I feel most sensibly, but at present I have no wants; and I hope soon to be in that state of complete independence, which you so really wish. But 'a friend in need is a friend indeed' is an old adage, but not the less true, and I am truly thankful and grateful for all your kindness. I am just got to work on the Copenhagen business, and I hope to get from Mr. Addington 50 or £60,000. for the captors, including the Holstein. Sir Hyde has given up the management of this matter to me. At another Board, they are still disputing, but the Secretary and myself are feeling towards each other as we ought (I do not choose to mention names). Yesterday I was at Colonel Despard's[1] trial, subpœnaed by him for a character. I think the plot deeper than was imagined; but as to the extent, nothing except the *Guards* has come out. I have been, and am, very bad in my eyesight, and am forbid writing; but I could not resist."[2]

At this time Nelson's eye was very bad, and he was forbidden to write; but in personal matters he could disregard injunctions. Mr. Bulkeley writes:—

"Ludlow, Thursday, February 17th, 1803.

"My dear Nelson,

"I am aware that I ought not to call upon your eyes to read my letter, after the restrictions of Moseley, and the account that you give of yourself, which I can with strict truth say *grieves me very much*, and though I don't desire you to answer me, but on the contrary, request you not to write, still I cannot impose silence on myself, and do so much injustice to my heart, as not to express my deep concern at

---
[1] See Vol. i. p. 12, *ante*.
[2] Dispatches and Letters, Vol. v. p. 42.

what gives you any serious cause for alarm, and which seems to threaten a severe misfortune to our country. My consolation in the present instance arises from my confidence in Moseley's skill, and my conviction that he will not trifle, or practise experiments, where so much is at stake, and I am sure that your resolution to withstand every temptation to deviate from his rules is sufficient to ensure him success. I shall be impatient to hear how you go on, and therefore beg that if any material change takes place, you will employ the pen of some one about you to communicate the intelligence to me, which I most ardently hope will be of the most pleasing kind.

"From every thing that the papers related as appearing upon the trials, I had no idea that the detestable conspiracy had gone the lengths which you seem to imagine, or involved in it any (poor Despard excepted) but of the lowest orders. I am sorry that you think it so extensive, and of so serious a nature; however, I still think and hope that the country at large is staunch to the constitution: in that case, the disaffection of a great majority of the Guards would not, I trust, when joined only to the rabble, without their officers, be able to effect more than partial evils, though certainly thousands on all sides might fall, and many families be reduced to penury.

"I rejoice that you have given your attention to the subject of our seamen; if we don't keep them in good humour, and *firm from principle,* our decline must be very rapid indeed. I can have no doubts of the Ministry paying every attention, and giving the greatest weight to your recommendations upon this subject. In all your systems you have shewn your preference for decision and vigour, and the good effects have been proved in all your actions. Even in matters of less moment I am an enemy to half and timid measures, and in the unfortunate executions which are to take place, I would have Government make all the parade which the case will admit of, and shew that it is undaunted. Despard ought not to be spared. The King owes to the country that the execution should take place.

"The Maltese is perfectly well, and recovered from the effects of his voyage. He is beautiful, and as fond of biting and kicking as any of his fraternity. Those of this country are all heavy and stupid looking, but this, on the contrary, is most playful, with a very animated eye.[1]

"Offer Mrs. Bulkeley's and my kind respects to Sir William and Lady Hamilton, Dr. and Mrs. Nelson, and believe me, my dear friend, most sincerely and affectionately,

"Yours,
"RICHARD BULKELEY."

The allusion made to Nelson's attention to the subject of seamen refers to a communication made by him to Earl St. Vincent, on the manning of the Navy.[2]

Sir John Acton wrote from Caserta:—

"Caserta, 2nd March, 1803.

"My Lord,

"A messenger arrived to Mr. Drummond, has brought to me your Lordship's kind favour of the 6th of February. I hear this moment that the same person goes back again in a few hours. I present these few words in answer. I shall employ my best cares and attentions in every respect for the welfare of your business in Sicily, and the success of your demands on the same. I have given the proper commissions for the best regulation and surest march of the propositions to come from Sicily on the same purposes. Your Lordship may be assured of my readiness to contribute to every wish that may afford you any satisfaction, if in my power.

"I have seen with sorrow what your Lordship mentions on treasons and spirit of revolutions still in agitation. I am sorry to hear that the Guards themselves could be corrupted in these times!!! So everywhere the same and horrid distemper has afflicted every class of men! It seems, however, that the principles which were the cause, and gave room to so many mischiefs, is at least out of mode and fashion at present.

---

[1] The asses of Malta are remarkable for their strength and beauty; they sell for a high price, and are called *Janets*.

[2] See Paper in the possession of Vice-Admiral Sir William Parker, Bart., and letter to the Right Honourable Sir William Scott, printed in Dispatches and Letters, Vol. v. pp. 44 and 61.

"What you favour to explain to me on the perfidious projects of Despard is horrible, and could that plan have its effects in England? I hope not, but many and many calamities might have taken room and affect the prosperity of the nation, but never, I confide, overcome its system of government at large. I am speaking on what I feel and desire, but find myself thoroughly unacquainted with the particular situation of that and my country.

"I hope that for some time peace will continue, though nobody can answer to that question certainly, whether we shall have peace or war as the things are at present. Buonaparte does not wish for war, though he detests the only nation which he could not subdue nor influence. He makes conquests in peace as well as in war. If however, a rupture takes room again, poor Italy is lost: no remedy can save it as the circumstances stand in the Continent at this moment. The more, however, that is left to operate to Buonaparte in the peaceable way, the more he seems to intricate himself in difficulties. He loses every day in the opinion of his people, and exposes himself to the highest danger—he cannot stop neither in his projects—his fall might happen every moment.

"I see that you have that ungrateful and dangerous woman the Belmonte, in London. I hope, by what you please to mention to me, that she will find there the same credit which she found established even at Paris, of a most horrid revolutionist. I am glad to hear that Sir William Hamilton is in a fair way as to his health. I beg Lady Hamilton to receive and agree my best compliments and wishes. I return you my thanks, my Lord, for what you are so good to tell me on my estates in Shropshire. I find that Mr. Haslewood of Bridgenorth, has given you proper informations. I think that I must go as soon as possible to visit that country with my little family, and judge better of my business on the spot. I shall have the pleasure then to see your Lordship, and rely much on this satisfaction. I shall be glad to be acquainted with those gentlemen of Shropshire which you are so good to recommend. I have agents, but could till now take very little care of those business of mine. All my cares have been taken for the best of Sovereigns, which I have the honour to serve. They have been glad to hear the news of your Lordship, and your loyal and cordial declaration on their regard.

"I beg your Lordship to be sure of my best wishes and constant sincere friendship, as well as of the highest regard and consideration of

"Your Lordship's
"Most obedient and most humble servant,
"JOHN ACTON."

Nothing can speak more favourably for the kindness of Nelson's nature than the repeated applications made to him by the parents of the officers who had served with him to promote the welfare of their families.

Captain Louis writes:—

"Chelston, Newton Abbott, March 8th, 1803.

"My Lord,

"The kindness with which your Lordship entered into my views respecting my son to India, induces me to be troublesome to you again on his behalf. I doubt how far I might attempt getting him into one of the public offices to bring him forward in the diplomatic line, which would be my next wish to that of India.

"If that is not practicable I think of placing him at Woolwich, could I obtain from my Lord Chatham an appointment of a Cadet. He is now fourteen, and in order to lose no time, I have written my Lord Chatham on the subject. I am well aware, at the same time, how very essential a line from your Lordship would be to strengthen my application to Lord Chatham, which, I make no doubt, would procure the desired appointment. I have two sons unprovided for, and I am sorry to say, although my services during my life have been devoted to the public, that I find the greatest difficulty in getting my sons forward; but I shall ever feel most grateful to your Lordship for the kindness and attention with which you have endeavoured to assist me. My best wishes attend all at Merton, and believe me with every respect,

"Your Lordship's faithful humble servant,
"THOMAS LOUIS."

The following relates to the widow of Colonel Despard:—

"Ludlow, Wednesday, 9th March, 1803.

"My dear Friend,

"Your last letter gave me great concern, because it speaks of your suffering eye, but is perfectly silent as to any probability of speedy relief. Do, my good friend, tell me who you have consulted besides Moseley, who though an *excellent physician*, is not, I apprehend, a *professed oculist*. And you have given so much reason to the country, to look with confidence for essential advantages from your future services, that it has some right to require of you to seek for every aid, and to do every thing in your power to preserve your health. Let that claim then which your country has upon you, call forth your utmost exertions.

"I highly approve of your withholding the money which I intended for an object, who as I conceived *you interested yourself about*, I concluded *might be deserving*, and if you think her so, my donation is still at your service to appropriate as you think proper, but I am by no means ambitious of classing myself, or being a contributor with her late husband's associates, or with such villains as *Citizen Hardy*.

"I find that the Board of Admiralty has established *Club Law*, and that the First Lord has a most *powerful support* in a man who has often proved his readiness and courage in a more honourable way than that of frightening an emaciated Secretary. Ministers would, by all accounts, gladly get rid of the Earl, but he loves power and patronage too well to indulge them by *taking miff*. Have we any chance, in case of a vacancy, of seeing the place filled by a man who would most ably and honourably execute the duties of the office, and who I wish to see gratified in every desire of his heart? You can't be at a loss to guess who I mean, you know my sentiments too well, and that I am at all times,

"My dear Nelson,

"Your Lordship's very affectionate and sincere,

"RICHARD BULKELEY.

"P. S. I just understand that the Amphion is ordered to Ireland to receive seamen. Give my compliments to Sir William and Lady Hamilton."

The following is a good sailor's letter:—

"Le Renard, Waterford,
March 17, 1803.

"My Lord,

"I take the liberty of writing to solicit your Lordship to have the goodness (should a war take place, which God forbid there should be a doubt of) to do me the honour of applying for Le Renard to be under your Lordship's command, as I trust you would find her a *tolerable* fast sailer, and I hope at least as prompt as her neighbours in executing any orders it may be her good fortune to receive.

"We are at present at Waterford, twenty miles up the river Suir, employed day and night pressing.

"For the trade carried on (which except in the Salt Provision line is very trifling, there being only thirty vessels here) have been fortunate. I have ready to ship for his Majesty's service fifty prime seamen, and about thirty ordinary and landsmen. The seamen are all White Haven men, which in my opinion enhances their value, though I must say I found the potatoe diggers very quiet. Le Renard is full and well manned.

"They were so *nice* at Plymouth as to reject some of my new raised men, because their *wrists* were too small, and they had had broken shins. Some of those men on their return I entered for Renard, and I have found them as good as ever came into a ship.

"I beg leave to transcribe a part of my last letter to the Admiralty, which I wrote fearing they might charge the expense of these rejected men against my wages, which would not have been very agreeable entertainment to me. 'I beg leave to add that the volunteers are all raw potatoe diggers, lightermen, &c. I believe to get them without broken shins and mutilated carcases must remain among the desiderata; as by my experience here, I can affirm, those complaints to be their general *characteristics*. The volunteers that were rejected at Plymouth from this place, were the best to be procured, being only slightly afflicted with the above-mentioned *maladies*.'

"I will conclude by begging your Lordship to excuse the liberty I have taken in addressing this scrawl to you, and after adding that it is my most fervent prayer soon to have the happiness of seeing Renard's *answering Jack* to signals addressed her by *blue at the fore*, will subscribe myself ever

"Your Lordship's
"Obliged humble servant,
"W. CATHCART."

The applications to Nelson to accompany him, should he go to sea, were most numerous. Even the Chaplain was anxious to quit his living and attend him:—

"Southminster, Essex, March 20th, 1803.

"My Lord,

"Under the impression that your Lordship would take me with you to the Mediterranean, I hastened to take possession of my living here; intending as soon as that was secured, to mention the matter to you: I am sorry to say that ill health detained me a day and night at Chelmsford, and this circumstance will prevent my getting through the necessary forms and ceremonies so soon as I anxiously desire. I am out of the world here, and know not what turn things take, but I will not lose a moment in getting to London as soon as I possibly can, where I hope to pay my respects to your Lordship.

"I have likewise to beg your Lordship, when at leisure, to send the certificate which I took the liberty to request of you, to Mr. George Rose, of Palace Yard, and to repeat to your Lordship how devotedly

"I am, with respect, your faithful humble servant,

"A. J. SCOTT."

Sir Edward Berry was desirous of again sailing under Nelson:—

"Catton, near Norwich, 21st March, 1803.

"My dear Lord,

"Seeing the continual reports in the newspapers of your Lordship having an appointment to a command, I can no longer resist again offering myself as a candidate to serve with you, either *temporary* or *permanent*, in any way your Lordship will accept of my exertions in the event of war. I have hardly thought it probable that we actually should again commence hostilities, I have therefore not made any application to the Board, from an idea that I should be put to some expense and a great deal of trouble for nothing, by being turned to the right-about again in a few months.

" When you can spare time, pray have the goodness to give me a line on the subject. By a letter from Tyson the other day, he says you are not very well; I hope it is nothing material. Every body here is complaining of *La Grippe*. I am but so-so. Pray remember me kindly to Sir William and Lady Hamilton, and believe me ever

" Your Lordship's
" Faithful and obliged
" E. BERRY.

" I am in great distress about a berth for a Midshipman, a relation of mine, a very good young man. I wrote to Hardy about him, but fear he sailed before my letter reached. Can your Lordship assist me? I would see the Admiralty folks at Bagdad before I ask them. Is the *Arch Jesuit* (as the Duke of Clarence calls him) going out?"

Reports of Lord Nelson's appointment to be Commander-in-chief of the Mediterranean were rife, but it did not take place until May 16th. Mr. Bulkeley writes:—

" Ludlow, Wednesday, 23rd March, 1803.

" My dear Friend,

" This infernal threat of war, and consequent bustle, I am sure, has entirely engaged all your time and thoughts; therefore, from the moment that the subject was announced officially, I knew that I was not to expect to know any thing about you but through the newspapers. Satisfied as I am as to your dislike to writing, and knowing that it is not an easy task with the left hand, and that you have at such a time no leisure for letter-writing, still my anxious friendship and desire to be acquainted with every thing that concerns you, has made me look with impatient hope for the arrival of every post for the last fortnight.

"You have proved yourself too true a prophet, for you have said ever since the peace, that it could not be of long duration; and though I hoped you might be mistaken, still I had my fears, and now confess that if war was inevitable, in the course of a very few years from the peace, I am better satisfied that we should *embrace* the first *justifiable* cause for war, while our *brilliant achievements* in the last are fresh upon our own and that of our enemies' memories, and whilst the breasts of every *effective* sailor burns with desire to follow the *unexampled example that you have set them*. Tell me, my dear Nelson, when you can, all you can, (consistently with *State secrecy*) as to your own probable destination. Poor Vardon is gone to town to offer; I wish that he had his *flag* and at quiet in Ludlow. He is a very venerable and good *old man*. I offered during the late war, repeatedly, my poor services without *fee* or *reward*. I was coolly thanked, but not accepted, and I did not think it necessary to exert much interest to put myself to great inconvenience by undertaking the training and commanding a set of fellows in a profession for which, in our country, I have the most thorough contempt, notwithstanding Lords Moira and Hutcheson's *figs to each other*. If I was a sailor, which I ought to have been, I would cut off both my arms rather than be idle at such a time. Can you tell me where the Amphion is gone? Dick is now old enough to enter into the glory and honour of his profession. He must earn those laurels which his father missed, and perhaps was not equal to the attainment of.

"My best compliments to Sir William and Lady Hamilton.

"I am, my dear Nelson,

"Ever sincerely yours,

"RICHARD BULKELEY."

Dr. Baird recommended a Surgeon:—

"Portsmouth, 24th March, 1803.

"My Lord,

"My unexpected and hasty departure from London on Saturday night totally precluded me doing myself the honour of waiting on you, and since I have been here, I have been so engaged on board the Neptune, that I have scarcely time to write a daily report to the Admiralty. She is now, I trust, in good health, and the means pursued will preserve it. The newspapers of to-day announce the Victory commissioned for your Lordship, if so, Mr. Allen, the Surgeon of the Venerable, is the Surgeon I would reccommend, if Mr. Bell stays with Lord Keith—perhaps your Lordship might ask Lord Keith that question. I am solicitous that your Lordship may not think me forgetful of so necessary an appointment as a good Surgeon, and your Lordship may rest assured if it be your wish to delay on that head, that I shall not fail to accommodate you with an eligible person.

"I take the liberty of offering most respectful compliments to Sir William and Lady Hamilton. I have the honour to be, my Lord, with every sentiment of gratitude,
"Your Lordship's dutiful servant,
"ANDREW BAIRD."

The prospect of being with Nelson put them all alive; Captain Louis writes :—

"Plymouth Dock, March 23rd, 1803.

"My Lord,
"I have the pleasure to inform your Lordship of my having joined the Conqueror at Plymouth. I think her a very fine ship indeed, and equal to Minotaur. I have now only to hope that she may be as useful to your Lordship whenever you may be pleased to call upon her services, though I agree with you very much that I do not think we shall go to war; appearances are strong for it, and I only wish *Johnny* came forward to man us. Several ships here: Sir Edward Pellew, Murray, Buller, Sutton, and yesterday arrived Admiral Campbell, whose flag goes to Culloden. No doubt we shall soon hear when your Lordship moves. I hope you enjoy your health, as well as my good friends Sir William and Lady Hamilton, to whom I beg my best regards.
"I remain, my Lord,
"Your most obliged and faithful servant,
"THOMAS LOUIS.

"P.S Pray command me if I can serve in any shape whatever. Youngsters, or any thing else."

Lord Nelson turned his attention seriously to the state of his pecuniary affairs in the month of March, and forwarded a statement to the Right Hon. Henry Addington, by which it appeared that his whole real property did not amount to more than £10,000, and that, deducting from his income the amount apportioned to Lady Nelson, the interest due on money borrowed, the pension to his brother's widow, and the assistance he rendered towards the education of his nephews, that he had only the sum of £768 *per annum* to answer all demands made upon him. This sum, so far beneath that which his station and rank demanded, induced him to apply to the Government for an increase of means. The particulars given to shew the justice of such an appeal, are to be found in his letter to the First Lord of the Treasury.[1]

On the 9th of March, 1803, a Debate took place in the House of Lords on the King's message respecting military preparations in the ports of France. Nelson was present, but did not speak. He, however, watched narrowly what was going on, and retiring from the body of the House, he wrote the following laconic epistle to the Premier, the Hon. Henry Addington:—

"House of Lords, 4 o'clock, March 9th, 1803,

"Whenever it is necessary, I am *your* Admiral."

"NELSON AND BRONTÉ."[2]

Lord Nelson commenced the month of April by delivering his evidence upon oath before the Committee of Naval Enquiry, and gave his opinion on the conducting of Prize Money in future.[3]

Writing to Captain Murray on the 2nd, he congratulates him upon the anniversary of the Battle of Copenhagen, and says: "No man sets a more just value on your gallantry and

---

[1] Dispatches and Letters, Vol. v. p. 47. See also p. 59. From the original draft of this application now before me, the chief part appears to have been written by Sir George Rose, and is in his hand-writing; the latter part is in Lord Nelson's autograph.

[2] Life of Lord Sidmouth, Vol. ii. p. 170.

[3] A copy of the examination of Lord Nelson is preserved at the Admiralty. Certain passages within brackets have been supplied by Nelson himself, and written in his own hand. Sir Harris Nicolas has printed it in his Dispatches and Letters, Vol. v. p. 53.

important services than myself." To Captain Sutton he writes on the 4th, to tell him that the Victory (the ship destined for Nelson) was to be commissioned on the 7th or 8th, and that he had sent a list of six Lieutenants, which was enough to begin with. He was under much distress at this time on account of the serious illness of Sir William Hamilton, who died on the 6th in his and Lady Hamilton's arms. Lord Nelson sat up with Sir William Hamilton for six nights prior to his decease, upon the occurrence of which he removed into lodgings in Piccadilly. To his Royal Highness the Duke of Clarence he wrote : " My dear friend Sir William Hamilton died this morning : the world never lost a more upright and accomplished gentleman."

Among Nelson's papers is the following written by Lady Hamilton :—

"*April* 6th. Unhappy day for the forlorn Emma. Ten minutes past ten dear blessed Sir William left me."

Nelson appears from the following letter from Lord Melville, to have made some application relative to Lady Hamilton :—

"Wimbledon, 17th April, 1803.

" My dear Lord,

" I have received your Grace's letter, together with one from Lady Hamilton herself. I had an opportunity of speaking with Mr. Addington yesterday, agreeable to your and her wishes ; but I had no occasion to press any thing with importunity, as he seems fully possessed of the circumstances of the case, and disposed to give a favourable attention to them. I need not trouble Lady Hamilton with a separate letter, as your Grace will communicate to her the contents of this, and I remain, my dear Lord,

" Yours very truly,
"MELVILLE.

" I will take an opportunity soon of calling on Lady Hamilton."

The Marquis of Douglas and Clydesdale (now Duke of Hamilton) kindly sympathized with her :—

"The inclosed letter, my dear Lady Hamilton, I received

yesterday. It was my intention to have given it into your
own hands; but having been prevented, I think it my duty
to send it to you by the earliest opportunity. In the course
of the day I am in hopes of being able to call and inquire
after you. I shall hope to find that necessity will have begun
to work upon your mind, and that you will feel that whatever
are the misfortunes under which we labour, patience and
resignation are the only proper, only efficacious remedies. I
will not preach, because I feel myself inadequate to it. My
own love and affection for our much lamented friend far
supersedes any sensations that philosophy and reflection can
possibly suggest, and in uniting a sigh with yours, I only
bestow what my heart acknowledges, and my every thought
approves. Believe me, with regard, dear Lady Hamilton,

"Your affectionate friend and relative,
"DOUGLAS AND CLYDESDALE.

"April 19th, 1803."

Lord Nelson intended Murray for his Captain, but he was
already in the Spartiate: "You are fixed as fate my First
Captain, and it is only on that score that I can speak to the
Earl soon, if nothing is decided soon as to peace or war, to
beg that you may not be sent out of the way, and then, if
you authorize me, I will mention to him that if the Spartiate
is wanted to go to sea, that you submit to him whether it
would not be better to give her up—there are scores wanting
her. I congratulate you on the birth of a son; if one of his
names is not *Baltic*, I shall be very angry with you indeed—
he can be called nothing else."[1] Sutton and Hardy were,
however, his Captains. The Duke of Clarence wanted Lord
Nelson to take Lieutenant the Hon. Edward Rodney, the
son of Admiral Lord Rodney, but his number was complete,
and he had twenty on his list. "Had I known (he says)
that there had been this claimant, some of my own Lieutenants must have given way to such a name, and he should
have been placed in the Victory."[2]

On the 6th of May he was ordered for departure. He
went to Merton to settle his affairs there. He received his
appointment as Commander-in-chief on the Mediterranean

[1] Dispatches and Letters, Vol. v. p. 58.
[2] Clarke and McArthur, Vol. ii. p. 312.

station from the Admiralty on the 16th, and on the 18th set out for Portsmouth, where he hoisted his flag on board the Victory, and in communicating this to the Earl of St. Vincent, he says: "You may rely, my dear Lord, that nothing shall be left undone by me, by a vigorous and active exertion of the force under my command, to bring about a happy peace." His anxiety now was to get off, for on the following day, the 19th, he wrote to the Earl, "If the devil stands at the door, the Victory shall sail to-morrow forenoon."

Admiral Lord Gardner[1] was the Commander-in-chief at Portsmouth. Nelson saluted him with thirteen guns, and the salute was returned. He sailed on the 20th.

[1] Lord Gardner has been universally esteemed a Naval officer of distinguished ability. Lord Collingwood gave it as his opinion that there was no officer on the list who had the skill of Lord Gardner, and expressed his surprise in 1804 that he was not appointed to any situation of importance. The Right Hon. Alan Lord Gardner was born at Uttoxeter, April 12, 1742, and commenced his naval career under Captain Peter Denis of the Medway, 60 guns, in May, 1755. He was at the taking of the Raisonable by the Dorsetshire in 1758, and in 1759 in the action off Belleisle between Sir Edward Hawke and Marshal de Conflans. He was made Lieutenant in 1760, and appointed to the Bellona; was at the capture of Le Courageux of 74 guns, and in 1762 made a Commander. He was made Post in 1766, and sent to the West Indies in the Preston, the flag-ship of Rear-Admiral Parry. He returned to England in 1771, but in 1775 was again sent to Jamaica, and in 1778 cruised off the coast of America in the Maidstone of 28 guns, in which he captured the Lion of 40 guns. Arriving at Antigua he was appointed to the Sultan, 74 guns, and was in the action with Count D'Estaing in 1779, distinguishing himself by his intrepid conduct. In 1781 he was ordered to join Sir George Rodney's fleet in the West Indies, and was engaged on the 12th of April, 1782, being the first to have the honour of breaking through the enemy's line. In 1785 he was appointed Commander-in-chief on the Jamaica station, where he remained three years. In 1790 he was appointed to Le Courageux, and afterwards made one of the Commissioners for executing the office of Lord High Admiral, and remained at the Admiralty Board until 1795. In 1796 he was elected one of the Representatives in Parliament for Westminster, having previously sat for the Borough of Plymouth. At the commencement of the Revolutionary war he was made a Rear-Admiral, and appointed to the command of a squadron in the West Indies. He hoisted his flag in the Queen, 98 guns, and afterwards joined the Channel Fleet under Earl Howe, and was in the glorious 1st of June; was appointed Major-General of the Marines, and was made Vice-Admiral of the White, June 1, 1795, and created a Baronet, on the 6th of August. He was second in command in Lord Bridport's action with Admiral Villaret de Joyeuse off Port L'Orient. In 1797 he was appointed to the Royal Sovereign of 110 guns, and was active in suppressing the mutiny in the Channel Fleet. In 1799 he was made Vice-Admiral of the Blue, and in the following year Commander-in-chief on the coast of Ireland. He was created Baron Gardner of Uttoxeter, a Peer of Ireland. He died January 1, 1809, at Bath, in the 66th year of his age.

Three days previously to Nelson's departure, an Order of Council was published, directing that reprisals be granted against the ships, goods, and subjects of the French Republic, and a proclamation was issued for an embargo on the French and Batavian vessels in British ports. On the 18th, the Papers forming the Diplomatic Correspondence between France and England, from the Peace of Amiens, were laid before Parliament. A Royal declaration was also issued on the subjects of complaint against France; it especially noticed and repudiated the opinion of Buonaparte that Great Britain had no right to take an interest in the affairs of the Continent, or to interfere with the proceedings of France in any point which did not constitute part of the stipulations in the Treaty of Amiens, and demonstrated the incompatibility of such a principle with the spirit of treaties in general, and the national law of Europe. The sentiments of the King, and the Declaration, were approved by the Parliament on the 23rd. In June, additional forces were raised, and a Bill was brought in by Mr. Yorke to enable the King to raise a levy *en masse*, in case of invasion, which was carried *nem. con.* The King's Speech and debates thereupon, excited the rage of the First Consul, and after many conferences with the Minister Talleyrand, and also with the First Consul, and a variety of subterfuges employed to cause delay, the English Ambassador obtained his passports and quitted France. Two days after Lord Whitworth's return, an Order of Council for granting reprisals and letters of marque, and a proclamation for an embargo, were issued, and the detention and capture of French and Dutch vessels, estimated at the value of three millions sterling, were effected. The First Consul ordered all English *of every condition* in the French territory, to be considered as prisoners of war, and not less than 10,000 British subjects were thus detained. The Peace was thus at an end.

## CHAPTER VII.

### 1803.

On his road to Portsmouth, at Kingston, Lord Nelson wrote a few lines to Lady Hamilton, and upon his arrival:—

"May 18th, 1803, (Portsmouth).

" My dearest Emma,

" I wrote you a line from Kingston by the Duke's servant, and having breakfasted at Liphock, arrived here almost smothered with dust exactly at one o'clock. I found Hardy and Sutton waiting for me. They both agreeing with me my flag is hoisted in the Victory, to prevent, without the service absolutely requires it, the indelicate removal of an Admiral. To-morrow night or Friday morning at daylight she sails. My things only begin to arrive this evening, and till noon to-morrow. Lord Gardner dining out, I have Hardy, Sutton, Mr. Scott, and Murray to dine with me—but what a change—it will not bear thinking of, except in the sweet hope of again returning to the society of those we so sincerely love. Either my ideas are altered or Portsmouth, it is a place the picture of desolation and misery, but perhaps it is the contrast to what I have been used to. Hardy is in good health and spirits. The Victory lays so far off that I can hardly see her, and the Amphion is beyond my vision. I am writing to the Admiralty—must keep them in good humour. When you see my élève, which you will when you receive this letter, give her a kiss for me, and tell her that I never shall forget either her or her dear good mother, and do you believe me,

" Yours,

" Nelson and Bronté.

"Write to the Duke of Queensberry and say how truly sensible I am of all his kindness. When I am on board I will write him a line; and say every thing for me to the Duke of Hamilton, and the Marquis of Douglas, Mr. Este, &c.: and to the Doctor and my sisters you will say every thing that is kind, and never forget me to your good mother."

And at the moment of departure:—
"BY MESSENGER.

"May 20th, 1803.

"My dearest Emma,

"The boat is on shore, and five minutes sets me afloat. I can only pray that the great God of heaven may bless and preserve you, and that we may meet again in peace and in true happiness. I have no fears. Your dear kind letters are just come.

"Yours,
"NELSON AND BRONTÉ."

When arrived on board the Victory he penned another letter, and again on the 21st.

"Victory, May 21st, 1803.

"My dearest Emma,

"This morning we stopped a Dutch ship from Surinam, of some value. Hardy carries her into Plymouth. We have a fine wind. I have only a moment to say, God in heaven keep you.

"Yours,
"NELSON AND BRONTÉ."

"May 22nd, 1803.
Eight o'clock in the morning.

"My dearest Emma,

"We are now in sight of Ushant, and shall see Admiral Cornwallis in an hour. I am not in a little fret, on the idea that he may keep the Victory, and turn us all into the Amphion. It will make it truly uncomfortable; but I cannot help myself. We are very comfortable. Mr. Elliot is happy, has quite recovered his spirits; he was very low at Portsmouth. George Elliot is very well; say so to Lord Minto. Murray, Sutton, in short every body in the ship, seems happy; and if we should fall in with a French man-of-war, I have no fears but they will do as we used to do. Hardy has gone into Plymouth to see our Dutchman safe. I think she will turn out a good prize.

"Gaetano desires his duty to Miledi! He is a good man; and, I dare say, will come back: for, I think, it cannot be a long war; just enough to make me independent in pecuniary matters. If the wind stands, on Tuesday we shall be on the coast of Portugal; and before next Sunday, in the Mediterranean.

"I shall now stop till I have been on board the Admiral."

"May 23rd.

"We were close in with Brest yesterday, and found by a frigate that Admiral Cornwallis had a rendezvous at sea, thither we went, but to this hour cannot find him. It blows strong. What wind we are losing! If I cannot find the Admiral by six o'clock, we must all go into the Amphion, and leave the Victory to my great mortification. So much for the wisdom of my superiors.

"I keep my letter open to the last, for I still hope; and I am sure, there is no good reason for my not going out in the Victory. I am just embarking in the Amphion: cannot find Admiral Cornwallis.

"May God in heaven bless you! prays your most sincere,

"NELSON AND BRONTÉ.

"Stephens's[1] publication I should like to have. I have left my silver seal; at least I cannot find it."

[1] Alexander Stephens, Esq., author of a "History of the Wars of the French Revolution," 2 vols. 4to. Lond. 1803. He applied to Lord Nelson for information relating to the proceedings in the Bay of Naples. The following is printed from the draft of Nelson's reply, and is in Lady Hamilton's hand-writing:--

"23, Piccadilly, February 10th, 1803.

"Sir,

"By your letter, I believe that you wish to be correct in your History, and therefore desire to be informed of a transaction relative to Naples. I cannot, at this moment, enter at large into the subject to which you allude; but I shall briefly say, that neither Cardinal Ruffo, Captain Foote, nor any other person had any power vested in them to enter into any Treaty with the rebels—that even the paper which they so improperly signed, was not acted upon, as I very happily arrived at Naples, and prevented such an infamous transaction from taking place. I put aside the dishonourable Treaty, and sent the rebels notice of it; therefore, when the rebels surrendered, they came out of the castles as they ought, without any honours of war, and trusting to the judgment of their Sovereign.

"If you allude to Mrs. Williams's book, I can assure you that nearly all she writes relative to Naples, is either entirely destitute of foundation, or falsely represented. If you wish to have any conversation with me on this subject, I am at home every morning at 10 o'clock, and am, Sir, your most obedient servant,

"NELSON AND BRONTÉ."

The Mrs. Williams alluded to by Lord Nelson, was Miss Helen Maria Williams, author of "Sketches of Manners and Opinions in the French Republic," 2 vols. 8vo. and has been well described in the Pictorial History of England (Vol. viii.

"May 25th, 1803.

"My dearest Emma,

"Here we are in the middle of the Bay of Biscay—nothing to be seen but the sky and water. I left the Victory at eight o'clock last night, a reflection I think on those who ordered me, for I am sure she is not wanted off Brest. Hardy takes good care of us, and the Amphion is very comfortable.

"*May 26th.* We have now got a foul wind, thanks to the Admiralty and our not finding Admiral Cornwallis off Brest, for we could with ease have been round Cape St. Vincent, when this would have been a fair wind. Not a vessel is to be seen on the face of the waters.

"*May 30th.* Our wind has been foul, blowing fresh and a nasty sea. We are still off Cape Finisterre. We have seen some Spaniards but not one Frenchman. We speak nothing for I am very anxious to get to my station. This is all lost time, and the sooner I get to work, the sooner, if it please God, I shall return. Perhaps by my being delayed much harm may arise, and even Sicily may fall into the hands of the French, but we are carrying sail, doing our utmost. Patience is a virtue at sea. Your dear picture and Horatia's are hung up, it revives me even to look upon them. Your health is as regularly drank as ever—the third toast, and that is all we drink. Sutton was in desperation when we left the Victory. As to news, you will not expect after what I have told you that we have not spoken a vessel. Gaetano has been tolerable—William very sea-sick.

"*June 2nd.* We have just passed the rock at Lisbon, and with a gentle fair wind, if it holds, we shall be off Cape St. Vincent in the night.

"*June 3rd.* We have had a fresh breeze and fair; at this moment, two o'clock, we are entering the Straits of Gibraltar, having run more than 100 leagues since eight o'clock yesterday morning. I have caught a little cold, but am otherwise very well. I am anxious to hear what is passing. I hope that we shall anchor at Gibraltar at eight o'clock.

"*June 4th.* I am sailing at one o'clock, having just been

---

p. 16), as "a rabid Republicaness, a vain, conceited, heartless woman, who had fixed her abode in France as a new and enlarged Goshen, and who had scribbled and printed a stupendous quantity of nonsense in praise of the whole Revolution, and in dispraise of all Kingly Governments, and all Kings, whether constitutional or despotic."

to pay my respects to the Governor. We captured a brig from the West Indies yesterday, and our boats another brig this morning. Buonaparte's brother, Jerome, passed a few days ago in a ship of the line from Martinique.

"Yours,
"NELSON AND BRONTÉ.

"I am much hurried, for they know nothing of the war."

The following from John Scott, Esq., Lord Nelson's Secretary, to Lady Hamilton, explains his removal from the Victory into the Amphion.

"Amphion in Gibraltar Bay,
8 o'clock, P.M. 3rd June, 1803.

"Dear Madam,

"We have this moment anchored here, and I have the pleasure of acquainting your Ladyship that Lord Nelson is in excellent good health and spirits. We were hopeful when we left Spithead to have fallen in with Admiral Cornwallis off Brest, and that he would have allowed the Victory to have gone on with us, but we were much disappointed at not finding the Commander-in-chief, particularly as his Lordship considered it proper to leave the Victory to *add* to the *show* off Brest, and proceed in this ship. This change gave a good deal of trouble, besides the many inconveniencies which must be submitted to before the Victory may join. His Lordship left his steward with *all* his stock, &c., a few trunks of linen excepted, on board that ship, so that until we get her, we shall not be able to commence regular *house*keeping, but I beg to assure your Ladyship, the moment that is the case, the most strict regard shall be paid to everything that concerns his Lordship's interests. We only remain here a few hours, so that I shall not be able to give your Ladyship the news of the Rock till my next. His Lordship has been particularly anxious to get here, but I am happy to observe that his health has not been in any degree affected by it, nor has it brought on any internal complaint; I have the remedy ready in case it should be wanted, and have directed Gaetano to watch narrowly the least appearance of any indisposition. His Lordship's life is so valuable and dear to his friends and country, that I trust Providence will ever guard and defend him from all danger; if the assistance of man can contribute to his happiness, or avert any danger, I am sure his Lordship will be in the full possession of the former, and never in any risk of the latter, for every one about him appears more anxious than another for his welfare. I have the pleasure of seeing your Ladyship's picture, it is hung up in the cabin, it is an excellent likeness, and one of the handsomest I ever saw. We have the honour every day of drinking a bumper to the health of the original, as our Guardian Angel, and I sincerely hope our wishes may contribute to that desirable end. I have many thanks to return your Ladyship for the kind and polite attention I had the honour to receive from you when in London, and to assure you that I shall ever think of it with grateful remembrance, and be particularly happy if it shall ever be in my power to shew your Ladyship how sensibly I feel your much respected kindness. I hope Dr. Nelson and his good family are well: may I presume on your Ladyship's kindness to make offer of my best compliments when you write them. With every wish for your Ladyship's health and happiness, I have the honour to be with great and due regard,

"Dear Madam,
"Your most obedient and faithful humble servant,
"JOHN SCOTT."

Nelson's correspondence with Lady Hamilton thus continues:—

"June 10th, twenty leagues east of Algiers.

"My dearest Emma,

"We left Gibraltar at three o'clock, June 4th. The next day we took a French brig from Cette, and a Dutch one from the same place. We have had foul winds, but by exertion are got so far on our voyage, and at present our wind is favourable, but with a nasty sea. The Admiral has had a severe cold, and is a little feverish. I really believe from anxiety to get on his station. Mr. Elliot, if this wind continues, leaves us to-morrow, as he passes over to Sardinia, and we inside the island of Galeta, passing Turin and Cape Bon. Gaetano will go in the Maidstone, and I hope return in her; but I think that very doubtful, when he once gets with his wife and family.

"How this letter will get home I know not. It will be read by every post office from Naples to London.

"The Admiral does not mean to stay at Malta more than twenty-four hours, for he is very anxious to get off Toulon. News I can tell you none, except from vessels spoke. We find that it was the Jemappe, seventy-four, passed the Straits a little before us, she was in a calm off Majorca, the 31st of May, so that if we had proceeded direct in the Victory, we should have had her to a certainty. This letter will probably find you returning from Hilborough, where my fancy tells me you are thinking of setting out, for it will amuse you by change of scene. I have wrote Gibbs a long letter to know something about Bronté—this is a matter I am determined to settle as speedily as possible, for the Admiral says it is shameful the way it has been managed. I have also wrote about your things at Malta. You forgot to give me the order, but I suppose they will believe me.

"*June* 11*th.* Mr. Elliot just leaving us, but this letter I send to Gibbs to send by the post, therefore I cannot write all I wish, but when the Admiral gets off Toulon, he intends sending a vessel direct to England.

"Yours, &c."

Nelson wrote the same day to Sir John Acton, and communicated to him his orders in regard to Naples, viz. :—
"Your Lordship is to be very attentive in observing if the French have any design of attacking the kingdoms of Naples or Sicily, and your Lordship is to exert yourself to counteract it, and to take, sink, burn, or destroy any ships or vessels which may be so employed, and to afford to his Sicilian Majesty and his subjects, all the protection and assistance may be in your power, consistently with a due attention to the other important objects entrusted to your care."[1]

He also wrote to the King and the Queen of the Two Sicilies. The Ambassador left the Amphion on the 11th. The Queen wrote thus to Lord Nelson :—

"July 6, 1803.

"I have read your letter, my worthy and respected Lord, addressed to General Acton and to Elliot, which has pro-

[1] Dispatches and Letters, Vol. v. p. 82.

duced a lively sensation. You enter into our position and circumstances perfectly, in prudently employing the strictest vigilance both by sea and land, so that we may not be compromised, and no pretext supplied to the destroyers of the human race for devouring us. You render us the most essential service, and have another claim on our eternal gratitude—depend on our vigilance, which is excited by a complete mistrust, and knowledge of the activity and perfidity of those we watch, and you shall be informed of every thing. What you send me increases my gratitude towards your loyal Government, and my satisfaction at their having chosen your worthy self for the command in the Mediterranean is infinite, and adds greatly to my tranquillity and safety. The stationing a ship constantly in the Gulf of Naples to be ready for any occasion augments the obligations of my family and myself towards you. You know that the Algerines have dared to declare war against the British flag, which renders the navigation still more difficult. I should be infinitely obliged could you send a first-rate frigate to Naples, which cruising the Adriatic would observe Tarento, Otranto, and carry the letters to Trieste, and our Minister to Vienna, the Commander Ruffo, without such protection, has no safe means of proceeding to his appointment. Pardon these demands and inconveniences, but I know your obliging attention. Rely also upon my esteem and eternal gratitude. Your sincere and very attached friend,

"CHARLOTTE.

"The King my husband, and all my dear children desire me to present their compliments and assurance of eternal esteem and gratitude."

Nelson wrote on the 14th to the Capitan Pacha, and acquainted his Highness of his appointment as Commander-in-chief of the Fleet in the Mediterranean, and that he had instructions to prevent the French from disturbing the tranquillity of the Ottoman empire, and to give every assistance in his power to the Sublime Porte and its subjects. He also addressed the Government of the Republic of the Seven Isles to the same effect, and referred to Mr. Spiridion Foresti for the sentiments of respect he entertained towards them, recollecting very vividly the testimony offered to him by the Presidents of the island of Zante, after the Battle of the Nile. He directed Captain William Edward Cracraft,[1] of the Anson, to cruise between Cape Matapan, and the south-west end of Candia, for the protection of commerce, and the destruction of the enemy, having received information that the French had a squadron of frigates in the Archipelago. The Maidstone, Captain Mowbray,[2] was dispatched with Mr. Elliot to Naples, and in her passage captured a French brig, L'Arabe,

---

[1] This officer commanded the Sea Fencibles on the coast of Sussex, and died at Chichester after a few days illness, in 1810, at the age of 48 years.

[2] Richard Hussey Mowbray was a native of Plymouth, born March 16th, 1776, and related to Sir Richard Bickerton, with whom he first went to sea in 1789. He served on the Newfoundland, Channel, and Jamaica stations. He had an opportunity of seeing much service, and was soon made a Lieutenant, and appointed to the Magicienne of 32 guns, and was at the taking of Port-au-Prince, after which, in 1794, he commanded the Fly, and brought home the bearers of the Dispatches on that occasion. He afterwards conveyed His Royal Highness the Duke of York from Helvoetsluys to Harwich, and assisted at the capture of two Dutch line-of-battle ships, one frigate, two sloops of war, nine East Indiamen, and about sixty other vessels in Plymouth Sound. In April, 1797, he was made a Post-Captain, and served as a volunteer with Sir Richard Bickerton in the Ramillies and the Terrible. In 1801, he was commissioned to the Maidstone frigate, and sent to the Mediterranean with information of the Peace of Amiens. Conveying the Russian Ambassador from Naples to Constantinople, he received a pelisse from the Grand Vizir. In 1803, he captured the brig L'Arabe with the antiquities as above stated, and in August of this year Lord Nelson appointed him to the Active, and stationed him as a frigate of observation off Toulon. In 1805, he, together with the Seahorse, Capt. the Hon. Courtenay Boyle, was chased by the French fleet, but they effected their escape. He afterwards cruised on the Irish station, and in 1807 accompanied Sir J. T. Duckworth to the Dardanelles, and most gallantly distinguished himself in the battle off Point Pesquies. On the return through the Dardanelles, his ship received one of those tremendous granite balls already mentioned, weighing 800lbs., and measuring six feet and a half in circumference. It struck the vessel two feet above the water, lodged on the orlop deck close to the magazine scuttle, without injuring any one! Proceeding to Malta with the Russian Ambassador, the Active was repaired, and afterwards employed in the Adriatic. He then commanded the Montague of 74 guns, and was at the reduction of Santa Maura. In 1811, he was employed in the Repulse in the in-shore squadron off Toulon, and then in arduous service with Rear-Admiral Hallowell. Off Port Morjean and in the Gulf of Genoa, he subsequently rendered much service, and in 1814 escorted a fleet of merchantmen from Malta to England. In 1815, he was made C.B., attained the rank of Rear-Admiral, July 19, 1821, and died Senior Vice-Admiral of the Red, and K.C.B. in November 1842.

which had on board several cases of antiquities from Athens, supposed to be for Buonaparte and the French Republic. They were, however, for the Count de Choiseul Gouffier,[1] as appears by the following letter :—

"Aux Eaux de Baréges,
1st Sept. 1803.

" My dear Lord,

" I am informed that a number of antiquities, &c. belonging to the Comte de Choiseul Gouffier, formerly French Ambassador at Constantinople, have lately been captured on board a French corvette, which was taken by an English frigate off Sicily. Your Lordship can be in no doubt what these vessels were, though I am ignorant of their names. But as I take upon myself to assure your Lordship, that the articles claimed by the Comte de Choiseul are really his private property, and as I had occasion to witness the treachery and losses to which he was subjected in regard to similar matters, from his countrymen and dependents in Turkey, I feel anxious to recommend his case, in a particular manner, to your Lordship's goodness.

" I am aware that these effects must be disposed of according to the general rules of the service; still, I am confident your Lordship will have the kindness to order every indulgence

---

[1] Count de Choiseul Gouffier, an eminent scholar and antiquary, was born at Paris, Sept. 27, 1752. He studied under the Abbé Barthélémy, from whom he derived his taste for learning, and the study of history and antiquities. He visited many countries, travelled in 1776 through Greece and Asia Minor, and commenced the publication of the results of his studies upon his return to France in 1782, in a splendid volume, entitled, " Voyage Pittoresque de la Grèce." Louis XVI. named him his Ambassador to Constantinople in 1784, where he erected an observatory, and established a printing press. Corresponding with Louis XVI. his papers were seized in 1792, and he was proscribed. He sought an asylum in Russia, and was protected by the Empress Catherine II. The Emperor Paul named him a Counsellor of State, and Director of the Academy of Arts, and of the Imperial Library. In 1802, he returned to France, and although deprived of the principal part of his fortune, he collected around him many friends of arts and letters, and in 1809, published the first part of the second volume of his splendid work, the remaining portion of which appeared after his death, under the editorship of M. M. Barbié du Bocage and Letronne. Upon the restoration of the Bourbons, Choiseul Gouffier was made a Peer of France, a Minister of State, and Privy Counsellor. In 1816, he returned to his former seat in the Royal Academy, and contributed to the transactions of that learned body. He died of an attack of apoplexy at Aix-la-Chapelle, June 20, 1817.

to be shewn to the Comte which can be granted to him. If they are necessarily to be sold, it would be an essential obligation to him, that the purchase could be made *for him* agreeably to the instructions he may send for the purpose. If the purchase were better made in the name of an Englishman, I would then beg you to authorize its being transacted on my account, according to the Comte's instructions, and to be paid for by his agent, or by drafts, on Messrs. Coutts, for my behoof, which will be immediately honoured. The unfortunate situation in which I stand will apologize to your Lordship for my not adding more than the expression of my very best wishes which ever attend you, and with which, I have the honour to remain,

"Most faithfully and truly yours,
"ELGIN.

"It were, I am sure, unnecessary for me to recommend to your friendship and assistance the several matters in which Sir Richard Bickerton, and my other friends, had taken a warm interest for me. I am confident of your Lordship's kindness."

Arrived at Gibraltar, Lord Nelson had the Guerrier fitted up for the reception of between 3 and 400 prisoners, and suggested to the Admiralty the appointment of a Lieutenant, Purser, and proper officers to her as a guard of safety. He suggested also the propriety of a similar establishment at Malta. He was much pleased with the Amphion, and described her to Captain Sutton as one of the nicest frigates he had seen. Off Messina he heard with much displeasure that a breach of neutrality had been committed by Captain Fyffe of the Cyclops, and by the Experiment, in the Bay of Naples, at anchor, in sending their boats to capture two French vessels coming into the port. One was immediately restored, and the other directed to be so when it should arrive at Malta. Nelson was very rigid in observing a strict neutrality, and would not allow it to be broken with impunity. He had upon his arrival at Malta, on the 15th, been enthusiastically received. He left it on the 17th, and as the following letter shews, was in the passage of the Faro on the 20th:—

"June 20th, 1803.

"My dear Emma,

"I am now in the passage of the Pharo. Charles is with me, and Captain Capel says behaves very well. I dare not say more, for I never expect you will ever receive this letter from

"Yours."

On June 25th:—[1]

"June 25th, off Capri.

"My dearest Emma,

"Close to Capri the view of Vesuvius calls so many circumstances to my mind, that it almost overpowers my feelings. I do not believe that I shall have any opportunity of sending this letter to Naples, and if I did, Lord Nelson does not believe Mr. Elliot would have any opportunity of sending it safely to England, therefore I can tell you little more than here we are. We arrived at Malta June 15th, in the afternoon, and sailed Thursday in the night, Lord Nelson being so very anxious to join the fleet off Toulon. Sir A. Ball is very well, but I think he looks melancholy. It was so hot that I was glad to breathe the sea air again. I saw the Marquis Testefatte—I think that is the name; he inquired after you. What is going on in Italy I cannot tell you, and if I could, dare not by this conveyance. The Admiral tells me that very soon he shall have a good and safe opportunity, therefore believe all the kind things I would say, and your fertile imagination come up to them.

"Yours.

"Charles is very well. The Maidstone is just in sight from Naples, where she went with Mr. Elliot. Reports say, by the Maidstone, that all at Naples have great confidence in Lord Nelson."

---

[1] This, and the preceding letters, are without signature, and from the mode in which they were written, display his caution in a correspondence through the post.

Nelson was now much occupied in corresponding with Mr. Elliot and Sir John Acton as to the conduct to be pursued in order to preserve the Two Sicilies. Lord Nelson was charged by the Government with the exercise of his discretion as to the steps to be taken with regard to the Two Sicilies and to the possession of the Citadel and Fort of Messina. He was anxious to prepare against any accident; and to secure an asylum and safe retreat to the royal family, he proposed to leave either a ship of the line or a frigate always at Naples. In a private letter to Sir John Acton he says, "If I know myself, it is to know that the more my friends are in distress, the more I am anxious to save them. A mouse assisted a lion, which is the only comparison I can make in arrogating to myself the power of assisting a King of the House of Bourbon; and I am sorry to say, the only one who has strictly preserved his honour, or dignity and fidelity to his Allies, and I shall feel proud in aiding you, my dear Sir John, in saving these two fine kingdoms, and Mr. Elliot will join us most cordially in this good work. All we must take care of is, not to run the risk of Sicily, beyond the line of prudence; on this point, we rely (as the seaman's phrase is) on your Excellency's look out. You must be aware of our distance, and be in time. I will, if you send to me off Toulon, either attend myself, or send Sir Richard Bickerton."[1]

Lord Nelson upon quitting Capri furnished his Excellency Mr. Elliot with an order, directed to the Senior Captain of His Majesty's ships in the Bay of Naples, to take on board, upon its presentation, the King, Queen, and Royal family of Naples and convey them to Palermo or such other place as the King might choose to proceed to. The order also extended to His Majesty's Minister and suite, and also to afford as much protection as possible to British subjects and their property. Nelson ordered Captain Richardson[2] of the Juno, to cruise off Cape Spartivento and on the coast towards Tarento for the purpose of interrupting French troops which Nelson suspected would be conveyed along shore. His orders were to take, sink, burn, and destroy them without

---

[1] From a copy in the Elliot Papers; Dispatches and Letters, Vol. v. p. 99.

[2] This officer died after a long illness, December 28th, 1815.

regard to their being in any ship or vessel bearing a Neutral flag. This determined measure arose from the French having taken possession of Pescara, Brindisi, Otranto and Tarento, and his fears that troops might thence be sent into Sicily or on the coast of Calabria opposite. He also issued orders to Captain Schomberg[1] of the Madras, or the Senior Officer of the ships at Malta to give any assistance that might be required by General Villettes to convey troops from Malta into Sicily. The importance of a Commander-in-chief of Nelson's vigour and capacity was strongly manifested at this time. His paper[2] to the Right Hon. Henry Addington, giving in brief the condition of Gibraltar, Algiers, Malta, Sicily, Sardinia, Rome, Tuscany, Genoa or Liguria, and the Morea, and his suggestions to the Government as to measures which it might be deemed advisable to adopt, exhibits Nelson's powers in a very prominent and effective manner. The Rev. Mr. Scott, Lord Nelson's chaplain and translator,

---

[1] Charles Marsh Schomberg was the son of Sir Alexander Schomberg, born at Dublin, and went to sea with his father. He was in active service during the Revolutionary war under Admiral Macbride with whom he continued until he was made a Lieutenant in 1795. He served under Captain Louis of the Minotaur, and with the Fleet off Cadiz was engaged in various daring enterprises with the Spanish flotilla and land batteries. In 1798 he went to the Mediterranean and was at the Battle of the Nile, where he took possession of the Aquilon. He was afterwards actively engaged on the coast of Italy, as already described in the account of Captain Louis's proceedings in the Minotaur. Lieutenant Schomberg accompanied Lord Keith to Egypt in the Foudroyant, and was Flag Lieutenant on that occasion. Advanced to the rank of Commander, he was appointed to the Termagant sloop, and received the gold medal of the Imperial Ottoman Order of the Crescent. After the evacuation of Egypt, he went to Tunis, and obtained the thanks of Governor Ball, and the present of a piece of plate for his services. Upon his return to England he was appointed to the Hibernia, and went to the Tagus. In 1810 he commanded the Astrea, went to the Cape of Good Hope, was detached to the Mauritius and fought an action with a French squadron near Madagascar, May 21, 1811. In 1813, he was appointed to the Nisus, sent to Brazil, and convoyed home a large fleet of merchantmen. In 1815, he was made C.B. and appointed to the Rochfort, 80 guns, the Flag ship of Sir Graham Moore in 1820. He returned in four years and was paid off at Chatham. He attained the rank of Rear-Admiral, was, in addition to the Companionship of the Bath, a Knight Commander of the Guelphic Order, and of the Royal Portuguese Order of the Tower and Sword. He died Lieutenant-Governor of Dominica, January 1st, 1835.

[2] See Dispatches and Letters, Vol. v. p. 106-11; from Autograph in the Sidmouth Papers.

says, that the services in which Lord Nelson was at this time engaged, were so complicated and harassing, and requiring so much untiring patience and watchfulness, that they gave full and anxious employment not only to himself but to all who were in his confidential service.

Off Monte Christo on the 1st of July, Lord Nelson ordered Captain Hardy of the Amphion to seize all vessels and property belonging to Genoa or the Ligurian Republic, the Government of the Republic having adopted the wishes of the French Minister as acts of their own Government, and thereby become hostile to Great Britain. He transmitted intelligence of these transactions to Sir Evan Nepean, Bart. for the Admiralty, and strongly advised an immediate blockade of Genoa in order to cut off supplies for the southern part of France and the northern parts of Italy. On his course from Monte Christo to Toulon, which voyage was unusually slow from the frequent calms and contrary winds, Nelson wrote the following letter to Lady Hamilton:—

"July, 1803.

"My dearest Emma,

"Although I have wrote letters from various places, merely to say 'Here I am,' and 'There I am,'—yet, as I have no doubt but they would all be read, it was impossible for me to say more than 'Here I am, and well,' and I see no prospect of any certain mode of conveyance, but by sea; which, with the means the Admiralty has given me, of small vessels, can be but seldom.

"Our passages have been enormously long. From Gibraltar to Malta, we were eleven days, arriving the 15th in the evening, and sailing in the night of the 16th, that is, three in the morning of the 17th, and it was the 26th before we got off Capri; where I had ordered the frigate, which carried Mr. Elliot to Naples, to join me.

"I send you copies of the King and Queen's letters. I am vexed that she did not mention you! I can only account for it, by her's being a political letter. You will only shew the King and Queen's letters to some few particular friends. The

King is very low; lives mostly at Belvidere; Mr. Elliot had not seen either him or the Queen, from the 17th, the day of his arrival, to the 21st. On the next day he was to be presented.

"I have made up my mind, that it is part of the plan of that Corsican scoundrel, to conquer the kingdom of Naples. He has marched 13,000 men into the kingdom, on the Adriatic side; and he will take possession with as much shadow of right of Gaeta and Naples: and if the poor King remonstrates, or allows us to secure Sicily, he will call it war, and declare a conquest.

"I have cautioned General Acton, not to risk the Royal family too long, but Naples will be conquered, sooner or later, as it may suit Buonaparte's convenience. The Morea and Egypt are likewise in his eye. An army of full 70,000 men are assembling in Italy. I am, you may believe, very anxious to get off Toulon, to join the Fleet. Sir R. Bickerton went from off Naples, the day I left Gibraltar. We passed Monte Christo, Bastia, and Cape Corse, yesterday; and am now moving slowly direct for Toulon. What force they have I know not; indeed, I am totally ignorant, some say nine sail of the line, some say seven, some five. If the former, they will come out, for we have only the same number, including sixty-fours, and very shortly manned. However, I hope they will come out, and let us settle the matter. You know I hate being kept in suspense.

"*July 8th.*—I left this note, to put down what force the French have at Toulon. Seven sail of the line ready, five frigates, and six corvettes. One or two more in about a week. We to-day, eight sail of the line, to-morrow, seven, including two sixty-four gun ships.

"I have not mentioned my Bronté affairs to Acton, as yet; but, if Naples remains much longer, I shall ask the question. But I expect nothing from them. I believe, even Acton wishes himself well and safely removed. I think from what I hear that the King's spirits are so much depressed, that he will give up the reins of Naples, at least to his son, and retire to Sicily. Sir William, you know, always thought that he would end his life so. Certainly, his situation must be heart-breaking.

"We joined this morning the fleet. The men in the ships are good; but the ships themselves are a little the worse for wear, and very short of their complements of men. We shall never be better: therefore, let them come, the sooner the better.

"I shall write a line to the Duke,[1] that he may see I do not forget my friends, and I rely on your saying every kind thing for me to the Doctor, Mrs. Nelson, &c. &c.

"Yours,
"NELSON AND BRONTÉ."[2]

The following appears to be the letter of the King of Naples to Lord Nelson, referred to in the preceding letter:—

"Admiral Nelson, Duke of Bronté,
"Your letter of the 10th of June gave me the liveliest satisfaction, which would have been complete, could I have had the pleasure of seeing you, but the reasons which induce you to abstain from granting it to me I quite appreciate. I recognize in that attention another proof of the constant attachment which I have experienced on so many other critical occasions. The hand of Providence again weighs on me and on my people. I see no hope or consolation but in the friendship of your august Sovereign, who was always my faithful and sincere ally. His support is certain, since he has appointed you to the command in these seas. I shall assuredly be under new obligations, and shall receive new succour from your valour and activity, to which I am infinitely indebted, as well as to the friendship of the British nation. I must solicit your immediate consideration of my position. I may lose the Kingdom of Naples, and must act with circumspection, in saving one part, not to risk the whole of the kingdom. You are too attached, and see too clearly all the circumstances, for me to fear being compromised, whilst I am also assured of being supported and perhaps saved a second time. I am very desirous of making Monsr.

---

[1] Queensberry.   [2] Collection of Letters, Vol. i. p. 123.

Elliot's acquaintance. I knew his excellent father, and have heard his praises spoken of. I trust in his intelligence, and in yours. You know my mode of thinking, it will remain the same to my last moment. Receive my wishes for all that interests you in every respect; and I pray God to have you, Admiral Nelson, Duke of Bronté, in his holy keeping.

"Your affectionate
"FERDINANDO B.

"At Naples, the 20th June, 1803."

Lord Nelson also wrote to his Royal Highness the Duke of Clarence, and observed:—

"It is, perhaps, very difficult for any one to say what are the plans of Buonaparte; he is assembling a very large army in Italy, and has already placed 13,000 men in the kingdom of Naples. I think it can only be with a view to conquer it, when it may, on some pretence or other, suit his convenience. The Morea, and ultimately Egypt, are in his view; therefore, his assembling so many troops in Italy—they say full 80,000—can only be for the purpose of removing them across the Adriatic. With this idea, I fully expect that the French fleet from Brest will assuredly come into the Mediterranean, to protect his army across the water, and along-shore from Genoa, Leghorn, &c. which are full of troops. We must keep a good look-out, both here and off Brest; and if I have the means, I shall try and fight one party or the other, before they form a junction."[1]

On the 8th Lord Nelson joined the fleet with Sir Richard Bickerton; he found them looking well, but short of men. Sir Richard was desirous of remaining with Nelson in the Mediterranean, and requested him to communicate the same to Earl St. Vincent, which he did, adding that he had no objection, as he had always heard him spoken highly of as an officer.

Captain Gore, of the Medusa, gave Nelson information of

[1] Clarke and McArthur, Vol. ii. p. 313.

the strength of the French fleet in the harbour of Toulon, and he determined on watching their movements most strictly.

The following interesting letter to Lady Hamilton is from Lord Nelson's Secretary :—

"Amphion, off Toulon, 8th July, 1803.

"Dear Madam,

"I had the honour of writing your Ladyship on the 3rd ultimo, and in order that I might not be too late, sealed up my letter just as we were going into Gibraltar Bay, on that evening. His Lordship went on shore next morning at five o'clock, after breakfast, to examine the state of the Yard, and pay his respects to the Governor. He returned about twelve, and after having finished his public dispatches, we left the Rock at four in the afternoon. I had not an opportunity of getting on shore to see the beauties of that place, nor did I much desire it. War was considered there as inevitable, but they had no account of it till our arrival; there was no news on the Rock. His Royal Highness the Duke of Kent had been some time gone previous to our arrival; Sir Thomas Trigge, notwithstanding, continues to act under his Sign Manual, but is now and then obliged to suspend some of his orders (which, however well they may answer, with Royalty to enforce them, are not perhaps so well calculated for another officer). His Royal Highness's aides-de-camp consider his return as certain; it is not, however, the public opinion, that such a desirable event is likely to take place, and therefore they are endeavouring to reconcile themselves to the absence of that illustrious military character. I forgot to mention to your Ladyship that we captured a French merchant brig off Tangier, and carried her into Gibraltar; she is supposed to be worth about £8000. On the 5th ultimo we captured another French merchant brig and a Dutch ship, and sent them to Malta. On the 11th his Lordship sent the Maidstone to Naples with his Excellency Mr. Elliot, who is really a pleasant, well-informed man. Gaetano went with him to see his wife, and was in very high spirits on the occasion. What a remarkable proof of his Lordship's

goodness of heart to part with a man, even for a short time,
so essentially necessary to his comfort, as a servant. We did
not get to Malta till the 15th, about four in the afternoon.
Sir Richard Bickerton had left that place on the 18th of May,
in consequence of the enemy's movements, and was informed
of the war on the 4th of June, by the Niger from Naples, the
French Minister at that Court having received the official
account of it some days previous to that, and long before it
was known through any other channel. It was not known
at Malta till we went there. We left that place on the 17th
ultimo, early in the morning. It is certainly one of the best
fortified towns in the world, and is worth every sacrifice we
have made to possess ourselves of it. I hope we shall never
give it up; its local advantages to England are incalculable,
although the possessing it may cost a considerable sum. We
got off Naples on the 20th of June, and were joined by the
Maidstone, who brought Gaetano back; this is a wonderful
proof of his attachment, and really more than I expected.
William did his best in the interval, though I fear was very
deficient in many instances. We are now on our way to
Toulon, where I hope we may soon arrive, and find the Victory before us, for although Captain Hardy's kind attention
cannot be excelled, yet the comfort of a large ship in this
climate is so desirable, that we are all wonderfully anxious to
fall in with her, and get settled. His Lordship, I have the
pleasure to tell your Ladyship, is quite well, and in excellent
health; he has been very anxious (and no wonder, when it is
considered how necessary his presence is off Toulon,) to join
Sir Richard Bickerton. I have heard much of Lord Nelson's
abilities as an Officer and Statesman, but the account of the
latter is infinitely short. In my travels through the service
I have met with no character in any degree equal to his Lordship; his penetration is quick, judgment clear, wisdom great,
and his decisions correct and decided: nor does he in company appear to bear any weight on his mind, so cheerful and
pleasant that it is a happiness to be about his hand; in fact,
he is a great and wonderful character, and very glad and
happy shall I be, if in the discharge of my duty, private and
public, I have the good fortune to meet his Lordship's appro-

bation. With every wish for your Ladyship's health and happiness, I have the honour to remain, with great regard,
"Dear Madam,
"Your most obedient and faithful humble servant,
"JOHN SCOTT.

"P.S. We arrived off here yesterday forenoon, and this morning, 8th of July, fell in with Sir Richard Bickerton and his squadron. We hear the Victory is in this country. I hope in fourteen days she will be with us."

Lord Nelson also wrote to Lady Hamilton on the 12th:—

"Amphion, July 12th, 1803.

"My dearest Emma,

"'Tis now near two months since my departure, and thanks to the Admiralty, nothing is yet arrived, nor have I heard the least bit of English news. It is my intention, the first money I get, to pay off Mr. Graves' £2000 mortgage, which is due 1st October next, and after that Mr. Davison; then I shall have Mr. Matcham's mortgage money lodged, after which I shall send you some to begin next spring our alterations; but first I will, if I can, get out of debt. I am talking as if I had made a fortune, and God knows, as yet I have not received one farthing of Prize Money. Some vessels are taken, but they, even if they are condemned, will not give me much. Prize Money does not seem my lot. However, time must give me something handsome, and I shall keep everybody alive, and on the look-out; for although money may not absolutely constitute the whole of happiness, yet we both know that happiness sits much more easy when we have a purse of money to resort to, and we must allow that there is great comfort in it.

"*July* 18*th*. Off Toulon. We have just had a three days gale, but we are close off Toulon, looking at them. I have not seen a single vessel these five days, except our own fleet; therefore, I neither can tell you news, nor have received any. The happiness of keeping a station is always to have a foul wind, and never to hear the delightful sound, *Steady*. Victory, I hope, will soon join. I have heard Sutton has made £8000. in her in his way to join me, but I fear with my usual prize luck I shall not share for his prizes; but perseverance will do wonders, and some day I shall get very rich. Hardy has been very unwell, indeed I was afraid that he would have been obliged to go home, but he is much better. His loss would have been a most serious one to me. Rev. Dr. Scott[1] is very busy translating; his health is much recovered. Murray, Hardy, and Mr. Scott are on a Court Martial, so I have all the ship to myself. My Secretary I esteem a treasure; he is not only a clever man, but indefatigable in his business, and an extraordinary well behaved, modest man; in short, I feel very well mounted at present, and I trust shall have no reason to wish for any alteration. I long to hear of your Norfolk excursion, and everything you have been about, for I ever am most warmly interested in all your actions.

"*July* 21*st*. We have not seen a vessel these many days. The Medusa and Termagant have been up the Gulf of Lyons, they spoke some Spaniards from Marseilles who tell them that all the seamen are sent to Toulon, and the merchant ships laid up. We are anxious for the Victory joining, as we are almost eating salt beef. Make my kind regards to Mrs. Cadogan, and all our friends, and be assured I ever am,

"Yours,

"NELSON AND BRONTÉ."

On the 17th, Captain Langford, who was wounded at the attack upon the Boulogne flotilla, wrote to Lady Hamilton:—

"H. M. Ship Fury,
Downs, July 17th, 1803.

"My dear Lady,

"Your kind mention of me to my family, believe me, is very flattering to me, and has made me both proud and grateful. I trust you will do me the justice to suppose I should lose no opportunity in assuring you of my respects, as well as informing you the moment I have any intimation of following our noble Admiral to the Mediterranean—for this you may guess I am extremely anxious. But I guess Lord St. Vincent, in his great goodness, does not think the

---

[1] The Chaplain, not a Doctor at that time. See Appendix, No. II.

*Fury's* services absolutely necessary in that quarter. After having so long followed the fortunes of our noble friend, I confess I do not feel a relish for serving under any other. I intend writing to Lord St. Vincent on the subject, and any service you can be to me on the part of Lord Nelson, in *this* case, I shall ever acknowledge with much gratitude. I am grieved to find Sir William Bolton is still unemployed; I had expected from the Earl's *promises*, he would immediately on the *war* have been called on.

"I am sure he must be happy in *governing* his *present* command. I have not been as yet very successful; in fact, the station I am on (which is the Downs) does not admit of it, being too far to the eastward to get prizes. I have had a *brush* with our friends the *Boulognese*—but no mischief done. My protegée is doing very well. I am much obliged to you for your good intentions towards him.

' I hope you found the great County of *Norfolk* agreeable. I am no friend to it. Pray assure every body under your roof of my respects, and believe me ever,

"Your much obliged,
"FRED. LANGFORD."

Nelson was full of activity and eagerness regarding the French fleet, and on the 21st wrote to Captain Gore, of the Medusa, to gain every information respecting their movements, fearing they might be joined by a squadron from the West Indies or from Brest.

Sir Alexander Ball wrote to Lady Hamilton on the 23rd:—

"Malta, 23rd July, 1803.

"My dear Lady Hamilton,

"I was happy to hear from our most worthy Nelson that you were in good health, and supporting with as much fortitude as possible the greatest loss which could happen to you, but which you must have foreseen, and knowing it to be unavoidable, your mind would be gradually preparing for the awful event. I hope that you will now be many years without meeting any misfortune to interrupt your peace of mind.

"I have great satisfaction in acquainting you that Lord

Nelson never looked in better health than when here. He will, I trust, return soon to his favourite spot with additional honours and wealth. If you should have any person coming here to whom I can be of use, pray command me, and consider me among your zealous friends. I have had a great deal of plague with the Foreign Ministers here. I found the Prince of Pantellaria disaffected to his Sicilian Majesty's Ministers, and very unfriendly to the English; he seemed devoted to the French.

"My family enjoy good health here. My son is grown very much, and desires to be respectfully remembered to you. Adieu, my dear Lady Hamilton. Believe me, with every wish, your obliged and affectionate friend,

"ALEXANDER JOHN BALL."

The Queen of Naples wrote to Lady Hamilton at this time:—

"My dear Lady,

"I take advantage of the departure of Mr. A'Court[1] to write to you. It is really so difficult now to find an opportunity of communicating with England, that one is glad to seize any offer. I embrace this in order to assure you of my constant and unchanging sentiments towards you. I learnt with great interest and regret the loss you have sustained of the good Chevalier, and what much distresses me is, that you are left so indifferently provided for: that, I am really much grieved to hear, for I take the liveliest interest in all that concerns you. My health is always ailing; that of my dear children, thank God, is good. We all recall with gratitude the many attentions you bestowed upon us, and only desire to be able to shew you how we appreciate them. The command in the Mediterranean being given to the brave and virtuous Lord Nelson has filled us with joy, and we already feel the happy results of it. Adieu, my dear Lady; let me have news of you sometimes, and believe me for life your grateful friend,

"CHARLOTTE.

"The 26th July, 1803."

[1] Afterwards Lord Heytesbury.

Lord Nelson wrote to her Majesty the same day:—

"Off Toulon, July 26, 1803.

"Madam,

"The first great object which is always nearest my heart is the safety of the persons of your Majesties, and of all the Royal Family. The second, so far as it is in my power, is that of the Kingdom of Naples, which is a very difficult affair.

"If your Majesty were to act with all the circumspection in your power, either the French would feel themselves offended, or, what is worse, if possible, their assistance would be given by force to the King, for the *preservation* of Sicily. The great wisdom of your Majesty will know all that I could allege upon this subject. I shall therefore only say, that if Sicily is lost, Europe will blame the councils of his Sicilian Majesty, and Lord Nelson, for having been so weak as to pay attention to, or credit what is reported by the agents of the present French Government.

"I have written to the English Government, declaring fully the unhappy position of the Kingdom of Naples; regretting the orders given for the return of the army of Egypt, and setting forth with energy the necessity for sending troops not only to assist in the defence of Sicily, but in sufficient numbers to place garrisons in Gaeta, in the castles of Naples, if it should be expedient, and to send a body of men into Calabria, to support the loyal and brave inhabitants of that country of mountains, in case the French should be too imperious in their demands.

"His Excellency, Mr. Elliot, will inform your Majesty of the difficulty I have in leaving a ship of the line at Naples, considering the present state of the enemy's fleet at Toulon; but I will never permit my personal feelings to weigh against the sacred interest which I shall always take in the safety and well-being of your Majesties, and of all the Royal Family; and I assure your Majesty that I am always

"Your most devoted and faithful servant,

"NELSON AND BRONTÉ."[1]

[1] Life of the Rev. Dr. Scott, p. 111.

Nelson was rendered unhappy at this time by intelligence that his friend Mr. Davison had got into trouble, and been prosecuted for bribery at the Ilchester election, and for which in April, 1804, he was sentenced by the Court of King's Bench to twelve months imprisonment in the Marshalsea prison. In a letter of the 27th, Nelson says, "I hope in God, my dear Davison, that you will get over these damned prosecutions for the election. It has, and does give me very serious uneasiness."[1] And on the 24th August: "I was glad to hear, and hope it will prove true, that your damned electioneering business will be got quit of. It has cost me many bitter pangs: and without those feelings for our friends, there can be no friendship."[2]

On the 1st of August, Lord Nelson wrote off Toulon to Lady Hamilton:—

"Victory, off Toulon, August 1, 1803.

"My dearest Emma,

"Your letter of May 31. which came under cover to Mr. Noble, of Naples, inclosing Davison's correspondence with Plymouth, arrived by the Phœbe two days ago; and this is the only scrap of a pen which has been received by any person in the fleet since we sailed from England. You will readily conceive the sensations which the sight and reading even your few lines [occasioned]. Sutton joined me yesterday, and we are all got into the Victory, and a few days will put us in order. Everybody gives a very excellent character of Mr. Chevalier, the servant recommended by Mr. Davison; and I shall certainly live as frugal as my situation will admit. I have known the pinch, and shall endeavour never to know it again. I want £2000. to pay off Mr. Greaves,[3] on October 1st, but I have not received one farthing; I hope to receive some soon. Mr. Haslewood promised to see this matter kept right for me.

"Hardy is now busy, hanging up your and Horatia's picture; and I trust soon to see the other two safe arrived from

---

[1] Dispatches and Letters, Vol. v. p. 143. From an autograph in the possession of Colonel Davison.  [2] Ibid. p. 175.
[3] On account of the purchase of Merton.

the Exhibition. You will not expect much news from us. We see nothing. I have great fear that all Naples will fall into the hands of the French; and, if Acton does not take care, Sicily also. However, I have given my final advice so fully and strongly, that, let what will happen, they cannot blame me. Captain Capel says, Mr. Elliot cannot bear Naples. I have no doubt but that it is very different to your time.

"The Queen, I fancy by the seal, has sent a letter to Castelcicala; her letter to me is only thanks for my attention to the safety of the kingdom. If Dr. Scott has time, and is able, he shall write a copy for you. The King is very much retired. He would not see the French General St. Cyr; who came to Naples, *to settle the contribution for the payment of the French army.* The Queen was ordered to give him and the French Minister a dinner, but the King staid at Belvidere. I think he will give it up soon, and retire to Sicily, if the French will allow him. Acton has never dared give Mr. Elliot, or one Englishman, a dinner.

"The fleet are ready to come forth; but they will not come for the sake of fighting me. I have this day made George Elliot, Post; Lieutenant Pettit, a Master and Commander; and Mr. Hindmarsh, the gunner's son of the Bellerophon, who behaved so well this day five years, a Lieutenant. I reckon to have lost two French seventy-fours by my not coming out in the Victory; but I hope they will come soon, with interest. This goes to Gibraltar, by Sutton, in the Amphion. I shall write the Doctor in a day or two. I see by the French papers he has kissed hands. With regards, &c. &c.

"Yours,
"NELSON AND BRONTÉ."[1]

Lord Nelson dispatched Captain Sutton of the Amphion to cruise from Cape Spartel towards Madeira, and thence to Cape St. Vincent and to Cape Spartel, to gain information of the French fleet, and acquainted the Admiralty that the enemy's force consisted of seven sail of the line, five or six frigates, and six or seven corvettes. At Genoa there were three Genoese vessels of war, about forty sail of merchant

---

[1] Collection of Letters, Vol. i. p. 129.

ships, and three Dutch merchantmen; and at Marseilles, he learnt from vessels that had been spoken with, they were putting in requisition eighty or ninety sail of vessels of about forty tons each, to be fitted as gun-boats, and to proceed by the Canal of Languedoc to Bordeaux. He directed Captain Sir Richard Strachan, Bart., of the Donegal, to proceed to the Straits of Gibraltar, and look after a French seventy-four and some frigates at Cadiz, impeding our trade.

To Lady Hamilton he wrote on the 10th:—

"Victory, off Toulon, August 10th, 1803.

" My dearest Emma,

" I take the opportunity of Mr. A'Court's going through Spain with Mr. Elliot's dispatches for England, to send this letter: for I would not for the world, miss any opportunity of sending you a line.

" By Gibraltar I wrote you as lately as the 4th; but all our ways of communicating with England are very uncertain; and I believe the Admiralty must have forgot us; for not a vessel of any kind or sort has joined us since I left Spithead. News I absolutely am ignorant of; except that a schooner, belonging to me, put her nose into Toulon; and four frigates popped out and have taken her, and a transport loaded with water for the fleet. However, I hope to have an opportunity, very soon, of paying them the debt with interest.

" Mr. A'Court says, at Naples they hope that the mediation of Russia will save them: but I doubt if Russia will go to war with the French for any kingdom; and they, poor souls! relying on a broken reed will lose Sicily.

" As for getting anything for Bronté, I cannot expect it; for the finances of Naples are worse than ever. *Patienza*, however, I will.

" I see many Bishops are dead. Is my brother tired of Canterbury? I wish I could make him a Bishop. If you see him, or write, say that I have not ten minutes to send away Mr. A'Court, who cannot be detained.

" I hope Lord St. Vincent has sent out Sir William Bolton. As soon as I know who is first Lord, I will write him."[1]

[1] Collection of Letters, Vol. i. p. 130.

Lord Nelson ordered Captain Cracraft of the Anson to proceed off Cape Spartiento, and between that and the entrance of the Adriatic, learning that the French intended sending a squadron of frigates into the Adriatic to protect their army at the heel of Italy. He lost no opportunity with, it must be admitted, very inadequate means, to protect our commerce in every direction.

In this month he endeavoured to effect an exchange of prisoners with the French Admiral, but his letter was refused acceptance. His offer was again made to Admiral La Touche, and the reply to this was, from the singular course adopted by the French Admiral by sending it through Paris, only received by Lord Nelson by the attention of Lambton Este, Esq. who addressed his Lordship as follows :—

"Malta, July 7th, 1804.

"My Lord,

"While searching, this morning, the old papers at the Post Office for certain letters of my own, concerning which not any accurate account could be given, I accidentally met with the inclosed; from the signature on the direction, perceiving it to be on public service, I can feel but doubly assiduous in forwarding it to your Lordship.

"The letter brought by the Italian post from Sicily to Malta, about the middle of the month of May, has been laying at the office ever since, and but for a mere chance might have continued there to remain.

"This instance, one among very many others it has been my fate to witness generally through the Mediterranean during the Egyptian expedition, no less than in the course of my present voyage, may serve to convince your Lordship, how from want of arrangement and regularity, the general service may suffer; while scarcely any individual can escape the inconveniences occasioned thereby.

"I venture thus to trouble your Lordship, as in the course of my various voyages at different periods, and in different parts of the Mediterranean, with the greatest deference to your Lordship's better judgment and opinion, it has ever appeared that were the general inspections and superintendence of the posts given in charge to some active intelligent person well acquainted with the Mediterranean, the service might be materially benefited, and every individual embarked in its different departments, not only at Gibraltar and Malta, but generally; while such as are engaged in civil and commercial pursuits, along the Barbarese-Levant and Adriatic, together with the former, might thence derive most material and important accommodation.

"I have the honour to remain,
"My Lord,
"With the greatest consideration and profound respect,
"Your Lordship's most humble and obedient servant,
"LAMBTON ESTE.
"Private Secretary to the Consul General in Egypt.

"Vice-Admiral Lord Viscount Nelson,
&c. &c. &c."

This was acknowledged by Lord Nelson, August 3rd, 1804: "I feel very much obliged by your letter of July 7th, and for Monsieur La Touche's letter, who, I suppose, not knowing *where to find me*, directed to Malta. I most perfectly agree with you on the great irregularity of our Post Offices in this country, but the mending them does not only not rest with me, but, probably, if I was to meddle or recommend, it might make *bad worse*. I hope you left your worthy father well: do little wonder that you are not at your post in Egypt. I had a line from Mr. Lock from Naples: reports say that he is first going to Constantinople."[1]

---

[1] Mr. now Dr. Lambton Este, was the son of the Rev. C. Este, well known to Lady Hamilton, and was introduced to Lord Nelson by the following letter:—

"My most dear and greatly to be honoured Lord, I cannot help troubling you with a line or two, for a beloved son of mine, who once dined with you at Merton, is again going through the Mediterranean to Egypt. When there before he was one of the Surgeons to the Guards. Now he goes with the mission of Mr. Lock as the Secretary and Physician. In the strange vicissitudes of Time and Chance it may so happen that he may come into your notice and correspondence: if it should be so, my dear Lord, I will answer for his manly conduct and unoffending manners; for the faithfulness and good affections of his heart.

"Adieu, adieu, Sir, the time and my spirits fail me to say more, than that the order for going to Portsmouth came with cruel abruptness but a few hours ago, and that my Lady, the most noble creature living, has been writing for us ever

In the exercise of these great and unwearied exertions requiring incessant attention and watchfulness, Nelson pre-

since. With kind emotions more than I can utter, and with esteem and admiration too, my most dear Lord, again and again, very tenderly adieu.

"Your most obliged servant,
"C. Este."

"Feb. 3, 1804, at midnight."

Mr. Este thus acknowledges Lord Nelson's letter:—

"Malta, August 20th, 1804.

"My Lord,

"Your Lordship's favour of the 3rd of August, I had the honour of receiving duly by the Amazon; not at all surprised that Monsieur Latouche Tréville should be endeavouring to find your Lordship any where where your Lordship does not happen to be—cannot abandon hope that your Lordship may yet have fair opportunity of letting him know, and in the most unequivocal manner, precisely where it is, your Lordship may, occasionally, be met with, in order not to leave room for mistakes in future.

"The administration of the posts—I never should have ventured to mention to your Lordship—had the inconveniences thereof been confined to myself or to my friends. But in the course of present and preceding voyages, I never remember meeting a single individual in any rank or situation, who had not been to greater or less degree a sufferer.

"Under such an impression, and the remembrance of certain observations, not in the way of every person to make, I felt it incumbent upon myself, as a kind of duty, to communicate the result of my experience to your Lordship; especially on an opportunity, and an act of irregularity, like that of Monsieur Latouche Tréville's letter.

"The inclosed will afford further confirmation of any thing that may have been before mentioned; no account is given of it—the present letter did not appear at the Post Office till very lately—probably came from Gibraltar in the Termagant, and for some trivial reason or other had been thrown into that part of the office, commonly called in England, the Dead Letter Office, whence I have the honour of redeeming and of forwarding it.

"My father, concerning whom your Lordship makes such kind inquiries, I parted with in high health in London; on leaving him he put the annexed into my hand, and desired me to deliver the same unto your Lordship—I have since been preserving it, under vain but flattering expectations that the chapter of accidents might have afforded me the satisfaction of so doing.

"Mr. Lock on the 19th of June, with Captain Vincent of the Arrow, sailed for Smyrna. Captain Vincent has since written to announce their speedy voyage. Mr. Lock may be expected daily, on return to Malta before taking a fresh departure for the Levant, or will send such instructions as will determine and guide the movements of,

"My Lord,
"With the greatest consideration and respect,
"Your Lordship's
"Most humble and most obedient servant,
"Lambton Este."

served his health and spirits, as appears from the following letter from his Chaplain to Lady Hamilton:—

"August 18th, 1803.

"Dear Lady Hamilton,

"I have the pleasure to assure you upon my honour that Lord Nelson is well both in health and spirits, hoping as he does most sanguinely to meet the enemy's fleet, and gather some more laurels. I have just read your letter, and can solemnly declare no one circumstance for years past has given me so much pleasure as this proof of your remembrance of me. In attaching myself to Lord Nelson I really considered you, as it were a part of him, and to say truth was sorry you did not, as I thought, like me enough. You have written to me, and I am contented. If you knew me long, you would rely upon my word, when I assure you that I hold as sacred this profession of attachment to you and Lord Nelson.

"I ought, perhaps, to have written to your Ladyship in a more distant and formal manner, but as it comes from the very bottom of my heart, you will pardon me on account of my sincerity. I am happy to hear all the family are well, and hope they will remember me, and accept of my best wishes and respects.

"I am ever,
"With the most devoted regard,
"Your Ladyship's faithful friend and humble servant,
"A. J. Scott.

"I have been so delighted with hearing from your Ladyship, that I have not thanked you for the verses, which are excellent.

"Addio! e qualche volte almeno
"Ricordati di me."

---

"Lazaretto, Malta, September 18th, 1804.
"My Lord,

"The inclosed dispatch, left open for your Lordship's perusal, contains the particulars of the unhappy fate of Charles Lock, Esq. late Consul-General in Egypt. Again, my Lord, I remain,

"&c. &c. &c.
"Lambton Este."

Mr. Lock died of the Plague in the Lazaretto at Malta, September 12, 1804. Mr. Este placed himself in the Lazaretto, and attended him and two of his suite, who also fell victims to the pestilence.

On the 21st Lord Nelson wrote to Lady Hamilton:—

"August 21st, 1803.

"We have had, my dearest Emma, two days pretty strong gales. The Canopus has lost her fore-yard, but we shall put her in order again. This is the fourth gale we have had since July 6th, but the Victory is so easy at sea, that I trust we shall never receive any material damage. It is never my intention, if I can help it, to go into any port—my business is to be at sea, and get hold of the French fleet, and so I shall by patience and perseverance. As for Malta you know what I said about it in Parliament—it is useless to us for the blockade of Toulon, and nothing but an action, and probably not that, can ever make me go there—it takes upon the average seven weeks to get an answer to a letter. Malta and Toulon are entirely different services. It struck me that it was a horrid place, and all the captains who have been laid up there detest it. Our friend Ball, if I am not mistaken, wishes himself afloat, but he is too proud to own it. *He* is, I can assure you, a great man, and on many occasions appears to forget that he *was* a seaman, he is bit with the dignity of the Corps Diplomatique; but I differ with no one, however I can think a little, and can see *a* little into a mill-stone.

"I entreat that you will let nothing fret you, only believe me, once for all, that I am ever your own Nelson. I have not a thought except on you and the French fleet—all my thoughts, plans, and toils tend to those two objects, and I will embrace them both so close when I can lay hold of either one or the other, that the devil himself should not separate us. Don't laugh at my putting you and the French fleet together, but you cannot be separated. I long to see you both in your proper places, the French fleet at sea, you at dear Merton, which in every sense of the word, I expect to find a paradise. I send you a copy of Gibbs's letter, my answer, and my letter to Mr. Noble about your things, and I will take all care that they shall get home safe."

Lord Nelson was anxious that Mr. Abraham Gibbs of Palermo should undertake the management of his Bronté estate, and wrote to him on the subject August 11th, 12th, and

13th. It appears from some fragments of letters among his papers that his property at Bronté had been much mismanaged. In one of these he says:—

"I see that Græffer has pensioned some man that is said to have gained my cause, 65 ounces a year, and Gibbs recommends me to buy him off. This is one thing that I never heard of before, however I have sent Gibbs an order to receive this year's rents, and to sell the stock on the farm, that the debts may be paid as soon as possible. You may rely that I shall take care and settle something, if possible, *solid* before I leave this country. It is more than two months since I have heard from Naples, and till yesterday five weeks since I heard from Malta. I had a letter from poor Macaulay, he desires to be most kindly remembered to you. I hear Mr. Elliot does not like Naples, indeed I can conceive it is very different to what it was in our time. Do you ever hear from the Queen? I fear that she is a time-serving woman, and cares for no one except for those at the moment who may be useful to her. However, *time will shew*. I am every day taking care of them. It is seven weeks since I heard from Gibraltar, for I have no small vessels to send about. We are cruising here in hopes some day to get hold of the French fleet, and that will repay us for all our toils."

In another fragment he writes that he is determined to lay out no more, and adds:—

"They say the house which is fitted up is ridiculous. Instead of a farm house it is a palace—quite a folly in Græffer.

"I had yesterday Charles on board to dine with me; he is not much grown, but Captain Capel says he behaves very well. I want to know what changes have taken place at the Admiralty—the French papers have announced Lord Castlereagh. I have wrote to Mr. Booth, and to Mr. Haslewood, and ordered home from Gibraltar £2100. to pay off Mr. Greaves, and I hope it will arrive before the 1st of October, but if it should not, I trust that Haslewood will manage that I get into no scrape. It is the first-fruits of prize-money, not much you will say, but I am not over fortunate in that respect. Be so good as to write a note to Haslewood. I long to be out of debt. I see by the papers that my cause has been argued and judgment deferred, I hope I shall get it, I long to know Haslewood's opinion. You will be sorry but not surprised to hear of Lord Bristol's death.[1] We are all well, and with kindest regards to Mrs. Cadogan, and all friends, believe me,

" Yours,
" NELSON AND BRONTÉ."

The following is Mr. Gibbs's reply to Lord Nelson :—

" Palermo, 12th September, 1803.

" My Lord,

" I have had the honour of receiving your Lordship's kind letters, 11th, 12th, and 13th ultimo, which are highly flattering to me. Allow me to assure your Lordship, that I regard the Bronté estate as if it belonged to myself, and have the satisfaction to acquaint you, that by the pressing orders given since my arrival, matters are already in a great state of forwardness. The old accounts are under examination, part of the unnecessary expenses diminished, the Baschetto farmed out, and the debt of four thousand ounces to the Archbishop of Bronté ordered to be discharged from this year's rents.

" Your Lordship is right, that nothing was repaid of the seven thousand ounces borrowed, which, with interest from the first period, is swelled to near eight thousand ounces. The occasion of there being no money resulting from the estate was, that poor Græffer employed three years' rent for fitting up the house and improving the farm, instead of two years' rent as first intended, for reasons that he wrote your Lordship at the time. I have thought, therefore, that these four thousand ounces might as well be paid out of the full rental due next August, 1804, and there would remain over at that period another thousand pounds to remit to your

---

[1] This nobleman before mentioned was fourth Earl of Bristol, and also Bishop of Derry. He died on the 8th of July, 1803. To avoid any superstitious exhibition on the part of sailors, who entertain a dread of having a corpse on board, his Lordship's body was packed up in a case, and shipped as an antique statue ! Could he have anticipated such a circumstance, it would have afforded him a capital subject to have written upon.

banker, when the estate will be quite clear, so as to enable you to have the full rental of the year 1805, unless, however, it should be your Lordship's pleasure to accept of the best offer made for the hire of the farm for a certain *number* of years.

"I have written last past to Mr. Broadbent to entreat him to renew his offer, that it may be in my power to decide upon the plan most suitable to your Lordship's interest, and as soon as Sir John Acton may have been pleased to communicate to me his Sicilian Majesty's determination relative to your Lordship's desire, to receive the *value* of the estate. I addressed Sir John the 9th instant upon the subject, in the manner you directed me, and sent my letter under cover to Cavaliere Gerardi, who is his present secretary, and my friend. I flatter myself therefore, that I shall shortly have the pleasure of sending your Lordship some satisfactory answer from Sir John Acton.

"In the event of the estate being hired, I shall be mindful of all your Lordship's orders; but supposing his Majesty should insinuate your Lordship's selling the estate to the best bidder, and that I should be able to find an equitable offer for it, would this be anyways against your Lordship's inclination?[1]

"I expect hither Mrs. Græffer every hour from Bronté; her presence will facilitate the classing of the past concerns, she is very desirous of remaining some time longer at Bronté, and considers it would be for your Lordship's interest.

"How very fortunate it was my landing dear Lady Hamilton's cases at Girgenti from the vessel that was taken in returning to Malta, and sent to Tunis: I had a foresight of this accident, owing to the number of French privateers in the south parts of Sicily; I expect the cases are embarked for Malta at this hour to Mr. Noble's care (either by the Spider brig or Cyclops), who writes me that he had received your Lordship's directions to forward them to England.

"The Arms of Bronté[2] are ordered, and will be sent to your Lordship immediately. Those of your Lordship are

---

[1] Lord Nelson has written '*Quite the contrary*,' against this paragraph.
[2] Lord Nelson was desirous of having them for the Herald's College.

sought for here to be placed among the rest of the nobility of the island, and at Bronté particularly.

"Mr. Taught and me, and Mrs. Porcelli are extremely flattered by your Lordship's remembrance; the former lost his wife the 9th instant. Your godchild really grows a fine boy, and is the comfort of the family.

"We can have no news here but what is known to your Lordship through Mr. Elliot.

"I hope I have not trespassed upon your Lordship's time, and have the honour to be, my Lord,

"Your Lordship's most obedient, and
"Most humble servant,
"ABRAHAM GIBBS.

"The Right Hon. Lord Nelson, K.B.
Duke of Bronté, &c. &c. &c."

On the 24th, Lord Nelson wrote to Lady Hamilton:—

"Victory, August 24th, 1803.

"My dearest Emma,

"Yesterday brought me letters from Mrs. Græffer, *via* Malta. As far as my own private concerns can occupy my attention in these times, they have made me angry, but I have done. I am glad I wrote to Gibbs; if I have time I will send you copies. In one part, she says, that if I had been there, I should have spent more; that might be, and yet very improper for them. She says, the house cost so much. Why did it? it was not my ordering. Græffer thought that I approved giving to the poor; so I am to be held forth as angry at a few ounces given to the poor, but I have done; what I have promised shall be punctually and regularly paid. From some expression in her letter, I think she means to say that she cannot live for £200. a-year. I suppose she will say something of it to you. She intends to reside at Palermo, and she wants me to apply to the Court for a pension. Do you know the King never knew of my wish to resign Bronté; it is said, Acton dare not tell him, and now I fear the French will have Sicily, so that I shall be well off. If that does not happen, I shall hope to get regularly £2000. a-year—that will be a pretty addition to our housekeeping.

"Mr. A'Court told me that Casteleicala was as great a favourite as ever with the Queen, and that if Acton went away she would try and have him Prime Minister—then I believe the kingdom would be well governed. If she has not wrote you she is an ungrateful ——. Admiral Campbell[1] is on board, and desires his best compliments. He has made a large fortune in the Channel Fleet—so much the better—the more we take from the French the less they have, and the sooner, I hope, we shall have peace. I have given Mrs. Johnson's letter to the lad South, and have promised him my protection if he is a good boy. Whenever young Faddy comes, he shall be promoted.

"Ever yours,
"NELSON AND BRONTÉ."

Small as was the amount of prize-money Lord Nelson was so fortunate as to obtain, the appointment of Agents seems to have given him no little trouble. The following fragment of a letter applies to one of these occasions:—

"To say the truth, I am so situated between Davison and Mr. Marsh that I do not think I ever can name an Agent again. I have had many and great obligations to both of them, and I never put a sixpence into Mr. Marsh's pocket—to Davison it has been twice in my power. Say he has touched (besides the use of the money, which you may lay at £10,000), full £15,000, and when I told Davison how I was situated with Mr. Marsh, and that I wished to name them together, Davison declined it, and said, 'Whatever you do, let me stand alone.' I may never have the power of naming one alone, for Secretaries and other Admirals will naturally look to the compliment being also paid them of joining together; therefore, if Davison will never be joined, I see but little chance of my being able to name him alone, and indeed, Captains have naturally so many friends of their own, that it is not to be expected. I have wrote Davison pretty near as much some time ago, but he may be assured that I shall never omit an opportunity when it can be done with propriety, and I am sure he is too much my friend to wish to place me in difficulties; but keep this to yourself. I will for a moment suppose a case which may happen: We take the French fleet, the

---

[1] Sir George Campbell, G.C.B., attained the rank of Admiral of the White, was appointed Commander-in-chief at Portsmouth, and in a fit of derangement, shot himself, January 23, 1821.

Captains name the three Secretaries, and pay me, perhaps, the compliment of asking me to name a person in England to do the business. I should, of course, wish to join Mr. Davison and Mr. Marsh; it would hurt me for him to refuse to be joined to Mr. Marsh and the Secretaries here, and yet he would do it. I know he would give up the proportion, and only ask to have his name stand alone, but neither the captors nor the other parties would agree to it; therefore, I know of no other way but not taking the French fleet, and that would be very hard upon me; but I have done with that subject. What is it that Mrs. Denis thinks that I can be useful to Mr. Denis in at Civita Vecchia; no prizes can be carried in there; even if the Pope would allow it, nobody would trust their property under the Pope's care, therefore, I know of nothing. I shall never have any communication with that place now Lord Bristol is dead. It cannot be an object for them to go out, the pay will not hire their lodgings, and there can be no trade till the Peace.

"N. & B."

On the 26th he again wrote to Lady Hamilton:—

"August 26th, 1803.

"My dearest Emma,

"By the Canopus, Admiral Campbell, I have received all your truly kind and affectionate letters, from May 20th to July 3rd, with the exception of one dated May 31st, sent to Naples.

"This is the first communication I have had with England since we sailed.

"I do not think it can be a long war; and I believe it will be much shorter than people expect: and I shall hope to find the new room built; the grounds laid out, neatly but not expensively; new Piccadilly gates; kitchen garden, &c. Only let us have a peace, and then all will go on well. It will be a great source of amusement to you; and Horatia shall plant a tree. I dare say she will be very busy. Mrs. Nelson, or Mrs. Bolton, &c. will be with you; and time will pass away till I have the happiness of ariving at Merton.

"I feel all your good mother's kindness; and, I trust, that we shall turn rich by being economists. Spending money to please a pack of people is folly, and without thanks. I desire that you will say every kind thing from me to her, and make her a present of something in my name.

"Dr. Scott[1] is gone with my mission to Algiers, or I would send you a copy of the King and Queen's letter. I send you one from the Queen. Both King, Queen, and Acton, were very civil to Sir William Bolton. He dined with Acton.

"Bolton does very well in his brig; but he has made not a farthing of prize-money. If I knew where to send him for some, he should go; but, unless we have a Spanish war, I shall live here at a great expense; although Mr. Chevalier[2] takes every care, and I have great reason to be satisfied.

"I have just asked William, who behaves very well, whether he chooses to remit any of his wages to his father; it does not appear he *does* at present. He is paid, by the King, eighteen pounds a-year, as one of my retinue; therefore, I have nothing to pay. I have told him, whenever he chooses to send any, to tell Mr. Scott, or Captain Hardy, and he will receive a remittance bill; so he may now act as he pleases.

"*Apropos* of Mr. Scott.[3] He is very much obliged to you for your news of Mrs. Scott's being brought to bed. No letters came in the cutter but to me, and he was very uneasy. He is a very excellent good man; and I am very fortunate in having such a one.

"I admire your kindness to my dear sister Bolton. I have wrote her that certainly I will assist Tom Bolton at College. It is better, as I tell her, not to promise more than I am sure I can perform. It is only doing them an injury. I tell her, if *vacancies*, please God, should happen, that my income will be much increased.

"With respect to Mr. Bolton—every body knows, that I have no interest; nobody cares for me: but, if he will point out what he wants, I will try what can be done. But I am sure, he will not be half so well off as at present. Supposing he could get a place of a few hundreds a-year, he would be a ten times poorer man than he is at present. I could convince you of it, in a moment; but if I was to begin then it would be said I wanted inclination to render them a service.

---

[1] His Chaplain and Private Secretary.
[2] His Steward.    [3] His Secretary.

"I should like to see Sir Home Popham's book. I cannot conceive how a man that is reported to have been so extravagant of Government's money, to say no worse, can make a good story.

"I wish Mr. Addington would give you five hundred pounds a-year; then, you would be better able to give away than at present. But your purse, my dear Emma, will always be empty: your heart is generous beyond your means.

"Your good mother is always sure of my sincerest regard; pray tell her so. Connor is getting on very well: but, I cannot ask Captain Capel to rate him; that must depend upon the boy's fitness, and Capel's kindness. I have placed another year's allowance of thirty pounds in Capel's hands, and given Connor a present.

"I have wrote to Dumouriez; therefore, I will only trouble you to say how much I respect him. I fancy he must have suffered great distress at Altona. However, I hope he will now be comfortable for life. He is a very clever man, and beats our Generals, out and out. Don't they feel his coming? Advise him not to make *enemies* by shewing he knows more than some of us. Envy knows no bounds to its persecution. He has seen the world, and will be on his guard.

"I put Suckling into a frigate, with a very good man, who has a schoolmaster; he does very well. Bulkeley will be a most excellent sea officer; it is a pity he has not served his time. I have answered Mr. Suckling's letter.

"Mr. Denis's relation has been long in the Victory; but, if the Admiralty will not promote my Lieutenants, they must all make a retrograde motion. But, I hope, they will not do such a cruel thing. I have had a very affectionate letter from Lord Minto. I hope George will be confirmed; but the Earl will not answer his application. I shall send you some sherry, and a cask of paxoretti, by the convoy. Perhaps it had better go to Merton at once, or to Davison's cellar, where the wine-cooper can draw it off. I have two pipes of sherry that is bad; but, if you like, you can send the Doctor a hogshead of that which is coming. Davison will pay all the duties. Send it entirely free, even to the *carriage*. You know, doing the thing well, is twice doing it; for, sometimes, carriage is more thought off than the prime cost.

"The paxoretti I have given to Davison; and ordered one hogshead of sherry to Canterbury, and one to dear Merton.
"N. & B."[1]

Captain Donnelly, afterwards Rear-Admiral Sir Ross Donnelly,[2] K.C.B., was ordered by Lord Nelson to repair in the

---

[1] Collection of Letters, Vol. i. p. 146.
[2] Ross Donnelly, a distinguished officer, entered the Navy early in the American war, under Vice-Admiral Arbuthnot, and was at the siege of Charlestown in 1780. He had the misfortune, after the capture of that place, to be taken prisoner, and was inhumanly turned adrift, with his crew, in an open boat, without either sails or provisions; but he fortunately reached Trepassay, almost exhausted, after a pull of two days and a night. On the Newfoundland station in the following year, he was made a Lieutenant, and appointed to the Morning Star of 16 guns, after which, he served in the Cygnet and the Mediator to the end of the war. In 1785, out of employ in the Navy, he became mate of an East Indiaman, and continued in this service until the revolutionary war commenced, when he was appointed First Lieutenant of the Montague of 74 guns, was in the battle of the 1st of June, 1794, and honourably mentioned by Earl Howe on this occasion. In 1795, he was made Post Captain, and during the remainder of the war commanded the Pegasus and Maidstone frigates. The merchants of Oporto voted him a handsome piece of plate, for his protection of their trade, and his escort of a large homeward bound fleet to England; but as he had not had an opportunity of fighting any of the numerous privateers then hovering about, he, much to his honour, declined accepting their generous offer. 32,000 pipes of wine, the largest quantity ever imported at one time into this country, were conveyed by this fleet. In 1801, he was appointed to the Narcissus of 32 guns, and took out the Algerine Ambassador and his suite, receiving from the Dey a handsome sabre. He then went for Malta and the Archipelago, and was engaged in a survey of the principal islands. Discovering some pirates off Miconi, he landed his men and secured thirty-six, whom he placed at the disposal of Lord Elgin, the British Ambassador then on board the Narcissus. The Capitan Pacha rewarded him with a Damascus sword for this service—it was presented by him to the Prince of Orange three days before the Battle of Waterloo, and used by the Prince on that memorable occasion. At Alexandria he hoisted a broad pendant, and after the evacuation of that place, he escorted General Stuart's army, and the French prisoners, to Malta. He afterwards went to Toulon and thence to Palermo, where he entertained the King of the Two Sicilies and his Court. Off Sardinia, in 1803, he captured L'Alcion, and was afterwards entrusted by Lord Nelson to watch off Toulon, and he possessed the Admiral's confidence in no small degree. He was employed on several missions to the Barbary States, and succeeded in obtaining the liberation of several English merchantmen that had been taken by the Corsairs. Under Sir Home Popham, he went to the Cape of Good Hope, took several vessels, and upon the subjugation of the Cape, accompanied Sir Home Popham to the Rio de la Plata, and brought home the dispatches giving an account of the capture of Buenos Ayres, and the specie, amounting to 1,086,208 dollars, found in the treasury of that place. He was immediately appointed to the Ardent of 64 guns, and took out a reinforcement of troops to

Narcissus to interrupt the French, and prevent them landing or forming a junction with the Corsicans at Ajaccio, and should they escape, he was directed to pursue them, even into the port of Sardinia. This order was given in consequence of a report which had reached him, that an embarkation of troops at Toulon or Marseilles was intended to join the Corsicans and invade Sardinia.

Sir N. Harris Nicolas has printed from White's Memoirs of Nelson, a letter supposed to have been written about the 6th of September to Mr. Haslewood, Lord Nelson's Solicitor, in which he inclosed him a codicil to his will to be drawn up properly and sent to him for execution. The following letter of the 8th will shew the nature of the intended instrument:—

"Victory, off Toulon, September 8th, 1803.

"I have, my dearest Emma, done what I thank God I have had the power of doing—left £4000. to my dear Horatia, and desire that she may be acknowledged as my adopted daughter, and I have made you her sole guardian; the interest of the money to be paid you until she is eighteen years of age. I trust, my dearest friend, that you will (if it should please God to take me out of this world) execute this great charge for me and the dear little innocent, for it would add comforts to my last moments to think that she would be educated in the paths of religion and virtue, and receive as far as she is capable, some of those brilliant accomplishments which so much adorn you. You must not allow your good heart to think that although I have left you this important charge I fancy myself nearer being knocked off by the French Admiral. I believe it will be quite the contrary, that

La Plata, but before his arrival, Buenos Ayres had been retaken by the enemy. Monte Video was therefore invested, and Captain Donnelly co-operated with the army in this service. In 1808 he commanded the Invincible of 74 guns, and fitted out in the short time of eight days the Spanish fleet at the Caraccas, and thereby prevented them falling into the possession of the French. He then joined Lord Collingwood off Toulon, and, from the failure of his eyesight, was compelled to retire from service for a time. Upon recovering, he was appointed to the Devonshire of 74 guns, but Peace being made, he did not again go to sea. He was made a Rear-Admiral in 1814, and died Admiral of the Blue, and K.C.B., September 30th, 1840.

God Almighty will again and again bless our just cause with victory, and that I shall live to receive your kind and affectionate congratulations on a brilliant victory. But be that as it may, I shall support, with God's help, my unblemished character to the last, and be

" Yours,
" Nelson and Bronté."

Lord Nelson having ascertained that French privateers had, under colours of the Bey of Tunis captured the Pomona, he sent Captain Donnelly to represent the same, and to claim the restitution of the ship. At the same time the Bey was to be informed that if Tunisian vessels were permitted to carry cargo belonging to the French, such property could not be respected, though conveyed in vessels belonging to the Bey.

The foresight of Nelson was remarkable: whether it related to the victualling or the repairing of the ships, or to the health of the seamen, it was always considered by him, and as far as means would permit, provided for. By this conduct he kept his fleet in as good condition as possible, and often under adverse circumstances there would not be a single man sick in the whole fleet. Contemplating the necessity of being at sea during the whole of the winter, at this period he wrote to the Admiralty to obtain a supply of topmasts, topsail-yards, and spare sails, as the Gulf of Lyons was remarkable for the number and severity and suddenness of its gales. To these gales the following letter alludes:—

"September 26th, 1803.

" My dearest Emma,

" We have had, for these fourteen days past, nothing but gales of wind and a heavy sea. However, as our ships have suffered no damage, I hope to be able to keep the sea all winter. Nothing but dire necessity shall force me to that out-of-the-way place, Malta. If I had depended on that island for supplies for the fleet, we must all have been knocked up long ago, for Sir Richard Bickerton sailed from Malta the same day I left Portsmouth; so that we have been a pretty long cruise; and if I had only to look to Malta for supplies, our ships' companies would have been done for long ago.

However, by management, I have got supplies from Spain and also from *France*, but it appears that we are almost shut out from Spain, for they begin to be very uncivil to our ships. However, I suppose by this time, something is settled; but I never hear from England. My last letters are July 6th, near three months; but as I get French newspapers occasionally, we guess how matters are going on. I have wrote Mr. Gibbs again a long history about Bronté, and I hope, if General Acton will do nothing for me, that he will settle something, but I know whatever is settled, I shall be the loser.

"N. & B."[1]

Lord Nelson's chief thoughts were directed to attacking the French fleet. Taking of prizes with him, much as he stood in need of money, was a secondary consideration. In a letter to Alexander Davison, Esq., he says: " I am truly sensible of your good wishes for my prosperity. I believe I attend more to the French fleet than making captures; but what I have, I can say as old Haddock[2] said, 'it never cost a sailor a tear, or the nation a farthing.' This thought is far better than prize-money;—not that I despise money—quite the contrary, I wish I had 100,000 pounds this moment, and I will do every thing consistent with my good name to obtain it. We are healthy beyond example, and in great good humour with ourselves, and so sharp set, that I would not be a French Admiral in the way of any of our ships for something. I believe we are in the right fighting trim, let them come as soon as they please. I never saw a fleet altogether so well officered and manned; would to God the ships were half as good, but they are what we call *crazy*."[3] The fact is, as stated by Nelson in a letter to Earl St. Vincent: " All the ships have expected every day before the war to go to England; therefore, when the war came, they wanted for everything, *more especially to go to England*. However, a good deal of that fever is worn off, and we are really got to a state of health which is rarely witnessed. I have exerted myself to get all

---

[1] Collection of Letters, Vol. i. p. 154.
[2] Admiral Sir Richard Haddock, of the reign of William III.
[3] Dispatches and Letters, Vol. v. p. 219.

the good things we could from Spain, and latterly our cattle and onions have been procured from France; but from the apparent incivilities of the Spaniards, I suppose we are on the eve of being shut out. Our length of passage from Malta is terrible. We have not procured one single article of refreshment from them since the fleet sailed (May 18th); therefore, if a fleet here had only Malta to trust to, the fleet must go to Malta, for the good things of Malta could never come to us; and in that case the French might do as they pleased between here and Gibraltar for two months together. At this moment I think the squadron, as far as relates to me, are fit to go to Madras. Their *hulls* want docking. I hope to be able to keep the sea all the winter—in short, to stay at sea till the French choose to come to sea; and then I hope to send many of our ships who want what I cannot give them to England, towing a line-of-battle ship. I believe we are uncommonly well disposed to give the French a thrashing, and we are keen; for I have not seen a French flag on the sea since I joined the squadron. A fortnight ago, three or four sail of the line were under sail, and some had got a few miles from Sepet, but I believe it was only for an exercise. Reports say, they are hard at work, fitting out two new 80-gun-ships; their lower rigging is over the mast-heads. I wish they would make haste, for our gales of wind, Admiral Campbell says, are harder and more frequent than ever. I believe them much the same—always very violent, and a heavy sea."[1]

The following letter from Lord Elgin was received by Lord Nelson:—

"Aux Eaux de Baréges,
September 30th, 1803.

" My dear Lord,

" As Prince Maurice and Prince Louis Lichtenstein may endeavour to visit Malta in the course of this winter, I wish to introduce them to your Lordship's acquaintance, and to mention, that I have recommended them to any British officers they may find cruising off the coast of Italy, and who may be able to give them a passage to La Valetta, in a British man-of-war.

[1] Dispatches and Letters, Vol. v. p. 214.

"They are officers of distinguished merit in the Austrian service, travelling on account of severe wounds; and having passed two months with them here, previous to their going southward, which their health obliges them to, I have advised their going to Malta as not less worthy notice than Italian antiquities. I hope they may have the good fortune to fall in with your Lordship. If they have that good fortune they will mention to you the melancholy situation to which Lady Elgin and I are reduced—God knows where or how it may terminate.

"Your Lordship will have learnt the nature and circumstances of the interests I have left behind me in the Levant. I am confident of your kind concern to objects so important to me, and that you will have been so very obliging as to give me essential and effectual assistance at Cenjo, and in the various points on which Sir Richard Bickerton, as well as Sir A. Ball and Mr. Macaulay are well informed.

"Wishing your Lordship success, which can add to your glory and comfort, I remain,

"My dear Lord,
"Most faithfully,
"Your humble and obedient servant,
"ELGIN."

And Lord Nelson wrote to Lady Hamilton on the 5th and 6th of October:—

"Victory, off Toulon, October 5th, 1803.

"By a letter from Davison of the 15th of August, sent by Lisbon, which reached me on the 1st of this month, I was made truly happy by hearing that my dearest Emma was at Southend and well, and last night I had the happiness of receiving your letters of June 26th from Hilborough, and of August 3rd from Southend, and most sincerely do I thank God that it has been of so much service to your general health. You desire to know my opinion of your coming to Malta or Sicily, &c. &c. I will tell you as I told you before my situation here, therefore you must let your own good sense have fair play. You may readily believe how happy I should be to have peace and live quietly at Merton. At this moment I can have no home but the Victory, and wherever the French fleet may go, there will the Victory be found. As to Malta or Sicily, or Naples, they are places which I may see from some extraordinary occasion, such as an action, a landing in Sicily, and then probably only for a few days; but should the French fleet travel westward, then I shall never see either Malta or Sicily. I assure you that Merton has a greater chance of seeing me sooner than Malta. How would you feel to be at that nasty place Malta, with nothing but soldiers and diplomatic nonsense, and to hear that the fleet has gone out of the Straits? The time will come, must come, that I shall see Merton, if God spares me. Malta, it is possible, I never may see, unless after a battle, and then that is not certain, for if it takes place down the Mediterranean it would be Gibraltar; in short, I can see nothing but uncomfortableness for you by such a voyage, and however much we feel, and I believe mutually the pain of being separated, yet the call of our country makes it indispensable for both our honours—the country looks up to the services of the poorest individual, much more to me, and are you not a sharer of my glory? These things must have their due weight in your mind, and therefore I shall only assure you that I am

" Yours,
" NELSON AND BRONTÉ."

" October 6th, 1803.

" My dearest Emma,

" I have had a letter from Mr. George Moyston, who is at Naples, and a very kind one. He has been to the Cataracts in Upper Egypt, through Syria, Palestine, Greece, &c. but has nearly died two or three times, and is now a prisoner on parole to the French, being in quarantine at Otranto when the French went there.

" I beg that you will not give credit to any reports which will reach England of the battle—trust to Providence that it will be propitious to your most sanguine wishes, and I hope that Captain Murray will be the bearer of a letter from me to you. Never fear, our cause is just and honourable. From Davison's letter of August 15th, I expect a ship of war every moment; it is now three months I see by the papers that Bolton has got the Childers. Had he been here he would have been Post. The Admiralty will send him out of course, and if I know how, I must try and put £5000 in his pocket. Don't you laugh. How I talk of thousands when I do not know how, or rather have not tried, to put money in my own pocket, but they will come. I wish you would have the plan made for the new entrance at the corner. Mr. Linton should give up that field this winter, and in the spring it should be planted very thick to the eastward, and a moderate thickness to the north. The plan for filling up the water on the south and east sides of the house [is good], but care must be taken that the house is not made damp for want of drains. A covered passage from *Downings* must be made beyond the present trees, and rails, and chains, in a line with it to keep carriages from the house. An opening can be left with a post, that foot-passengers may go to the kitchen. This may be done even before you begin the room, it will amuse you, and be of no great expense.

"Yours,

"NELSON AND BRONTÉ."

The representations made to the Government by Lord Nelson with regard to Genoa occasioned orders to be sent out in accordance with his suggestion for a blockade of that port and of Port Especia. He was also instructed to demand the delivery of all Maltese taken by the Algerine cruisers. The intelligence given by Nelson to the Government was so highly estimated and his judgment so regarded, that he was now requested to transmit his correspondence upon all political subjects to Lord Hobart, one of the Secretaries of State, direct, that they might be laid before the King, and his Majesty's commands taken thereon. This was highly gratifying to Nelson, who writes to Sir John Acton on the 8th:—"I have the pleasure also to inform your Excellency of his Majesty's most full and entire approbation of my conduct, and that he places full confidence in all my actions for the honour of his crown, and the advantage of his faithful friends. The testimonies of private confidence and approbation from the other Members of the Cabinet, are too flattering for me to repeat; therefore I shall only request your Excellency to lay me with all humility at the feet of the King and Queen, and assure them of my eternal fidelity and vigilance for their safety."[1]

On the 4th of October, Lord Nelson issued orders to the Fleet in the Mediterranean, announcing the establishment of the blockade. The condition of his men at this time was remarkable. "Never (he writes to Mr. Elliot) was health equal to this squadron; it has been within ten days of five months at sea, and we have not a man confined to his bed."

On the 13th Lord Hood wrote to Lord Nelson.

"Royal College, Greenwich,
October 13th, 1803.

"My dear Lord Duke,

"I give your Lordship a thousand thanks for your very affectionate letter of the 21st of August, am happy to hear you enjoy health, and flatter myself the day is not far distant when we shall be informed of your having taken or destroyed the greatest part of the Toulon fleet.

"I had much satisfaction in being somewhat useful to Mr. Nelson, whenever I have given a promise, I bear in constant remembrance the fulfilling of it.

"I am too sore, my dear Lord, from the harsh and unmerited treatment I have experienced with respect to my late Secretary, to say a word upon the subject with any degree of temper, and have been so accustomed to mortifying disappointments in all my views for the last eight years, that I have constantly expected them, am therefore become callous, but feel some consolation that I have mustered sufficient fortitude and resolution to enable me to bear up against them. Your Lordship will hear from all quarters that Buonaparte threatens us hard, and perceive that his Majesty's Ministers, and in consequence the nation in general, believe he will certainly attempt to carry them into execution; but I am very confident he will fail. At the same time, however, I am free to confess, that should he by good luck make a landing with any considerable force, either in England, Scotland, or Ireland,

[1] Dispatches and Letters, Vol. v. p. 241. From a copy in the Nelson Papers.

the country would be thrown into such confusion, there is no saying to what extent the evil might go. We are, I am happy to tell you, well prepared, and are improving daily.

"I am grieved to inform your Lordship that my dear Lady Hood still continues a very great invalid. She has not been out of her house but for an hour in a day in her coach since you left England; she is however better to-day than she has been for many weeks past, but I cannot flatter myself with any hopes of her being well enough to enjoy the society of her friends again.

"I saw Mr. Addington yesterday, and we had a good deal of conversation about you; he is in high health and good spirits.

"Lady Hood most cordially unites, as does Mrs. Hodwell in all kind wishes for your Lordship's health and success, with,

"My dear Lord,
"Your very affectionate and faithful,
"HOOD.

"P. S. Mr. Hood is at Southampton with his corps of Yeomanry and Wheler is Aide-de-camp to General Grosvenor, in the neighbourhood of Exeter."

Another old friend's letter he acknowledged on the 14th.

"TO ADMIRAL SIR PETER PARKER.

"14th October, 1803.

"Your grandson[1] came to me with your kind letter of August 20th on October 6th, nothing could be more grateful to my feelings than receiving him. I have kept him as Lieutenant of the Victory, and shall not part with him until I can make him a Post Captain; which you may be assured I shall lose no time in doing. It is the only opportunity ever offered me, of shewing that my feelings of gratitude to you are as warm and alive as when you first took me by the hand: I owe all my honours to you, and I am proud to acknowledge it to all the world. Lord St. Vincent has most strongly and kindly

---

[1] Afterwards Captain Sir Peter Parker, Bart. who fell at the storming of an American camp near Baltimore, August 30th, 1814.

desired your grandson's promotion; therefore I can only be the instrument of expediting it. Believe me ever, my dear Sir Peter, your most grateful and sincerely attached friend,

"NELSON AND BRONTÉ."[1]

To his Royal Highness the Duke of Clarence he wrote on the 15th, described the bad state of the weather, and expressed his hope of soon falling in with the French fleet: "Your Royal Highness will readily imagine my feelings, although I cannot bring my mind to believe they are actually out; but to miss them—God forbid! They are my superior in numbers, but in every thing else, I believe, I have the happiness of commanding the finest squadron in the world—Victory, Kent, Superb, Triumph, Belleisle, and Renown. Admiral Campbell is gone to Sardinia, and I have been anxiously expecting him these ten days. If I should miss these fellows, my heart will break: I am actually only now recovering the shock of missing them in 1798, when they were going to Egypt. If I miss them, I will give up the cudgels to some more fortunate commander; God knows I only serve to fight those scoundrels; and if I cannot do that, I should be better on shore."[2]

The destruction of the French fleet was a matter of much uncertainty. Lord Nelson wrote to Lord Hobart: "What the real destination of the French fleet may be is very difficult for me to guess. Mr. Elliot thinks they will try to have Sicily previous to their going to Egypt; others think they may go to Trieste to cover the army across to the Morea; others, that in the present unsettled state of Egypt, they may push with 10,000 men to Alexandria, and they may be bound outside the Mediterranean. Plausible reasons may certainly be given for every one of these plans, but I think one of the two last is their great object; and to those two points my whole attention is turned. If they put to sea, I hope to fall in with them, and then I have every reason to believe that all their plans will be frustrated."[3]

[1] Clarke and McArthur, Vol. ii. p. 330.   [2] Ibid.
[3] Dispatches and Letters, Vol. v. p. 249. From the Original in the Colonial Office.

Lord Nelson wrote to Lady Hamilton on the 18th :—

"Victory off Toulon, October 18th, 1803.

"My dearest Emma,

"Your truly kind letters from July 17th to August 24th, all arrived safe in the Childers, the 6th of this month. Since September the 1st, we have not had four fine days; and, if the French do not come out soon, I fear some of my ships will cry out. You know that I am never well when it blows hard. Therefore, imagine what a cruise off Toulon is; even in summer time, we have a hard gale every week, and two days heavy swell. The other day we had a report that the French were out, and seen steering to the westward. We were as far as Minorca, when the alarm proved false.

"I have received your letter with Lord William's and Mr. Kemble's about Mr. Palmer: he is also recommended by the Duke of Clarence, and he says, by desire of the Prince of Wales. I have, without him, twenty-six to be made Captains, and list every day increasing. It is not *one* whole French fleet that can get through it. I shall probably offend many more than I can oblige. Such is always the case: like the tickets— those who get them, feel they have a right to them; and those (who) do not get them, feel offended for ever. But I cannot help it, I shall endeavour to do what is right, in every situation; and some ball may soon close all my accounts with this world of care and vexation.

"Naples, I fancy, is in a very bad way, in regard to money. They have not, or pretend not to have enough to pay their officers; and I verily believe, if Acton was to give up his place, that it would become a province of France. Only think of Buonaparte's writing to the Queen, to desire her influence to turn out Acton! She answered properly; at least, so says Mr. Elliot, who *knows more of Naples* than any of us; God help him! and General Acton has, I believe, more power than ever.

"Our friend, Sir Alexander, is a very great diplomatic character, and even an Admiral must not know what he is negotiating about: although you will scarcely believe, that the Bey of Tunis sent the man at my desire.

"You shall judge, *viz.* 'The Tunisian Envoy is still here,

negotiating. He is a moderate man; and, apparently, the best disposed of any I ever did business with.' Could even the oldest diplomatic character be drier? I hate such parade of nonsense! But I will turn from such stuff.

"N. & B."[1]

On the 21st of October Lord Nelson wrote his first letter to his child, addressing it to Miss Horatia Nelson Thomson :—

"Victory, off Toulon, Oct. 21, 1803.

"My dear Child,

"Receive this first letter from your most affectionate father. If I live, it will be my pride to see you virtuously brought up; but if it pleases God to call me, I trust to Himself, in that case, I have left Lady Hamilton your guardian. I therefore charge you, my child, on the value of a father's blessing, to be obedient and attentive to all her kind admonitions and instructions. At this moment I have left you, in a Codicil dated the 6th of September, the sum of £4000. sterling, the interest of which is to be paid to your guardian for your maintenance and education. I shall only say, my dear child, may God Almighty bless you and make you an ornament to your sex, which I am sure you will be if you attend to all Lady Hamilton's kind instructions; and be assured that I am, my dear Horatia, your most affectionate father,

"NELSON AND BRONTÉ."[2]

On the same day Sir John Acton wrote the following to Lord Nelson:—

"Palermo, Oct. 21st. 1803.

"My dear Lord,

"I must return your Lordship my best thanks for the copies of the letters wrote to her Majesty and to Mr. Elliot. The Queen has sent me the original, but the secret shall be kept of your kindness to me, as well as with Mr. Elliot. I return your Lordship the copy of this last.

[1] Collection of Letters, Vol. i. p. 168.
[2] Dispatches and Letters, Vol. v. p. 260. From an autograph in the possession of Mrs. Horatia Nelson Ward.

"Your reflections, my Lord, are just in every respect on our position, and the general situation indeed of all Europe.

"I hope most earnestly, my Lord, that we may see you soon in these seas again, where your presence is so much desired, and with so very true and interested reasons.

"I am glad that Mr. Este was satisfied with this country for the short time that he favoured us with his company.

"Every thing that may depend on me, my Lord, shall be employed with energy in regard to your intentions and desires about Bronté. In the mean time I shall with pleasure concur on my part with whatever Mr. Gibbs shall desire for the management of these manors. I have inclosed a letter in the article of Sir Thomas Troubridge. Lady Acton begs leave to present her best wishes to your Lordship for your health and general satisfaction. I join with her, and so shall for ever do. Give me leave to repeat this assertion, and with the most faithful and sincere attachment,

"Your Lordship's
"Most obedient and most humble servant,
"J. Acton."

The Queen also wrote to Lord Nelson:—

"My dear and worthy Lord,

"I hasten with great satisfaction on the present occasion to renew my sentiments of esteem, attachment and gratitude for all that you have already done, and continue to do for us, not only having saved us from being compromised, by the painful and disagreeable circumstances in which we were placed, but also for continuing with your usual vigilance to watch over our safety. We are on the eve of a great crisis, may heaven vouchsafe our prayers, and your great nation reap the advantage and glory that my heart desires for it, which would have an important influence on our situation, and that of all Europe—ours is always dangerous and painful, having pretended friends but real enemies in the centre of our kingdoms practising injustice solely. I place our interests in your worthy hands, my Lord. I rely on your care, prudence and friendship, and I pray you to believe in my eternal gratitude and esteem, which my dear family desire me to assure you they also feel, and believe me for life, my very worthy and respected Lord, your attached and grateful friend,

"CHARLOTTE.

"10th December, 1803."

To this Lord Nelson replied:—

"Victory, December 29, 1803.

"Madam,

"Yesterday evening I had the honour of receiving your Majesty's gracious and flattering letter of the 10th of December, and it is only possible for me to repeat my assurances, that my orders for the safety of the Two Sicilies will be always exactly executed, and to this end my whole soul goes in unison with my orders. The Gibraltar shall not be sent away, for I would rather fight twice our number of forces, than risk for a moment the seeing your royal person and family fall into the hands of the French. I see no hope of a permanent peace for Europe during the life of Buonaparte. I ardently wish, therefore, that it would please God to take him from the world.

"Your Majesty's letter to my dear and good Lady Hamilton, shall set out by the first opportunity. Her attachment to your Majesty is as lively as ever. Her heart is incapable of the slightest change; and whether in prosperity or in adversity, she is always your devoted servant; and such, permit me to say, remains your faithful

"NELSON AND BRONTÉ.

"I beg to be allowed to present my humble respects to the Princesses, and to the Prince Leopold."[1]

Her Majesty replied on the 2nd January, 1804:—

"My dear and very worthy Lord and Friend,

"I received your two letters; penetrated with the liveliest gratitude I trace in each line, the grandeur and attachment of your soul, and am deeply grateful. I should have wished to have sent you twelve others of your own ships with the Gibraltar, but that grand quality (so well known) with which

[1] Life of the Rev. Dr. Scott, p. 113.

you inspire others, as so often witnessed, has no need of numbers. My vows will be offered to heaven for your complete success and happiness. We are always in a painful position, but which, thanks to the friendship of your Sovereign and Government, and your care and attention is only painful, not dangerous. Receive with the new year, my dear and worthy Lord, my wishes for your perfect happiness. The happiness of all Europe, and of all the right thinking is blended with it. May the wishes I form for you be fully realized, and your toils and cares be crowned with full success. Such are the wishes formed for you by her who is, and will be all her life, with the highest esteem and sincere gratitude, your very attached and true friend,

"CHARLOTTE.

"The 2nd January, 1804.

"My children, son and daughters, desire me to assure you of their eternal gratitude, esteem and attachment."

Whilst in the Bay of Rosas, where the ships had gone for wood and water, several seamen deserted from the fleet. The following admirable memorandum addressed to the Captains and Commanders of the ships and vessels on the Mediterranean station was issued by Lord Nelson: "When British seamen and marines so far degrade themselves in time of war, as to desert from the service of their own country, and enter into that of Spain; when they leave 1s per day, and plenty of the very best provisions, with every comfort that can be thought of for them—for 2d a day, black bread, horse beans, and stinking oil for their food;—when British seamen or marines turn Spanish soldiers, I blush for them: they forfeit, in their own opinion, I am sure, that character of love of their own country, which foreigners are taught to admire. A Briton to put himself under the lash of a Frenchman or Spaniard must be more degrading to any man of spirit than any punishment I could inflict on their bodies. I shall leave the punishment to their own feelings, which, if they have any, and are still Englishmen, must be very great. But, as they thought proper to abandon voluntarily, their wives, fathers, mothers, and every endearing tie, and also, all prospect of returning to their native country, I shall make them remain out of that country, which they do not wish to see, and allow others, who love their country, and are attached to their families, to return in their stead. And as they have also thought proper to resign all their pay, I shall take care that it is not returned to them, nor their 'R.'[1] taken off; but it shall be noted against their names, 'Deserted to the Spaniards,' or 'Entered as a Spanish soldier,' as the case was.

"NELSON AND BRONTÉ.

"The above memorandum respecting the desertion of British seamen or marines is to be read to the respective companies of his Majesty's ships and vessels under my command, and copies thereof to be stuck up in the most public places of the ships, in order that the magnitude of the crime may be properly impressed on their minds.

"NELSON AND BRONTÉ."[2]

The sum of forty shillings was allowed by him to Mr. Gibert the Vice-Consul at Barcelona for the apprehension of every deserter, with an allowance of ninepence *per diem* for the subsistence of each while in custody. The foregoing excellent address did not, however, it would appear, put a stop to desertion, for at the Madalena Islands, November 7th, he issued another memorandum:—"Lord Nelson is very sorry to find that notwithstanding his forgiveness of the men who deserted in Spain, it has failed to have its proper effect, and that there are still men who so far forget their duty to their King and Country, as to desert the service, at a time when every man in England is in arms to defend it against the French. Therefore Lord Nelson desires that it may be perfectly understood, that if any man be so infamous as to desert from the service in future, he will not only be brought to a Court Martial, but that if the sentence should be *death*, it will be most assuredly carried into execution.

"NELSON AND BRONTÉ."[3]

---

[1] Otherwise Run, the mark affixed in the ship's books against the names of those who have deserted.

[2] From a copy in the Nelson Papers.

[3] Ibid.

At the end of October, Lord Nelson left for the Madalena Islands to wood, water, obtain oxen, sheep, onions, &c. for the squadron, and Captain Donnelly was entrusted to watch the enemy off Toulon during his absence. On the 10th of November Lord Nelson sailed for Toulon, and on the 24th advised Sir John Acton that he had ascertained the French fleet to consist of eight sail of the line, eight frigates, and several corvettes. He describes them as being in high feather, as fine as paint could make them; but doubts not that his weather-beaten ships would make their sides like a plum-pudding. On the 4th of December he renewed his application to the French Admiral for an exchange of prisoners, which he had before ineffectually made. He also offered to allow a number of French officers to return on their parole of honour until they should be regularly exchanged by their Governments. At the end of November he had again put to sea, intending to proceed with the squadron to St. Pierre, near the island of Sardinia, leaving Captain Mowbray in the Active to watch the enemy. On the 7th of December he was again off Toulon, and wrote to his Royal Highness the Duke of Clarence: "The French fleet kept us waiting for them during a long and severe winter's cruise; and such a place as all the Gulf of Lyons, for gales of wind from the north-west to north-east, I never saw; but by always going about large, we generally lose much of their force, and the heavy sea of the Gulf, however, by the great care and attention of every Captain, we have suffered much less than could have been expected."[1]

On the 10th he departed for the Madalena Islands to complete the necessaries for his ships. He preferred the Gulf of Parma to St. Pierre, and was there on the 11th, whence he wrote to Mr. Davison, and therein states that he had signed his proxy for Lord Moira, and in doing it had broken through a resolution he had made never to give a proxy, nor could any thing have induced him to swerve from it but to such a man as Lord Moira: "Whether he is in or out of office (says Lord Nelson), my opinion of him is formed for ability, honour, and strict integrity, which nothing can shake, even should ever we unfortunately differ on any particular

---

[1] Clarke and McArthur, Vol. ii. p. 341.

point." In this letter he also speaks of the state of his fleet and of his own personal condition: "My crazy fleet are getting in a very indifferent state, and others will soon follow. The finest ships in the service will soon be destroyed. I know well enough that if I was to go into Malta, I should save the ships during this bad season; but if I am to watch the French, I must be at sea, and if at sea, must have bad weather; and if the ships are not fit to stand bad weather, they are useless. I do not say much, but I do not believe that Lord St. Vincent would have kept the sea with such ships. But my time of service is nearly over. A natural anxiety, of course, must attend my station; but my dear friend, my eye-sight fails me most dreadfully. I firmly believe that, in a very few years, I shall be stone blind. It is this only, of all my maladies, that makes me unhappy; but God's will be done. If I am successful against the French, I shall ask my retreat; and if I am not, I hope I shall never live to see it; for no personal exertion on my part shall be spared."

To his brother, the Rev. Dr. Nelson, he also wrote on the 14th: "The mind and body both wear out, and my eye is every month visibly getting worse, and, I much fear, it will end in total blindness. The moment the battle is over, if I am victorious, I shall ask for my retreat—if, unfortunately, the contrary, I hope never to live to see it. In that case, you will get an early seat in the House of Lords. If Mr. Addington does not give me the same pension as Government gave to the rich Lord St. Vincent and Duncan, I shall consider no great favour done to me, and the country never could avoid giving the pension to you: therefore, unless the other is tasked to it, I would not give thanks or sixpence to have it brought before Parliament to benefit Lord St. Vincent's heirs, and certainly, from circumstances, not mine. The putting the stone over poor Maurice was well done, and I approve very much. I do not know that you owe me any thing respecting Hilborough; but if you do, I fully acquit you of the debt, and so let it be considered."[1]

On the 19th December, Lord Nelson quitted the Gulf of

[1] From an autograph in the Nelson Papers. Dispatches and Letters, Vol. v. p. 311.

Parma, " the finest open roadstead he had ever seen ;" was again at the Madalena Islands on the 24th, whence he wrote the following to Lady Hamilton :—

"Victory, Madalena, December 26th, 1803.

"My dearest Emma,

"After closing my dispatches the weather was so bad, that we could not unload our transports at sea, therefore I anchored here on Saturday, and hope to get to sea on Wednesday. The Phœbe joined me here, and carries my letters to Gibraltar. I had Charles on board yesterday to dinner. Capel gives a very good account of him, and I have impressed upon his mind that if he behaves well, he will never want a protector in you and me. He had about three months ago, something wrong in his head. The killing a Lieutenant and some men belonging to the Phœbe, made such an impression, that he fancied he saw a ghost, &c. but Dr. Snipe thinks it is gone off. Was any of his family in that way? He is clever, and I believe Capel has been kind to him. I have had violent colds, and now and then a spasm, but Dr. Snipe takes care of me, and would give me more physic, but he says I am a bad patient; but I trust I shall do very well till the battle, and after that, if it pleases God I survive, I shall certainly ask permission to go home to recruit, and in this world nothing will give me so much pleasure as to see my dear Emma, being most faithfully,

"NELSON AND BRONTÉ."

At the close of this month he was busily engaged in making proper arrangements for the new Naval Hospital established at Malta, and entered minutely into every particular for its perfection. He was much impressed with the importance of Sardinia, and wrote to the Secretary of State thus : " God knows if we could possess one island, Sardinia, we should want neither Malta, nor any other; this, which is the finest island in the Mediterranean, possesses harbours fit for arsenals, and of a capacity to hold our navy, within twenty-four hours sail of Toulon. Bays to ride our fleets in, and to watch both Italy and Toulon; no fleet could pass to the eastward between Sicily and the Coast of Barbary, nor through the Faro of Messina : Malta, in point of position, is not to be named the same year with Sardinia. All the fine ports of Sicily are situated on the eastern side of the island, consequently of no use to watch any thing but the Faro of Messina. And, my Lord, I venture to predict, that if we do not—from delicacy or commiseration of the lot of the unfortunate King of Sardinia—the French will get possession of that island. Sardinia is very little known. It was the policy of Piedmont to keep it in the back ground, and whoever it has belonged to, it seems to have been their maxim to rule the inhabitants with severity, in loading its produce with such duties as prevented the growth. I will only mention one circumstance as a proof: half a cheese was seized because the poor man was selling it to our boats, and it had not paid the duty. Fowls, eggs, beef, and every article, are most heavily taxed. The Court of Sardinia certainly wants every penny to maintain itself; and yet I am told after the wretched establishment of the island is paid, that the King does not receive £5000 sterling a year. The country is fruitful beyond idea, and abounds in cattle and sheep, and would in corn, wine and oil. It has no manufactories. In the hands of a liberal government, and freed from the dread of the Barbary States, there is no telling what its produce would not amount to. It is worth any money to obtain, and I pledge my existence it could be held for as little as Malta in its establishment, and produce a large revenue."[1]

[1] Clarke and McArthur, Vol. ii. p. 344.

## CHAPTER VIII.

### 1804.

ON the 4th of January 1804, Lord Nelson again quitted the Madalena Islands with his squadron; writing to Lord Hobart,[1] that his heart was warm, his hand firm, but his body unequal to his wishes. It is astonishing the patience he exhibited in watching for the French fleet, exposed as he was at such a season of the year to all the vicissitudes of the sea. With small means he yet contrived to dispatch his officers to observe in various places, and to be alive to any circumstance that might occur. Every one was on the look out for intelligence. The political position of the different countries, particularly Sardinia and Sicily, escaped not his intelligent observation. The former place, as already stated, was of much advantage in his estimation, and his zeal in the cause of the King and Queen of the Two Sicilies, rendered him willing to undertake any measures for the defence of the latter. He was sensible of the misgovernment of both these countries and lamented their impoverished state. He received information of an intended attack by the French in Corsica upon Sardinia, and he did all within his power to check it, and to afford assistance should it take place. The invasion, however, was not undertaken—other views actuated Buonaparte, and to be master of the Continent was evidently his ambition. Nelson, however, offered his aid to the Viceroy his Royal Highness Prince Charles Felix Joseph, Duke of Génévois in Savoy,[2] from whom he received the following letters:—

[1] Afterwards the Earl of Buckinghamshire.
[2] Charles Felix of Savoy, brother of Victor Emanuel, the then reigning King of Sardinia. In 1792, and the succeeding year, the Sardinians under Victor Amadeus III. bravely resisted the French and repulsed their invaders with considerable loss. The state of the elements likewise favoured them, for the French fleet was dispersed by a furious hurricane, and Truguet, the Admiral, was compelled to seek shelter in the Gulf of Palmas, where with eleven sail of the line

"De Cagliari, 17th December, 1803.

"Sir,

"Accept my thanks for your attention in acquainting me with the motive which induced you to anchor your fleet in the Gulf of Palma, which I regret that bad weather should

he was detained nearly a month. The King of Sardinia though delighted at the brave conduct of the Sards, and the success attending their exertions, was yet unwilling, and absolutely refused to yield to their constitutional demands. These were five in number :—1. The Convocation of the Stamenti. 2. The confirmation of their laws, customs, and privileges. 3. The exclusive right of holding the national offices. 4. The establishment of a Council instead of a Secretary of State, to advise the Viceroy. 5. The permission to send a Minister to reside at the Court of Turin. The refusal to grant these requests irritated the people and disposed them to rebel, but after a slight émeute in April 1794, they were reduced to submission, and a new form of Government established, which stipulated that the Viceroy and the Piedmontese should immediately return to the Continent and the reins of Government be confided in the interim to the native members of the Royal Audience and the Stamenti according to the old constitution of the island. Another rising, however, took place on the 6th of July 1795, from the conduct of the Court; and Cavalier Pitzoln, the Intendant General, was dragged forth from his confinement in the Elephant tower and shot in the castle square. The proceedings had thus assumed a sanguinary character, and a remonstrance was sent to Turin in some measure to exculpate the people. An investigation followed, the Archbishop of Cagliari was dispatched to the Pope of Rome, and on the 8th of June, 1796, a diploma was obtained, which gave a general act of oblivion on the late events, the ratification of their laws, customs, and privileges, and the exclusion of foreigners from all public offices, except that of Viceroy. The finances of the kingdom were, at this time, exhausted by the expense attending the army, which had been much increased by this monarch, who was fond of great military parade. By the storms of the Revolution, Savoy and Nice had been lost in 1792, and Oneglia in 1794. An expensive warfare along the line of the Alps was continued for two years, and although the Piedmontese displayed great valour, the French ultimately succeeded by passing the Ligurian Apennines, and thus poured down into the plains of the Po. A hasty peace was the consequence, and the dominions were principally at the mercy of the French. Victor Amadeus died in October, 1796.

Savoy, Nice, and Oneglia thus lost, and Piedmont overrun by the French, a deplorable position of affairs presented itself when Charles Emanuel ascended the throne. The French in the course of two years gained admission into the strongest fortresses of the island. Emissaries and propagandists were actively employed by Buonaparte to work discontent in Cagliari and urge the people to an union with the French Republic, and his subjects favouring republicanism, demanded the abdication of the King. His Majesty went to Leghorn and received the deputies of the Stamenti of Sardinia, who assured him of the fidelity of the Sards. The Royal family and suite arrived at Cagliari, March 3, 1799, conveyed by an English frigate, and were enthusiastically welcomed; but the King was induced to return to the Continent, and hearing of the Battle of Marengo, determined to remain in the South of Italy. His Queen Clotilde, sister of Louis XVI. dying

have rendered necessary. The bearer will inform you of the condition of the country, and of the threats of our neighbours, but whatever may occur, I shall rely on receiving your aid, convinced that it will be employed with skilfulness to meet the actual circumstances of the King my brother, and begging you to give me an opportunity of proving to you the sentiments of esteem which animate me, I am, with the highest consideration, my Lord,

" Your good friend,

*Charles Felix de Savoye*

" De Cagliari, 14th January, 1804.

" Sir,

" By your letter of the 2nd current I learn with less surprise than indignation the contents of the letter from the French Minister at War to the General of Ajaccio, and I may confidently inform you that the conduct of the Commissary-General for commercial affairs here, tends to confirm, I think, your suspicions as to a project for attacking this island. Firm to my duty of executing on all occasions the orders of the King, my brother, I shall neglect nothing

in March 1802, he became inconsolable for her loss, abdicated the throne, resigning, as he said, "a crown of thorns," in favour of his brother Victor Emanuel at that time a resident at Naples. Having withdrawn from the toils and exertions of royalty, Charles Emanuel lived in great privacy, devoted himself to pious exercises at Rome, became totally blind, and died in 1819.

Victor Emanuel relied upon British assistance to regain his Continental dominions. He remained in Italy, but the Peace agreed upon at Amiens being at an end, and the French advanced upon Naples, he embarked for Sardinia in February 1806. His endeavours were directed to improve the country by attention to its agriculture, whilst at the same time he was organizing the forces of the island and improving the administration, but his means were very limited to effect such objects. In the year 1814 he went to Turin. An insurrection in Piedmont, excited by the constitutionalists, induced him to abdicate in 1821, in favour of his brother, Charles Felix, who, supported by Austria, quelled the insurrection, introduced many improvements benefiting his country, and became popular with his people. His reign was distinguished by mildness and an attention to the culture of the natural products of the country. He established an Agrarian Society, and also a Museum of Antiquities, and the Natural History of Cagliari. He died April 27, 1831, and having no male issue was succeeded by his collateral relative, Charles Albert of Carignano, the present Sovereign.

for the defence of all now remaining to him, and which he has confided to me; but I will not conceal from you that my means are very feeble, being equally deprived of money and troops. In consequence of which I can only rely upon your generous offers, persuaded that in such circumstances you will display the same interest that you have always manifested in favour of the King and of our family, and that to you we shall owe the safety of this state. Accept in anticipation, the assurance of the liveliest gratitude, and the expression of my sentiments of perfect esteem and of the highest consideration with which I am, my Lord,

"Your good friend,
"CHARLES FELIX DE SAVOYE.

"P.S. There is no doubt that the General Colli spoken of is an old Piedmontese officer, a bad man, but very intelligent. It would be very desirable if you could furnish me with the order of the Minister of War to give rations and and pay to the Sardinian refugees, who in fact are but revolutionists; that commission would enable me to expose to the King and his friends how the good faith with which he has always acted is responded to."

"25th February, 1804.

"Sir,
"I hasten to reply to your letter of the 17th current, and to thank you for the interest you take in the defence of Sardinia, and the counsels you are pleased to give me respecting it, assuring you that it will always be a great pleasure to me to act according to your advice. I indeed expect the King's galley from Cività Vecchia, and two half galleys which have been ceded to us by the King of Naples, their destination is to destroy Bonefaccio. I can rely upon the merit and zeal of the officers commanding them, and am persuaded that nothing will be neglected on their part to ensure the execution of the orders given to them—I should have wished to put them directly under the orders of the Commander of the English corvette which your Lordship may appoint to the station of that Straits, but as we are not openly at war with France, I cannot take such a step on my own authority; it rests with the King, but it appears to me that the best measures for

opposing the enemy might be secretly concerted with the
officers charged with your instructions, for which object I
shall send my orders to the Brigadier commanding the galley,
Baron Desgenays. The report is current that you have
seized a packet of French correspondence addressed to Sardinian Jacobins, and that some of the letters were for persons of consequence, and that you have sent them to me.
As I know nothing of this affair I cannot give the least
credence to it, but nevertheless think it better to mention it
to you in case you really have written to me and the packet
has been lost. If the bad weather has detained you in the
same anchorage, doubtless you have seen Major Lowe,[1] who
came from Naples to Cagliari, and afterwards crossed the
kingdom to rejoin you. I agree entirely with what he will
tell you respecting us, and am persuaded that you will furnish us with every thing requisite, and procure for us that
assistance so indispensable to us in this emergency. I conclude by assuring you of my undivided sentiments of esteem,
and of the very high consideration with which I am, my
Lord,

"Your very good friend,
"CHARLES FELIX DE SAVOYE."

The importance of Sardinia dwelt strongly on Lord Nelson's
mind: most of his letters at this period allude to it. To
Lord Hobart we have seen he pointed out the advantages of
this island. To Earl St. Vincent he says, " in addition to my
other cares, Sardinia must be guarded; the French most
assuredly mean to invade it, first, I suppose, under a pretext
for keeping us out of it; and then they will have it ceded to
them. I have written to Lord Hobart on the importance of
Sardinia, it is worth one hundred Malta's in position, and has
the finest man-of-war harbour in Europe; they tell me it is
superior to Beerhaven—in short, it has nothing but advantages; the mode of getting it is to be considered by
Ministers, but money will do any thing in these days. To
keep it, could not in the first instance cost half so much as
Malta. I can have no reserves—I venture my opinion,

[1] The late Sir Hudson Lowe.

Ministers are not bound to follow it: I can have no views, but to benefit my country by telling all I know of situations, and how far they can be useful."[1]

To Lord Minto he also writes, "Sardinia, if we do not take it very soon, the French will have it, and then we lose the most important island, as a naval and military station in the Mediterranean. It possesses at the northern end, the finest harbour in the world; it equals Trincomalee. It is twenty-four hours sail from Toulon; it covers Italy; it is a position that the wind which carries the French to the westward is fair for you to follow. In passing to the southward they go close to you. In short, it covers Egypt, Italy, and Turkey. Malta must not be mentioned in the same century. I delivered my opinion on the inutility of Malta as a naval station for watching Toulon. A fleet would sooner pass from St. Helen's to Toulon than from Malta. If I lose Sardinia, I lose the French fleet; and to keep it, it could not, in the first instance, cost half so much as Malta, and be of all the use of Malta, and ten thousand times as much. I have told Lord Hobart fully my opinion on this subject. I can have no reserves. I venture my opinion. Ministers are not bound to follow it. I can have no views but to benefit my country by telling all I know of situations, and how far they can be useful."[2]

To Lord Hawkesbury also: "Either France or England must have it. The loss to us will be great indeed. I do not think that the fleet can then be kept at sea. From Sardinia we get water and fresh provisions; the loss of it would cut us off from Naples except by a circuitous route, for all the purposes of getting refreshment, even were Naples able to supply us. I have hitherto watched Sardinia; but at this moment, when from the bad condition of many of the ships under my command, I can barely keep a sufficient force at sea to attend to the French fleet, I have not ships to send to Madalena: not less, my Lord, than ten frigates, and as many good sloops, would enable me to do what I wish, and what, of course, I think absolutely necessary. But I am aware of the great

---

[1] Clarke and McArthur, Vol. ii. p. 352.
[2] Dispatches and Letters, Vol. v. p. 365. From an Autograph in the Minto Papers.

want of them in England, and that other services must be starved to take care of home. If I were at your Lordship's elbow, I think I could say so much upon the subject of Sardinia, that attempts would be made to obtain it; for this I hold as clear, that the King of Sardinia cannot keep it, and, if he would, that it is of no use to him; that if France gets it, she commands the Mediterranean; and that by us it would be kept at a much smaller expense than Malta: from its position, it is worth fifty Malta's."[1]

Upon the Earl Camden being appointed to succeed Lord Hobart as Secretary of State for the Colonial and War Department, his Lordship wrote to Lord Nelson on his often repeated communications on the value of Sardinia. The opinions expressed by Lord Nelson would appear from this letter to have been duly appreciated by the Government, and a proper weight given to his authority. To prevent the island of Sardinia from falling into the hands of the French, the English Government considered as of the first importance. Captain Leake[2] (so well known by his admirable works on Albania, Morea, &c.), had been sent by Lord Harrowby to make inquiries into military matters connected with this subject, and Lord Nelson was requested to aid him in his objects to the utmost of his power, and to take him under his own orders if thought necessary. Lord Nelson was very favourably impressed by Captain Leake's zeal and ability, and solicited assistance for him from Sir Alexander Ball, General Villettes, and other distinguished persons. Lord Camden solicited a continuance of the correspondence Lord Nelson had maintained with his predecessor in office so useful to the public service. In a private letter to Lord Nelson, Earl Camden, in repeating this solicitation, adds, " in entrusting to me your Lordship's sentiments on the political subjects connected with the Mediterranean, you repose them in a person who justly appreciates your opinions, and has the highest admiration of your character." Lord Harrowby also wrote to Lord Nelson requesting a continuation of his correspondence as with Lord Hawkesbury, and introducing Captain Leake to him, who was instructed to act according

[1] Clarke and McArthur, Vol. ii. p. 374.
[2] Colonel Leake, F.R.S.

to Lord Nelson's directions. Lord Nelson's information with regard to Sardinia, was so complete, that it was not thought necessary to send Captain Leake thither, and he accordingly departed for Malta, Corfu, &c.

In the month of January Lord Nelson departed, as he said, "to settle a little account with the Dey of Algiers." He held that it was better to be at open war than to be insulted, which he considered we had been by the Dey, who had sent off Mr. Falcon, the Consul-General, to Algiers. A great offence had been committed by Mr. Falcon, it appears, in having admitted some Moorish women into his house. The Algerine cruisers had also taken some Maltese vessels, and their crews considered as belonging to his Majesty's subjects, and other vessels having English passports, and conveying provisions to his Majesty's Maltese subjects. These acts had excited Lord Nelson's indignation, and he sent Captain Keats[1]

[1] Sir Richard Goodwin Keats was the son of a Clergyman in Devonshire, and Head Master of the Free Grammar School at Tiverton. Entering the Navy at an early age he served as Lieutenant of the Ramillies in the action with the Count D'Orvilliers in 1778, and afterwards was in the Prince George, 98 guns, bearing the Flag of Rear-Admiral Digby. Promoted to the rank of Commander in 1782 he served on the American station, and was made Post Captain June 24th, 1789, and afterwards commanded the Southampton and the Niger. In 1793 he was appointed to the London. In 1795 he sailed under Sir J. B. Warren to Quiberon, and was at the taking of L'Etoile and four sail of French merchantmen. In the Galatia, to which he was appointed in 1794, he continued until 1797, when he removed into the Boadicea frigate, and cruised in search of French privateers. With Sir Charles Pole in 1799 he commanded the frigates of the squadron, covering an attack by some bomb vessels on the Spanish squadron under the batteries of Aix, and was afterwards in the Superb, 74, with Sir James Saumarez off Cadiz. He distinguished himself in the second attack off Algeziras, and by Nelson, in 1804, he was sent off Algiers, there performing very important service. He was subsequently engaged in pursuit of the French fleet. In November, 1805, he was made Colonel of Marines, and was sent to seek the squadron of the French sent to the succour of St. Domingo. In the action of the 6th February, 1806, he gave a proof of his admiration of Nelson in suspending his portrait to the mizen-stay of his vessel the Superb. The Captain and his men fought gallantly, and the Patriotic Fund voted to him a vase or sword. Nelson entertained a very high opinion of Keats. In a letter to him, August 24, 1805, he says, "Nothing, I do assure you, could give me more pleasure than to have you at all times near me, for without a compliment, I believe your head is as judicious as your heart is brave, and neither, I believe, can be exceeded." He was afterwards engaged against Copenhagen, and on the 2nd October, 1807, was made a Rear-Admiral. He then went to the relief of the Spanish army in the North of Europe, and brought off the Marquis de la Romana from Denmark, for which he was

of the Superb, to demand apology for sending away the Consul, and restitution of the vessels, their crews and cargoes. Nelson was very explicit to Captain Keats in his instructions on these several points, and directed him particularly as to the mode of conducting himself, and upholding the dignity of a British officer. Nelson also wrote to the Dey, and afterwards determined himself upon going thither to have the matter definitively settled. He felt that the Government had reposed great confidence in him, and no man could be more jealous of the honour of his country, or more determined to maintain her dignity and interests.

The negotiation by Captain Keats was unsuccessful. Lord Nelson wrote to Sir Alexander Ball on the 19th of January: "The Dey is violent, and will yield no one point, therefore I have no further business here. Time and opportunity will make him repent." Nelson entirely approved Captain Keats's conduct. He wrote to him no less than four letters on the 17th [1] He also wrote to Lord Hobart concerning the failure of the negotiation and observed: "The insolence of the Dey is only to be checked (with due submission to whatever his Majesty may please to direct) by blockading Algiers, and his other ports of Bona, and Oran, and to capture his cruisers; for the more that is given up to him the more he will demand with insolence in future. Therefore, I should propose, that, on the 28th day of April next, when, if he means to send his cruisers to sea, they will be out, that on that day, every ship under my command should have strict orders (to open on that day), to take, sink, burn, and destroy every Algerine, and that, on that day, the ports of Algiers should be declared in a state of blockade. Thus, the Dey could get neither commerce, presents, or plunder; and, although the other powers may rejoice at the war with us, yet, my Lord, I am

---

created a Knight of the Order of the Bath. In 1809 he was engaged in the Scheldt, then commanded off Cadiz, and in 1811 went to the Mediterranean in the Hibernia, 120 guns, being then second in command on that station. He was made a Vice-Admiral in 1810, and in 1813 appointed Commander-in-chief and Governor of Newfoundland. He also succeeded Sir George Hope as Major-General of Marines in 1818, and Sir John Colpoys as Governor of Greenwich Hospital in 1821. He died Admiral of the White and G.C.B. April 5th, 1834.

[1] See Dispatches and Letters, Vol. v. pp. 376-77.

firmly persuaded that it will be most advantageous to us (and humiliating to the other powers whom he will squeeze), for the next one hundred years. If I should find his cruisers at sea before that time, in consequence of what has passed, I shall of course, take them, but my wish is to make a grand *coup*."[1] He wrote also to the Earl St. Vincent, " Before the summer is out, I dare say the Dey of Algiers will be sick of his insolence, and perhaps have his head cut off. I have recommended Mr. Falcon to go to England, and then, he will be able to explain every part of his conduct; but it appears to me that Mr. Falcon's conduct has been spirited, but perfectly correct, and that the two women found in his house was greedily seized as the pretext for getting rid of a clear-headed, spirited man. I should do great injustice to my own feelings, if I did not state my opinion to your Lordship, and other his Majesty's Ministers."[2]

Lord Nelson's conduct and that of Captain Keats obtained the commendation of the Government, and in May, Lord Nelson received a letter from Lord Hobart upon the subject, recommending, that provided the Dey would express regret at the manner in which Mr. Falcon had been sent away, another Consul should be appointed. Captain Keats was sent by Lord Nelson to negotiate with the Dey upon the subject. The Dey made the *amende honorable* for his conduct to Mr. Falcon, and Mr. McDonough was sent under certain conditions to fill his place. These, however, were not complied with. They related to the restoration or the value of the English vessel, the Ape. The Consul would be sent, only upon this condition being complied with. Captain Donnelly was dispatched with a strong letter to the Dey at the end of August; but it was not until December that Lord Nelson received replies to his dispatches from Earl Camden, signifying to him the entire approbation of his conduct in the affairs of the Dey of Algiers, and recommending that in future regular passports should be given to British vessels to prevent misunderstanding. Mr. Cartwright was

---

[1] From an Autograph in the Colonial Office. Dispatches and Letters, Vol. v. p. 378.

[2] Dispatches and Letters, Vol v. p. 379. From an Autograph in the possession of Vice-Admiral Sir W. Parker, Bart. G.C.B.

appointed Consul-General at Algiers, but he was not to be landed unless the Ape and her crew were restored.

About this time Lord Nelson was much elated by receiving intelligence of the successful issue of a law-suit, nominally Nelson v. Tucker, but really Nelson v. St. Vincent. It related to a sum of Prize-money which had occasioned much discussion. Tucker was the Agent for Prizes taken by the Mediterranean fleet under Earl St. Vincent in 1799. The action was to recover £13,000, one-eighth share of the prizes taken by Captain Digby belonging to the Earl's squadron, after the Commander-in-chief had quitted his station and returned to England, leaving Lord Nelson in command. In the first instance judgment was given for Earl St. Vincent, but upon a writ of error the Lord Chief Justice of the Common Pleas, Lord Ellenborough, reversed the decision by delivering the opinion of the Court, that " the moment a superior officer left his station, the right of the next Flag officer commenced; and, consequently, that Lord St. Vincent having returned to England, the enterprize and conduct of the fleet devolved on Lord Nelson, judgment was accordingly given in favour of Lord Nelson, who thereby becomes entitled to the whole of the Admiral's share of the Prize-money." This decision put Lord Nelson out of debt, and allowed him to think of improvements at Merton, of which he wrote to his friend Mr. Davison.

On the 20th of January 1804, from the Dispatches and Letters published by Sir N. Harris Nicolas, it will be perceived that Lord Nelson wrote no less than nine letters. To these he added the two following: The first is addressed to the care of Lady Hamilton for his child, then three years of age. The second is to Lady Hamilton :—

'Victory, January 20th, 1804.

"My dear Horatia,

"I send you a watch, which I give you permission to wear on Sundays, and on very particular days, when you are dressed and have behaved exceedingly well and obedient. I have kissed it, and send it with the affectionate BLESSING of YOUR

"NELSON AND BRONTÉ."[1]

[1] In the fragment of a letter, Nelson writes to Lady Hamilton : " You have sent me in that lock of beautiful hair, a far richer present than any monarch in

"Victory, January 20th, 1804.

"My dear Emma,

"I send a very neat watch for our god-child, and you will see it is by a good maker, that is I suppose it will *tick* for a year instead of a month or two. You will impress her that it is only to be worn when she behaves well and is obedient. I am very sorry that your comb is not arrived, the brig is at Malta, but I daresay it will arrive sometime and you shall have it the first opportunity. I send you Mr. Falconet's letter. You will see how very civil both of them are. Mr. Elliot is a great Minister, but I doubt whether the Queen has much real friendship for him. *Acton* has him fast, but I believe that Mr. Elliot had rather that Acton and the King and the Queen looked to him for my services, than applying to myself, but circumstanced as I have been and am with that Court, Sir William Hamilton gave it up, and no other person shall deprive me of the immediate communication. No, my dear Emma, what I do for them shall be from myself and not through him. They are in very great fears at this moment.

"I have been towards Algiers, where I sent a ship with Mr. Falcon our Consul, whom the Dey turned away, but the Dey has been made so insolent by Mr. North's conduct in giving him £30,000, that nothing I suppose but a flogging will put him in order, and with the French fleet ready to put to sea that I have not time for. I have been but very indifferent, a violent cold upon my breast. Asses milk would have done me much service, but I am better, and I hope to continue so till the battle is over, then I hope my business here will be finished: that it may be soon is the sincere wish of

"Yours,
"NELSON AND BRONTÉ."

On the 23rd Lord Nelson sailed for the Madalena Islands, leaving Captain Mowbray of the Active to look after the French fleet. His anxiety increased about the French fleet,

Europe could if he was so inclined. Your description of the dear angel makes me happy. I have sent to Mr. Falconet to buy me a watch, and told him if it does but tick, and the chain full of trinkets, that is all which is wanted. He is very civil, and Mrs. Falconet has sent word that she will do her best in choosing any thing I may want."

which he anticipated having shortly to encounter, and on the 10th of February wrote thus to Lady Hamilton:—

"Victory, February 10th, 1804, Madalena.

"My dearest Friend,

"We were blown in here on the 8th, in the heaviest gale of wind at N.E. and snow storm that I almost ever felt, but all your letters to December 27th I found just arrived. I cannot tell you all I wish, as Lord Nelson has enjoined the fleet not to write politics. We are on the eve of a battle, and I have no doubt but it will be a glorious one; at least it shall be such a one that shall never bring a blush on the cheeks of my dearest friend, when my name is mentioned. Our fleet is healthy, our men spirited, our Commanders brave and judicious, and for our numbers the finest fleet in the world. I only hope our dearest friends are well, and happily past *all* danger. May God in heaven bless and protect you! my last sigh will be, my dearest Emma, for your felicity, for I am to the last moment,

"Yours.

"Best regards to all friends. I have received all letters and papers."

About this time Sir William Bolton wrote to Lady Hamilton:—

"Dear Madam,

"I will flatter myself that a few lines may be worth the trouble of breaking the seal, since they inform your Ladyship my noble patron was in good health when the Seahorse left the fleet, which was then off Minorca, on its return from Algiers.

"The English letters by the Diana frigate went up to the fleet eight or ten days ago. I have several letters for his Lordship, which I received from Mr. Locker, which, as I sail to-morrow to join him, I hope his Lordship will soon get. Captain Sutton of the Amphion here, had a singular piece of good fortune; he fell in with, apparently, a Dutch ship off Cape St Vincent, all her masts gone, not a soul on board, but what was fairly worth the whole, a valuable cargo, estimated at twenty-two thousand pounds, nine thousand of which he has already received. Not long ago, all Lord Nelson's friends were rejoiced to read in a newspaper that the long depending cause between him and St. Vincent was decided in his favour. But it is peculiar to Lord Nelson to carry his point, whatever cause he engages in.

"Your Ladyship will impute it to my vanity—I have had the honour of being introduced to your Ladyship's friends, their Sicilian Majesties.

"I will trespass no longer on your patience, than to return your Ladyship many thanks for your kind attentions to my wife, and pray for your health and happiness; being ever,

"Dear Madam,

"Your faithful servant,

"W. BOLTON.[1]

"Gibraltar, February 2nd."

To Captain Gore of the Medusa he wrote on the 17th:—

"The Admiralty seem to think that the Spaniards may be hostile to us, and therefore have put me on my guard. Do not let it escape your lips; I am determined to have the first blow; even if they come with their whole eighteen they shall not join the French. If they come up the Mediterranean, and you have a mind for a shooting party, come with your frigates. Every part of your conduct is like yourself, perfect."[2]

To Lady Hamilton, on the 25th, Lord Nelson wrote thus:—

[1] Sir William Bolton was the eldest son of the Rev. William Bolton, the brother of Thomas Bolton, Esq. who married Susannah, sister of Lord Nelson. Under the protection of his Lordship he entered and proceeded in the naval service, as will be seen from the letters printed in these volumes. He was made Commander in 1801, and appointed to the Childers in 1803, but he was not made Post Captain until April 10, 1805. He commanded the Eurydice, the Druid, the Endymion, and the Forth in the Mediterranean, and in the Irish Channel and North American stations. He received the honour of knighthood, acting as proxy for Lord Nelson at his installation as a Knight of the Bath. He married his cousin Catherine, second daughter of Thomas Bolton, Esq. He died in December, 1830.

[2] Clarke and McArthur, Vol. ii. p. 359.

"February 25th, 1804.

"As Lord Nelson tells me that it is very probable this letter may not only be read, but never arrive to your hands, I only write this line to say, here we are, and have for the whole of this month experienced such a series of bad weather, that I have seldom seen the like. I am anxious in the extreme to hear that you are perfectly recovered from your late indisposition. Lord Nelson has heard very lately from Naples. The French army is prepared for service, and have a month's bread baked in readiness; an embargo is laid at Genoa and Leghorn, and all the vessels seized as transports; so that we must have some work very soon. I only hope to keep my health till the battle is over, but my spasms have been very bad lately. We saw the French fleet very safe on the 22nd, at evening. Lord Nelson rather expects the ships from Ferrol in the Mediterranean. With my kindest love and affection to all I hold dear, believe me,

"Yours.

"This goes by Spain."

In March, Lord Nelson received from Dr. Moseley, of Chelsea Hospital, a present of a copy of the fourth edition of his work on Tropical Diseases, to which Nelson had furnished some particulars. It was thus acknowledged:—

"Victory, March 11th, 1804.

"My dear Dr. Moseley,

"Yesterday brought me the favour of your invaluable book and most kind letter, and although I know myself not equal to your praises, yet I feel that my honest intentions for the good of the service have ever been the same, and I feel as I grow in rank that my exertions double.

"The great thing is health, and you will agree with me, that it is easier for an officer to keep men healthy than for a surgeon to cure them, situated as this fleet has been, without a real friendly port where we could get all the things so necessary for us. Yet I have, by changing the cruising ground, not allowing the sameness of prospect to satiate the mind, sometimes looking at Toulon, Ville Franche; sometimes Barcelona, Rosas; running round Minorca, Majorca, Sardinia, and

Corsica, and two or three times anchoring for a few days sending a ship to this place for *onions*, which I find the best thing which can be given to seamen, having always good mutton for the sick; cattle, when we can get it, and plenty of fresh water. In the winter, giving half the allowance of grog instead of all wine. These things are for the Commander-in-chief to look to; and shut very nearly out from Spain, and only getting refreshments by stealth from other places, my task has been an arduous one. Cornwallis has great merit for his persevering cruise, but he has everything sent him—we have nothing—we seem forgot by the great folks at home. But our men's minds are always kept up with the daily hope of meeting the enemy. I send you as a curiosity, an account of our deaths and sent to the hospital out of 6000 men. The fleet put to sea, May 18th, 1803, and is still at sea, not a ship has been refitted or recruited, except what we have done at sea.

"You will readily believe that all this must have shook me. My sight is getting very bad, but *I must not* be sick till after the French fleet is taken; after which, I shall soon hope to take you by the hand. I am glad always to hear good accounts of our dear good Lady Hamilton; that she should be universally beloved does not surprise me; the contrary would very much. I am sure she feels most sensibly all your kindness. Believe me for ever, my dear Doctor,

"Your much obliged friend,
"NELSON AND BRONTÉ.

"To Dr. Moseley."[1]

He wrote to Lady Hamilton on the 14th respecting Merton, and it is curious to perceive into what details he entered relating to it whilst his mind was so deeply engaged upon the French fleet:—

---

[2] This letter has been printed in Harrison's Life of Nelson, (Vol. ii. p. 418), and copied into the 5th volume of Sir Harris Nicolas's Dispatches, &c., but it has been dressed up, and although the orthography of Nelson's letters is not always correct, I hold it much better to print them as they were written, for the hurry and circumstances attending which, the reader is always ready to make proper allowance. The above is taken from the autograph in the possession of Dr. Moseley's executor, my old and esteemed friend, William Luxmoore, Esq.

"I would not have you lay out more than is necessary at Merton. The rooms, and the new entrance, will take a good deal of money. The entrance by the corner I would have certainly done; a common white gate will do for the present; and one of the cottages, which is in the barn, can be put up, as a temporary lodge. The road can be made to a temporary bridge; for that part of the *Nile,* one day, shall be filled up. Downing's canvas awning will do for a passage. For the winter, the carriage can be put into the barn; and, giving up Mr. Bennett's premises, will save £50. a-year; and, another year we can fit up the coach-house and stables which are in the barn. The footpath should be turned. I did shew Mr. Haslewood the way I wished it done; and Mr. —— will have no objections if we make it better than ever it has been; and, I also beg, as my dear Horatia is to be at Merton, that a strong netting, about three feet high, may be placed round the Nile, that the little thing may not tumble in; and then, you may have ducks again in it. I forget at what place we saw the netting; and either Mr. Perry or Mr. Goldsmid, told us where it was to be bought. I shall be very anxious till I know this is done.

"I have had no very late opportunities of sending to Naples: but *viâ* Malta. I wrote to Gibbs, to desire he would send over the *armoisins.* They will arrive in time. I hope the watch is arrived safe. The expenses of the alterations at Merton *you are* not to pay from the income. Let it all be put to a separate account, and I will provide a fund for the payment. Sir William Bolton was on board yesterday. He looks thin. The fag in a brig is very great; and I see no prospect of his either making prize-money, or being made Post, at present: but I shall omit no opportunity.

"Ever yours,
"NELSON AND BRONTÉ."[1]

Suspicions were, at the commencement of 1804, beginning to be entertained with regard to hostile preparations on the part of Spain, and Government sent to Nelson the Royal Sovereign of 100 guns, to be followed by the Leviathan, to

[1] Collection of Letters, Vol. ii. p. 16.

strengthen his squadron. He removed Sir Richard Bickerton into the Royal Sovereign. To the Russian gentlemen on board this vessel, he addressed the following:—

"Victory at sea, 16th March, 1804.

"Gentlemen,

"Far removed from your country and relations, and placed to serve in the fleet under my command, I desire that you will, on every occasion, both in private and public concerns, consult with me, and let me know your wants and wishes, and always consider me as

"Your sincere friend,
"NELSON AND BRONTÉ."[1]

In March also he received a letter from Lord Hobart, conveying to him the King's approbation of his conduct in regard to Algiers, Tripoli, and Naples. Of the French fleet, he writes to Sir Thomas Troubridge: "The French want to get out, and we want them out. Yesterday, two of their frigates were outside the Hières, peeping to know if we were gone to the devil. Ball is sure they are going to Egypt; the Turks are sure they are going to the Morea; Mr. Elliot, at Naples, to Sicily; and the King of Sardinia, to his only spot."[2] To Hugh Elliot, Esq. he wrote: "I have no doubts but that the French fleet would long ago have sailed from Toulon, but for the commotions in France."

At this time, he was sorely troubled about his eye-sight, which was very bad, and he was under great apprehensions of becoming blind, a fear that frequently harassed him much. He directed Captain Richardson, of the Juno, to communicate with Mr. Gibert, the Consul at Barcelona, and learn the probable course of things in Spain towards England.

The activity of his mind and the comprehensiveness of its character, led him to reflect seriously on every thing around, and the probable views entertained by the different Powers. He wrote to Sir John Acton: "Will Russia come forth as she ought, or are her plans only preparative to the taking possession of Greece, and of course Constantinople? This is

[1] Dispatches and Letters, Vol. v. p. 448. From the Letter Book.
[2] Clarke and Mc'Arthur, Vol. ii. p. 360.

a subject I have no business at present to enter into, although it is seriously in my mind;"[1] and at the same time to Spiridion Foresti, Esq.: "The ultimate views of Russia become every hour more distinct; how long the mask may be kept on I cannot say, but sooner or later, the Morea will come by conquest to Russia. What part Great Britain may take, the connexions which Russia may form will point out. However, we are at present on the most friendly terms with the Emperor, and I hope we shall always continue so. I have said enough to so sensible a man as yourself."[2] He appointed Lieutenant Woodman[3] to the charge of the transports, and wrote to him thus: "I have thought proper to send you, and must recommend to your serious attention the circumstances in general that are passing in the Black Sea, on the part of Russia, who, it is said, is forming an armament to a very considerable extent; and although there is not the most distant idea that this armament will direct its operations against the interests of Great Britain, yet it is essentially necessary that its real intentions should be discovered as early as possible, and, therefore, you will let no opportunity escape you of obtaining all the information you may be able to collect on this important subject. And I must desire that you will endeavour to gain a particular account of the Naval force which Russia may have at Sebastapol and Cherson (their two principal naval ports in the Black Sea), and to what extent they are arming there. You will likewise endeavour to obtain a knowledge of their fortifications, and what number of guns is mounted on their different batteries, and whether they are able to protect their trade. It will be advisable to ascertain whether these armaments are with a view to check and oppose the measures of the French, should they attempt to possess themselves of the Morea. You will also endeavour to gain information of the trade and manufactures carried on by the Russians in the ports above mentioned—what supplies of provisions and naval stores might be drawn from that country, and upon what terms. In order to obtain a perfect knowledge of the local situation of the Russian territory in the Black Sea, you are to procure a chart of their country, which

---

[1] Clarke and McArthur, Vol. ii. p. 361.  [2] Ibid.
[3] He died a Lieutenant in 1811.

will assist you in forming a more clear idea of the places of principal importance, and endeavour, by every means, to obtain information of their present and future intentions with regard to England, transmitting me a very full and correct account of your observations, and, on your return to Malta, for the information of the Lords Commissioners of the Admiralty."[1]

These instructions exhibit Lord Nelson's exceeding adaptation to the conduct of affairs.

Towards the end of March he again repaired to the Madalena islands. "Day by day (he now writes to his friend Mr. Davison), I am expecting the French fleet to put to sea—every day, hour, and moment; and you may rely that if it is within the power of man to get at them, it shall be done; and, I am sure, that all my brethren look to that day as the finish of our laborious cruise. The event no man can say exactly, but I must think, or render great injustice to those under me, that let the battle be when it may, it will never have been surpassed. My shattered frame, if I survive, that day, will require rest, and that is all I shall ask for. If I fall on such a glorious occasion, it shall be my pride to take care that my friends shall not blush for me. These things are in the hands of a wise and just Providence, and HIS WILL be done. I have got some trifle, thank God, to leave those I hold most dear, and I have taken *care* not to neglect it. Do not think I am low-spirited on this account, or fancy anything is to happen to me. Quite the contrary: my mind is calm, and I have only to think of destroying our inveterate foe. *April 7th.*—A frigate has just brought me an account that she saw the French fleet outside Toulon, thirty-four hours ago, and she does not know that they are returned. I have two frigates gone for more information, and we all hope for a meeting with the enemy. Nothing can be finer than the fleet under my command."[2]

On the 2nd of April, he sailed from the Madalena Islands, and wrote to William Marsden, Esq., who had succeeded Sir Evan Nepean, Bart. as Secretary of the Admiralty

---

[1] Dispatches and Letters, Vol. v. p. 470. From the Letter Book.
[2] Ibid. p. 475. From an Autograph in the possession of Colonel Davison.

at this period. Captain Layman,[1] of the Weazle, (which was lost, and for which he was tried by a Court-Martial

[1] This officer, when only a Midshipman in the Myrmidon, scuttled the lower deck of the vessel in a very heavy gale, and to this proceeding the preservation of the ship was attributed. His Royal Highness the Duke of Clarence entertained a very high opinion of his abilities. He paid great attention to the growth of timber and the building of ships, as will be seen in Appendix, No. IV. In 1800, he was made a Lieutenant, and joined Earl St. Vincent's flag ship, and presented to the Earl a plan for annually building a frigate at Bombay, which was carried into execution. Shortly before the battle of Copenhagen, April 2, 1801, he solicited Lord Nelson to employ him in the event of boat duty being required, either for boarding, towing off the enemy's fire-ships, and other dangerous service His Commander gave him, when at Merton, a testimonial in regard to his services, observing, "You were always ready to go on every service I am sure; for the only favour you ever asked of me was, to be sent on all services of danger and difficulties, and I always understood you acquitted yourself as an able officer and seaman." He does not appear to have received the promotion his gallant conduct deserved. During the Peace of Amiens, he made some valuable suggestions to Government with regard to the cultivation of Trinidad, and the establishment of Chinese husbandmen in the island of Ceylon. In 1803, he was again with Nelson, and in 1804 was in the command of the Weazle at Gibraltar. In this vessel he kept the Straits free of French privateers, but he unfortunately lost his sloop on the rocks off Cabritta Point. He was appointed to the Raven, which was fitted up at Woolwich under his direction in a peculiar manner, giving great advantages under a chase, in clearing an enemy's coast, &c. In 1805, he was a prisoner of war at Puerto-Santa-Maria, near Cadiz. This circumstance, and the loss of his vessel, in which he was conveying dispatches for Sir John Orde and Lord Nelson, arose from the negligence of the officers to whom he had entrusted the safety of the vessel; he was ready to substantiate these assertions, but under the recommendation of Lord Nelson, induced by feelings of humanity towards those officers, he suppressed the allusions in regard to them, and was unhappily censured for the loss of his ship, and put at the bottom of the list. On hearing this, Nelson exclaimed, "I did not expect this, but it's all my fault; never mind, I'll get you over it." Nelson immediately wrote to Viscount Melville, at that time head of the Admiralty, strongly recommending Mr. Layman, and vouching for his bravery, zeal, judgment, and activity, and to strengthen his case, declared that if he had been censured every time he had run ships or fleets under his command into great danger, he should long ago have been out of the service, and never in the House of Peers. Commander Layman arrived at Portsmouth in May, 1805, and Nelson still urged his merits. He took him to the Admiralty, and a promise was given that he should be sent out to the Mediterranean, but, to use the words of Layman, "the next month terminating his Lordship's glorious career, the promise was forgot, and my offer of service rejected." He offered to prevent premature decay in our ships, to divulge a plan rendering forest trees fit for immediate use, provided he should be entrusted with the measure, but his applications were disregarded. He published some works, the Precursor, and others connected with this subject, but could not get his suggestions adopted. He is said to have terminated his existence in 1826.

and acquitted of all blame, presented himself with Dispatches to Earl St. Vincent, and was soon after appointed to the Raven sloop), conveyed the following letter to Lady Hamilton :—

"Victory, (April) 7th, 1804.

"My dearest Emma,

"I send this by Captain Layman; he is a good man, and an excellent officer, and he is attached to me. I have given him a strong caution not to say too much at the Admiralty. If he was dumb, and could not write, it would, upon the whole, be better for him. Do you caution him not to talk too much. He will tell you of my determination not to be *absent* from Merton on Christmas-day. Nothing, I can assure you, but events which I cannot foresee, can prevent me, and if I have the pleasure of meeting the French fleet, which I expect every hour, I shall certainly ask for *rest*, let who will be at the Admiralty, it is the same thing to me.

"*April 9th.* Whilst I was writing, a frigate communicated to me that, thirty-four hours before, she saw the French fleet outside Toulon, standing off; that in the evening they stood inshore again. Yesterday we saw some French ships of war, and they are now in sight, working into Toulon. Captain Layman will tell you my anxiety. I was in great hopes that all my fag was near being brought to a close, and that I should visit dear Merton.

"Yours,
"NELSON AND BRONTÉ."

Nelson wrote again on the 10th :—

"Victory, off Toulon, April 10th, 1804.

"My dearest Emma,

"I have received all your truly kind and affectionate letters to January 25th, by the Thisbe; and last night your letter of January 13th, by Naples. The *armoisins* will go under the care of Captain Layman, who unfortunately lost his sloop; but with much credit to himself, he has been acquitted of all blame.

"I rejoice that dear Horatia is got well; and also that you are recovered of your severe indisposition. In our present situation with Spain, this letter, probably, may never reach you. I have wrote fully; and intend to send them by the Argus, who I expect to join every minute. Elphi Bey, I hear, has had all his fine things taken from him. He escaped into the Desert, and is pursued; probably his head is off long before this time. The French fleet came out on the 5th, but went in again the next morning. Yesterday a Rear-Admiral and seven sail of ships, including frigates, put their nose outside the harbour. If they go on playing this game, some day we shall lay salt upon their tails; and so end the campaign of, my dearest Emma, your most faithful and affectionate."[1]

On the 19th:—

"Victory, April 19th, 1804.

"My dearest Emma,

"I had wrote you a line, intended for the Swift cutter, but instead of her joining me, I had the mortification, not only to hear that she was taken, but that *all* the dispatches and letters had fallen into the hands of the enemy: a very pretty piece of work! I am not surprised at the capture; but am very much so that any dispatches should be sent in a vessel with twenty-three men, not equal to cope with any row boat privateer. The loss of the Hindostan was great enough; but for importance, it is lost, in comparison to the probable knowledge the enemy will obtain of our connections with foreign countries! Foreigners for ever say—and it is true— 'We dare not trust England; one way or other we are sure to be committed!' However, it is now too late to launch out on this subject. Not a thing has been saved out of the Hindostan, not a second shirt for any one; and it has been by extraordinary exertions that the people's lives were saved.

"Captain Hallowell is so good as to take home for me, wine, as by the inclosed list; and if I can, some honey. The Spanish honey is so precious, that if [any one has] a cut, or sore throat, it is used to cure it. I mention this, in case you should wish to give the Duke a jar. The smell is wonderful! It is to be produced no where, but in the mountains near Rosas. The Cyprus wine, one hogshead, was for Buonaparte. I would recommend the wine-cooper drawing it off; and you

[1] Collection of Letters, Vol. ii. p. 26.

can send a few dozens to the Duke; who I know takes a glass every day at two o'clock. I wish I had any thing else to send you, but, my dearest Emma, you must take the will for the deed.

"I am pleased with Charlotte's letter; and as she loves my dear Horatia, I shall always like her. What hearts those must have who do not! But, thank God, she shall not be dependent on any of them.

"Yours,
"NELSON AND BRONTÉ."[1]

And on the 21st:—

"Victory, April 21st, 1804.

"My dearest Emma,

"We have had a hard gale of wind for two days, and it is now lulling for a moment. I am getting Hallowell on board to give him my dispatches. We shall be under Corsica to-morrow morning. I never saw such a continuation of bad weather. I received the inclosed from Charles. I did not, you may believe, let him go to the hospital. There has been, several times within this year, something very odd about him. Capel has been always very kind to him. I have had Dr. Snipe to examine him; he complains of a violent pain in the back of his head; it comes on occasionally. Has any of his family been so? He does not at other times, Capel says, want for abilities, and he is as well kept in money and clothes as any Mid. in the fleet. It has vexed me upon your account, for I know you will be sorry. I hope he will grow out of it. Remember me kindly to good Mrs. Cadogan, and believe me,

"Yours,
"NELSON AND BRONTÉ."

In this month the Swift hired cutter employed to convey dispatches to Lord Nelson (alluded to in his letter to Lady Hamilton, April 19th), was taken by a French privateer, and he was exceedingly annoyed at their having been sent in so inefficient a vessel. He wrote to Lord Hobart a private letter,

[1] Collection of Letters, Vol. ii. p. 29.

saying, "I rely with confidence that, although the Admiralty for ever send their dispatches, of whatever consequence, without the use of cypher, and trust to their being thrown overboard in case of capture, yet, as I know the other departments of Government always use cypher if of importance, and although Admirals are never intrusted with cyphers, yet I rely that your Lordship would not trust any dispatch of consequence in a vessel with twenty-three men, much less commit the interests and schemes of other powers to such a conveyance. This is the only consolation I derive from all the dispatches being this day read by the First Consul; I wish they were in his throat. I think a great deal on this matter, but it may be prudent to hold my tongue."[1]

Also to Hugh Elliot, Esq.: "The capture of the Swift cutter of four or six guns, and twenty-three men, with all the dispatches, is a loss which ages cannot do away. I only hope, but I have my *great fears*, that not only the secrets of our own country are exposed, but that, perhaps, Naples, Russia, Sardinia, and Egypt, may be mentioned. How the Admiralty could send out such a vessel is astonishing! I wish it to be known at Petersburgh and Constantinople, in case any plan has been agreed upon by our Courts, for the French will, of course, strike a blow instantly. Naples will keep on her guard, for we must prepare for the worst which may have happened. It has made me very uneasy and unwell."[2]

On the 26th he dispatched a secret and confidential letter to Captain Pulteney Malcolm[3] of the Kent, in which he says:

---

[1] Dispatches and Letters, Vol. v. p. 107. From an Autograph in the Colonial Office.

[2] From an autograph in the Elliot Papers.

[3] This distinguished officer was born at Douglas near Langholm, February 20, 1768. At the age of ten years he entered the Navy as a Midshipman on board the Sybil frigate, which was commanded by his uncle Sir Thomas Pasley, Bart. and his first voyage was to the Cape of Good Hope. He was afterwards engaged in the affair at Porto Praya, and at the taking of a fleet of Dutch Indiamen in Saldanha Bay. He was engaged in various services, from 1782 to 1793, in the Jupiter, the Formidable, the Scipio, the Pegasus, the Bellerophon, the Vengeance, and the Penelope, in which vessel he had much arduous duty in cutting out vessels in the port of St. Domingo. He was made Lieutenant March 3, 1783, and a Commander in the Jack Tar, April 3, 1794. His commission as Post Captain is

"You are hereby required and directed, on this order being delivered to you, to receive on board, or to convey them if they embark on board their own ships, the King, Queen, and Royal family of Naples, to Palermo, or such other place as the King may choose to proceed to, and you will afford every protection and assistance to all those who may wish to follow their Majesties (and that they approve of). And you will also receive his Majesty's Minister and suite, and afford such other protection as in your power to all British subjects and their property, as the urgency of the case may require."[1]

dated October 22, 1794, and he was appointed to the Fox frigate. In the following year he escorted a fleet of merchantmen to the Mediterranean, and afterwards served at Quebec, and in the North Sea, and then in the East Indies, and the China seas. In the Suffolk and the Victorious he served as Flag Captain to Vice-Admiral Rainier, Commander-in-chief in the Indian seas, and upon his return to England in 1803 the latter vessel was in such bad condition that she was obliged to be broken up, and he came back in a vessel hired at Lisbon for his conveyance. In 1804 he was appointed to the Royal Sovereign, proceeded to the Mediterranean, removed into the Kent, and joined Lord Nelson as above. He was afterwards in the Renown, and in 1805 in the Donegal, which he commanded for six years. In this vessel he was with Nelson in his pursuit of the combined French and Spanish fleets to the West Indies, and then returned to the Channel, and was sent by Sir Robert Calder to reinforce Vice-Admiral Collingwood off Cadiz. He aided this officer in the capture of El Rayo, which had escaped at the Battle of Trafalgar. He was then, after very meritorious exertions and humane conduct towards the Spanish prisoners, brought to Gibraltar, placed under the orders of Sir J. T. Duckworth, sailed to the West Indies, and was in the battle at St. Domingo, February 6, 1806. He proceeded with the prizes to England, and suffered much from a very heavy gale of wind. The Patriotic Fund presented him with a vase of the value of £100. In 1808 he was engaged to escort the army under Sir Arthur Wellesley to Portugal, then attached to the Channel Fleet under Lord Gambier. In 1811 he was appointed to the Royal Oak, and in 1812 to the San Josef as Captain of the Channel Fleet, then under Lord Keith. He was made a Colonel of Marines, August 12, 1812, and a Rear-Admiral, December 4, 1813. He hoisted his flag in 1814 in the Royal Oak, and took the troops under Brigadier-General Ross from Bourdeaux to North America. He was with Sir Alexander Cochrane in the Chesapeake expedition, and obtained the warmest acknowledgements from the Commander-in-chief for his services. In 1815 he was made K.C.B. and upon his arrival in England Sir Pulteney was ordered to co-operate with the Duke of Wellington in the proceedings against France. He struck his flag September 26th, but upon Napoleon Buonaparte's being sent to St. Helena, Sir Pulteney was made Commander-in-chief on that station, where he gained the respect and confidence of the ex-Emperor. He was promoted to the rank of Vice-Admiral, July 19, 1821, and died Admiral of the Blue, June 28, 1838.

[1] From an Autograph in the Elliot Papers.

At this time the King and Queen of Naples addressed the following to Lord Nelson :—

"Portici, 22nd of May, 1804.

"My dear Lord Duke Nelson,

"I am anxious that my letter should reach you as soon as possible to inform you of what has happened to me, and depose in your heart and friendship the pain and grief which I undergo. After innumerable sacrifices made to procure me peace, and after the peace to procure me the quiet and tranquillity of my subjects, I receive fresh insults, threats, and inexpressible demands from the French Government; my loyalty and constant mode of proceeding have kept me from yielding, but such conduct on my part has excited against me the animosity and hatred of the First Consul, in such a manner as to cause it to be signified to me, by several occasions that I must remove from about my person, the worthy and well-deserving General Acton. As there was no founded grievance, no precise facts to be brought against him, Buonaparte alleges his nationality as a motive, and attributes to him as being English, every kind of disposition to favour his own country alone. He has been attacked with fury, so far as to have had personal altercations with the French Ambassador, not a single circumstance could be produced as a subject of just remonstrance. But great power cannot be restrained, and at this moment in France the abuse of force is arrived at its height. It is demanded of me to send away this Minister, and I am menaced with war, if I do not comply with this extraordinary demand. Orders will arrive in a few days to Alquier, the French Ambasssdor, to go away, in case Acton shall not already be gone. The latter has thought it his duty to prevent a war, to which I was exposed: he goes therefore into Sicily, but possessing all my faith and just confidence. The present circumstances, and not having a numerous English force by hand, the Russians in Corfu not being in sufficient number, compel me still to temporise, so much the more, as such is the opinion of Lord Hawkesbury given lately to Castelcicala, and such likewise the sentiments of the Emperor of Russia, from whom I have letters of the 22nd of April. I must therefore submit, against my will, to the hard step which the moment demands, in order that I may not by anticipation mislead the ideas of your Court and that of Russia. When these shall come and assist me with effective bodies of troops, I will take up another position for this kingdom: in the mean time I am thinking equally for the safety of Sicily, which is furnished with every thing for that effect. To you, my dear Lord Nelson, I recommend myself again whatever may occur in case of the war's renewal: the ship which you leave me becomes more and more necessary in this Bay. My wife, son, and I shall divide ourselves. She will take upon her the defence of Naples, my son that of Calabria, and I shall go to Sicily, while the rest of the family will remove to Gaeta; I reclaim, however, your assistance at all events. Acton will continue to inform you of every thing from Palermo, whither I shall write him at whatsoever time any thing occurs, and shall avail myself always of his lights and counsels, which I have experienced to be constantly useful, firm and wise. I have mentioned to you what my two friendly Courts advise me in the case of Buonaparte's endeavouring to exercise his rage against me and my family; I have no other line of conduct to follow than that which they hold out to me, reposing upon their aid and friendship.

"To you, my Lord, I continue to recommend my fate, and that of the kingdom which you have once before saved: I will take care that you shall be exactly informed of every thing in time, so that you may assist me without provoking an attack from the troops, which I have the misfortune to see in my dominions, but which hitherto do not pass over the line marked out. Enjoy, my dear Duke, the best health which your constantly affectionate friend wishes you.

"FERDINANDO B."

"My dear and very worthy Lord and Admiral,

"The King and our worthy Minister will explain to you in detail what occasions the present dispatch, and plunges me in the deepest affliction, but I can assure you that our real sentiments will never be changed by any thing, but are confirmed daily. The King, my husband, has consented, at the repeated solicitations of General Acton, to give up temporarily the direction of affairs, to avoid any pretext on the part of the Imperial usurper for violent measures. It is a deep sacrifice he has made in acceding to the continual demands of his honest Minister, and to tranquillize the fears of his subjects, who dread deplorable events: besides England and Russia counsel temporising, and waiting the result, so he has felt himself compelled, without in any point changing his sentiments, and it is to assure you of this that he sends you this vessel. You know, my worthy Admiral, the truth and sincerity of my mode of thinking, which would ever prevent my asserting a fact, of which I was not perfectly sure. Continue, then, to be always our defender, protector, and guard, from the insidious treatment of those who have neither law nor faith. We confide totally in your Government and your achievements. You will be informed duly of all, and believe that I trust only in your brave loyal nation, and in you, my worthy Lord. Preserve the same sentiments always towards us, believe that we merit them, being, until death, your grateful and very attached friends, myself your affectionate friend,

"CHARLOTTE.

"The 22nd May, 1804.

"The Prince, my son, who thinks entirely as we do, desires me to present his compliments to you, as also all my other children."

On the 28th and on the 3rd of May Nelson wrote to Lady Hamilton:—

"Victory, April 28th, 1804.

"My dearest Emma,

"I have been for some days, and am still, very unwell, without being seriously ill, but I fret absolutely like a fool for the faults of others. It was no fault of mine that the dispatches were taken, but of those who sent them in a vessel not fit to trust my old shoes in; nor is it my fault that the Kent, the finest ship in the fleet, is kept so long from England, notwithstanding my representations that she is now obliged to leave the fleet, to lay guard-ship at Naples, and more will very soon be in as bad a plight. My only wish is for the coming out of the French fleet to finish all my uneasinesses. But I yet trust that the reign of Buonaparte will be soon over, and then that we shall have a few years of peace and quietness.

"Remember me kindly to all we hold most dear, and believe me,

"Yours,

"NELSON AND BRONTÉ.

"Captain Layman, Captain Hallowell, and I believe another packet of letters for you, are now at Gibraltar."

"Victory, May 3rd, 1804.

"Since I wrote you on the 28th April, we have not had the smallest communication with any vessel, but as I am sending a letter to Madrid, I cannot let the opportunity slip of saying we are alive this day. Events, and great ones, must soon take place. France seems prepared in all quarters, and if they do not attempt something, they must feel their own disgrace, and as Buonaparte cares not for the lives of Frenchmen, something must be done to keep up his Government, which, notwithstanding all that is said abroad, I believe is in very great jeopardy at home. God send a finish to it, for the benefit of mankind. I have not been very well lately, and I have only to wish for a battle with the French fleet, when probably my career will be finished. I only serve, you know, for the pleasure of fighting them; that over, I shall ask for rest for a little time, but I most sincerely hope that by the destruction of Buonaparte, that wars with all nations will cease. Sir William Bolton is now on board very well.

"Yours.

"Kiss Horatia for me. Admiral Campbell is on board, and desires his kind regards; so does Lord Nelson."

Lord Nelson dispatched Captain Sir William Bolton in the Childers, in quest of three French privateers off Tunis, interrupting our trade, and he again brought the subject of Sardinia under Lord Hobart's notice: "The question (he says) is not, shall the King of Sardinia keep it? that is out of the question;

he cannot, for any length of time. If France possesses it, Sicily is not safe an hour; and the passage to the Levant is completely blocked up. Pardon me, my Lord, for bringing this important subject again before you: but I really think that I should not do my duty to my country if I did not."[1]

On the 5th of May he wrote the following to Lady Hamilton:—

"Victory, May 5th, 1804.

"I find, my dearest Emma, that your picture is very much admired by the French Consul at Barcelona; and that he has not sent it to be admired—which I am sure it would be, by Buonaparte. They pretend that there were three pictures taken—I wish I had them: but they are all gone,[2] as irretrievably as the dispatches; unless we may read them in a book, as we printed their correspondence from Egypt. Dr. Scott went to Barcelona, to try to get the private letters; but I fancy they are all gone to Paris. The Swedish and American Consuls told him, that the French Consul had your picture, and read your letters; and Doctor thinks one of them, probably, read the letters.

"By the master's account of the cutter, I would not have trusted a pair of old shoes in her. He tells me she did not sail, but was a good sea boat. I hope Mr. Marsden will not trust any more of my private letters in such a conveyance; if they choose to trust the affairs of the public in such a thing, I cannot help it. I long for the invasion being over, it must finish the war, and I have no fears for the event."[3]

On the 11th he again departed for the Madalena Islands to complete the wood and water, and obtain other necessary supplies for the squadron, leaving Captain Mowbray in the Active to keep a watch on the French fleet. On the 22nd and 30th he again addressed Lady Hamilton:—

[1] From an Autograph in the Colonial Office.
[2] Taken in the Swift cutter.
[3] Collection of Letters, Vol. ii. p. 36.

"Victory, May 22nd, 1804.

"My dearest Emma,

"Your two letters *via* Lisbon arrived the same day with those in the Leviathan. I do not deserve your scolding. I have looked at my log, and I find that the Phœbe sailed for Gibraltar with the English letters on December 27th, and that all the English letters went in her; therefore no signal for English letters could be flying on the 28th, as you state. Your letter was dated the 26th. The Cameleon went to Naples, but I never have, nor intend to write by such a very uncertain route when I could write by a better at the same time, and we may be sure that all my letters would be read; not that I care, but I shall be more careful how I write a word of the fleet, as I see that extracts from my letters get into the newspapers. Davison is very wrong ever to quote a word I write, but I shall not scold him now, as I fear, poor fellow, he is in the King's Bench. I am quite hurt about his getting into such a scrape; he always told me: 'Oh! I know my ground—let me alone—I cannot be deceived.' It often turns out that these very clever men are oftener deceived than other people. Now let me put you right about Mr. Marsh. He did what was most perfectly right, and it was very hard upon me to force the money out of his hands. You *know* how £4000 was meant to be disposed of, but never mind. I never meant but to pay Davison, with many, many thanks, and a due sense of the obligations I owe him. I had hopes, if we got the Dutch ship given to the Victory, that, with a little more I should be out of his debt; and I do assure you that I should have ordered the money to have been paid to him, but that he begged me not to *think of it*. I feel it all, I would not have acted so by him had I been so rich; so finishes that matter.

"With respect to the improvements at Merton, I never meant that they should be paid out of the £1200 a year, and I send you an order that Davison will pay the bills, as I wish to know exactly what the alterations cost. With respect to the room, I hardly know how to find the money; but if it is to be done this year, it is begun before this time; it is too late to say a word now. I have wrote to Sir John

Acton on the subject you wished me, but that person is now so much French, that I doubt the effect if she does write— so it is said, but I cannot believe it. I have not heard of the arrival of the watch for Horatia, or a little box for you, but I suppose they went in the British Fair cutter, and the answers came out in the *Swift*. I shall write by Gibraltar in a few days. This goes through Spain by the care of Friend Gayner.

" Yours."

" Victory, May 30th, 1804.

" I see Lord Stafford is going to oppose Mr. Addington; the present Ministry cannot stand. I wish Mr. Addington had given you the pension; Pitt, and hard-hearted Grenville never will. What a fortune the death of Lord Camelford gives him!

"Every thing you tell me about my dear Horatia charms me. I think I see her, hear her, and admire her, but she is like her dear, dear mother. I wish I could but be at dear Merton, to assist in making the alterations. I think I should have persuaded you to have kept the pike and a clear stream, and to have put all the carp, tench, and fish who muddy the water into the pond. But as you like, I am content. Only take care that my darling does not fall in and get drowned. I begged you to get the little netting along the edge; and particularly on the bridges.

"I have only one more word—Do not believe a syllable the newspapers say, or what you hear. Mankind seems fond of telling lies.

"Remember me kindly to Mrs. Cadogan, and all our mutual friends: and be assured I am for ever your most faithful,

" NELSON AND BRONTÉ.

" George Campbell desires me always to present his best respects, and make mine to good Mr. Yonge; and when you see Sir William Scott, make my best regards acceptable to him. There is no man I have a higher opinion of, both as a public and private character."[1]

---

[1] Collection of Letters, Vol. ii. p. 39.

"Victory, May 30th, 1804.

"My dearest Emma,

"I am writing this day by way of Gibraltar and Barcelona; to take both chances. I wrote you on the 22nd through Friend Gayner, the Quaker at Rosas. We have nothing in the least new here. We cruise, cruise, and one day so like another, that they are hardly distinguishable, but *hopes*, blessed *hopes*, keeps us up, that some happy day the French may come out, then I shall consider my duty to my country fulfilled. I have been but so so, and am not so well as I could wish, a slow nasty fever hangs upon me, but I have a good medical man in the Surgeon of the Victory, Dr. Snipe being absent at Malta. I am not seriously ill, but am not quite in rude health. For God's sake and my sake do not believe anything that newspapers may tell you; I can tell my own tale; or conn over every word in my letter. My saying we are on the eve of a battle could only be intended to convey my belief that the French intended to put to sea, and so they did on April the 5th, and had we not been near, probably they would have pushed for their destination, therefore do not fancy this, that, or the other, as how, where, or when, I can get at them. I cannot do impossibilities, or go into Toulon, but all that man can do shall be done, and the sooner it is done the sooner I shall certainly be at dear Merton. Kiss my dearest Horatia for me. I shall hope to see her at Merton on my arrival. I think the election of Buonaparte to be Emperor will give us Peace, and the Ministry seems going. I hope Mr. Addington has given you a pension—it is shameful if he has not, however nothing shall be wanting from me. I will give you two-thirds of the last bit of bread I have. I have wrote Admiral Lutwidge, by Gibraltar. Say every kind thing for me to all friends. I have sent you a case of macaroni by the Agincourt, and will send for more from Naples this very day. I have not heard from Gibbs this age, nor of Bronté, but I hope he will do well for me. Gaetano desires his duty, he says he is afraid you have forgot him. I do not hear of William having any inclination to send home any part of his wages. Don't you give any, for it will come out of my pocket, which is not necessary, as his pay is £18. a year."

The fever alluded to in this letter is more particularly described by Lord Nelson in a letter to Dr. Baird. He says:—" The health of this fleet cannot be exceeded ; and I really believe that my shattered carcass is in the worst plight of the whole fleet. I have had a sort of rheumatic fever, they tell me; but I have felt the blood gushing up the left side of my head, and the moment it covers the brain, I am fast asleep: I am now better of that; and with violent pain in my side, and night sweats, with heat in the evening, and quite flushed. The pain in my head, nor spasms, I have not had for some time. Mr. (now Sir George) Magrath, whom I admire for his great abilities every day I live, gives me excellent remedies; but we must lose such men from our service, if the army goes on encouraging medical men, whilst we do nothing. I am sure much ought to be done for our Naval Surgeons, or how can we expect to keep valuable men? I look to you not only to propose it, but to enforce it to Lord St. Vincent, who must be anxious to preserve such a valuable set of men to the navy."[1]

He wrote to Lady Hamilton, June 6th, 10th, and 17th :—

" Victory, June 6th, 1804.

" Since I wrote you, my dearest Emma, on the 30th and 31st of May, nothing new has happened except our hearing the *feu de joie* at Toulon, for the declaration of Emperor. What a capricious nation those French must be ! However, I think it must in any way be advantageous to England. There ends for a century all republics! By vessels from Marseilles, the French think it will be a peace, and they say that several of their merchant ships are fitting out, I earnestly pray that it may be so; and, that we may have a few years of rest.

" I rather believe, my antagonist at Toulon, begins to be angry with me, at least, I am trying to make him so, and then he may come out and beat me, as he says he did off Boulogne. He is the Admiral that went to Naples, in December, 1792, La Touche Tréville, who landed the grenadiers. I owe him something for that.

[1] Clarke and McArthur, Vol. ii. p. 367.

"I am better, my dear Emma, than I have been, and shall get through the summer very well.

"Would you conceive it possible! but it is now from April 2nd since I have heard from Ball. The average time for a frigate to go and return, is from six to seven weeks. Sir William Bolton joined last night; and received his letters announcing his being called *papa*. He is got a very fine young man and good officer. Lord St. Vincent has desired he may have the first Admiralty vacancy for Post; but nobody will die, or go home.

"Apropos! I believe you should buy a piece of plate value fifty pounds, for our god-daughter of Lady Bolton: and something of twenty or thirty pounds value, for Colonel Suckling's. But my Emma you are not to pay for them, let it rest for me; or, if the amount is sent me, I will order payment."[1]

"Victory, June 10th, 1804.

"My dearest Emma,

"I wrote to you on the 6th *viâ* Rosas: this goes by Barcelona: to which place I am sending Sir William Bolton, to fetch Dr. Scott, who is gone there, poor fellow, for the benefit of his health.

"I have just had very melancholy letters from the King and Queen of Naples, on account of General Acton's going to Sicily. The insolence of Buonaparte was not to be parried without a war; for which they are unable, if unassisted. I have letters from Acton, May 28th, on board the Archimedes, just going into Palermo. He will probably return to Naples, unless new events arise and that may be; for a Minister, once out, may find some difficulty in renewing his post. He has acted with great and becoming spirit.

"I am better, but I have been very unwell. It blows here as much as ever. Yesterday was a little hurricane of wind. I dare say Prince Castelcicala knows it by express; if not you may tell him, with my best respects. He and every one else may be sure of my attachment to those good Sovereigns. By this route I do not choose to say more on this subject.

[1] Collection of Letters, Vol. ii. p. 48.

"I fear Sardinia will be invaded from Corsica before you get this letter. I have not small ships to send there or any where else; not in the proportion of one to five. You may communicate this to Mr. Addington, if you think that he does not know it; but to no one else except Castelcicala, of what relates to Naples.

"I have very flattering letters from the Grand Vizir, in the name of the Sultan, and from Cadir now Capitan Pacha."[1]

"Victory, June 17th, 1804.

"Not the least alteration has taken place in the fleet since I wrote you last on the 10th *viâ* Barcelona. By the French accounts I see therefore almost a total change of Administration. I sincerely wish that Mr. Addington may have rendered you justice in granting the pension before he left office, if not, I fear it will never be done, for although Dundas would express his wishes for your success, when he had but little, if anything, to say, yet you will find now he has much to say that he will say less. My last letters from England are April 5th, going on for three months in total ignorance of what is passing, but as Doctor Scott has continued through Spain to get the Paris papers, we know all the great events which are passing. I still think that we have a fair prospect of Peace. Pitt can have no objection to treat with a French Monarchy, and I should think that the new Emperor would wish very much for one. My friend Monsieur La Touche has got his fleet fully manned—he sometimes plays bo-peep in and out of Toulon, like a mouse at the edge of her hole; but as these playful tricks, which mean nothing serious, may be magnified by nonsensical letters, of which too many are wrote, I desire and beg that you will never give any credit to them. You are sure that when any one can write from the fleet that I can, and you are sure that I should to you. I very much doubt now your female friend at Naples has got Acton removed, whether he will be able to return. The male friend of ours says he will go to Sicily, and as neither Russia nor England can trust either Gallo or Micheroux

[1] Collection of Letters, Vol. ii. p. 53.

who want the place, and who, we know, are both French in heart; this is the only chance he has at seventy-three of being again Prime Minister, and the Queen cannot, I fancy, do now so well without him as formerly. My state of health is such that if I could fight the French fleet to-morrow, I should certainly solicit permission to come home for a few months rest, and I must do it before the winter, or I shall be *hors de combat*, and they ought to make some allowance for my maimed carcass. Kiss dear Horatia for me, and remember me to all our friends. Charles is very near perfectly recovered, and he behaves very well. I long to hear how poor Davison gets on. I hope he is out of prison, for I fear he has been in one before this time. Again and again bless you.

"*June* 18. Dr. Scott has just brought me from Barcelona one of your dear prints, the French Consul had it framed and glazed, the other he sent to Paris.

"Yours,
"NELSON."

## CHAPTER IX.

### 1804.

On the 14th of June in this year, the French fleet of eight ships of the line, and six frigates, came out of Toulon. Nelson was off Hières with five ships, and chased the fleet into Toulon again. He thought the French Admiral meant nothing beyond a gasconade. Monsieur La Touche, the French Admiral, put a very different version on this affair, and highly excited the indignation of Lord Nelson. His letter to Paris is as follows:—

"Abord du Bucentaure, en rade de Toulon, le 26 Prairial An XII.

"Général,

"J'ai l'honneur de vous rendre compte de le sortie de toute l'escadre à mes ordres. Sur l'avis que j' avais reçu que plusieurs corsaires Anglais infestaient la côte et les iles d'Hières, je donnai l'ordre, il y a trois jours, aux frégates l'Incorruptible et la Syrène, et le brick le Furet, de se rendre dans la baie d'Hières. Le vent d'est les ayant contrariées elles mouillèrent sous le château de Porqueroles. Hier matin, les ennemis en eurent connaissance. Vers midi, ils détachèrent deux frégates et un vaisseau, qui entrèrent par la grande passe, dans l'intention de couper la retraite à nos frégates. Du moment où je m'apperçus de sa manœuvre, je fis signal d'appareiller à toute l'escadre ; ce qui fut exécuté. En 14 minutes, tout était sous voiles, et je fis porter sur l'ennemi pour lui couper le chemin de la petite passe, et dans le dessein de l'y suivre, s'il avait tenté d'y passer ; mais l'Amiral Anglais ne tarda pas à renoncer à son projet, rappela son vaisseau et ses deux frégates engagés dans les isles et prit chasse. Je l'ai poursuivi jusqu'à la nuit ; il courait au sud-est. Le matin, au jour, je n'en ai eu aucune connoissance. Je vous salue avec respect,

"La Touche Treville."

Lord Nelson frequently referred to this letter in his correspondence. To Mr. Davison, he says, that he has only to hope M. La Touche will give him an opportunity of settling his account before he goes home. To Sir Evan Nepean, "All my wishes now rest that I may meet M. La Touche before October is over." To his brother, the Rev. Dr. Nelson, "You will have seen Monsieur La Touche's letter of how he chased me, and how I *ran*. I keep it; and, by God, if I take him, he shall *eat* it." To Mr. Davison, on the 9th of August, "I am expecting Monsieur La Touche (as he has wrote a letter that I ran away), to come out of his nest. The whole history is too contemptible for my notice, but I have thought it right, not upon my own account, but for the satisfaction of the Admiralty, &c. &c. to send a copy of the Victory's log: for if my character for *not* running away, is not fixed by this time, it is not worth my trouble to put the world right at my time of life; and if any Englishman has believed for one moment the story, I may, to my friend, say, without fear of being thought arrogant, that they do not deserve to have me serve them; but I have kept Mr. La Touche's letter; and if I take him, I shall never see him, or, if I do, *make him eat* his letter—perhaps, sovereign contempt is the best."[1]

His letter to the Secretary of the Admiralty run thus:—

"Although I most certainly never thought of writing a line of Mons. Touche's having cut a caper a few miles outside of Toulon, on the 14th of June, where he well knew I could not get at him without placing the ships under the batteries which surrounded that port; and that, had I attacked him in that position, he could retire into his secure nest whenever he pleased, yet, as the gentleman has thought proper to write a letter, stating that the fleet under my command ran away, and that he pursued it, perhaps it may be thought necessary for me to say something. But I do assure you, Sir, that I know not what to say, except by a flat contradiction; for if my character is not established by this time for not being apt to run away, 'tis not worth my time to attempt to put the world right. It is not, therefore, I do assure your Lordships, with any such intention that I stain my paper with a vaunting man's name, and, therefore, I shall only state, that the

[1] From autograph in the possession of Colonel Davison.

fleet I have the honour and happiness to command, is in the highest state of discipline, good order, good humour, and good health, and that the united wishes of all are, I am sure, to meet Mons. La Touche at sea: then I ought not to doubt that I should be able to write a letter equally satisfactory to my King, my country, and myself."[1] "Such a liar," (he writes to Sir Alexander Ball), "is below my notice, except to thrash him, which will be done if in the power of, my dear Ball, your sincere friend, NELSON AND BRONTÉ." And in another letter to Mr. Davison: "I dare say, Mons. La Touche will have a different sort of letter to write, if I can once get a shake at him. Whether the world thinks that I ran away or no, is to me a matter of great indifference. If my character is not fixed by this time, it is useless for me to try to fix it at my time of life." Monsieur La Touche, however, did not survive to feel Nelson's vengeance. He died on the 18th of August, at Toulon. Nelson wrote to General Villettes: "La Touche has given me the slip—he died of the colic; perhaps Buonaparte's, for they say he was a rank Republican. Dumanoir is the Rear-Admiral at present in Toulon." And to Sir Alexander Ball: "He is gone, and all his lies with him. The French papers say, he died in consequence of walking so often up to the signal post, upon Sepet, to watch us: I always pronounced that that would be his death."

The capture of the Swift cutter, induced Lord Nelson to alter the sheet of signals, and he communicated the same to the Admiralty. He determined likewise to cut off all commerce between Italy and the enemy's ports at Marseilles and Toulon, and therefore ordered Captain Mowbray of the Active to repair to the Hières islands, and cruise between these and Cape Taillat. Captain Donnelly of the Narcissus relieved Captain Mowbray on this service on the 23rd, the Active being ordered to join Lord Nelson. The vessels at this time cruising with Lord Nelson, were the Victory, Royal Sovereign, Canopus, Donegal, Belleisle, Triumph, Leviathan, Renown, Seahorse, Active, Amazon, Maidstone, Childers,

---

[1] Dispatches and Letters, Vol. vi. p. 150. From the original in the Admiralty, and autograph drafts in the possession of the Rev. Henry Girdlestone, and of James Young, Esq. of Wells.

Cameleon, thunder-bomb; the Medusa and Amphion were cruising outside the Straits, for the protection of trade into the Mediterranean; the Halcyon and La Sophie between Ceuta and Cape Spartel, for the protection of trade in the Straits of Gibraltar; the Anson, Arrow, Bittern, Morgiana, and Jalouse from the mouth of the Archipelago, along the Adriatic as far as Ancona, for the protection of trade, and to prevent the enemy sending troops into the Morea; the Juno off Cape Sebastian to communicate with Barcelona, and gain intelligence of Spanish affairs; the Agincourt and Argo, at Gibraltar; the Kent at Naples, to relieve the Gibraltar, for the protection of the Royal Family of Naples; the Superb and Niger at Malta; the Gibraltar to repair at Gibraltar; the Termagant to Naples with dispatches; the Narcissus at Madalena Islands to repair; the Excellent to Porto Conte in Sardinia, to assist in victualling, and in obtaining wood and water; the Phœbe and Thetis at the Bay of Rosas for the same; the Acheron bomb, with public dispatches for the Minister at Naples; the Ætna bomb at Malta, for provisions; the Spider brig, and Renard schooner at Malta, to protect the trade; L'Hirondelle at Malta to be under the directions of Sir Alexander Ball, and the Madras as a prison ship at Malta. Such was the disposition of the Mediterranean fleet under the command of Lord Nelson towards the end of June.

The Queen of Naples again addressed Lord Nelson in the following letter:—

"My very worthy, dear Lord,

"I seize the present opportunity of writing to you to assure you in the name of the King, and from myself, our unchanged, fixed, sentiments towards you, your Government, and great nation. Our position is very painful and disagreeable; we are surrounded by open and concealed enemies, and by treason of every kind, even the Pope, they say, at the instigation of the upstart Emperor, wishes to embarrass us as far as he has the means, but nothing will embarrass or make us waver from our fixed principles. I always rely with confidence on your friendship and interest in us. All that occurs is so contrary to all reason, that one can only sigh and detest a life so replete with horrors. Take care of your health my respected

Admiral, continue your support, aid, and care to my husband and children, and to our unfortunate and ungrateful subjects, and rely on the gratitude which will terminate only with life, of your very sincere, attached and grateful friend,

" CHARLOTTE.

" 14th June, 1804."

Her Majesty also wrote on the 28th, as appears from the following letter of Lord Nelson :—

" Victory, 10th July, 1804.

" Madam,

" I have been honoured by your Majesty's gracious and condescending letter of June 28th. I have no other reply to make to such flattering expressions of confidence, than to offer my most devoted thanks, and my assurances of always studying to merit your Majesty's favourable sentiments, and those of my benefactor the King.

" It would be presumptuous on my part to venture to speak of political matters, in a letter to your Majesty; but I cannot help wishing that Europe, was like a handful of rods against France. If it be proper to give way to the times, let us temporise: if to make war, let us all make it. On this principle, I could have wished that Russia had avoided war, unless she had been joined by Austria. Then, acting honourably side by side, there would have been some hope from such a coalition.

" If Russia sends men, and vessels to the Ionian Republic, and into the Morea only, I have no hesitation in saying, that she compromises Naples much more, than if she had, for the moment, bent to the storm. At least 50,000 troops (it should be 100,000) are necessary to answer for the safety of Italy. To say the truth, I do not believe we had in the last war, and according to all appearance, we shall not have in the present one either, plans, of a sufficiently grand scale to force France to keep within her proper limits. Small measures produce only small results. I dare not let my pen run on: the intelligent mind of your Majesty will readily comprehend the great things which might be effected in the Mediterranean, on this side Buonaparte is the most vulnerable. It is from here that it would be most easy to mortify his pride, and so far humble him, as to make him accept reasonable conditions of peace. I entreat your Majesty's pardon for having expressed my sentiments with such boldness.

"Mr. Elliot has informed me, by writing, of what your Majesty wished to say on the subject of writing to the Minister, respecting the pension for your Emma. Poor Sir William Hamilton believed that it would have been granted, or it would have been unpardonable in him to have left his widow with so little means. Your Majesty well knows, that it was her capacity and conduct which sustained his diplomatic character, during the last years in which he was at Naples. It is unnecessary for me to speak more of it. It only remains for me—begging pardon for having occupied your Majesty's time so long—to subscribe myself,

"Your Majesty's faithful and devoted servant,
"NELSON AND BRONTÉ."[1]

This letter is acknowledged by the Queen in the following:—

"My very worthy and respected Lord,

"I received with much gratitude your skilful, perfect letter of the 10th of July. I think entirely as you do, that trifling and partial attacks are only mischievous, contributing cheap laurels to the modern Emperor. I always wait with impatience your interesting news, and pray sincerely for the preservation of your health, and that for the sake of our safety and tranquillity you may remain in the Mediterranean, my confidence in you being perfect. God grant that a loyal, sincere union between the great Powers may stem the devastating torrent, and plans of conquest and aggrandisement of the despot of Europe, but, to obtain a durable peace, it requires to be prepared to enforce it. You may feel assured that I shall do all that depends on me for a friend in whom I am so greatly interested. Continue to favour me with news. May heaven accord to you all the prosperity I desire for you, and believe me for life, with sincere esteem, your very grateful, confiding, attached friend,

"CHARLOTTE.

"26th July, 1804."

[1] Life of the Rev. Dr. Scott, p. 114.

Lord Nelson received the following from Mr. Elliot:—

"Naples, June 15th, 1804.

"My dear Lord,

"Accept of my most grateful thanks, and of those of Mrs. Elliot, for your kindness to our dear boy. We rely with confidence, that if God spares your life, you will in time be as useful to those of our children who embrace your honourable profession, as their good conduct may deserve. I am certain you have placed William as advantageously as possible, and I trust he will prove worthy of your protection.

"The Queen asked me for your letter to Sir John Acton, as he had left directions for her Majesty and the King to open those which might come for him. The next day they were sent to me to be translated—that of the 1st of June, I did translate without hesitation in writing; but the other I only read to the Queen, as I can see no use of leaving copies of them in her hands. The originals will be sent by the first opportunity to Palermo.

"There are many things to say about the Queen, which I do not wish to commit to paper. She is in many respects so completely biassed in her attachments, by the *sad favourite* of the day, that her heart and her understanding are equally the dupe of this weakness.

"I understand that the Courts of Berlin and of Vienna, will without hesitation acknowledge the validity of Buonaparte's new title. This Court will follow their example.

"From Spain I have no news of a later date than what is mentioned in your Lordship's letter. It is the fashion here to believe, that the King of Spain will continue to avoid the war. But I speak from no authority concerning a topic which belongs to Mr. Frere. The King of Sardinia, thinking himself no longer safe in the Roman States, is expected to come to Gaeta in the course of this month. I have not failed to convey the kind expressions of your Lordship towards him through the proper channel. Ever most truly,

"Your Lordship's faithful and humble servant,

"H. ELLIOT."

On the 27th, Lord Nelson wrote to Lady Hamilton :—

"Victory, June 27th, 1804.

"Last night, my dearest Emma, I received your three letters of April 13th and 22nd, and May 13th, by way of Naples. It is the only scrap of a pen we have had from England since April 5th, by Leviathan. You must not complain of my not writing, for I never miss an opportunity, as the following list will shew. February 25th by Barcelona, March 2nd, 15th, by Rosas ; 19th, by Gibraltar ; April 10th, by Rosas ; 14th, by Captain Layman ; 19th, 21st, 23rd, by the Argo ; 20th, by Rosas ; May 3rd, by Barcelona ; 5th, by Rosas ; 12th, by Rosas ; 30th, 31st, by Gibraltar ; June 6th, by Rosas ; 10th, by Barcelona ; 19th, by Rosas. You will see, and I have wrote Davison to pay every bill relating to the alterations at Merton, and that nothing is to be touched on that business from the £100. a month. I also wrote to him to pay, if I can afford it, poor blind Mrs. Nelson's debts. The change of Ministry can do us no harm, and if Lord Melville is a true friend he may now get it[1] for you ; but my dear Emma, all their promises are pie-crusts, made to be broken. I hope to get out of debt and to have my income clear, and then we shall do very well with prudence. I am not surprised at the time poor Davison is to be confined, after what passed in Parliament, I did not expect so little, and I fear he has a heavy fine to pay besides. He would only consult Lord Moira and such clever folks, but an ignoramus like me, could only warn him not to touch Boroughs. He has, poor fellow, been completely duped, and who cares ? not one of those great folks. I am most sincerely sorry for him, but a year will soon pass away. Have not I been shut up in a ship without any one comfort ? He is ashore, with his friends round him, and even you to go to see him. I would change with him with much pleasure. I shall write him a line, he must not kill himself, that his enemies would rejoice at, and I hope he will live to plague them. Acton being gone to Sicily, the Queen had authority to open his letters. Mr. Elliot explained the one relative to her writing to Mr. Addington. She said, as Mr. Elliot writes me, as Mr. Addington is

[1] The pension.

out of office the application to him from her would no longer meet your purpose, and as to a letter to his successor, she must be regulated in that by your future explanation upon the subject. I can think a great deal. Mr. Elliot likes to class you in such a way as may make a precedent—that you recollect was always his plan, but I shall write Acton and the Queen to say, that there can be no harm in her writing to Mr. Pitt. Your eminent services, and her personal obligations to you, &c. &c. But you know enough of the world not to be surprised at any forgetfulness from even great folks. How delighted I shall be with Merton, and I shall hope to find Horatia fixed there. Why not? kiss her for me, and may God bless her. I am always glad to hear that Charlotte behaves well to you. She would be very ungrateful if she did not. Remember me kindly to Mrs. Cadogan and all our friends. I shall, if it pleases God, eat my Christmas dinner at dear Merton. My health absolutely requires a few months rest, even if my services are required again. Pray God in heaven bless and preserve you.

"Yours."

On the 1st of July, the two following letters:—

"Victory, July 1st, 1801.

"Although I have wrote you, my dearest Emma, a letter by Rosas, of June 27th, not yet gone, the weather, being so very bad, that ships cannot get across the gulf of Lyons, yet I will [not] miss the opportunity of writing by Gibraltar. You must not, my Emma, think of hearing from me by way of Malta; it takes as long to send a letter to Malta as to England. Your letters of April 13th, 22nd, and May 13th, through Mr. Falconet, came safe a few days ago; Mr. Falconet is the French banker; and he dare not buy a little macaroni for me, or let an Englishman into his house!

"What our friends are after at Naples, they best know. The poor King is miserable at the loss of Acton. The Queen writes me about honest Acton, &c. &c., and I hear, that she has been the cause of ousting him: and they say—her enemies—that her conduct is all French. That, I do not believe, although she is likely to be the dupe of French emigrés, who always beset her. I doubt much, my dear Emma, even her constancy of real friendship to you; although, in my letter to Acton, which Mr. Elliot says he read to her, I mentioned the obligations she was under to you, &c. in very strong terms.

"You will not hear of my making prize-money. I have not paid my expenses these last nine months. I shall expect to eat my Christmas dinner at Merton; unless those events happen which I can neither foresee nor prevent. I am not well: and must have rest for a few months, even if the country [want me], which is very likely they will not. News, I can have none. *April 9th.*—Leviathan sailed, so Government don't care much for us.

"NELSON AND BRONTÉ."[1]

"Victory, July 1st, 1804.

"My dearest Emma,

"I have a moment, and but a moment, to write you a line through Spain. I wrote you yesterday by Gibraltar, and sent you the first Bill of Exchange for £100. for you, and £100. for poor Mrs. Bolton. I take this opportunity of sending the second, as I dare say that this will be home months before the other. Nothing from England since April 5th.

"Yours.

"All my public dispatches go for Gibraltar this day."

At the beginning of this month, Lord Nelson learnt that the enemy was collecting troops and stores at Porto Ferrajo to make a descent on Sardinia, and he therefore sent off the Hon. Captain Capel in the Phœbe, together with the Cameleon, to cruise between that Port and Leghorn, and capture or destroy any vessels or transports he might meet with. On the 9th, he wrote to Lady Hamilton:—

"Victory, July 9th, 1804.

"Last night, my dearest Emma, I received your most kind letter of May 24th, and I feel very much distressed that my numerous letters do not get quicker to your hand, but I can

[1] Collection of Letters, Vol. ii. p. 56.

only write and send off, and indeed, I dare say, if I was the carrier, they would not be so long in travelling. I have mentioned the date of every letter, and how they went, in a letter sent a few days ago by Barcelona; in March, three; in April, six; in May, five; in June to the 19th, three; June 27th, July 1st. I must not write a word of any political matter, for as I send this through Mr. Falconet, I have assured him that nothing which can in any manner commit him in his employ with the French Government, shall be put in the letter. This, I am sure I may say, that we have had no summer here. For the last four days not a boat could pass. Before many months I shall certainly see all your improvements, and if Government, after some rest, want my services, they shall have them, but I must have a change of air, for always shut up in the Victory's cabin, cannot be very good for the constitution. I think you will find me grown thin, but never mind. Your trip to Canterbury I should suppose the very worst you could take; for, on any alarm, there you must stay, and in a town filled with soldiers; but if you like it I am content. However, we know to June 18th, all was safe. What a long letter Sir Sidney Smith has wrote. Well, this is an odd war—not a battle! Admiral Campbell always inquires after you, and desires to be kindly remembered. I have little to say—one day is so like another, and having long ago given you one day there is no difference but the arrival of a letter or newspapers; the same faces, and almost the same conversation. Remember me kindly to all our friends, and be assured, I am,

"Yours.

"Kiss dear Horatia for me."

"*July* 11*th.*—We have the French news to June 28th. I have wrote to the great lady at Naples about your pension. I think she must try and do something. God bless you.

"*July* 12*th.*—We have Paris papers to June 27th. I believe we are never to hear from England again."

The boats of the Narcissus, Seahorse, and Maidstone, made an attack on some of the enemy's vessels at La Vandour, in Hières Bay, on the night of the 10th of July, at the reports upon which, from Captain Donnelly and **Lieutenant Thompson**, Nelson was highly pleased, and he wrote to the former as follows:—" Lord Nelson has received with much satisfaction the report of Captain Donnelly, of the gallant conduct of the officers and men employed in destroying the enemy's vessels at La Vendura. The judicious arrangement of Lieutenant Thompson merits my praise, for without that, bravery would be useless; and the example of Lieutenant Parker,[1] Lumley,[2] and Moore,[3] was such as to insure the bravery of the inferior officers and men; for I never knew the superior officers to lead on well, but that they were always bravely supported by the men under their orders. Wounds must be expected in fighting the enemy. They are marks of honour, and our grateful country is not unmindful of the sufferings of her gallant defenders. A regular list will be sent to the Patriotic Fund at Lloyd's, and the Captains are to give each man a certificate before he leaves the ship, describing his wound, signed by the Captain and Surgeon."[4] He soon after ordered Captain Donnelly, in the Narcissus, and with the Maidstone, off to the Port of Genoa, having received information that the enemy were in the habit of sending their privateers, and other vessels of war, from Corsica, thither.

On the 14th, Lord Nelson wrote to **Lady Hamilton** —

"Victory, July 14th, 1804.

" I wrote you my dearest Emma, on the 8th, a letter dated

---

[1] Hyde Parker, now a Rear-Admiral of the White, is the son of the late Admiral Sir Hyde Parker, Knight, who so gallantly fought the Dutch squadron off the Dogger Bank. Admiral Donnelly had a very high opinion of his merits. He was made a Lieutenant, September 24th, 1804, a Commander, January 22nd, 1806, Post Captain, October 13th, 1807, and Rear-Admiral of the White, November 23rd, 1841. He distinguished himself early, as above stated; afterwards commanded the Prometheus fire-ship, and in 1812, the Tenedos frigate. He was actively employed on the North American station, and assisted in the taking of the President in January, 1815. He subsequently commanded the Iphigenia at Quebec, and on the Jamaica and Mediterranean stations, and was put out of Commission in June, 1821.

[2] Richard John Lumley, died a Post Captain, July 23, 1821.

[3] Lieut. Ogle Moore, died on half-pay in 1817.

[4] Dispatches and Letters, Vol. vi. p. 108. From autograph draft and Order Book.

June 27th, and July 4th, by way of Barcelona, and 9th and 12th by way of Naples. I begin very much to suspect that my letters from Rosas go directly into France. You must only rely that I omit no opportunity of writing. Although it will be frost and snow when I see dear Merton, yet good fires and your charming society, will make my heart warm, and asses milk will set me up again. In due time I shall write to the Admiralty, but this you will keep to yourself. Rest I ought to have for a few months, even should they want my poor services, but there will be so many desirous of getting the Mediterranean command, that I cannot expect they will allow me to return to it; but all this keep to yourself. It is time enough for the multitude to know of my movements by my arrival, whether it will be in frigate, brig, or leaky 74, I cannot say; that will depend on the Admiralty, but I yet hope before my departure that the French fleet will come out, indeed I expect the Brest fleet into the Mediterranean, and that this will be the great scene of action this autumn and winter. All I beg, my dearest Emma, that you will not believe any idle stories in newspapers. I am perfectly prepared how to act with either a superior or an inferior force. My mind is firm as a rock, and my plans for every event fixed in my mind. May God in heaven bless and preserve you.

"Yours.

"Remember me to all our joint friends."

Lord Nelson was apprehensive that part of the French fleet had got out, the idea of which he describes to Rear-Admiral Campbell, as giving him "half a fever." He wrote also to Sir Richard Bickerton, "I have been in a little alarm at the idea of Mons. La Touche having given me the slip, and it is not quite cleared up. I am sending Active and Thunder off Marseilles for information; for I am sure if that Admiral were to cheat me out of my hopes of meeting him, it would kill me much easier than one of his balls."[1]

The following from General Dumouriez was written in this month:—

[1] Clarke and McArthur. Vol. ii. p. 376.

"Le 20 Juillet, 1804.

"My dear Nelson,

"I love you as a brother, and agree with me the extreme enjoyment I would find in holding you fast in my arms, but I am so intimately convinced of the necessity of your assistance at the head of the Mediterranean fleet, that I heard with the greatest sorrow the tale of your removal of your important station. I hope you received the posterior orders sent of the new Ministry, and will remain to give us account of the Toulon fleet that is under your inspection. I consent to adjourn after the peace the very moment to live with you, except the case of being myself sent in Italy to partake your labours, and join in your glory: that is the hearty answer I return to your kind letter of the 31st May.

"I expect no answer of her Majesty, if even the Minister did faithfully return in her hands the letter, I dared to write for the public sake. The Sovereigns are all of them afraid or apathetic, and will remain so, till God judges convenient to awaken them, and strengthen their debased hearts.

"I see with horror the Corsican tyrant invested with an imperial mantle, impurpled with Bourbon's blood. I hope the Providence to be weary of so much impudence of one side, and meekness of the other. I hope the instant of revenge will soon come, my greatest desire is to be with you, an instrument of the catastrophe that is impendent upon that nefarious head. These are the indelible sentiments of your admirer and faithful friend,

"LE GENERAL DUMOURIEZ.

"A Milord Nelson, Duke de Bronté,
&c. &c. &c."

The month of August commenced with a letter which does great credit to Lord Nelson, and shews how superior he was to any feelings of jealousy or envy towards those officers who had the gratification of serving with him. The Corporation of London voted to Lord Nelson their thanks as Commander of the fleet blockading Toulon. On the copy of Lord Nelson's reply to this Lady Hamilton wrote: "The following is a copy of Admiral Lord Nelson's answer to the vote of thanks of the Corporation of London. It breathes a most noble and generous spirit, and does his Lordship as much honour as a victory."

"TO THE RIGHT HONOURABLE THE LORD MAYOR.

"Victory, August 1st, 1804.

"My Lord,

"This day I am honoured with your Lordship's letter of April 9th, transmitting me the resolutions of the Corporation of London, thanking me as commanding the fleet blockading Toulon. I do assure your Lordship, that there is not a man breathing who sets a higher value upon the thanks of his fellow citizens of London than myself; but I should feel as much ashamed to receive them for a particular service, marked in the resolution, if I felt that I did not come within that line of service, as I should feel hurt at having a great victory passed over without notice. I beg to inform your Lordship, that the port of Toulon has never been blockaded by me; quite the reverse—every opportunity has been offered the enemy to put to sea, for it is there that we hope to realize the hopes and expectations of our country, and I trust that they will not be disappointed. Your Lordship will judge of my feelings upon seeing that all the junior Flag Officers of other fleets, and even some of the Captains have received the thanks of the Corporation of London, whilst the junior Flag Officers of the Mediterranean fleet are entirely omitted. I own it has struck me very forcibly, for where the information of the junior Flag Officers and Captains of other fleets was obtained, the same information could have been given of the Flag Officers of this fleet and the Captains; and it is my duty to state that more able and zealous Flag Officers and Captains do not grace the British Navy than those I have the honour and happiness to command. It likewise appears, my Lord, a most extraordinary circumstance, that Rear-Admiral Sir Richard Bickerton should have been, as second in command in the Mediterranean fleets, twice passed over by the Corporation of London: once after the Egyptian expedition, when the first and third in command were thanked, and now again.

"Consciousness of high desert instead of neglect made the Rear-Admiral resolve to let the matter rest, until he could have an opportunity personally to call on the Lord Mayor to account for such an extraordinary omission; but from this second omission, I owe it to that excellent Officer not to pass it by.

"And I do assure your Lordship, that the constant, zealous, and cordial support I have had in my command from both Rear-Admiral Sir Richard Bickerton, and Rear-Admiral Campbell has been such as calls forth all my thanks and approbation. We have shared together the constant attention of being more than fourteen months at sea, and are ready to share the dangers and glory of a day of battle; therefore it is impossible that I can ever allow myself to be separated in thanks from such supporters. I have the honour to remain, with the very highest respect, your Lordship's most faithful and obedient servant,

"NELSON AND BRONTÉ."

From Prince Charles Felix of Savoy Lord Nelson received the following:—

"Cagliari, 9th August, 1804.

"My Lord,

"I have not replied sooner to the letter you politely wrote me, because I thought you must have quitted the anchorage at Palma to return again to the coasts of France, but having the pleasure of seeing you take a situation within sight of this town, I hasten to write to thank you, my Lord, for the trouble you have taken in chastising the insolence of the English Corsairs, as well as for the kindness with which you sent me the pretended Sardinian, whom you found on board a vessel coming from Marseilles, but as it proves that he does not belong to that nation, I intend transferring him to the English Consul, in order that he may be sent back to you (to do with him as you think fit) as soon as I have had his papers examined, which cannot be done until the Corsair, he was put on board of, has finished her cruise. I hope that your proximity to this town will permit of your landing and dining with me, that I may have the pleasure of making the personal acquaintance of so distinguished a person, an interview which would also enable me to make some communications which cannot be easily written. Deign to accept my assurance, my Lord, that I shall seize every occasion to convince you of the sentiments of esteem and perfect consideration with which I am, my Lord,

" Your very good friend,
" CHARLES FELIX OF SAVOYE."

In this month Lord Nelson received intelligence from the Admiralty of having been appointed Vice-Admiral of the White, the highest rank he lived to attain in the service. He wrote to Lady Hamilton on the 13th :—

" Victory, August 13th, 1804.

"The Ambuscade brought me your letters to June 5th, *viz.* April 9th, 15th, 18th, May 14, 22, 30, *via* Lisbon. May 10, 18, 29, June 1, 4, 6, by sea. The box you mention is not arrived, nor have I a scrap of a pen or newspaper from Davison.

" I do not believe one syllable of the intention of the late Admiralty to remove me without my own application. I verily believe so much the contrary, that I much doubt that they would have suffered me to come home without much contesting the point. I have every reason to believe that as a Board, my whole conduct met their entire approbation, and to say the truth, the old Earl was led wrong against his better judgment many a time. I am not so vexed with him as with the others. I am sure he would have promoted Bolton if they had mentioned him, but never mind, the late Admiralty have the execrations of the service for destroying as much as in them lay *the Navy*."

The number of gales of wind, and the long continuance of the vessels at sea, severely deteriorated the condition of the ships forming his squadron. The Gibraltar was to be sent home—the Kent was in a miserable state—the Superb could not be expected to keep the sea in the winter—the Renown and the Triumph were only fit to be sent home—the Maidstone and Narcissus were also out of repair. In August, he wrote to his Royal Highness the Duke of Clarence that they had an uniform sameness, day after day, and month after month—gales of wind for ever. " In July, we had seventeen days very severe weather; the Mediterranean seems altered. However, with nursing our ships, we have roughed it out better than could have been expected. I have always made it a rule never to contend with the gales; and either to run to the southward to escape its violence, or furl all the sails, and make the ships as easy as possible. Our friend Keats is quite well; in his own person, he is equal, in my estimation, to an additional 74; his life is a valuable one to the State, and it is impossible that your Royal Highness could ever have a better choice of a sea-friend, or counsellor, if you go to the Admiralty. Keats will never give that counsel which would not be good for the service."[1]

Nelson's health began to suffer, and he wrote to Mr. Marsden to communicate to the Admiralty the necessity of a few months quiet to enable him to serve in the next spring. A winter like that which had passed, he felt unable to withstand. He had much regret in making this application, as he says, " No officer could be placed in a more enviable command than the one I have the honour to be placed in, and no command ever produced so much happiness to a Commander-in-chief, whether in Flag Officers, the Captains, or the good conduct of the crews of every ship in this fleet; and the constant marks of approbation for my conduct which I have received from every Court in the Mediterranean, leave me nothing to wish for but a better state of health. I have thought it necessary to state this much, that their Lordships might not for a moment suppose that I had any uneasiness of mind upon any account. On the contrary, every person, of all ranks and descriptions, seems only desirous to meet my wishes, and to give me satisfaction. I must, therefore, entreat their Lordship's permission to return to England for the re-establishment of my health, and that their consent may reach me as soon as possible, for I have deferred my application already too long."[2]

To Viscount Melville, the First Lord of the Admiralty, he also wrote on the necessity of returning home to recover his

[1] Clarke and McArthur, Vol. ii. p. 381.
[2] Dispatches and Letters, Vol. vi. p. 157. From the original in the Admiralty.

health, and spoke highly of the talents of Sir Richard Bickerton, the second in command in the Mediterranean, and as being eminently qualified to command a fleet. He, however, hoped to get hold of the French fleet before the arrival of his successor—that he said would add ten years to his life. He determined upon enticing them out. He directed Captain Donnelly to proceed to the west end of Porquerolle, whilst he would get into the Gulf of Lyons and push round Cape Sicie the first favourable wind. He thought the appearance of the Narcissus might tempt the French fleet to come out and stand to the eastward, or to anchor in Hières Bay, which would afford his squadron an opportunity of bringing them to action.

Their Sicilian Majesties were not a little alarmed at the announced intention of Nelson to return home, as appears from the following letter from Hugh Elliot, Esq. :—

"September 8, 1804.

"My Lord,—I cannot sufficiently express the infinite regret with which their Sicilian Majesties have learnt your determination of quitting your command in the Mediterranean, and of going to England this winter for the re-establishment of your health. Their Sicilian Majesties are in this not more concerned for your indisposition, than they are anxious from the evil effects which they apprehend must ensue to their interest, in consequence of your Lordship's absence from the Mediterranean. I know it is the King's intention to write to the Prince of Castelcicala, to apply to the British Government for your Lordship's speedy return to these seas, in order to resume the high command you have hitherto exercised, with no less credit to yourself than advantage to the many countries, whose future security rests entirely upon the skill by which a British Admiral may be enabled to maintain the superiority of the British fleet over that of the enemy in the Mediterranean. When such great interests are concerned, I shall not presume to dwell upon my own feelings, although I cannot but recall to your Lordship, that I only consented to depart as abruptly as I did from England, to undertake this arduous and ruinous mission, from the expectation that my efforts to direct the councils of this kingdom would have been seconded by your pre-eminent talents and judgment. Allow me, however, my Lord, in this emergency, to propose to your consideration a plan, concerning which I have already had much conversation with the Queen, and which, if it can be adopted, will obviate many of the misfortunes to which we should be exposed by your absence. As your Lordship's health requires that you should not be exposed to the rigours of another winter's cruise in the Gulf of Lyons, it is the sincere wish of this Court that you would spend the severe months of the year either here or at Palermo, without abandoning your chief command in the Mediterranean. I only do my duty in suggesting this idea to your Lordship, without venturing to press upon you the many arguments by which, I think, I could prove its expediency. You must be sensible, my Lord, that no Admiral who is not as well acquainted as yourself with the political state of these Kingdoms, or other Eastern countries, and of Russia, can possibly act with the same effect that you can do, when there is every reason to expect that the Emperor of Russia, and perhaps even the Ottoman Porte, will ultimately co-operate with us in our endeavours to set bounds to the lawless ambition of France. May my representations upon this subject not come too late, as I am certain that your departure from the Mediterranean will not less tend to encourage our enemies, than to diminish the confidence of those friendly Powers, who look towards your Lordship's abilities as the surest means of success.

"I have the honour to be,

"&c. &c. &c.

"H. Elliot."[1]

On the 20th Lord Nelson wrote to Charles Connor:—

"Victory, August 20th, 1804.

"Dear Charles,

"As Captain Hillyar has been so good as to say that he would rate you Mid., I sincerely hope that your conduct will ever continue to deserve his kind notice and protection, by a strict and very active attention to your duty. If you deserve well, you are sure of my assistance.

---

[1] From the original in the Elliot Papers.

"Mr. Scott will supply you with money to begin your mess, and I shall allow you £30 a year, if it is necessary, which Captain Hillyar will supply you with; and as you this day start in the world as a man, I trust that your future conduct in life will prove you both an officer and a gentleman; and recollect, that you must be a seaman to be an officer, and also that you cannot be a good officer without being a gentleman.

"I am always, with most sincere good wishes,
"Your true friend,
"NELSON AND BRONTÉ.

"If you follow Mr. Magrath's advice, your eye will be as well as ever.

"Mr. Charles Connor,
"Mid. of H.M. Ship Niger."

He also wrote to Lady Hamilton:—

"Victory, August 22nd, 1804.

"My dearest Emma,

"The ship was gone for Rosas, when the Spencer yesterday, nineteen days from Plymouth, joined us, by whom I had the happiness of receiving your letters of *vîâ* Lisbon, June 28th, and one without a date through Mr. Marsden, July 4th, 7th, 10th, and 19th. I think it impossible that my friend the banker, I don't mention names, would allow me to be distressed by loss of money in his banking house. I cannot believe it, and why Haslewood in some measure forced the £5000 from Marsh and Creed's hands, who lay out every farthing as they get it in the funds, never keeping more than £50 in hand; but I hope the best, and I am sure, poor as I am, if the money I have in the house would save my friend, he should be welcome to it, but why should my all go to serve a parcel of people that I never saw or care one farthing about. I sincerely hope that the bathing has quite set you up again. The Kent will, I have no doubt, have a very short passage, and as she carries my request to come home for the restoration of my health, which a few months may set up, and fit me, if the Admiralty pleases, to return to this command; but there are so many my seniors who are using every exertion for employment, that when once it is gone from me I stand no chance of getting it back again. The more likelihood of a Spanish war, the less chance for me. You will know from Mr. Marsden what the Admiralty intend.

"I wish my proxy had never been given. I am not clear I should have voted on that side, but I have not read the debate. I hate the Grenvilles—cold-hearted. If Lord Moira was to be First Minister, and I First Lord of the Admiralty, it would be my duty to support, but I am to expect nothing from them; and to make enemies of those who are in, I'll be damned if I do. I will stand upon my own bottom, and be none of their tools. When I come home I shall make myself understood. I like both Pitt and Lord Melville, and why should I oppose them? I am free and independent. I have not heard from Davison more than six months. I shall write him a line, poor fellow; I wish his time was out. My kindest love to those we hold most dear—Horatia; and regards to good Mrs. Cadogan, Charlotte, &c. &c. &c. Don't forget old Oliver. God bless you. Amen, Amen, Amen. In a few days I shall write by Gibraltar."

"Victory, August 27th, 1804.

"My dearest Emma,

"Your kind letters by Friend Gayner, of June 22nd, and July 10th, are just received, and those by Spencer to July 19th. I do not believe that there is any danger of Davison's failure—I mean the house, for if they set off with a capital of £500,000, no speculation could have injured them, especially last winter, by the time the house was formed. As I wrote you, Marsh and Creed were the only authorized persons to receive the Prize-money from Mr. Tucker, and neither Davison nor Haslewood had a right to bully my agents. Nor do I believe that they ever said I was in their debt, unless it was to save the money for me; when that was received, I was £3800 in Davison's debt. He had wrote me never to think of his debt, for if it was never paid it was nothing to him. My agents put every farthing out to interest. God knows, it is not much. I dare say the banking house has done no such thing for me, but I shall be soon at home, and settle all my affairs; and if I do serve again for an expedition or another year, I shall be able to leave all my affairs in a better plight than at present. I am settling my Bronté affairs, and next year my net income from thence will be as sure as any estate in England; but I have very much to weed away; the gross amount is large, but the salaries for Governor, Campieras, the College fees, &c. &c. &c. with Mrs. Græffer's pension, will not be less than £800 sterling a year. I am now working to know why all this expense. If I allow Mrs. Græffer £100 a year, I think I shall do well, although I dare say not half satisfy her. In case of any accident happening to me, I have given you £500 sterling a year out of the estate, but I hope we shall live many years. The moment I get home, I shall put it out of your power to spend dear Horatia's money; I shall settle it in trustees' hands, and leave nothing to chance. If Horace[1] behaves well, he shall marry her. Mr. Elliot seems to think they will all go to the devil at Naples, that it is perceptibly getting to be French. I do not see things in so black a light as he does. Mr. Elliot says both King and Queen are in desperation at my going away; they say that I have so uniformly protected them, and never in the smallest instance committed them, notwithstanding what Castelcicala said. I have letters from Acton of August 9th. The lady, I hear, wishes to go to England, and Acton says so, but I am sure that he has no such intention, and that he will die in Italy. He longs to get to his house at Castel-à-Mare, in short, that he may be near the Court, and he thinks he can direct Circello, but I doubt whether the Queen will permit him even to come to the Kingdom of Naples, unless she finds that she is involved in difficulties, and cannot get out of them. Respecting your business he says, ' I see what you tell me, my Lord, on Lady Hamilton's settlement by Sir William; I think it very just that she should be helped. I have wrote to her Majesty on the subject, and she is pleased to answer me that she will do whatever is in her power on the subject, and has acquainted your Lordship lately by one of her letters.' I suppose, my dear Emma, that letter is the one which I sent you, and if her application through Castelcicala is as cold, I do not expect much from it; never mind.

"The letters you send with yours are many of them interest-

---

[1] His nephew, afterwards Viscount Trafalgar.

ing. What a fool Sir E. H. must be to tell; but tittle-tattle is almost all that the men of the present day can talk about. To marry into the family of the Macnamaras, what a prospect! As for Captain Macnamara, it is not difficult to foresee that he will be shot; he seems to lay himself out for it, and after what has happened no one will pity him. Our friend Mr. Davison seems to think him a *nonsuch*. Every scrap of your letters are so interesting, that flattering fancy for the moment *wafts* me home. Triumph and Narcissus leave the fleet this day to join the Maidstone, therefore do not expect letters by those two; this goes by Triumph. If Davison has not paid poor Mrs. Nelson's debts, which you say are £90, I shall be very sorry; if he has not, I will do it when I come home. You will not have time to answer this letter before you will see

"Yours,
"NELSON AND BRONTÉ.

"We have just reports from a vessel spoke that our fleet has gained a great victory. God send it may be true, and give us peace. Faddy[1] is confirmed, he is lucky, and Sir R. Barlow speaks highly of him."

"Victory, August 31st, 1804.

"My dearest Emma,

"Yesterday I wrote to you through Spain; this goes by Naples. Mr. Falconet, I think, will send it; although I am sure he feels great fear from the French Minister, for having anything to do with us. The Admiralty proceedings towards me, you will know much sooner than I shall. I hope they will do the thing handsomely, and allow of my return in the spring; but I do not expect it.

"I am very uneasy at your and Horatia being on the coast, for you cannot move, if the French make the attempt; which, I am told, they have done, and been repulsed. Pray God it may be true! I shall rejoice to hear you and Horatia are safe at Merton; and happy shall I be the day I join you. This is written within three miles of the fleet in Toulon, who are looking very tempting. Captain Hardy has not been very well: and I fancy Admiral Murray will not be sorry to see England, especially since he has been promoted."[2]

[1] Lieutenant William Faddy died in 1811, at the Leeward Islands.
[2] Collection of Letters, Vol. ii. p. 67.

"Victory, September 9th, 1804.

"Since I wrote you, my dearest Emma, on August 30th, not the least change has taken place, nor have I received a letter from any place. I have lost my opponent Mons. La Touche. I grieve to think he died a natural death—it was more than I bargained for, however, I hope not to follow his example for many years to come. You will know long before me what are Lord Melville's intentions towards me—who comes, and how I am likely to get home. If Captain Keats will allow me a passage with my numerous suite, I wish to go home in the Superb, but if the Admiralty send out a senior Admiral I must be subject to his will and pleasure—all that I hope is, that the Admiralty will not keep me in quarantine at farthest beyond the return of the post, for we shall be well crowded, seven or eight to sleep in one cabin, but I cannot help it, it was the same and very uncomfortable coming out in the Amphion, but then I shall look, my dear Emma, for happier moments, for I shall not stay three minutes at Portsmouth, but fly to dear Merton, where all in this world which is dearest to me resides; and, therefore, I would have you remain at Merton, being assured I shall lose no time in coming to you. I have only a moment to scrawl this line, but be assured I am,

"Yours,
"NELSON AND BRONTÉ.

"The box you mentioned sending May 18th, has never arrived, nor my arms from Mr. Nayler. I wish Mr. Spinks may please you in building, but he is a drunken fellow. I dare say you have made the subterraneous passage so as to stop the kitchen door and windows, or you will find the smell of the kitchen I fear very bad; but I think you have provided against that."

"Victory, September 22nd, 1804.

"Your two letters of August 7th and 13th I have received. I am not sure whether I gave the Spanish dresses to Captain Layman, or sent them to the Admiralty; the pieces of Armoisins and Naples shawls I gave him open, or there might be difficulty in getting them on shore. I have been expecting a ship from Naples and Palermo these several days, perhaps the Queen or Acton from Palermo might say something about you, but I can no longer defer sending off my dispatches to catch the Triumph at Gibraltar. Report says, she and the King are likely at last to have a serious rupture, Circello, who is Acton's man, will not give into her wants and wishes. However, I never trouble myself with these matters, they may settle their own affairs, they are *old* enough. Acton will get back to Castel à Mare, and by degrees try to get into office again, he will never go to England if he can help it. I am sure it is not his inclination. Your disposition is too generous to insult a fallen man, however much we may detest the principles which guide his conduct, and I am sure nine-tenths of those who now abuse the Earl and Troubridge were, and would be again, their most abject flatterers were they again in office—for me, I feel myself above them in every way, and they are below my abuse of them; now no longer in power, I care nothing about them, and now they can do no harm to any one I shall not abuse them. Sir William Bolton is going to Gibraltar to refit the Childers. I see no prospect of making him Post. When I come home I will speak to some of the Admiralty about Tom Bowen, but I must stick to Sir William Bolton, for if I ask many favours I may get none. Charles is rated on board the Niger, and I hope he will do well. I have talked much to him and he promises fair. When you receive this letter I shall most probably be upon my passage, in what ship, &c. &c. must be left to the Admiralty or the Admiral who they may send out. I have plenty of candidates for taking me to England. Gore of the Medusa writes in desperation, but I am not my own master. Superb I think will be the ship. God bless you. Kiss dear Horatia for me, and be assured I am,

"Yours, &c.

"NELSON AND BRONTÉ."

"Don't fix anything about Linton's farm till my arrival, perhaps some of it may be sold.

"I am anxious to hear from Gibbs and to settle Bronté, then that will be off my mind. It ought to have brought me £3000. a year, instead of a little more than £2000, when all is paid however. However, I have been a great fool in that business, but never mind. God bless us. Amen."

In October he wrote on the 2nd, the 5th, the 7th, the 10th, and on the 12th.

"Victory, October 2nd, 1804.

"It was only yesterday, my dearest Emma, that I received your letter of July 1st, it having travelled in a Spanish smuggling boat to the coast of Italy and returned again to Spain, the boat not having met any of our ships. I am anxious to put you right about my proxy, and that Lord Moira's having it could have had no influence against Mr. Addington, not having done anything for me or my friends; you will see that it was entrusted to support Mr. Addington. Perhaps Davison has been the innocent cause of any one having my proxy, for I never liked giving it. Lord Moira, in his letter to Davison, says,—'being intrusted by him with the charge of repelling any attack which envy might even aim at his character, I will give myself the pride of being ostensibly confided in by him, and in Political questions I shall hold myself bound to give his vote as his relation to the Ministry requires, though it may be in contradiction to my own.'

"On January 13th, 1804, I signed the Proxy and sent it to Davison with the following extract: 'I have intrusted him with what I did not believe I would have intrusted any man, and I hope he will be a firm supporter of Mr. Addington's Administration.' This did not get home till March, therefore no vote was given in Mr. Addington's administration, but you see if any had, it would have been to support Mr. Addington, therefore it could have had no influence upon Mr. Addington if his inclination had led him to do anything; but the fact is, that if my pension was entailed so would Lord St. Vincent's, and at a time he was to be turned out for misconduct, that I take to be the reason. I think I should not have given my vote against Pitt. I am no party man as a tool, if I am to be a part of Administration it alters the case. If Pitt is attentive to me he shall have my vote. I have told you all this that you might see my conduct had nothing to do with *Addington's* conduct.

"I have kept myself in this letter entirely to the subject of yours. You see Lord Moira bound himself to support Addington. God bless you."

"Victory, October 5th, 1804.

"My dearest Emma,

"Hallowell is just arrived with your dear letters, and although I have not in fact one moment of time, still I send a line to thank you for them. I have only hastily run over them. I never could have thought you did not give enough to poor Mrs. Bolton. I must have meant that you should hold your generous hand, for if you have a fault, it is that you give away much more than you can afford; but respecting her and Tom, &c. &c. I will regulate those things to the full extent of what I ought to afford, upon due consideration, and that shall be regularly paid. I can only touch hastily upon several subjects. I have letters from Mr. Elliot and the Queen. The King is also in desperation at the thoughts of my going home. The King offered me houses either at Palermo or Naples. A messenger is now near England with a letter for Castelcicala, to present to the King, begging that I may be desired to return in the spring, but I do not expect that Pitt will accord with their wishes, although I receive from every part of Administration the most flattering marks of confidence. Acton is also very uncomfortable at the thoughts of my going away—he was very kind to Dr. Scott. I much fear without great management Naples will be lost, I fear the Emperor of Germany is too closely allied to Buonaparte to mind his relations at Naples. The Queen is very angry. I have much to tell you when we meet upon all those subjects. Your brother Ball desires to be remembered to his *Sister* Emma. You will not have time to answer this. Letters are on the average five weeks getting *viâ* Lisbon to Rosas. Gibbs is doing I believe all he can for me at Bronté. Mrs. Græffer will be allowed £100. a year. I see I must do it, and then it can never be said but that I have done nobly by her. Gibbs wants to get her to England, and I can see by his letter that he means something.

" I must just write a line by post to Davison to thank him for his letters. He says every thing shall be done according to my desires, therefore I hope you will have no more trouble about paying for the improvements. Sir William Bolton is gone to heave down to Gibraltar, he is a very good young man. I wish I could make him Post, and into a good frigate. I shall write by Gibraltar in a few days."

"Victory, October 10th, 1804.

" This, my dearest Emma, will, I dare say, be the last letter you will receive before you see me. Whatever arrangements are made about me by the Ministers, it is all settled long before this time. You will know from the Admiralty about my quarantine, but I dare say it will not be longer than return of post. I would wish you to remain at Merton. You are sure I shall lose no time, and it is possible, if I have leave, to strike my flag at that same moment that I get pratique. I shall not land at Portsmouth. As I wrote you before, I think the Superb will carry me, but if a senior Admiral comes out, I am subject to his will and pleasure. If all our house is not finished it can be done next summer, and we shall get through the winter very comfortable I have no doubt. Your last letters were to August 27th. You write so naturally that I fancy myself almost, not *quite*, in your company, but that will soon be, and I hope you have fixed Horatia at Merton. We have had much bad weather, and it has disagreed very much with me. I have much to say to you,

" Yours,
" N. & B."

"Victory, October 13th, 1804.

" My dearest Emma,

" The dreadful effects of the yellow fever at Gibraltar and many parts of Spain, will naturally give you much uneasiness, till you hear that, thank God, we are entirely free from it, and in the most perfect health, not one man being ill in the fleet. The cold weather will I hope cure the disorder. Whilst I am writing this letter, a cutter is arrived from England with strong indications of a Spanish war. I hope from my heart that it will not prove one. But, however that is, my die is cast: and long before this time, I expect, another Admiral is far on his way to supersede me; Lord Keith, I think, a very likely man.

"I should for your sake, and for many of our friends, have liked an odd hundred thousand pounds; but never mind. If they give me the choice of staying a few months longer, it will be very handsome; and for the sake of others we would give up, my dear Emma, very much of our own felicity. If they do not, we shall be happy with each other, and with dear Horatia."[1]

On the 13th Lord Nelson received a secret Admiralty letter, inclosing instructions issued to the Honourable Admiral Cornwallis to continue the strict blockade of the Port of Ferrol, to prevent the escape of the French ships, and to oppose any hostile attempts on the part of the Government or subjects of Spain against his Majesty's dominions. Lord Nelson dispatched his instructions therefore to Captain Sir Richard Strachan, Bart. of the Donegal, to proceed immediately outside the Straits of Gibraltar, together with the Medusa, Amphion, Sophia, and Halcyon.

Captain Sutton wrote to Lady Hamilton:—

"Amphion, Plymouth,
20th October, 1804.

"My dear Lady Hamilton,

"I am very unexpectedly come to England, having in charge one of the Spanish frigates taken off Cadiz on the 5th instant, for the particulars I refer you to Captain Moore's[1] public letter to the Admiralty. They are very valuable, having on board nearly one million sterling in specie, besides cochineal and other valuable merchandise. I hope it will turn out a good thing for that great and good man Lord

---

[1] Collection of Letters, Vol. ii. p. 79.
[2] Captain Graham Moore of the Indefatigable, which with the Medusa, Captain Gore; the Amphion, Captain Sutton; and the Lively, Captain Hamond, fell in with four Spanish vessels from South America. Captain Moore resolved to detain these vessels, and an action commenced. One was blown up, and the remaining three were taken. Spain being at peace with England, at this time, great indignation was expressed, and the conflict led to a Spanish war.

Nelson, as well as for myself. The frigate I was opposed to took fire and blew up in action. I could only save one officer and forty-four men. Thirteen ladies, passengers from South America, were lost in the ship. On the 2nd instant off Gibraltar I spoke the Childers, Sir William Bolton, who left Lord Nelson on the 22nd of September off Toulon. Bolton told me his Lordship meant to leave the fleet in a few days afterwards in the Superb for England, so that if this Spanish business does not prevent him from quitting the command, his arrival may be very shortly looked for. I hope your Ladyship has enjoyed good health since I had the pleasure of seeing you. I never was better, it could not be otherwise with me, for Lord Nelson's kindness has been unbounded to me. When the Childers left the fleet his Lordship was tolerably well. I have no idea of what is to become of the Amphion; but wherever Lord Nelson is employed I hope I shall be so happy as to be with him. May I hope for the honour of hearing from you, for believe me to be, with great respect and regard,

"Your Ladyship's
"Most obedient and faithful servant,
"SAMUEL SUTTON.

"Two of the frigates present on this occasion belonged to Admiral Cornwallis, the other two to Lord Nelson, so that it prevents any dispute as to right to share prize-money."

Mr. Bulkeley writes:—

"Pencombe, Bromyard, 20th October, 1804.

"A thousand thanks to you, my dear Lady Hamilton, for your kind and immediate reply to my last letter. I had just sent it off when the post brought me one from my son, and one from my most esteemed Nelson, in which he speaks of being in England before Christmas. I congratulate you on so certain a prospect of a happy meeting, but I join with you most sincerely in lamenting (as I am sure you do) the *cause* of his return, and most ardently hope that a few weeks quiet at Merton, and the society of those he loves, will restore him to vigour of body equal to the ardour of his mind.

Our country can't spare him, and you know as well as I do, that he can experience no wretchedness equal to that which he would feel at being compelled to withdraw his arm and most gigantic mind from the service of Old England, therefore I hope that your care of him (as it has upon other occasions), will soon enable him to resume his station, and once more to *extort* clamorous admiration even from those who burst with envy, from a consciousness that they can never be put in the same page with him.

"Nelson did right to tell the dirty City Scrubs of their neglect. I wish he had got some of those *rich Spaniards*. Mrs. Bulkeley desires her best compliments to you, and I am very truly yours,

"RICHARD BULKELEY."

Mr. Davison to the same:—

"My dear Madam,

"I was greatly disappointed in not seeing you on Friday, and was fearful some accident had happened; but your letter on Saturday explained.

"The Admiralty could do nothing short of behaving handsomely. If they are not attentive and kind to Lord Nelson, to whom should they shew respect? I hold his character to be such as not only to demand civility from every department of Government, but the nicest and most scrupulous consideration from every individual in this country. For to whom are we all so much indebted as to him—to whom does the nation owe so much—to none, so much as to him. And I am satisfied in my own mind, whoever is in or out of Administration, it will be precisely the same to him, and he will be beloved and admired wherever he is. I only now wish that he was at home to enjoy the comforts of his own fireside for a few months, and endeavour to regain that health which has nearly been destroyed in the service of his country. You would read his letter to the Lord Mayor which appeared in all the papers, it staggered the high dignitaries in the City. The Lord Mayor came to me on receipt of our dear Lord's letter. I told him it was such a rebuke as the City merited, and such as he could only expect from the pen of such a character as Lord Nelson, who thought more for the honour of his officers than for himself.

"You ask me if our dear friend shares in the prizes taken? There can be *no doubt* of his participating in them, as Captains Gore and Sutton were under his orders. I hope these prizes never will be given up, but condemned as legal capture—which would put a very handsome sum into the pocket of our best friend—a week or ten days will determine it.

"The wines, citrons, &c. that came home by the Kent, arrived from Portsmouth on Saturday. I have given orders for them all to be sent to Merton this morning, which I hope you will receive safe. When you are well enough to take an airing, a ride even to a prison will do you no harm and me much good.

"Your very sincere and faithful,
"A. DAVISON.

"Monday Morning, 22nd October."

Understanding that the enemy intended sending three privateers from Ajaccio with 100 men to surprise and take possession of the town of Madalena, Lord Nelson directed Captain George Cocks[1] of the bomb vessel Thunder, to proceed to the town and anchor in such situation as he might deem best calculated to prevent the invasion of the enemy, and to render to the governor every assistance in his power. He received the following from Prince Charles Felix of Savoy:—

"Cagliari, 28th October, 1804."

"My Lord,
"It is always with the greatest pleasure that I hear of your being in the Sardinian waters, I only regret being unable to testify my attachment and esteem in such a manner as I should wish, and you are entitled to. I shall not fail to inform the King, my brother, of the last instructions you have received from his Majesty, both for his safety, and that of all our family, and also of Sardinia, as well as of the obliging manner in which on all occasions you fulfil them, which augments my

---

[1] This officer commanded the Thunder bomb, at the siege of Copenhagen, in 1807, and received the thanks of Admiral Gambier and Lord Cathcart, for his bravery and effective service. He was made Post Captain, Oct. 13, 1807.

gratitude to you, and my obligations towards your King, to whom I beg you to represent my feelings. I doubt not but your pressing statements respecting our pecuniary necessities in Sardinia, will produce the desired result in England. Meanwhile I rely upon your vigilance and the wise measures which you will take for the safety of the country. I beg to observe I have not received your letter of the 20th August, of which you speak, and assuring you of my sentiments of esteem, and of high consideration, I am, your very good friend,

"CHARLES FELIX DE SAVOYE."

To Lady Hamilton Lord Nelson wrote :—

"Victory, October 31st, 1804.

"My dearest Emma,

"Various circumstances make me rather believe that it will not be possible to land this letter in Spain, and if it is landed, I hardly think it will ever reach Lisbon. However, as I never miss an occasion of writing, I take the chance of saying a very few words. I have prepared every thing for my successor be he who he will, and a few hours will suffice me to give him up the cudgels. The fleet is perfection, not one man ill of any complaint, a great thing to say in these dreadful times of sickness. I have got Mr. Este's son on board —he wants to get to England, but through Spain it is impossible, as no one is allowed to travel from one town to another. I purpose sending him *viâ* Gibraltar, if we hear more favourable accounts of the fever, and from thence he intends to get to Lisbon, and so go home by the packet; but if my superiors comply with my request, I may probably be in England sooner than this letter. The French fleet all well the 29th. Sir William Bolton is at Malta, therefore I have not sent his letter. I have much to tell you on many subjects, and what I can tell the great people (you understand me) will, if I return again, be most useful to them, if not too great to hear what I know. God in heaven bless you, and send us a meeting at dear Merton. My cough is so so. Love to Horatia.

"Yours,
"&c. &c. &c."

"Victory, November, 1804.

"I yesterday, my dearest Emma, had the happiness of receiving your letters of September 16th, 20th, 27th, and October 1st. I cannot but think that I shall see you before you read this letter; it goes by way of Lisbon, where I am sending Mr. Este, who is very anxious to get to England. I have been, you will believe, as attentive to him as I could. I am glad that you have had so pleasant a trip into Norfolk. That you have made them all happy I have no doubt, but you have made yourself poor. I do not believe that Pitt will give you a pension any more than Addington who I supported to the last moment of his Ministry. There is no gratitude in any of them, however if they do not do it I will give it you out of Brontë. You will see what effect your Queen's letter has through Castelcicala—a very pretty channel. She has made Roger Dumas, Commander-in-chief, and some other Frenchman something else, against both the King's and Acton's consent, but I fear she is ruling not so well as we could wish. I did not hear from her by the last vessel from Naples; perhaps she is angry at my ill health and going home for a few months to save my life. The china that we heard so much about was never ordered. I have very attentive letters from General Acton, but he has no more the *Power*; the Queen has got clear of him, and never whilst she rules will he be suffered to even enter the kingdom. I send you his private letter, his public one goes to Lord Camden. Gibbs writes me of the difficulty of settling all my affairs at Brontë. He is anxious to remove Mrs. Græffer. I shall allow the £100. a-year and have done with her. If she intends to go to England, I have wrote to Captain Lamb, Agent of Transports to find her a passage, which he has promised me to do. I shall get nothing from Brontë *but accounts* till next year's crop, and when I let it the rents will be raised one-third at least, and I not benefited till eight years are expired.

"You may tell Davison, and truly, that I have so much fever and head-ache, that if I had the King's ransom I could not write to him, but remember me kindly to him, and compliments to Haslewood. Love to Mrs. Cadogan, Charlotte, &c. &c."

To Lady Hamilton, Lord Nelson again writes:—

"Victory, Nov. 6th, 1804.

"Although I have wrote you by the Admiralty, yet I will not allow Mr. Este to leave me without carrying a line from me. I think his father's and his own inclination, will induce him to call upon you and deliver this letter. He will be able to tell you how I am, not very stout, although perhaps not very ill. The Kent must have been arrived several days when you wrote October 1st. I am momentarily expecting a vessel from the Admiralty with either another Admiral, or permission or refusal for my return to England.

"As Mr. Este is first to go by Lisbon, instead of sharing my fate, I have sent the Termagant to land him there, but I tell him that he had better stay, for that I shall be in England before him, which that God may grant, is the fervent prayer of

"Yours,

"NELSON AND BRONTÉ.

"I have this day appointed Mr. Westphaling's friend, Mr. Roberts, to the Anson, it will most probably be my last act of attention during my present command."

The Admiralty issued an order to Lord Nelson on the 31st of July: "to hold in readiness, in such port as may be agreed upon by you and Mr. Jackson, one of the ships under your command, for the purpose of conveying his Sardinian Majesty to such port in the Mediterranean as he may appoint; and to adopt such measures for the naval defence of the island of Sardinia as may be best calculated for that purpose, and as may be consistent with the other services entrusted to your care." He dispatched Captain Henry Richardson of the Juno to Gaeta, to receive, if necessary, his Majesty, and to convey him to any place in the Mediterranean he might think proper. Captain Richardson therefore proceeded with his dispatches and letters to the King, who transmitted the following to Lord Nelson:—

"My Lord,

"I received the letter you forwarded to me by Captain Richardson of the Juno, who entered this port this morning.

It is a fresh proof of the interest taken in and felt for me by the King, your master, and also of that which you yourself never cease taking. Your sentiments towards me and my family excite all my gratitude. The formation of a French camp at Velletri has really been discussed; French troops have defiled towards the kingdom of Naples, but the firm measures taken by the King of Naples, who has increased his army, supported by the declaration of Oubril on quitting France, that any new enterprise of the French disturbing the peace of Europe, or directly opposed to Russia, or to her allies, would be regarded as a declaration of war by Buonaparte against Russia, has had an effect, so that 5000 French who were marching by Romagna towards this kingdom, have had orders to retrograde, and the army of St. Cyr, that occupied Fogia, and other places in the interior, have taken up their old position so as to avoid a rupture with Russia at present. A French regiment of artillery, which was at Alexandria and Liguria, has received orders with other troops to quit Italy for Toulon. It appears, therefore, that there is nothing to fear for this kingdom at present, but they seem to have some special object in view at Toulon, where they have assembled a large force without any known reason. As you are in those seas, I am not at all uneasy as to what the French fleet might attempt to do. Your name is dreaded as it ought to be in the French Navy, the French will never forget Egypt. I have had much conversation about you with Captain Richardson, who is a very intelligent man, and of great merit apparently, and both myself and the Queen are deeply sensible of your solicitude and attention in such a critical moment as the present, but not wishing to infringe upon it, and seeing no immediate danger, flattering myself also that events may in some way place me in a position of proving by action the desire I feel to render some service to my good friends, and being besides in a strong fortress, well provisioned, and commanded by a good soldier, who would know how to defend it in case of an attack, and whom I could assist in case of need, having already combatted with those who might attack it, I have thought it best to remain still here, as being more likely to realize my desires. I have, therefore, left Captain Richardson at liberty to follow his ulterior orders, reserving the privilege of having recourse to you again, should my situation require it. I shall with great pleasure take charge of the letter from you for Mr. Jackson, brought by Captain Richardson, and I conclude by renewing to you my very sincere thanks, as well as those of the Queen, and assuring you of the sentiments of esteem with which I am, my Lord,

"Your good friend,
"V. EMANUEL.

"Gaeta, November 12, 1804."

Nelson's uncertainty from the dispatches he had received of the reality of a war with Spain,[1] determined him to proceed to Barcelona, where he arrived on the 15th of November, and received from Mr. Frere orders for the general seizure of all Spanish vessels, whether of war or merchandise. On this day he boarded an Imperial ship from Barcelona, having a complete regiment going to Minorca, and issued his orders to the Captains of the respective vessels of his fleet to take or destroy all Spanish ships they might fall in with. He wrote to Lady Hamilton :—

[1] When the declaration of war was made against France by the British Government, Holland was included, but not Spain, though this country was at that time occupied by French arms. It, however, soon transpired that an armament was fitting out in the port of Ferrol, that a large Spanish force was there collected, and that a junction of the French was immediately expected. This intelligence induced our Government to send out a Commodore[2] with a small squadron to intercept four Spanish frigates which were known to be laden with specie, and bound for that port from Monte Video. The Commodore selected for this lucrative mission was Captain Graham Moore (the brother of the celebrated General Sir John Moore), who in the Indefatigable of forty-four guns, and three other frigates, the Amphion, the Lively, and the Medusa, formed this squadron. The Spanish vessels were under the command of Don José Bustamente, and were descried by the British when making all sail to get into Cadiz bay. Upon being hailed, and unsatisfactory answers given, Captain Moore directed a fire upon the Spaniards. One of the Spanish vessels, the Mercedes, blew up; another, La Fama, surrendered, as did also the Medea and the Clara. The value of these prizes amounted to little short of a million of money. The knowledge of this capture excited great commotion at Madrid, and orders were immediately given to make reprisals on English property. This action took place on the 5th of October, 1804, and on the 12th of December the King of Spain formally declared war against Great Britain.

[2] See page 428 note, *ante*.

"Victory, November 23rd, 1804.

"As all our communication with Spain is at an end, I can now only expect to hear by the very slow mode of Admiralty vessels, and it is now more than two months since the John Bull sailed. I much fear something has been taken; for they never would, I am sure, have kept me so long in the dark. However, by management, and a portion of good luck, I got the account from Madrid in a much shorter space of time than I could have hoped for; and I have set the whole Mediterranean to work, and think the fleet cannot fail of being successful; and if I had had the spare troops at Malta at my disposal, Minorca would at this moment have had English colours flying.

"Where is my successor? I am not a little surprised at his not arriving. A Spanish war I thought would have hastened him. Ministers could not have thought that I wanted to fly the service, my whole life has proved the contrary; and, if they refuse me now, I shall most certainly leave this country in March or April; for a few months' rest I must have, very soon. If I am in my grave, what are the mines of Peru to me!

"But to say the truth, I have no idea of killing myself. I may, with care, live yet to do good service to the State. My cough is very bad, and my side, where I was struck on the 14th of February,[1] is very much swelled; at times a lump as large as my fist, brought on occasionally by violent coughing; but I hope and believe my lungs are yet safe.

"Sir William Bolton is just arrived from Malta. I am preparing to send him a cruise, where he will have the best chance I can give him of making ten thousand pounds. He is a very attentive, good young man. I have not heard from Naples this age. I have, in fact, no small craft to send for news. If I am soon to go home, I shall be with you before this letter. As our means of communicating are cut off, I have only to beg that you will not believe the idle rumours of battles, &c. &c. &c.

"NELSON AND BRONTÉ."[2]

---

[1] The battle off Cape St. Vincent.
[2] Collection of Letters, Vol. ii. p. 83.

Vice-Admiral Sir John Orde came out as Commander-in-chief of a squadron off Cadiz, which had previously formed a portion of Lord Nelson's command. Nelson wrote to Lady Hamilton :—

"Victory, December 4th, 1804.

"If any one could have told me that Admiral Campbell would have sailed for England before me I should not have believed him, but his state of health is come to that crisis, that probably his life would be lost if he was kept here even forty-eight hours longer, therefore he proceeds this day in the Ambuscade, and poor fellow I hope he will arrive safe. I have for several months thought that his mind[1] was debilitated, but we tried to laugh him out of it. I send you his letter when I announced to him, in consequence of his application, that a frigate should carry him to England immediately. All my things are on board the Superb, and if my successor would arrive I could be off in two hours. We have reports that Sir John Orde is the man, which has thrown a gloom over all the fleet, but I hope unnecessarily, for six years upon the shelf, may have taught him a little moderation towards officers. I have made up my mind to overwhelm him with respect and attention, and to even make an offer, as Admiral Campbell has gone home, to serve till the Admiralty can send out another Flag-officer. I have wrote to Lord Melville that I should make such an offer, and that I entreated him to send out a Flag-officer as soon as possible, but I dare say Sir John Orde is too great a man to want my poor services, and that he will reject them ; be that as it may, you will, I am sure, agree with me, that I shall shew my superiority to him by such an offer, and the world will see what a sacrifice I am ready to make for the service of my King and Country, for what greater sacrifice could I make, than serving for a moment under Sir John Orde, and giving up for that moment the society of all I hold dear in this world. Many here think that he is sent out off Cadiz to take a fortune out of my mouth, that would be very curious. The late Admiralty directed Admiral Cornwallis to send Campbell to cruise at the mouth of the Straits, and he took all my sweets, and now this Admiralty sends and takes all my golden harvest ; it is very

[1] See page 336 note, *ante*.

odd—surely I never served faithfully, I have only dreamt I have done my duty to the advantage of my country, but I am above them, *I feel it*, although not one farthing richer than when I left England. It is this day seventy-five days since my letters were dated in London from the Admiralty. Kiss dear Horatia for me, and give my kindest regards to Mrs. Cadogan, Charlotte, and all our friends.

" Yours,

" NELSON AND BRONTÉ."

From Captain Staines,[1] Lord Nelson received the following :—

" Cameleon, Trieste, 5th Dec. 1804.

" My Lord,

" I am extremely sorry to say that my visit to the Adriatic has not been attended with that success, which I am perfectly persuaded it was your Lordship's good wishes it should

[1] Captain Thomas Staines was a native of Kent, born near Margate in 1776, and in 1790 entered the Navy as a Midshipman in the Solebay frigate, Captain Matthew Squire. He proceeded to the West Indies, and remained there during two years, was afterwards in the Mediterranean with Captain Cunningham, and at the surrender of Calvi in 1794. In the Victory, with Lord Hood, he was at the destruction of L'Alcide, and afterwards mate of signals under Sir John Jervis, who made him a Lieutenant in 1796, and was appointed to the Peterel, in which he saw much service, and experienced considerable danger off the coast of Portugal. In this vessel he was taken prisoner by four Spanish frigates, and very ill-treated, but the vessel was fortunately retaken by the Argo. In 1799, in this vessel, under the command of Captain Austen, he communicated the intelligence to Nelson at Palermo, that the Brest fleet having eluded the vigilance of Lord Bridport, had passed the Straits of Gibraltar, and the zeal with which he performed this duty insured the regard of Nelson. He became Third Lieutenant of the Foudroyant, the flag-ship of Nelson, in which he assisted in the capture of the two French Rear-Admirals, Perrée and Decrès, on the 15th of February and the 30th of March, 1800. Lieutenant Staines afterwards served in the Foudroyant with Lord Keith to the end of the Egyptian campaign. He received the Order of the Crescent. In 1801 he was made Commander of the Romulus, and afterwards of the Cameleon, in which vessel, in 1803, he joined Lord Nelson off Toulon, and was sent by him upon a confidential mission. He distinguished himself along the coasts of Italy and Provence. He also cruised in the Adriatic, and afterwards protected the Levant trade. He was paid off at Portsmouth in September, 1805, and had the honour to dine with Nelson, together with Mr. Canning and Mr. George Rose, prior to his departure for his last battle. Captain Staines was made Post-Captain in 1806, commanded the Cyané, fought an action with a French squadron in the Bay of Naples in June, 1809, prior to which he was in all the operations which led to the capitulation of Copenhagen ; afterwards blockaded Zea-

be; but, notwithstanding my failure of making captures, the arrival of his Majesty's sloop Cameleon in these seas, in combination with other circumstances, has certainly tended to rid this coast most completely of the numerous French privateers which have lately infested it. The Anson and Bittern having been in the Adriatic just previous to the Cameleon's arrival, and the liberation of the British ship taken by one of the French privateers, with costs against the captors, are the circumstances which I allude to, independent of the fear which they might have entertained of our retaliating by capturing them under the same circumstances, in defiance of neutral protection. The effect of that combination is not only proved by my not having seen, or even having heard, of one of those depredators since my arrival in this port, but also by the late arrival of the Morgiana, with a convoy for Trieste; which, although it was separated for several days among the small islands, and on the coast of Istria (which was most particularly the scene of their depredations), yet they all arrived in safety at this port without any annoyance or the least appearance of hostile intention.

"My endeavour has been to search into all the small islands, and in every other part wherein I thought it most probable they might still be lurking, but all without effect. I am perfectly well convinced, however, that your Lordship's liberality of sentiment will not for a moment allow my failure

---

land, then protected the trade in the Baltic, and was employed on the south coast of Spain. In the performance of those and subsequent duties, in which Captain Staines was so unfortunate as to lose his left arm, he obtained the marked approbation of Admiral Martin and Lord Collingwood, and received the honour of knighthood, together with permission to wear the Order of St. Ferdinand and Merit, which had been conferred on him by the King of Sicily for his conduct in his dominions. In 1810 he was appointed to the Hamadryad, went to Newfoundland, escorted troops, &c. to the Tagus, cruised on the Irish station, then in the Briton, in the Bay of Biscay, during a variety of service. In 1813 he sailed for the East Indies, convoyed a disabled Indiaman to Rio Janeiro, then went round Cape Horn, to Valparaiso. He proceeded to Callao, Paita, the Gallopagas, and Marquesas islands. Returning from the latter to Valparaiso he came upon Pitcairn's island, and thereby ascertained the manner in which the ship Bounty had been disposed of. (An account of this may be found in Marshall's Naval Biography, Suppl. Part I. pp. 96—104.) He returned to England in 1815, was made K.C.B. In 1823 he was appointed to the Superb of 78 guns, and afterwards visited Barbadoes, St. Vincent, Dominica, Bermuda, and Lisbon. He was paid off in December, 1825, and died near Margate, July 13, 1830.

in this pursuit to be attributed to inertness or deficiency of exertion on my part, and I am also well aware of the good construction which your Lordship has ever been in the habit of putting on circumstances, although wearing the most unfavourable appearances: but I am still very anxious to have everything of that nature perfectly undoubted, and much more so, to retain your Lordship's good opinion, which constitutes the summit of my ambition, and the most effective spur to my endeavours.

" I am waiting here, my Lord, since the 29th of November, from an application which the Consul has made to me to convoy three English vessels to Venice, which will be ready in two days, and from thence I proceed immediately to Malta, with the liberated ship under my convoy, she being ready laden for that destination. I am to continue in quarantine at this place, from having had communication with the island of Lissa, and many other parts which are not at this moment considered in liberal pratique.

" The Mareschino which your Lordship expressed a wish for, I have procured in four cases of two dozen bottles each, the bottle containing about a pint and a half, which I shall take the earliest opportunity of forwarding to England. May I request your Lordship will do me the honour of presenting my best respects to Lady Hamilton, which liberty I am induced to take from her Ladyship having been a shipmate of mine in the Foudroyant.

" I have the honour to be,
" Your Lordship's
" Most obliged, most obedient, humble servant,
" T. Staines."

From Prince Charles Felix:—

" Cagliari, Dec. 15th, 1804.

" My Lord,

" I regret that circumstances have deprived me of the pleasure of making your acquaintance, as I should have been highly gratified by your intimacy, and by an interview in which several important subjects would have been discussed. Having met Mr. Scott this morning, and knowing that he enjoys your confidence, I have explained to him the disastrous situation of this country, which I do not repeat, as I am persuaded he will lay before you full particulars of our unfortunate situation. He assures me, that you wrote urgently to your Court upon the subject, in consequence of my communications some months back, and I flatter myself that your representation will be attended with success, but I beg you to observe, that delay is likely to be equally prejudicial to England, for the occupation of Sardinia by the French will deprive her of several advantageous ports for the purpose of watching the operations of the enemy from Toulon, and if unfortunately she once falls into their power, a reconquest will be very difficult, even if twenty times the amount were expended, which would now suffice to protect her. As soon as I knew you had anchored at Poula, I determined to send Baron Desgenais, Commander in the Royal Navy, to convey to you what Mr. Scott will now say. The interest you take in the welfare of our family, will induce you, my Lord, I trust, to aid us to the extent of your power, and be assured of the gratitude of him who subscribes himself truly,

" My Lord,
" Your good friend,
" CHARLES FELIX DE SAVOYE.

" P.S.—I beg you not to lose sight of Madaleine Island. I suspect the French have a project to seize it, either to deprive the English of that anchorage, or that they may with more facility invade Sardinia. Some light ships cruising there would probably suffice to secure it."

" Cagliari, Dec. 26, 1804.

" My Lord,
" Up to the present moment I have received no report as to the French fleet having been seen from any part of the coasts of Sardinia, and consequently am unable to give you any information. I hope you will speedily meet it, and achieve success to your own satisfaction, and that of him who begs to reiterate the assurance of his sentiments, and subscribes himself,

" My Lord,
" Your good friend,
" CHARLES FELIX DE SAVOYE."

On the 19th December Nelson wrote to Lady Hamilton:—

"Victory, December 19th, 1804."

"My dearest Emma,

"Since I wrote you by the Ambuscade, when I was every moment expecting the arrival of the great Sir John Orde, I have received a letter from him, telling me that he was in the chief command of a squadron outside the Straits, &c. &c. He has treated my ships a little harshly, but never mind, he will get all the money, and your poor Nelson all the hard blows. Am I to take this act as a proof of Lord Melville's regard for me? but I submit patiently, but I feel. I have not had a scrap of a pen from England ninety days this day, it is rather long in these critical times. I send this through Mr. Falconet at Naples, and as it will be read by the French, and many others, I do not choose to say any thing more than I care for all the world knowing. I keep every thing packed up, and two hours would finish every thing I can have to do with my successor, who must certainly be near at hand; or is Sir John, after he has got riches, to come here and get glory? I have certainly much to arrange when I get home, and the situation of Mrs. Bolton shall have serious consideration, but such a place as Tyson's would very soon involve Mr. Bolton in difficulties; however, I will ask, and I fear I shall be refused. My cough is still very, very bad, and I ought at this moment to have been snug at Merton, but I look forward for that day with much pleasure, and please God it will arrive soon. You may tell Lord Melville that the French fleet was safe the 12th December, but my reporter says, that they are certainly embarking troops, but I hope to meet them, and to realize the fond wishes of my country.

"Yours, &c.

"Remember me kindly to all our friends. I wish I could be with you all this Christmas, which I fully expected."

In relation to the appointment of Sir John Orde, which it is evident from the preceding letters rankled in Nelson's breast, Mr. Coleridge has made some pertinent remarks. After beautifully alluding to the love of him entertained by the whole fleet, and the unexampled harmony which constantly reigned among them under circumstances that might well have undermined the patience of the best balanced dispositions, much more of men with the impetuous character of British sailors, he observes: "Year after year, the same dull duties of a wearisome blockade, of doubtful policy—little if any opportunity of making prizes; and a few prizes, which accident might throw in the way, of little or no value—and when at last the occasion presented itself which would have compensated for all, then a disappointment as sudden as it was unjust and cruel, and the cup dashed from their lips; add to these trials the sense of enterprises checked by a feebleness and timidity elsewhere, not omitting the tiresomeness of the Mediterranean sea, sky, and climate; and the unjarring and cheerful spirit of affectionate brotherhood, which linked together the hearts of that whole squadron, will appear not less wonderful to us than admirable and affecting. When the resolution was taken of commencing hostilities against Spain, before any intelligence was sent to Lord Nelson, another Admiral, with two or three ships of the line, was sent into the Mediterranean, and stationed before Cadiz, for the express purpose of intercepting the Spanish prizes. The Admiral dispatched on this lucrative service gave no information to Lord Nelson of his arrival in the same sea, and five weeks elapsed before his Lordship became acquainted with the circumstance. The prizes thus taken were immense. A month or two sufficed to enrich the Commander and Officers of this small and highly favoured squadron, while to Nelson and his fleet the sense of having done their duty, and the consciousness of the glorious services which they had performed, were considered, it must be presumed, as an abundant remuneration for all their toils and long sufferings! It was, indeed, an unexampled circumstance, that a small squadron should be sent to the station which had been long occupied by a large fleet, commanded by the darling of the Navy, and the glory of the British Empire; to the station where this fleet had for years been wearing away in the most barren, repulsive, and spirit-trying service in which the Navy can be employed! and that this minor squadron should be sent independent of, and without any communication with the Commander of the former fleet, for the express and solitary purpose of stepping between it and the Spanish prizes, and as soon as this short and pleasant service was performed, of bringing home the unshared booty with all possible caution and dispatch. The *substantial* advantages of naval service were perhaps deemed of too *gross* a nature for men already rewarded with the grateful affections of their own countrymen, and the admiration of the whole world! They were to be awarded, therefore, on a principle of compensation, to a Commander less rich in fame, and whose laurels, though not scanty, were not yet sufficiently luxuriant to hide the *golden* crown which is the appropriate ornament of victory in the bloodless war of commercial capture! Of all the wounds which were ever inflicted on Nelson's feelings (and these were not a few) this was the deepest! this rankled most! 'I had thought,' said the gallant man, in a letter written on the first feelings of the affront, ' I fancied—but nay, it must have been a dream, an idle dream—yet, I confess it, I *did* fancy, that I had done my country service—and thus they use me. It was not enough to have robbed me once before of my West India harvest—now they have taken away the Spanish—and under what circumstances, and with what pointed aggravation! Yet, if I know my own thoughts, it is not for myself, or on my own account chiefly, that I feel the sting and the disappointment: no! it is for my brave Officers; for my noble-minded friends and commanders—such a gallant set of fellows! such a band of brothers! My heart swells at the thought of them!' "[1]

The Admiralty approved Lord Nelson's recommendation of Sir Richard Bickerton's remaining in command of the squadron, and on the 25th of December he received the dispatches of the date of October 6th. He replied to the Admiralty, that the moment another Admiral in the room of Admiral Campbell joined the fleet, (unless the enemy's fleet should be at sea, when he should not think of quitting his command until after the battle), he should avail himself of the permission granted him to return to England.

On the 30th he wrote to Lady Hamilton :—

" Victory, December 30th, 1804.

" My dearest Emma,

" I received by the Swiftsure your letters to October 29th, on your return from your long expedition into Norfolk, on Christmas-day, the day I had devoted to spend most happily

[1] The Friend, Essay vi. p. 358.

with you and our dear adopted Horatia at dear Merton. I received the Admiralty's permission to go to England for the re-establishment of my health, and I think that a few months may enable me to serve another year, and then, except for an expedition, I shall most likely never serve again. The winter has been quite different to the last. We have not had a cold day, nor near so many gales of wind, but my cough is very troublesome, particularly from two in the morning until I have had my breakfast; but a little of your good nursing will set me up again. The Niger has been sent home, I fear by Sir John Orde, who has not behaved very civil towards any of my squadron, therefore I am afraid Mr. Charles Connor will lose his kind protector in Captain Hillyar, which will be a serious misfortune to him, for he was rated Midshipman, and forced by Captain Hillyar to study, which he was not very fond of. The going home of George Campbell has protracted my departure till another Admiral comes out, which may very well be in January, then unless the French fleet is actually at sea, nothing will keep me two hours. I have not heard from Naples for some time, but I hear the French are oppressing both the Sovereigns and the people very much. I wrote you on the 19th through Mr. Falconet.

"I have wrote to Lord Melville as strong as possible, and in fact have sold myself to him, if he complies with my desires for Mr. Bolton, but my dear kind hearted Emma, I do not believe he will give me any thing. I only wish I had the power myself, and so I might if the station had not been taken from me, and given to that great officer who has served so much and so well; but as I have asked favours of Lord Melville, I must not grumble. The end of February, or the first week in March, I shall certainly be in England in the Superb, and I only hope that we shall have a very short quarantine, for I shall certainly not communicate with Gibraltar, I cannot say what I would wish in this letter, for it goes by way of Lisbon in the Admiralty packet, and will be smoked, cut, &c. &c. before it gets to you, and I may very probably be with you before the letter, which will give inexpressible happiness to

"Yours,
"NELSON AND BRONTÉ.

"Kiss dear Horatia for me."

At the close of this year Lord Nelson wrote to Lord Melville, complaining of the want of frigates in the Mediterranean, and the following was directed to the Hon. Captain Boyle:—[1]

"Victory, December 30th, 1804.

"Dear Boyle,

" I am most exceedingly hurt at your not having joined the fleet, as you must know my distress for frigates, and I am much displeased with Captain Mowbray for interfering with your orders. I sincerely hope this will not find you at Gibraltar, but should it unfortunately, I desire you will not lose one moment in joining the fleet.

"Ever yours faithfully,
"NELSON AND BRONTÉ."

[1] The Hon. Courtenay Boyle was the third son of Edmund Earl of Cork and Orrery, born September 3, 1769, and served as a Midshipman under Sir Hyde Parker in the Latona frigate. Having received an accident from a fall from the booms to the orlop, he was obliged to go on shore for recovery; he afterwards served in the Goliath, and studied in the Naval College at Portsmouth, whence he came under the auspices of Nelson in the Boreas in 1784, and went to the West Indies. He afterwards served on board the Barfleur, bearing Lord Hood's flag, then in the Leander, L'Aquilon, the Vanguard, and the Roebuck. In the Revolutionary war he was in the Egmont of 74 guns. Lord Hood appointed Lieutenant Boyle to the Fox cutter, and he afterwards was in the Excellent and the Saturn. He brought over the Princess Caroline of Brunswick from Cuxhaven, and was made Commander, appointed to the Kangaroo, and placed on the Lisbon and Irish stations. He was made Post Captain in 1797. In 1799 he was appointed to the Cormorant, attended upon the Royal Family at Weymouth, went to the Mediterranean, captured a Spanish brig, and retook an English West Indiaman. In March, 1800, however, he was so unfortunate as to be wrecked off Damietta, when on his way to Alexandria, with dispatches of the ratification of the Treaty of El Arish. General Menou treated him in a savage manner, he was kept confined three months. Recovering his liberty he joined Sir Sidney Smith at Cyprus, whence he proceeded to Minorca, was tried for the loss of his ship, and honourably acquitted, it being proved to have arisen from an error in the reckoning, occasioned by the incorrectness of the Charts. He remained unemployed until 1803, when he was appointed to the Seahorse, and ordered to the Mediterranean, where he was placed under the orders of Nelson, who liked him much, and in 1787, in a letter to his father, described him as "amiable in the truest sense of the word; and I feel great regret in parting from him. In his professional line he is inferior to none: his virtues are superior to most." In 1805 he exchanged into the Amphitrite, and in 1806 to the Royal William. In 1809 he was made a Commissioner of Transports, and had the control of the Dockyard of Sheerness in 1814; subsequently he had a seat at the Navy Board. He lived to attain the rank of Vice-Admiral of the Red, was K.C.H. and died in May, 1844.

## CHAPTER X.

### 1805.

LADY Hamilton received the following account of Nelson at the commencement of 1805 :—

"Sunday Evening, 6th January, 1805.

" My dear Madam,

" I presume you have received letters from your dear Lord; but should that not be the case, I cannot delay a moment in acquainting you that he was *quite* well on the 4th of December. His private letter to Lord Melville I have heard read, and which gives as good an account of himself as you could wish. Admiral Campbell is come home in consequence of bad health, and Sir Richard Bickerton is but so, so. Your dear Lord says he cannot afford to be ill. I was rejoiced to know he was so well, and he writes in great spirits. I had a conversation about yourself, and am sure it will afford you great satisfaction to know how much Lord Melville interests himself in your favour. He tells me he has spoken to Mr. Pitt of the propriety of your having a pension settled upon you of £500. per annum, and that he will speak to him again very shortly about it. I asked Lord Melville if I might say as much to you. He immediately said, 'Yes, certainly.' He spoke very handsomely of you, and of your services in favour of this country when in Naples. It is needless to repeat the just compliments he paid to *our* gallant Nelson, who is reinforced with four ships-of-the-line, and now *must* make his fortune. Spain has declared war, and *now* will here be announced publicly, I presume, on Tuesday.

"Sir John (General) Moore is returned from Portugal, and looks better than he did ten years ago.

" Lord Melville told me that he would dispatch a letter or two for the Mediterranean, so that you must immediately set to work, and write your dispatches. I shall begin mine tomorrow morning. Yours, my dear Madam,

" Most faithfully,

" ALEXANDER DAVISON."

At this time Lord Nelson received information from his Excellency, Hugh Elliot, Esq. as to the state of affairs at Naples. In reply Nelson expresses his satisfaction at the spirited part the Queen took in the defence of Naples, and hoped she would not be depressed by hearing that the French are at sea, as if they never came out she could not enjoy the spectacle of a battle in the Bay of Naples. "Nothing," he added, " shall be wanting on my part to make it superior to the Nile, which it may be; and could any thing add to my exertions against the enemy, it would be the additional pleasure of knowing that I was fighting for the existence of the monarchy of my benefactors. But let who will command this fleet, they cannot go wrong: only get close enough."[1]

On the same day, the 13th January, he wrote a secret letter to Mr. Elliot, saying, " Sir John Orde brought me out my leave to go to England, for the re-establishment of my health, and many suppose that, the moment I had passed the Straits, he would take upon him the command. Others suppose, Sir John Colpoys will be my successor; and there are others that think, I shall return, if my health permits, and that my services will continue to be acceptable. However, I have kept my permission a profound *secret* in the fleet. Everybody expects that it will come; therefore do not mention my having received it, to either Captain Sotheron or Captain Malcolm, although you may to the King and Queen. I do assure you, that nothing has kept me here, but the fear for the escape of the French fleet, and that they should get to either Naples or Sicily in the short days; and that when I go, I shall leave such instructions with Sir Richard Bickerton (who, I am sure, will follow them up) to guard the Two Sicilies, as he would the apple of his eye; and nothing but gratitude, to those good Sovereigns, could have induced me to stay one moment after Sir John Orde's extraordinary command, for his general conduct towards me is not such as I had a right to expect."[2]

On the following day, he instructed Captain Frank

---

[1] Dispatches and Letters, Vol. vi. p. 317. From an Autograph in the Elliot Papers. [2] Ibid.

Sotheron,[1] of the Excellent, to hold himself in readiness to convey, if necessary, the King, Queen, and Royal family of Naples to Palermo, or such other place, as his Majesty might choose to proceed to, and to afford protection to all who might accompany their Majesties, and the English Minister and his suite, as well as to afford protection to British property and British subjects.

The opinion expressed in Mr. Davison's letter, to Lady Hamilton, (see *ante*, p. 448) of the improvement of Nelson's health is confirmed by the following :—

"Victory, January 14th, 1805.

"Although, my dearest Emma, I have not heard that Mr. Falconet forwarded my other letter of December 19th, yet I shall take the chance of another crossing the Continent, just to say I am not so unwell as I have been. The French are certainly preparing for an expedition. I only fear they will defer it till my departure. All our friends at Naples are pressing me to stay and save them, and certainly their situation becomes every day more critical. The Usurper has made most unjust demands upon them, and held out threats, but the Queen is firm. I must not go on with this subject,

---

[1] Captain Frank Sotheron, a native of Yorkshire, was born in 1765, and entered the navy at the age of eleven, as a midshipman, in the Bienfaisant, under Admiral M'Bride, with whom he remained during six years. He was lent to the Arethusa, and was in the action with La Belle Poule, in 1778, and afterwards in the action off Ushant, between Keppel and D'Orvilliers. He was also present at the capture of the Caraccas convoy, the defeat of Don Juan de Langara, and the relief of Gibraltar, under Sir George Rodney. He was also at the taking of the Comte d'Artois, of 64 guns, and the Comtesse d'Artois, a French privateer. The former was considered one of the finest vessels of her class in the world, and Mr. Sotheron moved with his Commander into her, engaged in watching the Dutch squadron, and in the action off the Dogger Bank, and in the captures of the Hercules and Mars, two Dutch privateers. He was sent to the Irish coast, and then to Newfoundland, where, in 1783, Admiral Campbell made him a Lieutenant. In 1792, he was First Lieutenant of the Romney, and afterwards in the Fury. In the following year, he was made a Post Captain, and appointed to the Monarch, of 74 guns, but moved into the Romney again, and was at Newfoundland. In 1799, he was in the Latona, sent against the Helder, and then continued in the North Sea. In 1802, he went abroad with dispatches, &c. in the Excellent, joined Nelson in the Mediterranean, and was entrusted with the defence of the Bay of Naples. He was made Rear-Admiral, August 1, 1811. He was promoted to be Vice-Admiral, August 12, 1819. He represented Nottinghamshire in Parliament, and having arrived at the rank of Admiral of the White, died in February, 1839.

for Lord Nelson insists that I shall put nothing of politics in my letter, therefore I can only assure my dear Emma of my truest affection and love for you.

"I shall probably be at home long before this letter, therefore shall only say, God bless and preserve you, for your own faithful

"J. T."[1]

The anxiety of the King and Queen of Naples for Lord Nelson's presence is seen in the following:—

"Belvidere, 19th January, 1805.

"My dear Duke de Bronté,

"I take advantage of the return of the vessel to reply to your letter of the 19th of December last; pleased as I have been by all you say to me in it, on the other hand, I am grieved to hear that the weakened state of your health renders it necessary that you should give up the command of the Mediterranean squadron, and return to your country; and particularly at a period, and under circumstances so critical for me, my family, and this kingdom, threatened with the same unhappy lot which has befallen so many others. A repetition of your sentiments is superfluous, since they are engraven on my grateful and affectionate heart, and will remain so till death. Every thing will certainly be done to sustain the good cause, and to raise up, protect, and defend the innocent and oppressed; but it is impossible that I should ever find such another true friend as the brave and attached Nelson. May God be with you in all your undertakings, increasing your glory, and crowning you with the happiness and blessings which you merit, and which I desire for you.

"Your ever affectionate and grateful friend,

"FERDINANDO B."

"January 19, 1805.

"I have received, my worthy Lord, your letter of December, and I profit of the departure of the man-of-war to write to you I cannot express to you, my worthy Admiral, how much both the King and I consider your departure from the command in the Mediterranean as a real calamity, added to

[1] Lord Nelson's fictitious signature.

the misfortunes that already oppress us. Your sensibility, your attachment, your great bravery; your name inspires that confidence which expectation had justified. You can never be replaced! Thus I must regard it as a real misfortune, and should be very happy if this could change, or at least retard it. I am convinced the crisis is fast approaching that will confirm the indolence of Europe, or great events arise. The ambition and immoderate good fortune of the Corsican has just created his brother Joseph hereditary King of Lombardy, or to speak more truly, its scourge. This must awaken the Sovereigns of Europe from their slumber, or consolidate their slavery. It is in these moments of struggle and indecision, when our dangers are infinitely increased, that our earnest desire is augmented to see you, my worthy and respectable friend, fixed near us. Consider, with your usual discernment, the present situation of affairs; above all, consult with your own heart, and you will acknowledge the justice of my wishes. In a word, my worthy and respectable friend, continue to be our saviour, and be assured of the eternal and sincere gratitude of those who deserve and feel they ought to live in an age different from this degenerate one. The trusty Elliot will better explain to you our painful circumstances. I confine myself to express our ardent desire that you will not quit us, and may you be once more our saviour. I know that the King, my innocent family, and all good people, prefer the same wishes. May they be realised! It will augment the gratitude with which I am, and ought to be for life, your

"Much attached and grateful friend,
"CHARLOTTE."

The following are copies of Napoleon's communications to the King and Queen of Naples, found among Nelson's papers:—

"Sir, my Brother,
"I reply to the letter of your Majesty. The French troops are in the kingdom of Naples, in consequence of the Treaty of Florence, and will remain there as long as the affairs of the Levant are unsettled; and I must so consider them until Malta shall be evacuated by the English, and Corfu by the

Russians. Had not those Russian troops been sent to Corfu at the special solicitations of your Majesty's Minister, I should have diminished the number of the French troops, leaving at Tarento only the four or five thousand men necessary for the occupation of that post; their arrival, on the contrary, compelled me to augment the number. If your Majesty will permit me to say so, you have been badly counselled, and follow a system pernicious to the interests of your house. Paris, Madrid, and Vienna, are the real supports of your Majesty. Your Majesty is more interested in peace than any other Prince. Reject the perfidious counsels with which England enthrals you. You have preserved your kingdom intact in the midst of the overthrow of social order; do not risk the loss of it now that social order is settled. The world, tranquil and pacific for a moment, will perhaps suddenly resume its accustomed politics and practice. I have provided for the payment of the French troops, which by the Treaty of Florence your Majesty engaged to do, wishing by it, to give you a proof of my desire to respond, as much as is reconcileable with general politics, to the sentiments that you express towards me. This said, I pray God to have you, Sir, my brother, in his holy keeping.

" Your good brother,
" NAPOLEON.

" Paris (Nivose), January, 1805."

### BUONAPARTE TO THE QUEEN OF NAPLES.

" Madam,

" Your Majesty's letter has been handed to me by the Marquis de Gallo. It is difficult to me to reconcile the sentiments it contains with the hostile projects apparently entertained at Naples—I have several of your Majesty's letters in my hands, which leave no doubt as to your real secret intentions. What must be the hatred your Majesty bears to France, that after the experience you have had, neither your conjugal love, nor your parental, nor love of your family, nor subjects, induce you to forbear a little, and adopt a policy more conformable with their interests. Is your Majesty's mind, so distinguished amongst women, unable to divest itself of the prejudices of sex, treating of affairs of state as if they were matters of the heart. You have already lost your kingdom once, and have twice been the cause of a war, which has shaken and ruined your paternal house to its foundation—do you wish to be the cause of a third? Already at the solicitations of your Ambassador at St. Petersburg, ten thousand Russians have been sent to Corfu. What! is your hatred so vigorous? Is your love for England so uncontrolled, that you would (although certain to be the first victim) set the Continent in a blaze, and work a fortunate diversion for England? I confess I should admire in some degree such strong passions, if the simplest reasoning did not make me feel their frivolity and impotence. Your nephew, the Emperor of Austria, does not partake these sentiments, and does not wish to renew a war, the results of which could not be very satisfactory to him; even Russia, who has yielded to the solicitations of your Majesty's Minister so much as to send ten thousand men to Corfu, is very sensible that war against France would be very different from that, and the feelings of Alexander I. are not warlike. But supposing that the overthrow of your family and throne were effected, and Russia and Austria were on that account induced to arm, can your Majesty, who has such a good opinion of me, think that I should remain inactive, and fall into subjection to my neighbours? Let your Majesty listen to this prophecy without impatience—In the first war caused by you, you and your posterity will cease to reign, your children will wander, begging in the different countries of Europe for assistance for their parents—by an inexplicable conduct your Majesty will have caused the ruin of your family, which providence and my moderation would have preserved to you. Would you thus renounce one of the finest kingdoms of the universe? I should be sorry, however, that your Majesty should view my frankness as threats. No, if it had entered into my plans to make war upon the King of Naples, I should have done it on the entrance of the first Russian in Corfu, agreeably to a wary policy, but I wish for peace with Naples, with Europe entire, with England even, and I do not fear war with any one. I am in a condition to make it with whoever provokes me, and to punish the Court of Naples without fearing the resentment of any one whatever. May your Majesty listen to the advice of a good brother, recall from St. Petersburg a Minister whose measures serve no end but to damage the affairs of Naples, and plunge them into imminent danger. Send back M. Elliot, who only weaves plots of assassination and excites all the movements in Naples. Give your confidence to the head of your house; and I venture to say it, to me, and do not be so much your own enemy as to lose a kingdom you have kept in the midst of the great confusion in which so many States have perished. I do not flatter your Majesty in this letter—it will be disagreeable, but it is also a proof of my esteem—it is only to a person of a strong character and above the common that I would give myself the trouble to write such truths. This said, I pray God, Madam, my sister and cousin, to have you in his holy keeping.

"NAPOLEON.

"Paris Nivose l'an 13.
January, 1805."

In the early part of January Lord Nelson was off Toulon. On the 12th he was at the Madalena Islands, where on the 19th, by the Active and Seahorse, he learnt that the French fleet had got out of Toulon the day preceding. Nelson conceived them to be bound round the south end of Sardinia, and resolved to intercept them by proceeding to the southward. He received the intelligence of the departure of the French fleet at 3 P.M. of the 19th, and by 6 P.M. the whole English fleet was at sea.

M. de la Gravière gives the following testimony to Nelson's extraordinary activity and zeal in the pursuit of the French fleet at this time :—

"On January 19th, 1805, Nelson was at anchor in Agincourt Roads, when two of his frigates, the Active and Seahorse, appeared at the entrance of the Straits of Bonifacio, under a press of sail, with the long expected signal, 'The enemy is at sea.' It was at three o'clock in the afternoon when they anchored near the Victory, and at half-past four the English fleet was under sail. It becomes dark there about five o'clock at that time of the year: the wind was blowing strong from the westward, and the fleet could not work to windward against it, so that it was necessary to go through one of the eastern passages which open into the Tuscan sea. Though it was now completely dark, Nelson took the lead in the Victory, and resolved to conduct his eleven ships of the line between the rocks of Biscia and the north-east extremity of Sardinia. This passage, whose breadth does not exceed a quarter of a mile, has never since been attempted by any fleet. The English squadron cleared it; formed in a single line a-head; each ship shewing a light astern, to guide the one which followed."[1]

This generous testimony to Nelson's zeal and determination, will be found to agree with what has been stated, and it remains to observe, that a heavy gale arrested their progress on the 20th, and by the 22nd they had only reached sixteen leagues east of Cape Carbonara. Nelson then dispatched frigates to Cagliari and St. Pierre, to obtain information of the position of the enemy, and another frigate to Sir John Acton at Palermo, that Sicily might not be surprised, and that intelligence might be conveyed to Naples of the movement that had been made. He wrote also to Sir Alexander Ball, that he might send to every position in which information was likely to be obtained: "What would I give to know where they are bound to, or to see them!—the result of the meeting I should be a wretch to doubt." From the Hon. Captain Boyle he learnt that a French frigate had been standing in for Pula, but the weather was too thick to enable him to perceive the fleet. Nelson therefore thought if Cagliari was their object, he should be in time to protect the Sards.

Off the Island of Serpentari on the 25th, he wrote to Sir John Acton, expressive of the state of uncertainty in which he was placed, as to the course taken by the enemy, and of his great anxiety, which was such that he had neither ate, drank, or slept with any comfort for several days. "I hope, (he writes) the Governor of Augusta will not give up the post to the French fleet, but if he does, I shall go in and attack them, for I consider the destruction of the enemy's fleet of so much consequence, that I would willingly have half of mine burnt to effect their destruction. I am in a fever. God send

---

[1] Plunkett's History of the last Naval War, Vol. ii. p. 169.

I may find them!"[1]  Failing in gaining any intelligence, he began to conceive that the French fleet had been crippled by the gales and put back to Toulon, and he wrote his suspicions to the Admiralty on the 29th. He wrote the same to Sir Alexander Ball, suspecting they might have put into different ports. He accordingly sent off to Elba, St. Fiorenzo, Malta, Tunis, Pantolaria, &c., in short, by different vessels in every direction to ascertain their situation. "Celerity in my movements (he says), may catch those fellows yet." At the same time he anxiously directed his attention to keeping the fleet together as much as possible.

In the Dispatches and Letters,[2] Sir H. Nicolas has printed a letter of Lord Nelson's addressed to Samuel Briggs, Esq., British Consul at Alexandria. Of this there is a duplicate in the present collection of papers, from which the following is printed: and I am enabled to add to it the letter referred to, addressed to Major Misset, British Resident at Cairo, and also one to the Governor of Alexandria, which was sent written in the Italian language, the translation from the English having been made by the Rev. Mr. Scott.

"Victory, February 4th, 1805.

"Sir,

"If the French are arrived before me, you will of course not receive this letter; if they are not arrived, it is my opinion, they are dispersed and crippled in the bad weather they have experienced since their leaving Toulon.

"I have wrote to the Governor of Alexandria to be upon his guard against a visit from those gentry, for as a week ago they had not either arrived at Sardinia, Naples or Sicily, I still think their destination is either Egypt or the Morea. I may chance to fall in with them on my return, for I shall pursue the route I think they will take, but as the Governor is now put upon his guard, I hope he will take every means in his power for the defence of Alexandria, and in particular to have vessels ready to sink to prevent the entrance of the French fleet into the old port until the obstructions were removed, which would give me time to get at them.

[1] Dispatches and Letters, Vol. vi. p. 331. From a copy in the Elliot Papers.
[2] Vol. vi. p. 336.

"The French fleet sailed on the 18th of January, with from 8000 to 10,000 troops embarked. On the 19th they had a very heavy gale of wind to the westward of Corsica and Sardinia. One ship of eighty guns put into Ajaccio crippled—three others were seen steering for St. Fiorenzo. On the 21st some of them were seen off the south end of Sardinia, but I know that on the 28th, they had neither been in Sardinia nor Naples, and I was at Messina on the 30th, therefore they are either returned to Toulon, or are, I fear, arrived in Egypt, but even in that case, if Alexandria is properly defended, it cannot have yet fallen into their hands, or their fleet got into the port. If the enemy is not here I shall not remain one moment on the coast, you will therefore by the return of the boat, give me all the information you have. I shall be much obliged to you to send my letter when opportunity offers to Major Misset at Cairo.

"I am, Sir, with great respect,
"Your most obedient servant,
"NELSON AND BRONTÉ."

"Samuel Briggs, Esq., Pro-Consul."

"Victory, February 4th, 1805.

"Sir,

"The French fleet having sailed on July 18th, with from 8000 to 10,000 troops embarked, their destination not known, but generally believed to be either the Morea or Egypt, a very heavy gale of wind separated some of their ships, one of eighty guns put into Ajaccio in Corsica, and three were steering for St. Fiorenzo in the same island, the remainder of the fleet I have not heard of since they were off the south end of Sardinia, on the 21st or the 28th they had not gone to Naples. On the 31st they had not been in Sicily when I passed the Faro of Messina. The weather has been too bad for me to communicate with the Morea, although I was on the 2nd off Coron, and sent a frigate to the Pacha of that place, I have, therefore, but little doubt but that their destination is to take possession of Alexandria, when the French Consul writes that all Egypt would declare for the French against the Turks, therefore even should they not be arrived, but forced to return into port from the very bad weather they have had, yet I would strongly recommend to you to urge the Vizir or Pacha of Egypt, whatever he is called, to be upon his guard, and, in particular, to strengthen Alexandria by every means in his power, for Egypt, he may rely, is one of Buonaparte's favourite objects.

"I am come a long voyage, in search of the French, hoping to either find them in the act of attacking Alexandria, for they cannot have taken it, if it is defended, or should the French fleet be dispersed, I have shewn the obedience to my orders, in endeavouring, to the utmost of my power, to defend the Turkish dominions from the attacks of the French, and I hope they will in future be entirely upon their guard against an attack.

"You will, Sir, I am sure, enforce this matter with all your power, in the opportunities which may be offered to you, with the great men in Egypt, and I am, Sir, with great respect,

"Your most obedient servant,
"NELSON AND BRONTÉ.

"Major Misset, British Resident in Cairo."

"Victory, February 4, 1805.

"Vice-Admiral Lord Nelson, Duke of Bronté, to the much respected Governor of Alexandria:—

"Sir,

"The French fleet put to sea from Toulon, on January 18th, with from 8000 to 10,000 troops embarked in their ships of war. Their destination was unknown, but it was very generally credited, that either the Morea or Egypt was their destination. For several days after their departure, it blew a strong gale of wind, and several of the ships put into different ports. An 80-gun ship put into Ajaccio, in Corsica, and three others were seen steering for St. Fiorenzo, in the same island.

"Whether the rest of the fleet have been separated I know not, for I was too anxious, in case any part of the Turkish dominions was the object of their attack, to hasten to the assistance of the ally of my most gracious Sovereign, the mighty Sultan of the Ottoman Empire. As the French, should Alexandria be their object, could only have arrived a very few days before me, I hope it will have been defended until my arrival, when I have no doubt but the whole French armament would be destroyed; but as the fleet may have been dispersed, in the late heavy gales of wind, I most strongly recommend to your Excellency to be upon your guard against such an attack. If there is an Admiral in the port, I would strongly recommend his having vessels ready to sink in the channel, so as to prevent the French fleet from entering the harbour of Alexandria, which they certainly will endeavour to do. May victory crown your endeavours against those common enemies, is the most sincere wish of your Excellency's most faithful and obedient servant,

"NELSON AND BRONTÉ."

In a letter to Sir Alexander Ball, Lord Nelson states his reasons for considering Egypt to have been the destination of the French fleet. On the 7th of February, he was off Alexandria, having conducted the fleet through the Faro of Messina, "a thing (he says) unprecedented in nautical history; but although the danger from the rapidity of the current was great, yet so was the object of my pursuit; and I relied, with confidence, on the zeal and ability of the fleet under my command." Disappointed in his object, he felt deeply the responsibility he had incurred by the course taken in search of the enemy, and wrote to Viscount Melville on the subject; and on the 18th of February, the following to Lady Hamilton:—

"Victory, February 18th, 1805.

"My dear Emma,

"When we passed the Faro, on January 31st, I sent friend Broadbent a letter for you, and begged him to forward it to England. Your good heart will readily believe what an anxious time I have had from that period to this moment, and it is still continuing, for I have, as yet, got no tidings of the French fleet. I fear they got crippled, and returned to Toulon, for they were not used to encounter a Gulf of Lyons gale, which we have been in the practice of for these twenty months past. If they are got back, no man regrets the accident which may have happened to them more than myself, for I looked upon my meeting the French Admiral, as the end of all my toil. No man commands a fleet, more anxious to fulfil the wishes of its Chief, than the one I at present command. For this month, I have neither eat nor slept one moment in comfort. However, both the King of Naples and the Turk are obliged, by my care of their dominions. John Bull, we know, calculates nothing right that does not place the British fleet alongside that of France. By the events are we judged; however, I feel that I have done right in going to Egypt, for at this moment, I as firmly believe, that was their destination, as I believed it before, and they have now a much better chance of holding Egypt, with a few men, than they had before, when they landed 40,000, for now, every inhabitant is for them, and they were then against them, and so are the Mamelukes. I have now traversed 1000 leagues of sea after them. Our passage from Messina, round by the Morea to Alexandria, was seven days. I am, at this moment, forty-six leagues from Malta, where I shall communicate to-morrow, but not shorten a rag of canvas. French fleet, French fleet, is all I want to have answered me. I shall never rest till I find them, and they shall neither, if I can get at them. You will believe that this anxiety has not done my general health much good, but had I been absent, and the French fleet put to sea, it would have gone hard to kill me, and anxious as I am sure we are to meet, I am sure you agree with me. But I do not despair of yet getting hold of these fellows, and they shall reward me for all my trouble. Your last letter was November 2nd, since when I have not heard a scrap from England. How is Horatia? Neither she or you are ever absent from my thoughts, and all my glory will serve to give you both real happiness. God send it may be so, and soon.

"*February* 20*th*. Yesterday I was off Malta, in a gale of wind, at south-east, so that a boat could only get to one of the fleet, which brought me intelligence of the return of the French fleet, in a most crippled state, to Toulon, except one ship of the line, which is on shore at Ajaccio, and one frigate dismasted and gone to Genoa. This news was grievous enough for me, but, to-day, I received the further mortifying news, of the capture of a convoy, which sailed from Malta, January 4th. This has hurt me more than the other, but I cannot help it; no blame, I feel, attaches itself to me, whatever may be said, my conduct will bear a scrutiny. I have not heard from Naples how they take my going to Egypt; perhaps the Queen thinks it only necessary for me to look to their safety, and that I have never neglected. I do not think that she and Mr. Elliot exactly hit it off. The Court of Naples ought to be most grateful for my constant and unwearied attention to them. I am now off Maritimo, in dreadful bad weather, beating to get off Toulon. Either the enemy will be near putting to sea again, or the summer will, in a few weeks, be so far advanced, that they will not venture to move, when I shall embrace the permission of the Admiralty, and return to England for a few months, but it shall never be said of me, as it has been of another Commander-in-chief, that I gave up the command, when the enemy's fleet was actually at sea. No, I would die 10,000 deaths before such a stigma should be cast upon my character. You may believe my anxiety, not for myself, for I have nothing to reproach myself with, but I cannot bear that the French fleet should have been out and got back again.

"Yours,

"NELSON AND BRONTÉ."

For three weeks after this time, the weather was most stormy and severe. Nelson declared it the worst he had ever seen, and was only enabled to anchor in the Gulf of Palma on the 8th of March. The following day, he wrote to Lady Hamilton :—

"Victory, March 9th, 1805.

"I do assure you, my dearest Emma, that nothing can be more miserable, or unhappy, than your poor Nelson. From the 19th of February, have we been beating from Malta to off Palma, where I am now anchored, the wind and sea being so very contrary and bad. But I cannot help myself, and no one in the fleet can feel what I do: and to mend my fate,

yesterday Captain Layman arrived—to my great surprise—
not in his brig, but in a Spanish cartel, he having been
wrecked off Cadiz, and lost all the dispatches and letters.
You will conceive my disappointment! It is now from November 2nd, that I have had a line from England. Captain
Layman says, he is sure the letters are sunk, never to rise
again; but as they were not thrown overboard until the
vessel struck the rock, I have much fear that they may have
fallen into the hands of the Dons. My reports from off
Toulon state the French as still in port: but I shall ever be
uneasy at not having fallen in with them.

"I know, my dear Emma, that it is in vain to repine; but
my feelings are alive to meeting those fellows after near two
years' hard service. What a time! I could not have thought
it possible that I should have been so long absent; unwell
and uncomfortable in many respects. However, when I calculate upon the French fleet not coming to sea for this summer, I shall certainly go for dear England. Captain Layman
is now upon his trial. I hope he will come clear, with honour.
I fear it was too great confidence in his own judgment that
got him in the scrape; but it was impossible that any person
living could have exerted himself more, when in a most
trying and difficult situation."

"March 10th.

"Poor Captain Layman has been censured by the Court,
but I have my own opinion; I sincerely pity him, and have
wrote to Lord Melville and Sir Evan Nepean, to try what can
be done. Altogether, I am much unhinged.

"To-morrow, if the wind lasts, I shall be off Toulon. Sir
William Bolton is safe, I heard of him this morning. I hear
that a ship is coming out for him; but, as this is only rumour,
I cannot keep him from this opportunity of being made Post,
and I dare say, he will cause by his delay, such a tumult, that
Louis's son, who I have appointed to the Childers, will lose
his promotion, and then Sir Billy will be wished at the devil!
But, I have done with this subject; the whole history has hurt
me. Hardy has talked enough to him to rouse his lethargic
disposition.

"I have been much hurt at the loss of poor Mr. Girdlestone!¹ He was a good man; but there will be an end of us all.

"N. & B."²

His opinion was unchanged with regard to the intended destination of the French fleet having been Egypt, and he wrote to Lord Melville : "To what other country could they want to carry saddles and arms? I yet hope to meet them before I go hence ; I would die 10,000 deaths, rather than give up my command when the enemy is expected every day to be at sea."³ To Mr. Marsden, Secretary of the Admiralty, he also wrote on the 13th : "Their Lordships are fully aware of my reasons for not attending to my own health, since I have received their permission to return to England for its re-establishment. I do assure you, that no consideration for self could come into my mind when the enemy's fleet was sure of putting to sea, and they are now perfectly ready in appearance to put to sea again. Therefore, though I have suffered very much from anxiety and the very stormy winter, yet I shall either stay to fight them, which I expect every hour, or until I believe they will not come to sea for the summer, when I shall embrace their Lordship's permission, and return to England for a few months for the re-establishment of a very shattered constitution." This is printed from an autograph copy on the back of the following letter to Lady Hamilton :—

"Victory, March 13th, 1805,
off Toulon, but not in sight.

"Last night, my dearest Emma, I received your letters of September 12th by way of Naples, November 27th, December 18th, 27th, 29th, and January 8th, sent by Amphion— all those by Layman are lost. When I see you are hurt at my non-arrival, I only wish that you would for one moment call your *good* sense before you, and see if it was possible. You know I never say a thing which I do not mean, and everybody knows that all my things are on board of the Superb, and there they remain. I expected Sir John Orde was come

---

¹ A relation by marriage Eliza, a daughter of Mrs. Bolton, Lord Nelson's sister, married the Rev. Henry Girdlestone.
² Collection the Letters, Vol. ii. p. 87.
³ Clarke and McArthur, Vol. ii. p. 397.

out to relieve me, for I never could have supposed that any Admiralty would have sent any Admiral to take from me every prospect of prize-money, but my soul is beyond that consideration, compared to getting at the French fleet. But to the point, and I have done ; my leave of absence, although given the 6th of October, came to me on December 25th, Christmas-day. Before that period, I could not go, and from that moment I was well assured that the French fleet would put to sea. They did so, and only yesterday I returned off here from the pursuit of them to Egypt. I now find them ready for sea, and the troops embarked, and I am in momentary hopes of their putting to sea. Call these circumstances before you, and *judge* me.

"You will see both the King and Queen of Naples are angry with me, but I cannot help it. When I am dead, I am of no use to them, or any one else.

"Sir William Bolton is got out of the way, I made him into the Amphitrite, and he goes directly to England. I shall recommend him to Lord Melville for immediate employment. He is unlucky, not having taken a single vessel. You will remember me most kindly to Mrs. Cadogan ; I am truly sensible of her worth and attention to our interest at Merton. You cannot imagine how I long to see it, but I fear the kitchen will smell, if so, I shall build one separate from the house, and make the present one a servants' hall. I have it all in my head if I have but the money. I am glad you have seen Captain Hillyar, he would be able to tell you about Charles. I hope he will behave well, and set himself on in the world."

Nelson wrote to Collingwood from the Victory, March 13th, 1805 :—

"My dear Friend,

"Many, many thanks for your kind remembrance of me, and for your friendly good wishes, which from my heart, I can say are reciprocal. I am certainly near going to England; for my constitution is much shook, and nothing has kept me here so long but the expectation of getting at the French fleet. I am told the Rochfort squadron sailed the same day as that from Toulon. Buonaparte has often made his boast that our fleet would be worn out by keeping the sea, and that his was kept in order and increasing by staying in port: but he now finds, I fancy, if Emperors hear truth, that his fleet suffers more in a night than ours in one year. However, thank God, the Toulon fleet is got in order again, and, I hear, the troops embarked; and I hope they will come to sea in fine weather. The moment the battle is over I shall cut: and I must do the same, if I think after some weeks, they do not intend to come out for the summer. We have had a very dull war, but I agree with you that it must change for a more active one. I beg, my dear Collingwood, that you will present my most respectful compliments to Mrs. Collingwood; and believe me, for ever, and as ever,

"Your most sincere and truly attached friend,
"NELSON AND BRONTÉ."[1]

And to Lady Hamilton, on the 30th :—

"Victory, March 30th, 1805.

"Your letters, my dear Emma, by the Ambuscade, to February 15th, came to me on the 26th; and now Louis is arrived, I shall, the moment I think that the French fleet will not come to sea for the summer, put myself into the Superb, from which my things never have been taken from the time I expected the great and rich Sir John Orde. I fix in my own mind to start May 1st, for if they are not at sea in April, I think they will lay fast, unless a very superior fleet should come into the Mediterranean, when I am readier to start from England than being here, at least for actual service, but keep my intended movements to yourself, for folks like to chatter. You are sure, my Emma, that I am as anxious to see you as you can be to see me; therefore I shall say no more upon that subject. I admire dear Horatia's writing. I think her hand will soon be like her dear mother's, and if she is but as clever, I shall be content. You may rely that when I come home, I shall do what I can for Mrs. Bolton, but before I can fix a sum I must see what I have; at all events I shall be able to keep Tom[2] at College without any expense to his father; that I will certainly do, and I must economise in something at home. My letter to Lord Melville was strong

---

[1] Memoirs of Lord Collingwood, Vol. i. p. 142.
[2] Afterwards second Earl Nelson.

about Mr. Bolton, but I have had no answer; in short, I never had any interest."

Lord Nelson sailed from Pula roads on the 3rd of April, and on the 4th learnt, by the Phœbe, that the French fleet had put to sea on the 30th of March. According to the Victory's log, the ship was cleared for action on this day at 10 A.M. He, however, was unsuccessful in meeting with the French fleet, as anxiously expressed by him in the following letters to Lady Hamilton:—

"Victory, April 4th, 1805.

"My Emma, Sir W. Bolton has lost his frigate, Amphitrite,[1] and perhaps a month or two's rank as Post, but I have waited three weeks for his joining me, and the service will not admit of my waiting any longer. Luckily for him, Lord Melville has wrote me that he will send out a Post-ship for him, and therefore I hope he will suffer no harm, but it vexes me. Unless the French fleet should be at sea, or a certainty of its putting to sea, I shall move to the Superb on the day I have before told you. I shall take care not to speak any thing which may subject me to quarantine, therefore I hope a return of post, or at least two, will liberate me. Our dear Horatia, how I long to settle what I intend upon her, and not leave her to the mercy of any one, or even to any foolish thing I may do in my old age. Adieu for a very short time, and may the Heavens bless you, and give us a happy meeting, prays

"Yours,
"NELSON AND BRONTÉ."

"Victory, 9 p. m. April 5th, 1805.

"My dearest Emma,

"You will easily conceive my anxiety, and indeed misery, at not yet having fallen in with these French rascals, but I sincerely hope an end may soon be put to my misery. You shall ever glory in your Nelson, whether living or dead. I could not exist long in this dreadful suspense, but I am doing

---

[1] Captain Corbet, of the Bittern, was appointed by Lord Nelson Captain of the Amphitrite, in the room of Sir W. Bolton, and Captain Louis was transferred to the Bittern.

what man can do to find them out. God send that I may soon meet them. The ship parts. Adieu,

"Yours,

"NELSON AND BRONTÉ."

He placed frigates on the coast of Barbary, and off Toro, and laid himself half way between Galita and Sardinia, being certain that should the French fleet be bound that way, they could not have passed before that time. To Lord Melville he wrote: "I must leave as little as possible to chance, and I shall make sure they are to the eastward of me, before I risk either Sardinia, Sicily, or Naples; for they may delay their time of coming even this distance, from an expectation that I shall push for Egypt, and thus leave them at liberty to act against Sardinia, Sicily, or Naples. I have taken every thing into my most serious consideration; and although I may err in my judgment, yet your Lordship may rely, that I will do what I think is best for the honour of my King and country, and for the protection of his Majesty's Allies. I will not say more."[1] To Sir Alexander Ball he also wrote by a transport to Malta: "I am, in truth, half dead; but what man can do to find them out, shall be done; but I must not make more haste than good speed, and leave Sardinia, Sicily, or Naples for them to take, should I go either to the eastward or westward, without knowing something more about them. Ambuscade has been sent to Galita; Active to the coast of Africa; and last night, I sent Moucheron to cruise between Galita and the shore, and to go to Tunis for information; Seahorse and Ætna are off Toro; Hydra is gone along the east side of Corsica, to find out if they passed through the Straits of Bonifaccio; Ambuscade is now in sight, but not having any signal flying, of course has seen nothing; Amazon will go to Naples the moment Active joins, which I expect will be to-night or to-morrow morning; and if I still get no information, Phœbe will go off St. Sebastian, to speak my look-out ship there, and try to find out where they are—[?] to examine Toulon. I shall take a position off Istria, ready to communicate with the vessels which will join me; and by this position, to be ready to push for Naples, should they be

[1] Clarke and McArthur, Vol. ii. p. 401.

gone there, or to protect Sicily. I am very uneasy and unwell; therefore I cannot write more."[1]

His letters and orders to his Captains at this time manifest his deep anxiety, and display his extraordinary activity. He was, notwithstanding, doomed to continued disappointment, which he denominated a "severe affliction."

"Victory, April 19th, 1805.

" You will I am sure, my dearest Emma, feel for my cruel disappointment in not meeting with the French fleet, but I could not divide myself and guard Sardinia, Naples, Sicily, the Morea, and Egypt at the same time. Had I gone west, and they east, twenty-four hours start of me would have lost any of those places, and England never could have regained them. To the westward they could only get out of the Straits, and abandon the Mediterranean, in which, with their Toulon fleet, they found they could not get a move a-head of me. I may be abused by some blockheads, but I do assure you, that upon a revision of my own conduct, that *I approve*, and that is a great thing: for if a man does not approve of his own conduct, it is certain nobody else can. Sir William Bolton is now with me, waiting impatiently for the Post-ship which Lord Melville promised to send him, but I am not sure that he may have an opportunity of writing. I have received your letters by the Decade. I think it very probable that a very few days will clear me of the Mediterranean, and draw me nearer to dear Merton, my dear Emma, and Horatia.

" Yours,
" NELSON AND BRONTÉ."

His impatience breaks out in a letter to Sir Alexander Ball, written on the same day as the preceding : " My good fortune seems flown away. I cannot get a fair wind, or even a side wind. Dead foul!—dead foul! But my mind is fully made up what to do when I leave the Straits, supposing there is no certain information of the enemy's destination. The Officer who commands the prize sent from Gibraltar will tell you all the news. I believe this ill luck will go near to kill me; but

---

[1] Dispatches and Letters, Vol. vi. p. 399 ; from an autograph in the possession of Sir W. Keith Ball, Bart.

as these are times for exertions, I must not be cast down, whatever I feel."[1]

To Lieutenant-General Fox on the 20th: " Broken-hearted as I am, Sir, at the escape of the Toulon fleet, yet it cannot prevent my thinking of all the points entrusted to my care, amongst which Gibraltar stands prominent. I wish you to consider me as particularly desirous to give every comfort to the old Rock."[2] His determination upheld him, and to Lord Melville, about the same time, he wrote : " I am not made to despair—what man can do shall be done. I have marked out for myself a decided line of conduct, and I shall follow it well up; although I have now before me a letter from the Physician of the fleet, enforcing my return to England before the hot months. Therefore, notwithstanding, I shall pursue the enemy to the East or West Indies, if I know that to have been their destination, yet, if the Mediterranean fleet joins the Channel, I shall request, with that order, permission to go on shore."[3]

On the 18th he was off Toro, and on the 4th of May at Tetuan, whence he wrote the following :—

" Victory, Tetuan Bay, May 4th, 1805.

" Your poor dear Nelson is, my dearest Emma, very, very unwell. After a two years hard fag, it has been mortifying the not being able to get at the enemy—as yet I can get no information about them. At Lisbon this day week they knew nothing about them; but it is now generally believed that they are gone to the West Indies. My movements must be guided by the best judgment I am able to form—John Bull may be angry, but he never had an officer who has served him more faithfully ; but Providence truly will yet crown my never-failing exertions with success, and that it has only been a hard trial of my fortitude in bearing up against untoward events.

"NELSON AND BRONTÉ."

On the 6th he was in Gibraltar Bay, and wrote his esteemed Surgeon as follows :—

---

[1] Dispatches and Letters, Vol. vi. p. 410 ; from an autograph in the possession of John Darlington, Esq.

[2] Clarke and M'Arthur, Vol. ii. p. 404.   [3] Ibid.

"Victory, May 6th, 1805.

"Dear Sir,

"I send you Dr. Harness's letter relative to Mr. Gardner's appointment to Gibraltar Hospital. I am not only sorry for your disappointment, but also, that however able Mr. Gardner may be, I well know you would have been an invaluable acquisition to the Rock. However, I hope you will soon get some other appointment equally pleasant, and tell me if one of those Hospital (appointments) in England would be acceptable, or what you would like, and I will try what I can do, being, dear Sir, with the greatest esteem, your most faithful servant,

"NELSON AND BRONTÉ.

"I have been, and am still very, very unwell, with my sciatic complaint—return Dr. Harness's letter."

"Mr. Magrath."[1]

On the 9th he reached Lagos Bay, and on the 10th was employed in getting provisions from the Transports. Previous to his arrival here he wrote to Lady Hamilton:—

"Victory, May 9th, off Cape St. Vincent.

"My dearest Emma,

"I think myself a little better, but I can neither drink porter nor eat cheese, and that is enough to satisfy me that I am far from well; but I take no physic, bark in all ways disagrees with me, but I submit myself to the care of a good Providence, and if it is His pleasure I shall soon be restored. I have wrote Nepean[2] that they must, if I go to the West Indies send out an Admiral, for I am not able to remain there, not that I fear the country, it would agree with me as well as any other. Half the people kill themselves from fear of the climate. I hope to God I shall get hold of the French fleet. I got through the Gut on the night of the 6th, and am now anxiously waiting the return of the Amazon from Lisbon, when my final route will be determined upon.

"I approve very much the plan of the kitchen, and I hope we shall live many years to enjoy it. I send you a bill for £300., £200 of which is for yourself, and the other £100.

---

[1] Sir George Magrath, M.D., K.H., F.R.S., a retired Inspector of Hospitals and Fleets. [2] Then one of the Lords of the Admiralty.

make into little presents for me to those about you. I have sent Mrs. Bolton her £100. so nothing is necessary to be given to her. You see Lord Melville is out, and given away a Commissionership of both the Navy and Victualling Office without considering me—they none of them care for me. I may be poor, but I am honest. I could say much on that subject, but I hope we shall soon talk upon that and many other subjects. I have sent two Codicils in which you are deeply interested to Mr. Haslewood, to be placed with my Will and other Codicils, for if I kept them on board ship they might be lost, and then you and my Horatia would not get what I intend, which would embitter my last moments. May Heaven bless you.

"*Noon.* Captain Sutton has just joined. Nothing is known of the French fleet, and my destination is the West Indies, and I only wait to see the troops under Admiral Knight[1] round the Cape. I have wrote to Nepean that I must be relieved. The Lively, Captain Hamond,[2] I find has passed the fleet for Gibraltar. Once more God bless you,

"Yours,

"NELSON AND BRONTÉ."

---

[1] Sir John Knight accompanied his father, Rear-Admiral Knight, to sea in 1758, and served in the Tartar frigate in the expeditions against Cancelle, Cherbourg, &c. He was in the squadron with Lord Anson, escorting Queen Charlotte to this country in 1761, and was engaged on the maritime survey of the coast of North America. In the Falcon he assisted in covering the attack on Bunker's Hill, soon after which he was taken prisoner and detained several months in Massachusetts. In 1777, he was appointed by Lord Howe to the Haerlem, and afterwards to the Eagle, bearing the flag of his Lordship. He was then made First Lieutenant of the Barfleur, the flag-ship of Sir Samuel Hood; was made Post Captain, September 21st, 1781, and appointed to the Shrewsbury of 74 guns. He was in all the exploits of Sir Samuel Hood in 1781 and 1782, and in the battle with the Count de Grasse, was moved from the Shrewsbury into the Barfleur with the Admiral. In this vessel Prince William Henry served as Midshipman, and formed great intimacy with Captain Knight, under whose tuition he was placed. In 1790 he was Flag Captain to Lord Hood in the Victory, and in the Revolutionary War was in the Mediterranean. Here he saw much service, and in 1797 was appointed to the Montagu, one of the ships whose company mutinied at Spithead. The spirit of insubordination subdued, Captain Knight had a command on the coast of Ireland; then in the Channel Fleet, and on the Mediterranean Station under Lords St. Vincent, Bridport, and Keith. He then commanded a squadron off Brest. On January 1st, 1801, he was made a Rear-Admiral; Vice-Admiral, December 4th, 1813; and K.C.B. January 2nd, 1815. He died Admiral of the Red, June 16th, 1832.

[2] Admiral Sir Graham Eden Hamond, Bart., K.C.B, is the present senior

"My dearest Emma,

"In case any thing should happen to the Wasp who is going to England with my dispatches and your letters, I send a duplicate of the draft upon Marsh and Creed, and I beg you to send Mrs. Bolton's to her. I have wrote her a line by the Wasp. We are hard at work victualling the fleet to five months, and hope to start to-morrow. May God be propitious to my wishes, and send me a victor—then, and not till then, can I be happy. Kiss my dear Horatia for me.

"Yours,

"NELSON AND BRONTË."

The letter to Mrs. Bolton is printed in Sir H. Nicolas's collection of Dispatches and Letters,[2] and runs thus:—

"Victory, May 9th, 1805.

"My dear Sister,

"God only knows where I may be on July 1st, and, therefore, I send you a bill for £100; and when I get home, I hope to be able to keep Tom at College without one farthing's expense to Mr. Bolton; and both you and him may be assured, that I would do more if in my power. I should have been a very rich, instead of a very poor man, if Lord

---

Admiral of the Blue, and is the son of Sir A. S. Hamond, Bart. (See Vol. I. p. 110, note). He was born in London in 1779, and saw much service with his father, and his cousin, Sir A. S. Douglas. He was made Lieutenant in the Britannia of 100 guns, July 23rd, 1795, and November 30th, 1798, made a Post Captain. He distinguished himself greatly in the Blanche at Copenhagen in 1801; returned to England with Sir Hyde Parker, was then attached to the Channel Fleet with Admiral Cornwallis, and after the Peace of Amiens engaged on the coast of Cornwall and Devonshire to suppress smuggling. He attended upon the Royal family at Weymouth, and afterwards visited France. In 1803 in the Plantagenet, he captured the Courier de Terre Neuve, and the Atalante, and returned to England from ill health. In 1804 he was appointed to the Lively, and joined Admiral Cornwallis off Brest, and afterwards had a rencontre with some Spanish ships. He was then stationed off Cadiz, and off Cape St. Vincent captured the San Miguel, a most valuable prize. He brought home in March, 1805, all the specie and bullion that had been captured from the Spaniards, amounting to near five millions of dollars, and arrived safely at Spithead on the 15th of April. In 1808 he was in command of the Victorious, and assisted at the capture of Flushing. His health had become so much impaired, that he was under the necessity of returning to England.

[2] Vol. vi. p. 429.

Melville had not given the galleons to Sir John Orde. God bless you, Mr. Bolton, and family; and believe me ever,

"Your most affectionate Brother,
"NELSON AND BRONTÉ."

He sailed on the 11th for the West Indies, thus pursuing the French fleet, which consisted of 18 sail of the line, with only 10 sail of the line. He wrote again to Lady Hamilton :—

"Victory, May 13th, 1805.
70 Leagues W.S.W. from Cape St. Vincent.

"My dearest Emma,

"No letter from any person for England could have left the Victory from the day we passed the Faro, January 31st to March 16th, when the Renown went to Gibraltar. Mr. Marsden, when you recollect his situation, cannot tell you any thing, and if he did, as has been the case at present, he must pretend to know exactly where I was, or it would soon get over London and to France. He is very much hurt that you are offended with him, for not telling you if I am alive or dead, and when he makes a story on purpose, as he thinks, to please you, by telling you I am well, &c. &c. &c., then you are angry. You should have known that it was impossible that I could write *alone* to him; but I will have done with this subject which, under my present cruel situation, almost cut my feeble thread of life.

"The Marquis Circello and Abbé Campbell came on board for a minute in a gale of wind, and with them your letters. I do assure you, that both my health and the arrangement of my affairs, independent of my inclination, demand my serious consideration. I know I am most deeply in debt to Davison, and I want his account that I may close it, for it must not run on in the way it has done, but I cannot get it, nor do I know how I stand with their banking house, I get no account; but things will be on a new footing when I get to dear Merton. I suppose if I do not find the French fleet that I shall be tried. They may do as they please, they will find none who has served them more faithfully, and this going to the West Indies ought to be a proof it, for it must be everything but a party of pleasure to me, but I am sure you will approve of my conduct, however we may feel the consequences. I write this in case of meeting any vessel bound to England, when I shall close it.

"*May* 20*th.* Nothing yet have we seen, we are running nine miles *per hour*, 700 leagues from Barbadoes. Sutton, of the Amphion, is with us. I am, as you will believe, very, very uneasy and anxious, but I hope it will all end well. Kiss dear Horatia for me, I never forget for a moment either you or her.

"NELSON AND BRONTÉ."

As he had anticipated he arrived at Barbadoes on the 4th of June, and then was informed that the French fleet was in the West Indies. He wrote to Lady Hamilton:—

"Victory, off Carlisle Bay, Barbadoes,
June 4th, 1805.

"My dearest Emma,

"I find myself within six days of the enemy, and I have every reason to hope that the 6th of June will immortalize your own Nelson. May God send me victory, and us a happy and speedy meeting. Admiral Cochrane is sending home a vessel this day, therefore only pray for my success.

"Yours,
"NELSON AND BRONTÉ.

"The enemy's fleet and army are supposed to have attacked Tobago and Trinidad, and are now about landing."

Lady Hamilton received a Barbadoes Gazette of the date of the 5th, having the following lines:—

"*Barbadoes Gazette*, 5*th June*, 1805.

"Whisper but Nelson in a Frenchman's ear,
And straight from head to foot he quakes with fear.
Sailors and soldiers all agree together,
To run away, and never mind the weather.
Their very ships, spontaneous crowd each sail.
Their anchors leave, and scud before the gale.
From Isle to Isle no more they dare to roam,
And their fixed rudders steer no course but home.
Villeneuve,[1] a second time, declines the fight,
And saves himself by ignominious flight."

[1] Ran away from Lord Nelson at the Nile, in the Guillaume Tell of 84 guns.

Nelson's expectations were however to be sadly crushed. When he arrived at Barbadoes, he received letters of information which had been sent to Lieutenant-General Sir William Myers,[1] Commander-in-chief in the Leeward Islands, from Dominica and St. Lucia, and stated, "I have this moment received a report from the windward side of Gros Islet, that the enemy's fleet, of twenty-eight sail in all, passed there last night. Their destination, I should suppose, must be either Barbadoes or Trinidad. R. BRERETON." The above passage which formed a P. S. to a letter, was written by Major Myers, the General's Secretary, and the Major said that he had no doubt but that the intelligence might be relied on. The General offered to embark 2000 troops, which offer Nelson readily accepted. Lord Nelson highly eulogised General Myers' conduct, saying, in a letter to the Earl Camden: "However unhappy I may feel at not having got up with the enemy's fleet, yet I should think myself very remiss if I failed to inform your Lordship, and to request you to inform his Majesty, of the very spirited conduct of Lieutenant-General Sir William Myers, who offered to embark on board the fleet 2000 troops, in order to try and annihilate both the enemy's fleet and army, had we fortunately found them in any of our islands. The zeal of the Lieutenant-General, and the whole body of troops, was such as could not be exceeded, and it is a matter of sincere regret that we have not met with the enemy. But great merit is not less due to the Lieutenant-General, for the expedition with which the troops were collected from different parts of Barbadoes, and to the officers and men for the cheerfulness with which they embarked."[2]

On the 5th of June Lord Nelson made the general signal to prepare for battle. On the 6th at 6-10 A.M. a schooner made signal for the enemy being at Trinidad. This arose from an accident which is detailed in Clarke and McArthur's Life of Lord Nelson:—

"On the 6th of June the fleet arrived off Great Courland Bay, Tobago; and Captain Henderson of the Pheasant sloop was directed to proceed with all expedition to Port Toko in

---

[1] He died in July, 1825.
[2] Clarke and McArthur, Vol. ii. p. 411.

Trinidad, to send a boat on shore with Sir William Myers' letters, for information whether the enemy were in the Gulf of Paria, and to communicate by signal with the Admiral in the morning. At Tobago all was bustle and apparent uncertainty, when in addition the following singular occurrence took place. A Merchant, particularly anxious to ascertain whether the fleet was that of a friend or enemy, had prevailed on his Clerk, with whom he had also agreed respecting signals, to embark in a schooner, and to stand towards it; and it unfortunately happened, that the very signal made by the Clerk corresponded with the affirmative signal which had been agreed on by Colonel Shipley, of the enemy being at Trinidad. It was the close of the day, and no opportunity occurred of discovering the mistake. An American merchant brig also had been spoken with, the same day, by the Curieux, probably sent to mislead, whose Master reported that he had been boarded a few days before by the French fleet off Granada, standing towards the Bocaz of Trinidad. No doubts were any longer entertained, the news flew throughout the British squadron, the ships were ready for action before daybreak, and Nelson anticipated a second Aboukir in the Bay of Paria. If further confirmation was necessary, it appeared in the seeming conflagration of one of our outposts at daylight, and the party retreating towards the citadel. The Admiral and Officers of his squadron, after such corroboration, felt it difficult to believe the evidence of their senses, when, on entering the Gulf of Paria on the 7th, no enemy was to be seen, nor had any been there."[1]

Off St. Lucia, on the 10th, he wrote to Lady Hamilton:—

"Victory, off St. Lucia, June 10th, 1805.

"Your own dear Nelson, my Emma, is very sad—the French fleet have again escaped me. It appears hard to have had the cup at my lip, and to have it dashed from me. When I wrote you a line from Barbadoes, I would not have given one farthing to have assured a battle. The information from St. Lucia, as you will see by the newspaper, was doubted by none. How I grieve at the arrival of that news, nothing could have prevented my getting at them on the 6th; long

[1] Vol. ii. p. 409.

ago it would have been all over, and your Nelson have added, I doubt not, another sprig of laurel to his brow, or his memory; but it has pleased God to order it otherwise. I sailed at eight o'clock in the morning of the 5th, with Lieutenant-General Sir W. Myers, and 2000 troops on board. On the 6th we were at Tobago, where they had heard of the enemy being at sea, and they supposed them to have arrived at Trinidad on the day before. I now was sure, and every thing was fully prepared to decide the contest, twelve to eighteen; but lo! on the 7th, when the fleet got into the Gulf of Paria, the enemy were not there, but we received an express that they were to sail from Martinico on the 5th for Granada and Trinidad. They did sail in the night of the 5th, but not for Granada, but I fancy to try and effect their escape. On the 8th at daylight, I sailed from Trinidad, and on the 9th at noon, I was at St. George's, Granada, where I received the mortifying news that on the 6th the enemy, eighteen sail of the line, six frigates and three brigs and schooners, were under Dominica; on the 7th they were under Guadaloupe. I am carrying every rag, but my hopes are very faint, although I must not despair. If they should attempt Antigua I shall be up with them, and if they run I may, by good fortune, overtake them before they get to Europe. However mortified I may individually feel at not fighting them, yet my happy arrival has saved all our West India islands and commerce. My services have benefited the country, although it brings neither honour nor riches to me—the latter is given by two Admiraltys' to others, how well deserved to have been taken from me time will shew. You will talk of this letter with prudence, for the public must not know, at least from you, of my movements; but I know my Emma is to be trusted with any secret. I shall fill this up as we get on, and write you another line before the vessel parts from the fleet.

"*June* 11*th.*—We are under Montserratt, whence the enemy were seen beating to windward on Saturday. God knows their intention, but I still think it is to get out of my way: it has almost broke my heart. I shall hear from Antigua to-day.

"Yours,

"NELSON AND BRONTÉ."

"Victory, 7 P.M, June 12th, 1805."

" My own Emma,

" I have just anchored in St. John's road to land the troops, and the moment they are on shore I am after Gravina, and I really hope to catch him before he gets to Cadiz.

" Yours,

" NELSON AND BRONTÉ."

To Lord Robert Fitzgerald, the Minister at Lisbon, he gives a summary of his movements : " I arrived at Barbadoes, June 4th, where I found Lieutenant-General Sir William Myers, who the night before had received information from Brigadier General Brereton, at St. Lucia, that twenty-eight sail of the enemy's fleet had been seen to windward of St. Lucia, steering to the southward. As there was no reason to doubt this information, the General offered to embark himself, with 2000 troops, for the relief of either Tobago or Trinidad, which was supposed to be the intended objects of the enemy's attack. On the 6th, we were off Tobago ; on the 7th, at Trinidad ; on the 8th, I received an account that the enemy had not moved on the 4th from Port Royal, but were expected to sail that night for the attack on Granada. On the 9th, I was at Granada, when I received a letter from General Prevost to say, that the enemy had passed Dominica on the 6th, and standing to the northward, to the leeward of Antigua, and took that day a convoy of fourteen sail of sugar-loaded ships, which unfortunately left St. John's in the night, for England. On the 11th, I was at Montserratt, and, at sunset of the 12th, anchored at St. John's, Antigua, to land the troops, which was done on the morning of the 13th, and at noon I sailed in my pursuit of the enemy ; and I do not yet despair of getting up with them before they arrive at Cadiz or Toulon, to which ports I think they are bound, or, at least, in time to prevent them from having a moment's superiority. I have no reason to blame Dame Fortune. If either General Brereton could not have wrote, or his look-out man had been blind, nothing could have prevented my fighting them on June the 6th ; but such information, and from such a quarter, close to the enemy, could not be doubted."[1]

[1] Dispatches and Letters, Vol. vi. p. 456. From copies in the possession of the Right Honourable Sir George Rose, G.C.H., and Captain Gambier.

The vessel conveying the preceding letter carried also the following to London to Lady Hamilton :—

> "Victory, June 16th, 1805.
> 130 leagues from Antigua.

"As I am sending a vessel to Lisbon, and a letter to the Admiralty to tell them I am so far on my return, I would not, you are sure, omit writing you a line, although it will probably be a long while in reaching you. I yet hope that I shall send a frigate with good news, for why may I not at last be so fortunate as to get up with the enemy's fleet? Ah! my Emma, June 6th would have been a great day to me had I not been led astray by false information. It is not worth sixpence, and I have ever found, if I was left and acted as my poor noddle told me was right, I should seldom err. My genius carried me direct to the spot, and all would have been as well as heart could wish, when comes across the General Brereton's information. I shall give up the command to Sir Richard Bickerton, if they are arrived before me, and so I have wrote the Admiralty, and proceed to England. I may be abused and neglected, but I have served the country most faithfully.

"*June* 18*th*.—As my letters are closed to the Admiralty, I can tell you what no one knows, that the French fleet are at this moment not eighty leagues from me. May God Almighty send us up with them. My Emma shall not blush for the conduct of her faithful

"NELSON AND BRONTÉ.

"Kiss my Horatia. Farewell,—farewell."

To ascertain whether the enemy's fleet from the West Indies had entered the Mediterranean, Lord Nelson sent Captain Sutton, of the Amphion, to Tangier Bay, to gain intelligence of the Consul at Tangiers, whether they had passed the Straits or gone to Cadiz. He sent also Captain Parker, of the Amazon, by Cape St. Vincent, Cape St. Mary's, and off Cadiz, for the same purpose. But no French fleet. He was very sorrowful; miserable at not having fallen in with the enemy. On the 19th he arrived in Gibraltar Bay, and on the following day wrote to Lady Hamilton :—

"Victory, Gibraltar, July 20th, 1805.

"My dearest Emma,

"I am sure that you will feel my most severe affliction in not having met the enemy's fleet. My misery is extreme, but my heart and head tell me I have done right. Whatever may be the judgment of my country I bow to it with submission. Had I followed the decision of my own *noddle* I should have been right, but I was forced from circumstances to follow the information of others against my own better judgment. I tell you, my Emma, my feelings, but I know your dear affectionate sensible heart, will have felt all my misery. The moment the fleet is watered and victualled I shall get outside the Straits, and then when I know that the enemy is arrived in any port in Europe, I shall proceed to England, as I have this day wrote the Admiralty, for the re-establishment of my health.

"The Generals and Commissioner having been on board to make me a visit, I have been forced against my inclination to set my feet upon the Rock to return their visits. It took me three hours hard work, but, thank God, I am got into my cabin again, and my next step on shore will, I hope, be Portsmouth, and then to dear Merton.

"Yours,
"NELSON AND BRONTÉ.

"I find by letters from Naples that they are in a desperate state, and longing for my return to protect them. I have only a moment, this goes by a merchant brig. I shall write in a few days by Prévoyante, Mr. McCoy, who has executed his commission in shaking hands with me, as he said you desired him when you shook hands with him. All my letters are, I find, gone to England."

In his private diary Lord Nelson records: "I went on shore for the first time since the 16th of June, 1803; and from having my foot out of the Victory, two years, wanting ten days." On this occasion he was accompanied by his Chaplain, and paid visits to the Governor, Sir Richard Bickerton, General Drummond, and others. He now learnt that Lord Barham had been appointed First Lord of the Admiralty, in the room of Lord Melville, and he wrote to his Lordship suggesting the necessity of establishing some regular and permanent force at Gibraltar. Vice-Admiral Collingwood having conceived the views of the French to be directed towards Ireland, and that the French fleet had gone to the West Indies in order to draw off the naval force, Lord Nelson was very anxious to communicate with Collingwood on the subject. He wrote to Mr. Marsden in despair: "I am as completely miserable as my greatest enemy could wish me; but I neither blame fortune, nor my own judgment. Oh, General Brereton! General Brereton!" On the 23rd he wrote to Lord Barham: "The fleet is complete, and the first easterly wind, I shall pass the Straits. I have yet not a word of information of the enemy's fleet: it has almost broke my heart. But the name of General Brereton will never be forgot by this generation; but for him our battle would have been fought on June 6th. The event would have been in the hands of Providence; but we may without, I hope, vanity, believe that the enemy would have been fit for no active service after such a battle. All our losses which have happened, or may happen, are entirely to be attributed to his information."[1]

He wrote to Lady Hamilton on the 24th:—

"Victory, July 24th, off Ceuta.

"I wrote you on the 20th, my Emma, by a merchant brig, under cover to Mr. Marsden, and I think she will get home safe. All my toils will probably end in abuse, but I feel I do not deserve any censure. We have been to Tetuan to water the fleet, and to get some refreshments for our poor fellows who have much of the scurvy. I sailed this morning, and I hope in the night to pass through the Straits. The moment I find the enemy are safe in port, and out of my reach, that moment I shall set off for England, but I am dreadfully uneasy. I have reason to hate the name of General Brereton as long as I live, and perhaps our country for ever, but it is vain to repine and fret myself ill. I know this too well but I cannot help it. The name and circumstances absolutely haunt me.

"*July* 25*th*. This morning in the Gut, Captain Pettit of

[1] Dispatches and Letters, Vol vi p. 489. From a Press Copy in the possession of the Right Honourable John Wilson Croker.

the Termagant, brought an account that the French fleet had been seen standing to the northward. I am just going off Cadiz to give some orders to Admiral Collingwood, and to dispatch the Pickle schooner to the Admiralty, with an account that I am steering for Ireland or England, as I may hear my services may be most wanted.

"Yours,
"NELSON AND BRONTÉ."

Lady Hamilton received intelligence at this time from Mr. Gibbs of the good condition of the Bronté estate, the rent of which had been considerably increased without distressing the Brontese, and more money had been remitted to the bankers than in any preceding year.

Lord Nelson breaks out to his friend Mr. Davison at his ill luck in not meeting with the French fleet. He says: "I am as miserable as you can conceive. But for General Brereton's damned information, Nelson would have been, living or dead, the greatest man in his profession that England ever saw. Now alas! I am nothing—perhaps shall incur censure for misfortunes which may happen, and have happened. When I follow my own head, I am, in general, much more correct in my judgment than following the opinion of others. I resisted the opinion of General Brereton's information, till it would have been the height of presumption to have carried my disbelief further. I could not in the face of Generals and Admirals go north-west, when it was *apparently* clear that the enemy had gone south. But I am miserable. I now long to hear that they are arrived in some port in the Bay; for until they have arrived somewhere, I can do nothing but fret. Then I shall proceed to England. I can say nothing, or think of any thing, but the loss my country has sustained by General Brereton's unfortunate, ill-timed, false information."[1]

On the 24th, Lord Nelson learnt that the "Combined fleet had been seen by the Curieux brig, on the 19th, standing to the northward. Having passed the Straits on the 25th, and communicated with Admiral Collingwood, the squadron under Lord Nelson bore away to the westward, and then pro-

[1] From an autograph in the possession of Colonel Davison.

ceeded off Cape St. Vincent, with a view to go more northward, or to act as circumstances of intelligence might render necessary."

Failing thus in his endeavours to meet with the French fleet in the West Indies and other places to which he had directed his pursuit, he now made his way from Gibraltar to Ushant, having, as noted in his Diary, " run from Barbuda, day by day, 3459 miles: from Cape St. Vincent to Barbadoes, 3227 miles ; so that our run back was only 232 miles more than our run out—allowance being made for the difference of the latitudes and longitudes of Barbadoes and Barbuda ; average, *per diem*, thirty-four leagues, wanting nine miles." On the voyage home they celebrated the anniversary of the Battle of the Nile by the performance of a Play.

The following was addressed by Mr. Pearce[1] to Lady Hamilton :—

" Admiralty Office, 5th August, 1805.

" My dear Madam,

" The combined fleet has certainly steered to the southward. Sir Robert Calder's letters[2] of the 31st of July report that he has lost sight of them: they are not in Ferrol nor Rochfort; the opinion is, therefore, that they have pushed for Cadiz. With a heart anxious for the glory of England, and

---

[1] Chief Clerk in the Admiralty, and the Author of several Dramatic Pieces, among which may be mentioned, Netley Abbey, the Midnight Wanderers, Windsor Castle, Hartford Bridge, Arrived at Portsmouth, &c.

[2] Sir Robert Calder had, off Cape Finisterre, on the 22nd of July, had an action with the enemy, and captured two Spanish ships of the line. The Vice-Admiral was severely censured for not having renewed the action, and by a Court-Martial was sentenced to be severely reprimanded. The generosity of Nelson's character is strongly exhibited on this occasion, in a letter to Captain Fremantle. He says: " I was in truth bewildered by the account of Sir Robert Calder's victory, and the joy of the event ; together with the hearing that *John Bull* was not content, which I am sorry for. Who can, my dear Fremantle, command all the success which our country may wish ? We have fought together, and therefore well know what it is. I have had the best disposed fleet of friends, but who can say what will be the event of a battle ? And it most sincerely grieves me, that in any of the papers it should be insinuated, that Lord Nelson could have done better. I should have fought the enemy, so did my friend Calder ; but who can say that he will be more successful than another ? I only wish to stand upon my own merits, and not by comparison, one way or the other, upon the conduct of a brother officer. You will forgive this dissertation, but I feel upon the occasion."— (From a Press Copy in the possession of the Right Hon. J. W. Croker.)

sincerely attached to Lord Nelson, I entertain a strong hope that he may fall in with them. May every success that your ardent and anxious mind may predict attend our champion on the ocean.

"I remain, dear Madam,

"Your faithful and sincere servant,

"WILLIAM PEARCE.

"You will hear this information from other sources; but I write that you may have some confidence in it, and I will not omit further communication if necessary."

Sir William Bolton also wrote from Gibraltar:—

"H.M.S. Guerrier, Sept. 8th, 1805.

"Dear Madam,

"It is with heartfelt pleasure I learnt his Lordship's safe arrival in town, but I felt a stronger sensation at finding Cobbett, in his paper, directing the attention of the public to the virtues of a friend we all so deservedly venerate. I cannot help smiling at this singular beginning to your Ladyship, but, or I am mistaken, your Ladyship feels greater pleasure in the smallest addition to my noble Patron's glory, than in any compliment my weak pen can address to yourself. I will not, therefore, offer it an excuse.

"It is generally believed here, that his Lordship sails for this country some time this month; in which case a letter could not reach him in England. Should I, therefore, be out in my conjecture, I trust to your Ladyship's known goodness to present him my grateful respects. I am full of hopes from his Lordship's being in town, he will have it in his power (he ever had the will) to take me out of the Guerrier. I heard from my dear Lady Bolton about the middle of July. My letters from Norfolk are all full of the praises of my Emma. With so generous a friend as your Ladyship has approved yourself, and surrounded as they are by papas and mammas, to me absence seems deprived of half its *désagrément*, and should our own Admiral come to us again, I verily believe the remaining half would be felt no more: but your Ladyship will not be so cruel to tell Kate so. The Rock is still perfectly healthy, and every prospect of continuing so this summer, to the general satisfaction of the inhabitants.

Isolated as we are, I can have nothing in the shape of news to communicate, but remain,

"Dear Madam,
"Your most obliged,
"WILLIAM BOLTON."

On the 15th Lord Nelson joined the Channel Fleet under Admiral Cornwallis. His squadron, with the exception of the Victory and Superb, were left with the fleet, and he proceeded in the former to Spithead, where he arrived on the 18th. He then wrote the following:—

"Victory, Spithead, August 18th, 1805.

"I am, my dearest Emma, this moment anchored, and as the post will not go out until eight o'clock, and you not get the letter till eleven or twelve o'clock to-morrow, I have ordered a Post-office express to tell you of my arrival. I hope we shall be out of quarantine to-morrow, when I shall fly to dear Merton. You must believe all I would say, and fancy what I think; but I suppose this letter will be cut open, smoked, and perhaps read. I have not heard from you since last April by Abbé Campbell. I have brought home no honour for my country, only a most faithful servant; nor any riches —that the Administration took care to give to others—but I have brought home a most faithful and honourable heart. The boat is waiting, and I must finish. This day two years and three months I left you. God send us a happy meeting, as our parting was sorrowful.

"Ever yours,
"NELSON AND BRONTÉ."

The Duke of Queensberry, a near relation of Sir William Hamilton, was anxious immediately to receive him. But he, being in quarantine, could not proceed to London,[1] and on the 19th, wrote to Lady Hamilton:—

"Victory, Motherbank, August 19th, 1805.

"I am now, my dearest Emma, in quarantine, for the first

[1] During his last stay in England, he dined away from Merton Place only twice, once with the Duke of Queensberry, and once with Mr. Abraham Goldsmid at Morden.

time of my life, and I never could have been more mortified by it, but whatever we may feel, we must submit—*none* can come to us, nor we go to any one. I hope to be out of quarantine to-morrow forenoon, for we have not a sick man. You may believe I shall not stay ten minutes in Portsmouth, only to bow to the Commander-in-chief and the Commissioner, whilst the post-chaise is preparing. The Admiralty leave is arrived, but nothing can be done without an Order in Council, and I cannot be at Merton before nine o'clock, and not by that time if we have not Pratique, therefore do not expect me after that hour.

" I have this moment got yours of last night from Merton. I shall rejoice to see dear Horatia, Charlotte, and Ann and Eliza, and I would not have my Emma's relative go without my seeing her.

" Mr. Marsden has just sent me your letter of August 10th. I must write a line to the Doctor, as he is in Norfolk. I shall only say, may Heaven send us a speedy meeting, and a happy one.

" Ever yours,
" NELSON AND BRONTÉ."

To his brother he wrote: " You will have heard of our arrival, but I know you would like better to have it under my hand. I am but so, so—yet, what is very odd, the better for going to the West Indies, even with the anxiety. We must not talk of Sir Robert Calder's battle : I might not have done so much with my small force. If I had fallen in with them, you would probably have been a Lord before I wished; for I know they meant to make a dead set at the Victory."[1]

[1] Clarke and McArthur, Vol. ii. p. 419.

## CHAPTER XI.

### 1805.

LORD Nelson arrived at Merton, on the morning of the 20th, and Lady Hamilton received the following letter of congratulation from Mrs. Lutwidge, upon his arrival:—

"Holmrock, August 25th, 1805.

"A thousand congratulations to the charming Emma, upon the return of that dear friend, and very great hero, Lord Nelson. How my Admiral and self envy every person in the south, who have had the happiness of greeting his arrival; indeed, I know not a higher gratification than being blest with a sight (even had we not the happiness of knowing him) after the very signal and new act of service he has performed towards his country. Here, we look upon his having drove the French from the West Indies, as one of the greatest possible conquests,[1] and he has shewn the world, that he is able to perform as much by his name alone, as he has hitherto done by feats of arms. We sigh, at the impossibility of seeing this truly great man, and dear friend, at our humble mansion, because his country must look up to him, as its greatest support and protection, and, therefore, in times like these, he cannot be suffered to remain unemployed, but should the fates ever permit him to steer northward, the most welcome reception will attend him and the fascinating

---

[1] This opinion was entertained by a body most interested in, and most capable of forming an accurate judgment on the occasion. At a Meeting of West India Merchants, convened on the 23rd of August, Sir Richard Neave, Bart, in the Chair, it was unanimously agreed, "That the prompt determination of Lord Nelson, to quit the Mediterranean in search of the French fleet: his sagacity in judging of, and ascertaining, their course; and his bold and unwearied pursuit of the combined French and Spanish squadrons to the West Indies, and back again to Europe; have been very instrumental to the safety of the West India Islands in general, and well deserve the grateful acknowledgments of every individual connected with these colonies; and that a deputation from the Committee of Merchants of London, trading to the West Indies, be appointed to wait upon Vice-Admiral Lord Nelson, to express these their sentiments, and to offer him their unfeigned thanks."

Emma, also at Holmrock, and at Muncaster too. As English folk, that noble family feel the utmost admiration and gratitude towards Lord Nelson, and when they hear the Admiral and self talk of his Lordship, they love him very sincerely. We kept the glorious 1st, quite in style. All the neighbours round the country were assembled, *chez-nous*. My Admiral filled a great bumper, he was followed by Lord Muncaster and all the party. 'The Hero of the Nile,' was drank in three times three, with hip, hip, hip, and all the &c.'s. I believe my jollity, on the occasion, surprised some of my country neighbours; and now, my dearest Emma, I must tell you, that the Admiral and myself are dying with impatience to hear that Lord Nelson's health has not suffered from his exertions and fatigue, in his country's service; and you will much oblige us both, should you have a moment's leisure, with this comforting intelligence; in the mean time, have the goodness to remember us with every kind wish, most tenderly to his Lordship: and believe me, my dear Lady Hamilton, no person can more sincerely participate in his Lordship's return, and the joy it must cause, than your truly obliged and affectionate

"C. LUTWIDGE."

The following was addressed to Lord Nelson, from Mr. Bulkeley:—

"Pencombe, Bromyard, Monday 26th August, 1805.

"Many thanks to you, my dear friend, for your short but most comprehensive letter, mine to Captain Hardy was *conditional*, as to Richard's leave of absence, and the conditions, such as I suppose, from the present posture of affairs, will prevent his allowing him to visit me; but should he have complied, you may depend on my not detaining him from his duty, or exposing him to any risks from love. I must not omit, in this place, giving you Richard's own words, in his letter to me, on his arriving at Spithead. 'I solicit you to write directly to Lord Nelson, and return him your grateful thanks for the unexampled attention, conduct and fatherly affection, which he has marked towards me ever since I have had the honour of sailing with him, expressly mention how warmly I feel it.' Need I, my dear Lord, say more, the boy's sentiments correspond most perfectly with those that I feel.

"The last sentence in your letter grieves and vexes me; surely the crisis is sufficiently alarming for Ministers, in defiance of personal partiality or private interest, to prefer the country's good, and to give *its best hope* a *carte blanche*. You have put us out of conceit with all other Admirals. Look into your own acts and read the public papers for the last four months, then judge if John Bull will consent to give up *his sheet anchor*. We must not be imbecile at sea, as we are in the Cabinet.

"Pray tell me, if you received a book upon the subject of increasing seamen for the navy. I think I sent it by Captain Layman. Have you got any letter since your arrival at the Admiralty from me?

"All here join in best wishes and compliments to you. God bless you,—may we soon hear of your thunders.

"Your most affectionate and faithful friend,
"RICHARD BULKELEY."

The Duke of Clarence visited Lord Nelson at Merton. Mr. Beckford was very anxious to receive him:—

"Fonthill, 30th August, 1805.

"You may easily imagine, my dear Lady Hamilton, how anxiously I wish to catch sight of our glorious friend's benign and commanding countenance. To expect he could immediately, at such a moment as this, lift up its light at Fonthill is too much.

"I consider the pressure in ten thousand shapes of these imperious times; but see Lord Nelson I must, and it was not flourish or compliment, when I assured his Lordship, in my scrawl of the other day, that nothing but the apprehension of intruding upon any of the more sacred important hours he owes his country, kept me back. However, I am certain, his goodness is such that he will excuse my breaking in upon him, for a few minutes, and allow me to ask him, how he does, after his almost incredible exertions, and to tell him again and again, that if it were possible for him to bestow a day or two upon Fonthill, I should feel the proudest and happiest of beings.

"I am going to see Windsor with Wyatt, who has been passing a week here, and next Tuesday or Wednesday, at farthest, I propose reaching my old quarters, at the hotel, Berkeley Square.

"Will my dear Lady Hamilton have the goodness and graciousness to let me know where we can meet, and at what hour?

"Ever believe me, most constantly,
"Sincerely and affectionately yours,
"W. B."

The following was Lord Nelson's reply to Mr. Beckford's invitation:—

"Merton, August 31st, 1805.

"My dear Mr. Beckford,

"Many thanks for your kind letter. Nothing could give me more pleasure than paying my respects at Fonthill, but I cannot move at present, as all my family are with me, and my stay is very uncertain, besides, I have refused for the present, all invitations. Every ship, even the Victory, is ordered out, for there is an entire ignorance, whether the Ferrol fleet is coming to the northward, gone to the Mediterranean, or cruising for our valuable homeward bound fleet. I hope they will be met with, and annihilated. Lady Hamilton desires me to present her kind regards, and believe me, ever, my dear Mr. Beckford, your much obliged friend,

"NELSON AND BRONTÉ."

Admiral Louis wrote to Lord Nelson:—

"Canopus, off Cadiz, August 31st, 1805.

"My Lord,

"Here I am performing the great character off Cadiz with a part of your Lordship's squadron, keeping a watch upon the *enemy's* movements. They consist of thirty-five sail of the line, in all forty-six sail, frigates, &c. &c. I cannot help saying that I wish, and expect very soon, to see your Lordship's handwriting at the bottom of my order, believe me, it would be one of the first comforts I could name. Stopford,[1] Hallowell, Bayntun,[2] and Malcolm, form my party. You will say, I am a very fortunate fellow to have such valuable and good company. Believe me, my Lord, I feel it, and to complete the *whole* would be the sight of your Lordship's flag once more among us. I have inclosed the list of our party, and as we all stand in the line of battle, I want to see the Victory in the centre, then I think we should be just the thing for any party whatever. Sir Richard Bickerton, I am sorry to say,

---

[1] The Hon. Sir Robert Stopford was descended from an ancient and noble family, and born February 5, 1768. He entered the Navy at an early age, and in 1790 was in the command of the Lowestoffe, being at that time a Post Captain. He brought home Prince Augustus, Duke of Sussex, in the Aquilon, from the Mediterranean, was then attached to Lord Howe's fleet, and was in the battle of the 1st of June, 1794. Removed into the Phaeton in 1795, he formed part of the escort of the Princess Caroline of Brunswick to this country. He was afterwards at the capture of the eight ships with naval stores from Bordeaux, and then with Admiral Cornwallis, when he met with the French fleet near the Penmarks. In 1798 he joined Sir J. B. Warren, and in the following year was appointed to the Excellent of 74 guns, and captured the Arethusa and other French vessels. In 1803 he commanded the Spencer, and in 1804 joined Lord Nelson in the Mediterranean, accompanying him to the West Indies in pursuit of the French fleet. In 1805 he was made a Colonel of Marines. In 1806 he fought an action off St. Domingo, and was sent with the prizes to Jamaica. He was afterwards employed in the expedition against Copenhagen, and in 1808 made a Rear-Admiral, and had a command in the Channel Fleet. He blockaded the French squadron in the Aix Roads. In 1810 he went to the Cape of Good Hope, and thence to Java, to assist in the expedition against that place. He was made a Vice-Admiral August 12, 1812; K.C.B in 1815, afterwards G.C.B. and G.C.M.B. May 1st, 1841, he was appointed Governor of Greenwich Hospital, and died Admiral of the Red, June 25, 1847.

[2] Henry William Bayntun was employed as a Lieutenant at the reduction of Martinique in 1794, and made Commander by Sir John Jervis in the Avenger. He was made Post Captain, May 4, 1794, and appointed to the Undaunted, and placed on the West India station. Two years afterwards, in the Reunion, his ship was lost, and he was subsequently in the Quebec, the Thunderer, and the Cumberland. In 1803 he commanded a squadron off St. Domingo, and took a schooner, having on board 100 bloodhounds intended to be employed by the French against the blacks. In the Leviathan he joined Lord Nelson in the Mediterranean, and was with him at the battle of Trafalgar, passing through the enemy's line on that occasion. He was in 1806 engaged with Rear-Admiral Murray in reducing the province of Chili, and afterwards at Buenos Ayres. He then commanded the flotilla up the North River to Colonia. He was afterwards appointed to the Milford, and to the Royal Sovereign Yacht. He was made a Rear-Admiral, August 12, 1812; K.C.B. in 1815; G.C.B. in 1840; a Vice-Admiral in 1821; and died December 16, 1840.

has been very ill indeed, and the faculty advise his going to England. I think they say it is a liver complaint. I hope he will get the better of it, he is a valuable good man. Captain Hallowell is near me, and begs me to say he intended writing your Lordship, but as I am in the act of doing it, desires me to say every thing that is kind for him. He cannot help thinking your Lordship upon your passage out at this moment, and that my letter will miss you. I beg you will remember me very kindly to Lady Hamilton and all my friends at Merton. Accept my best wishes, and believe me, with every respect and esteem,

"Your Lordship's faithful and obliged friend,
"THOMAS LOUIS.

"P.S.—Captain Austen[1] begs his best respects. My son is gone to Naples with orders to Captain Sotheron."

[1] Frederic William Austen, a native of Hampshire, was born at Steventon, April 23, 1774, and studied in the Royal Naval Academy, whence from good conduct he was recommended for promotion, and served as Midshipman on board the Perseverance in 1788. In 1792 he was made Lieutenant, and served in various ships, conducting himself with great ability. He was made a Commander, appointed to the Peterel in 1799, and afforded protection to the trade in the Mediterranean. He was likewise at the capture of a French squadron returning from Egypt in that year. Off Marseilles, in 1800, he was engaged in a most gallant contest with three French vessels, and obtained Lord Keith's marked approbation. He then joined Sir Sidney Smith on the coast of Egypt, and for his services received from the Capitan Pasha a rich sabre and pelisse. In this year he was made Post Captain, and in 1801 he joined Vice-Admiral Gambier in the Neptune of 98 guns. In 1803 he commanded the Sea Fencibles at Ramsgate, and afterwards served in the Leopard off Boulogne. He then removed to the Canopus, and was on the Mediterranean station at the particular request of Lord Nelson. He accompanied his Lordship to the West Indies, and continued with him until August, 1805, when the junction with Admiral Cornwallis was formed off Ushant, and then with Sir Robert Calder. Captain Austen afterwards joined Vice Admiral Collingwood near Cadiz. He went with a detachment under Rear-Admiral Louis to obtain water and provisions, and was thus precluded being at the battle of Trafalgar. Captain Austen was afterwards with Sir J. T. Duckworth, and at the taking of three French sail of the line off St. Domingo, February 1, 1806. He received a gold medal, the Thanks of Parliament, and a vase of the value of £100 from the Patriotic Fund. In 1807 he convoyed five East Indiamen to the Cape of Good Hope, and returned with a valuable fleet of Chinamen. He took 2000 troops to Portugal in time to assist at the battle of Vimiera, superintended the embarkation of the wounded, and conveyed them to Oporto. In 1809 he again went to the East, and upon his return was with Lord Gambier cruising off the French coast. In 1811 he was attached to the North Sea fleet, and in 1813 put on half-pay. He is now an Admiral of the Blue and K C.B.

During his short stay at Merton, (from the 20th of August to the 13th of September) he was engaged in writing to Mr. Pitt on the importance of Sardinia, and to the Admiralty on a question of prize-money. Captain the Hon. Henry Blackwood of the Euryalus arrived at the Admiralty on the 2nd of September, with information that the combined fleet had put into Cadiz, and he had called on Lord Nelson on his road thither at 5 A. M., and found him at Merton up and dressed. Nelson felt assured Blackwood had brought him intelligence of the enemy's position, and expressed his conviction of giving "Monsieur Villeneuve a drubbing."[1] He followed Captain Blackwood to the Admiralty.

Lord Nelson was now all activity and in eagerness to depart. The Admiralty promised to send after him whatever ships he wished as soon as they were able, and he wrote to Mr. Davison: "I hope my absence will not be long, and that I shall soon meet the combined fleets, with a force sufficient to do the job well; for half a victory would but half content me. But I do not believe the Admiralty can give me a force within fifteen or sixteen sail-of-the-line of the enemy; and therefore, if every ship took her opponent, we should have to contend with a fresh fleet of fifteen or sixteen sail-of-the-line. But I will do my best; and I hope God Almighty will go with me. I have much to lose, but little to gain; and I go because it is right, and I will serve the country faithfully. I send you a memorandum, which I am sure you will comply with. Poor blind Mrs. Nelson I must assist this morning. Mr. Brande, an Apothecary, called upon me for £133. 2s 6d, as due from my brother Maurice to him. I shall refer him to you, and if it is a just demand, he must have it. I shall leave the bill in St. James's Square."[2] He wrote off to Vice-Admiral Collingwood: "I shall be with you in a very few days, and I hope you will remain second in command. You will change the Dreadnought for Royal Sovereign, which I hope you will like." At the solicitation of Captain Philip Charles Durham,[3] of the Defiance, Lord Nelson appointed

[1] See Blackwood's Magazine, July, 1833.
[2] From an Autograph in the possession of Colonel Davison.
[3] Sir Philip Charles Durham died Admiral of the Red, 1845, having received the Grand Cross of the Order of the Bath in November, 1830, and the Grand

him to put himself under his command. On the 11th he wrote the following to Earl Moira:—

"Merton, September 11th, 1805.

"My dear Lord,

"I find that my having intrusted my conscience to you (even under the greatest restrictions), who I hold to be the most honourable of men, and warmly attached to my honour, has both by the last and present Ministry, been perfectly misunderstood, therefore I am under the painful necessity of withdrawing this precious deposit, but I shall trust at present no other person with it; I must therefore, my dear Lord, beg you to consider my proxy as no longer in force. I am an officer serving, and therefore I believe you will think with many other friends, that I ought not to be considered as taking any party, except that of my King and country. I feel very much the idea of recalling what I had such pleasure in giving, but, my dear Lord, you are the only man who has ever had my proxy. I hear the Prince is coming to town, if he does before my departure, I shall endeavour to see him, and assure his Royal Highness of my attachment to his per-

---

Cross of the Order of Military Merit in France. He was made a Rear-Admiral in 1810, and Vice-Admiral in 1819. He was the son of James Durham, Esq. of Largo in Fifeshire, and a Lieutenant on board the Royal George when sunk at Spithead in 1782. He was fortunately picked up on that occasion, on which not less than 900 persons are supposed to have perished. In the Revolutionary war Captain Durham commanded the Spitfire, and in 1793 was made a Post Captain, and stationed in the Channel. He was appointed to the Hind, afterwards to the Anson, in which he served against Quiberon, and in the Bay of Biscay, where he made some captures. He was then placed off the coast of Ireland, and then in attendance on the Royal Family at Weymouth, who honoured a ball, given by Captain Durham, with their presence. He protected the trade from Portugal, and escorted a large fleet home from India, for which the Hon. East India Company presented him with a service of plate, of the value of 400 guineas. In 1803 he was appointed to the Defiance of 74 guns, and formed part of Sir Robert Calder's force in the action July 22, 1805. He was also at the Battle of Trafalgar, and was wounded on this occasion. Vice-Admiral Collingwood spoke in praise of his exertions after the battle to save L'Aigle from being wrecked. He had the honour to carry Nelson's Banner as K.B. on the day of his funeral. He afterwards commanded the Renown and the Colossus. In 1811 he was employed off the Scheldt, and then in the Channel. Appointed Commander-in-chief of the Leeward Islands, he went to his station in the Venerable, and on his passage with the Cyane captured the Alcmene and Iphigenia. In 1815 he co-operated in reducing the Island of Guadaloupe.

son. I am ever, my dear Lord, with the sincerest esteem and respect, your most faithful humble servant,

"NELSON AND BRONTÉ."

And on the same day he received the following from Carlton House :—

"Colonel McMahon presents his best respects to Lord Nelson, and is commanded by the Prince of Wales to say how miserable he shall feel if his Lordship were to take his departure without his Royal Highness having the happiness to see him, and to entreat for that pleasure to-morrow morning at any hour, however early, that Lord Nelson will have the goodness to appoint.
"Carlton House, Wednesday evening,
    September 11th, 1805."

In his private diary, he made the following entry, which is here printed from a copy made and subscribed by his Chaplain, the Rev. A. J. Scott, for Lady Hamilton, July 5th, 1806 :—

"Friday, Sept. 13th, 1805.

"'Friday night, at half-past ten, drove from dear, dear Merton, where I left all which I hold dear in this world, to go to serve my King and country. May the great God whom I adore, enable me to fulfil the expectations of my country, and if it is His good pleasure that I should return, my thanks will never cease being offered up to the throne of His mercy. If it is His good Providence to cut short my days upon earth, I bow with the greatest submission, relying that He will protect those so dear to me, that I may leave behind. His will be done. Amen, Amen, Amen.'

"A. J. SCOTT.
"Great Portland Street,
    No. 26, July 5th, 1806."

Lord Nelson's stay at Merton, as already told, continued only for the short period of twenty-four days, and his departure has been described in a very affecting manner. It is reported that before leaving this abode, which, independent of his deep-rooted and most absorbing love of country, contained all that was deeply interwoven with his most affectionate feelings, at ten o'clock at night, he visited the bedroom of his child Horatia, and kneeling down, prayed the protection and blessing of the Almighty for his offspring. He then bade adieu to Lady Hamilton, entered his chaise, and was on the road to Portsmouth.

Here he arrived at 6 A.M., and wrote the following:—

"My dearest Emma,

"I arrived here this moment, and Mr. Lancaster takes this. His coach is at the door, and only waits for my line. Victory is at St. Helen's, and, if possible, shall be at sea this day. God protect you and my dear Horatia, prays,

"Yours ever,
"NELSON AND BRONTÉ.

"6 o'clock, George Inn,
Sept. 14th, 1805."

He then arranged many things, and went on board the Victory at 2 P.M., having Mr. Rose and Mr. Canning with him to dinner, which he alludes to in the following letter, which is unfortunately imperfect:—

"Victory, Sept. 15th, 1805.

"My dearest Emma,

"Most probably some boat will come off to the ship before the tide suits us to weigh. Being obliged to anchor, it being calm, Messrs. Rose and Canning dined here yesterday; they seemed pleased, and I did not dislike letting out a little knowledge before Canning, who seems a very clever deep-headed man. I hope, and indeed think, Bolton will get something; but I entreat that Perry[1] will not say anything respecting my not having had any favour or honour conferred upon me. It can do no good, and may do harm. Rose was astonished at my not being rich, and he said he would tell the whole."

Southey states that Lord Nelson embarked from the beach where the bathing machines were placed, instead of the usual landing-place, "to elude the populace; and that a crowd col-

---

[1] Proprietor of the Morning Chronicle.

lected in his train, pressing forward to obtain sight of his face: many were in tears, and many knelt down before him, and blessed him as he passed. England has had many heroes, but never one who so entirely possessed the love of his fellow-countrymen as Nelson. All men knew that his heart was as humane as it was fearless: that there was not in his nature the slightest alloy of selfishness or cupidity; but that, with perfect and entire devotion, he served his country with all his heart, and with all his soul, and with all his strength; and therefore, they loved him as truly and as fervently as he loved England. They pressed upon the parapet to gaze after him when his barge pushed off, and he was returning their cheers by waving his hat. The sentinels who endeavoured to prevent them from trespassing upon this ground, were wedged among the crowd; and an officer, who, not very prudently upon such an occasion, ordered them to drive the people down with their bayonets, was compelled speedily to retreat; for the people would not be debarred from gazing till the last moment upon the hero—the darling hero of England!" This very affecting demonstration of love and regard, caused Nelson to exclaim to his Captain, Hardy, " I had their huzzas before —I have their hearts now!"

On the following day, he wrote:—

" My beloved Emma,

" I cannot even read your letter. We have fair wind, and God will, I hope, soon grant us a happy meeting. The wind is quite fair and fresh. We go too swift for the boat. May Heaven bless you and Horatia with all those who hold us dear to them. For a short time, farewell,

" Ever yours,

"NELSON AND BRONTÉ.

"Off Dunmore, Sept. 16th, 1805. 11 A.M."

He was exceedingly anxious for the proper adjustment of his accounts, and wrote to Mr. Davison:—" I regret most exceedingly, for many reasons, my not having had the pleasure of seeing you; but my fate is fixed, and I am gone, and beating down Channel with a foul wind. I am, my dear friend, so truly sensible of all your goodness to me, that I can only say, thanks, thanks: therefore, I will to business. I wish I could have been rich enough, with ease to myself, to have settled my account with you; but as that is not done, I wish for my sake, that you would have it closed, and receipts pass between us; and then I will give you a bond for the balance, as for money lent. Those bonds relative to Tucker, being all settled, should be returned to me. Be so good as to give them to Haslewood. If you and I live, no harm can happen; but should either of us drop, much confusion may arise to those we may leave behind. I have said enough. Haslewood will settle the account with all legal exactness. I have requested you to pay Chawner's account for work to be done in his line; and what is ordered, *viz.* the kitchen, anti-room, and for altering the dining-room, which you would have been provoked to see spoiled. The alteration will cost about three times as much as if it had been done at first. However, Chawner now knows all my plans and wishes. Poor blind Mrs. Nelson I have given £150 to pay her debts, and I intend to pay her house-rent in future, in addition to the £200 a-year, which I take will be about £40 a-year. I wished also to have seen you respecting my proxy, for as it passed through your hands without an immediate communication with Lord Moira, so it should have been returned that way. I ever was against giving my proxy to any man, and now I have it again, it will probably never be given again. Lord Moira made me break my intention; and as very few can equal our friend for honour and independence, it is not very likely that I shall give it, without strong reasons, again."[1]

He renewed his almost daily correspondence with Lady Hamilton:—

"Victory, off Portland, September 16th, 1805.
At noon, Wind West—foul.

"I have read, my dearest Emma, your kind and affectionate letters of Saturday. With God's blessing we shall soon meet again. Kiss dear Horatia a thousand times for

[1] From an autograph in the possession of Colonel Davison. Dispatches and Letters, Vol. vii. p. 38.

me. I write this letter, and I fear I shall too soon have an opportunity of sending it, for we are standing near Weymouth, the place of all others I should wish to avoid; but if it continues moderate I hope to escape without anchoring, but should I be forced, I shall act as a man, and your Nelson neither courting nor ashamed to hold up my head before the greatest monarch in the world. I have, thank God, nothing to be ashamed of.

"I have wrote a line to the Duke—he will shew it you, and I shall do it occasionally. I prepare this to be ready in case opportunity offers, and I am working very hard with Mr. Scott. If you see Sir William Scott, say how very sorry I am not to have seen him, but it was impossible. God bless you, and believe me, ever most faithfully,

"Yours,
"NELSON AND BRONTÉ."

"Victory, September 20th, 1805.
30 leagues S. W. from Sicily.

"My dearest Emma,

"A frigate is coming down, which we take to be the Decade, from the fleet off Cadiz. If the battle has been fought, I shall be sadly vexed, but I cannot help myself. We have had very indifferent weather, and it is still very dirty. Perseverance has got us thus far, and I trust will accomplish all our wishes. I write this line to put on board her, for if she has news, I have to write to the Admiralty. May heavens bless you. Kiss dear Horatia for

"Yours faithfully,
"NELSON AND BRONTÉ."

To the Right Honourable George Rose he wrote on the 17th, saying: "I will try to have a motto,—at least it shall be my watchword, ' *Touch and take.*' " On the 25th he was off Lisbon, and wrote :—

"Victory, off Lisbon, September 25th, 1805.

"My dearest Emma,

"We are now in sight of the Rock of Lisbon, and although we have very little wind, I hope to get round Cape St. Vincent to-morrow. We had only one day's real fair wind, but by perseverance we have done much. I am anxious to join the fleet, for it would add to my grief if any other man was to give them the Nelson touch, which WE say is warranted never to fail.

"I have read with much interest your letters, which I got at Merton, but I must have many others afloat. I do feel by myself what you must have felt at not hearing from me from January 29th to after May 18th. At first I fancied that they had been stopt by the Admiralty, as the account of Sir John Orde's joining the Channel fleet got to the Admiralty on the 3rd or 4th of May; but I now trace that my dispatches with Layman went home in the Avenger sloop, with a convoy, and that they had a very long passage; I mention all these circumstances that you should never think that Nelson neglects or forgets. I have this letter ready in case I should fall in with any thing from Lisbon homewards steering. May God bless you, and with my warmest affections to Horatia, be assured I am,

" Yours,
" NELSON AND BRONTÉ."

To the Consul at Lisbon, to Captain Sutton and others, he anxiously wrote to secure as many men as possible for the fleet. How truly gratifying it must have been to Nelson to receive assurances of desire to serve under him, and solicitations to that effect from so many brave and distinguished officers. The applications were numerous, and amongst them may be mentioned Admiral Sir John Thomas Duckworth, Captain Otway, Sir Edward Berry, Captain Durham, Lord Henry Paulet,[1] &c. The following letter from Sir Pulteney Malcolm is interesting:—

[1] The Right Hon. Lord Henry Paulet was the second son of George, twelfth Marquis of Winchester, and in the Revolutionary war, commanded the Nautilus. He was made Post Captain in 1794, and was at the reduction of Martinique. In the Channel fleet he commanded the Astrea, and in 1795 captured La Gloire. He was afterwards in the action off L'Orient, with Lord Bridport's fleet. In 1797 he was with Sir John Jervis on the 14th February, and after the battle employed on the Mediterranean station, taking several French and Spanish privateers. In the Defence he afterwards served in the Channel fleet, the Baltic, and on the coast of Spain. Upon the dissolution of the Peace of Amiens he was appointed to the Terrible, and employed in blockading the enemy's ports. In 1811 he was made a Colonel of Marines, and also a Rear-Admiral in the following year. He had a seat at the Board of Admiralty in 1813, which he resigned from ill health in 1816. He died a Vice-Admiral of the Red, and K.C.B. in January 1832.

"Donegal, off Cadiz, September 5th.

"My Lord,

"Admiral Louis conveyed to me your very handsome letter of thanks to the Officers and crews of the ships that had the honour to serve under your flag. I can assure your Lordship that the Donegals feel most particularly flattered by your good opinion, and it is their most anxious wish that they may again serve with you, and our hopes are very sanguine, for in such eventful times your Lordship will not be permitted to remain on shore, and we believe that if in your power, you will have your own old friends again with you. I fear there is little prospect that the Donegal will be docked; was her copper clean there would not be her superior in the service. Sir Richard sailed round us, and wrote me a complimentary note on her appearance. We are in wonderful health considering that we have had no refreshments since we sailed from Tetuan. I suppose our Chiefs have taken measures to procure supplies, but we are in the dark, for as they have done me the honour to place me near to the rear of the lee division, and as we keep open order, we know not what is done in the van. Since we joined Admiral Collingwood we have been detached with Admiral Louis inshore. The enemy appear ready for sea, that is, thirty-six sail of the line, and reports say they have embarked troops. If we are to blockade them, I fancy we must be very much on the alert, for they will be very active with their gun-boats. Last night I had the look out inshore—at daylight near twenty of them came out, and had the breeze not sprung up, they would have been within shot in an hour, as it was, they were at no great distance.

"If your Lordship is in London when you receive this, you will confer a singular obligation on me if opportunity offers, if you would mention to Lord Barham that my brother has been soliciting employment upwards of two years. Sir Thomas Pasley has applied very frequently, but I apprehend he is considered as past serving, and therefore not attended to (the more is the pity). I would not have troubled your Lordship, as I know you have so many such applications, but my anxiety for my brother induces me.

"I have the honour to remain with respect and esteem,

"Your Lordship's most faithful humble servant,

"PULTENEY MALCOLM."

On the 28th of September, according to Dr. (afterwards Sir William) Beatty's[1] Diary, Nelson saw the enemy's fleet in Cadiz: they amounted to thirty-five or thirty-six sail of the line, and he gave out the necessary orders to his fleet, and wrote on the 30th to Admiral Knight: "I was only twenty-five days, from dinner to dinner, absent from the Victory. In our several stations, my dear Admiral, we must all put our shoulders to the wheel, and make the great machine of the fleet entrusted to our charge go on smoothly."[2] Lord Nelson, it appears, was entrusted with a message to Sir Robert Calder, and he wrote on the 30th to the First Lord of the Admiralty:

"I did not fail, immediately on my arrival, to deliver your message to Sir Robert Calder; and it will give your Lordship pleasure to find, as it has me, that an inquiry is what the Vice-Admiral wishes, and that he had written to you by the Nautilus, which I detained, to say so. Sir Robert thinks that he can clearly prove, that it was not in his power to bring the combined squadrons again to battle. It would be only taking up your time were I to enter more at large on all our conversation; but Sir Robert felt so much, even at the idea of being removed from his own ship which he commanded, in the face of the fleet, that I much fear I shall incur the censure of the Board of Admiralty, without your Lordship's influence with the members of it. I may be thought wrong, as an officer, to disobey the orders of the Admiralty, by not insisting on Sir Robert Calder's quitting the Prince of Wales for the Dreadnought, and for parting with a 90-gun ship before the force arrives which their Lordships have judged necessary; but I trust that I shall be considered to have done right as a man, and to a brother officer in affliction—my heart would not stand it, and so the thing must rest. I shall submit to the wisdom of the Board to censure me or not, as to them may seem best for the service; I shall bow with all due respect to their decision."[3]

On this day he also wrote to Mr. Elliot, and desired his dutiful and humble respects to their Sicilian Majesties, from whom he had received the following letters:—

---

[1] The Surgeon of the Victory.
[2] Clarke and McArthur, Vol. ii. p. 425.
[3] Ibid. p. 426.

"My dear Duke and estimable Friend,

"I received your letter of the 18th of June, and see by it with great pleasure that you are returned into our vicinity. The difficult circumstances in which we are placed renders your presence in our seas a great consolation to me. You know me and the constancy of my sentiments which will last as long as I have life. I predict the greatest successes and glory for you always in our vicinity. All my family join with me equally in wishing you all possible success—believe me, my very dear Lord, with real esteem and gratitude, always

"Your constant, true, and affectionate friend,
"FERDINANDO B.

"Belvidere, 28th August, 1805."

"My very worthy Lord,

"I hasten to reply to the letter you wrote me from Gibraltar on the 21st of July. I cannot, my dear Admiral, sufficiently express to you the pleasure I derive from knowing that you are nearer to us, and I beseech you not to quit the Mediterranean whilst we are in such an emergency. The mere knowledge of our hero, Nelson's, being in the Mediterranean animates individual courage, and contributes to the success of all the operations in progress. I thank you for the productions of the various places you have visited, it being an additional proof of your great attention. My dear children, who all cherish and respect you, desire me to make their compliments; we offer our best wishes for your prosperity, glory, and happiness. I congratulate you upon the good condition of health your squadron enjoys after so tedious a voyage, which is the result of your attention and zeal. The general crisis is approaching, God grant it may be for good. Once more, I pray you not to quit the Mediterranean, for all our trust is in you, and believe me, for life, with the sincerest esteem and confidence, your eternally attached friend,

"CHARLOTTE.

"September 5th, 1805."

Lord Nelson also received the following from the Abbé Campbell, which was answered on the 9th:—

"Naples, September the 6th, 1805.
[Received October 6th, off Cadiz.]

"My dear Lord,

"I can't let escape the opportunity of the Bittern's sailing this evening from hence to join you without troubling your Lordship with a few lines, which in all probability will find you at Merton, where I sincerely wish to have the honour of seeing you and our dear friend Lady Hamilton, being certain of a friendly reception. How sorry I was that your Lordship did not meet with the combined fleets, we should have had a better account of them. Your friend the Marquis Circello has not been as yet officially appointed to any place, some attribute it to the fear of displeasing the French, whilst others think it is a cabal of Medici, the Duke St. Theodore, Cardito and Gallo against him; he, however, goes as Counsellor of State to all the Councils, and is extremely liked, particularly by the poor good King, the Queen likewise is very attentive to him. St. Clair is made Gentleman of the Chamber to the great scandal of every well meaning person of the country; Count and Countess de la Tour as a cloak to the former, are appointed one a Gentleman of the Bedchamber, and the other Lady of Honour, those last are mortal enemies to us English, even more so than St. Clair, because they are more clever.

"The French are very quiet here at present, but it is only momentary, as they are waiting for a force from the north of Italy to march into the kingdom whenever they can safely do it; they are now at Bari, and as I am informed will retreat to Pescara without risking a battle, in case either the English or Russians land in the kingdom, this is what I learn. The King comes to town to-night from Caserta, the Queen from Castel-à-Mare, and the Prince from Portici to assist at a popular feast near Possilippo, named Pie della Grotta.

"The Marquis and Marchioness of Circello desire their best respects to you. I have not heard from our dear Lady Hamilton since my arrival here, though I wrote twice to her. God for ever bless you, and believe me, my dear Lord,

"Ever your Lordship's
"Most faithful humble servant,
"HENRY CAMPBELL.

"P. S. Pray remember me to my brother Parson Scott, whom I like much."

On the 1st of October Lord Nelson wrote the following, which has been incorrectly printed:—[1]

"Victory, October 1st, 1805.

"My dearest Emma,

"It is a relief to me to take up the pen and write you a line, for I have had, about four o'clock this morning, one of my dreadful spasms, which has almost enervated me. It is very odd, I was hardly ever better than yesterday. Fremantle stayed with me till eight o'clock, and I slept uncommonly well, but was awoke with this disorder. My opinion of its effect some one day has never altered. However, it is entirely gone off, and I am only quite weak, but I do assure you, my Emma, that the uncertainty of human life makes the situation of you dearer to my affectionate heart.

"The good people of England will not believe that rest of body and mind is necessary for me, but perhaps this spasm may not come again these six months. I had been writing seven hours yesterday, perhaps that had some hand in bringing it upon me.

"I got round Cape St. Vincent the 26th, but it was the 28th before I got off Cadiz, and joined Admiral Collingwood, but it was so late that I did not communicate till next morning. I believe my arrival was most welcome, not only to the Commander of the fleet, but also to every individual in it, and when I came to explain to them the *Nelson touch*, it was like an electric shot. Some shed tears—all approved ' it was new—it was singular—it was simple,' and from Admirals downwards it was repeated, ' it must succeed if ever they will allow us to get at them! You are, my Lord, surrounded by friends whom you inspire with confidence.' Some, my dear Emma, may be Judas's, but the majority are certainly much pleased with my commanding them. The enemy's fleet is thirty-five or thirty-six sail-of-the-line in Cadiz. The French

[1] In the Collection of Lord Nelson's Letters to Lady Hamilton, Vol. ii. p. 100.

have given the Dons an old seventy-four to repair, and taken possession of the Santa Anna of 112 guns. Louis is going into Gibraltar and Tetuan to get supplies, of which the fleet is much in want; and Admiral Knight, as I am told, has almost made us quarrel with the Moors of Barbary; however, I am sending Mr. Ford[1] and money to put us right again. God bless you. Amen—Amen—Amen."

To another, apparently of the same date, he adds on the 2nd October:—

" And when Louis's squadron goes I shall have twenty-three sail-of-the-line to meet them, but we shall do very well. I am sensible that Ministry are sending me all the force they can, and I hope to use it.

" *October* 2*nd*. Last night I got your dear letters, September 18th, 19th, by Admiral Sutton. You must not complain of my short letters. I have had, as you will believe, a very distressing scene with poor Sir Robert Calder. He has wrote home to beg an inquiry, feeling confident that he can fully justify himself, I sincerely hope he may, but— I have given him the advice as to my dearest friend. He is in adversity, and if he ever has been my enemy, he now feels the pang of it, and finds me one of his best friends.

" Louis, Hallowell, Hoste, are all inquiring about you, and desire their kind regards. I am pressed beyond measure for time, for I cannot keep the vessel, as Vice-Admiral Collingwood's and Sir Robert Calder's dispatches were stopt by me off Cape St. Vincent on the 26th. May God bless you. Kiss Horatia for me a thousand times. I shall write to her very soon; in eight or ten days another vessel will be sent.

" Your most faithful,
" NELSON AND BRONTÉ."

---

[1] Richard Ford, Esq. was Agent Victualler afloat, to whom Lord Nelson, in a letter of the 2nd, (printed in the Gentleman's Magazine, New Series, Vol. vii. p. 158) says: " I have the firmest reliance upon your abilities and zeal, that this matter will be well terminated; and although no man wishes to be more economical of the public money than myself, yet in our present state, and with the sort of people with whom we have to manage these matters, care must be taken not to be *penny wise* and *pounds foolish*."

The ships were now getting short of provisions and water, and Nelson was obliged to detach a portion of his squadron, including Rear-Admiral Louis of the Canopus, who was fearful he should be prevented being present at the battle, and expressed the same to his Admiral, who replied: "My dear Louis, I have no other means of keeping my fleet complete in provisions and water, but by sending them in detachments to Gibraltar. The enemy *will* come out, and we shall fight them; but there will be time for you to get back first. I look upon Canopus as my right hand, and I send you the first to insure your being here to help beat them." Rear-Admiral Louis was right in his conjecture. He was not in the Battle of Trafalgar, and from the same cause Nelson's esteemed and attached officers, Austen, Stopford, and Hallowell were also absent.

In the Naval Chronicle[1] a letter addressed to some one, whose name has been suppressed, has been printed of the date of the 3rd of October, in which Nelson says: "The reception I met with on joining the fleet caused the sweetest sensation of my life. The Officers who came on board to welcome my return, forgot my rank as Commander-in-chief in the enthusiasm with which they greeted me. As soon as these emotions were past, I laid before them the plan I had previously arranged for attacking the enemy; and it was not only my pleasure to find it generally approved, but clearly perceived and understood. The enemy are still in port, but something must be immediately done to provoke or lure them to a battle. My duty to my country demands it, and the hopes centered in me, I hope in God, will be realized. In less than a fortnight expect to hear from me, or of me, for who can foresee the fate of battle? Put up your prayers for my success, and may God protect all my friends!"

The plan of attack alluded to in the preceding letter was not made generally known until the 9th or 10th, although he had formed it in his mind whilst in England, and had indeed, at an interview with Lord Sidmouth, sketched it out upon a small table after dining with him. The table was preserved by Lord Sidmouth, and had an appropriate inscription marked upon it. The particulars of this interesting fact are detailed

[1] Vol. v. p. 37.

in Dean Pellew's Life of Lord Sidmouth.[1] Nelson's attachment to Mr. Addington (afterwards Lord Sidmouth) has already been seen, and upon his arrival in town in August, before Lord Sidmouth could be able to visit him, as it was his intention to do at Merton, his Lordship called upon him in town.

"Nelson (Lord Sidmouth writes to his brother on the 24th August), surprised me yesterday in Clifford Street without my coat, just as I had undergone the operation of bleeding. He looked well, and we passed an hour together very comfortably. Our conversation will be renewed to-morrow, when he has promised to call here after church." Lord Sidmouth's serious indisposition, and Lord Nelson's numerous engagements, prevented their frequent meetings: when, therefore, the departure of the latter to command the fleet off Cadiz approached, Lord Sidmouth addressed a note to him on the 8th September, expressing the great mortification it would be to him to miss the pleasure of seeing his Lordship again whilst he remained on shore, and offering to call on him at Merton on the following day, if his Lordship could not take Richmond Park on his way to town, which would not be a great deal out of his way. The reply, dated on the same day, was carefully cherished by Lord Sidmouth as the last he ever received from the illustrious writer:—

"On Tuesday forenoon, if superior powers do not prevent me, I will be in Richmond Park, and shall be happy in taking you by the hand, and to wish you a most perfect restoration to health. I am ever, my dear Lord, your most obliged and faithful friend,

"NELSON AND BRONTÉ."

To the foot of this note Lord Sidmouth has appended the following words: "Lord Nelson came on that day, and passed some hours at Richmond Park. This was our last meeting." His Lordship was accustomed, in after years, to relate to his friends the interesting particulars of this interview. Amongst other things, Lord Nelson explained to him with his finger, on the little study table, the manner in which, should he be so fortunate as to meet the combined fleets, he

---

[1] Vol. ii. p. 380-2.

proposed to attack them : " Rodney," he said, "broke the line in one point; I will break it in two." "There," he said to Miss Halsted, whose pen has recorded the anecdote, "there is the table on which he drew the plan of the Battle of Trafalgar but five weeks before his death. It is strange that I should have used this valued relic for above thirty years, without having once thought of recording upon it a fact so interesting. Now," pointing to a brass plate inserted in the centre of the table, " I have perpetuated it by this brief record :—

" On the 10th day of September, 1805, Vice-Admiral Lord Viscount Nelson described to Lord Sidmouth, upon this table, the manner in which he intended to engage the combined fleets of France and Spain, which he expected shortly to meet. He stated that he should attack them in two lines, led by himself and Admiral Collingwood, and felt confident that he should capture either their van and centre, or their centre and rear. This he successfully effected, on the 21st of October following, in the glorious Battle of Trafalgar."

On the 6th of October Lord Nelson wrote thus to Lady Hamilton :—

" Victory, 16 leagues west from Cadiz,[1]
October 6th, 1805.

" My dearest Emma,

" I wrote you on the 2nd, by the Nimble, and if she acts up to her name, she will have a good passage. She will tell you of my arrival in the fleet, but as an opportunity now offers of sending a letter by way of Lisbon, I will not omit writing, although most probably other letters will get home before this, and perhaps those of the very greatest importance. The enemy are, I have not the smallest doubt, determined to put to sea, and our battle must soon be fought, although

---

[1] His reason for taking this position is given by Lord Nelson to Lord Barham, First Lord of the Admiralty. " The position I have taken for this month is from sixteen to eighteen leagues west of Cadiz; for although it is most desirable that the fleet should be well up in the easterly winds, yet I must guard against being caught with a westerly wind near Cadiz, as a fleet of ships, with so many three-deckers, would inevitably be forced into the Straits, and then Cadiz would be perfectly free for the enemy to come out with a westerly wind, as they served Lord Keith in the late war."—(Clarke and McArthur, Vol. ii. p. 431.)

they will be so very superior in numbers to my present force, yet I must do my best, and have no fears but that I shall spoil their voyage; but my wish is to do much more, and therefore hope the Admiralty have been active in sending me ships, for it is only numbers which can annihilate. A decisive stroke on their fleet would make half a peace; and, my Emma, if I can do that, I shall, as soon as possible, ask to come home and get my rest, at least for the winter, and if no other inducement was wanting for my exertion, this would be sufficient. To come to you a victor would be a victory twice gained. God bless you, and be assured I am yours most faithfully,

"NELSON AND BRONTÉ.

"Kiss dear Horatia, and remember me most kindly to all."

"*Oct. 7th.*—Since writing yesterday, I am more and more assured that the combined fleets will put to sea. Happy will they be who are present, and disappointed will those be who are absent. May God instruct us and Heavens bless. Defiance has just joined—it now blows fresh easterly, and a nasty sea. Bless you. Amen.

"Tell Mr. Bolton to be easy. I hope soon something will turn up for him; it is useless to complain. The best thing is to say nothing of any expectations."

To Captain the Hon. Henry Blackwood he wrote on the 4th of October:—"You estimate, as I do, the importance of not letting those rogues escape us without a fair fight, which I pant for by day, and dream of by night."

Nelson offered to Captain the Hon. Henry Blackwood the choice of a line-of-battle ship, but he preferred remaining in the Euryalus, in which, as senior officer of the frigates, he would necessarily have much to do. He kept up a constant communication with Nelson by signals, who writes: "The fleet will be from sixteen to eighteen leagues west of Cadiz; therefore, if you throw a frigate west from you, most probably, in fine weather, we shall communicate daily. In fresh breezes easterly, I shall work up for Cadiz, never getting to the northward of it; and in the event of hearing they are standing out of Cadiz, I shall carry a press of sail to the southward towards

Cape Spartel and Arrache, so that you will always know where to find me. I am writing out regular instructions for the frigates under your orders, but I am confident you will not let these gentry slip through our fingers, and then we shall give a good account of them, although they may be very superior in numbers."[1] Again, on the 8th: "I send Naiad to you, and will Phœbe and Weazle, as I can lay hands upon them. I am gratified (because it shews your soul is in your business), and obliged by all your communications. I see you feel how much my heart is set on getting at these fellows, whom I have hunted so long." On the 9th: "Let us have them out. The Weazle, I hope, has joined, although you don't mention her. Keep the schooner; she will be useful in the night close inshore; and as Weazle sails faster, you can send her to me with accounts, when you can't communicate by signals. I should never wish to be more than forty-eight hours without hearing from you." On the 10th: "Keep your five frigates, Weazle and Pickle, and let me know every movement. I rely on you, that we can't miss getting hold of them, and I will give them such a shaking as they never yet experienced; at least I will lay down my life in the attempt. We are a powerful fleet, and not to be held cheap. I have told Parker, and do you direct ships bringing information of their coming out, to fire guns every three minutes by the watch, and in the night, to fire off rockets, if they have them, from the masthead." On the 14th: "I hope we shall soon get our Cadiz friends out, and then we may (I hope) flatter ourselves that some of them will cruise on our side; but if they do not come forth soon, I shall then rather incline to think they will detach squadrons; but I trust either in the whole, or in part, we shall get at them. I am confident in your look-out upon them."[2]

Nelson's sole anxiety was to annihilate the combined fleets. He wrote to the Right Hon. George Rose on the 6th: "I verily believe the country will soon be put to some expense for my account, either a monument, or a new pension and honours; for I have not the very smallest doubt but that a very few days, almost hours, will put us in battle; the success no man

---

[1] Blackwood's Magazine for July, 1833, p. 8.   [2] Ibid.

can ensure, but to fighting them, if they are to be got at, I pledge myself, and if the force arrives which is intended. I am *very, very, very* anxious for its arrival, for the thing will be done if a few more days elapse; and I want, for the sake of our country, that it should be done so effectually as to have nothing to wish for; and what will signify the force the day after the battle? It is, as Mr. Pitt knows, annihilation that the country wants, and not merely a splendid victory of twenty-three to thirty-six—honourable to the parties concerned, but absolutely useless in the extended scale to bring Buonaparte to his marrow-bones: numbers can only annihilate."[1]

On the 9th of October, Lord Nelson sent to Vice-Admiral Collingwood his plan of attack, with the accompanying letter:—

"I send you Captain Blackwood's letter; and as I hope Weazle has joined, he will have five frigates and a brig. They surely cannot escape us. I wish we could get a fine day. I send you my plan of attack, as far as a man dare venture to guess at the very uncertain position the enemy may be found in: but, my dear friend, it is to place you perfectly at ease respecting my intentions, and to give full scope to your judgment for carrying them into effect. We can, my dear Coll., have no little jealousies: we have only one great object in view,—that of annihilating our enemies, and getting a glorious peace for our country. No man has more confidence in another than I have in you; and no man will render your services more justice than your very old friend,

"NELSON AND BRONTÉ."[2]

The following letter to the present Admiral the Hon. Sir T. B. Capel, K.C.B. Commander-in-chief at Portsmouth, is a good specimen of Lord Nelson's playful manner and style, and as such is highly prized by the distinguished officer to whom it is addressed, marking as it does the character of his mind at a time when it might be supposed he would be wholly engrossed with the great object of meeting the enemy:—

[1] Dispatches and Letters, Vol. vii. p. 80. From an autograph in the possession of the Right Hon. Sir George Rose, G.C.B.
[2] Memoirs of Collingwood, Vol. i. p. 162.

"Victory, October 10th, 1805.

"My dear Capel,

"Many thanks for your letter. I am sorry to hear such a bad account of Phœbe's movements. When we have done with those gentry in Cadiz, you must be sent home and coppered, but if they do not unfortunately move soon, write me a public letter, stating the situation of Phœbe's copper, and I will send it to the Admiralty. All our prize-money is in Cadiz; we have only to pass through a pretty hot fiery ordeal, and we shall be rich both in glory and money.

"Ever faithfully yours,
"NELSON AND BRONTÉ."

Lord Nelson's activity at this time is rendered very apparent by the numerous letters printed in the Dispatches and Letters (Vol. vii.) Of the 10th there are no less than twenty-three letters, and from the 1st to the 19th, sixty-eight letters. On the morning of the 19th, the combined fleets began to get under weigh. A signal was made at half-past nine, A.M. that the enemy's fleet were coming out of port; at three P.M. that they were at sea; and on the morning of the 20th, Nelson was made acquainted that nearly forty sail of ships of war had been seen outside Cadiz the previous evening.

Towards the close of this day, Nelson, fearful that the enemy might endeavour to avoid a general action by passing the Straits into the Mediterranean during the night, the weather appearing to promise darkness and squalls, he telegraphed Blackwood thus: "*I rely on you that I do not miss the enemy.*" This indefatigable Captain and most excellent officer, after placing the frigates and other vessels under his orders in the best position, stationed himself for the night not more than half a gun-shot from that ship which he conceived to be the flag-ship of the Admiral of the enemy, to secure attention to his great Commander's wishes. On the day of the battle Captain Blackwood wrote the particulars to his wife in the following letter, too interesting to be omitted in this narrative :—

"At this moment the enemy are coming out, and as if determined to have a fair fight; all night they have been making signals, and the morning shewed them to us getting under sail. They have thirty-four sail of the line, and five frigates. Lord Nelson has but twenty-seven sail of the line with him; the rest are at Gibraltar getting water. Not that he has not enough to bring them to close action; but I want him to have so many as to make this the most decisive battle that was ever fought, and which may bring us lasting peace, and all its blessings. Within two hours, though our fleet was sixteen leagues off, I have let Lord Nelson know of their coming out, and have been enabled to send a vessel to Gibraltar, which will bring Admiral Louis and the ships there. At this moment (happy sight) we are within four miles of the enemy, and talking to Lord Nelson by means of Sir H. Popham's signals, though so distant, but reached along by the rest of the frigates of the squadron. You see, dearest, I have time to write to you, and to assure you that to the latest moment of my breath, I shall be as much attached to you as man can be. It is odd how I have been dreaming all night of carrying home dispatches. God send me such good luck! The day is fine, and the sight magnificently beautiful. I expect before this hour to-morrow to carry General Decrès[1] on board the Victory in my barge, which I have just painted nicely for him.—*Monday Morning, 21st.* The last twenty-four hours has been most anxious work for me; but we have kept sight of them, and at this moment bearing up to come to action, Lord Nelson twenty-seven sail of the line. French thirty-three or thirty-four. I wish the six we have at Gibraltar were here. My signal just made on board the Victory: I hope to order me into a vacant line-of-battle ship."[2]

On the 19th, Lord Nelson wrote to Lady Hamilton:—

"Victory, October 19th, 1805.
"Noon, Cadiz, E.S.E. 16 leagues.

"My dearest beloved Emma, the dear friend of my bosom. The signal has been made that the enemy's combined fleet are coming out of port. We have very little wind, so that I have no hopes of seeing them before to-morrow. May the

---

[1] Villeneuve, not Decrès, as Blackwood thought. His dream was verified; he carried home the Dispatches.

[2] Blackwood's Magazine for July, 1833, p. 10.

God of battles crown my endeavours with success; at all events, I will take care that my name shall ever be most dear to you and Horatia, both of whom I love as much as my own life. And as my last writing, before the battle, will be to you, so I hope, in God, that I shall live to finish my letter after the battle. May Heaven bless you, prays your

"NELSON AND BRONTÉ."

"*October* 20*th.* In the morning we were close to the mouth of the Straits, but the wind had not come far enough to the westward, to allow the combined fleets to weather the shoals off Trafalgar; but they were counted as far as forty sail of ships of war, which I suppose to be thirty-four of the line, and six frigates. A group of them was seen off the lighthouse of Cadiz this morning, but it blows so very fresh, and thick weather, that I rather believe they will go into the harbour before night. May God Almighty give us success over these fellows, and enable us to get a peace."

To the above last writing of Lord Nelson, Lady Hamilton has added: "This letter was found open on *his* desk, and brought to Lady Hamilton, by Captain Hardy. Oh, miserable wretched Emma—Oh, glorious and happy Nelson." The envelope containing the letter is superscribed "The inclosed letters were found after the action, and sealed up in the presence of the Reverend Mr. Scott.

"T. M. HARDY.

"For Lady Hamilton."

And also to his daughter:—

"To MISS HORATIA NELSON THOMPSON.[1]

"Victory, October 19th, 1805.

"My dearest angel,

"I was made happy by the pleasure of receiving your letter of September 19th, and I rejoice to hear that you are so very good a girl, and love my dear Lady Hamilton, who

[1] From an autograph in the possession of Mrs. H. N. Ward, printed in Dispatches and Letters, Vol. vii. p. 132.

most dearly loves you. Give her a kiss for me. The combined fleets of the enemy, are now reported to be coming out of Cadiz; and therefore I answer your letter, my dearest Horatia, to mark to you that you are ever uppermost in my thoughts. I shall be sure of your prayers for my safety, conquest, and speedy return to dear Merton, and our dearest good Lady Hamilton. Be a good girl, mind what Miss Connor says to you. Receive, my dearest Horatia, the affectionate parental blessing of your father,

"NELSON AND BRONTÉ."

The British fleet consisted of three of 100 guns; four of 98; one of 80; sixteen of 74; and three of 64; being twenty-seven *sail of the line* together with four frigates, a schooner, and a cutter. The combined fleets consisted of French: four of 80 guns; and fourteen of 74. Spanish: one of 130; two of 112; one of 100; two of 80; eight of 74; and one of 64; making thirty-three *sail of the line*, and five French frigates, and two brigs.

The French Admiral Villeneuve, it is rather singular, received orders on the day of Nelson's arrival in the fleet (September 28) to put to sea, pass the Straits, land troops on the coast of Naples, and sweep the Mediterranean of our ships, after which services they were to put into Toulon.

On the morning of the 21st, Lord Nelson made signals to "form the order of sailing in two columns," and to "prepare for battle," and ten minutes after to "bear up." Sir William Beatty's statement of the dress in which Nelson appeared on the day of battle, contradicts the assertion so confidently and so repeatedly made by the biographers of the hero: "Soon after daylight, Lord Nelson came upon deck: he was dressed as usual in his Admiral's frock coat, bearing on the left breast four stars of different orders, which he always wore with his common apparel. He did not wear his sword in the battle of Trafalgar; it had been taken from the place where it hung up in his cabin, and was laid ready on his table; but it is supposed he forgot to call for it. This was the only action in which he ever appeared without a sword. He displayed excellent spirits, and expressed his pleasure at the prospect of giving a fatal blow to the naval power of France and Spain;

and spoke with confidence of obtaining a signal victory, notwithstanding the inferiority of the British fleet, declaring to Captain Hardy, " that he would not be contented with capturing less than twenty sail of the line."

Vice-Admiral Collingwood led the lee line of thirteen ships, and Lord Nelson the weather line of fourteen. Sir William Beatty says : " His Lordship had ascended the poop to have a better view of both lines of the British fleet, and while there, gave particular directions for taking down from his cabin the different fixtures, and for being very careful in removing the portrait of Lady Hamilton. 'Take care of my guardian angel,' said he, addressing himself to the persons to be employed in this business." Immediately after this he quitted the poop, and retired to his cabin, for a few minutes, where he wrote the following Prayer, and Codicil to his Will :—

### PRAYER.

" May the Great God, whom I worship, grant to my country, and for the benefit of Europe in general, a great and glorious victory ; and may no misconduct, in any one, tarnish it ; and may humanity after victory be the predominant feature in the British fleet. For myself, individually, I commit my life to Him who made me, and may his blessing light upon my endeavours for serving my country faithfully. To Him I resign myself and the just cause which is entrusted to me to defend. Amen, Amen, Amen."

### CODICIL TO LORD NELSON'S WILL.

" October the twenty-first, one thousand eight hundred and five, then in sight of the combined fleets of France and Spain, distant about ten miles.

" Whereas the eminent services of Emma Hamilton, widow of the Right Honourable Sir William Hamilton, have been of the very greatest service to our King and country, to my knowledge, without her receiving any reward from either our King or country :—first, that she obtained the King of Spain's letter, in 1796, to his brother, the King of Naples, acquainting him of his intention to declare war against England ; from which letter, the Ministry sent out orders to then Sir John Jervis, to strike a stroke, if opportunity offered, against either the arsenals of Spain, or her fleets. That neither of these was done, is not the fault of Lady Hamilton. The opportunity might have been offered. Secondly, the British fleet, under my command, could never have returned the second time to Egypt, had not Lady Hamilton's influence with the Queen of Naples, caused letters to be wrote to the Governor of Syracuse, that he was to encourage the fleet being supplied with every thing, should they put into any port in Sicily. We put into Syracuse, and received every supply, went to Egypt, and destroyed the French fleet. Could I have rewarded these services, I would not now call upon my country; but as that has not been in my power, I leave Emma, Lady Hamilton, therefore, a legacy to my King and country, that they will give her an ample provision to maintain her rank in life. I also leave to the beneficence of my country, my adopted daughter, Horatia Nelson Thompson; and I desire she will use, in future, the name of Nelson only.[1] These are the only favours I ask of my King and country, at this moment, when I am going to fight their battle. May God bless my King and country, and all those who I hold dear. My relations, it is needless to mention, they will, of course, be amply provided for.

"NELSON AND BRONTÉ.

" Witness—HENRY BLACKWOOD,
T. M. HARDY."

Sir N. Harris Nicolas has given a very interesting anecdote connected with the foregoing Prayer, derived from Captain John Pasco, who acted as signal Lieutenant of the Victory, though senior Lieutenant in rank :—

"About 11, A.M, of the 21st of October, Lieutenant Pasco had to make a report to Lord Nelson, and intended at the same time to have represented to him that he considered himself very unfortunate, on so glorious an occasion, to be doing duty in an inferior station, instead of that to which his seniority entitled him. 'On entering the cabin,' says Captain Pasco, 'I discovered his Lordship on his knees writing. He was then penning that beautiful prayer. I waited until he rose, and communicated what I had to report, but could not at such a moment, disturb his mind with any grievances of

---

[1] The grant under the King's sign manual, by which Horatia took the name of Nelson only, bears date Sept. 30, 1806.

mine.' Captain Pasco considers, that but for this delicacy on his part, he should have been directed to assume his position as *First* Lieutenant, and thereby have been made a Post Captain instead of a Commander for the battle, as Lieutenant Quilliam, his junior in rank, who acted as *First* Lieutenant of the Victory, was posted in December, 1805, together with the two Lieutenants who commanded the Ajax and Thunderer, in the absence of their Captains."

The Battle of Trafalgar, and every particular connected with it, has been so frequently detailed, that it would be supererogatory to give more than a sketch of the events in this place, as a necessary portion of the history endeavoured to be connected together in these pages in relation to the original correspondence included in them.

The ships and Commanders engaged in this celebrated action were as follows:—

### British Fleet.

| GUNS. | | | |
|---|---|---|---|
| 100 | Victory | | Vice-Admiral (W) Lord Nelson, K. B. <br> Captain Thomas Masterman Hardy |
| | Royal Sovereign | | Vice-Admiral (B) Cuthbert Collingwood <br> Captain Edward Rotheram |
| | Britannia | | Rear-Admiral (W) the Earl of Northesk <br> Captain Charles Bullen. |
| 98 | Téméraire | | " Eliab Harvey. |
| | Prince | | " Richard Grindall. |
| | Neptune | | " Thomas Francis Fremantle. |
| | Dreadnought | | " John Conn. |
| 80 | Tonnant | | " Charles Tyler. |
| 74 | Belleisle | | " William Hargood. |
| | Revenge | | " Robert Moorsom. |
| | Mars | | " George Duff. |
| | Spartiate | | " Sir Francis Laforey, Bart. |
| | Defiance | | " Philip Charles Durham. |
| | Conqueror | | " Israel Pellew. |
| | Defence | | " George Hope. |
| | Colossus | | " James Nicoll Morris. |
| | Leviathan | | " Henry William Bayntun. |
| | Achille | | " Richard King. |
| | Bellerophon | | " John Cooke. |
| | Minotaur | | " Charles John Moore Mansfield. |
| | Orion | | " Edward Codrington. |
| | Swiftsure | | " William George Rutherford. |
| | Ajax | | Lieutenant John Pilford. } Acting. |
| | Thunderer | | " John Stockham. } |
| 64 | Polyphemus | | Captain Robert Redmill. |
| | Africa | | " Henry Digby. |
| | Agamemnon | | " Sir Edward Berry. |

1805.]  LORD VISCOUNT NELSON.  521

*Frigates*, Euryalus, Naïad, Phœbe, and Sirius, Captains the Hon. Henry Blackwood, Thos. Dundas, the Hon. Thomas Bladen Capel, and William Prowse.

*Schooner*, Pickle, Lieutenant John Richard Lapenotiere: and *Cutter*, Entreprenante, Lieutenant Robert Benjamin Young.

### Enemy's Fleet.
#### French.

| GUNS. | | |
|---|---|---|
| 80 | Bucentaure | Vice-Admiral P. Ch. J. B. S. Villeneuve. <br> Captain Jean Jacques Magendie. |
| | Formidable | Rear-Ad. P. R. M. E. Dumanoir le Pelley. <br> Captain Jean Marie Letellier. |
| | Neptune | Commodore Esprit Tranquille Maistral. |
| | Indomptable | "   Jean Joseph Hubert. |
| 74 | Algesiras | Rear-Admiral Charles Magon. <br> Captain Gabriel August Bouard. |
| | Pluton | Commodore Julian Marie Cosmao Kerjulein. |
| | Mont Blanc | "   Guill. Jean Noël le Villegris. |
| | Intrépide | "   Louis Antoine Cyprien Infernet. |
| | Swiftsure | Captain C. E. L'Hospitalier Villemadrin. |
| | Aigle | "   Pierre Paul Gourrège. |
| | Scipion | "   Charles Berenger. |
| | Duguay-Trouin | "   Claude Touffet. |
| | Berwick | "   Jeane Gilles Filhol Camas. |
| | Argonaute | "   Jacques Epron. |
| | Achille | "   Gabriel Denieport. |
| | Redoutable | "   Jean Jacques Etienne Lucas. |
| | Fougueux | "   Louis Alexis Beaudouin. |
| | Héros | "   Jean Bap. Jos. Reiné Poulain. |

#### Spanish.

| | | |
|---|---|---|
| 130 | Santissima Trinidad | Rear-Admiral Don B. Hildago Cisneros. <br> Commodore Don Francisco de Uriarte. |
| 112 | Principe de Asturias <br> Santa Anna | Admiral Don Federico Gravina. <br> Rear-Admiral Don Antonio Escano. <br> Vice-Admiral Don Tyn. Maria de Alava. |
| 100 | Rayo | Captain Don Josef Gardoqui. |
| | | Commodore Don Enrique Macdoull. |
| 80 | Neptuno <br> Argonauta | "   Don Cayetano Valdés. <br> "   Don Antonio Parejas. |
| 74 | Bahama | Captain Don Dionisio Galiano. |
| | Montanas | "   Don Josef Salzedo. |
| | San Augustin | "   Don Felipe Xado Cagigal. |
| | San Ildefonso | "   Don Josef Bargas. |
| | S. Jeun Nepomuano | "   Don Cosme Churruca. |
| | Monarca | "   Don Teodoro Argusnosa. |
| | S. Francisco de Asis | "   Don Luis de Flores. |
| | San Justo | "   Don Miguel Gaston. |
| 64 | San Leandro | "   Don Josef Quevedo. |

*Frigates*, (all French) Cornélie, Hermione, Hortense, Rhin, Thémis.
*Brigs*, Argus and Furet.

At half-past eleven A.M. Lord Nelson made his celebrated signal "ENGLAND EXPECTS THAT EVERY MAN WILL DO HIS DUTY;" a signal, than which no one was ever more judiciously chosen—a signal, which appealed to the heart of every man in the fleet, serving, not only to light up every spark of patriotic feeling, and bring forth in all its power the natural love of country existing in the bosom of every Briton; but also to direct his thoughts towards his individual home, with all its delightful and overwhelming associations. It has been truly regarded as the noblest appeal to national feeling ever made by a warrior to warriors, and it was received by a glorious shout of three cheers from the whole fleet. The Honorable Captain Blackwood describes the effect as truly sublime.[1]

Dr. Beatty says: "It is impossible adequately to describe by any language, the lively emotions excited in the crew of the Victory when this propitious communication was made known to them: confidence and resolution were strongly pourtrayed in the countenance of all; and the sentiment

---

[1] M. Thiers forms an exception to every other writer upon the Battle of Trafalgar, by omitting to notice the celebrated signal. His account is most exceptionable and inaccurate both as regards the number of guns and the loss of men. M. de la Gravière,[2] who has written with a much more impartial spirit, and whose object appears to have been to inquire into the cause of the immense superiority of the English naval power over that of the French, as shewn particularly in Nelson's battles of the Nile and Trafalgar, states the number of guns on the latter occasion to have been as follows: British, 2148; French, 2626. Thiers, however, is compelled to admit that the English had the glory of skill, and of experience, combined with incontestable bravery, and he also says, that from that day Napoleon thought less of the navy, and wished every body else to think less of it too. Buonaparte desired, it seems, that little should be said about Trafalgar in the French newspapers, and that it should be mentioned as an imprudent fight, in which they had suffered more from the tempest than the enemy. "Ils avoient la gloire de l'habileté, de l'expérience, unies à une incontestable bravoure." (Hist. du Consulat. tom. vi. liv. xxii. p. 173.) "A partir de ce jour, Napoléon pensa moins à la marine, et voulut que tout le monde y pensât moins aussi." (Ib. p. 183.) "Il voulut, qu'on parlât peu de Trafalgar dans les journaux français, et qu'on en fit mention comme d'un combat imprudent dans lequel nous avions plus souffert de la tempête que l'ennemi." (Ibid.)

---

[2] Papers in the Revue des Deux Mondes, translated by the Hon. Captain Plunkett, and published as "Sketches of the Last Naval War."

generally expressed to each other was, that they would prove to their country that day, how well British seamen *could* 'do their duty' when led to battle by their renowned Admiral."[1]

"Now (said Lord Nelson) I can do no more. We must trust to the Great Disposer of all events, and the justice of our cause. I thank God for this great opportunity of doing my duty." Nelson's presentiment of death seems to have been strong. When Captain Blackwood took leave of him and quitted the Victory for his own vessel the Euryalus, he said, " I trust, my Lord, that on my return to the Victory, which will be as soon as possible, I shall find your Lordship well, and in possession of twenty prizes." To which Nelson replied, "God bless you, Blackwood, I shall never speak to you again."

Sir W. Beatty states that " Lord Nelson often talked with Captain Hardy on the subject of his being killed in battle, it was a favourite topic of conversation with him, and it was the most ambitious wish of his soul to die in the fight, and in the very hour of a great and signal victory." It was said of Sir Ralph Abercromby, "When death *must* come, it never comes better than disguised as glory. Such ashes should rather be revered than deplored." And Lord Sidmouth finely remarked: " I cannot so dishonour Nelson as to weep over him. He has left a name the most splendid in our annals." If Nelson's desire was as stated, it was strictly accomplished—it was in the hour of victory, and one of, if not the greatest, ever obtained by any country at sea, that he fell, and to the last moment of his life retained his knowledge of the event and his own position.

At the main top-gallant-mast head of the Victory was fast belayed Nelson's customary signal on going into action: No. 16. " Engage the enemy more closely." At noon the action may be said to have commenced by a firing direct from the Fougueux upon the Royal Sovereign, and that vessel engaged the Santa Anna, firing with such precision with her double-shotted guns that, as afterwards appeared by the testimony of the Spanish officers, nearly 400 men were killed and wounded,

[1] Narrative, p. 24.

and 14 guns disabled. The Royal Sovereign also raked the Fougueux, which had commenced the attack, but with little effect, in consequence of her distance and the quantity of smoke. Nelson was delighted with Collingwood's conduct, and exclaimed: "See how that noble fellow Collingwood carries his ship into action." The Royal Sovereign was most severely engaged, for not only were the Santa Anna and the Fougueux opposed to her, but she had also to contend with the San Leandro, the San Justo, and the Indomptable. The shots from those vessels frequently met together, and this, added to the approach of some British ships to the relief of the Royal Sovereign, induced the ships to drop off and leave her and the Santa Anna to combat with each other.

Lord Nelson's chief anxiety was to find out in what ship the French Admiral was placed.[1] Every glass on board the Victory was put in requisition to ascertain this point, but no decisive information could be obtained. According to the Victory's log, she opened her fire on the enemy's van, at four minutes past twelve, and in attempting to pass through their line, she fell on board the 10th and 11th ships, when the action became general. As soon as the enemy ascertained the Victory to be within reach of shot, at least seven or eight of the weathermost ships opened a fire upon her—such a fire as is said had scarcely before been directed at any single ship. The Rev. Dr. Scott says that before the Victory returned a shot, she had fifty killed and wounded. Lord Nelson's Secretary, Mr. Scott, was killed whilst conversing with Captain Hardy. The Victory sustained much damage from the firing of the Santissima Trinidad, the Bucentaure, and

[1] The practice of French Admirals removing from their ships into a frigate when going into action, was adopted by order of the French Government, after the capture of the Comte de Grasse in the Ville de Paris by Rodney. M. de la Gravière says that Nelson was urged to do the same, the better to watch events and transmit orders; but that he refused to do so, conceiving nothing in battle so important as example. This writer, and French naval officer, does not seem to be aware that it has never been the practice in the English navy for an Admiral to quit his ship, unless the peculiarities of the situation in which he should be placed would not admit of his being effective in her, as was the case at Copenhagen with Nelson, when he removed from the St. George into the Elephant, the water being too shallow, and the navigation rendering it impossible for the former vessel to proceed to the spot at which his presence was required.

the Redoutable, without being able to make any return. The mizen-top-mast was shot away, about two-thirds up, and the wheel was also knocked away, so that the ship was obliged to be steered from the gun-room by the First Lieutenant and the Master. Eight marines on the poop having been killed by a double-headed shot, Nelson ordered the men to be more dispersed, and soon after a shot which had carried away part of the larboard quarter of the launch, as she lay on her booms, passed between Lord Nelson and Captain Hardy, and a splinter bruised the left foot of the latter and tore away the buckle from his shoe. Sir William Beatty says, they both instantly stopped, and were observed by the officers on deck to survey each other with inquiring looks, each supposing the other to be wounded. His Lordship then smiled and said, 'This is too warm work, Hardy, to last long;' and declared that, through all the battles he had been in, he had never witnessed more cool courage than was displayed by the Victory's crew on this occasion. The Victory now fired into the Bucentaure. Mr. James, from whose narrative the following summary account is principally taken, says, "At one, P. M. the 68-pounder carronade on the larboard side of the Victory's forecastle, containing its customary charge of one round shot and a keg filled with 500 musket-balls, was fired right into the cabin windows of the Bucentaure. As the Victory slowly moved ahead, every gun of the remaining fifty upon her broadside, all double, and some of them treble-shotted, was deliberately discharged in the same raking manner. So close were the ships, that the larboard main-yard arm of the British three-decker, as she rolled, touched the vangs of her opponent's gaff: so close indeed, that had there been wind enough to blow it out, the large French ensign trailing at the Bucentaure's peak might, even at this early period of the action, have been a trophy in the hands of the Victory's crew. While listening, with characteristic avidity, to the deafening crash made by their shot in the French ship's hull, the British crew were nearly suffocated with clouds of black smoke that entered the Victory's port-holes; and Lord Nelson, Captain Hardy, and others who were walking the quarter-deck, had their clothes covered with the dust which issued from the crumbled wood-work of

the Bucentaure's stern. Although the work of scarcely two
minutes, and although not a mast or yard of the Bucentaure
was seen to come down, the effects of the British three-
decker's broadside upon the *personnel* of the French ship, as
acknowledged a day or two afterwards by Vice-Admiral
Villeneuve, and long subsequently by his Flag Captain, M.
Magendie, was of the same destructive character as the
broadside poured by the Royal Sovereign into the stern of
the Santa Anna. The account which the Bucentaure's
officers gave, as the extent of their loss in killed and wounded
by the Victory's fire, was 'nearly 400 men.' They represented, also, that twenty of their guns were dismounted by
it, and that the Bucentaure was reduced to a comparatively
defenceless state."

The Neptune came to the relief of the Bucentaure, and did
much injury to the Victory. Fearing, however, this vessel
running on board of her, the Neptune ranged ahead, and the
Victory came in the direction of the Redoutable, of which
she ran foul, and the two ships dropped alongside each other.
They were, indeed, held together, the Victory's starboard fore-
topmast studding-sail boom-iron, as the ships were in the act
of rebounding off, having hooked itself into the leech of the
Redoutable's fore-topsail. The boatswain of the Victory,
Mr. William Willmet, soon cleared the gangways of the
Redoutable by firing the starboard 68-pounder carronade,
loaded as the larboard one had been, right upon the Redoutable's decks. "The guns of the middle and lower decks
were also occasionally fired into the Redoutable, but very few
of the 12-pounders, on account chiefly of the heavy loss
among those who had been stationed at them. The Redoutable, on her part, fired her main deck guns into the Victory,
and used musketry, as well through her ports into those of
the Victory, as from her three tops down upon the latter's
deck. In her fore and main-tops, also, the Redoutable had
some brass cohorns which, loaded with langridge, were frequently fired with destructive effect upon the Victory's forecastle. The larboard guns of the Victory were fired occasionally at the Bucentaure; but it was with little or no effect,
the latter ship continuing to move to the northward, while
the Victory and Redoutable kept inclining their heads to the

eastward. The Santissima Trinidad also received into her starboard or lee quarter, and stern, a portion of the Victory's fire.

"Never allowing mere personal comfort to interfere with what he considered to be the good of the service, Lord Nelson, when the Victory was fitting to receive his flag, ordered the large sky-light over his cabin to be removed, and the space planked up, so as to afford him a walk amid-ships, clear of the guns and ropes. Here, along an extent of deck of about twenty-one feet in length, bounded abaft by the stancheon of the wheel, and forward by the combings of the cabin ladder-way, were the Admiral and Captain Hardy, during the whole of the operations just detailed, taking their customary promenade, at about one hour, twenty-five minutes, P.M., just as the two had arrived within one pace of the regular turning spot at the cabin ladder-way, Lord Nelson, who, regardless of quarter-deck etiquette, was walking on the larboard side, suddenly faced left about. Captain Hardy, as soon as he had taken the other step, turned also, and saw the Admiral in the act of falling. He was then on his knees, with his left hand just touching the deck. The arm giving way, Lord Nelson fell on his left side, exactly upon the spot where his Secretary, Mr. Scott, had breathed his last, and with whose blood his Lordship's clothes were soiled.

"On Captain Hardy's expressing a hope that he was not severely wounded, Lord Nelson replied: 'They have done for me at last, Hardy.' 'I hope not,' replied Captain Hardy. 'Yes,' replied his Lordship, 'my back bone is shot through.' The wound was by a musket ball, which had entered the left shoulder, through the fore part of the epaulette, and, descending, had lodged in the spine. That the wound had been given by some one stationed in the Redoutable's mizen-top was rendered certain, not only from the nearness (about fifteen yards) and situation of the mizen-top in reference to the course of the ball, but from the circumstance that the French ship's main-top was screened by a portion of the Victory's main-sail as it hung when clewed up. That the ball was intended for Lord Nelson is doubtful, because, when the aim must have been taken, he was walking on the outer side, concealed in a great measure from view by a much taller and stouter man. Admitting also (which is very doubtful), that the French seaman or marine, whose shot had proved so fatal, had selected for his object, as the British Commander-in-chief, the best dressed officer of the two, he would most probably have fixed upon Captain Hardy, or, indeed, such was Lord Nelson's habitual carelessless, upon any one of the Victory's Lieutenants who might be walking by the side of him.

"Serjeant-Major Secker of the marines, and two seamen, who had come up on seeing the Admiral fall, now by Captain Hardy's direction, bore their revered and much lamented Chief to the cockpit."

Dr. Beatty states that there were only two Frenchmen left alive in the mizen-top of the Redoutable at the time of Lord Nelson being wounded, and by the hands of one of these he must have fallen. They continued firing at the officers on the poop of the Victory for some time afterwards; one of them was at length killed, and the other, endeavouring to effect his escape from the top down the rigging, was shot by Mr. Pollard, a Midshipman, not more than sixteen years of age, and he fell dead from the shrouds. The same authority acquaints us, that several of the officers on board the Victory had communicated to each other their sentiments of anxiety for Lord Nelson's safety, to which every other consideration seemed to give way. No one, it appears, entertained any apprehension of defeat, but all were anxious for the preservation of the Admiral. The Surgeon made known to the Rev. Dr. Scott, his fears that his Lordship might be the object of the enemy's marksmen, having his stars affixed to his coat, and a desire was expressed that some one should entreat his Lordship to cover them with his handkerchief. Dr. Scott and Mr. Scott observed that this would be without effect, and that it might incur his displeasure. The Surgeon, however, determined to do so when making his sick report for the day, and remained on deck for the purpose, but the opportunity did not occur. The Admiral was too much engaged with his Captains to allow of the report being made, and all persons were ordered to retire to their proper quarters.

The fire from the Redoutable's tops upon the Victory was

very destructive. The Téméraire wreaked her vengeance on the enemy. When the guns on the deck of the Victory were run out, their muzzles came in contact with the side of the Redoutable, there was therefore great reason to fear the vessel taking fire, by which not only the enemy's ship, but the Victory and the Téméraire would be also endangered. To obviate this a fireman was to be seen standing at each gun with a bucket full of water ready upon the discharge, immediately to dash into the hole its contents, and prevent a conflagration.

Mr. James records:—

"Most of the few effective men left upon the Victory's upper deck after the Redoutable's destructive fire, formerly noticed, being employed in carrying their wounded comrades to the cockpit, Captain Hardy, Captain Adair of the marines, and one or two other officers, were nearly all that remained upon the quarter-deck and poop. The men in the Redoutable's mizen-top soon made this known to the officers below; and a considerable portion of the French crew quickly assembled in the chains and along the gangway of their ship, in order to board the British three-decker; whose defenceless state they inferred, not merely from her abandoned upper deck, but from the temporary silence of her guns on the decks below, occasioned by a supposition that the Redoutable, having discontinued her fire, was on the eve of surrendering. A party of the Victory's officers and men quickly ascended from the middle and lower decks; and after an interchange of musketry, the French crew, who, in addition to the unexpected opposition they experienced, found that the curve in the hulls of the two ships prevented their stepping from one to the other, retired within-board. The repulse of this very gallant assault cost the Victory dearly. Captain Adair and eighteen men were killed, and one Lieutenant (William Ram,[1] mortally), one Midshipman (George Augustus Westphal[2]), and twenty men wounded. Captain Adair met his

[1] Lieutenant W. A. Ram was a native of Hampshire, and son of Colonel Ram, M.P. for Wexford. His brother, also a Lieutenant in the navy, was drowned in 1809, at Bermuda, by the upsetting of a boat.

[2] Now Captain Sir George Augustus Westphal, being made Post, August 12th, 1819. After the action of Trafalgar he was made senior Lieutenant of the

death by a musket ball received at the back of the neck, while standing upon the Victory's gangway encouraging his men, and several seamen and marines were also killed by the French musketry; but the Lieutenant and Midshipman, and four or five seamen standing near them, were struck by a round shot, or the splinters it occasioned, which shot had come obliquely through the quarter-deck, and must have been fired from one of the Redoutable's main-deck guns, pointed upwards."

Further hostility on the part of the Redoutable now ceased, and she was afterwards quietly taken possession of by Lieutenant John Wallace, Second Lieutenant of the Téméraire.

But to return to our Hero:—Sir William Beatty, the Surgeon, to whose care he was now consigned, has furnished us with every particular in relation to his condition, and this cannot be stated better than in the narrator's own words.[1] Nelson received his mortal wound about a quarter past one o'clock.

"Captain Hardy ordered the seamen to carry the Admiral to the cockpit; and now two incidents occurred strikingly characteristic of this great man, and strongly marking that energy and reflection which, in his heroic mind, rose superior even to the immediate consideration of his present awful

---

Belleisle, 74 guns, commanded by Captain Sir George Cockburn, and was present during an attack on Flushing, having the command of a sub-division of gun-boats from the 8th to the 15th of August, 1809. In 1810 he was appointed to the Implacable, and landed the Baron de Kolli at Quiberon Bay, when proceeding to facilitate the escape of Ferdinand VII. He was afterwards employed in the expulsion of the enemy from Moguer, a town on the Huebla, and received the approbation of his commander, Sir George Cockburn, as expressed in his Dispatches to Rear-Admiral Sir R. G. Keats. On the North American station, with the same commander—but now Rear-Admiral—he was engaged at the Chesapeake in 1813, and again merited high commendation. In his service on this station he received a shot through his hand at Havre de Grace, but with the other brought in as a prisoner a Captain of Militia. In the Sceptre, of 74 guns, he continued to distinguish himself, and captured a fine brig, the Anaconda, and a schooner. Having obtained his Post rank, he was appointed to the Jupiter, of 60 guns, and took out Lord Amherst to Bengal in 1822. Upon his return to England he received the honour of Knighthood, and in 1846 made Aide-de-camp to the Queen.

[1] " Authentic Narrative of the Death of Lord Nelson, by William Beatty, M.D. Surgeon to the Victory, at the Battle of Trafalgar, and now Physician to the Fleet under the command of the Earl of St. Vincent, K.B. &c. &c." Lond. 1807. 8vo.

condition. While the men were carrying him down the ladder from the middle deck, his Lordship observed that the tiller ropes were not yet replaced; and desired one of the Midshipmen stationed there, to go upon the quarter-deck, and remind Captain Hardy of that circumstance, and request that new ones should be immediately rove. Having delivered this order, he took his handkerchief from his pocket and covered his face with it, that he might be conveyed to the cockpit at this crisis unnoticed by the crew.

"Several wounded officers, and about forty men, were likewise carried to the Surgeon for assistance just at this time; and some others had breathed their last during their conveyance below. Among the latter were Lieutenant William Andrew Ram, and Mr. Whipple, Captain's Clerk. The Surgeon had just examined these two officers, and found that they were dead, when his attention was arrested by several of the wounded calling to him, 'Mr. Beatty, Lord Nelson is here: Mr. Beatty, the Admiral is wounded.' The Surgeon now, on looking round, saw the handkerchief fall from his Lordship's face; when the stars on his coat, which also had been covered by it, appeared. Mr. Burke, the Purser, and the Surgeon ran immediately to the assistance of his Lordship, and took him from the arms of the seamen who had carried him below. In conveying him to one of the Midshipmen's berths, they stumbled, but recovered themselves without falling. Lord Nelson then inquired who were supporting him; and when the Surgeon informed him, his Lordship replied, 'Ah, Mr. Beatty, you can do nothing for me. I have but a short time to live: my back is shot through.' The Surgeon said, 'he hoped the wound was not so dangerous as his Lordship imagined, and that he might still survive long to enjoy his glorious victory.' The Rev. Dr. Scott, who had been absent in another part of the cockpit administering lemonade to the wounded, now came instantly to his Lordship; and in his anguish of grief wrung his hands, and said: 'Alas, Beatty, how prophetic you were!' alluding to the apprehensions expressed by the Surgeon for his Lordship's safety previous to the battle.

"His Lordship was laid upon a bed, stripped of his clothes, and covered with a sheet. While this was effecting, he said to Dr. Scott, 'Doctor, I told you so. Doctor, I am gone;' and after a short pause, he added in a low voice, 'I have to leave Lady Hamilton, and my adopted daughter Horatia, as a legacy to my country.' The Surgeon then examined the wound, assuring his Lordship that he would not put him to much pain in endeavouring to discover the course of the ball; which he soon found had penetrated deep into the chest, and had probably lodged in the spine. This being explained to his Lordship, he replied, 'he was confident his back was shot through.' The back was then examined externally, but without any injury being perceived; on which his Lordship was requested by the Surgeon to make him acquainted with all his sensations. He replied, 'that he felt a gush of blood every minute within his breast: that he had no feeling in the lower part of his body: and that his breathing was difficult, and attended with very severe pain about that part of the spine where he was confident that the ball had struck; for,' said he, 'I felt it break my back.'

"These symptoms, but more particularly the gush of blood which his Lordship complained of, together with the state of his pulse, indicated to the Surgeon the hopeless situation of the case; but till after the victory was ascertained and announced to his Lordship, the true nature of his wound was concealed by the Surgeon from all on board, except only Captain Hardy, Doctor Scott, Mr. Burke, and Messrs. Smith and Westemburg, the Assistant-Surgeons.

"The Victory's crew cheered whenever they observed an enemy's ship surrender. On one of these occasions, Lord Nelson anxiously inquired what was the cause of it; when Lieutenant Pasco, who lay wounded at some distance from his Lordship, raised himself up, and told him that another ship had struck, which appeared to give him much satisfaction. He now felt an ardent thirst, and frequently called for drink, and to be fanned with paper, making use of these words: 'fan, fan.' and 'drink, drink.' This he continued to repeat, when he wished for drink, and the refreshment of cool air, till a very few minutes before he expired. Lemonade, and wine and water were given to him occasionally. He evinced great solicitude for the event of the battle, and fears for the safety of his friend Captain Hardy. Dr. Scott, and Mr.

Burke used every argument they could suggest to relieve his anxiety. Mr. Burke told him 'the enemy were decisively defeated, and that he hoped his Lordship would still live to be himself the bearer of the joyful tidings to his country.' He replied, 'It is nonsense, Mr. Burke, to suppose I can live: my sufferings are great, but they will all be soon over.' Dr. Scott entreated his Lordship 'not to despair of living,' and said, 'he trusted that Divine Providence would restore him once more to his dear country and friends.' 'Ah, Doctor!' replied his Lordship, 'it is all over; it is all over.'

"Many messages were sent to Captain Hardy by the Surgeon, requesting his attendance on his Lordship; who became impatient to see him, and often exclaimed: 'Will no one bring Hardy to me? He must be killed: he is surely destroyed.' The Captain's Aide-de-camp, Mr. Bulkeley, now came below, and stated that 'circumstances respecting the fleet required Captain Hardy's presence on deck, but that he would avail himself of the first favourable moment to visit his Lordship.' On hearing him deliver this message to the Surgeon, his Lordship inquired who had brought it. Mr. Burke answered, 'It is Mr. Bulkeley, my Lord.' 'It is his voice,' replied his Lordship: he then said to the young gentleman, 'Remember me to your father.'

"An hour and ten minutes however elapsed, from the time of his Lordship being wounded, before Captain Hardy's first subsequent interview with him; the particulars of which are nearly as follows: they shook hands affectionately, and Lord Nelson said: 'Well, Hardy, how goes the battle? How goes the day with us?' 'Very well, my Lord,' replied Captain Hardy: 'we have got twelve or fourteen of the enemy's ships in our possession; but five of their van have tacked, and shew an intention of bearing down upon the Victory. I have therefore called two or three of our fresh ships round us, and have no doubt of giving them a drubbing.' 'I hope,' said his Lordship, 'none of *our* ships have struck, Hardy.' 'No, my Lord,' replied Captain Hardy, 'there is no fear of that.' Lord Nelson then said: 'I am a dead man, Hardy. I am going fast: it will be all over with me soon. Come nearer to me. Pray let my dear Lady Hamilton have my hair, and all other things belonging to me.' Mr. Burke was about to withdraw at the commencement of this conversation; but his Lordship perceiving his intention, desired he would remain. Captain Hardy observed, that 'he hoped Mr. Beatty could yet hold out some prospect of life.' 'Oh! no,' answered his Lordship; 'it is impossible. My back is shot through. Beatty will tell you so.' Captain Hardy then returned on deck, and at parting shook hands again with his revered friend and Commander.

"His Lordship now requested the Surgeon, who had been previously absent a short time attending Mr. Rivers,[1] to return to the wounded, and give his assistance to such of them as he could be useful to; for, said he, 'you can do nothing for me.' The Surgeon assured him, that the Assistant-Surgeons were doing everything that could be effected for those unfortunate men; but on his Lordship several times repeating his injunctions to that purpose, he left him, surrounded by Doctor Scott, Mr. Burke, and two of his Lordship's domestics. After the Surgeon had been absent a few minutes, attending Lieutenant Peake, and Reeves, of the Marines, who were wounded, he was called by Doctor Scott to his Lordship, who said: 'Ah, Mr. Beatty! I have sent for you to say, what I forgot to tell you before, that all power of motion and feeling below my breast are gone; and *you*,' continued he, 'very well *know*, I can live but a short time.' The emphatic manner in which he pronounced these last words, left no doubt in the Surgeon's mind, that he adverted to the case of a man who had some months before received a mortal injury of the spine, on board the Victory, and had laboured under similar privation of sense and muscular motion. The case had made a great impression on Lord Nelson: he was anxious to know the cause of such symptoms, which was accordingly explained to him; and he now appeared to apply the situation and fate of this man to himself. The Surgeon answered, 'My Lord, you told me so before:' but he now examined the extremities, to ascertain the fact; when his Lordship said, 'Ah, Beatty! I am too certain of it: Scott and Burke have tried it already. *You know* I am gone.' The Surgeon replied: 'My Lord,

---

[1] James Elphinstone Rivers, died Second Lieutenant of the East India Company's surveying ship Minto, of a fever, at Chowinghee, the 16th of June, 1814, at the early age of twenty-two years.

unhappily for our country, nothing can be done for you;' and
having made this declaration, he was so much affected, that
he turned round and withdrew a few steps, to conceal his
emotions. His Lordship said: 'I know it. I feel something
rising in my breast,' putting his hand on his left side, 'which
tells me I am gone.' Drink was recommended liberally, and
Doctor Scott and Mr. Burke fanned him with paper. He
often exclaimed, ' God be praised, I have done my duty;' and
upon the Surgeon's inquiring whether his pain was still
very great, he declared, ' it continued so very severe, that he
wished he was dead. Yet,' said he, in a low voice, ' one would
like to live a little longer, too?' and after a pause of a few
minutes, he added, in the same tone, ' What would become of
poor Lady Hamilton, if she knew my situation!'

Captain Hardy now came to the cockpit to see his Lordship a second time, which was after an interval of about fifty minutes from the conclusion of his first visit. Before he quitted the deck, he sent Lieutenant Hill to acquaint Admiral Collingwood with the lamentable circumstance of Lord Nelson's being wounded. Lord Nelson and Captain Hardy shook hands again, and while the Captain retained his Lordship's hand, he congratulated him, even in the arms of death, on his brilliant victory; 'which,' he said, 'was complete; though he did not know how many of the enemy were captured, as it was impossible to perceive every ship distinctly. He was certain, however, of fourteen or fifteen having surrendered.' His Lordship answered, 'That is well, but I bargained for twenty:' and then emphatically exclaimed, '*Anchor*, Hardy, *anchor!*' To this the Captain replied, 'I suppose, my Lord, Admiral Collingwood will now take upon himself the direction of affairs.' ' Not while I live, I hope, Hardy!' cried the dying Chief; and at that moment, endeavoured ineffectually to raise himself from the bed. 'No,' added he; 'do *you* anchor, Hardy.' Captain Hardy then said, 'Shall *we* make the signal, Sir?'—' Yes,' answered his Lordship, ' for if I live, I'll anchor.' The energetic manner in which he uttered these his last orders to Captain Hardy, accompanied with his efforts to raise himself, evinced his determination never to resign the command while he retained the exercise of his transcendent faculties, and that he expected Captain Hardy still to carry into effect the suggestions of his exalted mind; a sense of his duty overcoming the pains of death. He then told Captain Hardy, 'he felt that in a few minutes he should be no more;' adding in a low tone, 'Don't throw me overboard, Hardy.' The Captain answered: 'Oh! no, certainly not.' 'Then,' replied his Lordship, 'you know what to do: and,' continued he, 'take care of my dear Lady Hamilton, Hardy: take care of poor Lady Hamilton. Kiss me, Hardy.' The Captain now knelt down, and kissed his cheek; when his Lordship said, 'Now I am satisfied. Thank God, I have done my duty.' Captain Hardy stood for a minute or two in silent contemplation: he knelt down again, and kissed his Lordship's forehead. His Lordship said: 'Who is that?' The Captain answered: 'It is Hardy;' to which his Lordship replied, 'God bless you, Hardy!' After this affecting scene Captain Hardy withdrew, and returned to the quarter-deck, having spent about eight minutes in this his last interview with his dying friend.

"Lord Nelson now desired Mr. Chevalier, his steward, to turn him upon his right side; which being effected, his Lordship said: 'I wish I had not left the deck, for I shall soon be gone.' He afterwards became very low; his breathing was oppressed, and his voice faint. He said to Doctor Scott: 'Doctor, I have *not* been a *great* sinner;' and after a short pause, '*Remember*, that I leave Lady Hamilton and my daughter Horatia as a legacy to my country; and,' added he, 'never forget Horatia.' His thirst now increased, and he called for 'drink, drink,' 'fan, fan,' and 'rub, rub,' addressing himself in the last case to Doctor Scott, who had been rubbing his Lordship's breast with his hand, from which he found some relief. These words he spoke in a very rapid manner, which rendered his articulation difficult: but he every now and then, with evident increase of pain, made a greater effort with his vocal powers, and pronounced distinctly these last words: 'Thank God, I have done my duty;' and this great sentiment he continued to repeat as long as he was able to give it utterance.

"His Lordship became speechless in about fifteen minutes after Captain Hardy left him. Dr. Scott and Mr. Burke, who had all along sustained the bed under his shoulders (which raised him in nearly a semi-recumbent posture, the only one that was supportable to him), forbore to disturb him by speaking to him; and when he had remained speechless about five minutes, his Lordship's steward went to the Surgeon, who had been a short time occupied with the wounded in another part of the cockpit, and stated his apprehension that his Lordship was dying. The Surgeon immediately repaired to him, and found him on the verge of dissolution. He knelt down by his side, and took up his hand, which was cold, and the pulse gone from the wrist. On the Surgeon feeling his forehead, which was likewise cold, his Lordship opened his eyes, looked up, and shut them again. The Surgeon again left him, and returned to the wounded, who required his assistance; but was not absent five minutes before the steward announced to him, that 'he believed his Lordship had expired.' The Surgeon returned, and found that the report was but too well founded: his Lordship had breathed his last, at thirty minutes past four o'clock; at which period Doctor Scott was in the act of rubbing his Lordship's breast, and Mr. Burke supporting the bed under his shoulders."[1]

His body was deposited in a cask, called a leaguer, there being no lead on board capable of being made into a coffin, and the cask was filled with brandy. It was placed on the middle deck, and a sentinel stationed over it. On the arrival of the Victory at Gibraltar, on the 28th of October, spirits of wine was substituted for the brandy. The wounded of the crew of the Victory were sent on shore to the Naval Hospital at this place, and the damage done to the ship in the action so far repaired, as to enable her to go to England. A tedious passage of five weeks from Gibraltar to Spithead was occasioned by adverse winds and tempestuous weather. No orders with respect to the body of Nelson having been received at Portsmouth, and the Victory being ordered to proceed to the Nore, and reports being current of an intention that the Hero should lie in state, and that his remains would be exposed to the public view in Greenwich Hospital, Dr. Beatty inspected the body on the 11th of December, whilst proceeding from

---

[1] Dr. Beatty's Narrative, pp. 34-51.

Spithead to the Nore, and it was found to have been well preserved. At this time also the ball was discovered, having, after passing through the lung and spine, lodged itself in the muscles of the back, below the shoulder-blade, carrying with it a portion of the gold lace, pad, lining of the epaulette, and piece of the coat through which it passed.[1] The body was enveloped in cotton bandages, and placed in a leaden coffin, which was filled with brandy, in which camphor and myrrh were dissolved. For the leaden coffin was substituted that made from the mainmast of the French ship, L'Orient, and presented to him by Captain Hallowell, after the battle of the Nile.[2] His directions were thus complied with—the coffin was placed in a leaden one and soldered up—then in a wooden shell, and was thus conveyed from the Victory into Commissioner Grey's yacht, and taken to Greenwich Hospital by his Chaplain, the Rev. Mr. Scott, Mr. Tyson, and Mr. Whitby.

Lord Nelson was buried in the Cathedral of St. Paul's on the 9th of January, 1806. The funeral was conducted at the public expense, and accompanied by all military honours. The body which, upon its arrival at Greenwich, had been placed in the Record Room, was removed to the Painted Hall, where it laid in state for three days, after which it was conveyed to the Admiralty by water, and attended by the Lord Mayor and Corporation of London in their state barges, and a large number of naval officers who had enjoyed the friendship of the deceased. A procession was formed from the Painted Hall to the water side, and the Dead March in Saul was executed. Five hundred of the Greenwich Pensioners preceded the officers and the body, and constituted a truly affecting sight. The venerable Sir Peter Parker, the Admiral of the Fleet, the early patron and constant friend of Lord Nelson, the officer to whom he was always so anxious to pour forth expressions of gratitude was chief mourner on this occasion, and was supported by the Admirals Lords Hood and Radstock. The body was conveyed in the Admiral's own barge, in which, by its own crew, it was safely taken to Whitehall, and thence to the Admiralty.

---

[1] The fatal ball is now in the possession of her Majesty the Queen Victoria. The coat has been presented to Greenwich Hospital, by his Royal Highness the Prince Albert.   [2] See Vol. i. p. 132.

On the 9th of January the funeral took place. It moved at noon from the Admiralty, the streets were lined by the volunteers, and in the procession were not less than 10,000 troops, who chiefly belonged to regiments that had been engaged in service in Egypt. The military bands performed solemn music. Thus was the first or military part of the procession constituted; the second consisted of the carriages of the nobility and gentry, then the private carriages of the Royal Family and the Princes of the Blood Royal. The third part of the procession was headed by the Greenwich Pensioners and the crew of the Victory, and formed altogether the most interesting part of the ceremonial. The sailors of the Victory wore crape hatbands in addition to their naval dress. The flag of the Victory which followed, and was pierced by numerous balls and stained with the blood of the hero, formed no inconsiderable feature on the occasion. The coffin was exposed to view upon a bier or car, now to be seen in Greenwich Hospital, ornamented with various emblems, and the escutcheons of the deceased, and was attended by the heralds carrying the emblems of his rank, whilst the pall was supported by four Admirals. Then followed the mourners, Sir Peter Parker being the principal, and his train borne by the Hon. Captain Blackwood, followed by Captain Hardy, Captain Bayntun, and Lieutenants King and Bligh. Arriving at the Cathedral the procession was again formed, and the burial service read by the Dean of St. Paul's, the whole terminating with the Anthem, "HIS BODY IS BURIED IN PEACE, BUT HIS NAME LIVETH EVERMORE." Parliament voted a monument to his memory, and it was placed in St. Paul's, executed by Flaxman. The inscription on it was written by Richard Brinsley Sheridan, Esq., M.P. Other public monuments were erected at Edinburgh, Glasgow, Dublin, Liverpool, Birmingham, Yarmouth, &c. At Portsdown Hill a pillar was raised as a landmark by the subscription of those who had shared in the dangers and glories of Trafalgar. A singular monument, deserving of notice, is also mentioned by Lady Chatterton, in her interesting "Rambles in the South of Ireland." "Sometimes we caught glimpses of the distant rocky headlands which render this part of the coast so magnificent. At the summit of one, is a lofty arch, erected to the memory of Nelson by a party of officers. It is formed of large stones without cement, and I was told it was entirely constructed after Church one Sunday. If this account be true, it reminds one of the marvellous tale related in Ireland of every colossal structure, that it was the work of a night! This wonderful arch, however, forms a fine object in most of the views about Castle Townsend, and as I first saw it towering above the mist which concealed the base of the mountain height on which it stood, its appearance was supernatural."[1]

The Government proposed and Parliament granted honours and emoluments to the family of the departed hero. An Earldom was permanently annexed to the family, and conferred upon his brother the Rev. Dr. William Nelson, with a pension of £5000 *per annum* attached to the Earldom, and a gift of £120,000 in money. From this grant, an estate in Wiltshire, which formerly belonged to the ancestors of the first Countess Nelson, was purchased, and named after the celebrated victory "Trafalgar." The present Horatio Earl Nelson, who now resides there, is descended from the Boltons, being the son of Thomas Bolton, second Earl, and is therefore the grandson of Lord Nelson's sister, and succeeded to the title November 1, 1835, upon the death of his father. He was born August 7, 1823. £90,000 was destined for the purchase of the mansion and lands, and £10,000 to the reparations or improvements adjudged necessary; whilst the remaining £20,000 was to be divided between Lord Nelson's sisters, Mrs. Bolton and Mrs. Matcham. It was in a great measure through the exertions of Mr. Abraham Goldsmid that the sums mentioned were appropriated to Mrs. Bolton and Mrs. Matcham, and the following extract from a letter addressed to Lady Hamilton by this truly benevolent and excellent man will shew his zeal and anxiety on the occasion, and that he endeavoured to induce the Government to double the amount to Mrs. Bolton:—

"Finsbury Square, April 8, 1806.

"I had the pleasure yesterday to receive a few lines from you, and am happy you are well, but am sorry your spirits are not yet recovered. I hope shortly to see you, and to tell you that it is the will of Providence, and to him it is our duty to content ourselves; and on mature reflection you will

---

[1] Vol. i. p. 40.

be convinced that it was for the good of those he esteemed, and his time was to die, and if not by a shot you might have lost him by sickness, and then his feelings would not have been fulfilled according to his own wishes, which to me I am sure of. Now for business, and please to keep it to yourself and Mrs. Bolton. I have seen and conversed with all the parties and pushed all I could. The answer from Lord Grenville was, he meant to give Mr. Bolton £10,000 at his disposal, and £10,000 to Mr. Matcham for his disposal. My answer was, that as to Mr. Matcham there might be an apology for such a sum, but as to Mr. Bolton I hoped and trusted they would give at least £20,000 ready money, exclusive of a respectable place under Government for Mr. Bolton. Mr. Vansittart's answer was that he admired my zeal in the promotion of the welfare of the late Lord Nelson's family, but they had a deal to contend with, &c. &c.

" Your affectionate friend,
" ABRAHAM GOLDSMID."

Parliament also voted £320,000 to the victors of Trafalgar, as compensation for the prizes taken, but lost in or destroyed by the gales subsequent to the action.

Large subscriptions were entered into, and the Patriotic Fund voted a vase of £500 value as a relic to the Viscountess Nelson, and similar ones to Earl Nelson, and Admiral, now Lord Collingwood. Vases of £300 value were voted to Rear-Admirals Earl Northesk and Sir Richard Strachan, Bart. Swords of the value of £100 were voted to the several Captains and Commanders of the different ships engaged in the battle, and £100 in money to each of the Lieutenants of the Navy, Captains of the Royal Marines, and other officers wounded severely on the occasion, whilst £50 to each of those slightly injured was determined to be given. To different classes of the service were also allotted various sums according to the usual distribution of prize-money, and the money collected at the Churches and Chapels on the Day of Thanksgiving for the Victory, was appropriated exclusively to the relief of the seamen, soldiers, marines, and volunteers wounded, and to the widows, orphans, and relations of those who had fallen in the action.

## CHAPTER XII.

### 1805-1806.

HAVING, in the preceding Chapters, traced the Hero through his brilliant career, and attended his loved remains to the tomb, the following letters written to Lady Hamilton, on occasion of Lord Nelson's decease and the transit of his remains to the Admiralty, cannot but be interesting to the reader :—

From Captain Sir William Bolton :—

"H. M. S. Eurydice, November 3rd, Gibraltar.

" My dear, honoured Lady Hamilton,

" Most sincerely do I hope this letter will not be ill-timed, for I should ever feel self-reproach did I for a moment delay writing to your Ladyship my feelings on our late so dreadful calamity

" With a heart and mind deeply impressed with gratitude for your Ladyship's generous attention to me and mine ; still more so with the inestimable value of *such a friend ;* I humbly request, with a true heart, request you will not deprive me of the almost sole consolation left—your regard. In faithfulness, none shall exceed me ; in attachment and esteem, none ; if my ability equals not my will, I must *indeed* regret it ; but it shall be a spur, to incite me to the exertion of my abilities in the situation our saint has placed me. With fervent prayers to that good God (with whom he is) for your consolation and future peace of mind, I for ever subscribe myself your Ladyship's most faithful friend,

"W. BOLTON."

Sir Andrew Snape Hamond, Bart., Comptroller of the Navy, to Lady Hamilton :—

"Admiralty, 6th Nov. 1805.

" The Hero of the Nile has again achieved more than ever fell to the lot of man. He fought the combined fleet of

France and Spain of thirty-three sail of the line, on the 21st October, with twenty-seven on his part, and gained a most complete and decisive victory, depriving the enemy of twenty ships. This he did for his country; but, alas! what has that country paid for it!!!

"How shall I relate the rest. The noblest and most magnanimous of mankind fell in the conflict, but not till he knew the victory was gained, and that he had accomplished the most ardent wish of his heart.

"Let us, my dear Madam, bear this severe stroke of fortune as becomes us. We have both lost our most beloved friend, but we must submit to the will of Providence, and believe that the Almighty has ordered this for the wisest purposes.

"Adieu,

"Your faithful and afflicted friend,

"A. S. HAMOND."

From Rear-Admiral Sir Thomas Louis, Bart:—[1]

"Canopus, off Cadiz,
Nov. 9th, 1805.

"Dear Lady Hamilton,

"The painful task I am now about to undertake is truly distressing to me—still, after the many repeated marks of attention and friendship from you and yours, when abroad, as well as in England, I should think myself very deficient indeed, at a moment like this, not to offer my condolence with yours, for the loss of our *gallant, valuable,* and much to be lamented Lord Nelson. To enter upon my sufferings upon this awful occasion must give pain to both, and every one that knew his value. Never was a man more beloved by all, nor a loss so much regretted. He died truly the hero in the arms of victory. Such a loss can never be replaced. Could I suppose, when I last parted with him, it was never to meet again? Surely not, nor would I have parted from him had a thought of the kind entered my head, although I might have received his displeasure at the moment in objecting; but if

---

[1] This officer was not created a Baronet until March 29, 1806, but I have preferred in this, as in the following letters in this Chapter, to designate the writers in accordance with the position they afterwards attained in the service.

was my lot to be detached with a division to receive supplies at Gibraltar, and water at Tetuan, after which, to protect a valuable convoy, with a considerable sum on board, clear of the Carthagena squadron. I could not help remarking to my most worthy and good friend, Lord Nelson, that I feared the enemy would come out while we were absent. His reply, '*Don't mind, Louis, they won't come out yet, and my fleet must be completed; the sooner you go the better.*' Now what must all our distress and sufferings be, after following him close upon the enemy, and to be prevented the honour of closing the day with the *man* we all so much adored, and what was still more distressing, to lose him on that ever-to-be-remembered day. Poor Captains Hallowell and Stopford were of my party: the former, you know full well the regard they had for each other. The grand consolation now left, is, that after the severe wound he received, had he lived, he might have lingered a life of existence only, painful to himself, and equally, or more so, as very distressing to those who knew and loved him.

"It would be a great gratification to me to have something that was once really *his*, as a token of remembrance and regard for the man I loved and had the highest respect for, which shall be handed down to my posterity. I never made such a request before, nor ever shall again, for no man can ever have the warmth of my heart and soul so strong and sincere. I don't care what it is, you will oblige me much by sending it, directed to Mrs. Louis, Cadwell, Newton Bushell, Devon. She will take care of it until my return. God bless you, my dear Lady Hamilton. Had I shared the honours of the day, I might have seen you earlier than it appears *likely* at present I shall, but whenever I come to England, I shall not lose time in paying my respects, and to assure you, how much obliged I feel for every mark of attention and kindness from you, and how much I regret the loss of my dear and valuable friend, Lord Nelson.

"My best wishes attend you, Mrs. Cadogan, and Miss Charlotte, to whom I beg particularly to be remembered, and believe me, with respect and esteem,

"Your obliged and faithful friend,

"Thomas Louis."

From Captain Sir William Hoste, Bart:—

"Amphion, Gibraltar Bay,
November 9th, 1805.

"My dear Lady Hamilton,

"I should have wrote you before this, and by the Victory, but I had not arrived from Algiers when she sailed from Gibraltar. Even now I am at a loss what to write, and the gloomy disposition of my mind at this moment leaves me in a sad wretched state. The chief purport of my writing is, I believe, to beg that Lady Hamilton, the best and dearest friend of that great man, Lord Nelson, will endeavour to bear up against the late most severe and irreparable loss, and to assure herself that to be considered as one who she will condescend to call amongst the numerous circle of her friends, will now be the first wish of, my dear Madam,

"Your ever faithful and sincere friend,
"W. Hoste."

From Lady Elizabeth Bentinck to Miss (afterwards Lady Charlotte) Nelson, now Lady Bridport:—

"Sunday, Ramsgate.

"My dear Miss Nelson,

"Our anxiety to hear how my friend, Lady Hamilton, supports herself, must plead my excuse for troubling you at a time like this. I shall not say more of my feelings on this *great* but *truly lamentable* occasion, than that they are sincerely affected with adoration and regret, and that I have unceasingly thought of the sufferings poor Lady Hamilton must endure. Favour me, then, with one line just to say how she is, and tender her my best love and condolence. Lord Edward joins me in every kind sentiment of esteem to you and yours, and I pray you to believe me, very affectionately

"Yours,
"Elizabeth Bentinck."

From the Right Hon. Sir George Rose, Secretary of the Treasury:—

"Dear Madam,

"There are occasions on which silence is more expressive than words. If I were to attempt to convey what I feel, and shall to the end of my life, at the irreparable loss the country, and the friends of the glorious hero have sustained, I should utterly fail.

"In the beginning of September he wrote to inform me, from London, on my entreating him to sit to Edridge for me, that he would certainly do so if he should not be ordered to sea *very, very* soon. When I saw him on board the Victory, I did not ask him whether he had done so; lest, if he had not, he should be at all uncomfortable; but since the melancholy news was received, I wrote to Mr. Edridge, and learn from him that I am disappointed. I recollect an admirable portrait, by Sir William Beechey, to whom I wrote to learn where it is, in the hope of getting a small whole-length by Bone from it, but Sir William Beechey tells me it is in the Great Hall at Norwich. In this state of despair I entreat you will help me in the best way you can; I dare not hope that any one who has an original painting, or the rougher sketch of a drawing, would let me have it, though I should set a value on it above all price: it occurs to me, however, that you may be able to assist me, and afford me the highest gratification (next to possessing *any thing* original), by procuring me the loan of a good portrait of him, to have one done by Bone. I will make no apology for this intrusion on you.

"I am, dear Madam,
"Your most obedient and humble servant,
"GEORGE ROSE.
"Christ Church, November 17th, 1805.

"I return to Cuffnells on Wednesday.

"I have this instant a letter from my incomparable and ever-to-be-lamented friend, in which (when he was hourly expecting the action) he says, 'I verily believe the country will soon be put to some expense on my account, either a monument or new pension.'"

From Admiral Sir Richard Goodwin Keats:—

"Superb, off Cadiz, 19th November, 1805.

"Dear Lady Hamilton,
"I will not pretend to express to you the feelings I experienced on the news of the melancholy event which has caused

you so much sorrow, and which occasions my returning to your Ladyship the accompanying letters.[1] As well as your Ladyship I too have lost a friend I loved and adored, to whom I owe obligations that can never be effaced from my bosom. I will not dwell on a subject that has caused you such sincere grief, but I cannot conclude without expressing my hope that the Hero's last wishes may meet with their fullest accomplishment in a handsome provision for your Ladyship by Government, and that if my trifling but zealous services can any how prove convenient or useful in this part of the world to your Ladyship, or any of his family, I should have sincere pleasure in being employed. As the Chiffonne frigate, by which I forwarded from Portsmouth some letters from your Ladyship did not arrive in time, I shall not fail to make the most particular inquiries for them; in order that if they have not already, they may be safely returned.

"I have the honour to be,
"Your Ladyship's
"Faithful and very obedient humble servant,
"R. G. KEATS.

"I send by the Téméraire two covers of letters addressed to your Ladyship."

From Richard Bulkeley, Esq. :—

"Pencombe, Bromyard, 28th November, 1805.

"My dear Lady Hamilton,

"From the moment that the much-dreaded and ever-to-be-lamented tidings reached me, I have been overwhelmed by the deepest and sincerest grief, in which you have often recurred to my mind. The public has lost its greatest and favourite hero,—society has lost a man endowed by nature with every quality the most endearing, and which no individual that ever I knew possessed in an equal degree to my dear friend Nelson. You have lost what must be irreparable to you, that which any woman in any age and situation would have been proud to possess, a friend, who, in all his actions, was governed by the purest feelings, and whose mind was in-

---

[1] Letters addressed by Lady Hamilton to Lord Nelson.

capable, under any circumstances, of forgetting those who had in the slightest degree marked kindness towards him. To you, therefore, who had served and *saved* him when no common exertions could have availed, it was quite natural that his attachment should have been (as it was) the most tender and unbounded. Such an attachment from such a man was a blessing, which nothing in this world can ever equal, and I feel the magnitude of your misfortune. I would, if I knew how, offer comfort to your agonized heart, and if the certainty that you possess the sympathy of one who loved our dear departed hero as he deserved, can be a soothing reflection, you may at all times rely upon mine, and assure yourself that I shall always feel interested in the concerns of one so dear to the friend whose memory I shall, so long as I live, dwell upon with admiration and affection. I entreat that you will let me hear from you as soon as possible.

"The fate of my poor boy[1] is still unknown to me, and though I anxiously expect, yet I dread the arrival of every post, lest it should bring me an accumulation of affliction. Mrs. Bulkeley joins me in compliments of condolence to you, and I beg you to offer them to the family at Merton. I have endeavoured, through Mr. Davison, to set on foot a measure which, if adopted as I wish, will be highly beneficial to those who fought so nobly for us, and to the immediate heir and family of our inestimable Nelson. If you wish to know the particulars, ask Mr. Davison to shew you my letter, and believe me,

"Your faithful and sincere friend,
"RICHARD BULKELEY."

From the Hon. Lady Blackwood, and Admiral the Hon Sir Henry Blackwood, Bart.:—

"Portsmouth, Friday, December the 6th.

"Madam,

"It was Captain Blackwood's wish to have had the pleasure of addressing you himself, but the great hurry of accumulated business, on his arrival at Portsmouth, will, I hope,

---

[1] Richard Bulkeley, Midshipman on board the Victory, and wounded at the battle of Trafalgar.

apologize for his thus deputing me his secretary. Captain Blackwood is anxious to communicate to your mind the relief which, allow me to say, *we* trust the purport of this letter may afford you, in informing your Ladyship that he saw Captain Hardy this morning, who has in his possession papers of the *last* will of this ever-to-be-regretted Commander, which will prove highly gratifying and satisfactory to you ; that it is Captain Hardy's determination not to deliver any of them up to *any* person until he has seen you, which in the course of a few days he hopes to do, in town : that Captain Hardy will most steadily endeavour to fulfil the wishes of his departed friend by his best exertions, and utmost efforts to assist your interest and promote your wishes in every possible way he can. Captain Hardy this morning set off early for Mr. Rose's at Cuffnells, upon business of importance. What I have taken the liberty of expressing was expressed by Captain Hardy in the most friendly and zealous manner towards your Ladyship.

"I am, Madam,
"Your very obedient humble servant,
"HARRIET BLACKWOOD."

"Dear Lady Hamilton,
"Hardy may have spoken his mind on former occasions more freely than you could have wished; but depend upon it that the last words of our lamented friend will influence his conduct. He desires me, in the most unequivocal manner, to assure you of his good intentions towards you. This, I hope, will ease your mind.

"Sincerely in haste,
"Your friend,
"HENRY BLACKWOOD."

From Admiral Sir Thomas Masterman Hardy, Bart. :—

"Victory, December 8th, 1805.

"My dear Lady Hamilton,
"I am quite sorry to hear of Chevalier's[1] conduct, and what could induce him to request you not to mention to

[1] Steward of the Victory.

Earl Nelson his having given you my letter I know not (for I had no idea of its being kept a secret). Such is his story to me; and, as the Earl was not pleased with him for having detected him in something like a *falsehood*, he did not return to you. However, I shall keep a strict look out over him and all the rest of the servants. I have requested Sutton to speak to you on the subject, and write to me at Deal, where I expect to be on Wednesday next, as we sail for the Downs to-morrow evening. Every thing shall be preserved for you that you can wish; and it shall be my constant study to meet your wishes, as it was our ever dear Lord's last request to be kind to you, which, I trust, I never shall forget. As his dear body is in spirits, I think it would be wrong for you to think of seeing him, and do let me beg of you to give up the idea; but should you still be determined, I certainly shall not oppose it; and I would recommend you to consult Sutton on the subject. I have his hair, lockets, rings, breast-pin, and all your Ladyship's pictures in a box by themselves, and they shall be delivered to no one but yourself. Every thing shall be done to meet Earl Nelson's wishes, and I have no doubt but he will be satisfied with my conduct. I beg of you, my dear Lady Hamilton, to keep up your spirits under this most melancholy and trying occasion; and you may be sure of always meeting a most sincere friend in

"T. M. HARDY."

From the Rev. Alexander John Scott, D.D., Chaplain and Private Secretary to Lord Nelson:—

"My very dearly respected Lady Hamilton,

"I did not get your letter before yesterday afternoon, too late to answer you from hence—indeed, now it is such weather, I doubt if I can get my letter on shore. I cannot come to London yet; nothing upon earth, however, would prevent me but the duty I owe the remains of the best beloved and most interesting of human beings. I will not go on shore but with them, after which my next duty will be to pay my respects to you. In offering you my services, for the first time in my life, I regret my own insignificance; I am devoted to you, however, sincerely.

"Admiral Collingwood sent home dispatches, without giving us an opportunity of writing. A gale of wind had

separated us from the fleet, otherwise I had taken precautions to write to you. I hope you do not think me either negligent or forgetful. Have the goodness to remember me to all the family, Lord Nelson, Lady Nelson, and Lady Charlotte.
"Believe me ever while I live,
"Your most sincerely attached friend,
"And most respectful humble servant,
"A. J. SCOTT."

"My dearly respected Lady Hamilton,
"I take the liberty of writing to you only to say, that, with the blessing of God, the remains of your beloved, incomparable, and invaluable friend are safe, and will be on shore at Greenwich by to-morrow. I would wait upon you to-morrow, but it does not agree with the principle I have adopted of not leaving the place where he is until I lose sight of him for ever; I know you will approve of this. God bless you, my dearest Madam. Accept the warmest prayers of my heart for your repose and welfare. I am ever while I live, with zeal and attachment,
"Your faithful and devoted servant,
"A. J. SCOTT."

"Commissioners' Yacht, passing Gravesend,
"December 23, 1805.

"Mr. Tyson is here; Mr. Nayler, &c."

"Dear Lady Hamilton,
"The body of my dear Lord was last night deposited in the Board Room of Greenwich Hospital, which will not be opened until his removal to the Painted Chamber. I need not tell you how sorry I was to quit it. I have taken lodgings here, and shall remain until the procession goes from hence to London. In all things you may command me, and I really wish for your approbation in every thing, considering you as a still surviving part of my blessed and beloved Friend. God bless you, my dear Madam, and give you happier days than these. With sincere respect, I am,
"Your devoted servant and most attached friend,
"A. J. SCOTT."

"Dec. 25th, 1805, Park Row, Greenwich,
No. 21, near the East Gate of the Hospital."

"Wednesday night,
Admiralty, half-past twelve o'clock.

"My dear Lady Hamilton,

"I am sorry not to be able to write oftener to you, and more at length—however, just now I sent Mr. Beckwith, foreman to Mr. France,[1] who has throughout conducted the business—he can tell you every thing minutely. I hope he will get in, though it is now very late. Nothing ever was equal to the affection shewn for your poor hero. One trait I must tell you, the very beggars left their stands, neglected the passing crowd, and seemed to pay tribute to his memory by a look—many did I see, tattered and on crutches, shaking their heads with plain signs of sorrow—this must be truly the unbought affection of the heart.

"I should never have made any request of the kind to the Earl, but merely as a tribute of affection to the name of Nelson—to no other nobleman in the land would I be Chaplain, nor indeed could I, with any propriety, ask the Prince of Wales to be Chaplain to any one else; without whose particular leave no Chaplain of his could presume to belong to any one else also. Your poor Nelson, upon his first vacancy, intended to speak to the Prince about it, and to have nominated me. I wished it earnestly, not for any nasty material good of this world, but because it drew my connexion closer with him, it was a matter, therefore, I did press with him, as he knew it could be no advantage to me, already Chaplain to the Prince, and entitled therefore to all privileges which it affords. But, indeed, my dear Lady Hamilton, I would never have talked on this subject while dear Lord Nelson remained unburied, but for the information I had that the Earl was already arranging his Chaplains. Meeting him, I wished to put him on his guard, as he might otherwise have forgot my *prior* claim to any one—but in all this do you but approve of my conduct, and I care little for the rest in this world.

"Sir Evan Nepean was here just now, and cried very much—most sincerely, had the man not been in office, I would have taken him by the hand for it, nay, embraced him. Every thought and word I have is about your dear Nelson. I have him now before me—dear Lady Hamilton—here lies Bayard

---

[1] The Undertaker employed by Government.

—but Bayard victorious—*sans peur et sans réproche*. This is my motto for an emblem to be worn by those who cherish his memory—it might be interwoven in a sprig of gold laurel—dear Lady Hamilton speak to some of your sex about it. *Sans peur et sans réproche.* So help me God, as I think he was a true knight and worthy the age of chivalry—one may say—*lui même fait le siècle*—for where shall we see another? When I think, setting aside his heroism, what an affectionate fascinating little fellow he was, how dignified and pure his mind, how kind and condescending his manners, I become stupid with grief for what I have lost. Pardon my scrawl.

"Your devoted servant,
"A. J. Scott."

"My dear Madam,

"Mr. Beckwith has just come back, and I learn he did not see you from the lateness of the hour. I sent him only to give you a minute detail of every thing which he must be better acquainted with than any one else. I came from Greenwich with our dearest Lord in the same boat. I am grievously vexed that to-morrow I am all day so far removed from him by my place in the procession. I cannot with ease bear this separation; but there is no help for it. To the last I could have wished to have been near him. God bless you and give you rest.

"With respect,
"Your devoted servant,
"A. J. Scott.

"Wednesday night—rather Thursday morning."

"No. 21, Park Row, Greenwich,
January 1st, 1806.

"Dear and much respected Lady Hamilton,

"Why, my dearest Madam, do you not order one of your young folks to write to me, and let me know your health and spirits are improving? I do not expect you should trouble yourself with writing to me. No human being is more sincerely interested in your happiness and welfare than I am. I have not moved out of these lodgings but to go to the Hospital over the way. I saw Mr. Tyson yesterday, who had enjoyed the good fortune to see you. I cannot—unless you expressly wish it—until after the funeral. When the scene is closed for ever with my valuable and incomparable friend, I am devoted to your service. Good God! how does the country want him now!

"I do not mean to speak to you in worldly terms, my dearest Madam, while I live with the deepest respect, regard, and attachment, I am your servant,
"A. J. Scott."

"January 3rd, 1806,
No. 21, Park Row, Greenwich.

"My dearly respected Madam,

"I received this morning your very kind note, and although I am flattered, I feel grateful for the manner in which you speak to me, still I am sorry you should have troubled yourself to write. Earl Nelson and Horace[1] were here to-day—the latter was very much affected, and wept a great deal—I can truly say he won my heart by it, and I hope to God he will never one day of his life forget his uncle.

"Had you not mentioned it, I should most certainly have waited on you immediately after the ceremony—it is a duty, and with me a sacred one, to do all and every thing which he could wish, were it possible for him to look down and direct. My heart pays a grateful tribute to the kind expressions in your letter. I honour your feelings, and I respect you, dear Lady Hamilton, for ever.
"A. J. Scott."

From the Abbé Campbell:—

"Naples, Dec. the 8th, 1805.

"My ever beloved Friend,

"It is with a heart full of anguish, grief, and sorrow, I commiserate and condole with you for the loss of our ever dear and beloved friend and hero—excuse me, I cannot write a word more on the subject. I truly pity you from my soul, and only wish to be near you, to participate with you the agonies of your heart, and mix our tears together. The only consolation remaining is, that his name shall be for ever immortal. The news only arrived here the 2nd instant.

[1] Viscount Trafalgar.

Judge of my feelings—not only of mine but of every person's here, where he was adored. I have not had the courage to see their Majesties since, but have been told they are much afflicted. I received a letter, and alas! the last letter from our late dear friend, dated off Cadiz, the 9th of October; in the postscript of which he said, 'I have letters from my dear Lady Hamilton of September the 20th. I am sure you will forgive her writing when you consider all she suffered on my tour to the West Indies;' that he was only twenty-five days from the Victory, and that he intended to repose his wearied bones this winter at Merton; but that he could not resist the cry of his country for him to go to beat their enemy, &c. &c. This letter we shall, if God spares us life, read together, as it contains something which I cannot commit to paper.

"This country never was in such danger of being for ever lost as it is at this moment. You know they made a treaty of neutrality lately with the French, in consequence of which they evacuated the kingdom. It was stipulated that Damas should not be employed; he, however, in a week's time, was recalled here from Messina, and put at the head of the Neapolitan army; a few days after the English and Russians disembarked here, in consequence of which the French Ambassador quits, and swears vengeance against the treachery of the country. I must observe to you, that all this has happened within these fifteen days past. After the disasters in Germany, when there were no further hopes from that quarter, I ask you if they wanted to lose the country—if they could have taken a more efficacious method than what they have done? How can 22,000 Russians and English withstand all the force of France now, as they have nothing more to do in Germany?—They will march into the country, and that soon, and destroy it. I am very sorry for all these circumstances, as I shall be a sufferer with many others. I have not seen the Queen these many months—I suppose they will all go to Sicily. For God's sake don't mention this to any soul living. I have written to the Duke, but as I have had no answer, I don't wish to trouble him more. Pray remember me most kindly to him and Lord William, Doctor Nelson and his lady, Miss Charlotte and Horace. If I can serve them in any way respecting the Bronté estate, they may command me freely. May I hope you have been left that for life? God grant it, I am sure I wish it; and pray let me know every particular concerning yourself. Poor Nudy[1] is with me, he is very sad for my poor Lord; he desires a thousand compliments with mine to your good mother. God for ever bless you, and believe me ever

"Your constant friend,
"H. CAMPBELL."

From William Hayley, Esq. the Biographer of Romney:—

"January 31st, 1806.

"My dear Lady,

"If I have ever been a *source of good* to you in any period of your life, I rejoice in the idea; but I shall be *much more so*, if you allow me to suggest to you, what bitter and long experience has *taught me*, and what I consider as an *inestimable acquisition*—I mean *the habit* of making affectionate justice to departed excellence a source of the purest delight. My meaning will be more forcibly impressed, perhaps, on your feeling heart, by my transcribing for you (*in confidential privacy*) a few verses, of which I have already cited to you a single line.

> "Blest be this hallowed movement of the heart,
> Affection for the dead! It has a charm,
> A tender, awful, melancholy charm,
> Source of aspiring thoughts, and fair designs!
> That gratify the feeling soul, beyond
> The towering transport, and the gaudy pride,
> That gayer passions boast!—'Tis my delight
> On Heaven-descended Contemplation's seat
> To sit me down, before the gates of death,
> And with fond aid from faithful memory,
> Muse o'er the virtues of each dearer friend,
> Who passed that solemn portal.—How sublime!
> How sweet such converse with departed worth!
> Then free from all Mortality's dark mist,
> Its doubts, its troubles, its infirmities,
> True goodness (finding in the grave a shrine,
> That hides not, but refines, its sacred light)
> Pours its full lustre to enrich the mind
> Of friendship, in whose sight the buried live!

[1] The Physician.

"If these lines prove half as soothing to your heart as they have been to my own, you will deem them worth your acceptance. I now scrawl in extreme haste to give you the quickest assurance in my power, that I most heartily wish to reanimate your wounded spirit, and excite you to display that angelic fortitude, through every earthly trial, which the heroic angel, whose flight from earth we ought not *too deeply* to lament, must wish and expect from your *elevated and inspiring mind.*

"You kindly say you are very sorry you have promised Earl Nelson *to give him your letters;* probably because you imagine I *should wish* them to be imparted to the biographer I mentioned, but, as *your very sincere friend,* I should advise you to retain these letters in your own custody, and not suffer *even me,* your old and faithful friend, to persuade you to impart them to the public, except at some distant day, as a *legacy to your country, from yourself.*

"More of this at our greater leisure! I can only add, that on all occasions you may command the sincerest advice, and every service within the power of

"Your affectionate
"Hermit."

"June 7, 1806.

"Believe me, dear Emma, the most valuable of all victories are those we obtain over ourselves! Self-conquest is the summit of real heroism. Remember, your country has reason to expect from you the most *serene* and *sublime magnanimity* as the confidential friend of her favourite hero! The highest compliment that you can pay to his memory is to prove yourself worthy of his praise. You tell me you are *most unhappy.* No! you *must not be so.* You must allow your friendly Hermit to lead you to discover, and to enjoy, perhaps, the very sweetest of cordial gratifications. In a pilgrimage of threescore years on earth, I have learnt that the most soothing and satisfactory of all human pleasures may be found in discharging our affectionate duties to the dead; and particularly in acting, upon all occasions, as the pure Spirits of the Just made perfect, must wish their surviving friends to act.

Now, dear Emma, you have abundance of such delightful duties (as I have mentioned) to furnish you with the most animating occupation. I conjure you, therefore, to let *no sort of trouble depress the native energy of your mind.* I perfectly conceive the charm you find in the scenery of Merton. A poet of your acquaintance has said :—

> " Ye, who have loved, and lost your soul's delight,
> Ye know what value, in Affection's sight,
> Trifles may gain ; a tree, or rural shed,
> That once were favourites of the honoured dead !

" These lines I have just recollected from a private unfinished poem, in several cantos, begun many years ago ; in which (by the way) something like a portrait of Emma herself may also be found ; for I remember, in describing the heroine of the poem, I had present to my fancy the wonderfully expressive features of my friend Emma, as she used to display them in a variety of characters to me and our beloved Romney. If we ever meet again, you shall hear some of the lines I allude to. At present I scrawl in *extreme haste* to return you most cordial, though hasty, thanks for your kind letter, and to assure you, that I shall receive with the most lively gratitude, all the dates and anecdotes that you may be so good as to send with the promised list of your pictures.

" I charge you, *be not dispirited!* Can you be so with a just remembrance of Nelson ? No—rather say to yourself

> " Di quella Fronte un raggio,
> Tinto di Morte ancora,
> M'inspirerà Coraggio,
> M'insignerà Virtù."

"Adopt these charming words of Metastasio to the sublimest notes you can ! and sing them as an act of devotion every day ! This is a *medicinal prescription* against *low spirits,* that you will find *most efficacious,* if you follow the friendly advice of

" Your affectionate,
" HERMIT."

From Sir Alexander John Ball, Bart., Governor of Malta :—

"My dear Lady Hamilton,

"By the time this will probably reach your Ladyship,[1] I hope you will, in some measure, have recovered from the shock caused by the irreparable loss of our immortal Nelson. In him we have to bewail the death of our best friend, and the public that of their greatest hero. The nation was sensible of his inestimable talents and worth before he was snatched from us. I cannot but lament that it was not ordained that he should live a few years with us, and witness the plaudits of a grateful nation, and enjoy the society of his much attached friends. I have to entreat you to continue to command my services whenever they can be useful.

"Their Sicilian Majesties are once more doomed to quit the Neapolitan dominions, and take refuge at Palermo. They will now more deeply feel the loss of their confidential friends, the Hamiltons and Nelson.

"I hope you will do me the favour of answering this, and that you will be assured of the respect and esteem of

"Your sincere and obedient,

"ALEXANDER JOHN BALL."

From Mrs. Lutwidge, wife of Admiral Lutwidge :—

"Holm Rock, Whitehaven,
January 10th, 1806.

"I have long wished to write to you, my dearest and beloved Emma, but had not courage to take up my pen; but there has not a day passed in which my Admiral and self have not thought of you. Our hearts bleed for your sufferings, and, had it been possible to have alleviated your sorrow, dearest Emma, we should not thus long have remained silent; but we could only add our tears to yours for the loss of the greatest hero and best of men that ever existed. From the bottom of our hearts do we most truly feel for and compassionate your situation, and beg to assure you of our tenderest sympathy.

"The last sad, sad duty, has been paid ere this to the

---

[1] Post mark, March 31, 1806.

remains of that immortal hero, whom we shall ever most feelingly deplore. My Admiral was most anxious to attend this awful ceremony, but was really unable—indeed he never has been well since the fatal news reached us, and, I am sorry to say, is threatened with the loss of sight. His eyes are in so weak a state he is unable to write, else, my dearest Emma, he would have added a few lines to this letter. I long to hear from yourself how you are, how you support yourself during the scene of anguish and affliction with which you are overwhelmed. From others I have heard of you, or I could not have borne the degree of anxiety I experienced. Mrs. Cookson, who frequently saw Mrs. Denis, never failed to give me constant accounts, and I have twice heard by means of Captain Blackwood; but it is from yourself, dearest Emma, I long to be informed how you are, and, when you feel yourself able, I hope you will not deny me the consolation of a line.

"I cannot yet hear the loved name of Nelson without torrents of tears, and *entre nous*, my dear friend, most truly regret that any one should bear the same title. We have all here mourned both in hearts and habit, and the house of Muncaster, as well as ourselves, put their family in deep mourning. What a dreadful loss the country has sustained! and who shall support us?—but I will not rend your heart by longer dwelling on this subject, and yet I cannot think of any other. Tell me, my beloved Emma, that you will take care of yourself for the sake of the interesting little being consigned to your care, and with such a public testimony of *his* high sense of all those great and good qualities you eminently possess. I own, my dear Emma, I shall have no small curiosity to know who this dear little being is, who is so distinguished. Adieu, my dearest friend; with the tenderest, affectionate, and most grateful regard, in which my Admiral begs most cordially to unite, I am now, and for ever,

"Your most faithful,
"C. LUTWIDGE.

"We beg to be kindly remembered to Lady Charlotte and all the friends by whom you are surrounded."

From Admiral Lord Collingwood:—

"Queen, March 3rd, 1806.

"Madam,

"I most sincerely condole with you on the great and irreparable loss that we have met with; but particularly those who had the happiness of his friendship, in the death of my most excellent and beloved friend Lord Nelson, and hope that time will soften your sorrows for him, to a pleasing remembrance of all that was good and great in nature. I have thought it extraordinary that not one private letter has ever come to me, addressed to Lord Nelson; indeed, it happened, that no ship came from England, for some time after the action, except those which sailed after the event was known; but should any letter be found, bearing his address, your Ladyship may trust that I will forward it as you desire, to Mr. Davison, in Saint James's Square.

"Your Ladyship mentions Mr. Davison, as having been the Prize Agent for Lord Nelson's fleet, on former occasions, and he has told me he expected to have been on this. I am exceedingly sorry he should have met with any disappointment; but I assure your Ladyship I never heard of such a proposal from Lord Nelson. I do not think his Lordship interfered in the agency of Captains, and for the Flag shares, Mr. Scott, the Secretary, was appointed the Agent, and, if I am not mistaken, I signed his power on board the Victory. On his death, the Captains of the fleet wrote to me a letter, to say, if I approved of it, they had resolved to appoint my Secretary their agent, which I received as a great compliment to me, for they knew, that wherever money is to be managed, I never recommend, or interfere in any way, but leave to the Captains the sole management of their own affairs.

"I beg your Ladyship's pardon for entering into a detail of this business; but I am really very much hurt that there should have been any cause of disappointment to Mr. Davison, and I wished to explain to your Ladyship, that it is a subject I have never, in any way, interfered in.

"I have the honor to be,
"Your Ladyship's,
"Most obedient humble servant,
"COLLINGWOOD."

## CHAPTER XIII.

#### CONCLUSION.

Thus gloriously fell Lord Nelson—in the hour of victory, and with a full consciousness of the glorious achievement by which, with other daring and heroic deeds, his name was to descend to posterity. "A name and an example, which are at this hour inspiring thousands of the youth of England—a name which is our pride, and an example which will continue to be our shield and our strength."[1]

The estimate formed by his country of his military talents, and the love entertained for him personally, has been fully exemplified in the preceding pages, and it will not be, I trust, an unsatisfactory conclusion to a narrative of the life and exploits of the Hero, to bring together some of the principal features of his character and portraitures which have been drawn of him by those who have rendered themselves illustrious, either in the Senate, on the Ocean, or in the Republic of Letters.

Contemplation of Nelson's career admits of no pause—it was one of incessant activity. He had a mind adequate to any emergency—to every exigency—his promptitude in action was as remarkable as his judgment was distinguished. Nothing escaped his attention. He is an example of decided genius in his profession, for, whilst he could enter into a consideration of even the most minute and particular details, his grasp of intellect was such as enabled him to embrace and embody the whole view and entire object, and determine upon the consequences of action. The consideration given to the Battles of the Nile, Copenhagen, and Trafalgar, was complete, long ere they were entered upon; the particulars had been so frequently and so fully discussed by him with his Captains, that signals of direction were scarcely needed, and the results following those glorious achievements prove how just were the principles upon which they had been

[1] Southey.

formed. The moment a conception was engendered, it engrossed all his thoughts, and not an instant was lost in the contemplation of the means calculated to ensure its success. His energies were proportioned to the greatness of the object to be achieved, and nothing was left to the possibility of temporary necessity or accident. He was too heroic to feel difficulty an opposition to his progress, and nothing affecting either individual or national honour was with him a matter of indifference.

" Gifted by nature with undaunted courage, indomitable resolution, and undecaying energy, Nelson (Alison observes) was also possessed of the eagle glance, the quick determination, and coolness in danger, which constitute the rarest qualities of a consummate Commander. Generous, open-hearted, and enthusiastic, the whole energies of his soul were concentrated in the love of his country; like the youth in Tacitus, he loved danger itself, not the rewards of courage; he was incessantly consumed by that passion for great achievements, that sacred fire, which is the invariable characteristic of heroic minds. His soul was constantly striving for historic exploits; generosity and magnanimity in danger were so natural to him, that they arose unbidden on every occasion calculated to call them forth."[1]

Coleridge roundly says: " Lord Nelson was an Admiral every inch of him. He looked at every thing, not merely in its possible relations to the naval service in general, but in its immediate bearings on his own squadron; to his officers, his men, to the particular ships themselves, his affections were as strong and ardent as those of a lover. Hence, though his temper was constitutionally irritable and uneven, yet never was a Commander so enthusiastically loved by men of all ranks, from the Captain of the fleet to the youngest ship-boy. Hence, too, the unexampled harmony which reigned in his fleet, year after year, under circumstances that might well have undermined the patience of the best balanced dispositions, much more of men with the impetuous character of British sailors."

Nelson possessed every qualification necessary to form a great Admiral. In no profession, perhaps, is there demanded

[1] History of Europe, Vol. iii. p. 281, 5th edition.

more coolness, presence of mind, self-denial, energy, intrepidity, humanity and decision, than in the naval service, and in the possession of these high qualities no individual stands so eminent as Lord Nelson. No injustice to his memory can be greater than the opinion expressed by M. Thiers, that Nelson was in fact only qualified to fight (n'était propre qu' à combattre). Noticing his being second in command in the Baltic, this author looks upon him as merely placed there to act when battle was necessary; yet he cannot deny to him the possession of a happy instinct for warfare, and at the same time is compelled to admit that he reasoned ably upon subjects connected with his profession. The genius of Nelson, however, was of a far more extensive character. No subject whatever belonging to the naval service failed to occupy his attention, and to receive from him proper consideration and regard. He was a great Commander in every sense of the word. He was alike distinguished in every variety of service, whether as a negotiator, a naval Commander, a general Officer on shore, a superintendent of transports, or as a director for the embarkation and landing of troops. Nelson's quickness and sagacity in every thing were very remarkable. The Rev. Dr. Scott, who acted as his Chaplain and Foreign Secretary, and who made translations of the dispatches and communications directed by Lord Nelson to the functionaries of the different Powers, tells us that he had the newspapers, French, Italian, Spanish, &c. which were regularly transmitted to the fleet, scanned and read over to him, as well as pamphlets of a very ephemeral nature; that he never discarded any as unworthy notice, feeling persuaded that no man would put his hand to paper unless furnished with some matter of importance to communicate. He detected the drift of an author with marvellous quickness, for two or three pages were generally sufficient to put him in possession of the writer's aim and object. He was not less acute in discerning the talents of those about him; and M. de la Gravière has remarked that Nelson so well knew how to elicit the particular talents of each individual, that there was no officer so bad that he did not succeed in obtaining zealous and often valuable services from him.

His activity upon being appointed to a command is very strikingly illustrated, when named to the Agamemnon, in 1793; to the Saint George, in 1801; and in 1805, when only upon the 16th of May, a message from the King announced to Parliament, the necessity of immediate war with France, Nelson was on the following day, Commander-in-chief at Portsmouth, and ready to embark. His sagacity was equal to his quickness. In the Life of the Reverend Doctor Scott,[1] it is said, that the fleet which had been so long baffled by contrary winds, in the Mediterranean, suddenly experienced so unexpected a change, that the Officers and men had gone on shore, and the linen was landed to be washed. Nelson, however, observing, and weatherwise as he was, perceived an indication of a probable change of wind. Off went a gun from the Victory, and up went the blue peter, whilst the Admiral paced the deck in a hurry, with anxious steps and impatient of a moment's delay. The Officers looked upon this as "one of Nelson's mad pranks." But he proved to be right, the wind did become favourable, the linen was left on the shore, they cleared the Gut, and steered off for the West Indies.

Nothing but the genius of Nelson could have enabled him to sustain such personal fatigue as he experienced. Naturally delicate and feeble, known as physically weaker than his brothers even in his infancy he was yet able to perform all the duties required of him by the service, and often, voluntarily, to undertake others of considerable labour, to accomplish any object he conceived necessary or desirable. This feebleness of frame, united to a mind of such extraordinary activity, rendered him, at times, irritable and peevish; but the genuine kindness of his nature, added to his strict sense of justice, regulated his feelings, and never failed to restore his tranquillity. When at Naples, he admitted the irritability of his temper, and wrote to Lord St. Vincent, "I am very unwell, and the miserable conduct of the Court, is not likely to cool my *irritable* temper." He had, also, it must be admitted, many circumstances well calculated to try his temper, in the appointments of Sir Sidney Smith, Sir John Orde, Lord Keith, &c.

[1] Page 171.

Considering the personal disabilities under which Lord Nelson laboured, in the loss of an eye, in the exceeding weakness of the other, and in the deprivation of his right arm, it is remarkable what difficulties he subdued. The number of letters, under such circumstances, written by him is truly astonishing, often, from ten to twenty daily. Sir Harris Nicolas's collection, I believe, amounts to between three and four thousand, composed mostly under these circumstances. His occupations were incessant. Impetuosity was the evidence and consequence of his genius; he could not brook any delay, slow measures were ill suited to his capacity; he abhorred the regularity of military operations, and contrasted them with the direct proceedings of naval officers.

Nelson's character for extraordinary achievements must have manifested itself at a very early period, and been particularly striking, for Collingwood, one of his earliest and most intimate friends in the service, even in November, 1792, writes to him of the "respect and veneration," he entertained for his character.

Lord Hood, in 1782, referred his Royal Highness the Duke of Clarence, to Nelson, for information on naval tactics, as being, in his opinion, as competent as any officer in the fleet. The Honourable Captain Plunkett says, "were the names of Aboukir, St. Vincent, Copenhagen and Trafalgar, obliterated from Nelson's life, he would still stand before us as a consummate officer, whose eye and judgment, in critical circumstances, were equally sure, whose ardent courage always communicated itself to others, whose value was not less in subordinate stations than in the chief command, and whose zeal and activity were ever equal to the occasion."[1]

The battles of Nelson were perfect—annihilation of the enemy was his object, and never, until his time, were such numbers of vessels made prizes of, or destroyed. His mode of tactics was, especially, to break the line of the enemy, a measure first adopted by Sir George Rodney, and followed by St. Vincent and Nelson. The character of naval battles before the time of these commanders, was essentially different. Refer to the order of battle marked out by Earl Howe, on

---

[1] Last Naval War, p. 178.

the celebrated 1st of June, 1794—see the beautiful precision, yet slowness, with which the movements were executed—the formal manner with which the engagement was entered into, and contrast these with the vigorous and rapid proceedings at the Nile, and at Trafalgar, particularly the latter—the progress of Collingwood's, and other vessels, to divide the enemy's force, and bring them to the closest possible action. This constituted the great triumph of the modern over the prudent and cautious rules of the ancient school. The vigour of St. Vincent was eminently calculated to follow up the skill and bravery of Rodney. Nelson carried the principle still further, and was never satisfied whilst anything remained to be done.

No commander ever succeeded so perfectly in attaching to him those under his direction. This demonstrates the uniform kindness of his nature, and examples of tenderness and consideration on the one hand, and respect, regard, love and veneration on the other, might be cited from every part of the whole period of his service. His Midshipmen were constantly spoken of by him as his children, and he treated them as such. Lady Hughes, whom he took out to the West Indies, in the Boreas, in 1784, wrote to Nelson's brother-in-law, after his death, her recollections of his conduct towards the youngsters:—

"As a woman, I can only be a judge of those things that I could comprehend—such as his attention to the young gentlemen who had the happiness of being on his quarter-deck. It may reasonably be supposed, that among the number of thirty, there must be timid as well as bold: the timid he never rebuked, but always wished to shew them he desired nothing of them that he would not instantly do himself: and I have known him say—' Well, Sir, I am going a race to the mast-head, and beg I may meet you there.' No denial could be given to such a wish, and the poor fellow instantly began his march. His Lordship never took the least notice with what alacrity it was done, but when he met in the top, instantly began speaking in the most cheerful manner, and, saying how much a person was to be pitied, that could fancy there was any danger, or even anything disagreeable, in the attempt. After this excellent example, I have seen the timid youth lead another, and rehearse his Captain's words. How wise and kind was such a proceeding! In like manner, he every day went into the schoolroom, and saw them do their nautical business, and at twelve o'clock, he was the first upon deck, with his quadrant. No one there could be behind-hand in their business, when their Captain set them so good an example. One other circumstance I must mention, which will close the subject, which was the day we landed at Barbadoes. We were to dine at the Governor's. Our dear Captain said, 'You must permit me, Lady Hughes, to carry one of my *aides-de-camp* with me:' and when he presented him to the Governor, he said, ' Your Excellency must excuse me for bringing one of my Midshipmen, as I make it a rule to introduce them to all the good company I can, as they have few to look up to besides myself, during the time they are at sea.' This kindness and attention made the young people adore him; and even his wishes, could they have been known, would have been instantly complied with."[1]

This admirable kindness and tenderness could not fail of exciting the affection of his young officers. He was greatly attached to young Hoste, and writes to his father upon leaving him in the Theseus in 1797: " I grieved to have left him, but it is necessary; and Lord St. Vincent will continue to be his kind protector and friend: his worth as a man and an officer exceeds all which the most sincere friend can say of him. I pray God to bless my dear William; happy father in such a son." How was this feeling reciprocated! Hoste writes to his father: " He has taken me by the hand from my first entrance into the service, and has never ceased his good offices till he has got me a Post Captain's commission. O that I may ever have it in my power to shew my gratitude! Next to my dearest father and family, who is there who has half so much claim to my gratitude and respect as Lord Nelson? Him I look upon as almost a second father, a sheet anchor, whom I shall always have to trust to." Again, " Grateful, I am sure, I shall always be, but it is not in the power of words to convey to you what I feel when I think of that most exalted character." When Hoste broke his leg in

[1] From Nelson Papers. Dispatches and Letters, Vol. i. p. 124, *note*.

Vado Bay, Nelson frequently visited him, and told him to get everything he wanted from him. Nelson wrote to his father in strong terms of approval of his conduct, and says he has "strongly recommended him not to break any more limbs." No wonder that everything connecting him with Nelson should have been so cherished. He speaks of his vessel thus: "My darling Amphion—my dear old Amphion. She was the last gift of my poor Lord Nelson. I hope I have not disgraced his memory in the care of her, though she is cruelly knocked about."

Sir Pulteney Malcolm, whose service made him not only acquainted with Buonaparte, but also the Duke of Wellington and Lord Nelson, says of the latter, "that he was the man to *love*." All about him entertained the same feelings in regard to him. His Chaplain writing, subsequent to the death of Nelson, to Miss Ryder, to whom he was afterwards married, says:—"I dare not mention with my name, in point of talent or purity, that great and innocent being—my dear Lord—but upon my life, Mary, that man possessed the wisdom of the serpent with the innocence of the dove. He taught me, if I did not think so before, that the most difficult things might be accomplished by talent, wisdom, and integrity."

His sense of justice was most rigid. He never failed to acknowledge merit; the services of his Officers were always recognized, and their claims made known to the Admiralty. His engaging to obtain medals for those who served in the Battle of Copenhagen, and his remonstrances with the Lord Mayor for the neglect of the City of London with respect to this achievement, could not but delight his brave companions in arms. He made common cause with them, and never failed to put forward their most reasonable demands. His regard to the memory of distinguished Officers who had fallen in the service of their country, and his respectful attention to their relatives, give great interest to Nelson's character. His exertions and liberal subscriptions to the erection of monuments to Lieutenant Moutray,[1] Captain Miller,[2] Captain Bowen,[3] &c., and his visit to Captain Westcott's[4] relations,

---

[1] Vol. i. page 60. [2] Ibid. page 99. [3] Ibid. page 108. [4] Ibid. page 144, 410.

are instances of the kindness of his nature, and reflect the highest honour on his memory.

But it was not only to the Officers about him that Nelson so endeared himself; he was alike beloved by the men. When his ship, the Albemarle, was paid off in 1783, the whole ship's company offered, if he could get a ship, to enter for her immediately. In 1797, also, when he hoisted his flag in the Theseus, such was the character he had raised, that the crew dropped a paper on the quarter-deck, expressive of their gratitude to him and Captain Miller, and that they were ready to shed their blood to support them, and render the Theseus as immortal for glorious deeds as his former ship, the Captain.[1] Poor John Sykes, his coxswain, who was killed by the bursting of a cannon in 1799, more than once interposed himself to save the life of his Commander, and was seriously wounded in his exertions.

That an Officer thus esteemed by his companions in arms should have few occasions in which it was necessary to resort to punishment, will readily be conceived; and corporal punishment was in Nelson's ships a matter of rarity; so also in Collingwood's, both were remarkable for their humanity, and in no vessels did seamen perform their duties with more alacrity and pleasure.

Sir John Barrow has remarked, that Howe and Nelson mostly agreed on points of naval service. Both were equally anxious of attaching their men to them; and no mutiny ever happened in ships under their command. It was the opinion of both, that if a Commander knew his own comfort, and valued his reputation, his first object should be to win the affection of those on whom his character, as well as his success in the service, must mainly depend.[2]

M. de la Gravière[3] states, that to magnanimous feelings Nelson joined that simplicity of manners, which, in a superior mind, is always an additional charm. He never thought he compromised his dignity by being communicative with those about him, and whose superiority he was willing to admit in the thousand little details which perplex the operations of war. In this manner he rendered justice to

[1] See Vol. i. page 98.   [2] Life of Earl Howe, p. 206.
[3] Last Naval War, page 182.

individual merit, and knew how to obtain information and suggestions which often threw fresh light upon his own views; for he considered that the free participation of all and each in the formation of definite plans, was the way to insure the better comprehension and execution of them.

Humanity was a leading feature in Nelson's character. To pass by his exertions when so seriously wounded at Santa Cruz to save those who were in the Fox cutter—his directions also, when wounded at the Battle of the Nile to preserve the sufferers from the blowing up of L'Orient—his flag of truce to stay useless bloodshed at Copenhagen—let us reflect upon his affectionate care of Captains Parker and Langford, when wounded in the attack on the Boulogne flotilla, and other minor incidents, which, as characteristic of the uniform tenor of his life, raise him so much in our estimation as a man. As a boy he felt severely for the suffering of a lamb; as a man he was sick and disgusted at beholding a Spanish Bull-feast. The sight of two men in irons who were supected of simulating derangement, on board the Swiftsure, distressed him exceedingly, and he wrote to Sir John Jervis: "If Mr. Weir (afterwards Dr. Weir, Physician to the Fleet), would look at them, I should be glad. The youth may, I hope, be saved, as he has intervals of sense; his countenance is most interesting. If any means can be devised for sending him home, I will, with pleasure, pay £50 to place him in some proper place for his recovery." Sir John Jervis considered the cases as deceptive, and Nelson again wrote to him: "I hope, for the poor men's sakes, that they are imposing on me; but depend on it, that God Almighty has afflicted them with the most dreadful of all diseases. They do not sham; indeed, you will find I am not mistaken, and all the Commissioners in the world cannot convince me of it. For what purpose can these poor wretches attempt to destroy themselves? for what purpose can one of them have spoken to me as rationally as any person can do? Do let Mr. Weir look at them: I am sure he will think with me; from the order to represent those who are objects unfit for the service, I could not do otherwise than I did; but if you think I have said too much, pray curtail my Report."[1]

[1] Clarke and Mc'Arthur, Vol. ii. p. 17.

John Jolly, a private marine, was tried by a Court Martial, for having struck Lieutenant Pearce while in the execution of his duty, and for threatening to shoot him as soon as he should be released, and was sentenced to death for his offence. This occurred in Naples Bay in July, 1799. Lord Nelson issued the order for carrying the sentence into effect, but at the same time wrote to Captain Troubridge to have every obedience shewn to his orders, and preparation made for the execution; and when all was gone through prior to the last act, then to acquaint the prisoner, that although there were no mitigating circumstances to check the operation of the law, yet, as he had reason to hope, the sparing of his life might have as beneficial an effect for the discipline of the service, as if he had suffered death, the sentence of death should be respited until his Majesty's pleasure could be known. He hoped that this exhibition of lenity would have its proper effect upon those under Troubridge's command, and serve as a beacon to them to avoid the crime of drunkenness, which often brought with it even the punishment of death. On other occasions he remitted portions of the punishment awarded, always declaring the principles upon which he acted, and which were for the honour and character of the service, as well as humanity to the accused. To prisoners of war also he was uniformly kind and sympathising. When at Malta, and provisions were exceedingly dear, and an order was given to supply the French prisoners with salt instead of fresh beef, he addressed the Commissioners of the Admiralty on the subject, calling to their attention that as they were not allowed wine, the giving them salt provisions, together with their confinement, might operate to produce disease and dangerous consequences, and suggested that, as Frenchmen were in the habit of drinking wine in their own country, they should be allowed a certain quantity each day.

Regard to health is a very necessary consideration with a Commander. It is truly astonishing how little sickness prevailed in Nelson's ships, and in the fleets commanded by him. The modes adopted by him for maintaining the health of the crews, were highly creditable to his judgment.[1] No less

---

[1] See Letter to Dr. Moseley, p. 375, *ante*.

regard was paid by him to the subject of Naval Hospitals—their defects were notorious—they served only to enrich contractors, and disgust the seamen who were so unfortunate as to become inmates of them.

When the Rev. Mr. Este expressed a wish to go out to Lord Nelson, his Lordship wrote thus to Lady Hamilton: "What can induce Mr. Este to want to come out—curiosity—he can be no inconvenience to me for a few months, but I think to a landsman, it must be a very heavy scene, nothing but the day we see the French fleet can make up for all our toils; however, I have a most serious respect and regard for him, and shall always be glad to see him in all times, places, and situations, even if Charles Fox was Minister, and he was my Lord Bishop.[1] My routine goes on so regular, that one day, except the motion of the ship, is the same as the other. We rise at five, walk the deck till near seven, send out ships to chase, refit our ships, &c. breakfast at seven precisely. Captains Murray, Hardy, Dr. Scott, as we call him, to distinguish him from the Secretary, Mr. Scott, Dr. Snipe, Officer of the watch, and two Mids. This is always with the addition of the Captain of a frigate or sloop, if I want to send off. From breakfast to dinner employed variously on the business of the fleet, writing, exercising the squadron, &c. Dine at three—in fine weather always some of the Captains, in general twelve at table. After coffee and tea, no more eating. I send, if I am so inclined, at half-past seven for my family to sit and talk half an hour or longer, and at a quarter or half-past eight go to bed, sleep and dream of what is nearest my heart, pull the bell three or four times for the Officer of the watch, and rise again the next morning. This is the life I lead, scarcely a shade of difference from day to day. You may easily credit that every one knows their place, and Dr. Scott, nor no other person comes into my apartment, unless sent for or upon duty. The poor Doctor will never get quite well, his intellects were too much shook by the lightning[2] for him ever to be perfectly well again. He has great abilities certainly, but at times very low and unconnected in his thoughts. Dr. Snipe prescribes for him, but nothing will

---

[1] Mr. Este was a staunch Whig.   [2] See Appendix, No. II.

entirely cure him, but he is better. My secretary is a treasure, and in every respect I am well mounted. Hardy is invaluable. Murray is very zealous and attentive, few if any Admiral, is better off."

That a man so humane as we find Nelson uniformly to have been should be generous, is perfectly natural. His whole life affords examples of his liberality to all connected with him, or having any claim whatever upon his benevolence. When at sea he never forgot home, the poor were thought of at all the festive seasons, and their wants endeavoured to be alleviated. Judgment and propriety always accompanied these exercises of benevolence. When directing his winter's gift to the poor of his native place, he says: "Fifty good large blankets, of the very best quality, and they will last for seven years at least. This will not take from anything the parish might give. I wish inquiry to be made, and the blankets ordered of some worthy man; they are to be at my father's disposal in November."

When Nelson received information on the 3rd of July, 1799, of the grant to him of £10,000. from the Hon. East India Company, for his regard to the interests of India, as exhibited by him in communicating an account of the Battle of the Nile, he immediately set about to see in what way he could benefit the different branches of his family. That they should all participate in his good fortune was on this, as on all other occasions, uppermost in his mind, and his generous nature in this case manifested itself by his drawing several drafts for £500 each, in favour of his venerable father, his brothers Maurice and William, and his sisters Mrs. Bolton and Mrs. Matcham.[1]

He expressed to Mr. Davison his thanks for his exertions in his behalf at the East India House, but added that his pride was, that at Constantinople, from the Grand Signior to

---

[1] Lady Nelson is reported (Harrison's Life, Vol. ii. p. 107), to have complained of these acts of generosity, and in such terms as to have induced Nelson's father to forego the acceptance of his allotted portion. No payment in favour of his father appears in his accounts, the other sums are entered. The £10,000. was received on the 24th of October, and the several payments of £500. made in November and December following.

the lowest Turk, the name of Nelson was familiar in their mouths.

When the estate of Bronté was given to him, with the Dukedom, by the King of Naples, his first feeling was to render the inhabitants the happiest in his Sicilian Majesty's dominions.

When his sister Ann died, he became entitled to a legacy. His brother William, on this occasion, thought it necessary to advise him " to take it, and not give it up to the rest." So also upon the death of his father, his brother again advises him thus: " As I know your great liberality, and that it sometimes outstrips itself, let me venture to give your Lordship one piece of advice on this occasion—and that is, *don't* throw your *share* into the common stock, to be divided amongst us all, it will be but a trifle to each, and do no good; but take it to yourself in the first instance; you may have occasion for it afterwards, to settle some of our father's affairs, or if not, you can always do as you please with it." His great liberality to his brother's widow is another strong evidence of his generous nature. Nelson was always anxious to requite services, and acknowledge obligations. His presents to Captain Gore, for his care of him in the Medusa, and to Dr. Baird for his attention to Captain Parker, are instances from many that might be adduced. He had a noble contempt for riches, except in as far as they enabled him to pay his debts, concerning which he uniformly expresses his great anxiety. He was not desirous of possessing beyond what was necessary for his position, and to enable him to assist those who he felt had a claim either by nature or service upon him. Desire for wealth was always subdued by his love of his country. In 1783 he writes to his friend, Hercules Ross, Esq.: " I have closed the war without a fortune: but, I trust, and from the attention that has been paid to me, believe that there is not a speck in my character. True honour, I hope, predominates in my mind far above riches."

To the same friend in 1788: " My integrity cannot be mended, I hope; but my fortune, God knows has grown worse for the service; so much for serving my country. But, the devil ever willing to tempt the virtuous, (pardon this flattery of myself) has made me offer, if any ships should be sent to destroy his Majesty of Morocco's posts, to be there; and I have some reason to think, that should any more come of it, my humble services will be accepted. I have invariably laid down, and followed close, a plan of what ought to be uppermost in the breast of an officer: that it is much better to serve an ungrateful country, than to give up his own fame. Posterity will do him justice: a uniform conduct of honour and integrity seldom fails of bringing a man to the goal of Fame at last."[1]

To Mrs. Nisbet, afterwards Lady Nelson, in 1786: "Duty is the great business of a sea officer; all private considerations must give way to it, however painful it is." Again, to the same, in 1794: "Corsica, in respect to prizes, produces nothing but honour, far above the consideration of wealth: not that I despise riches, quite the contrary, yet I would not sacrifice a good name to obtain them. Had I attended less than I have done to the service of my country, I might have made money too: however, I trust my name will stand on record, when the money-makers will be forgot." "If my father should at any time wish for any part that is in my Agent's hands, I beg he would always take it, for that would give me more real pleasure than buying house or land."

Nelson's inflexible honesty is apparent in all his dealings: he sold his diamonds, those diamonds which had been presented to him as memorials of gratitude from various Powers of the trophies he had gained, to pay his debts; and he wrote to his Agents: "*I take no shame to be poor; never for myself have I spent sixpence, it has all gone to do honour for my country.*"

Nelson's gratitude to all who had been kind to him was uniformly shewn. To the memory of his uncle Suckling, to Sir Peter Parker, Hercules Ross, Captain Locker, and others, he always rendered the warmest acknowledgments.

Humour constitutes one of the characteristics of a British seaman; Nelson possessed this naturally, or imbibed it at an early period as may be shewn in many instances. I have now a letter before me which has the post mark of Bungay, and is as follows:—

---

[1] Original draft in the Nelson Papers. Dispatches and Letters, Vol. i. p. 273.

"Admiral Nelson,

"May it please your Honour,

"As I am informed, you are going to *destroy* or bring *away* all the Swedes, Danes, and Russians, I take the opportunity to beg your Honour's goodness to bring over the Emperor Paul, and bestow him upon *me*, as I am a poor fellow, and wants an outlandish *wild beast* to carry about as a *show*, which I think will enable me to maintain a wife, and six small children.

"Your Honour's humble servant to command,
"THOMAS TUGBEAR.

" March 7th, 1801.
To the Right Hon. Admiral Lord Nelson, K.B.
Of his Majesty's Fleet, Yarmouth, or elsewhere."

Beneath this he has written :—

" Lord Nelson will do his best
To comply with Mr. Tugbear's request."

And dated this reply from the St. George, March 11th, 1801.

When at Bath for the recovery of his health in 1781, he wrote to Captain Locker: "I must wish you a good night, and drink your health in a draught of my physician's cordial and a bolus." At this time J. F. Rigaud, R.A. painted a portrait of Nelson, which he presented to Captain Locker, and alluding to his own weak condition of body, and the situation in which the picture was to be placed, he suggests that it should be between Sir George Montague and Sir Charles Morice Pole. He says: "I must be in the middle, for God knows, without good *supporters*, I shall fall to the ground." At Port Royal, writing to the same, and enumerating an exceeding disparity of force, and a likelihood of battle, he says: "I have very fairly stated to you our situation, and I leave you in England to judge what stand we shall make; I think you must not be surprised to hear of my learning to speak French."

To the Rev. Dixon Hoste, from Bath in 1797, he wrote, "As for myself, I suppose, I was getting well too fast; for I am beset with a physician, surgeon, and apothecary."

The French were reported in the revolutionary war to be providing their ships with forges for shot; Nelson expressed his hope that the *red-hot* gentlemen would come out.

In 1794 the first resolution of the Corsican Parliament,

after their union with England, was to declare they were Englishmen. Nelson remarked, " They might have been mistaken for Irishmen by their bull." At the siege of Calvi, where he lost his eye, he wrote to Mr. Pollard, of Leghorn, saying, " Hallowell and myself are both well, except my being half-blinded by these fellows, who have given me a smart slap on the face, for which I am their *debtor*, but hope not to be so long." On the same occasion, being of necessity so much on shore conducting operations, he says, " I have been four months landed, except a few days, when we were after the French fleet; and I feel almost qualified to pass my examination as a besieging general."

At the bombardment of Cadiz he learnt that much damage was done, and that a shell fell in a convent, and destroyed several priests; upon which he remarked, " that no harm, they will never be missed." To Sir John Jervis, at this time remarking upon the shyness of the Spaniards and their disinclination to come out of port, he says, " If the King of Spain goes on this way, and the Mexican fleet falls into our hands, he will be like Billy Pitt, give nothing but paper."

He often joked upon the loss of his arm at Santa Cruz; he assured the Duke of Clarence not a scrap of his ardour had been shot away: to his Majesty, who expressed concern at the loss he had sustained, he nobly replied to the King's observation that he had lost his right arm, " but not my right hand, as I have the honour of presenting Captain Berry; and, besides, may it please your Majesty, I can never think that a loss which the performance of my duty has occasioned." Mr. Twiss tells us that the King, after acknowledging his services, added, " But your country has a claim for a bit more of you." The loss of his eye, also, served him for the exercise of his humour. When Sir Hyde Parker made his signal to discontinue the action at Copenhagen, he inquired of Colonel Stewart whether he understood the meaning of No. 39; and, after explaining to him what it meant, observed to one of his Captains, " You know, Foley, I have only one eye—I have a right to be blind sometimes;" and, putting his glass to his blind eye, exclaimed, " I really do not see the signal."

When Lord Nelson dined at the Guildhall with the Lord Mayor and Corporation, the late Sir Benjamin Hobhouse, Bart., was seated near to him, and was asked by the former what the dish was which was before him? He replied that he thought it was a French pie; upon which the Admiral eagerly remarked, "Then have the goodness to stick your knife into the heart of it, and let me have a bit."

When the destination of the French fleet was so very uncertain, he wrote to Ball, "Whatever the French may intend to do, I trust, and with confidence, they are destined for *Spithead*."

In reference to some orders relative to soldiers when aboard ship, and whether it would be better for the navy to be subject to the same articles of war as the army, he wrote to Lord Melville, then First Lord of the Admiralty, that he thought we might take a lesson from the epitaph: "I was well—I would be better—and here I am:—let well alone."

Mr. Bedingfield, wounded in the Narcissus with Captain Donnelly, July 11, 1804, had been recommended to Nelson by his relative, the Rev. Robert Rolfe; and he writes to him, " Mr. Bedingfield has been wounded in the hand, which the Surgeons say will go off with only a stiff finger; in order to complete the cure I have given him a Lieutenant's commission."

To his friend Davison he wrote, in March, 1805, " I have had a very hard fag; I shall not talk of Sir John Orde, who must be the richest Admiral that ever England saw: he will torment the Admiralty enough. *How should he know* HOW *to behave—he never was at sea*." Sir Harris Nicolas has given the old anecdote to which this refers:—" A sailor, seeing a young prince of the blood royal on the quarter-deck with his hat on, while the Admiral, Captain, and other officers were uncovered, expressed his astonishment to his shipmate, who replied, ' Why, how should he know manners, seeing as how he's never been to sea!' "

Towards the close of Nelson's career, Captain, afterwards Admiral Sir Philip Durham, declined leaving him to give evidence on Sir Robert Calder's affair; and he communicated to Nelson that he had on board the Defiance a large sum in dollars, and, as the fleet was reported to be on the move, he requested to know what was to be done with them. Nelson's answer was, "If the Spaniards come out, fire the dollars at them, and pay them off in their own coin."

Southey has recorded Nelson's advice to his Midshipmen: "There are three things, young gentlemen, which you are constantly to bear in mind. First, you must always implicitly obey orders, without attempting to form any opinion of your own respecting their propriety. Secondly, you must consider every man your enemy who speaks ill of your King; and thirdly, you must hate a Frenchman, as you do the devil." He had a perfect Gallo-phobia. It breaks forth perpetually in his correspondence, and it was mixed up with all his discourses. To his brother, in 1784, he says, "I hate their country and their manners." To the Reverend Dixon Hoste, "I hate a Frenchman. They are equally objects of my detestation, whether royalists or republicans—in some points, I believe, the latter are the best." To Collingwood, when in Leghorn Roads, in 1796, "Except 1700 poor devils, all are gone to join the army. Sometimes I hope, and then despair of getting these starved Leghornese to cut the throats of this French crew. What an idea for a Christian! I hope there is a great latitude for us in the next world." To Captain Troubridge, "There is no way of dealing with a Frenchman, but to knock him down. To be civil to them, is only to be laughed at, when they are enemies." To the Honourable William Wyndham, "Thank God, the plague has got into both the French army, and into their shipping—God send it may finish those miscreants." To the Bey of Tunis, "For at this moment all wars should cease, and all the world should join in endeavouring to extirpate from off the face of the earth this race of murderers, oppressors, and unbelievers." To the Bashaw of Tripoli: "I was rejoiced to find that you had renounced the treaty you had so imprudently entered into with some emissaries of General Buonaparte—that man of blood, that despoiler of the weak, that enemy of all good Mussulmen; for, like Satan, he only flatters that he may the more easily destroy; and it is true, that since the year 1789, all Frenchmen are exactly of the same disposition." To his Royal Highness the Duke of Clarence: "To serve my King, and to destroy the French, I consider as the great order of all, from which little ones spring; and if one of those little ones militate against it, I go back to obey the great order and object, to *down, down*, with the damned French villains. Excuse my warmth; but my blood boils at the name of a Frenchman. I hate them all—royalists and republicans." To Hugh Elliot, Esq. Minister at Naples: "Whatever information you can get me, I shall be very thankful for; but not a Frenchman comes here. Forgive me; but my mother hated the French." To the same he also says, "You may safely rely that I never trust a Corsican or a Frenchman. I would give the devil ALL the good ones to take the remainder."

All these expressions of hatred appear very inconsistent when the evidences of his great piety are considered. Nelson had a deep sense of religion, and placed a firm reliance upon Providence. Upon his recovery, from the amputation of his arm, in 1797, he offered up his thanks at Saint George's Church, and immediately after the Battle of the Nile, caused a general Thanksgiving to be celebrated in the fleet, which had never before been done after a battle. He received Captain Hallowell's extraordinary present of the coffin, made from the mast of L'Orient, with a proper pious feeling, and nothing can more strongly mark his devotion than his celebrated letter to his wife, after the storm, in the Gulf of Lyons. To Lady Hamilton, during a gale, he also wrote, "I have no fear; I can take all the care which human foresight can, and then we must trust to Providence, who keeps a look-out for poor Jack." When he wrote to her Ladyship, also, on the night of the day on which the battle of Copenhagen was fought, he commences his letter, by "That same Deity, who has on many occasions protected Nelson, has once more crowned his endeavours with complete success." Again, "Your own Nelson will return safe, and under the hand of Providence is as safe as if walking London streets." When watching the French fleet off Toulon, in 1804, alluding to the probable battle, he wrote to Mr. Davison, "If I fall on such a glorious occasion, it shall be my pride to take care that my friends shall not blush for me. These things are in the hands of a wise and just Providence, and *His will* be done." And in another letter, to Lady Hamilton, he writes, "I own myself a *believer in God*, and if I have any merit in not fearing death, it is because I feel that *His* power can shelter me, when *He* pleases, and that I must fall when it is *His* good pleasure."

My late most estimable and lamented friend, Sir John Barrow, Bart. at the close of his Life of the Earl Howe, has depicted that which he conceived to be the characteristics of the three most distinguished officers of later times:—Howe, St. Vincent, and Nelson. His observations, the result of long acquaintance with naval men and naval affairs, are marked with too much justice to need any apology for their introduction in this place, he observes:—

" In the extensive sense of all three being skilful and accomplished Flag Officers, thoroughly experienced in every branch of the service—who, by their superior knowledge, energy, and zeal, in introducing and maintaining good order and discipline in the fleet—may be considered pretty nearly on an equality; it is perhaps not too much to say, they have done more towards elevating the character of the profession than any or all of their predecessors; perhaps it may also with truth be said, and not without a feeling of regret,

> 'Farewell, with them,
> The hope of such hereafter.'

" Howe, unquestionably, led the way. He was his sole instructor in naval matters—not brought up in any particular school—hardly, indeed, can it be said, there was any school in the early part of his career. Whatever he gained, from the various Commanders, under whom he served, must have been by comparison, observation, and reflection. At that time, there was very little system observed in the navy, and still less of science. Naval tactics, evolutions, and signals, were then but feebly creeping into use, in humble imitation of the French, and had made but slow progress—rarely attempted indeed, to be carried into practice, except by one individual—the talented and unfortunate Kempenfelt, who perished in the Royal George. After him, Howe seriously took them up, and never lost sight of those important objects, until he had completed a system which long bore the name of 'Howe's Signals.' In the perfecting of this system he was indefatigable—whether on shore or afloat, theoretically or practically, this favourite and most useful object was uppermost in his mind. It is scarcely necessary to repeat, that Howe was professionally and characteristically bold, cool, and decisive—a thorough seaman in theory and practice—and his knowledge was conveyed to others mostly by mildness, persuasion, and the force of example.

" In tactics, and in discipline, St. Vincent was a disciple of Howe. In giving his opinion, on the expediency of a night action with a superior enemy, the former decided against it, on the ground of being, in such a case, deprived of the great advantage of Howe's signals. In discipline the scholar may be said to have carried his mode of instruction beyond the master. Where Howe was patient, gentle, indulgent, and kind, by which he won the attachment of both Officers and seamen, St. Vincent was rigorous, peremptory, and resolute, rigidly maintaining, that the life and soul of naval discipline was obedience—his favourite word was *obedienza*. The one obtained his object by pursuing the *suaviter in modo*—the other by the *fortiter in re*. The mutinous seamen at Portsmouth, but half subdued, were at once completely reduced to order, by the kind and gentle treatment of, and the confidence they placed in, Lord Howe. The mutiny in the fleet off Cadiz, no sooner sprung up, than it was crushed by the prompt and vigorous measures of Lord St. Vincent, whose determined and resolute conduct, on that occasion, was absolutely necessary to prevent that spirit of insubordination from spreading, which had manifested itself in many of the ships employed in blockading a distant and an enemy's port.

" These two gallant Admirals, pursuing different modes of attaining the same ends, and of very different temperaments, had the greatest respect and deference for each other. St. Vincent always spoke of Howe in terms of the highest praise and regard. He used to say he was a man of few words, but what he said was always to the purpose, and well worthy to be remembered. The kindly feelings of men towards each other are frequently discovered in trifling incidents or expressions. Lord St. Vincent, on entering the breakfast-room, would often say, ' Well, I have got on my blue breeches this cold morning; Lord Howe wore blue breeches, and I love to follow his example even in my dress.'[1]  On the other hand, St. Vincent was considered by Howe as the first naval officer of his day. He was unquestionably a fearless and intelligent Commander, bold in design, and prompt in execution, free in his opinions, generous, and charitable, without ostentation; a keen observer of mankind; indulgent to minor offences, severe in those of an aggravated nature. In politics he was a Whig, firmly attached to his party; but his friends always maintained that he never allowed his political feelings to interfere with his professional duties. As an officer, his talents were certainly of the highest order, and many excellent commanders were educated and brought forward under his auspices. With all this merit, which public opinion duly appreciated, he is said (by one who knew him well), to have affected, as well when afloat as under circumstances on shore, the character of a blunt tar, obstinate in his resolutions, and rough in the manner of exercising his authority over the officers of his fleet; but, notwithstanding this, the features by which he was best known in society was that of a refined courtier, smooth and complimentary in his address. His professional character, however, was steady resolution and firmness of purpose.

"The character and conduct of Nelson were widely different from both of the above-mentioned officers. Without being a thorough seaman, he knew well how to stimulate exertions, and to animate zeal. He had the peculiar tact to make every officer, from the highest to the lowest, believe that his individual share in any enterprise contributed mainly to its success—thus giving encouragement and inspiring confidence to each in his own exertions. In the result, he was singularly fortunate: where he led, all were anxious to follow. Nelson was indeed a being *sui generis*—'none but himself could be his parallel'—and it may be feared he has left few of the same breed behind him. That he had his weak points cannot be denied, but what human being is exempt from them? He has been unjustly compared with an Anthony,

---

[1] George II. first gave to the Navy a fixed uniform dress. See anecdotes relating to this subject in the Journal of the British Archæological Association, Vol. ii. p. 76, by Mr. Planché, Mr. Barrow, Mr. T. C. Croker, and others, and also in Sir John Barrow's Life of Earl Howe, p. 68.

ready to sacrifice the world to another Cleopatra—than which
nothing can be more incorrect; with one unfortunate exception, which, in a moment of infatuation, has cast an indelible
stain on his memory, he never suffered the deplorable influence alluded to in any way to interfere with his professional
duties.[1] Whenever such demanded his presence, all pleasures
and indulgences gave way; neither those nor the least care
of life occupied for a moment a share in his thoughts. A
passionate and insatiable love of fame was the spur to Nelson's 'noble mind.' To be 'crowned with laurel, or covered
with cypress'—'a Peerage, or Westminster Abbey'—'Victory,
or Westminster Abbey'—these were the *words*, the signal
for each terrible conflict. He never anticipated defeat, but
went into battle with the full conviction he was to conquer or die. The *words* were the ebullition of that feeling,
which carried his feeble frame through exertions and energies, that nothing short of his ardent and spiritual nature
could have supported. The strength and elasticity of his
mind got complete controul over bodily pain and infirmity.
These, in the scale of human affliction, were to him as nothing,
when in sight or pursuit of an enemy. An ambitious love of
distinction, a thirst for the acquisition of honours, or a glorious death, was the ruling passion, and his destiny led him to
experience them all. Conqueror of 'a hundred fights,' he
died at last, as all true heroes would wish to do, in the arms
of victory! Howe, on the contrary, was exempt entirely
from ambition of that kind. He was less of an egotist than
almost any man in his station of life. The results of his
actions were considered by him in no other light than as they
affected his country; he speaks only of the duty he owes to
his King and his country, and to the good of the naval service.
The Earldom conferred on him was received with indifference;
the offer of a Marquisate was rejected as coming immediately
from the Minister, in lieu of an honour promised by his Sovereign; but the Garter he considered as an ostensible mark of
the King's approbation, and the medal and chain equally so,
and, therefore, felt it due to the Royal donor to wear them on

[1] For refutation of this so generally received opinion, see the Preface, and Vol. i. Chapter IX.

all occasions. Thus it also was with Lord St. Vincent's Star of the Bath, which he always wore on his morning as well as on his evening dress, as an honourable distinction conferred for his services by his Sovereign.

" Howe sought for no pension nor any remuneration of a pecuniary nature for his long and meritorious services, and murmured not at those who obtained rewards for deeds far less brilliant than his own. The only complaint he appears ever to have uttered, was on account of the neglect of the Admiralty towards the more humble, but not less valuable instruments who had faithfully served under him. Of his military character there never was, nor could there be, but one opinion. His moral conduct through life, his love of truth and sense of justice, were universally admitted ; he was generous, humane, kind-hearted, and charitable ; always manifesting an eagerness to do good. In politics, he was a Tory, but no party-man ; a true patriot, he was sensitively alive to the honour of his King and country. In one word, Lord Howe was a man in all the relations of social life—

" Integer Vitæ Scelerisque purus."[1]

Lord Malmesbury[2] has an entry in his diary on the death of Lord Nelson, whom he thus describes :—

" He added to genius, valour and energy, the singular power of electrifying all within his atmosphere, and making them only minor constellations to this most luminous planet. The confidence he inspired in his followers, and the terror of his name to our enemies, are what make his loss an irreparable one. Others may be great in many points ; nay, admit but another, like himself, might appear again amongst the disciples he has formed, there would yet be wanting *all he had done*, and all the *circumstances* of the times in which he *did* those wondrous deeds. Every victory was greater than the last. Every additional difficulty seemed only to bring out some new proof of the combination and powers of his mind, as well as the invincible force of his arms, and had he survived this last victory, the next and the next would have

[1] Pages 425-32.
[2] Diaries and Correspondence of James Harris, First Earl of Malmesbury, 4 vols. 8vo. Lond 1844.

still surpassed each other. *All this is sorrow for ourselves;* but still more deeply do I regret that *he* cannot see the effect his death produced. Not one individual who felt *joy* at this victory, so well-timed and so complete, but first had an instinctive feeling of *sorrow,* not *selfish sorrow,* (for it came before the reflection of the *consequences* of his loss to us), but the sorrow of affection and gratitude—for what he *had* done for us; and the first regret was, that *he* who did the deed should be deprived of the enjoyment which he, above all other men, from his character, would have derived from its effects.

" Could he have lived but long enough to have known that *no victory,* not even *his victories,* could weigh in the hearts of Englishmen against his most persevering life, it would have been some consolation. I never saw so little public joy. The illumination seemed dim, and, as it were, half clouded, by the desire of expressing the mixture of contending feelings. Every common person in the streets speaking *first* of their sorrow for *him;* and *then* of the victory.

" Collingwood's letter (which is admirable) proves that it was his art to make all under him love him, and own his superiority, without a ray of jealousy. He never was a *party man* himself, and there was never a party in his fleets. All were governed by *one mind,* and this made them invincible. He was a true patriot, which is nearly as rare a character as to be the hero he was. He had the aim and spirit of chivalry, and he was the most loyal subject; living and dying for his country, without reference to those who held the helm under that Sovereign, to whom, next to her, he considered himself most bound. This completes a character, which cannot, I fear, appear again in *our* time."[1]

The distinguished Nobleman just referred to, has also another paragraph relating to the death of Nelson, which is of exceeding interest:—

" On the receipt of the news of the memorable battle of Trafalgar I happened to dine with Pitt, and it was naturally the engrossing subject of our conversation. I shall *never forget* the eloquent manner in which he described his conflicting feelings, when roused in the night to read Collingwood's Dis-

---

[1] Vol. iv. p. 342.

patches. Pitt observed, that he had been called up at various hours in his eventful life by the arrival of news of various hues; but that, whether good or bad, he could always lay his head on his pillow and sink into sound sleep again. On *this occasion*, however, the great event announced brought with it so much to weep over, as well as to rejoice at, that he could not calm his thoughts, but at length got up, though it was three in the morning."[1]

Nothing could exceed the public distress for the loss of Nelson. The glory of the victory of Trafalgar, and joy at the happy consequences that must necessarily follow upon such an event, was a secondary consideration to the loss of the hero, and a feeling of exquisite tenderness and gratitude pervaded every bosom. Deeply impressed with this feeling, Coleridge has finely observed:—

"When he died it seemed as if no man was a stranger to another: for all were made acquaintances by the rights of a common anguish. In the fleet itself, many a private quarrel was forgotten, no more to be remembered; many, who had been alienated became once more good friends; yea, many a one was reconciled to his very enemy, and loved, and (as it were) thanked him, for the bitterness of his grief, as if it had been an act of consolation to himself in an intercourse of private sympathy. The tidings arrived at Naples on the day that I returned to that city from Calabria: and never can I forget the sorrow and consternation that lay on every countenance. Even to this day there are times when I seem to see, as in a vision, separate groups and individual faces of the picture. Numbers stopped and shook hands with me, because they had seen the tears on my cheek, and conjectured that I was an Englishman; and several, as they held my hand, burst, themselves, into tears. And though it may awaken a smile, yet it pleased and affected me, as a proof of the goodness of the human heart struggling to exercise its kindness in spite of prejudices the most obstinate, and eager to carry on its love and honour into the life beyond life; that it was whispered about Naples, that Lord Nelson had become a good Catholic before his death. The absurdity of the fiction

---

[1] Lord Fitzharris's Note Book, 1805. Vol. iv. p. 341. *Note.*

is a sort of measurement of the fond and affectionate esteem which had ripened the pious wish of some kind individual through all the gradations of possibility and probability into a confident assertion believed and affirmed by hundreds."[1]

The Hon. Captain Blackwood, the bearer of the Dispatches of the Battle of Trafalgar to England, writes to his wife:—" I am so depressed with both the public loss, and my own private loss in such a friend, that really the victory, and all the other advantages are lost in the mournful chasm, and cause for sorrow in the death of this great and much loved hero. I can scarcely credit he is no more, and that we have, in sight of the Spanish shore, so complete and unheard-of a victory. No man ever died more gloriously, or more sincerely regretted. He was the bravest, most generous, kindest of men!"

On the 8th of September, 1811, Sir James Mackintosh, according to his Diary (from which extracts are given by his son, in the Memoirs of the Life of his Father),[2] finished the perusal of Clarke and McArthur's Life of Lord Nelson. " Finished Nelson's Life. Let me now endeavour to say what I think of him as he originally was, before he was surrounded by that blaze of glory, which makes examination impossible. He seems to have been born with a quick good sense, an affectionate heart, and a high spirit; he was susceptible of the enthusiasm either of the tender or the proud feelings; he was easily melted or inflamed; to say that he was fearless, seems ridiculously unnecessary; he was not merely averse to falsehood or artifice, but he was in the highest degree simple and frank. These qualities of his heart are not mentioned for the idle purpose of panegyric; however singular it may sound, I will venture to affirm that they formed no small part of the genius of Nelson: they secured attachment and confidence, and they reconciled to him the feelings of other men—that great secret in the art of command, which reason alone can never disclose. His understanding was concentrated on his profession; and as danger must always excite where it does not disturb, it acted on his mind, in the moment of action, with the highest stimulant power, and roused his genius to exertions greater than the languor of

---

[1] The Friend, Essay vi.    [2] Vol. ii. p. 135.

tranquillity could have produced. Still, Windham certainly, and perhaps Fox, met Captain Nelson at Holkham, without suspecting that he was more than a lively and gallant officer.

"The nature of the service in the Mediterranean must have had an influence in expanding his character. He soon obtained a separate command, co-operating with an army acting on shore in situations full of military or maritime peril, calling forth all the resource, enterprise, and fortitude of an officer. The revolutionary character of the war had, doubtless, a powerful effect; he saw thrones subverted, revolutions effected, counter-revolutions projected, the fate of governments and nations immediately effected by operations in which he had some share. Scarcely emerged from his retreat at his father's parsonage, he began to negotiate with generals, ambassadors, and princes. If he had commanded a ship in a fleet on ordinary service, it is scarcely possible that his spirit should have been so much elevated, and his faculties so much strengthened. He must already have become an extraordinary man, when he was selected by the stern and shrewd St. Vincent for that service, which terminated with such glory.

"In this progress it is easy to see, by his correspondence, how his mind climbed from height to height, till he reached the summit, where the grand images of his country and of glory presented themselves to his view, and kindled that fierce flame of enthusiasm which converted his whole soul into genius. His passion for glory extended even to the most trivial of its outward badges. All the pomps and vanities of the world retained their power over him. Neither pleasantry, nor speculation, nor the familiarity of rank and wealth, had weakened the force of these illusions. He had not lived in that society where wit makes the gratification of vanity ridiculous, or where reason proves their emptiness, or where satiety rejects them with disgust; he came forth from the most humble privacy. Fame, with all her marks, and praise from every source, worked with irresistible efficacy on his fresh and simple mind. The love of glory, and even of praise and of honours; the indignant contempt of money; the sincerity and ardour of his character, and the simplicity and energy of his sayings; give him more the appearance of an ancient than a modern hero."

Similar opinions to those now referred to have been very generally entertained and expressed of the character of Nelson; but it would be uncandid and unjust were I to omit making mention of three points which have often been alluded to as spots upon his otherwise irreproachable name; these all refer to transactions at Naples. It is not without some degree of satisfaction, founded, I trust, upon reasonable grounds, that I venture to hope what has been stated in Chapters VIII. and IX. of the first volume of this work, and the royal papers and letters therein printed, may tend to remove much of the opprobrium which has attached to Nelson, for his repudiation of the Treaty of Capitulation of the Castles Nuovo and Uovo, and the orders given in reference to the trial and execution of Francisco Caracciolo; whilst I trust that the Supplementary Chapters on Lady Hamilton and Miss Horatia Nelson, will serve at least to palliate his conduct, though they may be insufficient to exculpate him from the charge of yielding, certainly under very peculiar circumstances, to the powerful fascinations of perhaps the most beautiful and interesting woman of the age in which she lived.

# SUPPLEMENTARY CHAPTERS.

### No. I.

#### LADY HAMILTON.

EMMA LADY HAMILTON, whose name has occurred so repeatedly in the preceding pages, and with whom Lord Nelson's correspondence was principally maintained, was of obscure birth, being the daughter of Henry Lyon or Lyons, a man living in a menial capacity at Preston, in the county of Lancashire. He dying when she was very young, her mother removed to Hawarden in Flintshire, and there maintained herself and family in habits of industry. It is obvious that the education of the daughter must have been of the most trifling description, and that whatever knowledge or accomplishments she attained were acquired in later years; and, as in the case of most persons who are educated only in advanced life, she never overcame the difficulties of orthography: although she maintained an extensive correspondence with many persons of very high station in society, and with many who were distinguished and will long be remembered in the world of letters by their attainments in science, arts, and literature, she never learnt to spell with accuracy, or to write with any degree of exactness. The precise date of her birth is unknown, but was probably April 26th, 1764. The earlier period of her life was passed in servitude, and without means to cultivate her intellectual faculties. She was first engaged in the capacity of nursery-maid in the family of Mr. Thomas of Hawarden, the brother-in-law of Mr. Alderman Boydell, and father of Mr. Honoratus Leigh Thomas, of Leicester-place, a distinguished Surgeon; and she filled a similar situation in the family of Dr. Budd, to whom I was known, residing in Chatham-place, Blackfriars, and one of the Physicians attached to St. Bartholomew's Hospital. It is not a little curious that at the time she was thus engaged in the family of Dr. Budd she had a fellow-servant, as housemaid, a companion, who afterwards became highly and deservedly popular as an actress at Drury Lane Theatre, the late Mrs. Powell. Among the papers now before me there is a letter[1] from Mrs. Powell, which shews that a certain, though qualified, intimacy was kept up by these two adventurers of fortune: and it is not a little singular to find that when Sir William Hamilton married Lady Hamilton, and that it was known to be their intention to be present at a performance at Drury Lane Theatre, where a large audience was assembled to see this remarkable woman, whose achievements, and whose conquests formed a common theme of conversation, the admiration of the house was shared by two beautiful women, the actress and the wife of the Minister whose early fortunes had thrown them together under such humble circumstances. Perhaps, at the time, this secret of their lives was known in the house only to themselves, and the feelings excited by this occurrence must necessarily have been of a very peculiar description.

Quitting her servitude as nursery-maid, Emma is reported to have engaged herself to a dealer in St. James's Market, where, by her appearance and manners, she attracted the attention of a lady of fashion, and by her was withdrawn from her obscurity, and invited to a situation more congenial to her feelings and disposition. Here she had opportunities of reading the novels and romances of that day. This lady was visited by the fashionable world and at her parties were numerous singers and other public performers, together with many of the writers for the stage. Emma has been known to express regret at the manner in which her time was here engaged. The reading of romances and books of light intelligence and character, only served to fire her imagination, excite a love of display, and distract her attention from the duties belonging to those in her sphere of life. The acquaintances here formed, and the deluge of flattery with which she was overwhelmed soon overcame her reason, and led her into habits of dissipation.

By all who had acquaintance with her, and I have met with many in my own circle of friends to whom she was well known, she has been described as of great beauty, of voluptuous form,

[1] "Dear Lady Hamilton,      "Southend,

"I cannot forbear writing a line to inform your Ladyship I am at this place, and to tell you how much your absence is regretted by all ranks of people. Would to Heaven you were here to enliven this (at present) dull scene. I have performed one night, and have promised to play six, but unless the houses are better must decline it. Please to remember me most kindly to your mother and every one at Merton,

"I am, dear Lady Hamilton,
"Your obliged,
"JANE POWELL."

of remarkable activity, having also a most powerful and charming voice, exquisite ear, and great powers of mimicry. It is not remarkable that with these possessions she should attract the notice of all who came in contact with her.

The exercise of a charitable disposition evinced in an attempt to obtain the release of either a friend or a relative, a native of Wales, who had been impressed on the river Thames at the commencement of the American War, seems first to have endangered her virtue. To Captain, afterwards Rear-Admiral John Willet Payne,[1] this application was made, and, by her manners, the seaman was so completely captivated, that he induced her to become his mistress. The rapidity with which one false step is succeeded by another was, as is common, illustrated in her case. She soon afterwards attracted the notice of Sir Harry Featherstonhaugh, Bart., of Up-Park, Sussex, who then became her protector. This Baronet's love of a

[1] This officer was the youngest son of the Hon. Mr. Payne, Governor of St. Christopher's Island, and was educated at the Royal Academy at Portsmouth. In 1769 he sailed in the Quebec to the Leeward Islands, whence he was transferred to the Montagu, Rear-Admiral Robert Man. Made Lieutenant, he was appointed to the Falcon sloop, and sailed in 1772 to St. Vincent, on the Carib expedition. A treaty of peace being made with the Caribs, and the dominion of his Majesty established, Lieutenant Payne returned to England in the Seahorse. He was soon afterwards appointed to the Rainbow, and with Commodore T. Collingwood, sailed to the coast of Guinea, whence he departed for Jamaica. At the commencement of the American War he joined Sir Peter Parker in the Bristol, and afterwards in the Eagle, where he acted as Aide-de-camp to the Admiral, Lord Howe, and was at the taking of New York. Pleased with his services, his Lordship named him Second Lieutenant of the Brune frigate, 32 guns, Captain James Ferguson. After much service on the North American station, he was appointed to the Phœnix, Captain Sir Hyde Parker, and went to the West Indies, and was in the action with Count D'Estaing. He then served in the Roebuck and the Romney, from which he was made Commander of the Cormorant, and on his way to Lisbon captured the Santa Margaretta, a Spanish frigate. In 1780 he was made a Post Captain. In the Enterprize he afterwards visited several parts of Europe and America, and for his bravery was appointed to the Leander, 50 guns, and then to the Princess Amelia of 80 guns, in which, at the conclusion of the war, he returned to England. He now enjoyed elegant society, was an especial favourite of the Prince of Wales, and universally beloved for his information and good humour. He was made Keeper of the Privy Seal to the Prince, and represented Huntingdon in Parliament. At the breaking out of the Revolutionary War he was appointed to the Russell, 74 guns, and was in Lord Howe's victory of the 1st of June, 1794. In the Jupiter, 50 guns, he was Commodore of the squadron to bring over the Princess Caroline of Brunswick to England. In 1796 he commanded the Impeteux, 80 guns, joined Admiral Colpoys, and afterwards Lord Bridport, and Sir J. B. Warren, in which services his health failed from excessive anxiety and fatigue. In 1797 he was made a Rear-Admiral of the Blue, and in 1799 appointed Treasurer of Greenwich Hospital, where he died of a fit of apoplexy, November 17, 1802.

country life and the sports of the field, gave to her opportunities for the display of equestrian talent, for which she became very remarkable, and, as may be expected under such circumstances, she soon joined in scenes of dissipation, which led to a derangement of the Baronet's resources, and a separation ensued. The manner, however, in which she deported herself to Sir Harry Featherstonhaugh, was such as to gain his esteem, for late in life he addressed letters to her of great propriety and good sense, and they evince the most respectful regard. Bankrupt in virtue—unfitted to return to servitude—without adequate means of subsistence—she was now thrown upon the world, and endured many privations. Threatened to be ejected from her lodgings by her landlord, she was induced by an empiric of great notoriety, a Dr. Graham, then delivering lectures in the Adelphi, to exhibit herself under his auspices as a perfect model of health and beauty. Her appearance at the meetings of the quack doubtless led to the admiration of her form by artists, and thus their attention was directed towards her as a model for their works. From the altar of the 'Goddess of Health' the transition to the studio of the Painter was easy. Romney, the Royal Academician, equally fascinated by the powers of her mind and the symmetry of her form, selected her as the subject of many of his most esteemed paintings. When Hayley was collecting materials for a life of Romney, he applied to Lady Hamilton, who seems to have equally captivated both painter and biographer.

The following is from the Biographer and Poet:—

" My dear Lady Hamilton,
" In looking over the letters of our dear departed Romney, it pleased me not a little to find my friend describing you as desirous that I should write a life of the artist, and expressing a very flattering wish that I should speak of you *as his model.* He told me, with great truth at the time, that I had made some preparation for such a work, by taking from his own lips many incidents of his younger days. I am now endeavouring to accomplish the affectionate desire of my friend in writing such a life of him, as I hope those who knew and loved him, as we did, may read with cordial satisfaction. You will oblige me infinitely by favouring me with a list of the various pictures (with *their dates*) which he finished or began from your lovely features in all their variations of character.

"You were not only *his model* but *his inspirer,* and he truly and gratefully said, that he owed a great part of his felicity, as a painter, to the angelic kindness and intelligence with which you used to animate his diffident and tremulous spirits to the grandest efforts of art. If you have any letters of his or verses of mine that may tend to illustrate his life, by ascertaining the date of his productions, pray indulge me with copies of them; for years of affliction and ill-health made me expect so little to survive my old friend, that I neglected to collect any materials for the work he wished me to execute.

"It has pleased Heaven to restore to me a better state of health than I had reason to expect, and the best use I can make of it is to render affectionate justice to the talents and virtues of those departed companions, whose memory is justly dear to me. In celebrating our beloved Romney, it will gratify me exceedingly to have the fullest information from you, which may enable me, in recording his works, to express how justly you were the object of our united idolatry for your beauty, your talents, and your benevolence. Continue, my dear Lady, to be kind, as you have ever been, to your affectionate admirer and sincere friend,

"W. HAYLEY.

"Felphan, near Chichester, May 17, 1804.

"I am grown such a hermit, that I never wander to London; but if you ever visit Bognor in the bathing season, you will be only a mile distant from my little marine cell, where I should be delighted to see and hear you: and where I can entertain you with a sight of yourself in *three enchanting personages, Cassandra, Serena,* and *Sensibility.* These three ladies are all *worth visiting,* whether the old hermit is so or not; so pray come to see us whenever you can.

" Adieu!"

In his Life of Romney, Hayley thus speaks of her:—

"The high and constant admiration with which Romney contemplated the personal and mental endowments of this lady, and the gratitude he felt for many proofs of her friendship, will appear in passages from his letters describing some memorable incidents, when their recent and pleasing impression on his mind and heart gave peculiar vivacity to his description. The talents which nature bestowed on the fair Emma, led her to delight in the two kindred arts of music and painting; in the first she acquired great practical ability; for the second she had exquisite taste, and such expressive powers as could furnish to an historical painter an inspiring model for the various characters, either delicate or sublime, that he might have occasion to represent. Her features, like the language of Shakespeare, could exhibit all the feelings of nature, and all the gradations of every passion with a most fascinating truth and felicity of expression. Romney delighted in observing the wonderful command she possessed over her eloquent features, and through the surprising vicissitudes of her destiny she ever took a generous pride in serving him as a model; her peculiar force and variations of feeling, countenance, and gesture, inspirited and ennobled the production of his art."[1]

On the 19th of June, 1791, the Painter wrote to his Biographer, saying, "At present, and the greatest part of the summer, I shall be engaged in painting pictures from the divine lady; I cannot give her any other epithet, for I think her superior to all womankind. I have two pictures to paint of her for the Prince of Wales." And on the 7th of July following:—"I dedicate my time to this charming lady; there is a prospect of her leaving town with Sir William for two or three weeks. They are very much hurried at present, as every thing is going on for their speedy marriage, and all the world following her and talking of her; so that if she had not more good sense than vanity, her brain must be turned. The pictures I have begun are Joan of Arc, a Magdalen, and a Bacchante for the Prince of Wales, and another I am to begin as a companion to the Bacchante. I am also to paint a picture of Constance for the Shakespeare Gallery."[2] The Joan of Arc is described by Hayley as having a countenance of most powerful expression. The head was thought one of the finest that he ever painted from the features of his favourite model, and gave rise to a sonnet by Hayley:[3]

---

[1] Life of George Romney, by W. Hayley. Chichester, 1809, 4to. page 118.
[2] Ibid. p. 159.

[3] SONNET.

"A bright atonement soothes that injured shade,
Who drew from Orleans her immortal fame;
Hark! hear you not the heroine exclaim?
'Now I renounce, by grateful honour swayed,
My fix'd abhorrence of the English name:
Here I at last am worthily portrayed,
And for this tribute to my glory paid,
Forgive all past indignity and shame.
No more I deem this isle a savage clime:
Her chiefs to me were barbarously base,
And Shakespeare, of her lofty bards the prime,
Drew a faint copy of my soul sublime:
But generous Romney, you my wrongs efface,
And crown my deathless form with dignity and grace."

In addition to the pictures above mentioned, Lady Hamilton was Romney's model for Cassandra, a Wood Nymph, a Calypso, the Pythian Priestess on her Tripod. St. Cecilia, Serena, Sensibility, and, I think, Miranda. To those who are familiar with the features of Lady Hamilton it is not difficult to trace his model in many other of the artist's fancy pictures.

In August, 1791, Romney wrote to Hayley: " In my last letter I think I informed you that I was going to dine with Sir William and his Lady. In the evening of that day there were collected several people of fashion to hear her sing; she performed, both in the serious and comic, to admiration both in singing and acting; but her Nina surpasses every thing I ever saw, and, I believe, as a piece of acting, nothing ever surpassed it. The whole company were in an agony of sorrow: her acting is simple, grand, terrible, and pathetic."[1] Again, August 29, 1791: " She performed in my house last week, singing and acting before some of the nobility with most astonishing powers: she is the talk of the whole town, and really surpasses every thing, both in singing and acting, that ever appeared. Gallini offered her two thousand pounds a-year, and two benefits, if she would engage with him; on which Sir William said, pleasantly, that he had engaged her for life."[2]

During the period alluded to, in which she was supporting herself by turning to advantage, for the maintenance of life, that beauty of form with which nature had endowed her, she formed an acquaintance with an honourable member of the House of Warwick, Mr. Charles Francis Greville, who saw her, and was immediately enamoured. This gentleman was well known for his taste in objects of art and vertù, probably derived from his communication with his uncle, Sir William Hamilton. No regular attempt at the cultivation of Emma's powers was undertaken, until she formed her connexion with Mr. Greville. He placed her under the tuition of various instructors, and in music she rapidly attained a wonderful perfection. Mr. Greville took her one night to Ranelagh, and there, exhilarated by the admiration bestowed on her form and manners, she became so excited, that she ventured, in public, to display her vocal powers, and thereby called forth the most rapturous applause. Mr. Greville had gone farther than he had intended, and became alarmed at her fondness for adulation, and ventured to reproach her for her indiscretion. She retired to her room, threw off the elegant attire in which

---

[1] Ibid. p. 162.    [2] Ibid. p. 165.

she was clothed, and presenting herself before him in a plain cottage dress, proposed to relieve him of her presence. This act, however, served only the more securely to bind him in his chains, and a reconciliation took place. By her connexion with Mr. Greville, she is reported to have had three children, named Eliza, Ann, and Charles. She always passed for their aunt, and took upon herself the name of Harte. In the splendid misery in which she lived, she hastened to call to her her mother, to whom she was through life most affectionate and attentive, and she passed by the name of Cadogan.

In 1789, the changes produced by the French Revolution, operated upon Mr. Greville's affairs, and he was under the necessity of reducing his establishment and making arrangements with his creditors. A separation became necessary. The Right Honourable Sir William Hamilton, K.B., and Ambassador to his Britannic Majesty at Naples, but now in London, at this time (probably not before) became acquainted with her, was passionately attached to her, and prevailed upon her to accompany him to Naples, whither she went, together with her mother, and he devoted still further attention to the cultivation of her mind and accomplishments. It is only charitable to suppose Sir William to have been ignorant of his nephew's connexion with Emma, but there have not been wanting reports, that the condition of the engagement between Sir William, and the lady, was the payment of his nephew's debts. Sir William Hamilton was a native of Scotland, born in 1730, and was Minister at Naples for the long period of thirty-six years. He was a distinguished antiquary, remarkable for his taste in, and appreciation of the Fine Arts. He possessed, also, scientific acquirements, and had some knowledge of mineralogy. He was a Trustee of the British Museum, a Fellow of the Royal Society, and a Vice-President of the Society of Antiquaries. He was, also, a distinguished Member of the Dilletanti Club, and appears among the portraits, in their room of meeting, at the Thatched House Tavern. A portrait of him by Sir Joshua Reynolds, one of his intimate friends, may be seen in the National Gallery. He is known as an author by his works.[1] With the King of Naples, he was a great favourite, and largely

---

[1] Antiquités Etrusques, Grecques, et Romaines, tirées du Cabinet de M. Hamilton; with Introductory Dissertations in English and French, by M. D'Harcanville, Naples, 1765-75. 4 vols. folio. A smaller edition was published at Paris, in 1787, in 5 vols. 8vo. by M. David.

Observations on Mount Vesuvius, Mount Ætna, and other Volcanoes of the Two Sicilies. London, 1772, 1774, 8vo.

shared with him the enjoyment of the chase and other sports, to which the Sovereign is well known to have been egregiously addicted.

Already familiarised to the studies of the painter, and according to Romney, and his biographer, no mean judge of the arts; with Sir William, she had, in Italy, many opportunities of displaying her taste, of improving herself, and also of imparting her knowledge. This she is said to have practically evinced, for with a common piece of stuff, she could so arrange it, and clothe herself, as to offer the most appropriate representations of a Jewess, a Roman matron, a Helen, Penelope, or Aspasia.[2] No character seemed foreign to her, and the grace she was in the habit of displaying, under such representations, excited the admiration of all who were fortunate enough to have been present on such occasions. The celebrated Shawl Dance, owes its origin to her invention; but it is admitted to have been executed by her with a grace and elegance, far surpassing that with which it has ever been rendered on the stage of any of our theatres.

Under the tuition and governance of Sir William Hamilton, she improved so greatly, and obtained such complete sway over him, that he resolved upon making her his wife. They came to England, and on the 6th of September, 1791, she writing the name of Emma Harte, he married her at the Church of St. George, Hanover Square, resolving to return with her to Naples, that she might there be recognised by the Neapolitan Court. But prior to quitting London to return to Naples, she was doomed to experience disappointment; for although she had, through the position of Sir William Hamilton, and his high connexions, together with her own attractions and accomplishments, gained admission into a very high circle of society, she was very properly refused admission to the Court of St. James's, which Sir William, in vain, endeavoured most assiduously to effect. In the society, however, in

Campi Phlegræi; or Observations on the Volcanoes of the Two Sicilies, English and French, Naples, 1776-7, 2 vols. folio. A Supplement: being an account of the Great Eruption of Mount Vesuvius, in August, 1779, folio.

Various Papers in the Philosophical Transactions of the Royal Society, and in the Archæologia of the Society of Antiquaries.

Sir William Hamilton died at the age of 72, on the 6th of April, 1803. His estates at Swansea, which he acquired by his former wife, were willed to his nephew, Charles F. Greville, with a charge of £700 *per annum*, as an annuity to Lady Hamilton, for her life. He was buried at Milford Haven, in Pembrokeshire, and from a letter before me from Mr. Greville to Lady Hamilton, April 7, 1807, it appears that Lady Hamilton, presented to the chapel at Milford, a piece of the wreck of L'Orient, the French vessel that was blown up at the Battle of the Nile. [1] See Vol. i. p. 406, *ante*.

which she now moved, she became distinguished for her great accomplishments, and the dulness of fashionable life was greatly relieved by her displays as a singer, and as an actress. The admiration she excited was universal. Mr. Richard Payne Knight, writing to Lady Hamilton, January 21st, 1795, says, " I frequently see and hear from Lord Moira. He is among the most constant and fervid of your admirers; for he scarcely ever writes or converses without saying something in your commendation. The having heard you sing, he reckons an epoch in his life, and often says, that you gave him ideas of the power of expression in music, which he should never otherwise have conceived."

It is said, that at first, upon the return of Sir William to Naples, there was some difficulty in the way of her introduction to the Queen, not having been received at the Court of her own country; that, however, was soon removed, and in a short time, she maintained the most confidential intercourse with her Majesty. That the Queen of Naples, should have become intimately attached to Lady Hamilton, cannot be a matter of surprise, when we recollect the calamities her family had sustained by the French Revolution. To seek consolation in the bosom of the wife of the English Minister, the Minister of that country which almost stood alone in its opposition to the principles and conduct of the French Revolution, seems natural. Friendship is often created by sympathetic associations, called forth under the pressure of affliction, and is sustained by the consolations of hope, derived from them. There are many letters in my possession, from the Queen of Naples to Lady Hamilton, breathing the most ardent attachment, the most unbounded friendship, and expressing eternal gratitude to her. The following letter, accompanied by a portrait of the Dauphin, will be read with interest:—

"February 9, 1793.

" My dear Lady,

" I am very grateful for the interest you took respecting the execrable deed the infamous French have committed. I send you the portrait of that innocent child, who implores assistance, vengeance, or if he is also sacrificed, his ashes, united to those of his parents, cry to the Eternal for speedy retribution; I rely the most on your generous nation to accomplish it. Pardon these distracted sentiments, of my afflicted heart, your attached friend,

" CHARLOTTE."[1]

---

[1] The Queen of Naples, who exercised so much influence upon, and took so active a part in the political affairs of the kingdom, as detailed in many of the

Sir William Hamilton was remarkable for the hospitable manner in which he received visitors at his mansion, and the

letters printed in the preceding biography, was Maria Caroline, daughter of Maria Theresa of Austria, known as one of the handsomest women of her day, and descended from the Counts of Hapsburgh. Her husband, Francis Duke of Lorraine and Bar, commonly known as Francis the First, Emperor of Germany, was also very handsome, and they had many children, among whom may be mentioned Joseph II., Leopold II., Maximilian, Ferdinand, Caroline, Marie Antoinette, Maria Amelia, Christina, Marianna, and Elizabeth.

On the accession of Charles III. to the throne of Spain, October 5th, 1759, Ferdinand, his son, who was born January 12th, 1751, ascended the throne of Naples, and April 7th, 1768, married Maria Caroline of Austria. She partook in no little degree of the beauty of her mother, and shared with her also in pride and haughtiness, which has been attributed to the tuition she received at the Austrian Court. All, however, admit her to have possessed a masculine understanding, to have had great natural and acquired powers of mind, a cool head in council, and great knowledge of men and manners.

General Pépé says (Memoirs, Vol. i. p. 9), that "although in the prime of youth, her mind was of the most powerful stamp, and her wit of the highest order. By nature she was both proud and haughty, and she nourished within her bosom the most inordinate love of power." Of Ferdinand, he says—" He was both by nature and education weak, strongly addicted to pleasure, and utterly incapable of opposing himself to the strong mind of the young Queen, who soon discovered the character of her husband." He further says, " She soon claimed the right of sitting in the State Council, and of having a voice in its deliberations." To this, it must be observed, she was entitled by the laws of Naples, having given birth to a son. This had been established from 1776, and was in conformity with the marriage treaty. Ferdinand IV. is well known to have thought of little else than pleasure, principally derived at excursions in hunting. Sir William Hamilton says in a letter, what is expressed by Lord Nelson in another to the same effect : " The King has killed eighty-one animals of one sort or other to-day, and amongst them a wolf and some stags. He fell asleep in the coach, and awaking told me he had been dreaming of shooting. One would have thought he had shed blood enough." Sir John Acton is reported to have said of Ferdinand, that he was a good sort of man, because nature had not supplied him with the faculties necessary to make a bad one.

The Queen gave more attention to state business than her husband. The active part she took, and the knowledge of the power she possessed is shewn by her letters in these volumes, and by the letter Napoleon Buonaparte addressed to her. Great hatred was entertained between these two Sovereigns, Buonaparte calling the Queen " Fredegonda,"[1] and she him, " Murderer of Princes, and Corsican tyrant." The condition of Naples during the whole of the revolu-

---

[1] Fredegonda was mistress, and afterwards wife of Chilperic I. King of the French, in the middle of the sixth century, whose reign was remarkable for cruelty, to which he is said to have been instigated by Fredegonda, who was also suspected of causing the assassination of the King himself. See, Sismondi Histoire des Français, tom. i. p. 371.

fascinating powers of Lady Hamilton, tended much to render the society agreeable and entertaining. His Royal Highness

tionary period, was very remarkable. Botta, an excellent authority, in his " History of Italy during the Consulate and Empire of Napoleon Buonaparte," says : " In coming to speak of Naples, I know not how to furnish myself with adequate expressions; for the people are like the climate, on the one side an extreme of benevolence, that borders on ideal virtue, on the other an extreme of hatred that borders on ferocity; conspiracies, civil war, foreign wars, conflagrations, devastation, treachery, executions of the virtuous, and of the infamous; but the sword of the executioner fell more frequently on the just than the unjust. To these we must add acts of heroism, of invincible courage, of perfect friendship even in misfortune, civic moderation even in want, the gentlest thought of happy humanity, the purest desires for the common good; now a kingdom agitated by conspiracies, now a republic contaminated by rapine, now a kingdom full of cruelty, and now the theatre of rapine also; Ferdinand twice driven away, again restored; a republic the slave of France, a monarchy the slave of England; a republic established by force through the agency of a soldier, a monarchy restored by force through the agency of a priest;[1] the first accomplished by an immense slaughter of Lazzaroni, the latter by an equal number of republicans. The same individuals who had fawned on Championnet the republican, and on Ferdinand the king, now crouched to the monarch Joseph; and on the other side might be beheld on the same field the cross of Christ in close alliance with the crescent of Mahomet. Altogether these things form a tale so marvellous, that when the eyes and the ears of those who have seen them, and have heard them, shall be closed, none could be found to give them credit, were not testimonies multiplied by the press."— (Vol. ii. p. 25.)

The course of affairs in Naples up to the time of the battle of Trafalgar has been traced in the preceding pages. Lord Collingwood visited Palermo, after the death of Lord Nelson, whom he succeeded as Commander-in-chief in the Mediterranean. He gives a melancholy picture of the state of Sicily, Calabria, and Naples. Of the first he says, " It is as weak as it can be. It is a kingdom that has nothing in it which constitutes the strength of a country; but divided councils; a king, who *ought* to rule, a queen who *will;* no army for its defence; its military works ruinous; without revenue, except just enough to support its gaieties; a nobility without attachment to a court, where foreigners find a preference; and a people, who, having nothing beyond their daily earnings, are indifferent as to who rules them, and look to a change for an amelioration of their condition. Every cause of weakness in a country is to be found here; factions alone are abundant." Of the King he speaks as having the appearance and manner of a worthy, honest country gentleman, living generally in the country, and amusing himself in planting trees and shooting. The Queen he describes to be " penetrating into the souls and minds of every body that comes near her, would be thought a deep politician, yet all her schemes miscarry."

The breach of neutrality on the part of Ferdinand, in admitting an English and Russian force into Naples in November, 1805, during the absence of General St. Cyr, in Upper Italy, carrying on operations with Marshal Massena,

---

[1] Cardinal Ruffo.

the Duke of Sussex and Mrs. Billington were of those parties, and I have often heard from his Royal Highness and others induced Buonaparte to issue a proclamation declaring the Bourbon dynasty to have ceased to reign in Naples. This was enforced by an army of not less than 60,000 men, against whom resistance was hopeless. Joseph Buonaparte was named by his brother, King of Naples. Ferdinand quitted his regal seat of Naples, January 23, 1806, and retired to Sicily; the Queen however remained until February 11th, when she with her daughters fled to join the King. On the 15th, Joseph Buonaparte entered Naples and assumed the reins of government. The Hereditary Prince Francis, and the Prince Leopold, had been sent by Ferdinand, the one into the Abruzzi, the other into Calabria to rouse the people, but although there was no deficiency of loyalty on the part of the peasantry, there was a want of means, which rendered them powerless. Upon the death of Sir John Acton, the Chevalier Medici succeeded as Minister of Finance. He was a man odious to the Sicilians, from his arbitrary character, and his being a Neapolitan, but he pleased Queen Caroline, who, according to Botta, " alone, uncontaminated by the general weakness of the nobles and the people, compensated by the boldness of her character for its fierceness." She never rested from disturbing the Napoleonic dynasty in Naples. She abetted the English in every thing in her power, to render the Jacobin government turbulent and insecure. The acts consequent upon this state of things, are marked by the greatest atrocity and cruelty. Thousands were massacred, Sicilians and Calabrians, and England, as a Power called to defend the people, could not escape a portion of the odium excited by the enormities which took place. Sicily by her part in these transactions, became weaker, receiving less defence from England. The Queen had become exceedingly unpopular, and England found it necessary to deliberate on the condition of affairs and apply a remedy to such disorders. The Duke of Ascoli, a feeble man, worthy associate of Ferdinand, having the same foibles and weakness of character, was made Prime Minister, by which the Queen obtained a further control or ascendancy over the King, and was the better enabled to repress any desire on his part to exercise his authority in opposition to her will. Public money was shamefully lavished on Neapolitans and Calabrese, and great discontent prevailed among the Sicilians. They appeared to reap no advantage by a most profligate expenditure, occasioned by different expeditions, directed against Castel-à-Mare, Procida, Ischia, and Capri. The treasury was nearly exhausted, the money taken from Naples to Palermo in the flight of the Royal family was expended, and the Queen, as a last resource, pawned her dowry jewels for a sum of about £5000 sterling. England at this time paid to the Sicilian Court £300,000 sterling in yearly subsidy, and no apparent benefit resulted from such an enormous expenditure. Suspicion arose that the money was dispensed in payments to Neapolitan spies and Calabrian homicides, and the character of the English nation began to suffer under such imputations. It was clear that the support of such an Ally produced disrespect, and it was thought necessary to dispossess the Queen of her authority, and thus put an end to such a state of affairs. In vain did England endeavour by constitutional means, through the Sicilian Parliament, which had been convoked by the King in 1810, to remedy these evils. In this Parliament the Chevalier Medici had gained over to him the Commons and the Clergy, but he had neglected the Barons, which as a body was the most powerful, and they opposed themselves to his measures. Amongst these, most conspicuously shone the Prince of Belmonte, who had by the machinations

of the wonderful effect produced by the combined vocal powers of Lady Hamilton and Mrs. Billington.

of Medici endured exile from court. Belmonte was both noble and wealthy; a man issuing from a distinguished lineage, and possessing much influence. Neither was he deficient in ability or wanting in generosity. His good qualities were, however, counterbalanced by great pride. He became the leader of the Barons, and was determined to avenge himself of Caroline and Medici. By his means, Parliament granted but small taxes in augmentation to the donatives; these being paid unwillingly by the Sicilians, and great dissatisfaction expressed. The Barons, by their conduct in suppressing irregularities and punishing offenders, rose into great favour with the people, and obtained much credit. Medici resigned his office, and was succeeded by a Sicilian, who proved ignorant of state affairs. He soon fell into disgrace, the taxes were with great difficulty collected, and the desperate state of affairs rendered it necessary to summon a second Parliament. The Court were not more successful with this assembly than the former, they refusing to grant larger amounts. Tommasi, who had been called to the Royal councils, suggested some expedients to relieve the Government from the embarrassed condition in which it was placed, but they failed of success, and even aggravated the discontent. Botta says, " The Queen, who, although she deserved praise for her firmness, merited censure for the means she employed, and the end she proposed, followed her usual line of conduct. The Barons were equally steady, nor were they men to let occasions pass them. The English now interposed; for they saw that the courses followed by the Government favoured the designs of the French, by rousing the ill-will of the people; and as they had proved that it was useless to give advice to the Queen, they were resolved to avail themselves of the new aspect which affairs had taken." (Vol. ii p. 330.)

A remonstrance to the King was presented by the Barons against two edicts which had been issued contrary to the principles of the Sicilian Constitution, as to the right of levying money. The Queen was resolute in her opposition to the Barons, and even prevailed upon the King to have them arrested. The Prince of Belmonte, the Princes of Aci, of Villamora, of Villa Franca, and the Duke of Anjou, were conducted to different islands and ill treated. Unable to control the Queen or suppress the anger of the people, the English made attempts by an union with the Barons to rule the island. Lord Amherst was at this time the British Ambassador, and he was recalled, that his place might be filled by one of a more indomitable spirit, which was found in the person of Lord William Bentinck. He immediately commenced negotiations with the Queen, and was met by her Majesty with her usual firmness and ability. In vain did he represent to her the dangers with which she was environed, and the necessity of reforming abuses which existed, which endangered not only the administration but the constitution of the kingdom. He demanded the revocation of the offensive edicts, the liberation of the five Barons, and impressed upon her the determination of compelling submission to those conditions, should they be rejected. Her obstinacy was increased as her pride was offended—she declared that Caroline and not Bentinck was sovereign, and wished to know by what right he obtruded himself into the affairs of the kingdom; intimating that he must have exceeded his credentials. She went so far as to demand the production of his mandate for interfering in the government of the kingdom of Sicily. She told him to confine himself to the duties of an Ambassador, and not to arrogate to himself the functions of a Prime Minister

It was in 1793 that Lady Hamilton first saw Nelson on occasion of his being sent by Lord Hood with dispatches for

or a King. Lord William had indeed gone beyond his instructions, and although unable to produce his authority for such an exercise of power, he replied, that if not possessed of the required mandate he would soon get one, and accordingly prepared to put his threats into practice. Perceiving her danger, the Queen resolved upon again seeing the Ambassador, but no conciliatory measure on either side was the result of the interview, and they parted, the Ambassador declaring, as he withdrew from the royal presence, " either a Constitution or a Revolution." He quitted Sicily, returned to London, and in three months was again in Sicily, vested with ample powers to carry his threat into execution. He had the command of all the English troops in the island. He endeavoured to persuade the Queen to submission, but she was inflexible; and at length he declared he would arrest both the King and Queen and send them to England, leaving the son of the Hereditary Prince Don Francisco, then a child of only two years of age, to govern under a Regency, to be composed of the Duke of Orleans, and the Prince of Belmonte. No less than 12,000 troops were brought from all parts into the vicinity of Palermo. The Queen summoned her Council, declared she would not yield to foreign domination, and determined upon repelling force by force. The Sicilian troops were however inefficient and unfit to be trusted; they were without clothing, rations or arms, and the issue of such an unequal contest, could therefore easily be calculated. Caroline was compelled to submit to the decision of her Council, and she withdrew to one of her country seats, at a short distance from the capital. Lord William Bentinck, thus successful in his endeavours, soon prevailed upon the King to resign the royal authority in favour of his son, the Hereditary Prince, as Vice-General of the kingdom. Lord William was elected Captain-General of Sicily, by which he united the command of the nation and the British force, and thus defeated the machinations of Buonaparte, in his views upon Sicily. The Barons were recalled, the Ministers of Caroline dismissed, the edicts relating to the levying of money annulled, Belmonte made Minister for Foreign Affairs, Villamora, of Finance, and Aci, of the Marine. The people rejoiced, and the fortunes of Sicily appeared to be retrieved. Many judicious measures were adopted, the executive power was vested in the King alone, whose person was regarded sacred and inviolable, the judges were made independent of the Parliament and the King, the Ministers held responsible. The Senate was divided into two chambers, the Peers and the Commons, the latter elected by the people, the former such as were ennobled by the King. In the King was vested the power of summoning Parliament, which he was bound to do once in every year; an ample revenue was secured to him by the nation, which took upon itself the administration of the crown lands. Person and property could only be affected through the operation of the laws as sanctioned by Parliament, judicial forms were established, and other measures approaching those of the British constitution were made as far as applicable to Sicily, in promotion of the public good. This Constitution gave great satisfaction. After many difficulties, and with much hesitation, the King divested himself of his regal authority, and his son, the Prince Vicar, ratified the decrees. The Queen is reported to have endeavoured to create confusion, and has been accused of various plots to disturb the public peace, and even endanger the lives of the Senators. The evidence is wanting sufficiently to substantiate these charges. Lord William Bentinck at length succeeded in

Sir William, to obtain troops from Naples to assist in the preservation of Toulon. Reference has been already made to the

removing the Queen from the vicinity of the Government to Castelvetrano, a distance of sixty miles from Palermo, and only awaited the spring to send her to Vienna.

A Lady of rank, who published, "Venice under the yoke of France and of Austria," states that Queen Caroline was confined at Palermo, and that a ship was ordered to be got ready to convey her from the island; this was an order from the British Commander-in-chief, in consequence of its having been discovered that the Queen had been concerned in a plot for the betrayal of the island and the British troops into the hands of the French! Her Majesty denied the truth of the allegations made against her, and insisted that she had given the English no reason for so acting, excepting that of continuing to govern, as she ever had done before she came to the island. Having disposed of all her jewels, she retired to the mountains, raised a party of peasants, and resolved upon recovering her former situation as an independent Queen, and to resist the banishment proposed by a Power she had called in to protect her against the aggression and violence experienced from another quarter. The situation she chose as her retreat was a mountainous one, occupied scarcely by any but goats. She collected together 800 or 900 men with instruments of husbandry only, as defensive or offensive weapons. Here she resolved to oppose Lord William Bentinck, and would accept of no terms of conciliation; she declared, that the King's restoration to power, and the total evacuation of Sicily by the British troops, were the only terms to which she would listen. She respected the English as Allies, but would not acknowledge them as masters. Lord William Bentinck ordered a sufficient number of troops to surround her place of refuge, and reduce her to submission. She was compelled to yield, and was confined in a palace a short distance from Palermo, and carefully watched, to prevent intrigue or further opposition. She was shipped off to the Ionian Islands, thence to Constantinople, and so on to Austria.

Soon after the deposal of the Queen, the King Ferdinand, it is conjectured, upon the urgent entreaties of the Queen, came unexpectedly to Palermo one morning, announced the perfect recovery of his health, and commanded a Proclamation to be posted up throughout the city, ordering *Te Deum* to be performed in all the churches for his convalescence, revoking his son's authority, and proclaiming his own resumption of the Government. The Duke of Orleans was sent by Lord William Bentinck immediately, to acquaint the King, that his palace would be surrounded by cannon, and himself made prisoner, and held responsible for all the mischief that might ensue, unless he immediately withdrew from the capital. The *Te Deum* was relinquished, and the King departed.

The King became an object of contempt with his people, but the Queen was looked upon in another view, for it was held by them, that she had never been favourable to placing them under the power of a foreign yoke. The determined conduct on the part of Lord William Bentinck, prevented any serious consequence arising from this unexpected movement. The step taken, however, rendered the removal of the Queen more than ever necessary, and means were immediately taken to convey her from Sicily. After adverse winds and many hardships she reached Vienna, was soon after taken suddenly ill, and expired, September 7th, 1814. Thus terminated the life of this extraordinary woman.

reception given to Nelson by the King and Royal family, and also by Sir William and Lady Hamilton.[1] From an expression in one of Nelson's letters to his wife, it has been endeavoured to be shewn that that unfortunate passion, which at a later period so lamentably predominated, had at this time its commencement; but there is no authority to justify a belief that an ardour beyond that which would naturally be lighted up in the bosom of a man of Nelson's simplicity and character, full of devotion to the interests of his country and the preservation of national honour and glory, had at this period any existence.

The correspondence of Nelson with his wife, and the style of address maintained by him in his communications to Lady Hamilton, even beyond 1798, when the battle of the Nile had been fought, forbid any such suspicion. By an extract from the Letter Book of Nelson already quoted (Vol. i. p. 126), it appears that through the exertions of Lady Hamilton, she obtained from the Queen of Naples a letter which gave permission to Nelson to water and victual the British fleet at Syracuse, and thus enabled him to seek out the French fleet, and fight the battle of the Nile. As it is principally upon the strength and importance of this service that he left in his will Lady Hamilton's claims upon the country to the notice of the

---

The lady of rank before referred to, who had been presented to Caroline when Queen reigning in Naples, saw her after she had been sent off for the Ionian Islands. At Zante, this lady, upon being ushered into the royal presence, offered as usual to kiss her Majesty's hand, which was remarkably handsome. Upon seeing her intention the Queen withdrew it, saying, "No, the ceremony would now be a mockery of royalty, and an insult to my present condition. The daughter of Maria Theresa—a wanderer and an outcast—must no longer receive those marks of distinction which were the prerogatives of the Queen of Naples. You behold me now in a very different situation to that in which you first saw me, when you presented me with the letters of my dear murdered sister." (Vol. ii. p. 71.) This remark naturally affected the lady much, and the Queen continued: "Do not imagine I mean to offend you. I know your respectful attentions are directed to my person; for, certainly, they cannot be interested at this moment, as I am no longer in a situation to reward you as such attention merits; but, when I reflect, that the only foreign nation for which I had a sincere regard has thus insulted me, and what is still worse, ruined me in the esteem of many of my friends, by calumniating me in the eyes of all Europe, I cannot help feeling a pleasure at the sight of one of that nation who, I am sure, will do me justice."

It is sufficient to add, that the good effects promised by Lord William Bentinck's Constitution, were not realized according to the expectations entertained, and that Ferdinand, upon his restoration to the throne of Naples, in 1814, abolished the Sicilian Constitution, without exciting either the opposition or regret of the people. Ferdinand, King of Naples, died of an attack of apoplexy, January 4th, 1825.

[1] See *ante*, Vol. i. p. 40.

Government, it is proper here to state her case somewhat in detail.

Immediately after the marriage of Sir William and Lady Hamilton, they departed for Naples. Arrived at Paris, they waited upon the Queen of France, then at the Tuilleries, who entrusted to Lady Hamilton the last letter she wrote to her sister, the Queen of Naples, a circumstance which naturally tended to attach the Queen to her, and probably led to an ascendancy in her esteem, which Lady Hamilton endeavoured, in every possible way, to turn to the advantage of the British interest. When Lord Hood had taken possession of Toulon, as above stated, and Sir John Jervis (afterwards Earl of St. Vincent) was employed upon the reduction of Corsica, the latter, who regarded and styled her the Patroness of the Navy, was in the practice of writing to Lady Hamilton for every thing he required from Naples, and in his letters to her he admits that the assistance she rendered him in these various services, contributed much, by the promptness with which it was afforded, to facilitate the reduction of that island. The influence of Lady Hamilton with the Queen operated favourably upon the King, who thereby became so opposed to French interests, and so attached to the English, that it was common to them both to say that Lady Hamilton had "De-Bourbonized them, and made them all English." By the cultivation of this influence, and untiring watchfulness to promote British interests, Lady Hamilton ascertained that a courier had brought to the King of Naples a private letter from the King of Spain, and such was her zeal for the interests of her country, and so great was her power with the Queen, that she absolutely prevailed upon her Majesty to abstract this communication from the King's possession. Upon examination it was found to contain the King of Spain's determination to withdraw from the coalition into which he had entered, and join the French against England. At this time Sir William Hamilton was lying dangerously ill, and unable to attend to his duties; but Lady Hamilton prevailed on the Queen to permit her to take a copy of the letter, and she immediately dispatched it by a messenger to Lord Grenville, taking the then very necessary precautions to insure its safe transit, to effect which cost her about £400, which she paid out of her own private purse.

The following Letters from the Queen to Lady Hamilton exhibit her great attachment to England:—

"My very dear Lady,        "April 29th, 1795.

"My head is so confused, and my spirits so agitated, that I

know not what to do. I hope to see you to-morrow morning about ten o'clock. I send you a letter in cypher, come from Spain, from Galatone, which must be returned before twelve o'clock, so that the King may have it. There are some facts very interesting to the English Government, which I wish to communicate to them, to shew my attachment to them, and the confidence I feel in the worthy Chevalier. I only beg of him not to compromise me. Villars has shewn at Genoa publicly, and privately to Ignasia Serra, Capano's brother, full powers to make peace with all the States of Italy, and afterwards they wish it particularly with the Two Sicilies; that shews their need of it. Adieu. We shall talk of many things to-morrow. Adieu. Believe me your sincere friend."

"April 30th, 1795.

" My dear Lady,

" I must go for the whole day to Carditello, my health and my feeble frame are unsuited for these long journeys, but one must obey. You will be very, very much occupied for me; rely on my sincerely felt gratitude. I have received my letters and seen all that you sent me yesterday. I hope that so much application will not be injurious to the Chevalier. I observe what you say of Gallo.[1] I think him honest and attached, but still young. Adieu, a thousand compliments to the Chevalier."

Various other matters of minor consideration were effected by the influence of Lady Hamilton, from this time until 1798, in affording assistance to the English fleets in those seas, to fully estimate the value of which, it must be borne in mind that at this period so high was French ascendancy and revolutionary principles in Naples, that it was absolutely dangerous for the British Minister even to go to Court.

In June, 1798, about three days after the French fleet had passed by for Malta, Sir William and Lady Hamilton were one morning awakened, about six o'clock, by the arrival of Captain Troubridge with a letter from Sir Horatio Nelson, then with the fleet lying off the Bay near to Capri, "requesting that the Ambassador would procure him permission to enter with his fleet into Naples, or any of the Sicilian Ports, to provision, water, &c., as otherwise he must run for Gibraltar, being in urgent want, and that, consequently, he would be obliged to give over all further pursuit of the French Fleet, which he had missed at Egypt on account of their having put

[1] The Marquis of Gallo afterwards became Ferdinand's Ambassador at Paris; then turned round to Napoleon, became Ambassador from Joseph Buonaparte, and afterwards his Minister for Foreign Affairs.

into Malta." At this time, Naples had made peace with France, and an Ambassador was resident then at Naples. One of the stipulations of the Treaty which had been entered into was to the effect that *no more than two English ships of war should enter into any of the Neapolitan or Sicilian ports.* However, Sir William Hamilton called up Sir John Acton, the Minister, who immediately convened a Council, at which the King was present. This was about half-past six. Lady Hamilton went immediately to the Queen, who received her in her bedroom. She represented to her Majesty that the safety of the Two Sicilies now depended upon her conduct, and that, should the Council, as she feared under the circumstances they must do, decide on negative or half measures, the Sicilies must be lost, if Nelson were not supplied agreeably to his request, by which he would be enabled to follow the great French force which had passed in that direction only a few days before. Nothing could exceed the alarm with which the Queen received this intelligence; she urged that the King was in Council, and would decide with his Ministers. Lady Hamilton prayed and implored on her knees to authorize the required assistance; the Queen was unable to withstand her entreaties and her arguments; pen, ink and paper were brought to her, Lady Hamilton dictated, and the Queen wrote a positive order, "directed to all Governors of the Two Sicilies, to receive with hospitality the British fleet to water, victual, and aid them." In every way, this order, as Lady Hamilton well knew, would be more respected than that which might emanate from the King. The Council did not break up until eight o'clock, and Lady Hamilton attended Captain Troubridge and her husband to their residence. The faces of the King, of Acton, and of Sir William, too plainly told the determination to which they had arrived, and that *they could not then break with France.* On the way home, Lady Hamilton told Sir William and Captain Troubridge that she had anticipated the result and had provided against it; that whilst they were in Council debating the application, she had been with the Queen, and had not without effect implored her Majesty to render the aid required. She then, to their great astonishment and delight, produced the order in question. Nothing could exceed the gladness this occasioned: Troubridge declared that it would "cheer Nelson to ecstasy," and that by this means they should be able to pursue and conquer the French fleet, otherwise they must have gone for Gibraltar. Sir William Hamilton wrote to Sir Horatio Nelson, communicating to him the formal decision of the Council, but added, "You will receive from Emma herself what will do the busi-

This letter I received
after I had sent
the Greens letter
for receiving on
ships together for
Nott — from the Queen
had (Aug 70) to ask
in apposition to the
King who would not
then break with
France & Mr
[illegible]

have gone
down to Gibraltar
I have hastened
to the people
& the Nile
war is not
have been
forgotten, for
the french fleet
wasn't have
got back to
[illegible]

My Dear Lady Hamilton

I have kissed the Queens letter pray say I hope for the honor of kissing her hand when no fears will intervene, assure her Majesty that no person has her felicity more than myself at heart, and that the sufferings of her family will be a Tower of strength on the day of Battle, care not the event, God is with us, God bless you and Sir William pray say I cannot try to answer his letter ever
yours faithfully
May 6th Horatio Nelson

ness, and procure all your wants." Lady Hamilton inclosed to the Admiral the order, praying him "that the Queen might be as little committed in the use of it as the glory and service of the country would admit of." To this, Nelson replied, that he received the precious order, and that if he gained a battle it should be called hers and the Queen's, for to Lady Hamilton he should owe his success, as, without the order, their return to Gibraltar was decided upon. But, he added, "I will now come back to you crowned with laurel, or covered with cypress."

The following letter[1] was written to Lady Hamilton on this occasion:—

"My dear Lady Hamilton,

"I have kissed the Queen's letter. Pray say I hope for the honour of kissing her hand when no fears will intervene. Assure her Majesty that no person has her felicity more at heart than myself, and that the sufferings of her family will be a tower of strength on the day of battle. Fear not the event: God is with us. God bless you and Sir William. Pray say I cannot stay to answer his letter.

"Ever yours faithfully,

"HORATIO NELSON.

"17th May, 6 P.M."

The month affixed to this letter is incorrect; it must have been written on the 17th of June not the 17th of May. On the back of it Lady Hamilton has written: "This letter I received after I had sent the Queen's letter for receiving our ships into their ports; for the Queen had decided to act in opposition to the King, who could not then break with France, and our fleet must have gone down to Gibraltar to have watered, and the Battle of the Nile would not have been fought, for the French fleet would have got back to Toulon." On the 17th of May Nelson was not off Naples but off Cape Sicie, and on that day wrote[2] to Earl St. Vincent to acquaint him that the Terpsichore had that morning captured a French corvette which came out of Toulon the previous night, and that from examination of the crew he found Buonaparte had arrived at Toulon, and had examined the troops which were embarking in transports; that troops frequently arrived from Marseilles, but that no one knew to what place the armament was destined. On the 24th of May he wrote the well-known letter to Lady Nelson from the island of St. Peter's in Sardinia, descriptive of the effects of the awful storm he had witnessed. On the

---

[1] See Fac-simile.    [2] Dispatches and Letters, Vol. iii. p. 15.

27th he was able, by great efforts, again to put to sea. On the 12th of June he was off Elba, and wrote to Sir William Hamilton, expressing his hope that he had arrived in good time to save Naples or Sicily from falling into the hands of the enemy, and wishing to know what co-operation was intended by the Court of Naples, and asking for information relative to the French fleet. On the 15th he was off the Ponza Islands, and wrote to the Earl of St. Vincent that not finding a cruiser, he should send Captain Troubridge into Naples to talk with Sir William Hamilton and General Acton. "Troubridge (he says) possesses my full confidence, and has been my honoured acquaintance of twenty-five years standing." On the 14th, being then off Civitá Vecchia, he sent Troubridge with a letter to Sir William Hamilton. On the 17th he was in the Bay of Naples, and Captain Troubridge must have returned on that day, for upon his arrival Nelson immediately put to sea. On the 18th he wrote the following note to Sir William Hamilton:—

(Private.)　　　　　　　" Vanguard, at Sea, 18th June, 1798.

" My dear Sir,

" I would not lose one moment of the breeze in answering your letter. The best sight (as an Irishman would say) was to see me out of sight; especially as I had not time to examine the Marquis de Gallo's note to you. I send you an extract of the Admiralty orders to Earl St. Vincent, by which it would appear as determined by the Cabinet to keep a superior Fleet to the enemy in the Mediterranean; for the Admiralty, you know, can give no such orders, but by an order from the Secretary of State. As for what depends on me, I beg, if you think it proper, to tell their Sicilian Majesties, and General Acton, that they may rest assured that I shall not withdraw the King's fleet but by positive orders, or the impossibility of *procuring supplies*. I wish them to depend upon me, and they shall not be disappointed. God forbid it should so happen that the enemy escape me and get into any port. You may rely, if I am properly supplied, that there they shall remain, a useless body, for this summer; but, if I have gun and mortar boats, with fire-ships, it is most probable they may be got at: for, although I hope the best, yet it is proper to be prepared for the worst (which, I am sure, all this fleet would feel), the escape of the enemy into port. My distress for frigates is extreme; but I cannot help myself, and no one will help me. But, thank God, I am not apt to feel difficulties.

" Pray present my best respects to Lady Hamilton: tell her I hope to be presented to her crowned with laurel or cypress.

But God is good, and to Him do I commit myself and our cause. Ever believe me, my dear Sir,

"Your obliged and faithful,
"HORATIO NELSON."

In a letter also to the Earl of St. Vincent, written at sea, June 29th, he says, "On the 17th, in the Bay of Naples, I received my first letter from Sir William Hamilton, and in two hours Captain Troubridge returned with information that the French fleet were off Malta on the 8th, going to attack it; that Naples was at peace with the French Republic, therefore could afford us no assistance in ships; but that, under the rose, they would give us the use of their ports, and sincerely wished us well, but did not promise the smallest information of what was, or likely to be, the future destination of the French armament."[1] On the 20th of July he anchored at Syracuse, and there watered and obtained fresh provisions, &c. On this day he wrote to the Earl of St. Vincent: "We are watering, and getting such refreshments as the place affords, and shall get to sea by the 25th."[2]

I have been thus particular with regard to this letter, because Sir N. H. Nicolas questions Nelson's knowledge of the Queen's letter to enable him to obtain supplies, and thinks the fact inconsistent with the letters addressed by him to Sir William and to Sir William and Lady Hamilton, both of the 22nd of July; the former taken from a copy in the State Paper Office, Admiralty and Letter Book, runs thus:—

"Vanguard, Syracuse, July 22, 1798.

"My dear Sir,

"I have had so much said about the King of Naples' orders only to admit three or four of the ships of our fleet into his ports, that I am astonished. I understood that private orders, at least, would have been given for our free admission. If we are to be refused supplies, pray send me by many vessels an account, that I may in good time take the King's fleet to Gibraltar. Our treatment is scandalous for a great nation to put up with, and the King's flag is insulted at every friendly port we look at.

"I am, with the greatest respect, &c.

"HORATIO NELSON.

"You will observe that I feel as a public man, and write as such. I have no complaint to make of private attention,

---

[1] Dispatches and Letters, Vol. iii. p. 39.     [2] Ibid. Vol. iii. p. 45.

quite the contrary. Every body of persons have been on board to offer me civilities."

To Sir William and Lady Hamilton:—

"22nd July, 1798.

"My dear Friends,

"Thanks to your exertions, we have victualled and watered; and surely watering at the Fountain of Arethusa, we must have victory. We shall sail with the first breeze, and be assured I will return either crowned with laurel or covered with cypress."[1]

To reconcile these we must refer to Nelson's letter to the Earl of St. Vincent of the 20th, before quoted, where it will be seen that he was at that time getting water and refreshments, although two days afterwards he writes to Sir William Hamilton as if they were to be refused to him, and on the same day acknowledges to Sir William and Lady Hamilton that they are victualled and watered, and attributes it to their exertions. The former letter to Sir William is clearly a *public* letter, perhaps thought necessary by Nelson, that the Queen should not be compromised, and the latter is a *private* letter to satisfy the British Minister and his Lady, that the object had been accomplished. That it was so accomplished, and that the supplies being so furnished occasioned the Chargé d'Affaires of the French Republic, Mons. La Cheze, to protest to the Marquis de Gallo, 17 Thermidor, An vi. (August 4, 1798), is well known and on record, and that it was effected by Lady Hamilton's exertions is admitted by Nelson in the most solemn document that could be written, no less than in that Codicil to his Will made at the moment he was (and under a presentiment of death) about to engage in battle with the enemy; Nelson abhorred a falsehood, and his affirmation on that subject is entitled to be received as proof.

On the 23rd of July he again wrote to Sir William Hamilton, and says, "The fleet is unmoored, and the moment the wind comes off the land, shall go out of this delightful harbour, where our present wants have been most amply supplied, and where every attention has been paid to us; but I have been tormented by no private orders being given to the Governors for our admission."[2]

Nelson returned after the Battle of the Nile to Naples, arriving there on the 20th of September, where not only was every assistance given to the repairing of our ships, but also to

---

[1] Harrison's Life of Nelson, Vol. i. p. 256.
[2] Dispatches and Letters, Vol. iii. p. 48.

the care of the wounded and to the general supply of the demands of the fleet. But, especially, was the broken health and wounded body of the valorous chief regarded. Nelson was taken into the British Minister's house, and there personally tended by her whose sympathies had been so awakened, and by whose attentions he was after a time restored to health.

The French Ambassador urged strongly upon the Neapolitan Court their breach of faith in supplying the British fleet at Syracuse contrary to treaty, and Lady Hamilton availed herself at this juncture, whilst the Court was flushed with joy at the Victory of the Nile, to exercise her influence still further with the Queen, and to urge upon her the benefits and honour likely to result by breaking boldly with the French, and dismissing their Ambassador altogether. She also urged the raising an army to oppose the threats of invasion, which were then put forth. The Queen, who had been obliged to cede to the necessity of receiving an Envoy from that nation, which was tinged with the blood of her sister, her brother-in-law, and her nephew, failed not to enter in the most lively manner into these proposals, and communicated them to the King. Lady Hamilton did the same to Sir William, and Sir Horatio Nelson, and the Minister, Sir John Acton, being brought into favour of the measure, the Council determined to dismiss the French Ambassador, who, together with his suite, was sent off at twenty-four hours notice. An army also of 35,000 men was raised in nearly a month. They marched from St. Germain's, under the command of General Mack, the King himself accompanying the army. On the 21st of November they opposed a scattered and inferior force, but not with success, and in the course of one month only from that time the Royal family were obliged to quit Naples, and embark for Palermo. Much difference of opinion as to the policy necessary to be adopted by the Neapolitan Court was entertained, the question being whether they should place themselves entirely under the French, or fly to Sicily and put themselves under British protection. The difficulties, however, attendant upon separation, and the impressions likely to be consequent upon the flight of the Court, offered strong inducements to abide at Naples under any circumstances. Lady Hamilton was mainly instrumental in effecting the departure of the Royal family—she urged upon the Queen the necessity of the measure, as the French army was rapidly advancing towards Naples. She failed not to paint to her Majesty's imagination all the horrors likely to succeed upon their arrival, and at length prevailed upon her and the King to adopt the measure. This was not, however, effected without difficulty, for the King was at first very averse to the proceeding. A hurried letter of Lady Hamilton's to Lord Nelson is now before me—it runs thus:—

" My dear Lord,
" I have this moment received a letter from my adorable Queen. She is arrived with the King. She had much to do to persuade him, but he approves of all *our projects*. She is worn out with fatigue—to-morrow I will send you her letter. God bless you.
" Yours, sincerely."
[No signature, but in Lady Hamilton's hand-writing.]

No little danger was connected with this proceeding, for the growth of French principles, together with the rapid march of their army upon the capital, made it too hazardous to trust the Neapolitans with any knowledge of the plan in contemplation for getting off the Royal family, the Court, and its treasures. The arrangements for this purpose have already been noticed (see Vol. I. pp. 174—185), and Lady Hamilton's exertions briefly stated. From notes now before me, she says: " I, however, began the work myself, and removed all the jewels, and then thirty-six barrels of gold, to our house; these I marked as *stores for Nelson*, being obliged to use every device to prevent the attendants having any idea of our proceedings. By many such stratagems I got those treasures embarked, and this point gained, the King's resolution of coming off was strengthened—the Queen I was sure of."

There can be no doubt of this having been effected by Lady Hamilton; no other individual was in a position capable of accomplishing such an object. Lord Nelson wrote to the First Lord of the Admiralty, and said, " Lady Hamilton seemed to be an angel dropt from Heaven for the preservation of the Royal family." To effect, however, the safe departure of the Royal family, together with the property which had thus been conveyed on board the ships, it is obvious many sacrifices must have been necessarily made. The Ambassador was obliged to abandon his house, together with all the valuables it contained, nor was he able to convey away a single article. The private property of Sir William and Lady Hamilton was voluntarily left to prevent discovery of the proceeding, and this Lady Hamilton estimated at £9000 on her own account, and not less than £30,000 on that of Sir William. To shew the caution and secresy required in thus getting away, Lady

Hamilton says:—" I had, on the night of our embarkation, to attend the party given by Kelim Effendi, who was sent by the Grand Signior to Naples, to present Nelson with the Chelongh, or Plume of Triumph! I had to steal from the party, leaving our carriages and equipage waiting at his house, and in about fifteen minutes to be at my post, where it was my task to conduct the Royal family through the subterraneous passage, to Nelson's boats, by that *moment* waiting for us on the shore! The season for this voyage was extremely hazardous, and our miraculous preservation is recorded by the Admiral upon our arrival at Palermo."

In 1799, Lord Keith missed the French squadron, and Lord Nelson sailed in quest of them from Palermo. Such was the confidence he reposed in Lady Hamilton, that he left directions for her to open all letters and dispatches for him, and to act in his behalf to the best of her power, governing herself by events. Sir Alexander Ball was at this time in possession of a part of the island of Malta, residing at St. Antonio. The French had possession of La Valetta. Sir Alexander sent six natives deputies to Nelson at Palermo, for a supply of grain, their necessity for provisions being so great, that the inhabitants were ready to join any sortie the French might attempt in the hope of getting relieved. Lady Hamilton received the deputies, opened their dispatches, and, without hesitation, went down to the port to try what could be done. She found several vessels lying there, laden with corn for Ragusa, and immediately purchased their cargoes and engaged the vessels to go with their loading and the deputies to Malta. This service Sir Alexander Ball, in his letters to Lady Hamilton, as well as to Lord Nelson, plainly states to have been the means whereby he was enabled to preserve that important island. To accomplish this, however, Lady Hamilton was under the necessity of borrowing a considerable sum, which she repaid with her own private money, and thus expended, as she says, nothing short of £5000, not a shilling of which, nor the interest, did she ever get returned.

In a previous Chapter[1] I have printed the letter of Lord Nelson to the Emperor Paul, in relation to the services rendered by Lady Hamilton to preserve Malta. These were amply recognized by the Emperor, and the Order of St. John of Jerusalem was accorded to her, the distinction being communicated to her by the Emperor himself. That his Imperial Majesty set a high value on the aid afforded by Lady Hamilton, and on the value of the testimony he bestowed on her on

[1] Vol. i. p. 324.

the occasion, may be inferred from the circumstance that he requested Lord Whitworth, then Ambassador of Great Britain at the Court of Russia, that the honour he had conferred might be registered in the King's College of Arms in Lady Hamilton's native country. This was, indeed, attended to, as the following letter from Sir George Nayler, then York Herald, but afterwards Garter King-at-Arms, will shew :—

" Heralds' College, London,<br>
31st August, 1805.

" My Lady,

" Enclosed are two paintings of Arms for your Ladyship's choice, subject to the approbation of the Kings of Arms, previous to being confirmed by patent, and registered in the College. The one marked A represents part of the Arms to the name of *Lyons*, with the Cross of Malta in chief; the other, marked B, is also part of the Arms borne by the name of Lyons, with a Fess charged with cinque foils and the Cross of Malta, in allusion to the Coat of Hamilton, and the aforesaid Order. I have also herewith enclosed a copy of the King's warrant to record the documents relating to the Order of Malta, given by the Emperor to Sir H. R. Popham, and a copy of his Grace the Earl Marshal's warrant for recording your Ladyship's Arms, and like honours in the said College, previous to which it will be necessary for your Ladyship to collect all the documents relating thereto for registration; and should it be the wish of your Ladyship to have the Order of Malta recognized by Royal Warrant similar to Sir H. Popham, I conceive it may easily be done. Your Ladyship, in transmitting me the necessary documents aforesaid, will be pleased to signify which of the two drawings, A or B, you should prefer having granted, in order that I may be enabled to proceed with the patent, and when completed will be borne on an Escutcheon of Pretence, the Arms of the late Sir William Hamilton, K.B.

" I have the honour to be, with respect,
" Your Ladyship's most obliged,
" And faithful humble servant,
" GEORGE NAYLER, York."

The following Arms were granted, by patent, dated 19th November, 1806, to Dame Emma Hamilton, of Clarges Street, Piccadilly, in the County of Middlesex, (only issue of Henry Lyons, of Preston, in the County of Lancashire), widow of the Right Honourable Sir William Hamilton, K.B., *viz*.: " Per pale Or and Argent, three Lions rampant, Gules on a chief Sable, a Cross of eight points of the second."

Lady Hamilton's services did not terminate with those just narrated, for upon the retaking of Naples in 1799, when Nelson brought (with the exception of the Queen) the King and Court back to their country, Sir William Hamilton was so exceedingly ill as to be quite unfit for business, particularly under such a pressing state of affairs. From the commencement of June until the middle of August, Lady Hamilton acted not only as interpreter, but also as secretary both to his Secretary and to Lord Nelson, writing for them from morning till night, and translating a great number of documents written in the Italian language, which they were unable to do; nor could persons in whom that degree of confidence necessary to be reposed be found for a knowledge of papers of so secret and confidential a nature. Her attention also to the two households at Palermo and Naples, obtained for her the repeated expressions of gratitude from the Queen. Her Majesty was indeed most desirous of testifying her sense of obligation in a substantial manner, for she was aware of the neglect of Lady Hamilton to her own interests, sacrificing all means of enriching herself to promote the public cause; and upon the recall of Sir William Hamilton from his embassy at Palermo in 1800, her Majesty having determined to travel with Lord Nelson, Sir William and Lady Hamilton, as far as Vienna to visit her daughter the Empress of Germany, she, upon parting with Lady Hamilton, put into her hands a paper, saying it was a conveyance of £1000 *per ann.*, that she had fixed to invest for her in the hands of Friez of the Government Bank at Vienna, lest by any possibility she should not be suitably compensated for the services she had rendered, the money she had generously expended, and the losses she had so voluntarily sustained for the benefit of the British nation and her own. Lady Hamilton, however, declined this generous proposal—the acceptance of such a reward from a Queen so circumstanced, she deemed unworthy her position as the wife of a British Minister, and with every expression of respect and gratitude—declined the gift, and destroyed the instrument conferring it, saying, England was ever just, and to her faithful servants generous, and that she should feel it unbecoming to her own beloved and magnanimous Sovereign to accept of meed or reward from any other hand.[1]

Upon their return to England Sir William Hamilton made many attempts to be reimbursed for his losses and rewarded for his services. He was indeed placed in a position of no little difficulty, and had need of assistance from private hands. I have papers shewing Lord Nelson to have lent to him various sums, and to have paid others of considerable amount (£3588.)

[1] See Vol. i. p. 389.

on his account. Lady Hamilton absolutely sold her jewels at a great loss for his support, but Sir William fully relied upon the generosity of the British Government and nation to compensate Lady Hamilton for the great services she had been able to render to her country. Lord Nelson was incessant in his statements of the value of these services, and above all considered the Battle of the Nile as having been achieved through her instrumentality. He strongly urged her claims upon Mr. Pitt, Mr. Canning, and Mr. Rose; and he fully relied upon their assurances that a suitable provision would have been made for her: had not the most confident expectation been entertained that the Government would recognize her claims and provide for her, it is scarcely likely that Sir William would have left her with so little to supply her wants. At the close of his life Sir William, in commissioning his nephew, the Hon. Mr. Greville, then Deputy Lord Chamberlain, upon his decease to deliver to his Majesty George the Third, the Insignia of the Order of the Bath, desired him to tell his Majesty that he died in the confident hope that his pension would be continued to her for her zeal and services. Those services were, however, unrecognized.

Through Sir John Acton, Lord Nelson, in a letter written in French (printed in Sir Nicholas Harris Nicolas's Dispatches and Letters of Lord Nelson, from a copy in the Elliot Papers), made a solicitation to gain the influence of the Queen of Naples with the English Premier in support of Lady Hamilton's claims, but that he did not feel very sanguine as to the success of this application, appears from a letter written to Mr. Davison, saying, that he much doubted whether the pension would ever be given, adding, " More shame for them ;" and the Right Honourable George Rose, who appears from the following letter to have been consulted by Lady Hamilton on the occasion, entertained little hope of obtaining it.

" Madam,

" In proposing to you to write the inclosed letter to Mr. Addington, I entreat I may not raise a hope in your mind that your doing so will be likely to produce any good to you; I have in conformity with the principles to which I have invariably adhered, been anxious from the first mention of your case to me, to prevent your forming an expectation of success from any application you might make to the Minister, lest I should in the remotest possible degree contribute to add disappointment to misfortune: but I think in your situation the attempt (however hopeless) is worth making. You will at least be put to a certainty, for I am persuaded if it does not succeed now it never will; and this sort of application will, I think, afford you as good a chance of success as any you can have: I sincerely and most heartily wish you had a better than I can wish to hope for.

"If you can prevail with either the Peer or the Knight you mentioned to me, to put your letter into Mr. Addington's hand, or to inclose it to him, I should strongly recommend your doing so, shewing them first the contents of it, but on no account mention my name, or allude to me, as I am quite sure that would not be useful to you. And when you have copied the letter to Mr. Addington, I must beg you will burn it.

"In the event of any thing wanting explanation, I will have the honour of waiting on you any morning you please between eleven and twelve o'clock, or a little later, if that shall suit you better.

"I am, Madam,
"Your most obedient and humble servant,
"GEORGE ROSE.

"Old Palace Yard, March 9th, 1804."

Lord Nelson wrote to Mr. Elliot on the 7th of July: "With respect to the Queen's writing to this minister or that, whether Addington or Pitt, it cannot matter. It depends upon her Majesty's feelings towards the best friend she ever had, and Lady Hamilton has had opportunities of serving her country, which can fall to the lot of very few, and therefore has those claims for personal services which few can have. As Sir William's wife, I believe, (indeed I am sure), they will give her not one farthing."[1] To the Queen of Naples he also wrote on the 10th: "Mr. Elliot has informed me, by writing, of what your Majesty wished to say on the subject of writing to the Minister respecting the pension for your Emma. Poor Sir William Hamilton believed that it would have been granted, or it would have been unpardonable in him to have left his widow with so little means. Your Majesty well knows that it was her capacity and conduct which sustained his diplomatic character during the last years in which he was at Naples. It is unnecessary for me to speak more of it."[2]

Nelson endeavoured on every occasion to substantiate the justice of her claim, and failing to obtain that for her which he felt she was justly entitled to, as the last and most powerful effort he could make, he appended a Codicil to his Will in the following terms:—

[1] Dispatches and Letters, Vol. vi. p. 99.
[2] Life of the Rev. Dr. Scott, p. 114.

"Victory, October the 21st, 1805, then in sight of the combined fleets of France and Spain, distant about ten miles.

"Whereas, the eminent services of Emma Hamilton, Widow of the Right Honourable Sir William Hamilton, have been of the very greatest service to our King and country, and, to my knowledge, without receiving any reward from either our King or country.

"First, that she obtained the King of Spain's letter in 1796 to his brother the King of Naples, acquainting him of his intention to declare war against England, and from which letter the Ministry sent out orders to the then Sir John Jervis to strike a stroke if opportunity offered, against either the Arsenals of Spain or her Fleets, that neither of them was done is not the fault of Lady Hamilton, the opportunity might have been offered. Secondly, the British Fleet under my command, would never have returned a second time to Egypt, had not Lady Hamilton's influence with the Queen of Naples caused letters to be wrote to the Governor of Syracuse, that he was to encourage the Fleet being supplied with everything should they put into that Port in Sicily. We put into Syracuse, and received every supply, went to Egypt, and destroyed the French Fleet; could I have rewarded those services, I would not *now* call upon my country, but as that has not been in my power, I leave Emma Lady Hamilton, therefore, a legacy to my King and country, that they will give her an ample provision to maintain her rank in life.

"I also leave to the beneficence of my country my adopted Daughter, Horatia Nelson Thompson, and I desire she will use in future the name of Nelson only. These are the only favours I ask of my King and country at this moment, when I am going to fight their battle.

"May God bless my King and country, and all those who I loved dear. My relations it is needless to mention; they will, of course, be amply provided for.

"NELSON AND BRONTÉ.

"Witness   HENRY BLACKWOOD,
         T. M. HARDY.

"The above is a true copy from the original, taken this day, Monday, the 16th of December, 1805.

"ALEXANDER DAVISON."

It is a remarkable circumstance, that this Codicil should not have been produced at the same time as the Will itself, and that it was not, reflects the greatest disgrace on the successor to the titles of the glorious conqueror. When Captain

Blackwood brought it home, after the Battle of Trafalgar, he gave it to the Reverend William, subsequently Earl Nelson, who with his wife and family were then with Lady Hamilton, and had, indeed, been living with her many months. To their son Horatio, afterwards Viscount Trafalgar, she was as attentive as a mother, and their daughter, Lady Charlotte, had been almost exclusively under her care and education for six years. The Earl, fearful that Lady Hamilton should be provided for in the sum Parliament was expected to grant to uphold the hero's name and family, kept the Codicil in his pocket, until the day £120,000 was voted for that purpose. On that day he dined with Lady Hamilton in Clarges Street, and hearing, at table, what had been done, he brought forth the Codicil, and throwing it to Lady Hamilton, coarsely said, she might now do with it as she pleased. She had it registered the next day at Doctors' Commons, where it is now to be seen.

From the commencement of Lord Nelson's influence, created by his services to his country, the conduct of his brother is exceedingly disgusting. Many letters, passing over several years, are now before me, and display him as an exceedingly avaricious man. The object of his life appears to have been the attainment of wealth and honours, and to acquire these he hesitated not to sacrifice his character and reputation. As a clergyman, he could not but feel the impropriety of Nelson's mode of life, with Lady Hamilton, yet he hesitated not to place his children under her roof, to entrust one of his daughters, at least, entirely to her guidance and controul, and to heap adulation upon her, in order that she might exercise the great influence she possessed over his brother for his advancement.

Lady Hamilton made many ineffectual attempts to obtain a recognition of her claims, and a reward for her services. In these efforts she was sanctioned and supported by several eminent individuals. The Right Honourable George Rose, continued solicitous in her behalf, and addressed to her the following:—

"Cuffnells, December 9th, 1805.

"Madam,

"Captain Hardy had the goodness to take the trouble, at much inconvenience to himself, to come over here soon after the Victory anchored at Spithead, to tell me what passed in the last moments of my late most invaluable friend, respecting whom I shall at no time attempt to express my feelings. But understanding that, in those moments, he manifested a confidence I would do all in my power to make effectual his last wishes, I shall consider it a sacred duty not to disappoint that expectation.

" You will learn from the Captain that Lord Nelson within the hour preceding the commencement of the action, in which he immortalized his name, made an entry in his Pocket Book,[1] strongly recommending a remuneration to you for your services to the country when the fleet under his command was in Sicily, after his first return from Egypt, on which subject he had spoken to me with great earnestness more than once. I cannot therefore delay assuring you I will take the earliest opportunity of a personal communication with Mr. Pitt, to enforce that solemn request upon him; and I am sure his respect for the memory of one of the greatest men that ever lived in any country, and his sense of what is right to be done in such a case, will incline him to listen attentively, and I trust favourably to the claim made for you, of which I never heard any thing till he went out of office in 1801.

" When I last had the honour of seeing you, during Mr. Addington's Administration, more than two years ago, I suggested the length of time since the service was performed as an obstacle; that objection is certainly not weakened; but considering the time when the solemn and earnest recommendation already alluded to, and the strong attestation of the importance of your interposition were given; and having in view the highly beneficial effect produced to the country so satisfactorily ascertained, I am not without a hope of success. I am extremely anxious, however, to guard you against entertaining a sanguine expectation on the subject, that I may not have the self-reproach of occasioning a disappointment to you. My application must be to Mr. Pitt, but the reward (to which I have not the slightest hesitation in saying, I think you are, both on principle and in policy, well entitled,) must, I conceive, be from the Foreign Secretary of State, on account of the nature

[1] The following is in the Earl Nelson's writing:—" Before Mr. Pitt's death it was determined that the memorandum book should be given or sent to him;—after that took place, as soon as conveniently could be, after Lord Grenville was fixed in his office of Prime Minister, it was the opinion of many persons of consequence, that as the said memorial contained secret matters relative to the part the Queen of Naples privately took in assisting our fleet at Syracuse before the Battle of the Nile, that no other person ought to have it but the Minister, accordingly Lord Nelson took it from Sir William Scott and gave it to Lord Grenville on the 15th of February last, and at the same time he read it to his Lordship, and strongly pointed out to him the *parts* relative to Lady Hamilton and the child, and in doing this Lord Nelson observed to Lord Grenville that he thought he was most effectually promoting the interest of Lady Hamilton, and doing his duty, in which Lord Grenville acquiesced."

of the service. I can promise nothing but zeal; how far *that*, acting upon the conviction of my mind, of the justice of your pretensions will be effectual, you shall know within a few days at the latest, after I shall see Mr. Pitt either at Bath or in London.

"I trouble you with no particulars about Mr. Bolton, as I have written to himself; the earnest manner in which Lord Nelson repeatedly spoke and wrote to me respecting him, will ensure to him my liveliest attention; he knows from me Mr. Pitt's positive engagement to provide for him.

"I have the honour to be,
"Madam,
"Your most obedient and very humble servant,
"GEORGE ROSE."

"Madam,

"Deeply as I am affected by the recent loss I have sustained in the death of Mr. Pitt, I cannot omit to express to you my sincere and deep regret that I had not a possible opportunity of fulfilling the engagement which the veneration I have for the memory of Lord Nelson induced me to make to you in my letter from Cuffnells, after I had seen Captain Hardy.

"I had no alarm about Mr. Pitt's health, till it was decided he should leave Bath; but on my seeing him at Putney Heath I found him so ill as to preclude my talking to him on any business whatever; Sir Walter Farquhar, indeed, had positively prohibited any one from doing so.

"I shall certainly not remain in office, and, respecting arrangements that are about to take place, I know nothing, no one can be in more utter ignorance of them than I am; but if it shall happen that any representation of mine to any of those who may fill the departments of government can have the remotest chance of being useful to you, it shall not be wanting. I am persuaded, however, Lord Nelson's last and solemn appeal to his country for justice to be done to your claim will be the best possible support to it.

"I will have the honour of waiting on you some morning in the course of next week.

"I have the honour to be,
"Madam,
"Your faithful and most obedient humble servant,
"GEORGE ROSE.

"Old Palace Yard, January 27th, 1806."

"Dear Madam,

"I have made arrangements for to-morrow that would render it really inconvenient for me to wait on you while you are in town; I would, however, break in upon those, and call in Clarges-street, if I could have a chance of being useful to you, but I am certain I cannot. What I have repeatedly suggested to you I am more and more confirmed in, that the difficulty in affording you relief is increased, to a great extent, by the length of time that has elapsed since your claim arose, in which period there have been three administrations. If you cannot obtain attention to it now, I am sure you had better think no more of it. I do not say this from indifference on the subject, but from an anxiety that you should not continue to entertain a hope that must (if you do not immediately obtain relief) end in disappointment. Lord Nelson's codicil, I think, affords a ground for making a last attempt.

" I am, dear Madam,
" Your very faithful humble servant,
" GEORGE ROSE.

" Old Palace Yard, July 3rd, 1806."

" Dear Madam,
" I had an opportunity of a very quiet conversation with Mr. Canning, on Sunday last, about the paper written by Lord Nelson just before he went into his last action, which has led to a further conversation on the subject. I repeat what I think I before said, that there is a perfect disposition in Mr. Canning's mind to give effect to that paper, but the difficulties are, I fear, insurmountable.

" I can most truly assure you that I have most anxiously and conscientiously discharged all that Lord Nelson could have expected from me if he were now alive, and I am *most sincerely grieved* that I have failed of success. The point is not absolutely decided, but I should be inexcusable if I were to give you any hope. I leave London to-morrow, and from Cuffnells I will write to Mr. Bolton on the affairs which interest him.

" I am your very faithful humble servant,
" G. ROSE.

" Old Palace Yard, July the 21st, 1808."

Lord Grenville, upon being referred to, he having been Foreign Secretary of State, at the time Lady Hamilton's services were rendered to the country, observed, that had the application for remuneration been made during the period, it would, certainly, have met with his attention. Lady Hamilton sought for remuneration from the Foreign Secret Service Fund, and she addressed the Earl of St. Vincent, to induce him to move a Parliamentary consideration of her claims. The following exhibits the effort she made on this occasion:—

"My dear Lord,

"A strong sense of the deep regard which you have ever shewn, for all that relates to the welfare of our country in general, and consequently to its naval glory in particular; with the tender recollection, how dear you thus rendered yourself to the heart of our immortal and incomparable hero, whose ardent wish it was to see your Lordship always at the head of the Admiralty, a sentiment that still pervades the bravest bosoms in the navy; have awakened in my heart a hope, after so many years of anxiety and cruel disappointment, that the public services of importance, which it was my pride as well as duty to perform, while the wife of his Majesty's Minister at the Court of Naples, may, possibly, through your Lordship's friendly and generous advice, and most able and active assistance, which I now most earnestly solicit, but a short time longer remain either unacknowledged, or unrewarded, by my King and country.

"I will not agonize the extreme sensibility of your Lordship's feeling breast, by any attempt to detail the various vicissitudes of my hapless fortunes, since the fatal day when dying Nelson bequeathed myself and his infant daughter, expressly left under my guardianship, to the munificent protection of our Sovereign and the nation. I will not arouse the just indignation of your Lordship's great and honourable mind, by reciting the many petty artifices, mean machinations, and basely deceptive tenders of friendship, which hitherto have prevented Lord Nelson's dying request from being duly heard, by those to whom it is so peculiarly and pathetically addressed.

"You, my Lord, cannot be insensible of the value of my public services; since it is to them alone, I have been so many years indebted for the proud boast of possessing your friendship. As the widow of Sir William Hamilton, more than thirty years Ambassador at the Courts of Naples and Palermo, had I never seized the opportunity, or even felt the inclination, to perform any one act of public service, I might still have expected a reasonable pension would be granted, if duly applied for, by the benevolent Monarch whom my husband had so long, so ably, and so faithfully served. Even the widow[1] of Mr. Lock, only about two years Consul at Palermo, a man not remarkable either for great loyalty, or the most correct attention to his official duties, had a pension assigned her, almost imme-

---

[1] A daughter of the Duchess of Leinster, by Mr. Ogilvie.

diately on his death, of £800 a year; while I, who have been seven years the widow of such a man as Sir William Hamilton, the foster brother of our Sovereign, and have constantly done all in my power to benefit my country, continue to be totally neglected. The widow of Mr. Fox, whose *services* to his country are, at best, very *problematical*, had instantly a grant of £1200, per annum; and even his natural daughter, Miss Willoughby, obtained a pension of £300 a year. Yet this *man of the people*, did not shed his blood for his King and country; and neither asked, nor could have expected, from them, when dying, like the noble and confiding Nelson, any such posthumous national support, as has humanely been extended to those who had thus lost their only protector. Surely, the daughter of Lord Nelson, now Miss Nelson, is not less an object worthy the attention of her King and country, than Miss Willoughby, the daughter of Mr. Fox.

"I have said, perhaps, more than enough; but the goodness of your Lordship's heart will excuse whatever may flow from mine, however irregularly, in the act of addressing, as my assured friend, the greatest stateman that the death of Mr. Pitt has left behind.

"Lamenting, as I feelingly, perhaps selfishly do, in common with all who have a just sense of your Lordship's transcendent abilities, and the exigencies of our country at this eventful period, that you are not in the proper situation to act more effectually for the national security and glory, I shall, in a few days, transmit you a printed copy of Lord Nelson's dying request, prefaced by his admirable prayer for his King and country, and accompanied by the Reverend Dr. Scott's attestation, as registered with this remarkable Codicil, in Doctors' Commons; and relying, with the most unbounded confidence, on your Lordship's judgment, as to what measures may be most advisable to be pursued, for the attainment of objects so important to Miss Nelson, as well as to myself, and so dear to the heart of Britain's greatest naval hero,

"I am, my dear Lord,
"With every sentiment of veneration,
"Esteem, and gratitude,
"Your Lordship's most affectionate,
"and obedient humble servant,
"EMMA HAMILTON."

Mr. Rose, in a letter addressed in 1807 to Lady Hamilton, among other things, and after having obtained the promise of a Pursership of an Indiaman, for some one who had suffered by the death of Lord Nelson, and in whom she was interested, exclaims: "Would to God, I could do so in instances more deeply interesting! I never exerted myself, on any occasion in my life, more with my whole heart, and I deeply lament my want of success."

Lady Charlotte Nelson, wrote from Canterbury, to Lady Hamilton: "Sir William Scott came on Friday, and left us on Monday. He slept at our house. He talked a great deal about you, and says that you have great claims on Government, and we all sincerely wish they would do what they ought."

Lady Hamilton petitioned the Prince Regent, in 1813, and received the following from Lord Sidmouth:—

"Whitehall, March 6th, 1813.

"Madam,

"It is very painful to me, to acquaint your Ladyship, that after a full communication, with Lord Liverpool, on the subject of your memorial to his Royal Highness, the Prince Regent, I am unable to encourage your hopes, that the object of it can be accomplished. His Lordship sincerely regrets the embarrassments which you have described, but upon comparing them with representations now before him of difficulty and distress, in many other quarters, and upon view of the circumstances with which they are attended, he finds it impossible so to administer the scanty means of relief and assistance, which, under the authority of the Prince Regent, are at his disposal, as to satisfy his own sense of justice to others, and at the same time give effect to your Ladyship's application.

"I have the honour to be, Madam,
"Your Ladyship's obedient humble servant,
"SIDMOUTH."

Notwithstanding the apparent justice of Lady Hamilton's claims, and the interests with which they were urged upon the Government, no success resulted. She, therefore, presented a petition to the King, but its prayer was disregarded.[1]

---

[1] The Memorial of Dame Emma Hamilton, widow of his Excellency, the late Sir William Hamilton, K.B. your Majesty's most faithful Ambassador at the Court of Naples.

Humbly sheweth,

That her late husband, Sir William Hamilton, in his liberal and munificent discharge of the honourable duties of that elevated situation to which he was exalted by the goodness of your most gracious Majesty, had so considerably encumbered his private fortune that he was incapable of making a sufficient provision for your Majesty's Memorialist to maintain, after his decease, the rank to which he had indulgently raised her; and which it was her constant study as much as possible to merit, by anxiously entering into all her husband's zealous

The expenses Lady Hamilton had incurred at Merton, and by her mode of living, compelled her now to seek some method

and enlarged views of diplomatic devotion to the true interests of our dear country, and the beloved Sovereign who had thus benignantly vouchsafed to honour him.

That it was the good fortune of your Majesty's Memorialist to acquire the confidential friendship of that great and august Princess, the Queen of Naples, your Majesty's most faithful and ardently attached Ally, at a period of peculiar peril; and when her august Consort, the Sovereign of the Two Sicilies, was unhappily constrained to profess a neutrality but little accordant with the feelings of his own excellent heart: by which means, your Majesty's Memorialist, among many inferior services, had an opportunity of obtaining, and actually did obtain, the King of Spain's letter to the King of Naples, expressive of his intention to declare war against England. This important document your Majesty's Memorialist delivered to her husband, Sir William Hamilton, who immediately transmitted it to your Majesty's Ministers.

That your Majesty's Memorialist, on a subsequent occasion, by means of the same confidential communication with that great and good woman, the Queen of Naples, had the unspeakable felicity of procuring a secret order for victualling and watering, at the port of Syracuse, the fleet of your most gracious Majesty, under the command of Admiral Nelson; by which means, that heroic man, the pride and glory of his King and country, was enabled to proceed the second time for Egypt, with a promptness and celerity which certainly hastened the glorious Battle of the Nile, and occasioned his good and grateful heart to admit your humble Memorialist, as well as the Queen of Naples, to a participation in the honour of that important victory.

That during the long blockade of Malta, your Majesty's humble Memorialist is well known, by all Europe, to have contributed her best assistance, as well as influence, in furnishing and procuring various necessaries for the distressed natives, that they might thus be animated and encouraged to resist as well the artifices as the arms of the enemy, and thereby prevent that important fortress from fatally falling under the entire domination of the French: services with which the Emperor of all the Russias, as your Majesty's Ally, and Grand Master of Malta, was so perfectly satisfied, that he actually transmitted to your Majesty's humble Memorialist, soon after the surrender of that island, the title and insignia of Lady of Malta, of the honourable order of the Petit Croix, accompanied by a cross of that order, and a very flattering letter signed by his Imperial Majesty's own hand.

That, in short, your Majesty's Memorialist, on all occasions—of which she possesses innumerable proofs, under the hands of Sovereign Powers in amity with your Majesty, as well as of the most exalted public and private characters of the age—has endeavoured to merit the regard of her King and country, by fostering every principle which might tend to promote their honour and welfare, as far as it was possible for her influence to accomplish this primary desire of her heart. In the Royal British Navy, your Majesty's Memorialist humbly presumes, where sincerity as well as valour is always pre-eminently found, the zeal and attachments to its glory which she has at all times peculiarly manifested, is a theme on which it may not become your Majesty's Memorialist to enlarge; but which many of the most illustrious characters by whom it has ever been graced, your Memorialist may be permitted proudly to assert, have generously acknow-

of retrieving her fortune. Her embarrassments were great, and in April, 1808, a valuation of the villa at Merton, of the furniture, &c. exclusive of books and wines, was made by Mr. Willock, of Golden Square, and estimated by him at the sum of £12,930.

In her embarrassment, she wrote the following to the Duke of Queensberry:—

"Richmond, September 4th, 1808."

"My dear Lord and friend,

"May I hope, that you will read this, for you are the only hope I have in this world, to assist and protect me, in this moment of unhappiness and distress. To you, therefore, I appeal. I do not wish to have more than what I have. I can live on that at Richmond, only that I may live free from fear —that every debt may be paid. I think and hope £15,000 will do for every thing. For my sake, for Nelson's sake, for the good I have done my country, purchase it [*i. e.* Merton]; take it, only giving me the portraits of Sir William, Nelson, and the Queen. All the rest shall go. I shall be free and at liberty. I can live at Richmond on what I have; you will be doing a deed that will make me happy, for lawyers will only involve me every day more and more—debts will increase new debts. You will save me by this act of kindness—the title deeds are all good, and ready to deliver up, and I wish not for more than what will pay my debts. I beseech you, my dear Duke, to imagine, that I only wish for you to do this, not to lose by it, but I see that I am lost, and most miserable, if *you* do not help me. My mind is made up to live on what I have. If I could but be free from Merton—all paid, and only one hundred pounds in my pocket, you will live to see me blessing you, my mother blessing you, Horatia blessing you. If you would not wish to keep Merton, perhaps it will sell

---

ledged, promulged, and applauded, in every part of the world where the British flag is triumphantly borne.

That the solemn recognition of such services, by that immortal man, the late Lord Viscount Nelson, and his pathetic call for their kind remuneration, at the moment when he was about to commence his last and fatal conflict with the enemies of his King and country, in whose battle, at the moment of victory, he so gloriously fell; bequeathing to the generosity of your Majesty and his country, the future fortunes of your humble Memorialist, must afford an everlasting proof that she is not altogether unworthy of being enabled, by the condescending bounty of your Majesty, with the generous concurrence of her country, to maintain that rank and dignity which she derived from the affections of a beloved husband; and which, it is humbly presumed, your Majesty's Memorialist has not, in any single instance, ever disgraced or abused.

And your Majesty's most humble Memorialist, and in duty she is bound to do, shall **ever** ardently pray, &c.

in the spring better—only let me pass my winter without
the idea of a prison. 'Tis true my imprudence has brought
it on me, and villany and ingratitude has helped to involve
me, but the sin be on them. Do not let my enemies trample
on me; for God's sake, then, dear Duke, good friend, think
'tis Nelson who asks you to befriend

"EMMA HAMILTON."

In vain, however, she attempted to dispose of Merton, and
at length, by repeated applications to her friends, a meeting
was held at the house of Alderman Sir John Perring, Bart.
on the 25th of November, at which were present Sir John
Perring, Sir Robert Barclay, Mr. Davison, Mr. Moore,
Mr. Gooch, Mr. Macklew, Mr. Abraham Goldsmid, Mr.
Nichol, Mr. Wilson, and Mr. Lavie, when Mr. Dawson, Lady
Hamilton's solicitor, laid before them a list of debts, amounting to £8000, exclusive of £10,000 required to pay off
annuities, and a valuation of her property at Merton, and
elsewhere, (taken at a low rate) amounting to £17,500.
An assignment of Merton and her effects was made to Sir
John Perring, Mr. Alexander Davison, Mr. Abraham Goldsmid, Mr. Richard Wilson, and Mr. Germain Lavie, and to
afford immediate relief, Mr. Davison and Mr. Goldsmid each
advanced £1000, Sir Robert Barclay, Mr. John Gooch, and
Mr. Wilson, each £500, and Sir John Perring, £200. The
Trustees were to go to market at the time and manner they
might think most advantageous, and they formed themselves
into a Committee to follow up her claim on Government.
Their efforts in the latter respect were unavailing. Lady
Hamilton removed to Richmond, and afterwards took lodgings in Bond Street. She was, however, soon obliged to
secrete herself from the pursuit of her creditors, but in 1813
was imprisoned in the King's Bench. From this confinement,
after ten months, she was liberated by the kind assistance of
Mr. Alderman Joshua Jonathan Smith, a man of most upright
conduct, and kind heart and disposition. Threatened with an
arrest on a coachmaker's bill, which was afterwards found to
be a fictitious claim, she, however, fled to Calais, remained
there in great obscurity, fell ill, of an attack of water in the
chest, and other ailments, of which she died, January 15th,
1815. She is reported by an anonymous foreigner to have
died in the bosom of the Roman Catholic Church, and to have
taken the sacraments on her death-bed. This writer affirms
Lady Hamilton to have embraced that faith a long time previous to her decease, and asserts also in the most positive manner, that a Roman Catholic priest had administered to her the
sacrament during her confinement in the King's Bench.

This statement is, however, unconfirmed, and from an account given to me by an English lady, Mrs. Hunter, of Brighton, whose kindness of heart and benevolence brought her in contact with Lady Hamilton in the closing hours of her life, I am not disposed to credit it. This excellent lady tells me, that at the time Lady Hamilton was at Calais, she was also there superintending the education of her son at the Academy of Mr. Mills. She resided in the "Grande Place," and became acquainted with Monsieur de Rheims, the English interpreter, who persuaded Mrs. Hunter to take up her residence with him in his château, which was visited by many English. When Lady Hamilton fled to Calais, Monsieur de Rheims gave to her one of his small houses to live in. It was very badly furnished. Mrs. Hunter was in the habit of ordering meat daily at a butcher's for a favourite little dog, and on one of these occasions was met by Monsieur de Rheims, who followed her, exclaiming, " Ah! Madame, Ah! Madame! I know you to be good to the English; there is a lady here that would be glad of the worst bit of meat you provide for your dog." When questioned as to who the lady was, and promising that she should not want for anything, he declined telling, saying that she was too proud to see any one, besides, he had promised her secresy. Mrs. Hunter begged him to provide her with everything she required, wine, &c. as if coming from himself, and she would pay for it. This he did for some time, until she became very ill, when he pressed her to see the lady that had been so kind to her, and upon hearing that her benefactress was not a person of title, she consented, saw her, thanked her, and blessed her. A few days after she ceased to live. This lady describes her to me as exceedingly beautiful even in death. She was anxious to have her interred according to English custom, for which, however, she was only laughed at, and poor Emma was put into a deal box without any inscription. All that this good lady states she was permitted to do, was, to make a kind of pall out of her black silk petticoat, stitched on a white curtain. Not an English Protestant Clergyman was to be found in all Calais, or its vicinity, and so distressed was this lady to find some one to read the Burial Service over her remains, that she went to an Irish half-pay officer in the Rue du Havre, whose wife was a well-informed Irish lady. He was absent at the time, but, being sent for, most kindly went and read the Service over the body. Lady Hamilton, according to the Register of Deaths preserved in the Town Hall, died in a house situate in the Rue Française, and was buried in a piece of ground in a spot just outside the town, formerly called the Gardens of the Duchess of Kingston, which had been consecrated and was used as a public cemetery till 1816. This ground, which had neither wall nor fence to protect it, was some years since converted into a timber-yard, and no traces of the graves now remain. Mrs. Hunter wished to have placed a head or footstone, but was refused. She, therefore, placed a piece of wood in the shape, as she describes it to me, of a battledore, handle downwards, on which was inscribed, "Emma Hamilton, England's Friend." This was speedily removed—another placed, and also removed; and the good lady was at length threatened to be shot by the sentinel if she persisted in those offices of charity. A small tombstone was, however, afterwards placed there, and was existing in 1833. Upon it, according to a little "Guide to Calais," compiled by an Englishman, was inscribed:—

. . . . . . QUÆ
. . . . . . CALESIÆ
VIA IN GALLICA VOCATA
ET IN DOMO. C. VI. OBIIT
DIE XV MENSIS JANUARII, A.D. MDCCCXV.
ÆTATIS SUÆ LI.

The Register of Burials commences only in 1819. The British Consulate contains no documents relating to Lady Hamilton, but in the office of the Juge de Paix there is an inventory of her effects, which were estimated at the value of two hundred and twenty-eight francs; besides fifteen francs found in a box with some articles of wearing apparel, and some duplicates of plate that had been pawned.

The Earl Nelson came over to demand Lady Hamilton's property, but found only the duplicates of trinkets, &c. pledged, and which he wished to take away without payment. He declined repaying any expenses that had been incurred.[1]

During a visit to Calais, upon his return from a residence in Germany in attendance upon his late Majesty William IV. and her Majesty the Queen Dowager, my estimable friend, Dr. William Beattie, visited the grave of poor Emma, and in the "Journal" published by him in 1831, has inserted some elegant and most feeling lines,[2] though without mention of the name of her to whom they apply, of which I avail myself of the following extracts:—

" And here is *one*—a nameless grave;— the grass
Waves rank and dismal o'er its crumbling mass

---

[1] There are various accounts relating to the payment of the funeral expenses. My friend Mr. Rothery tells me that his relative Mr. Cadogan, to whom Horatia was entrusted, and by whom she was taken, after the demise of Lady Hamilton, to Mrs. Matcham, made the payments on this occasion, and also afforded much assistance to Lady Hamilton prior to her decease. Alderman Smith was also generous on this occasion. [2] Vol. ii. p. 335.

Of mortal elements,—the wintry sedge
Weeps, drooping o'er the ramparts' watery edge ;—
The rustling reed—the darkly rippling wave—
Announce the tenant of that lowly grave !

Crush'd in a pauper's shell, the earth scarce heaves
Above that trodden breast ! the turf scarce leaves
One lingering token that the stranger found
' Ashes for hope ' in that unhallow'd ground ;
And ' dust for mourning !' Levelled with the soil
The wasting worm hath revelled in its spoil—
The spoil of beauty ! This the poor remains
Of one who, living, could command the strains
Of flattery's harp and pen ! whose incense, flung
From venal breath upon her altar, hung
A halo ; while in loveliness supreme,
She moved in brightness, like the embodied dream
Of some rapt minstrel's warm imaginings,
The more than form and face of earthly things !
Ah, when hath heart so warm, have hopes so fair,
Been crush'd amid the darkness of despair ?
With broken heart, and head in sorrow bow'd,
Hers was the midnight bier and borrow'd shroud !

Few bend them at thy bier, unhappy one !
All know thy shame, thy mental sufferings none ;
All know thy frailties,—all thou wast and art !
But thine were faults of circumstance—not heart !
Thy soul was form'd to bless and to be bless'd
With that immortal boon—a guiltless breast,
And *be* what others *seem*,—had bounteous Heaven
Less beauty lent, or stronger virtue given !
The frugal matron of some lowlier hearth,
Thou hadst not known the splendid woes of earth ;
Dispensing happiness, and happy—there
Thou hadst not known the curse of being fair !
But like yon lonely vesper star, thy light—
Thy love—had been as pure as it was bright !

I've met thy pictured bust in many lands ;
I've seen the stranger pause, with lifted hands,
In deep, mute admiration, while his eye
Dwelt sparkling on thy peerless symmetry !
I've seen the poet—painter—sculptor's gaze
Speak, with rapt glance, their eloquence of praise ;
I've seen thee, as a gem in royal halls,
Stoop like presiding angel from the walls,
And only less than worshipp'd ! Yet 'tis come
To this ! when all but slander's voice is dumb ;
And they who gazed upon thy living face,
Can hardly find thy mortal resting-place.''

## No. II.

## HORATIA NELSON.

IN the preceding chapter I have endeavoured, in a brief manner, to sketch the particulars, as far as I have been able to collect them, of the life of Emma Lady Hamilton. Of adventurers it has been pertinently said, "que les évènemens de leur vie peuvent être vrais et paraître merveilleux," and this is doubtless true of this extraordinary woman. With all her faults, all her weaknesses, and if it must be added, all her vices, she unquestionably rendered very important services to her country in a time of great peril, and exerted herself for the maintenance of social order and European civilization. Young and beautiful, with a knowledge of the world derived under circumstances, and attended by consequences any thing but agreeable to reflect upon, or calculated to excite satisfaction—versed in its most seductive fascinations, and intellectually gifted with taste for the fine arts, and with powers for the most effectual display of grace and beauty—enthusiastic in her devotion to noble and generous acts, and sensibly alive to the honour and glory of her country, it is not surprising that Nelson should have felt the power of her influence. Simple in his manners, and pure in his nature—warm and generous in his feelings—unskilled in the arts of the world—and, by his professional engagements, unaccustomed to any but the most limited society, it is not extraordinary that he should have fallen under the blandishments of a syren. From the documents I have most carefully examined, I am perfectly satisfied that Nelson was long ere he succumbed to the temptation. The religious principles in which he had been educated by his venerable father, served doubtless to operate for a time against the violation of his marriage promises and obligations. It is, however, incumbent upon me, as a faithful biographer, to enter, though not without reluctance, into a consideration of the particulars relating to the birth of a daughter, to whom Nelson's name descended, and who, to the last moment of his existence, was as dear to him as the offspring of a legitimate source.

Sir N. H. Nicolas has endeavoured to shew that the connexion which existed between his Lordship and Lady Hamilton was not "in the usual sense of the word of a criminal nature."[1]

---
[1] Dispatches and Letters, Vol. vii. p. 389.

This able writer has arrived at this conclusion, after a perusal of some of the letters and documents which formed a part of the collection embraced in these volumes. The examination of the entire correspondence leads me to adopt a totally different opinion, and one which permits of no question, as the parentage of the child Horatia is admitted by the parties concerned. Considering the mystery attaching to the child, whom Lord Nelson so solemnly " bequeathed to the beneficence of his country," I cannot but agree with Sir N. Harris Nicolas that all of her history which has been discovered ought to be stated.[1] The publication of a part leading to a conclusion contrary to truth on such a subject, and furnished to Sir Harris Nicolas by the Lady herself, relieves me of a delicacy I should otherwise have felt in printing any letters or portions of letters relating to this particular matter; nor do I now feel it at all either necessary or desirable to publish the whole, but merely sufficient to dispose of the question, and not unnecessarily or wantonly to expose the weakness of an otherwise noble, spotless, and heroic character. Justice to others demands this statement, as narratives have been put forth leading to the inference that an illustrious personage (unquestionably meaning the Queen of Naples), one " TOO GREAT to be mentioned," was the mother of the child.

Sir Harris Nicolas[2] has stated that he " is authorised by Mr. Haslewood, long the confidential friend and professional adviser of Lord Nelson, to declare, in the most positive manner, that *Lady Hamilton was not its mother*. The name of the mother (he adds) is known to Mr. Haslewood; but he is prevented by a sense of honour from disclosing it. Lady Hamilton always said that the child's mother was a person of high birth, and she has left a written declaration that she was " too great to be mentioned." Mrs. Salter possesses this paper which has been examined by Sir H. Nicolas, and is as follows:

" She is the daughter, the true and beloved daughter of Viscount Nelson, and if he had lived, she would have been all that his love and fortune could have made her; for nature has made her perfect, beautiful, good, and amiable. HER MOTHER was TOO GREAT TO BE MENTIONED, but her father, mother, and Horatia had a true and virtuous friend in EMMA HAMILTON."[3]

That Horatia was the daughter of Nelson no one has been disposed to entertain a doubt, but the evidence in connection with the birth of the child has been purposely obscured and mystified.

---

[1] Dispatches and Letters, Vol. vii. p. 369.
[2] Ibid. p. 369.
[3] Ibid. p. 389.

The intimacy from which resulted the illegitimate issue under consideration, appears to have taken place in the month of April, 1800, when Lord Nelson conveyed Sir William and Lady Hamilton, on board the Foudroyant, from Palermo to Syracuse, and thence to Malta. The voyage was passed with great festivity, and Lady Hamilton's birth-day, April 26th, was celebrated by music and singing. Miss Knight,[1] who was also on board, composed the following song on the occasion:—

Song, addressed to Lady Hamilton, on her Birthday, April the 26th, 1800, on board the Foudroyant, in a gale of wind.

BY MISS KNIGHT.

Come, cheer up, fair Emma, forget all thy grief,
For thy shipmates are brave, and a hero's their chief;
Look round on these trophies,[2] the pride of the Main,
They were snatched by their valour from Gallia and Spain.
     *Chorus*—Hearts of oak, &c.

Behold yonder fragment, 'tis sacred to fame,
'Mid the waves of old Nile it was saved from the flame:
The flame that destroyed all the glories of France,
When Providence vanquished the friends of blind chance.
     Hearts of oak, &c.

These arms the San Josef once claimed as her own,
Ere Nelson and Britons her pride had o'erthrown;
That plume too evinces that still they excel,
It was torn from the cap of the famed William Tell.
     Hearts of oak, &c.

Then, cheer up, fair Emma! remember thou'rt free,
And ploughing Britannia's old empire—the sea:
How many in Albion each sorrow would check,
Could they kiss but one plank of this conquering deck.
     Hearts of oak, &c.

Miss Knight also wrote three additional verses to God save the King:—

---

[1] Miss Knight was the daughter of Rear-Admiral Sir Joseph Knight. She was many years at Naples and Palermo, and returned to England with Lord Nelson and Sir William and Lady Hamilton, in the autumn of 1800. She was afterwards the Preceptress of Her Royal Highness the Princess Charlotte of Wales, and is favourably known as the author of "Marcus Flaminius," "Dinarbas," and a "Description of Latium." Sir N. Harris Nicolas has given some extracts from her Diary in his collection of the Dispatches and Letters of Lord Nelson.

[2] The cabin of the Foudroyant was ornamented with the Flagstaff of L'Orient, the Arms of the San Josef, and the Plume of the Guillaume Tell.

1. *For the Battle of the Nile.*
   Join we great Nelson's name
   First on the roll of fame;
    Him let us sing!
   Spread we his praise around,
   Honour of British ground:
   Who made Nile's shores resound.
    God save the King!

2. *For Le Généreux.*
   Lord, thou hast heard our vows!
   Fresh laurels deck the brows
    Of him we sing.
   Nelson has laid full low
   Once more the Gallic foe;
   Come let our bumpers flow!
    God save the King!

3. *For Le Guillaume Tell.*
   While thus we chaunt his praise,
   See what new glories blaze,
    New trophies spring!
   Nelson! thy task's complete;
   All their Egyptian fleet
   Bows at thy conquering feet,
    To GEORGE our King.

And Sir Edward Berry also contributed the following:—

   Then let's join hand in hand,
   Friends of great Nelson's band,
    Crown him and sing:
   Let us lay at his feet,
   Last of the Gallic fleet,
   His glory is complete!
    God save the King!

   France! haul thy standard down:
   Honour the laurel crown
    Of him we sing.
   No more in pride you swell,
   On him you us'd to dwell;
   We have your William Tell,
    And George our King!

Lord Nelson returned to Palermo on the 1st of June. At the middle of this month he was at Leghorn, where he struck his flag, and departed with the Queen of Naples, the three Princesses, Prince Leopold, Sir William and Lady Hamilton, for Vienna, whence he travelled with Sir William and Lady Hamilton to London, arriving at Yarmouth on the 6th of November. In the month of January, 1801, Sir William and Lady Hamilton inhabited a house, No. 23, in Piccadilly, while

Lord Nelson was in Arlington-street with Lady Nelson, until the 13th, on which day he finally separated from her Ladyship. An eye-witness on this occasion has given the following account, addressed to Sir N. Harris Nicolas:

"Kemp Town, Brighton, 13th April, 1846.

"Dear Sir,

"I was no less surprised than grieved, when you told me of a prevailing opinion, that Lord Nelson, of his own motion, withdrew from the society of his wife, and took up his residence altogether with Sir William and Lady Hamilton; and that you have never received from any member of his family an intimation to the contrary. His father, his brother, Dr. Nelson (afterwards Earl Nelson), his sisters, Mrs. Bolton and Mrs. Matcham, and their husbands, well knew, that the separation was unavoidable on Lord Nelson's part; and, as I happened to be present when the unhappy rupture took place, I have often talked over with all of them, but more especially with Mr. and Mrs. Matcham, the particulars which I proceed to relate, in justice to the memory of my illustrious friend, and in the hope of removing an erroneous impression from your mind.

"In the winter of 1800-1801, I was breakfasting with Lord and Lady Nelson, at their lodgings in Arlington-street, and a cheerful conversation was passing on indifferent subjects, when Lord Nelson spoke of something which had been done or said by 'dear Lady Hamilton;' upon which Lady Nelson rose from her chair, and exclaimed, with much vehemence, 'I am sick of hearing of dear Lady Hamilton, and am resolved that you shall give up either her or me.' Lord Nelson, with perfect calmness, said, 'Take care, Fanny, what you say: I love you sincerely; but I cannot forget my obligations to Lady Hamilton, or speak of her otherwise than with affection and admiration.' Without one soothing word or gesture, but muttering something about her mind being made up, Lady Nelson left the room, and shortly after drove from the house. They never lived together afterwards. I believe that Lord Nelson took a formal leave of her Ladyship before joining the fleet under Sir Hyde Parker; but that, to the day of her husband's glorious death, she never made any apology for her abrupt and ungentle conduct above related, or any overture towards a reconciliation. I am, dear Sir, your faithful servant,

"W. HASLEWOOD."

Lord Nelson gave to Lady Nelson an opportunity of reconciliation after the step she had taken, for he wrote from Southampton, that evening upon his arrival, the following letter, of which, however, it does not appear that any notice was taken:—

"Southampton, 13th January, 1801.

"My dear Fanny,
"We are arrived, and heartily tired; and, with kindest regards to my father and all the family, believe me,
Your affectionate,
"NELSON."

The last letter ever written by Lord Nelson to his wife is probably the following, from off Copenhagen:—

"St. George, March 4th, 1801.

"Josiah is to have another ship, and to go abroad, if the Thalia cannot soon be got ready. I have done *all* for him, and he may again, as he has often done before, wish me to break my neck, and be abetted in it by his friends, who are likewise my enemies; but I have done my duty as an honest, generous man, and I neither want or wish for any body to care what becomes of me, whether I return, or am left in the Baltic. Living, I have done all in my power for you, and if dead, you will find I have done the same; therefore my only wish is, to be left to myself: and wishing you every happiness, believe that I am, your affectionate,
"NELSON AND BRONTÉ."

That Lady Nelson's suspicions were not groundless will be evident from what follows; but that they had been excited some time ere foundation existed for them, is apparent to me from an attentive perusal of Lord Nelson's correspondence, and a close examination of the circumstances which took place. Lady Hamilton's manners attracted the admiration of all who were introduced to her society. Earl St. Vincent was scarcely less enthusiastic in her praise than Lord Nelson, who felt grateful to her for her attention to his step-son, Josiah Nisbet, in 1793.

Five years elapsed before Nelson and Lady Hamilton again met, and then it was to aid in effecting that most important Battle of the Nile. The part Lady Hamilton took on this occasion could not fail to render her an object of admiration with Nelson; nor could the reception given to him after the battle, nor the care bestowed on his deranged state of health, a care admitted by the Earl of St. Vincent,[1] serve otherwise than to demand his gratitude. Lord Nelson's unreserved and un-

---

[1] See Letter, Vol. i. p. 165.

constrained manner of describing to Lady Nelson the distinctions conferred upon him, the splendour of the fêtes given in his honour, &c., satisfy me that no feeling of an improper character at this time prevailed between them. The conduct of Lady Hamilton at the celebrated fête, induced Captain Nisbet to exceed the bounds of decorous attention due to his step-father, and it is not improbable that a communication from Captain Nisbet to his mother relative to this affair, may have laid the basis of those suspicions which took possession of Lady Nelson's mind: her Ladyship's letters were, unfortunately, too trivial and insignificant to command her husband's attention — her expressions for his return too cold for one of his ardent temperament, and he could not fail to draw a comparison unfavourable to Lady Nelson, when contrasted with that admiration of his glorious achievements entertained and bestowed upon him at Naples. It is much to be lamented that Lady Nelson was not at Yarmouth to receive her husband upon his return to England after nearly three years' absence, during which time he had rendered such signal services to his country, and had raised her to the rank of a Peeress. No display of eagerness to receive him to her bosom was manifested — she coolly waited at an hotel in London, and then gave to him a reception which has been described as "cold and chilling." Nothing could exceed the enthusiasm of all classes manifested upon the return of Nelson to England. Every town through which he passed offered its testimony to his character, his valour, and his greatness; from the partner of his bosom alone he received a cold and indifferent reception. The operation of this conduct on the mind of Nelson was calculated not to recall but to estrange him from his just and legitimate affections: the continued fascinations of Lady Hamilton had already done much, and the evil was confirmed by this conduct. It is much to be lamented that none of the family of Lord Nelson should have advised her to a different line of behaviour: his father, whose conduct and affections were of the most exemplary character, was unfortunately too old and infirm to take any active part on such an occasion, and his other relations seem rather to have attached themselves to Lady Hamilton.

Lord Nelson arrived in London on the 9th of November, 1800. On the 20th he took his seat in the House of Lords, and then finding his home with Lady Nelson exceedingly uncomfortable, he went an excursion to Salisbury, Fonthill, &c. with Sir William and Lady Hamilton, returning to London on the 29th of December, where he remained until the 13th of January, 1801, when, as before stated, he finally separated from

Lady Nelson, and immediately quitted to join his ship, the San Josef, at Plymouth, accompanied by his elder brother, the Reverend William Nelson. No attention had been paid by Lady Nelson to Lord Nelson's comforts for this voyage. His letters make complaint of the absence of all necessaries except those furnished by Lady Hamilton. At this time his mind was suffering no little anxiety on account of this lady's situation, and his daily correspondence with her both under her own name and the assumed one of Mrs. Thomson, exhibits the misery he endured.

On January 21, 1801, he writes: " I sincerely hope that your very serious cold will soon be better. I am so much interested in your health and happiness, that pray tell me all. I delivered to Mr. —— Mrs. Thomson's message and note; he desires me, poor fellow, to say, he is more scrupulous than if Mrs. T. was present. He says he does not write letters at this moment, as the object of his affections may be unwell, and others may open them."

On the 24th: " Pray tell Mrs. Thomson her kind friend is very uneasy about her, and prays most fervently for her safety."

On the 25th: " I delivered poor Mrs. T.'s note. Her friend is truly thankful and grateful for her kindness and your goodness. Who does not admire your benevolent heart? Poor man! he is very anxious, and begs you will, if she is not able, write a line just to comfort him. He appears to me to feel very much her situation; he is so agitated, and will be so for two or three days, that he says he cannot write, and that I must send his kind love and affectionate regard."

On the 26th: " My dear Lady Hamilton, when I consider that this day nine months was your birth-day, and that, although we had a gale of wind, yet I was happy, and sung ' *Come, cheer up, fair Emma,*' &c.\* even the thought, compared with this day, makes me melancholy. My heart some how is sunk within me. I long to hear you are well. The dearest friends must part; and we only part, I trust, to meet again.—Mrs. Thomson's friend is this moment come into my room; he desires me to thank you for your goodness to his dear friend. He appears almost as miserable as myself. He says you have always been kind to his dear Mrs. T.; and he hopes you will continue your goodness to her on this trying occasion. I have assured him of your innate worth and affectionate disposition : and he lives, as ever and for ever, your attached and truly affectionate friend,

" NELSON AND BRONTÉ."

---

\* See Miss Knight's Song, page 640, ante.

On the 27th, he writes in a similar strain, and requests her "to do everything which was right."

On the 28th: "I have this moment seen Mrs. Thomson's friend; poor fellow! he seems very uneasy and melancholy. He begs you to be kind to her. I have assured him of your readiness to relieve the dear, good woman."

On the 29th: "Pray, tell your friend, Mrs. T., that I have delivered her note to her friend; and he desires me to say, through your goodness, how sensible he is of her kindness. As the very particular business he is engaged upon will not be over for two or three days, he defers answering her note till that time. What a hard case these poor people's is! but, between your unparalleled goodness and my attention, I hope they will yet be happy and comfortable. In my opinion, neither of them can be happy as they are. May the great God of Heaven protect, comfort, and assist you, is the fervent wish of, my dear Lady, ever your affectionate friend,

"NELSON AND BRONTÉ."

Between the 29th and the 31st of January it is clear that the child was born; for,

On the 1st of February he writes:—"My dear Lady, I believe poor dear Mrs. Thomson's friend will go mad with joy. He cries, prays, and performs all tricks, yet dare not shew all or any of his feelings. He has only me to consult with. He swears he will drink your health this day in a bumper; and d—n me if I don't join him, in spite of all the doctors in Europe; for none regards you with truer affection than myself. You are a dear, good creature, and your kindness and attention to poor Mrs. T. stamps you higher than ever in my mind. I cannot write; I am so agitated by this young man at my elbow. I believe he is foolish: he does nothing but rave about you and her. I own I partake of his joy: I cannot write any thing."

On the 2nd: "All your letters are so good, so kind, so like yourself, that, had not your last been so excellent, and even far exceeding all the others, I should not have known which to have selected. *I have cut out two lines, and never will part with them.* I have no letters as yet to-day, except the returned one from Plymouth; therefore I shall not close this till after post is arrived. I dined yesterday with Troubridge, Darby, Hardy, my brother, and Parker, who all drank a bumper to your health; and I set all the doctors at defiance, till my brother said I should hurt myself; and Mrs. Thomson's friend drank two, because he said you had been so kind to his dear friend, who he loved more than life: such is the power of good and generous actions; they do good to the doer and the receiver. . . . That friend of our dear Mrs. T. is a good soul, and full of feeling. He wishes much to see her and her little one. If possible, I will get him leave for two or three days when I go to Portsmouth, and you will see his gratitude to you."

On the 3rd, though undated: "My dear Mrs. Thomson your good and dear friend, does not think it proper at present to write with his own hand, but he charges me to say how dear you are to him, and that you must, every opportunity, kiss and bless for him his dear little girl, which he wishes to be called Emma, out of gratitude to our dear, good Lady Hamilton; but whether it's from Lord Nelson, he says, or Lady Hamilton, he leaves to your judgment and choice. I have given Lord N. a hundred pounds this morning, for which he will give Lady H. an order on his agents; and I beg that you will distribute it amongst those who have been useful to you on the late occasion; and your friend, my dear Mrs. Thomson, may be sure of my care of him and his interests, which I consider as dearly as my own."

On the 4th the first mention of Horatia is made;

"San Josef, February 4th, 1801.

"My dear Lady Hamilton,

"It blows so very hard that I doubt if it will be possible to get a boat on shore, either to receive or send letters; but if it moderates in time for the post, of course mine shall go, and I hope from my heart to hear you are better. It has made my head ache stooping so much, as I have been making memorandums for my will, and, having regularly signed it, if I was to die this moment, I believe it would hold good. If I am not able to send it, as far as relates to you, this day, I will to-morrow. I have been obliged to be more particular than I wished, as a wife can have nothing, and it might be taken from you by will or the heirs of your husband. If you disapprove of any part say so, and I will alter it; but I think you must approve—I have done my best that you should. I shall now go to work and save a fortune. Say, shall I bequeath the £2000, owing me from Sir William for the same purpose? You must keep this letter till you receive a copy of my memorandum. . . . . Make my kindest regards to Mrs. Jenkins and Horatia, and ever believe me,

"Yours,

"N. & B.

"P.S.—We drink your health every day. Believe me your letters cannot be long or too minute of all particulars. My mind is a little easier, having perfect confidence."

On the 5th, the following copy of the will and letter were sent:—

"And as Emma Hamilton, the wife of the Right Honourable Sir William Hamilton, K.B., has been the great cause of my performing those services which have gained me honours and rewards, I give unto her, in case of the failure of male heirs, as directed by my will, the entire rental of the Brontë Estate for her particular use and benefit; and, in case of her death before she may come into the possession of the Estate of Brontë, she is to have the full power of naming any child she may have, in or out of wedlock, or any child, male or female, which she, the said Emma Hamilton, wife of the Right Honourable Sir William Hamilton, may choose to adopt and call her child, by her last will and testament, or by deed declaring her intent: and the sword given by his Sicilian Majesty is to be delivered on her coming to the estate, or to the person she may name, as directed by my said will: and I likewise give to the said Emma, wife of the Right Honourable Sir William Hamilton, K.B., &c., a picture of his Sicilian Majesty, set in diamonds, with the Queen's cypher on the opposite side, whom God preserve, with all the diamonds which surround it, as it is now lodged in a mahogany box, in the care of Alexander Davison, Esq., St. James's-square, London: and I give all my other boxes, lodged in the aforesaid box at Alexander Davison's, Esq., in which diamonds are placed; viz. one with the portrait of the Emperor Paul of Russia; one of the King of Sardinia, and the one, said to have been sent me by the mother of the Grand Signior, likewise to the said Emma Hamilton, wife of Sir William Hamilton, to be sold, if she pleases, and the income to be for her use during her natural life, and at her decease it is to be given to a child called ———, in whom I take a very particular interest; and as Emma Hamilton is the only person who knows the parents of this female child, I rely with the greatest confidence on her unspotted honour and integrity, that she will consider the child as mine, and be a guardian to it, shielding it from want and disgrace, and bringing it up as the child of her dear friend, Nelson and Brontë: and to this female child, of which Lady Hamilton shall only be the declarer that it is the one I mean, I give and bequeath all the money I shall be worth above the sum of twenty thousand pounds, the interest of it to be received by Lady Hamilton for the maintenance and education of this female child; the principal to be paid her at the death of Lady Hamilton, if she has attained the age of twenty-one years, or that she may marry; the guardians of my adopted child to be named by Lady Hamilton in her will.

"Such are my ideas, if you have no objection; if you have, I will endeavour to alter them to your wishes. I shall now begin and save a fortune for the little one.

"*Thursday Noon.* I have this moment received your letters of Tuesday; all that you have been so good as to write me have come safe. I have delivered the letter to Mrs. Thomson's friend, and he feels truly grateful for all your affectionate regards to poor dear Mrs. Thomson, who you say, and truly, is a pattern for all wives and mothers. I write the note for him, as he does not wish his hand to be known at present.

"I have letters from Dumouriez and Sir Brooke Boothby. Dumouriez says, 'pay my sincere compliments to the excellent Lord Hamilton and to his incomparable Lady. Let her remember the promise she made to send me the portrait of my dear Nelson and her own. Be so good as to be the interpreter of the Baronne de Bearant, who prays to her the most tender compliments.' Sir B. B. says, 'In the dreary times I have passed here, the passage of your party, which, I think, it would be difficult to match, seems like a bright dream in a long night. I beg of your Lordship to present my affectionate regards to Lady Hamilton (certainly one of the most *charming women in the world*). Nothing can please me so much as to have justice done you. Thank God, you want not the society of princes or dukes. If you happened to fall down and break your nose or knock out your eyes, you might go to the devil for what they care; but it is your good heart which attaches to you your faithful and affectionate,

"NELSON AND BRONTÉ.

"Troubridge desires his best regards; so does Hardy and Darby. Signal is just made to sail. Send me back the first half-sheet of paper, *as it is* clearer worded than the original memorandum."

On this day, also, Lord Nelson writes about the christening of the child :—

"My dear Mrs. Thomson,
"Your dear and excellent friend has desired me to say, that it is not usual to christen children till they are a month or six weeks old; and as Lord Nelson will probably be in town as well as myself, before we go to the Baltic, he proposes then, if you approve, to christen the child, and that myself and Lady Hamilton should be two of the sponsors. It can be christened at St. George's, Hanover-square; and, I believe, the parents being at the time out of the kingdom, if it is necessary, it can be stated born at Portsmouth or at sea. Its

name will be Horatia, daughter of Johem and Morata Etnorb.[1] If you read the surname backwards, and take the letters of the other names, it will make, very extraordinary, the names of your real and affectionate friends, Lady Hamilton and myself; but, my dear friend, consult Lady Hamilton. Your friend consults me, and I would not lead him wrong for the world; he has not been very well: I believe he has fretted, but his spirit is too high to own it. But, my dear Madam, both him, you, and your little one, must always believe me your affectionate

"NELSON AND BRONTÉ.

"The child, if you like it, can be named by any clergyman without its going to church."

From the following, apparently written on the next day, he acknowledges the receipt of a portion of the child's hair:—

"My dear Mrs. Thomson,

"Your good friend is very much obliged by your kind present of this morning; it is very like what I remember his. He has put it in a case with her dear mother's— for I almost love you as much as he does. He is sorry for the trouble you have had about the nurse; but he says children bring their cares and pleasures with them; but, however, you will rely on Lady Hamilton, her goodness and good advice cannot be too closely followed; she is the pattern I wish you to imitate. Respecting the naming and christening of the child he wrote to Lady Hamilton yesterday. He hopes to get leave for three days to come to town when the ship gets to Portsmouth.

"Ever your friend and unalterable friend,
"N. & B."

"San Josef, February 6th, 1801.

"It blows a gale of wind, but which only affects me as it may deprive me of my dear and much honoured friend's letters. Your letters are to me Gazettes, for as yet I have not fixed upon any, nor can they be half so interesting to my feelings, although you know I am not a little fond of a newspaper, and we have often almost quarrelled for a first reading, and I trust the time will soon arrive when we shall have those amicable squabbles again. I am now of course very much by myself, for none ever come to me except at meals, or I send for either Hardy or Parker, and they are both so modest and well behaved, that it is really a pleasure to have them on board. Parker boasts, whenever he drinks your health, which

[1] Emma and Horatio Bronté.

is at least once a day, that he had the honour of being your Aide-de-camp, and that he has given many messages by your orders. *Ah*, those were happy times! Would to God we were at this moment in the Bay of Naples, and all matters for those good monarchs going on as well as it did at that time.

"*Noon.*—This moment has brought me your two kind letters. You may rely I shall not open my mouth on poor dear Mrs. Thomson's business to any creature on this earth. You and I should be very unworthy, if we did any such thing, as all the secret of these two people rests solely in our bosoms. He desires me to say that he approves very much of the sum of money, and submits it to your discretion, if a small pension should not be promised if the secret is well kept, but desires that nothing should be given under handwriting. He also desires you will now and then give the nurse an additional guinea. He thinks it might be better to omit christening the child for the present, and even privately baptizing it, the clergyman would naturally ask its parents' names, which would put poor dear Mrs. T. in some trouble, or cause suspicion. But, in all this matter, he submits himself to your prudence and friendship. He will send you more money as Mrs. T. wants it, only let him know every thing. Poor fellow, he would have given any thing to have seen the child, especially in your charming company. To say the truth, this lad seems to love you not a little, but who does not, I am sure I do. *Saturday noon.*—Mr. Davison came whilst I was at dinner yesterday, and gave me your letter. He says you are grown thinner, but he thinks you look handsomer than ever. I know he is a very great admirer of yours. He says you told him to tell me not to send you any more advice about seeing company, for that you are determined not to allow the world to say a word against you; therefore, I will not say a word. I rest confident in your conduct. This morning brought me your letter of Thursday. I am sorry for all your trouble, but poor Mrs. T.'s friend will never forget the obligation.

"Ever, my dear Lady,
"Yours affectionately, and for ever. Amen.
"NELSON AND BRONTÉ."

On the 17th:—" I fear saying too much—I admire what you say of my god-child. If it is like its mother it will be very handsome, for I think her one, aye, the most beautiful woman of the age. Now, do not be angry at my praising this dear child's mother, for I have heard people say she is very like

you. My dear friend, I hope you will never receive any more cross letters, but always such as ought to be wrote by, my dear Lady, your obliged, unalterably attached and faithful
" NELSON AND BRONTÉ.

" I would steal white bread sooner than my god-child should want."

It is, I imagine, unnecessary to indulge in further extracts, and I shall therefore close this part of the evidence with the following avowal on the part of Lord Nelson, in a letter to Lady Hamilton, sent by a private hand that could be depended upon for its safe delivery:—

"*March* 1, 1801. Now my own dear Wife, for such you are in my eyes and in the face of heaven, I can give full scope to my feelings, for I dare say Oliver will faithfully deliver this letter. You know, my dearest Emma, that there is nothing in this world that I would not do for us to live together, and to have our dear little child with us. * * * I love, I never did love any one else, I never had a dear pledge of love till you gave me one, and you, thank my God, never gave one to any body else. I think before March is out you will either see us back, or so victorious that we shall insure a glorious issue to our toils. Think what my Emma will feel at seeing return safe, perhaps with a little more fame, her own dear loving Nelson. Never, if I can help it, will I dine out of my ship, or go on shore, except duty calls me. Let Sir Hyde have any glory he can catch—I envy him not. You, my beloved Emma, and my country, are the two dearest objects of my fond heart —*a heart susceptible and true*.[1] Only place confidence in me, and you never shall be disappointed. I burn all your dear letters, because it is right for your sake, and I wish you would burn all mine—they can do no good, and will do us both harm if any seizure of them, or the dropping even one of them, would fill the mouths of the world sooner than we intend. * * * I had a letter this day from the Reverend Mr. Holden, who we met on the Continent; he desired his kind compliments to you and Sir William: he sent me the letters of my name, and recommended it as my motto—*Honor est a Nilo*— HORATIO NELSON. May the Heavens bless you. N. & B.

" Monday morning—Oliver is just going on shore; the time will ere long arrive when Nelson will land to fly to his Emma, to be for ever with her. Let that hope keep us up under our present difficulties. Kiss and bless *our* dear Horatia —think of that."

[1] A reference to some lines written by Nelson.

Two verbal statements have been put forth on this subject, one said to have emanated from Tom Allen, Lord Nelson's servant, which is totally incorrect and undeserving of a single word—the other, by Mrs. Johnstone, the daughter of the nurse, Mrs. Gibson, to whom the child was entrusted by Lady Hamilton, which agrees with the documents now made public. Her statement runs thus, and it was made in 1828 to Captain Ward, of the 81st Regiment, brother of the Reverend Philip Ward, to whom Miss Horatia Nelson was married in 1822.

"Lady Hamilton brought the child to her mother's house in a hackney coach one night, and placed her under her charge, telling her that she should be handsomely remunerated. She was unattended, and did not give the nurse any information as to the child's parents. The nurse declared she was no more than eight days' old. This was either in the month of January or February; and Mrs. Gibson said she could never make out why her birth-day was kept in October. She remained with the nurse till she was five or six years old. Lady Hamilton constantly visited her: Lord Nelson was frequently her companion in her visits to her, and often came alone, and played for hours with the infant on the floor, calling her his own child."[1]

Sir Nicholas Harris Nicolas has printed several letters addressed to Lady Hamilton, alluding to Mrs. Thomson, and states the first time of that name occurring to be on the 28th January. I have, however, shewn that it was used as early as the 21st. He has also printed several notes of Lady Hamilton to the nurse, Mrs. Gibson, and I have the nurse's receipts, but they are not necessary to be particularized. In one of the letters, however, to Lady Hamilton, printed by Sir Harris Nicolas, of the date of the 16th of February, Lord Nelson says, "I send you a few lines wrote in the late gale, which I think you will not disapprove." Sir Harris questioned the genuineness of those lines, and felt disposed to attribute them to Harrison, the editor of the volumes in which they appeared, as Nelson was not known to have attempted to write verse. I have no doubt, however, that they are the productions of Nelson, and shall therefore here reprint them, together with another among the papers now in my possession, and also one written on the night of the attack on Copenhagen, which will be found in its proper place, April 2, 1801. (See p. 17, *ante*.)

> "Though ———'s[2] polished verse superior shine,
> Though sensibility grace every line;
> Though her soft Muse be far above all praise,
> And female tenderness inspire her lays;

---

[1] Dispatches and Letters, Vol. vii. p. 370.   [2] Emma's.

Deign to receive, though unadorned
  By the poetic art,
The rude expressions which bespeak
  A sailor's untaught heart.

A heart *susceptible*, sincere, and true ;
A heart, by fate and nature, torn in two ;
One half to duty and his country due,
The other, *better half,* to love and you !

Sooner shall Britain's sons resign
  The empire of the sea ;
Than Henry shall renounce his faith,
  AND PLIGHTED VOWS TO THEE !

And waves on waves shall cease to roll,
  And tides forget to flow ;
Ere thy true Henry's constant love
  Or ebb or change shall know.

---

## HENRY (OFF CADIZ) TO EMMA.

The storm,—is o'er,
  The troubled main,
Now, heaves no more,
  But, all is silent,—hushed,—and calm again,
Save in this bosom,—where a ceaseless storm,
Is raised—by love and Emma's beauteous form.

No calm,—at sea,
  This heart shall know,
While far from thee,
  Midst lengthening hours of absence, and of woe,
I gaze,—in sorrow, o'er the boundless deep,
With eyes,—which were they not ashamed would weep.

But, hark ! I hear
  The signal gun !
Farewell ! my dear !
  The Victory leads on ! The fight's begun !
Thy Picture, round this cannon's neck shall prove,
A pledge,—to valour ! sent by thee and love !

Should conquest smile,
  On Britain's Fleet,
(As at the Nile,)
  With joyful hearts, upon the beach, we'll meet !
No more, I'll tempt, the dangers of the sea,
But live, in Merton's groves, with love and thee !

The allusion made in the previous verses to Emma's polished verse, probably has reference to the following lines sent by Lady Hamilton to Nelson. The Blue Peter, it is scarcely necessary to remark, is a flag hoisted when a vessel is about to depart.

### BLUE PETER.

Silent grief, and sad forebodings
(Lest I ne'er should see him more,)
Fill my heart, when gallant Nelson,
Hoists BLUE PETER at the fore.

On his Pendant anxious gazing,
Fill with tears (mine eyes run o'er)
At each change of wind I tremble
While Blue Peter's at the fore.

All the live-long day I wander,
Sighing on the sea-beat shore;
But my sighs are all unheeded,
When Blue Peter's at the fore.

For when duty calls my hero
To far seas, where cannons roar,
Nelson (love and Emma leaving),
Hoists Blue Peter at the fore.

Oft he kiss'd my lips at parting,
And at every kiss he swore,
Nought could force him from my bosom,
Save Blue Peter at the fore.

Oh, that I might with my Nelson,
Sail the wide world o'er and o'er,
Never should I then with sorrow,
See Blue Peter at the fore.

But (ah me!) his ship's unmooring;
Nelson's last boat rows from shore,
Every sail is set and swelling,
And Blue Peter's seen no more.

EMMA.

To sum up the whole, it appears that the child, Horatia, is unquestionably the daughter of Lady Hamilton and Lord Nelson—that she was born between the 29th and 31st of January, 1801, in Piccadilly; on the 1st of February Lord Nelson acknowledges receipt of the information of the birth; on the 2nd determines to apply for two or three days' leave of absence to see the child; and on the 3rd expresses a desire that she should be called Emma, though he leaves it to the mother's judgment and choice. He sends £100 [1] to pay expenses attending the birth; on the 4th, the name Horatia is first mentioned; on the 5th, he makes a will in favour of Lady Hamilton and the child, and expresses his determination to set about saving a fortune for the little one. At apparently the same date, Lord Nelson writes relative to the christening of the child, and on the next day acknowledges a present of a lock of hair, which he places with her mother's in a case. In another, of the date of the 6th, he alludes to the secret being only deposited in their own bosoms, and submits the propriety of promising a small pension to the nurse; thinks it better to postpone the christening,[2] as it might lead to unpleasant inquiries; but leaves the matter entirely to Lady Hamilton's discretion; and on the 1st of March writes an absolute and distinct avowal of the parentage of the child, which sets the question completely at rest and beyond dispute.

[1] In Lord Nelson's account with his Agents, Messrs. Marsh, Page and Creed, I find an entry of the payment of a draft of this amount to Lady Hamilton; it is the first time her name occurs in the accounts. To Lady Nelson I find Lord Nelson drew for £400 on the 13th of January, 1801, the day he departed from London and separated from his wife. From this day to January 5, 1802, Lord Nelson paid to Lady Nelson's account, at different times, sums amounting to £2000, after which a quarterly allowance of £400 was regularly paid to Lady Nelson by his Lordship's agents.

[2] The baptism of the child was deferred until 1803; and in the register of the parish of Marylebone there is the following entry:—

"Baptisms, 1803.
May 13, Horatia Nelson Thompson,
B. 29 October, 1800."

# APPENDIX.

## No. I.

### BOULOGNE FLOTILLA.

*Force necessary.*

Eight flat boats to be fitted as fire boats.
Fifteen flat boats, with howitzers, and 24lb. carronades.
Ten launches with 18lb. carronades. Carcasses for these to be sent from Woolwich.
Forty rowing boats.

The flat boats to be paired,  made fast together with twelve fathoms of small chain, and towed by six boats. A light brig to be kept alongside the fire boats to light the combustibles. An artillery man or two, to attend each of the fire boats.

The eight flat boats to be sent from Sheerness to the Downs, but not till the last moment, with the chains, and twelve of Syder's compasses. The combustible matter, reeds, &c. to be sent in a warren hoy, to the Downs, or Dungeness, if I am not in the Downs.

Leyden . . 4
Iris . . . 4
Amazon . 4
Medusa . . 4
Discovery . 2
Ariadne . . 2

The bombs who have flat boats to send the crew, and a Lieutenant with them. Ships will be found likewise off to man the flat boats, and to furnish the other boats for the service.

Some other vessels to carry the other four.
Eight divisions of boats. Two fire boats; ten rowing boats to attend each fire boat.
Two howitzer boats; two flats, with carronades.
Two launches, with carronades.

658                                   APPENDIX.

| 3 boats 1 under a Capt. | 3 B 2 under Capt. | 3 B 3 under Capt. | 3 boats 4 under Capt. |
|---|---|---|---|
| ʃ - 6 . H . B | ʃ - b - | ʃ - b | ʃ - 6 . H . B |

under a Capt.
    1.
Astern of the fire boats. ⎫
    4.          ⎬ Do.      Do.      Do.
for protecting. ⎭

Each sub-division under a Captain.
Twelve Captains.  Boat compasses, H. sized.

The boats to put off from four ships, at the first of the flood or water.  Each separate sub-division of boats to be tied together, and to tow each other.  The divisions to be kept separated, but at not a greater distance than thirty fathoms.

On approaching the enemy's ships, the fire vessels will be laid across hawse.  The howitzer boats are to row close, and to fire as many carcasses into the ships as circumstances will admit.  The division No. 1, will attack the outer ship, the division No. 2, to attack the second, and so to the fourth ship.  The enemy may naturally be supposed to be alarmed, cutting their cables, &c. the commanders of the howitzer divisions are in that case to fire on them, and otherways annoy them as circumstances may point out to be most proper.

The fire vessels are to go in after the boats, and to endeavour to lay on board such of the enemy's ships as may be run aground, or which they may be able to grapple with, as the boats will all be furnished with grapnells.  They can be anchored if driving too far up the harbour, and the Commanders of divisions are to take care and come out of the harbour, at the first retiring of the ebb.

Upon a deliberate consideration with Captains Bedford, Sutton, and Campbell, we are of opinion, that although the risk may be great, from the circumstances of wind, setting of tides, uncertainty of finding the ships in a dark night, from their great distance, not much less than twelve miles, and many other incidental circumstances, yet the object is great, and will justify the attempt.  And we are of opinion, that an Admiral, or officer of high standing, in the Post Captains List, should command the whole.[1]

---

[1] The above constituted Lord Nelson's draft of the proposed attack; the precise order adopted may be seen in " The Dispatches and Letters, Vol. iv. p. 460," from a copy in the possession of the Right Honourable John Wilson Croker.

## No. II.

The Rev. Alexander John Scott, born in 1768, was the son of a half-pay Lieutenant in the Navy, who retired from the Service, and engaged in ship-building, and in the Russia and Danish trade. His uncle was a Rear-Admiral. Upon the nomination of George III., he was appointed to a scholarship on the foundation of the Charter House, and displayed much aptitude in the acquisition of languages and classical literature. Having taken his degree of B.A. at Cambridge, in 1791, he entered the Church, was ordained, and in 1793 became Chaplain of the Berwick, 74 guns. This vessel was commanded by Sir John Collins, and it was one which formed part of the first squadron of the Mediterranean fleet under Lord Hood, which gave to Mr. Scott the opportunity of being introduced to Captain Nelson of the Agamemnon. Upon the death of Sir John Collins, Nelson invited the Chaplain to come into his ship, but it being one of less force, as a matter of policy, it was judiciously declined. Nelson had, however, enjoyed opportunities of witnessing Mr. Scott's zeal, and had remarked upon his acquaintance with the Italian and Spanish languages, and formed a proper estimate of his value.

In 1795, Mr. Scott became Chaplain to Sir Hyde Parker in the St. George, of 98 guns, and a warm friendship subsisted between him and the Admiral. Sir Gilbert Elliot, Bart. offered to him the Chaplaincy of Bastia, and was desirous that he should reside in his family, and become the tutor to his sons; but this advantageous offer was also declined, Sir Hyde Parker entreating him to remain with him. Mr. Scott's acquirements extended to the Greek, Latin, French, Italian, Spanish, German, Danish and Russian languages. He translated a number of Italian papers of consequence for Sir John Jervis. Having returned to England with Sir Hyde Parker, he was made Chaplain to the Queen, and went out to the West Indies, where he was presented with the living of St. John's in Jamaica, estimated to be of the value of £500 *per annum*, through the interest of Sir Hyde Parker with the Governor of that island. When Sir Hyde Parker was relieved from his command by Lord Hugh Seymour, Mr. Scott returned with the Admiral to England, whom he afterwards joined in the Royal George, when Sir Hyde was appointed second in command of the Channel fleet; but upon his being named to the command of the fleet in the Baltic, in 1801, he again accompanied his Commander, and was thus again also brought into communication with Lord Nelson, who found him of great service in his correspondence with the Danes, from his knowledge of the language, and he was in consequence selected and sent on shore at Copenhagen, as Secretary to the Legation, where he displayed much diplomatic tact, as well as skill in the language. He drew up the articles agreed to at the Convention, and in so able a manner, that Lord Nelson urged him to affix his signature to them, which, however, from modesty, he declined doing, but which Nelson truly told him he would live to repent. Towards the close of this year, Nelson drew up a testimonial in favour of Mr. Scott, and strongly recommended him to the Governors of the Charter House, by whom he was presented with the Vicarage of Southminster in Essex. From his Jamaica living, he had been suspended by reason of his long absence. In proceeding to the West Indies, to endeavour to recover this living, he met with a serious accident, which is alluded to in one of Lord Nelson's letters to Lady Hamilton. The particulars of this accident are thus detailed in an unpretending little work, entitled, "Recollections of the Life of the Rev. A. J. Scott, D.D, Lord Nelson's Chaplain," published in 1842 by his daughter and son-in-law:—"On the passage, the ship, soon after midnight, was struck by lightning in a severe thunder-storm. The electric fluid rent the mizen-mast, killing and wounding fourteen men, and descending into the Captain's cabin, in which Mr. Scott was sleeping, communicated with some spare cartridges and powder horns, which lay on a shelf immediately over his head. By this means he sustained a double shock, the electric fluid struck his hand and arm, passing along the bell wire, with which they were in contact, and the gunpowder exploding at the same time knocked out some of his front teeth, and dreadfully lacerated his mouth and jaw. The lightning also melted the hooks to which the hammock was slung, and he fell to the ground, receiving a violent concussion of the brain. His cabin was found in flames, himself a sheet of fire, and he was taken up senseless, and apparently not likely to live. On landing, he was lodged in a convent, at Kingston, and by the excellent skill of Dr. Blair, Physician to the fleet in the West Indies, he soon recovered from his external injuries; but one side of his body was paralyzed for a length of time, his sight, hearing, and the powers of his mind were also impaired; the last so much so, as to cause general apprehension that he would never regain them; and the nervous system was so completely shattered by the accident, that he suffered from it for the remainder of his life."

Mr. Scott was unsuccessful in his attempts to regain his living, and upon his return to England, Lord Nelson, with his usual kindness and sympathy, hastened to visit him in his affliction, paid great attention to him, and finding him to be wholly unfit to attend to the duties of his living, situated in the marshes of Essex, prevailed upon him to accompany him when put in command of the Mediterranean fleet, and as his Chaplain and foreign and confidential Secretary, he joined him in the Victory, and remained with him until the death of the hero.

Mr. Scott was frequently employed by Lord Nelson in special missions, which, from his acquaintance with different languages, he could be well and safely engaged in, and in Spain, and at Naples, he was often apparently occupied in the pursuit of pleasure or of health, though in reality securing for his commander articles of fresh provisions, and frequently important intelligence.

In Sardinia he materially assisted in victualling the ships, and removed many impediments arising from the neutrality to which the Government was pledged with France. At length complaints were made by the French authorities, and the Sardes having no adequate means of defence against the threatened punishment by the French, the supplies were limited, but continued favourable to the English.

Mr. Scott returned to England with Nelson, and after passing a short time at Merton, becoming, as his relatives say, "a participator in the last happy domestic days Nelson was ever destined to know," he attended in Downing Street with Lord Nelson upon Mr. Pitt, and took his leave for Trafalgar. The horror occasioned to Mr. Scott by the crowded cockpit of the Victory with wounded and dying men at the memorable battle off this place, was so great, that it haunted him like a shocking dream for years afterwards. He is said never to have talked of it. The only remark on the subject extorted from him by the inquiries of a friend, soon after his return home was, that "it was like a butcher's shambles." A fine young Lieutenant was brought down and dressed by the Surgeons, when the poor fellow, learning the extent of the injury he had received, tore off the ligatures with which the vessels had been secured, and bled to death. Mr. Scott was so frenzied by this sight, that he quitted the cockpit and hurried to the deck, regardless of his own safety. "He rushed up the companion ladder—now slippery with gore—the scene above was all noise, confusion, and smoke; but he had hardly time to breathe there, when Lord Nelson himself fell, and this event at once sobered his disordered mind."[1] Having followed his Chief to the cockpit, he tended him to the last, and was indeed still rubbing his breast after life had fled.

With the death of Lord Nelson, his connexion with the Navy ceased. He received by Royal mandate the degree of D D.[2] at Cambridge, and he looked forward to having the prebendal stall at Canterbury, which, it was supposed, would be now vacated by Nelson's brother, who had been created an Earl with an adequate provision. He reasonably built this expectation from what Lord Nelson had said to him: "Only you remain quiet, let me get my brother a step, that is all, and you shall have his. I must not ask for both now, for the stall is a good thing to give up to get the deanery; but if I meet the French fleet I'll ask for both, and have them too."[3] The Earl was, however, very unwilling to resign, nor

---

[1] Page 186.

[2] The following letter was written by Mr. Scott at this time:—

"Feb. 19, 1806, St. John's College, Cambridge.

"My dear Lady Hamilton,

"I suppose you are well acquainted with my being at this place, which accounts for my non-appearance for some days. Supposing hourly I should set off for town, I have deferred writing to you to tell you that the University are about to petition the King to grant me a D.D. degree by mandamus. You will be delighted, I think, in knowing this, as it marks attention to the memory of our dear Lord. The matter has been some time in agitation, but I trust now is pretty well fixed; it was necessary that all should join in the business—I mean all the heads of Colleges—this thing they have now done. I remain for ten days longer, by which time it will be finished, and I shall return to you with all the dignity of a Doctor of Divinity. I thought the whole could not be completed before July, when the commencement is, and therefore was removing to London, but I now am given to understand that it can be done as soon as the King has signed the Mandate. So much for plans and projects, &c. &c. But I write chiefly to give some account of myself, and tell you that I constantly remember you, and that no selfish consideration can supersede the regard and attachment which I bear you.

"Pray kiss Horatia for me, and let her not forget the sound of my name. Make my respects to the Earl and Countess, Lady Charlotte, and those who recollect me. To Mr. Bolton and his wife, many kind and true expressions of regard, with Anne, Miss O'Connor, and Mrs. Voller if with you. With respect and affection ever

"Your devoted servant,

"A. J. SCOTT."

[3] Page 203.

could he be prevailed upon to do so until the proposed grant of £120,000 was settled, though urged by Lord Moira and the Prince of Wales. The disinclination of the Earl to attend to the claims of the worthy Chaplain, at length excited public notice, and was even alluded to in the House of Commons. An anonymous letter was written to Mr. Fuller, the well-known Member for Sussex, who had adverted to the subject, in which the writer endeavoured to falsify the pretensions of Mr. Scott, and accused him of being the author of various paragraphs which had appeared in the newspapers on the occasion. Upon being shewn this letter, Dr. Scott wrote to the Earl the following letter:—

"Great Portland Street, May 26, 1806.

"My Lord,

"I beg leave to assure your Lordship, that I have not, either directly or indirectly, written, or caused to be written, any paragraphs in the newspapers, neither have I been privy to, or countenanced them. I should not have thought it necessary to make such a declaration to your Lordship, but for an anonymous letter addressed to Mr. Fuller, M.P. for Sussex, in which I am accused as the author of them. As to any promise from my dear Lord, that you should resign your prebend in my favour; could I have submitted myself to the indignity of asserting such a falsehood, I could hardly have been guilty of the folly of it.

"What I have said to my friends, is what I have said to your Lordship, when I have solicited your resignation of the stall. 'That your brother's intentions were, if he could advance you a step higher in the Church, for me to succeed you in the stall. That he avowed such his wishes and intentions, and expressed his doubts of being able to accomplish both, adding, however, if he met the French fleet and gained another victory, that it certainly should be so.' Such were poor Lord Nelson's words; all promise to me from his Lordship was merely that of exerting himself in my favour, as soon as you, my Lord, should be better provided for. On those grounds alone I have solicited, and still most respectfully solicit your Lordship's resignation in my favour. On these grounds alone I have stated to friends my claim and pretensions.

"I have the honour to be, &c. &c.

"A. J. SCOTT."

Notwithstanding this appeal, the Earl retained possession, and Scott was doomed to neglect and disappointment, which was much aggravated by the receipt of letters from Captain Hardy, and others, congratulating him upon his supposed advancement.

He retired to his living in Essex, but the climate and its duties proved too much for his health. His friends made many ineffectual attempts to obtain preferment for him, and his spirit became almost broken by the neglect. His patron was gone, and his services were forgotten.

In 1807 he contracted marriage with an estimable lady, Miss Ryder, a niece of Sir Richard Croft, Bart., and then withdrew to the vicarage house of Burnham, a village adjoining Southminster, the curacy of which Dr. Scott held with his living. He had by this marriage three children, the first of whom was named after Nelson, Horatio. Mrs. Scott died in 1811, and her loss was sincerely bewailed, added to which, he now suffered much from the wound he had formerly received in the head, and a portion of bone exfoliated. After this he was better, but his fortunes were still adverse, and attempts he had made at farming to improve his very limited income, proved unsuccessful. He wisely directed himself to the improvement of his parishioners, and paid great attention to their welfare. His exertions to promote their happiness, and to forward the progress of religious education among the poor, obtained for him the hearty commendations of Dr. Howley, then Bishop of London. Through the interest of Lord Liverpool, the Prince Regent promoted him to the Crown living of Catterick in Yorkshire, which was represented in value as from £1000 to £1400 *per annum*. He was also named one of the King's Chaplains, in November, 1816. His former parishioners presented him with a silver salver, to mark their respect and gratitude for his services. The value of the living of Catterick, however, proved not to amount to more than one half of that which had been stated, and he also became involved in a law proceeding, in connexion with it, arising from the death of his predecessor. These proceedings embittered his life, and he reaped no enjoyment from his preferment. He lived in a secluded manner, occupying himself chiefly in the education of his children, in the indulgence of his literary habits, and in attention to his parochial duties. His parishioners held him in great and deserved respect. All his life he had been a book collector, and this taste brought with it his greatest comfort in his latter days. His chief time was spent in his library, which was of no inconsiderable extent, and he was most delighted when he could exhibit his curious volumes to an intelligent and kindred spirit.

Dr. Scott never visited London but to perform his duty at the Royal Chapel, and he was sensibly affected by King William IV.

recognizing him as Lord Nelson's Chaplain at a levee, and thanking him for his excellent sermon. He died July 24, 1840, having the day before completed his 72nd year. He was deeply regretted by his friends, and the late Lord Chief Justice Tindal truly said of him, " so much acquired learning, such goodness of heart, and such integrity of purpose, united in one man, can seldom be met with amongst his survivors, and the loss of these amiable and useful qualities, create a regret amongst his friends, which it will require a length of time to forget."

## No. III.

### Order of St. Joachim.

IN Sept. 1801, Le Commandeur Ivanovitz de Wittewode, Master of the Ceremonies of the Order of St. Joachim, addressed a letter to Lord Nelson, acquainting him that it was the desire of the Order, to nominate him a Knight Grand Commander. And on the 6th of Feb. 1802, Nelson, not having replied to the communication, Baron d'Eiker and Ekoffen, a Knight Grand Commander of the Order, and Chancellor Keeper of the Seals, of the most Illustrious Order; Equestrian Secular, and Capitular of St. Joachim; Knight of the Royal Order of Stanislaus, &c. &c. also addressed his Lordship, to state the wishes of the Order, and to communicate the nature of its constitutions, under which Lord Nelson would be honorarily admitted into its body. To this Lord Nelson replied :—

" Merton, Surrey, February 22, 1802.
" Sir,

" I certainly must have appeared very rude to yourself, and the Noble Order of St. Joachim, not to have answered your very polite letter of September last; but I trust that a few words of explanation, will mark that extraordinary respect for the Order, has in truth been the cause of my apparent inattention. Your letter was received in due time, when I had the command of a large portion of his Majesty's ships. I sent it immediately to Mr. Addington his Majesty's first Minister, in order that it might be laid before the King. From the business of the Peace, and other most important avocations, his Majesty's pleasure was not notified to me in form, until last Wednesday, the 17th February. *It was his Majesty's full and entire approbation and consent, that I might receive the honour of Knight Grand Commander of the Order of St. Joachim.*

"I have, now, therefore, only to assure the Noble Order, that I am deeply impressed with the great honour conferred upon me, and that it shall be the study of my life to endeavour, by future actions, to merit the continuance of their good opinion. I hold myself at the disposal of the Order, in what manner I am to be invested with this high dignity. I have further to request of you, Sir, to make use of words more adequate to my feelings than any in my power to write to the Order, my sense of the high honour and obligation conferred upon,

"Sir,
"Your most obliged and obedient Servant,
"NELSON AND BRONTÉ.

"I shall write to his Excellency, the Chancellor of the Order, to-morrow, through the hands of Mr. Rühl, writer in Chancery to the Order as desired.

"Le Commandeur Ivanowitz de Wittewode,
"Maitre des Cérémonies de dit Ordre."

This letter having been transmitted by Mr. Rühl, to his Excellency the Chancellor, the election of Lord Nelson took place, and upon receiving the Insignia of the Order, he addressed the following to the Count of Leiningen Westerbourg, the Grand Master of the Order :—

"TO HIS HIGHNESS MONSEIGNEUR COUNT OF LEININGEN.

"Merton, June 9th, 1802.

"Sir,
"I have deferred replying to the polite letter of April 3rd, which your Highness did me the honour of writing, until I received the Insignia of the Order, which I did on the 5th of June, and which I have now the honour of wearing. I can only say, that I will endeavour by my future conduct to merit the esteem of your Highness, and to do no discredit to the illustrious Order, which I have now the honour of belonging to. The fortitude with which your Highness bears the injustice done your venerable parent, and the loss of territory, establish you as the most proper character to fill your present illustrious station as head of the Order of St. Joachim, and a pattern for all classes of the Order. Wishing from my heart your Highness health, and every blessing that this world and the next can afford, I have the honour of subscribing myself with the highest respect,

"Your Highness's
"Most obliged and faithful humble servant,
"NELSON AND BRONTÉ."

## No. IV.

*Proposal for producing very superior Line of Battle Ships, at a small Expense to the Nation.*

"IF, from the great scarcity, and alarming *want* of naval timber in England, his Majesty's Ministers should deem it expedient to have most durable and superior men-of-war built in India, with Malabar teak; I humbly propose, with the support and under the direction of Government, to produce, in the first instance, two 74-gun ships of the *largest* class, exactly conformable to any draught and moulds with which I may be furnished, and barring unforeseen accidents, not only enter into the customary bond of security for the performance, but deliver the ships in the river Thames, *without any charge to Government for building them.* As the sending out the requisite establishment and materials for this undertaking, with the erecting of buildings, &c. would be attended with great expense to an individual, although to Government the cost would be comparatively trivial, I should require to have the *use* of an old 64-gun ship, that may be considered by the dock-yard officers, as not worth repair—together with a *decayed* sloop of war, in India, and such things as that country does not at present afford; which, including an overseer, builder, foreman, and sailing charges, would be the whole of the expense to Government, and every article allowed for, not exceed £17. 19s 6d per ton, for large ships.

"The furnishing durable and superior 74s, on such moderate terms to the State, it is conceived will be allowed a great national acquisition, and it falls in with the principle of this place, to produce them at the present period, even at a considerable reduction of the above sum. I, therefore, beg leave, with great deference to suggest, that if the Trident, or other old 64, now in India, should be brought home for no other purpose but to be broken up; or what may be found more prejudicial to the expenditure of timber and increase of expense, a thorough repair; to propose, with a small establishment, and at present, the use only of an unserviceable bomb ship, to furnish two of the largest third rates, of which the whole cost to the public, will be less than half the sum they can be built for in this country; namely, £10. 4s per ton, with every allowance for the officers' return, and consideration for employment of the people, if the unserviceable ships are paid off in India, and as the most convincing proof that these estimates are maturely weighed, although there are many cogent reasons against an individual engaging for every particular; I am willing, with the countenance I should no doubt receive from administration, on such occasion of consequence, to supply the principal part of the undertaking at the sums I have estimated.

"To accomplish a measure so beneficial to the nation at large; it is evident that I rely, not only upon my exertions, and the friends who are personally attached to me on the Malabar coast, but the local knowledge, which from experience and research, I particularly possess, of the resources of our Asiatic Provinces, for naval purposes, and as no emolument would accrue to myself, I depend upon an equivalent of rank and reward, when the first 74-gun ship arrives in England; for, on my return to India, I could produce a regular supply of the largest third-rates, at the comparative small cost to Government of £12. 19s 6d per ton, and amongst other considerations of magnitude, the larger the ships, the greater would not only be the augmentation of efficient force to our navy, of most durable and superior men of war, with a saving of £213,075, on every teak line-of-battle ship of 2000 tons, making an inconceivable decrease in the public expense of nearly £11,000,000 per ann.; but above all, the important national object obtained, of very considerably lessening the demand, and consequently consumption, of English timber.

"W. LAYMAN.

" Clapton, April 9th, 1802.

" *Note.*—As the preceding proposal is simply, in the first instance, the building of two seventy-four's, and for which only an unserviceable bomb-ship requires to be equipped, it may not be improper to state, that if she does not leave England by the end of May, or the beginning of June, the season for collecting timber on the Malabar coast will be past before her arrival there, which will be the loss of a monsoon, and consequently occasion an increase of expense."

THE END.

www.ingramcontent.com/pod-product-compliance
Lightning Source LLC
Chambersburg PA
CBHW031407230426
43668CB00007B/233